CLYMER
YAMAHA
FZ700, FZ750 & FAZER • 1985-1987

The world's finest publisher of mechanical how-to manuals

PRIMEDIA
Business Directories & Books

P.O. Box 12901, Overland Park, Kansas 66282-2901

Copyright ©1989 PRIMEDIA Business Magazines & Media Inc.

FIRST EDITION
First Printing April, 1989
Second Printing February, 1990
Third Printing January, 1993
Fourth Printing October, 1995
Fifth Printing July, 1998
Sixth Printing April, 2002

Printed in U.S.A.

CLYMER and colophon are registered trademarks of PRIMEDIA Business Magazines & Media Inc.

ISBN: 0-89287-438-4

COVER: *Mark Clifford Photography, Los Angeles, California*

AUTHOR: Ed Scott

TECHNICAL PHOTOGRAPHY: Ron Wright

PHOTOGRAPHIC ASSISTANCE: *Anaheim Motorcycles, Anaheim, California*

TECHNICAL ILLUSTRATION: Steve Amos

TOOLS AND EQUIPMENT: K&L Supply Co.

All rights reserved. Reproduction or use, without express permission, of editorial or pictorial content, in any manner, is prohibited. No patent liability is assumed with respect to the use of the information contained herein. While every precaution has been taken in the preparation of this book, the publisher assumes no responsibility for errors or omissions. Neither is any liability assumed for damages resulting from use of the information contained herein. Publication of the servicing information in this manual does not imply approval of the manufacturers of the products covered.

All instructions and diagrams have been checked for accuracy and ease of application; however, success and safety in working with tools depend to a great extent upon individual accuracy, skill and caution. For this reason, the publishers are not able to guarantee the result of any procedure contained herein. Nor can they assume responsibility for any damage to property or injury to persons occasioned from the procedures. Persons engaging in the procedure do so entirely at their own risk.

1
2
3
4
5
6
7
8
9
10
11
12
13
14
15

CLYMER PUBLICATIONS
PRIMEDIA Business Magazines & Media
Chief Executive Officer Timothy M. Andrews
President Ron Wall

EDITORIAL

Editors
Mike Hall
James Grooms

Technical Writers
Ron Wright
Ed Scott
George Parise
Mark Rolling
Michael Morlan
Jay Bogart
Rodney J. Rom

Production Supervisor
Dylan Goodwin

Lead Editorial Production Coordinator
Shirley Renicker

Editorial Production Coordinators
Greg Araujo
Shara Pierceall

Editorial Production Assistants
Susan Hartington
Holly Messinger
Darin Watson

Technical Illustrators
Steve Amos
Robert Caldwell
Mitzi McCarthy
Bob Meyer
Michael St. Clair
Mike Rose

MARKETING/SALES AND ADMINISTRATION

Vice President, PRIMEDIA Business Directories & Books
Rich Hathaway

Marketing Manager
Elda Starke

Advertising & Promotions Coordinator
Melissa Abbott

Associate Art Directors
Chris Paxton
Tony Barmann

Sales Manager/Marine
Dutch Sadler

Sales Manager/Motorcycles
Matt Tusken

Operations Manager
Patricia Kowalczewski

Sales Manager/Manuals
Ted Metzger

Customer Service Manager
Terri Cannon

Customer Service Supervisor
Ed McCarty

Customer Service Representatives
Susan Kohlmeyer
April LeBlond
Courtney Hollars
Jennifer Lassiter
Ernesto Suarez

Warehouse & Inventory Manager
Leah Hicks

The following books and guides are published by PRIMEDIA Business Directories & Books.

CLYMER® | I&T SHOP SERVICE | AC-U-KWIK | EC&M Books

EQUIPMENT WATCH™
www.equipmentwatch.com

The Electronics Source Book®

BLUE BOOK Values
National Market Reports™...Since 1911

WATERWAY GUIDE®

More information available at *primediabooks.com*

CONTENTS

QUICK REFERENCE DATA IX

CHAPTER ONE
GENERAL INFORMATION 1
    Manual organization
    Notes, cautions, and warnings
    Safety first
    Service hints
    Torque specifications
    Fasteners
    Lubricants
    Parts replacement
    Manufacturer's label
    Emission control information
    Basic hand tools
    Test equipment
    Mechanic's tips

CHAPTER TWO
TROUBLESHOOTING 18
    Operating requirements
    Troubleshooting instruments
    Troubleshooting
    Engine performance
    Engine noises
    Engine lubrication
    Clutch
    Transmission
    Electrical problems
    Excessive vibration
    Carburetor troubleshooting
    Front suspension and steering
    Brake problems

CHAPTER THREE
PERIODIC LUBRICATION, MAINTENANCE AND TUNE-UP 28
    Routine checks
    Maintenance intervals
    Tires
    Battery
    Periodic lubrication
    Periodic maintenance
    Suspension adjustment
    Tune-up
    Ignition timing
    Carburetor

CHAPTER FOUR
ENGINE 72

    Servicing engine in frame
    Engine principles
    Engine
    Cylinder head cover and camshafts
    Cam chain tensioner
    Cam case and cylinder head
    Valves and valve components
    Cylinder block
    Pistons and piston rings
    Oil pump and strainer
    Oil pressure relief valve
    Oil level switch
    Crankcase
    Crankshaft
    Connecting rods
    Starter clutch assembly
    Break-in

CHAPTER FIVE
CLUTCH 135

    Clutch cover
    Clutch
    Clutch hydraulic system
    Clutch master cylinder
    Slave cylinder
    Bleeding the clutch

CHAPTER SIX
TRANSMISSION 153

    Sprocket cover
    Neutral switch
    Engine sprocket
    External shift mechanism
    Transmission gears

CHAPTER SEVEN
FUEL, EMISSION CONTROL AND EXHAUST SYSTEMS 166

    Carburetor
    Fuel tank
    Fuel valve
    Fuel level sender
    Fuel filter
    Fuel pump
    Emission control
    Exhaust system

CHAPTER EIGHT
ELECTRICAL SYSTEM 187

    Charging system
    Ignition system
    Electric starter
    Lighting system
    Switches
    Wiring connectors
    Electrical components
    Fuel pump testing
    Fuses

CHAPTER NINE
COOLING SYSTEM **215**

- Cooling system inspection
- Coolant reservoir
- Radiator and fan
- Thermostat
- Water pump
- Hoses
- Thermostatic switch and water temperature sensor

CHAPTER TEN
FRONT SUSPENSION AND STEERING **225**

- Front wheel
- Front hub
- Wheel balance
- Tubeless tires
- Tubeless tire changing
- Handlebars
- Steering head
- Front fork

CHAPTER ELEVEN
REAR SUSPENSION **249**

- Rear wheel
- Rear hub
- Rear sprocket and coupling
- Drive chain
- Wheel balancing
- Tire changing and repair
- Rear shock absorber
- Swing arm

CHAPTER TWELVE
BRAKES **274**

- Disc brakes
- Brake pad replacement
- Brake calipers
- Front master cylinder
- Rear master cylinder
- Brake hose replacement
- Brake disc
- Bleeding the system

CHAPTER THIRTEEN
FAIRING **292**

- Lower fairing
- Upper fairing
- Windshield

INDEX **295**

WIRING DIAGRAMS **298**

QUICK REFERENCE DATA

MOTORCYCLE INFORMATION

MODEL:_____ YEAR:_____
VIN NUMBER:_____
ENGINE SERIAL NUMBER:_____
CARBURETOR SERIAL NUMBER OR I.D. MARK:_____

FUSES

	Amperage
Main	30 amp
Headlight	15 amp
Signal	10 amp
Ignition	10 amp
Fan	30 amp

ENGINE AND CHASSIS NUMBERS

Model No./year	Engine/chassis No. (start to end)
FZ740N/1985	1AE-000101-005100
FZ750S/1986	1AE-005101-on
FZ250SC/1986	1LJ-000101-on
FZ700T/1987	2KT-000101-on
FZ700TC/1987	2KU-000101-on
FZX700S/1986	IUF-000101-030100
FZX700SC/1986	1UH-000101-030100
FZX700T/1987	1UF-030101-on
FZX700TC/1987	1UH-003101-on

FZX700-RECOMMENDED FRONT FORK AND REAR SHOCK SETTINGS

Load	Front fork air pressure kg/cm2 (psi)	Rear shock absorber spring preload adjuster
Rider only	0.4-0.8 (5-7)	1-2
Rider plus passenger	0.4-0.8 (5-7)	3-5
and or luggage	0.6-1.0 (8.5-14)	3-5
Maximum vehicle load	0.8-1.2 (12.18)	5

FZ700-RECOMMENDED FRONT FORK AND REAR SHOCK SETTINGS

Load	Front fork spring preload adjuster	Rear shock spring length
Rider only	1, 2	12.5-16.5 mm (0.49-0.65 in.)
Rider plus passenger	2, 3	14.5-18.5 mm (0.57-0.73 in.)
Rider plus luggage	2, 3	14.5-18.5 mm (0.57-0.73 in.)
Maximum vehicle load	3, 4	16.5-20.5 mm (0.65-0.81 in.)

FZ750-RECOMMENDED FRONT FORK AND REAR SHOCK SETTINGS

Load	Front fork air pressure kg/cm² (psi)	Rear shock absorber Spring preload adjuster	Damper adjuster
Rider only	0-0.4 (0-5.7)	1, 2	1, 2
Rider plus passenger	0-0.4 (0-5.7)	3, 4	3, 4
Rider plus luggage	0-0.4 (0-5.7)	2, 3	2, 3
Maximum vehicle load limit	0-0.4 (0-5.7)	4, 5	4, 5

FRONT FORK AIR PRESSURE

Model	Standard kg/cm² (psi)	Maximum kg/cm² (psi)
FZX700	0.4 (5.7)	1.2 (17)
FZ750	0 (0)	0.4 (5.7)

TUNE-UP SPECIFICATIONS

Air filter element	Dry paper type
Ignition timing	Fixed
Valve clearance (cold)	
Intake	0.11-0.20 mm (0.0043-0.0079 in.)
Exhaust	0.21-0.30 mm (0.0083-0.0118 in.)
Spark plug	
Type	NGK DP8EA-9 or ND X24EP-U9
Gap	0.8-0.9 mm (0.031-0.035 in.)
Tightening torque	17.5 N•m (12.5 ft.-lb.)
Idle speed	950-1,050 rpm
Compression pressure (cold @ sea level)	
Standard	11 kg/cm² (156 psi)
Minimum	9 kg/cm² (128 psi)
Maximum	12 kg/cm² (171 psi)
Maximum difference between cylinders: 14 psi (1.0 kg/cm²)	

GENERAL TIGHTENING TORQUES *

Nut	Bolt	ft.-lb.	N•m
10 mm	6 mm	4.5	6
12 mm	8 mm	11	15
14 mm	10 mm	22	30
17 mm	12 mm	40	55
19 mm	14 mm	51	85
22 mm	16 mm	94	130

* This table lists general torque for standard fasteners with standard ISO pitch threads.

TIRE INFLATION PRESSURE (COLD)

Load	Psi (kg/cm^2)
FZX700	
Up to 198 lb. (90 kg) load	
Front	32 (2.3)
Rear	32 (2.3)
198-500 lb. (90-227 kg) load	
Front	32 (2.3)
Rear	36 (2.5)
FZ700 & FZ750	
Up to 198 lb. (90 kg) load	
Front	28 (2.0)
Rear	21 (2.3)
198-470 lb. (90-213) load	
Front	32 (2.3)
Rear	42 (2.9)
High speed riding (all models)	
Front	32 (2.3)
Rear	36 (2.5)

REPLACEMENT BULBS

Item	Wattage
Headlight	
FZX700 and FZ700	60/55W
FX750	35/35W
Tail/brakelight	8/27W
Flasher light	27W
Meter light	
FZX700	3.0W
FZ700 & FZ750	3.4W
License light	
FZX700	3.0W
FZ700 & FZ750	8W
Indicator lights	
FZX700	3.0W
FZ700 & FZ750	3.4W

RECOMMENDED LUBRICANTS

Engine oil	
Temperatures 40° F and below	SAE 10W/30 SE/SF
Temperatures 40° F and up	SAE 20W/40 SE/SF
Brake fluid	DOT 3
Battery refilling	Distilled water
Fork oil	10 weight
Cables and pivot points	Yamaha chain and cable lube or SAE 10W/30 motor oil
Fuel	Regular
Drive chain	SAE 30-50 motor oil
Coolant	High-quality ethylene glycol antifreeze compounded for aluminum engines

APPROXIMATE REFILL CAPACITIES

Engine oil	
With filter change	3,000 cc (3.1 qt.)
Without filter change	2,700 cc (2.7 qt.)
After engine rebuild	3,500 cc (3.7 qt.)
Front forks	
FZX700	294 cc (9.94 oz.)
FZ700	404 cc (13.7 oz.)
FZ750	408 cc (13.8 oz.)
Cooling system	
FZX700 and FZ750	2.3 liters (2.4 qt.)
FZ700	2.6 liters (2.7 qt.)
Fuel tank	
FZX700	13.0 liters (3.4 gal.)
FZ700	21.0 liters (5.6 gal.)
FZ750	22.0 liters (5.8 gal.)

CHAPTER ONE

GENERAL INFORMATION

This detailed, comprehensive manual covers Yamaha FZX700, FZ700 and FZ750 models. **Table 1** lists engine and chassis numbers for models covered in this manual.

Troubleshooting, tune-up, maintenance and repair are not difficult, if you know what tools and equipment to use and what to do. Anyone of average intelligence and with some mechanical ability can perform most of the procedures in this manual.

The manual is written simply and clearly enough for owners who have never worked on a motorcycle, but is complete enough for use by experienced mechanics.

Some of the procedures require the use of special tools. Using an inferior substitute tool for a special tool is not recommended as it can be dangerous to you and may damage the part. Special tools are described in the appropriate chapters and are available from Yamaha dealers or other manufacturers as indicated.

Metric and U.S. torque standards are used throughout this manual. Metric to U.S. conversion is given in **Table 2**.

MANUAL ORGANIZATION

This chapter provides general information and discusses equipment and tools useful both for preventive maintenance and troubleshooting.

Chapter Two provides methods and suggestions for quick and accurate diagnosis and repair of problems. Troubleshooting procedures discuss typical symptoms and logical methods to pinpoint the trouble.

Chapter Three explains all periodic lubrication and routine maintenance necessary to keep your Yamaha operating well. Chapter Three also includes recommended tune-up procedures, eliminating the need to constantly consult other chapters on the various assemblies.

Subsequent chapters describe specific systems such as the engine, clutch, transmission, fuel system, exhaust system, suspension, steering, brakes and fairing. Each chapter provides disassembly, repair and assembly procedures in simple step-by-step form. If a repair is impractical for a home mechanic, it is so indicated. It is usually faster and less expensive to take such repairs to a dealer or competent repair shop. Specifications concerning a particular system are included at the end of the appropriate chapter.

NOTES, CAUTIONS AND WARNINGS

The terms NOTE, CAUTION and WARNING have specific meanings in this manual. A NOTE provides additional information to make a step or procedure easier or clearer. Disregarding a NOTE could cause inconvenience, but would not cause damage or personal injury.

A CAUTION emphasizes areas where equipment damage could occur. Disregarding a CAUTION could cause permanent mechanical damage; however, personal injury is unlikely.

A WARNING emphasizes areas where personal injury or even death could result from negligence. Mechanical damage may also occur. WARNINGS *are to be taken seriously.* In some cases, serious injury and death has resulted from disregarding similar warnings.

SAFETY FIRST

Professional mechanics can work for years and never sustain a serious injury. If you observe a few rules of common sense and safety, you can enjoy many safe hours servicing your own machine. If you ignore these rules you can hurt yourself or damage the equipment.

1. Never use gasoline as a cleaning solvent.
2. Never smoke or use a torch in the vicinity of flammable liquids, such as cleaning solvent, in open containers.
3. If welding or brazing is required on the machine, remove the fuel tank and rear shock(s) to a safe distance, at least 50 feet away. Welding on a gas tank requires special safety precautions and must be performed by someone skilled in the process. Do not attempt to weld or braze a leaking gas tank.
4. Use the proper sized wrenches to avoid damage to fasteners and injury to yourself.
5. When loosening a tight or stuck nut, be guided by what would happen if the wrench should slip. Be careful; protect yourself accordingly.
6. When replacing a fastener, make sure to use one with the same measurements and strength as the old one. Incorrect or mismatched fasteners can result in damage to the vehicle and possible personal injury. Beware of fastener kits that are filled with cheap and poorly made nuts, bolts, washers and cotter pins. Refer to *Fasteners* in this chapter for additional information.
7. Keep all hand and power tools in good condition. Wipe greasy and oily tools after using them. They are difficult to hold and can cause injury. Replace or repair worn or damaged tools.
8. Keep your work area clean and uncluttered.
9. Wear safety goggles during all operations involving drilling, grinding, the use of a cold chisel or anytime you feel unsure about the safety of your eyes. Safety goggles should also be worn anytime compressed air is used to clean a part.
10. Keep an approved fire extinguisher nearby. Be sure it is rated for gasoline (Class B) and electrical (Class C) fires.
11. When drying bearings or other rotating parts with compressed air, never allow the air jet to rotate the bearing or part; the air jet is capable of rotating them at speeds far in excess of those for which they were designed. The bearing or rotating part is very likely to disintegrate and cause serious injury and damage.

SERVICE HINTS

Most of the service procedures covered are straightforward and can be performed by anyone reasonably handy with tools. It is suggested, however, that you consider your own capabilities carefully before attempting any operation involving major disassembly of the engine or transmission.

1. "Front," as used in this manual, refers to the front of the motorcycle; the front of any component is the end closest to the front of the motorcycle. The "left-" and "right-hand" sides refer to the position of the parts as viewed by a rider sitting on the seat facing forward. For example, the throttle control is on the right-hand side. These rules are simple, but confusion can cause a major inconvenience during service.
2. Whenever servicing the engine or transmission, or when removing a suspension component, the bike should be secured in a safe manner. If the bike is to be parked on its sidestand, check the stand to make sure it is secure and not damaged. Block the front and rear wheels if they remain on the ground. A small hydraulic jack and a block of wood can be used to raise the chassis. If the transmission is not

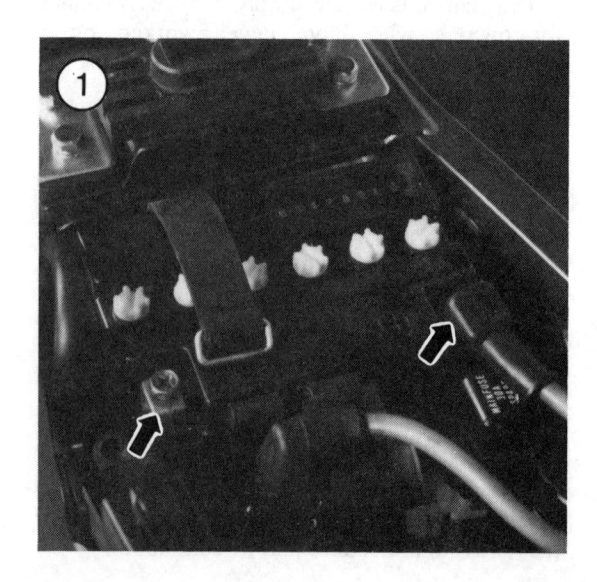

GENERAL INFORMATION

going to be worked on and the drive chain is connected to the rear wheel, shift the transmission into first gear.

3. Disconnect the negative battery cable when working on or near the electrical, clutch or starter systems and before disconnecting any wires. On models covered in this manual, the negative terminal will be marked with a minus (-) sign and the positive terminal with a plus (+) sign. See **Figure 1**.

4. When disassembling a part or assembly, it is a good practice to tag the parts for location and mark all parts which mate together. Small parts, such as bolts, can be identified by placing them in plastic sandwich bags. Seal the bags and label them with masking tape and a marking pen. When reassembly will take place immediately, an accepted practice is to place nuts and bolts in a cupcake tin or egg carton in the order of disassembly.

5. Finished surfaces should be protected from physical damage or corrosion. Keep gasoline and brake fluid off painted surfaces.

6. Use penetrating oil on frozen or tight bolts, then strike the bolt head a few times with a hammer and punch (use a screwdriver on screws). Avoid the use of heat where possible, as it can warp, melt or affect the temper of parts. Heat also ruins finishes, especially paint and plastics.

7. Keep flames and sparks away from a charging battery or flammable fluids and do not smoke near them. It is a good idea to have a fire extinguisher handy in the work area. Remember that many gas appliances in home garages (water heater, clothes drier, etc.) have pilot lights.

8. No parts removed or installed (other than bushings and bearings) in the procedures given in this manual should require unusual force during disassembly or assembly. If a part is difficult to remove or install, find out why before proceeding.

9. Cover all openings after removing parts or assemblies to prevent dirt, small tools, etc. from falling in.

10. Read each procedure *completely* while looking at the actual parts before starting a job. Make sure you *thoroughly* understand what is to be done and then carefully follow the procedure, step by step.

11. Recommendations are occasionally made to refer service or maintenance to a Yamaha dealer or a specialist in a particular field. In these cases, the work will be done more quickly and economically than if you performed the job yourself.

12. In procedural steps, the term "replace" means to discard a defective part and replace it with a new or exchange unit. "Overhaul" means to remove, disassemble, inspect, measure, repair, reassemble and install major systems or parts.

13. Some operations require the use of a hydraulic press. It would be wiser to have these operations performed by a shop equipped for such work, rather than to try the job yourself with makeshift equipment that may damage your machine.

14. Repairs go much faster and easier if your machine is clean before you begin work. There are many special cleaners on the market, like Bel-Ray Degreaser, for washing the engine and related parts. Follow the manufacturer's directions on the container for the best results. Clean all oily or greasy parts with cleaning solvent as you remove them.

WARNING
Never use gasoline as a cleaning agent. It presents an extreme fire hazard. Be sure to work in a well-ventilated area when using cleaning solvent. Keep a fire extinguisher, rated for gasoline fires, handy in any case.

15. Much of the labor charged for by dealers is for the time involved in the removal, disassembly, assembly, and reinstallation of other parts in order to reach the defective part. It is frequently possible to perform the preliminary operations yourself and then take the defective unit to the dealer for repair at considerable savings.

16. If special tools are required, make arrangements to get them before you start. It is frustrating and time-consuming to get partly into a job and then be unable to complete it.

17. Make diagrams (or take a Polaroid picture) wherever similar-appearing parts are found. For instance, crankcase bolts are often different lengths. You may think you can remember where everything came from—but mistakes are costly. There is also the possibility that you may be sidetracked and not return to work for days or even weeks—in which time the carefully laid out parts may have become disturbed.

18. When assembling parts, be sure all shims and washers are replaced exactly as they came out.

19. Whenever a rotating part butts against a stationary part, look for a shim or washer.

20. Use new gaskets if there is any doubt about the condition of the old ones. A thin coat of oil on non-pressure type gaskets may help them seal more effectively. If it is necessary to make a gasket and you do not have a suitable old gasket to use as a guide, apply engine oil to the gasket surface of the part. Then place the part on the new gasket

material and press the part slightly. The oil will leave a very accurate outline on the gasket material that can be cut around.

21. Heavy grease can be used to hold small parts in place if they tend to fall out during assembly. However, keep grease and oil away from electrical and brake components.

22. A carburetor is best cleaned by disassembling it and spraying the fuel and air orifices with a spray carburetor cleaner. Never soak gaskets and rubber parts in these cleaners. Never use wire to clean out jets and air passages. They are easily damaged. Use compressed air to blow out the carburetor only if the float has been removed first.

23. Take your time and do the job right. Don't forget that a newly rebuilt engine must be broken in just like a new one.

TORQUE SPECIFICATIONS

Torque specifications throughout this manual are given in Newton-meters (N•m) and foot-pounds (ft.-lb.).

Table 2 lists general torque specifications for nuts and bolts that are not listed in the respective chapters. To use the table, first determine the size of the nut or bolt. **Figure 2** and **Figure 3** show how this is done.

FASTENERS

The materials and designs of the various fasteners used on your Yamaha are not arrived at by chance or accident. Fastener design determines the type of tool required to work the fastener. Fastener material is carefully selected to decrease the possibility of physical failure.

Threads

Nuts, bolts and screws are manufactured in a wide range of thread patterns. To join a nut and bolt, the diameter of the bolt and the diameter of the hole in the nut must be the same. It is just as important that the threads on both be properly matched.

The best way to tell if the threads on 2 fasteners are matched is to turn the nut on the bolt (or the bolt into the threaded hole in a piece of equipment) with fingers only. Be sure both pieces are clean. If much force is required, check the thread condition on each fastener. If the thread condition is good but the fasteners jam, the threads are not compatible. A thread pitch gauge can also be used to determine pitch. Yamaha motorcycles are manufactured with metric standard fasteners. The threads are cut differently than those of American fasteners (**Figure 4**).

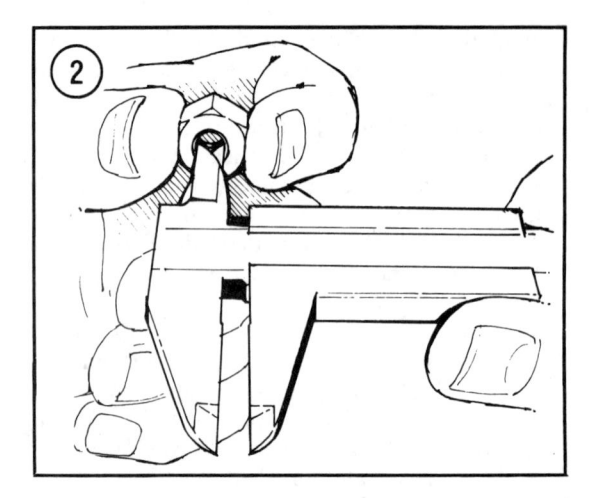

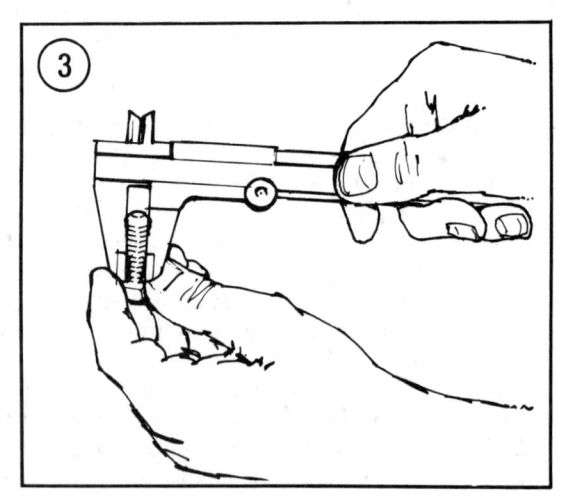

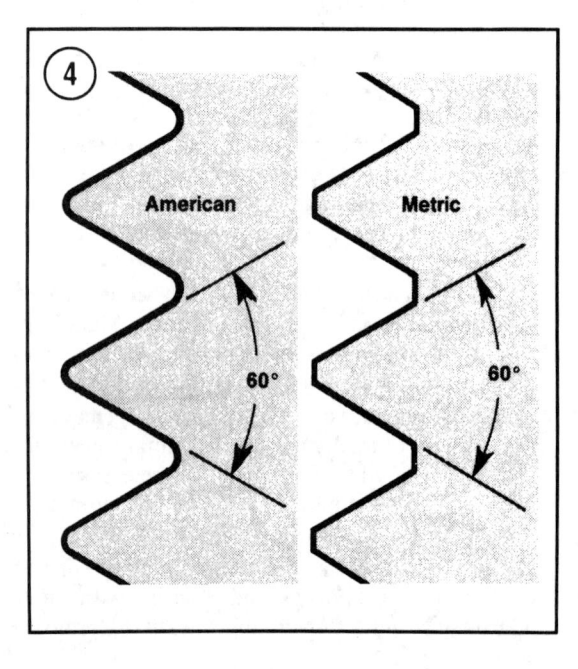

GENERAL INFORMATION

Most threads are cut so that the fastener must be turned clockwise to tighten it. These are called right-hand threads. Some fasteners have left-hand threads; they must be turned counterclockwise to be tightened. Left-hand threads are used in locations where normal rotation of the equipment would tend to loosen a right-hand threaded fastener.

Machine Screws

There are many different types of machine screws. **Figure 5** shows a number of screw heads requiring different types of turning tools. Heads are also designed to protrude above the metal (round) or to be slightly recessed in the metal (flat). See **Figure 6**.

Bolts

Commonly called bolts, the technical name for these fasteners is cap screw. Metric bolts are described by the diameter and pitch (or the distance between each thread). For example, an M8×1.25 bolt is one that has a diameter of 8 millimeters with a distance of 1.25 millimeters between each thread. The measurement across 2 flats on the head of the bolt indicates the proper wrench size to be used. **Figure 3** shows how to determine bolt diameter.

Nuts

Nuts are manufactured in a variety of types and sizes. Most are hexagonal (6-sided) and fit on bolts, screws and studs with the same diameter and pitch.

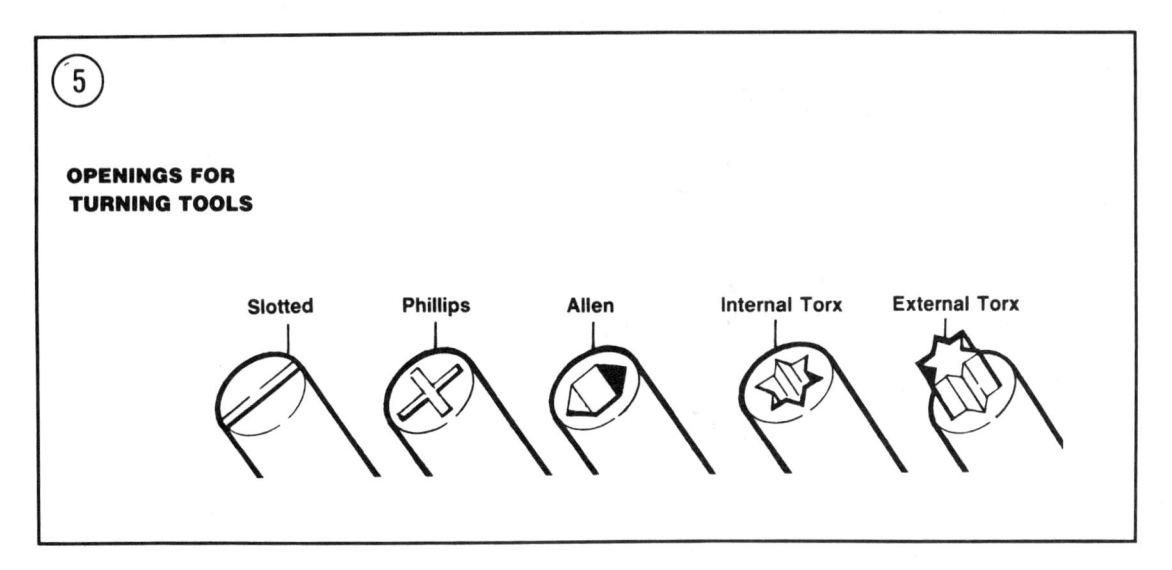

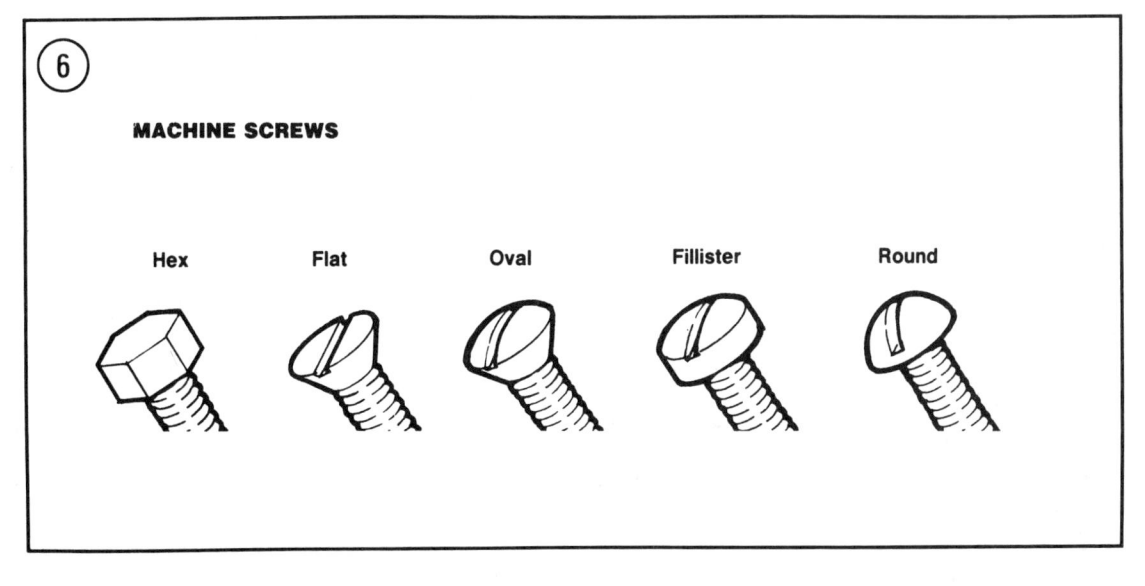

Figure 5 OPENINGS FOR TURNING TOOLS: Slotted, Phillips, Allen, Internal Torx, External Torx

Figure 6 MACHINE SCREWS: Hex, Flat, Oval, Fillister, Round

Figure 7 shows several types of nuts. The common nut is generally used with a lockwasher. Self-locking nuts have a nylon insert which prevents the nut from loosening; no lockwasher is required. Wing nuts are designed for fast removal by hand. Wing nuts are used for convenience in non-critical locations.

To indicate the size of a nut, manufacturers specify the diameter of the opening and the thread pitch. This is similar to bolt specifications, but without the length dimension. The measurement across 2 flats on the nut indicates the proper wrench size to be used.

Self-Locking Fasteners

Several types of bolts, screws and nuts incorporate a system that develops an interference between the bolt, screw, nut or tapped hole threads. Interference is achieved in various ways: by distorting threads, coating threads with dry adhesive or nylon, distorting the top of an all-metal nut, using a nylon insert in the center or at the top of a nut, etc.

Self-locking fasteners offer greater holding strength and better vibration resistance. Some self-locking fasteners can be reused if in good condition. Others, like the nylon insert nut, form an initial locking condition when the nut is first installed; the nylon forms closely to the bolt thread pattern, thus reducing any tendency for the nut to loosen. When the nut is removed, the locking efficiency is greatly reduced. For greatest safety, it is recommended that you install *new* self-locking fasteners whenever they are removed.

Washers

There are 2 basic types of washers: flat washers and lockwashers. Flat washers are simple discs with a hole to fit a screw or bolt. Lockwashers are designed to prevent a fastener from working loose due to vibration, expansion and contraction. **Figure 8** shows several types of washers. Washers are also used in the following functions:
   a. As spacers.
   b. To prevent galling or damage of the equipment by the fastener.
   c. To help distribute fastener load during torquing.
   d. As seals.

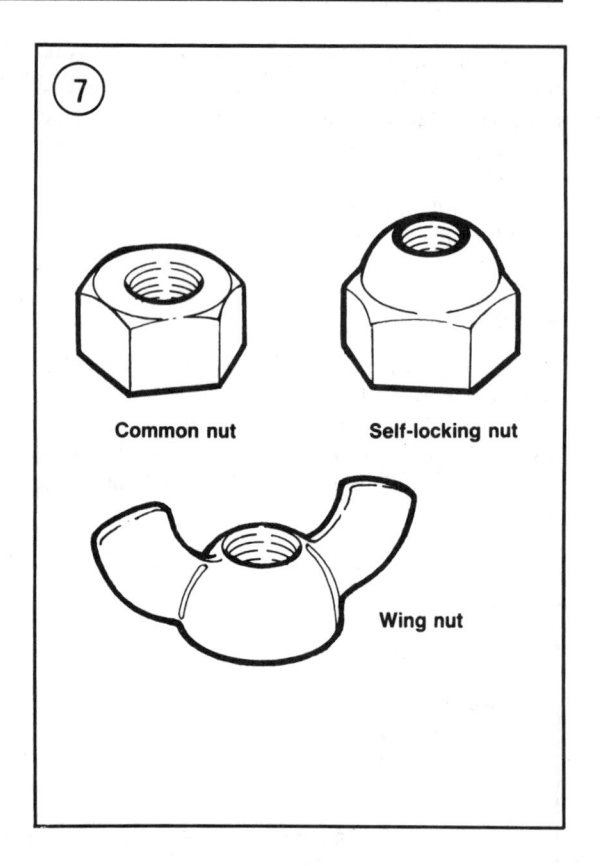

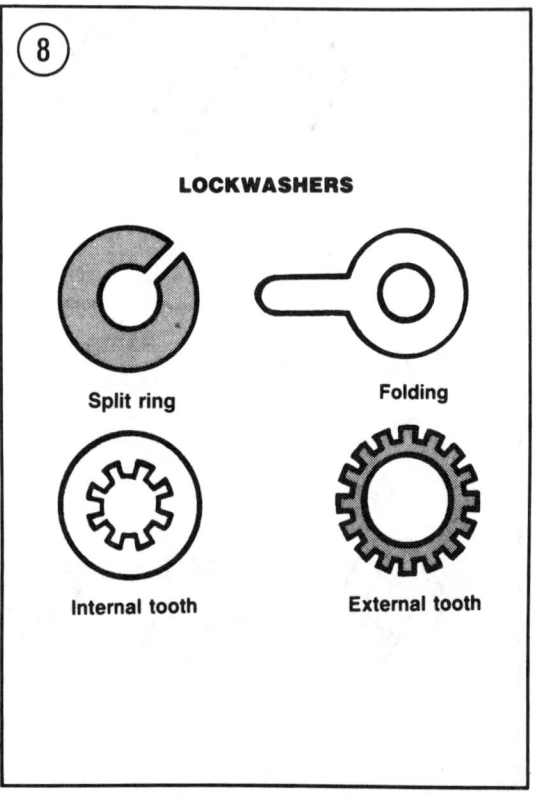

⑦
Common nut
Self-locking nut
Wing nut

⑧
LOCKWASHERS
Split ring
Folding
Internal tooth
External tooth

GENERAL INFORMATION

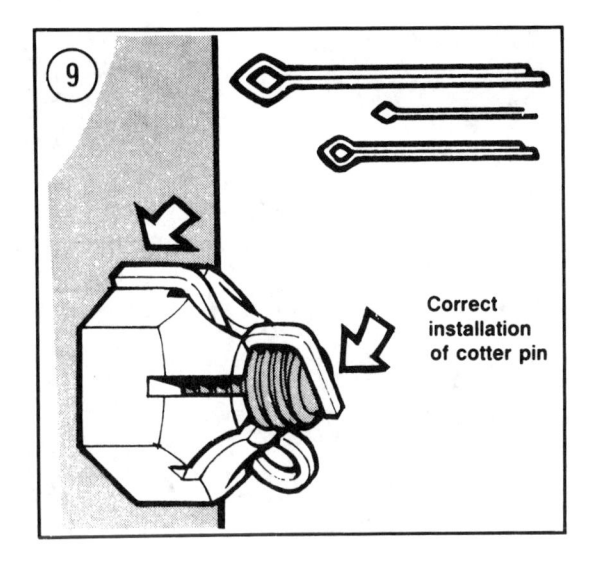

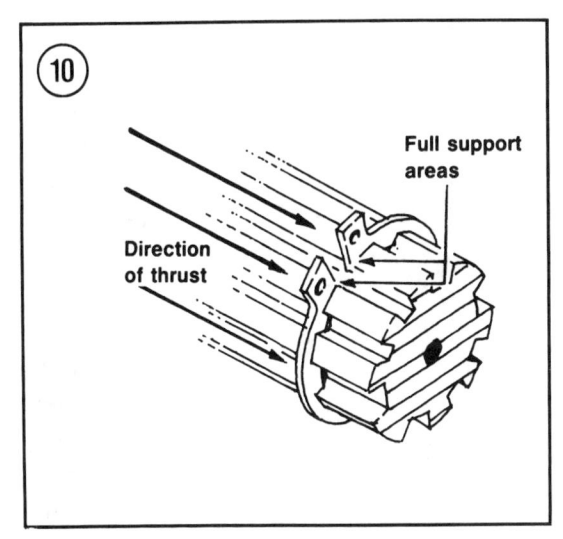

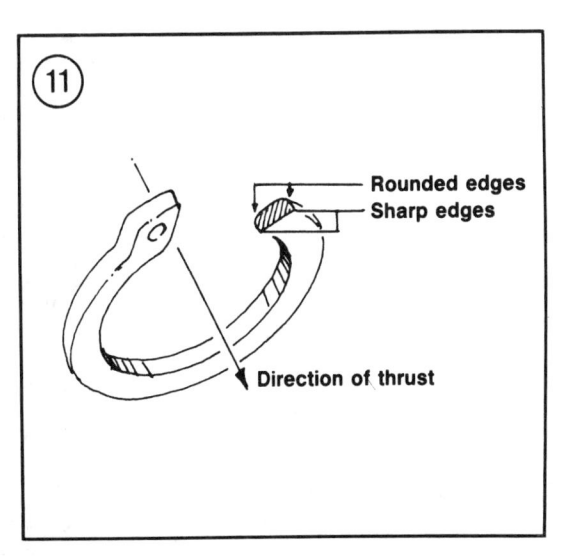

Figure 9 – Correct installation of cotter pin

Figure 10 – Direction of thrust; Full support areas

Figure 11 – Rounded edges; Sharp edges; Direction of thrust

Note that flat washers are often used between a lockwasher and a fastener to provide a smooth bearing surface. This allows the fastener to be turned easily with a tool.

CAUTION
Beware of washers sold with some nut and bolt storage kits. The washers in some kits are very thin. In use, these washers will distort and cause inaccurate torque readings.

Cotter Pins

Cotter pins (**Figure 9**) are used to secure special kinds of fasteners. The threaded stud must have a hole in it; the nut or nut lock piece has castellations around which the cotter pin ends wrap. Cotter pins should not be reused after removal.

Snap Rings

Snap rings can be internal or external design. They are used to retain items on shafts (external type) or within tubes (internal type). In some applications, snap rings of varying thicknesses are used to control the end play of parts assemblies. These are often called selective snap rings. Snap rings should be replaced during installation, as removal weakens and deforms them.

Two basic styles of snap rings are available: machined and stamped snap rings. Machined snap rings (**Figure 10**) can be installed in either direction (shaft or housing) because both faces are machined, thus creating two sharp edges. Stamped snap rings (**Figure 11**) are manufactured with one sharp edge and one rounded edge. When installing stamped snap rings in a thrust situation (transmission shafts, fork tubes, etc.), the sharp edge must face away from the part producing the thrust. When installing snap rings, observe the following:

  a. Compress or expand snap rings only enough to install them.
  b. After the snap ring is installed, make sure it is completely seated in its groove.

LUBRICANTS

Periodic lubrication assures long life for any type of equipment. The *type* of lubricant used is just as important as the lubrication service itself, although in an emergency the wrong type of lubricant is better than none at all. The following paragraphs describe the types of lubricants most often used on motorcycle equipment. Be sure to follow the manufacturer's recommendations for lubricant types.

Generally, all liquid lubricants are called "oil." They may be mineral-based (including petroleum bases), natural-based (vegetable and animal bases), synthetic-based or emulsions (mixtures). "Grease" is an oil to which a thickening base has been added so that the end product is semi-solid. Grease is often classified by the type of thickener added; lithium soap is commonly used.

Engine Oil

Oil for motorcycle and automotive engines is graded by the American Petroleum Institute (API) and the Society of Automotive Engineers (SAE) in several categories. Oil containers display these ratings on the top or label.

API oil grade is indicated by letters; oils for gasoline engines are identified by an "S." The engines covered in this manual require SE or SF graded oil.

Viscosity is an indication of the oil's thickness. The SAE uses numbers to indicate viscosity; thin oils have low numbers while thick oils have high numbers. A "W" after the number indicates that the viscosity testing was done at low temperature to simulate cold-weather operation such as 5W and 20W.

Multi-grade oils (for example 10W-40) are less viscous (thinner) at low temperatures and more viscous (thicker) at high temperatures. This allows the oil to perform efficiently across a wide range of engine operating conditions. The lower the number, the better the engine will start in cold climates. The higher numbers provide engine protection when running in hot weather conditions.

Grease

Greases are graded by the National Lubricating Grease Institute (NLGI). Greases are graded by number according to the consistency of the grease; these range from No. 000 to No. 6, with No. 6 being the most solid. A typical multipurpose grease is NLGI No. 2. For specific applications, equipment manufacturers may require grease with an additive such as molybdenum disulfide (MOS2).

PARTS REPLACEMENT

Yamaha makes frequent changes during a model year, some minor, some relatively major. When you order parts from the dealer or other parts distributor, always order by engine number (**Figure 12**) and vehicle identification numbers (**Figure 13**). Write the numbers down and carry them with you. Compare new parts to old before purchasing them.

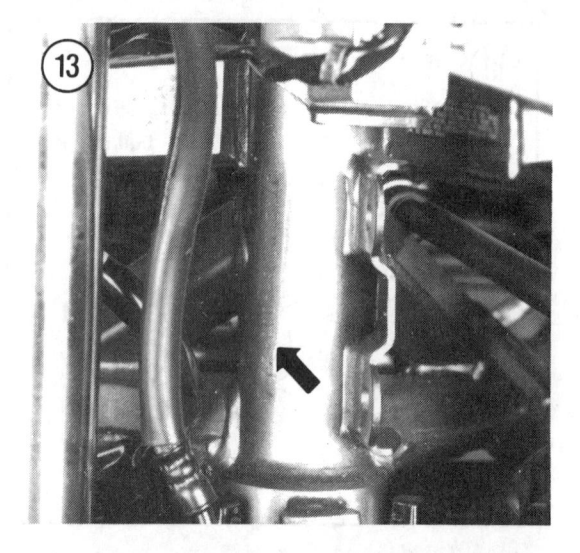

GENERAL INFORMATION

If they are not alike, have the parts manager explain the difference to you before buying the part.

MANUFACTURER'S LABEL

The manufacturer's label is fastened to either the steering head or on the upper right-hand frame tube (**Figure 14**). The label lists manufacturing date, the gross vehicle weight rating (GVWR) and gross axle weight rating (GAWR), tire size and pressure and the vehicle ID number.

EMISSION CONTROL INFORMATION

The vehicle emission control information decals (**Figure 15**) are mounted on the backside of one side cover. These list required tune-up information and fuel specifications.

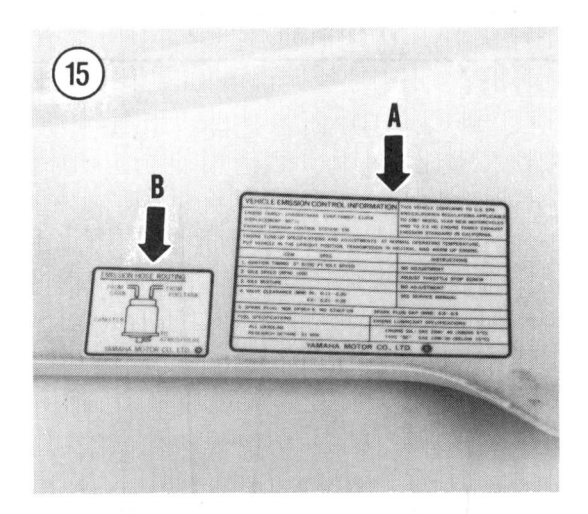

CALIFORNIA EMISSION CONTROL LABEL

All models sold in California are equipped with an evaporative emission control system. An emission control hose routing diagram is mounted on the backside of one side cover (B, **Figure 15**).

MOTORCYCLE NOISE EMISSION CONTROL INFORMATION

The motorcycle Noise Emission Control Information decal is mounted on a front frame tube (**Figure 16**). The decal lists EPA noise emission requirements that the motorcycle met at the time of manufacture.

BASIC HAND TOOLS

Many of the procedures in this manual can be carried out with simple hand tools and test equipment familiar to the average home mechanic. Keep your tools clean and in a tool box. Keep them organized with the sockets and related drives together, the open-end and combination wrenches together, etc. After using a tool, wipe off dirt and grease with a clean cloth and return the tool to its correct place.

Top quality tools are essential; they are also more economical in the long run. If you are now starting to build your tool collection, stay away from the "advertised specials" featured at some parts houses, discount stores and chain drug stores. These are usually a poor grade tool that can be sold cheaply and that is exactly what they are—*cheap*. They are usually made of inferior material, and are thick, heavy and clumsy. Their rough finish makes them difficult to clean and they usually don't last very long. If it is ever your misfortune to use such tools, you will probably find out that the wrenches do not fit the heads of bolts and nuts correctly and damage the fastener.

Quality tools are made of alloy steel and are heat treated for greater strength. They are lighter and better balanced than cheap ones. Their surface is smooth, making them a pleasure to work with and easy to clean. The initial cost of good quality tools may be more but they are cheaper in the long run.

The following tools are required to perform virtually any repair job. Each tool is described and the recommended size given for starting a tool collection. Additional tools and some duplicates may be added as you become familiar with the vehicle. Don't try to buy everything in all sized in the beginning; do it a little at a time until you have the necessary tools.

Yamaha motorcycles are built with metric standard fasteners—so if you are starting your collection now, buy metric sizes.

The screwdriver is a very basic tool, but if used improperly it will do more damage than good. The slot on a screw has a definite dimension and shape. A screwdriver must be selected to conform with that shape. Use a small screwdriver for small screws and a large one for large screws or the screw head will be damaged.

Two basic types of screwdriver are required: common (flat-blade) screwdrivers (**Figure 17**) and Phillips screwdrivers (**Figure 18**).

Screwdrivers are available in sets which often include an assortment of common and Phillips blades. If you buy them individually, buy at least the following:

a. Common screwdriver—5/16×6 in. blade.
b. Common screwdriver—3/8×12 in. blade.
c. Phillips screwdriver—size 2 tip, 6 in. blade.

Use screwdrivers only for driving screws. Never use a screwdriver for prying or chiseling metal. Do not try to remove a Phillips or Allen head screw

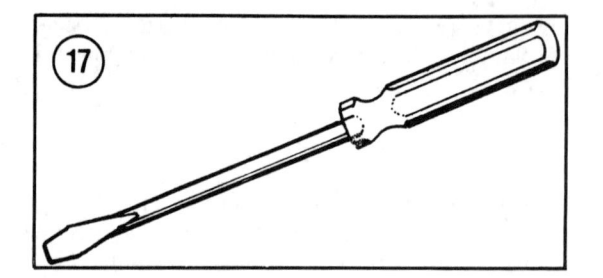

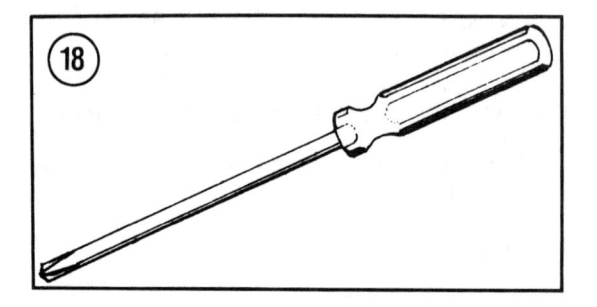

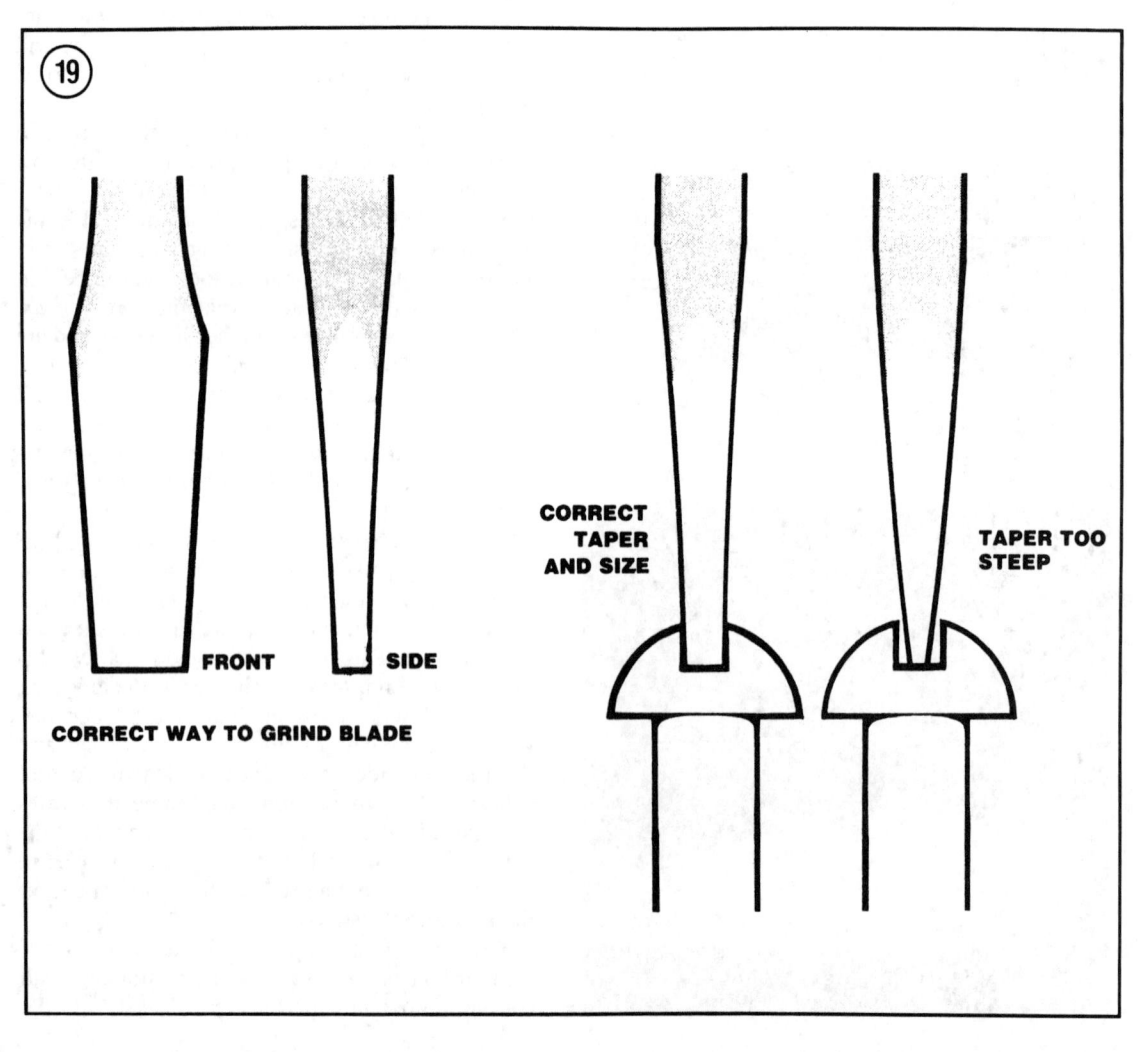

GENERAL INFORMATION

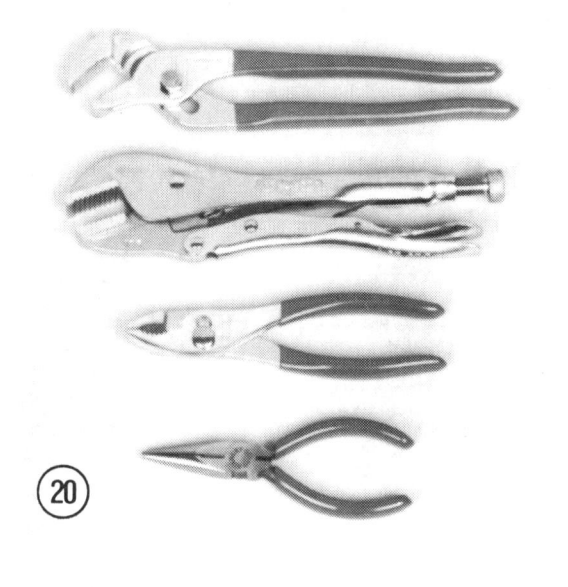

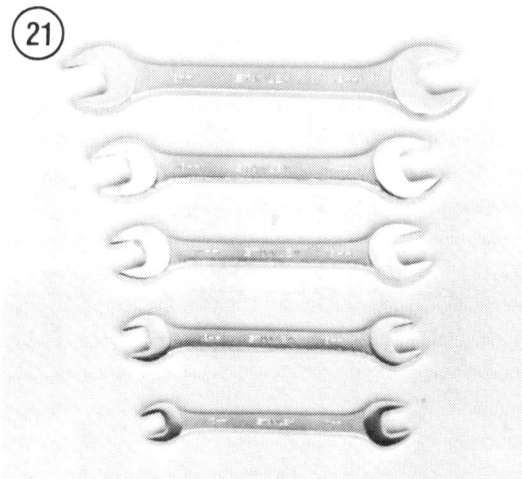

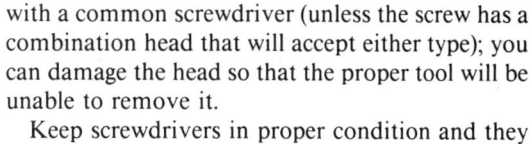

with a common screwdriver (unless the screw has a combination head that will accept either type); you can damage the head so that the proper tool will be unable to remove it.

Keep screwdrivers in proper condition and they will last longer and perform better. Always keep the tip of a common screwdriver in good condition. **Figure 19** shows how to grind the tip to the proper shape if it becomes damaged. Note the symmetrical sides of the tip.

Pliers

Pliers come in a wide range of types and sizes. Pliers are useful for cutting, bending and crimping. They should never be used to cut hardened objects or to turn bolts or nuts. **Figure 20** shows several pliers useful in motorcycle repairs.

Each type of pliers has a specialized function. Gas pliers are general purpose pliers and are used mainly for holding things and for bending. Vise Grips are used as pliers or to hold objects very tightly like a vise. Needlenose pliers are used to hold or bend small objects. Channel lock pliers can be adjusted to hold various sizes of objects; the

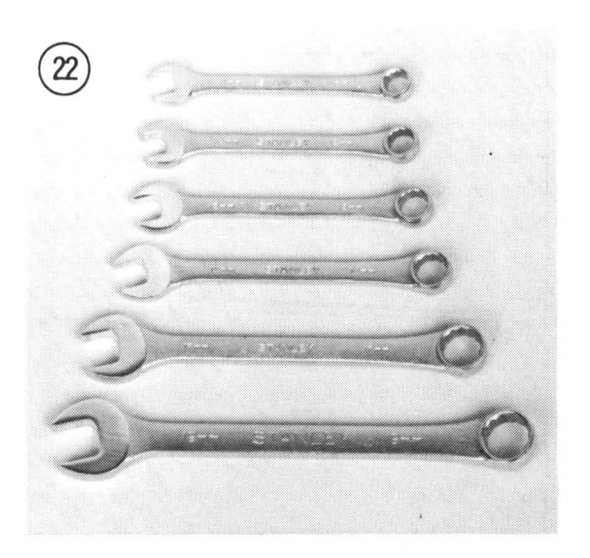

Box, Combination and Open-end Wrenches

Box, combination and open-end wrenches are available in sets or separately in a variety of sizes. The size number stamped near the end refers to the distance between 2 parallel flats on the hex head bolt or nut.

Box wrenches are usually superior to open-end wrenches (**Figure 21**). Open-end wrenches grip the nut on only 2 flats. Unless a wrench fits well, it may slip and round off the points on the nut. The box wrench grips on all 6 flats. Both 6-point and 12-point openings on box wrenches are available. The 6-point gives superior holding power; the 12-point allows a shorter swing.

Combination wrenches (**Figure 21**) which are open on one side and boxed on the other are also available. Both ends are the same size.

CHAPTER ONE

Adjustable Wrenches

An adjustable wrench can be adjusted to fit a variety of nuts or bolt heads (**Figure 23**). However, it can loosen and slip, causing damage to the nut and injury to your knuckles. Use an adjustable wrench only when other wrenches are not available.

Adjustable wrenches come in sizes ranging from 4-18 in. overall. A 6 or 8 in. wrench is recommended as an all-purpose wrench.

Socket Wrenches

This type is undoubtedly the fastest, safest and most convenient to use. Sockets which attach to a ratchet handle or extension (**Figure 24**) are available with 6-point or 12-point openings and 1/4, 3/8, 1/2 and 3/4 in. drives. The drive size indicates the size of the square hole which mates with the ratchet handle.

Torque Wrench

A torque wrench (**Figure 25**) is used with a socket to measure how tightly a nut or bolt is installed. They come in a wide price range and with either 3/8 or 1/2 in. square drive. The drive size indicates the size of the square drive which mates with the socket.

Impact Driver

This tool makes removal of tight fasteners easy and eliminates damage to bolts and screw slots. Impact drivers and interchangeable bits (**Figure 26**) are available at most large hardware and motorcycle dealers. Sockets can also be used with a hand impact driver. However, make sure the socket is designed for impact use. Do not use regular hand type sockets, as they may shatter.

Hammers

The correct hammer is necessary for repairs. Use only a hammer with a face (or head) of rubber or plastic or the soft-faced type that is filled with buckshot. These are sometimes necessary in engine teardowns. *Never* use a metal-faced hammer, as severe damage will result in most cases. You can always produce the same amount of force with a soft-faced hammer.

Feeler Gauge

This tool has both flat and wire measuring gauges and is used to measure spark plug gap. See **Figure 27**. Wire gauges are used to measure spark plug gap; flat gauges are used for all other measurements.

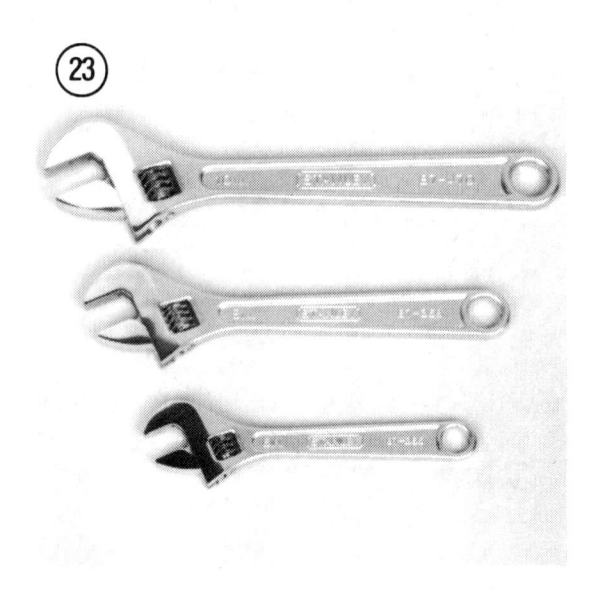

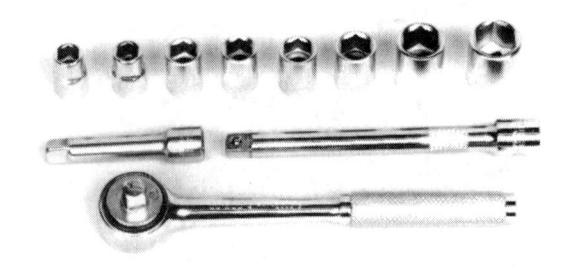

GENERAL INFORMATION

Vernier Caliper

This tool is invaluable when reading inside, outside and depth measurements to close precision. Some models list only metric or inch graduations while models can be purchased that list both. Vernier calipers can be purchased from large dealers or mail order houses. See **Figure 28**.

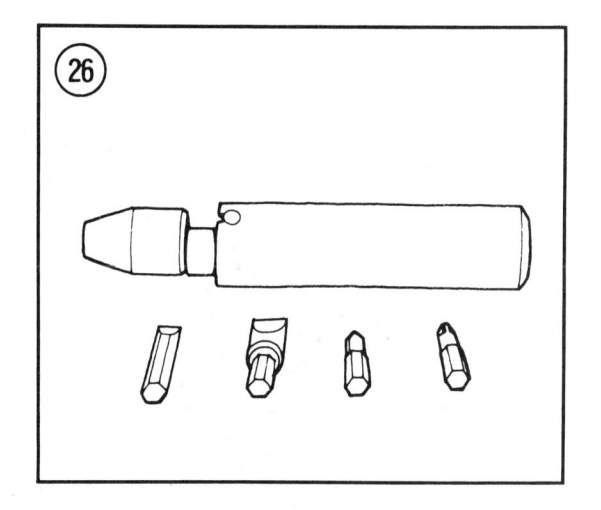

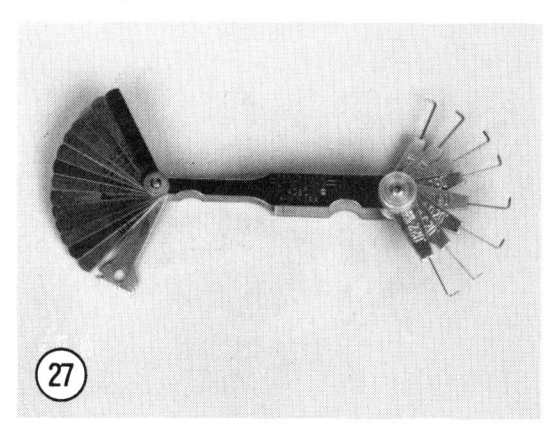

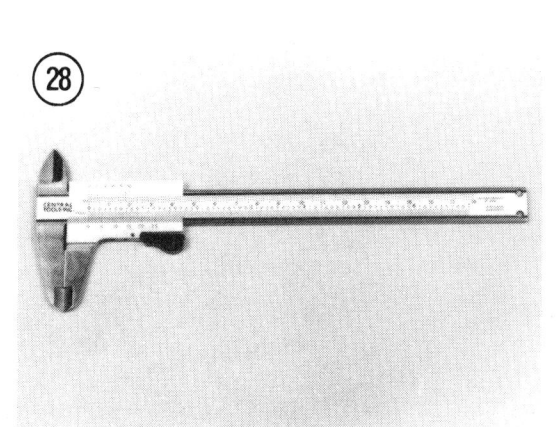

Special Tools

A few special tools may be required for major service. These are described in the appropriate chapters and are available from Yamaha dealers or other manufacturers as indicated.

TEST EQUIPMENT

Voltmeter, Ammeter and Ohmmeter

A good voltmeter is required for testing ignition and other electrical systems. Voltmeters are available with analog meter scales or digital readouts. An instrument covering 0-20 volts is satisfactory. It should also have a 0-2 volt scale for testing individual contacts where voltage drops are much smaller. Accuracy should be ±1/2 volt.

An ohmmeter measures electrical resistance. This instrument is useful in checking continuity (for open and short circuits) and testing lights. A self-powered 12-volt test light can often be used in its place.

The ammeter measures electrical current. These are useful for checking battery starting and charging currents.

Some manufacturers combine the 3 instruments into one unit called a multimeter or VOM. See **Figure 29**.

Compression Gauge

An engine with low compression cannot be properly tuned and will not develop full power. A compression gauge measures the amount of pressure present in the engine's combustion chambers during the compression stroke. This indicates general engine condition.

The Yamaha models described in this manual require the use of a 12 mm screw-in compression gauge that threads into the spark plug hole (**Figure 30**).

Dial Indicator

Dial indicators (**Figure 31**) are precision tools used to check dimension variations on machined parts such as transmission shafts and axles and to check crankshaft and axle shaft end play. Dial indicators are available with various dial types for different measuring requirements.

Strobe Timing Light

This instrument is necessary for checking ignition timing. By flashing a light at the precise instant the spark plug fires, the position of the timing mark can be seen. The flashing light makes a moving mark appear to stand still opposite a stationary mark.

Suitable lights range from inexpensive neon bulb types to powerful xenon strobe lights. See **Figure 32**. A light with an inductive pickup is recommended to eliminate any possible damage to ignition wiring.

Portable Tachometer

A portable tachometer is necessary for tuning. See **Figure 33**. Ignition timing and carburetor adjustments must be performed at the specified idle speed. The best instrument for this purpose is one with a low range of 0-1,000 or 0-2,000 rpm and a high range of 0-4,000 rpm. Extended range (0-6,000 or 0-8,000 rpm) instruments lack accuracy at lower speeds. The instrument should be capable of detecting changes of 25 rpm on the low range.

Expendable Supplies

Certain expendable supplies are also required. These include grease, oil, gasket cement, shop rags and cleaning solvent. Ask your dealer for the special locking compounds, silicone lubricants and lube products which make vehicle maintenance simpler and easier. Cleaning solvent is available at some service stations.

MECHANIC'S TIPS

Removing Frozen Nuts and Screws

When a fastener rusts and cannot be removed, several methods may be used to loosen it. First, apply penetrating oil such as Liquid Wrench or WD-40 (available at hardware or auto supply stores). Apply it liberally and let it penetrate for 10-15 minutes. Rap the fastener several times with

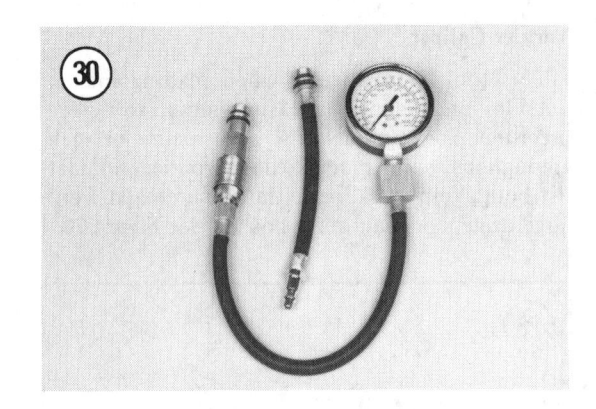

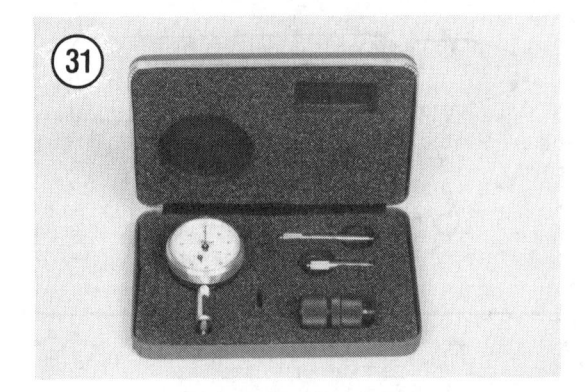

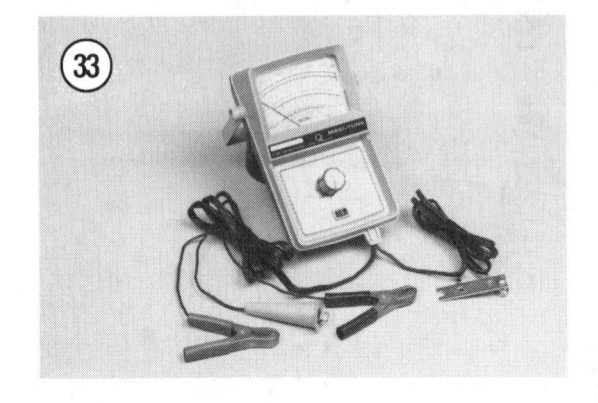

GENERAL INFORMATION

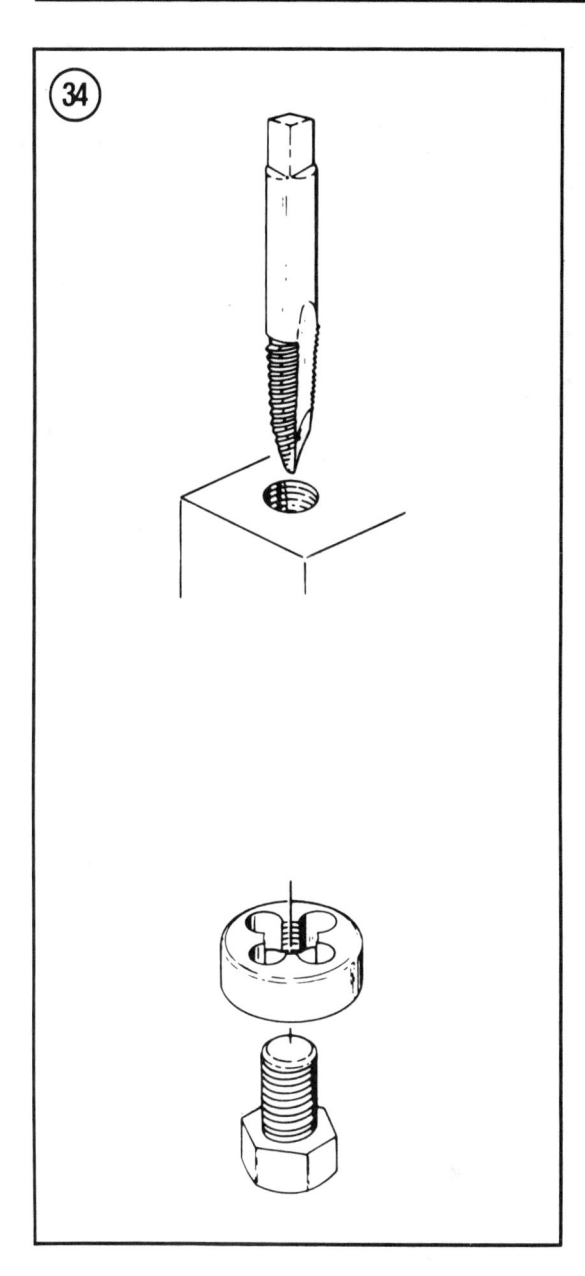

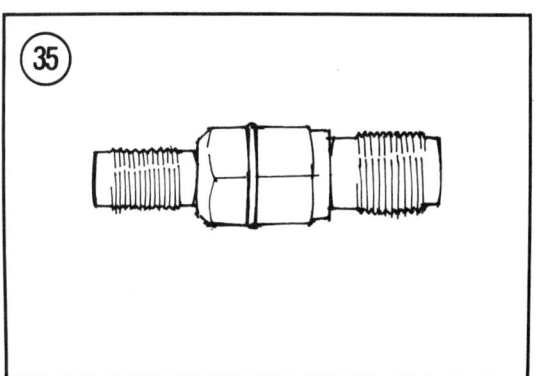

a small hammer; do not hit it hard enough to cause damage. Reapply the penetrating oil if necessary.

For frozen screws, apply penetrating oil as described, then insert a screwdriver in the slot and rap the top of the screwdriver with a hammer. This loosens the rust so the screw can be removed in the normal way. If the screw head is too chewed up to use this method, grip the head with Vise Grips pliers and twist the screw out.

Avoid applying heat unless specifically instructed, as it may melt, warp or remove the temper from parts.

Remedying Stripped Threads

Occasionally, threads are stripped through carelessness or impact damage. Often the threads can be cleaned up by running a tap (for internal threads on nuts) or die (for external threads on bolts) through the threads. See **Figure 34**. To clean or repair spark plug threads, a spark plug tap can be used (**Figure 35**).

Removing Broken Screws or Bolts

When the head breaks off a screw or bolt, several methods are available for removing the remaining portion.

If a large portion of the remainder projects out, try gripping it with Vise Grips. If the projecting portion is too small, file it to fit a wrench or cut a slot in it to fit a screwdriver. See **Figure 36**.

If the head breaks off flush, use a screw extractor. To do this, centerpunch the exact center of the remaining portion of the screw or bolt. Drill a small hole in the screw and tap the extractor into the hole. Back the screw out with a wrench on the extractor. See **Figure 37**.

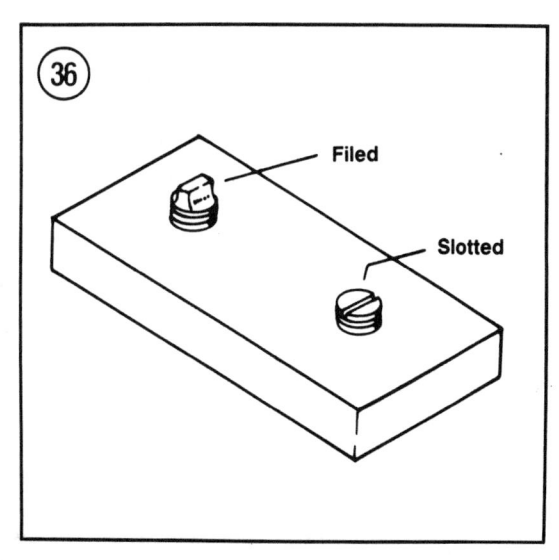

CHAPTER ONE

③⑦

REMOVING BROKEN SCREWS AND BOLTS

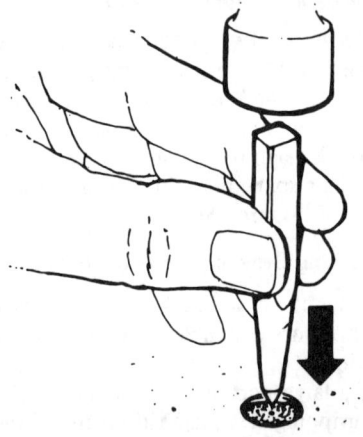

1. Center punch broken stud

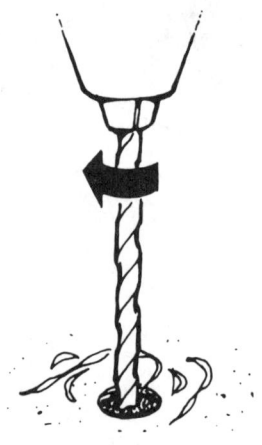

2. Drill hole in stud

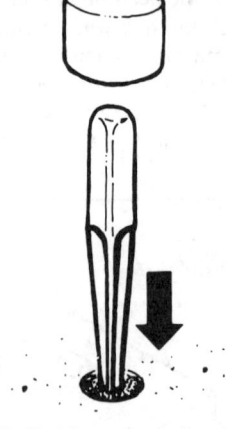

3. Tap in screw extractor

4. Remove broken stud

GENERAL INFORMATION

Table 1 ENGINE AND CHASSIS NUMBERS

Model No./year	Engine/chassis No. (start to end)
FZ750N/1985	1AE-000101-005100
FZ750S/1986	1AE-005101-on
FZ750SC/1986	1LJ-000101-on
FZ700T/1987	2KT-000101-on
FZ700TC/1987	2KU-000101-on
FZX700S/1986	IUF-000101-030100
FZX700SC/1986	1UH-000101-030100
FZX700T/1987	1UF-030101-on
FZX700TC/1987	1UH-003101-on

Table 2 GENERAL TIGHTENING TORQUES*

Nut	Bolt	ft.-lb.	N·m
10 mm	6 mm	4.5	6
12 mm	8 mm	11	15
14 mm	10 mm	22	30
17 mm	12 mm	40	55
19 mm	14 mm	51	85
22 mm	16 mm	94	130

* This table lists general torque for standard fasteners with standard ISO pitch threads.

CHAPTER TWO

TROUBLESHOOTING

Every motorcycle engine requires an uninterrupted supply of fuel and air, proper ignition and adequate compression. If any of these are lacking, the engine will not run.

Diagnosing mechanical problems is relatively simple if you use orderly procedures and keep a few basic principles in mind.

The troubleshooting procedures in this chapter analyze typical symptoms and show logical methods of isolating causes. These are not the only methods. There may be several ways to solve a problem, but only a systematic approach can guarantee success.

Never assume anything. Do not overlook the obvious. If you are riding along and the bike suddenly quits, check the easiest, most accessible problem spots first. Is there gasoline in the tank? Has a spark plug wire fallen off?

If nothing obvious turns up in a quick check, look a little further. Learning to recognize and describe symptoms will make repairs easier for you or a mechanic at the shop. Describe problems accurately and fully. Saying that "it won't run" isn't the same thing as saying "it quit at high speed and won't start," or that "it sat in my garage for 3 months and then wouldn't start."

Gather as many symptoms as possible to aid in diagnosis. Note whether the engine lost power gradually or all at once. Remember that the more complicated a machine is, the easier it is to troubleshoot because symptoms point to specific problems.

After the symptoms are defined, areas which could cause problems are tested and analyzed. Guessing at the cause of a problem may provide the solution, but it can easily lead to frustration, wasted time and a series of expensive, unnecessary parts replacements.

You do not need fancy equipment or complicated test gear to determine whether repairs can be attempted at home. A few simple checks could save a large repair bill and lost time while the bike sits in a dealer's service department. On the other hand, be realistic and don't attempt repairs beyond your abilities. Service departments tend to charge heavily for putting together a disassembled engine that may have been abused. Some won't even take on such a job—so use common sense and don't get in over your head.

OPERATING REQUIREMENTS

An engine needs 3 basics to run properly: correct fuel/air mixture, compression and a spark at the correct time. If one or more are missing, the engine will not run. Four-stroke engine operating principles are described under *Engine Principles* in Chapter Four. The electrical system is the weakest

TROUBLESHOOTING

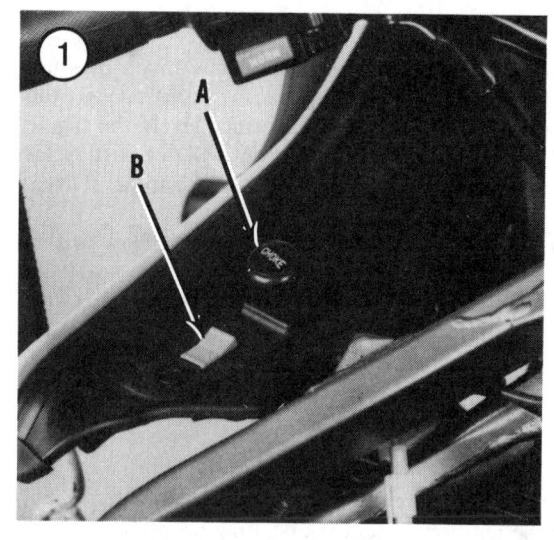

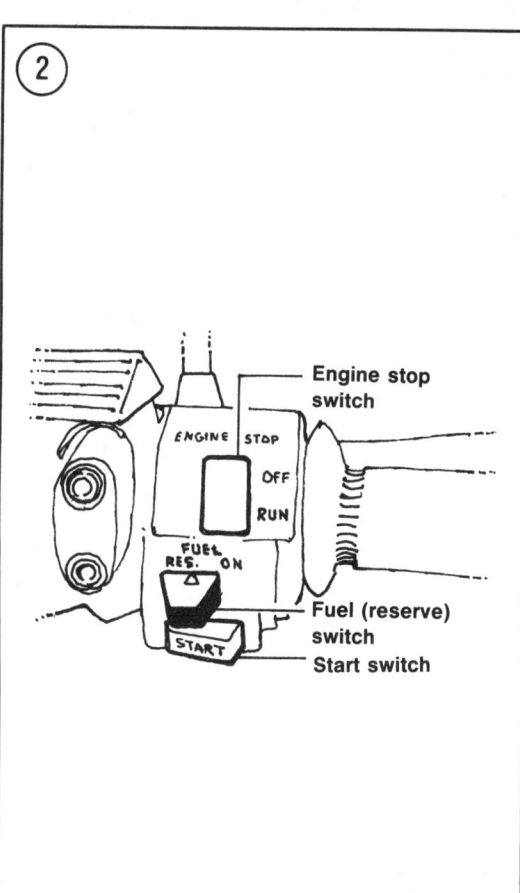

19

link of the 3 basics. More problems result from electrical breakdowns than from any other source. Keep that in mind before you begin tampering with carburetor adjustments and the like.

If the machine has been sitting for any length of time and refuses to start, check and clean the spark plugs and then look to the gasoline delivery system. This includes the fuel tank, fuel pump, fuel shutoff valve and fuel line to the carburetor. Gasoline deposits may have formed and gummed up the carburetor jets and air passages. Gasoline tends to lose its potency after standing for long periods. Condensation may contaminate the fuel with water. Drain the old fuel (fuel tank, fuel lines and carburetors) and try starting with a fresh tankful.

TROUBLESHOOTING INSTRUMENTS

Chapter One lists the instruments needed and gives instruction on their use.

TROUBLESHOOTING

When the bike is difficult to start, or won't start at all, it doesn't help to wear down the battery using the electric starter. Check for obvious problems even before getting out your tools. Go down the following list step by step. Do each one; you may be embarrassed to find the engine stop switch off, but that is better than wearing down the battery.

Engine Fails to Start

If the bike will not start, perform the following checks in order:
  a. Fuel system check.
  b. Compression check.
  c. Ignition system check.
  d. Battery check.

Fuel system check

All models are equipped with an electric fuel pump system.

1. Check position of the choke knob (A, **Figure 1**).
2. Is the fuel supply switch in the correct position? See **Figure 2** (FZX700) or B, **Figure 1** (FZ700 and FX750). Note the following:
  a. *FZX700*: When the fuel tank level drops below 3.0 L (0.8 U.S. gal.), the fuel indicator

light (**Figure 3**) will come on. Turn the fuel supply switch (**Figure 1**) to RES. If the indicator light does not operate correctly, refer to *Fuel Pump Testing* in Chapter Eight.
  b. *FZ700 and FZ750*: When the fuel tank level drops to 5.0 L (1.3 U.S. gal.), the fuel gauge needle will rest in the red zone (**Figure 4**). Turn the fuel supply switch (B, **Figure 2**) to RES. If the fuel gauge needle does not operate correctly, refer to *Fuel Pump Testing* in Chapter Eight.
  c. If the engine does not start, perform Step 2.

WARNING
Do not use an open flame to check in the tank. A serious explosion is certain to result.

3. Check fuel tank pressure by opening the fuel tank cap. A sound of rushing air should be present as soon as the cap is opened. Interpret results as follows:
  a. Normal: If the tank's pressure is okay and there is a sufficient supply of fuel in the tank, fuel is not getting to the carburetors. Check for a plugged fuel filter, fuel line or inoperative fuel pump system (Chapter Eight). If these are okay, refer to *Compression Check* in this chapter.

NOTE
A quick way of checking to see if fuel is getting from the carburetors to the engine is by removing the spark plugs immediately after trying to start the engine. The tips of the spark plugs should be wet.

  b. Abnormal: If the tank did not have any internal pressure, check the fuel tank breather tube for obstructions or other damage. Repair the tube and retest.

Compression check

A compression test shows how much pressure builds in a cylinder during starting. If the compression falls below specified levels, the engine will become difficult to start or will not start. Refer to *Compression Testing* in Chapter Three. Interpret results as follows:
  a. Normal: Perform the *Ignition Check* in this chapter.
  b. Abnormal: If the engine compression is low, perform the procedures listed under *Compression Testing* in Chapter Three.

Ignition check

Perform the following spark test to determine if the ignition system is operating properly.
1. Remove the fuel tank as described in Chapter Seven.
2. Remove one of the spark plugs.
3. Connect the spark plug wire and connector to the spark plug and touch the spark plug base to a good ground like the engine cylinder head. Position the spark plug so you can see the electrodes.

WARNING
During the next step, do not hold the spark plug, wire or connector with fingers or a serious electrical shock may result. If necessary, use a pair of insulated pliers to hold the spark plug or wire. The high voltage generated by the ignition system could produce serious or fatal shocks.

4. Crank the engine over with the starter. A fat blue spark should be evident across the spark plug electrodes.

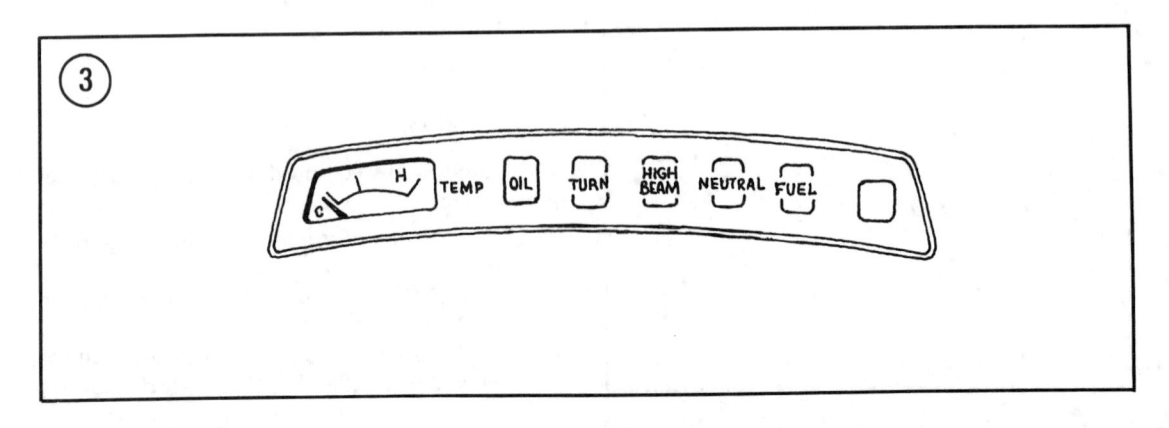

TROUBLESHOOTING

NOTE
*If the starter does not operate or if the starter motor rotates but the engine does not turn over, refer to **Engine Will Not Crank** in this section.*

5. If the spark is good, recheck the fuel and compression systems.
6. If the spark is not good, check for one or more of the following:
   a. Loose electrical connections.
   b. Dirty electrical connections.
   c. Loose or broken ignition coil ground wire.
   d. Blown fuse.
   e. Clutch or side stand switch malfunction.
   f. Ignition or engine stop switch malfunction.
   g. Broken or shorted high tension lead to the spark plug(s).
   h. IC igniter malfunction.

Battery Check

If ignition system tests okay, but the starter turns slowly, service the battery as described under *Battery* in Chapter Three.

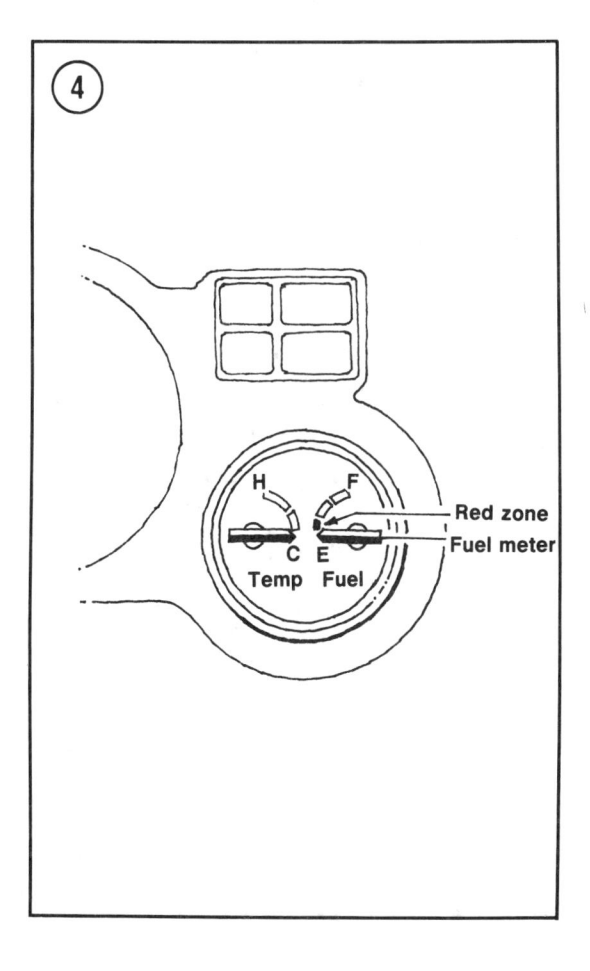

Engine is Difficult to Start

Check for one or more of the following possible malfunctions:
   a. Fouled spark plug(s).
   b. Improperly adjusted choke (FZ700 and FZ750).
   c. Intake manifold air leak.
   d. Contaminated fuel system.
   e. Improperly adjusted carburetor.
   f. Weak ignition unit.
   g. Weak ignition coil(s).
   h. Poor compression.
   i. Engine and transmission oil too heavy.

Engine Will Not Crank

Check for one or more of the following possible malfunctions:
   a. Blown fuse.
   b. Discharged battery.
   c. Side stand or clutch switch malfunction.
   d. Engine stop switch malfunction.
   e. Defective starter motor button and contact.
   f. Defective starter motor.
   g. Seized piston(s).
   h. Seized crankshaft bearings.
   i. Broken connecting rod.

ENGINE PERFORMANCE

In the following checklist, it is assumed that the engine runs, but is not operating at peak performance. This will serve as a starting point from which to isolate a performance malfunction.

Engine Will Not Idle

   a. Carburetor incorrectly adjusted.
   b. Fouled or improperly gapped spark plug(s).
   c. Leaking head gasket.
   d. Obstructed fuel line or fuel shutoff valve.
   e. Obstructed fuel filter.
   f. Fuel pump malfunction.
   g. Ignition timing incorrect due to defective ignition component(s).
   h. Valve clearance incorrect.

Engine Misses at High Speed

a. Fouled or improperly gapped spark plugs.
b. Improper carburetor main jet selection.
c. Ignition timing incorrect due to defective ignition component(s).
d. Weak ignition coil(s).
e. Obstructed fuel line or fuel shutoff valve.
f. Obstructed fuel filter.
g. Fuel pump malfunction.
h. Clogged carburetor jets.
i. Dirty air cleaner.

Engine Overheating

a. Incorrect carburetor adjustment or jet selection.
b. Ignition timing retarded due to defective ignition component(s).
c. Improper spark plug heat range.
d. Cooling system malfunction (see below).
e. Incorrect coolant level.
f. Oil level low.
g. Oil not circulating properly.
h. Valves leaking.
i. Heavy engine carbon deposits.
j. Dragging brake(s).
k. Clutch slipping.

Engine Overheating (Cooling System Malfunction)

Note the above, then proceed with the following items:

a. Clogged radiator.
b. Damaged thermostat.
c. Worn or damaged radiator cap.
d. Water pump worn or damaged.
e. Fan relay malfunction.
f. Thermostatic switch malfunction.
g. Damaged fan blade(s).

Black Smoke

a. Clogged air cleaner.
b. Incorrect carburetor fuel level (too high).
c. Choke stuck open.
d. Incorrect main jet (too large).

White Smoke

a. Worn valve guide.
b. Worn valve oil seal.
c. Worn piston ring oil ring.
d. Excessive cylinder and/or piston wear.

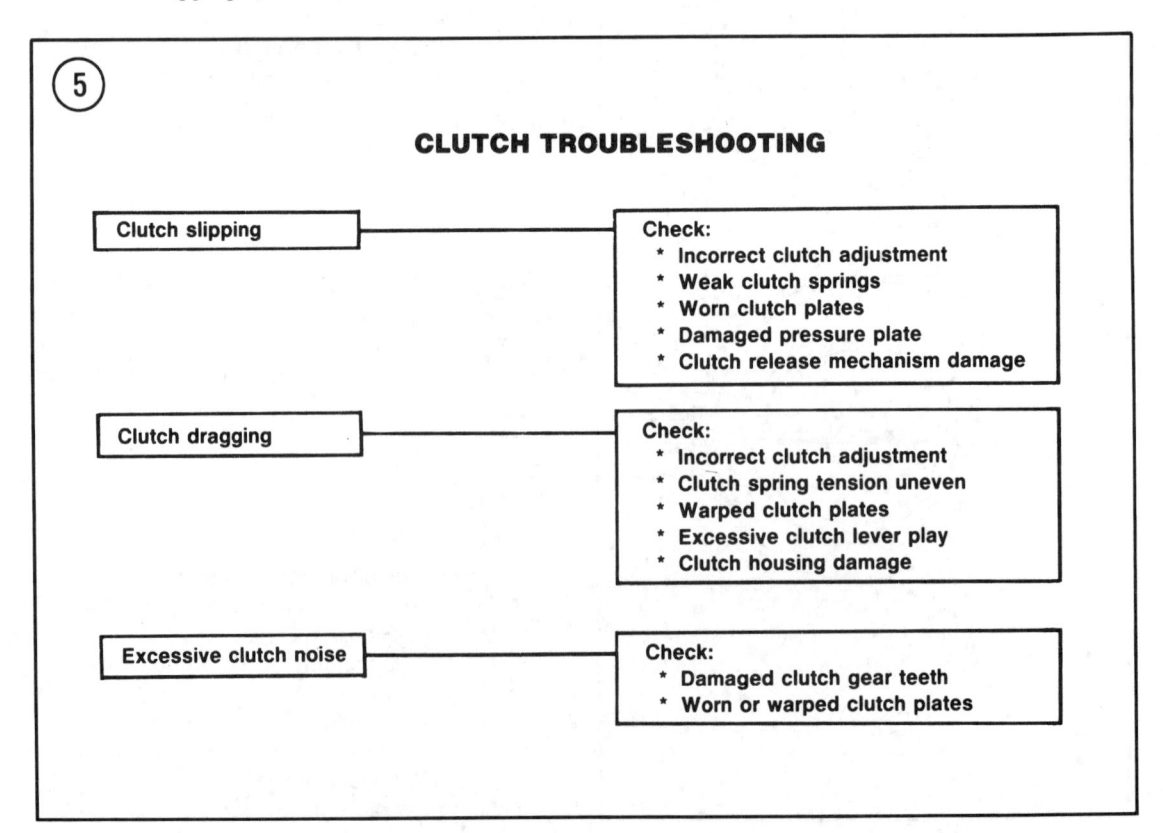

---

⑤

CLUTCH TROUBLESHOOTING

Clutch slipping — Check:
* Incorrect clutch adjustment
* Weak clutch springs
* Worn clutch plates
* Damaged pressure plate
* Clutch release mechanism damage

Clutch dragging — Check:
* Incorrect clutch adjustment
* Clutch spring tension uneven
* Warped clutch plates
* Excessive clutch lever play
* Clutch housing damage

Excessive clutch noise — Check:
* Damaged clutch gear teeth
* Worn or warped clutch plates

TROUBLESHOOTING

Smoky Exhaust and Engine Runs Roughly

  a. Clogged air filter element.
  b. Carburetor adjustment incorrect- mixture too rich.
  c. Choke not operating correctly.
  d. Water or other contaminants in fuel.
  e. Clogged fuel line.
  f. Spark plugs fouled.
  g. Ignition coil defective.
  h. IC igniter or pickup coil defective.
  i. Loose or defective ignition circuit wire.
  j. Short circuit from damaged wire insulation.
  k. Loose battery cable connection.
  l. Valve timing incorrect.
  m. Intake manifold or air cleaner air leak.

Engine Loses Power at Normal Riding Speed

  a. Carburetor incorrectly adjusted.
  b. Engine overheating.
  c. Ignition timing incorrect due to defective ignition component(s).
  d. Incorrectly gapped spark plugs.
  e. Obstructed muffler.
  f. Dragging brake(s).

Engine Lacks Acceleration

  a. Carburetor mixture too lean.
  b. Clogged fuel line.
  c. Ignition timing incorrect due to defective ignition component(s).
  d. Dragging brake(s).
  e. Slipping clutch.

ENGINE NOISES

Often the first evidence of an internal engine problem is a strange noise. That knocking, clicking or tapping sound which you never heard before may be warning you of impending trouble.

While engine noises can indicate problems, they are difficult to interpret correctly; inexperienced mechanics can be seriously misled by them.

Professional mechanics often use a special stethoscope (which looks like a doctor's stethoscope) for isolating engine noises. You can do nearly as well with a "sounding stick" which can be an ordinary piece of doweling, a length of broom handle or a section of small hose. By placing one end in contact with the area to which you want to listen and the other end near your ear, you can hear sounds emanating from that area. The first time you do this, you may be horrified at the strange sounds coming from even a normal engine. If you can, have an experienced friend or mechanic help you sort out the noises.

Consider the following when troubleshooting engine noises:

1. *Knocking or pinging during acceleration—* Caused by using a lower octane fuel than recommended. May also be caused by poor fuel. Pinging can also be caused by a spark plug of the wrong heat range or carbon buildup in the combustion chambers. Refer to *Correct Spark Plug Heat Range* and *Compression Test* in Chapter Three.

2. *Slapping or rattling noises at low speed or during acceleration—* May be caused by piston slap, i.e., excessive piston-cylinder wall clearance.

3. *Knocking or rapping while decelerating—* Usually caused by excessive rod bearing clearance.

4. *Persistent knocking and vibration—* Usually caused by worn main bearing(s).

5. *Rapid on-off squeal—* Compression leak around cylinder head gasket or spark plug(s).

6. *Valve train noise—* Check for the following:

  a. Valves adjusted incorrectly.
  b. Valve sticking in guide.
  c. Low oil pressure.

ENGINE LUBRICATION

An improperly operating engine lubrication system will quickly lead to engine seizure. The engine oil level should be checked weekly and topped up, as described in Chapter Three. Oil pump service is described in Chapter Four.

Oil Consumption High or Engine Smokes Excessively

  a. Worn valve guides.
  b. Worn or damaged piston rings.

Excessive Engine Oil Leaks

  a. Clogged air cleaner breather hose.
  b. Loose engine parts.
  c. Damaged gasket sealing surfaces.

CLUTCH

The three basic clutch troubles are:

a. Clutch noise.
b. Clutch slipping.
c. Improper clutch disengagement or dragging.

All clutch troubles, except adjustments, require partial clutch disassembly to identify and cure the problem. The troubleshooting chart in **Figure 5** lists clutch troubles and checks to make. Refer to Chapter Five for clutch service procedures.

TRANSMISSION

The basic transmission troubles are:
a. Excessive gear noise.
b. Difficult shifting.
c. Gears pop out of mesh.
d. Incorrect shift lever operation.

Transmission symptoms are sometimes hard to distinguish from clutch symptoms. The troubleshooting chart in **Figure 6** lists transmission troubles and checks to make. Refer to Chapter Six for transmission service procedures. Be sure that the clutch is not causing the trouble before working on the transmission.

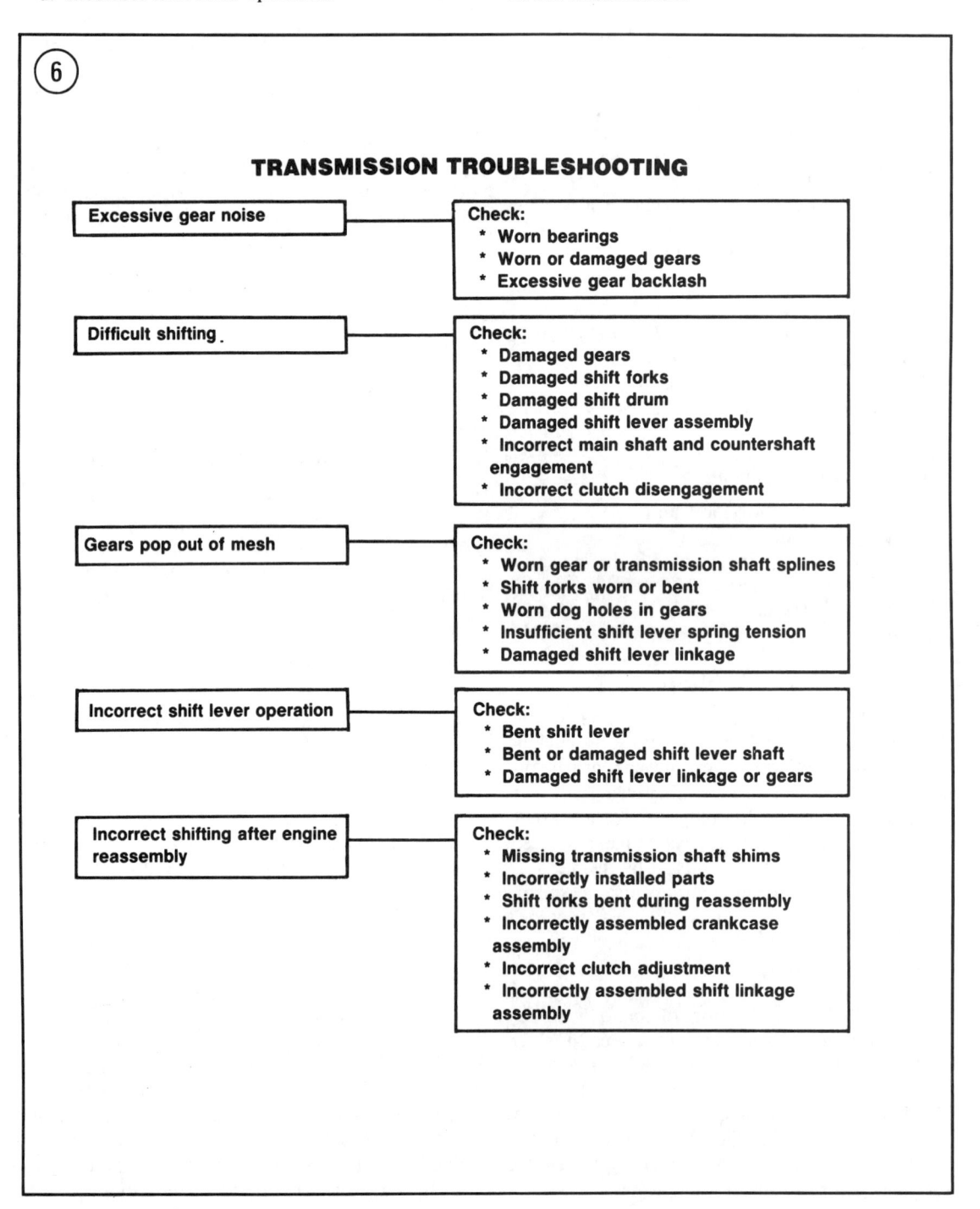

(6)

TRANSMISSION TROUBLESHOOTING

Excessive gear noise
Check:
* Worn bearings
* Worn or damaged gears
* Excessive gear backlash

Difficult shifting
Check:
* Damaged gears
* Damaged shift forks
* Damaged shift drum
* Damaged shift lever assembly
* Incorrect main shaft and countershaft engagement
* Incorrect clutch disengagement

Gears pop out of mesh
Check:
* Worn gear or transmission shaft splines
* Shift forks worn or bent
* Worn dog holes in gears
* Insufficient shift lever spring tension
* Damaged shift lever linkage

Incorrect shift lever operation
Check:
* Bent shift lever
* Bent or damaged shift lever shaft
* Damaged shift lever linkage or gears

Incorrect shifting after engine reassembly
Check:
* Missing transmission shaft shims
* Incorrectly installed parts
* Shift forks bent during reassembly
* Incorrectly assembled crankcase assembly
* Incorrect clutch adjustment
* Incorrectly assembled shift linkage assembly

TROUBLESHOOTING

ELECTRICAL PROBLEMS

If bulbs burn out frequently, the cause may be excessive vibration, loose connections that permit sudden current surges, or the installation of the wrong type of bulb.

Most light and ignition problems are caused by loose or corroded ground connections. Check these prior to replacing a bulb or electrical component.

EXCESSIVE VIBRATION

Usually this is caused by loose engine mounting hardware. If not, it can be difficult to find without disassembling the engine. High speed vibration may be due to a bent axle shaft or loose or faulty suspension components. Vibration can also be caused by the following conditions:
  a. Broken frame.
  b. Worn drive chain.
  c. Improperly balanced wheels.
  d. Defective or damaged wheels.
  e. Defective or damaged tires.
  f. Internal engine wear or damage.

CARBURETOR TROUBLESHOOTING

Basic carburetor troubleshooting procedures are found in **Figure 7**.

FRONT SUSPENSION AND STEERING

Poor handling may be caused by improper tire pressure, a damaged or bent frame or front steering components, worn wheel bearings or dragging brakes. Possible causes of suspension and steering malfunctions are listed below.

Irregular or Wobbly Steering

  a. Loose wheel axle nuts.
  b. Loose or worn steering head bearings.
  c. Excessive wheel hub bearing play.
  d. Damaged wheel.
  e. Unbalanced wheel assembly.
  f. Worn hub bearings.
  g. Incorrect wheel alignment.
  h. Bent or damaged steering stem or frame (at steering neck).
  i. Tire incorrectly seated on rim.
  j. Excessive front end loading from non-standard equipment.
  k. Damaged fairing assembly.
  l. Loose fairing mounts or brackets.

Stiff Steering

  a. Low front tire air pressure.
  b. Bent or damaged steering stem or frame (at steering neck).
  c. Loose or worn steering head bearings.

Stiff or Heavy Fork Operation

  a. Incorrect fork springs.
  b. Incorrect fork oil viscosity.
  c. Excessive amount of fork oil.
  d. Bent fork tubes.
  e. Excessive front fork air pressure.

Poor Fork Operation

  a. Worn or damaged fork tubes.
  b. Fork oil level low due to leaking fork seals.
  c. Bent or damaged fork tubes.
  d. Contaminated fork oil.
  e. Worn fork springs.
  f. Heavy front end loading from non-standard equipment.

Poor Rear Shock Absorber Operation

  a. Damper unit leaking.
  b. Incorrect rear shock adjustment.
  c. Heavy rear end loading from non-standard equipment.
  d. Incorrect loading.

BRAKE PROBLEMS

Sticking disc brakes may be caused by a stuck piston(s) in a caliper assembly, warped pad shim(s) or improper rear brake adjustment. See **Figure 8** for disc brake troubles and checks to make.

⑦ CARBURETOR TROUBLESHOOTING

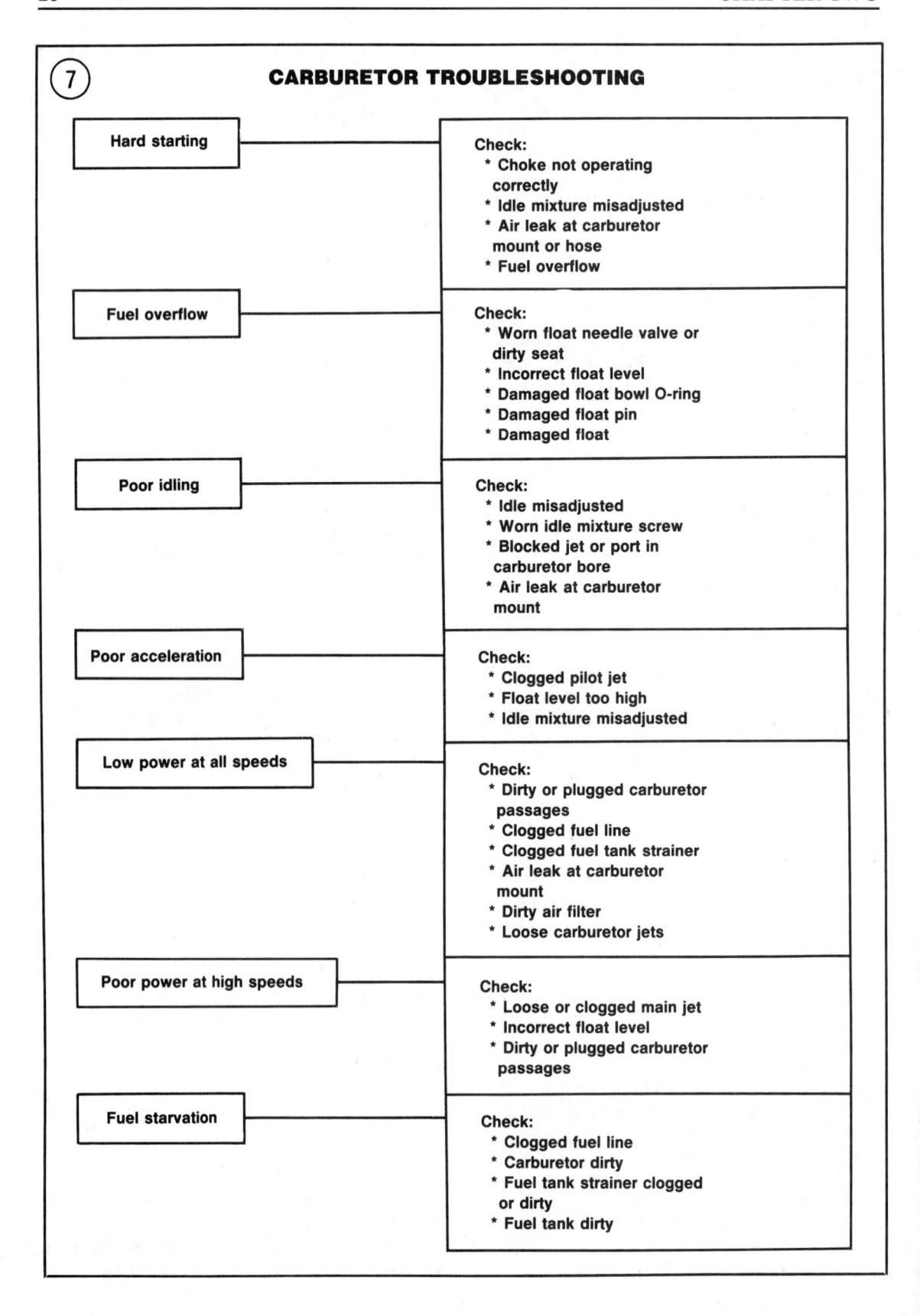

Hard starting	Check: * Choke not operating correctly * Idle mixture misadjusted * Air leak at carburetor mount or hose * Fuel overflow
Fuel overflow	Check: * Worn float needle valve or dirty seat * Incorrect float level * Damaged float bowl O-ring * Damaged float pin * Damaged float
Poor idling	Check: * Idle misadjusted * Worn idle mixture screw * Blocked jet or port in carburetor bore * Air leak at carburetor mount
Poor acceleration	Check: * Clogged pilot jet * Float level too high * Idle mixture misadjusted
Low power at all speeds	Check: * Dirty or plugged carburetor passages * Clogged fuel line * Clogged fuel tank strainer * Air leak at carburetor mount * Dirty air filter * Loose carburetor jets
Poor power at high speeds	Check: * Loose or clogged main jet * Incorrect float level * Dirty or plugged carburetor passages
Fuel starvation	Check: * Clogged fuel line * Carburetor dirty * Fuel tank strainer clogged or dirty * Fuel tank dirty

TROUBLESHOOTING

(8)

DISC BRAKE TROUBLESHOOTING

Disc brake fluid leakage	Check: * Loose or damaged line fittings * Worn caliper piston seals * Scored caliper piston and/or bore * Loose banjo bolts * Damaged sealing washers * Leaking master cylinder diaphragm * Leaking master cylinder secondary seal * Cracked master cylinder housing * Too high brake fluid level * Loose master cylinder cover
Brake overheating	Check: * Warped brake disc * Incorrect brake fluid * Caliper piston and/or brake pads hanging up * Riding brakes during riding
Brake chatter	Check: * Warped brake disc * Loose brake disc * Incorrect caliper alignment * Loose caliper mounting bolts * Loose front axle nut and/or clamps * Worn wheel bearings * Damaged front hub * Restricted brake hydraulic line * Contaminated brake pads
Brake locking	Check: * Incorrect brake fluid * Plugged passages in master cylinder * Incorrect front brake adjustment * Caliper piston and/or brake pads hanging up * Warped brake disc
Insufficient brakes	Check: * Air in brake lines * Worn brake pads * Low brake fluid level * Incorrect brake fluid * Worn brake disc * Worn caliper piston seals * Glazed brake pads * Leaking primary cup seal in master cylinder * Contaminated brake pads and/or disc
Brake squeal	Check: * Contaminated brake pads and/or disc * Dust or dirt collected behind brake pads * Loose parts

CHAPTER THREE

PERIODIC LUBRICATION, MAINTENANCE AND TUNE-UP

Your bike can be cared for by two methods: preventive and corrective maintenance. Because a motorcycle is subjected to tremendous heat, stress and vibration—even in normal use—preventive maintenance prevents costly and unexpected corrective maintenance. When neglected, any bike becomes unreliable and actually dangerous to ride. When properly maintained, your Yamaha is one of the most reliable bikes available and will give many miles and years of dependable, fast and safe riding. By maintaining a routine service schedule as described in this chapter, costly mechanical problems and unexpected breakdowns can be prevented.

The procedures presented in this chapter can be easily performed by anyone with average mechanical skills. **Table 1** is a suggested factory maintenance schedule. **Tables 1-10** are located at the end of this chapter.

ROUTINE CHECKS

The following simple checks should be carried out at each fuel stop.

Engine Oil Level

Refer to *Engine Oil Level Check* under *Periodic Lubrication* in this chapter.

Coolant Level

Check the coolant level when the engine is cool.
1. On FZ700 models, support the bike so that it is level.
2. Check the level through the level gauge in the coolant reserve tank. The level should be between the "FULL" and "LOW" marks (**Figure 1**). If necessary, add water to the reserve tank (not to the radiator) so the level is to the "FULL" mark.

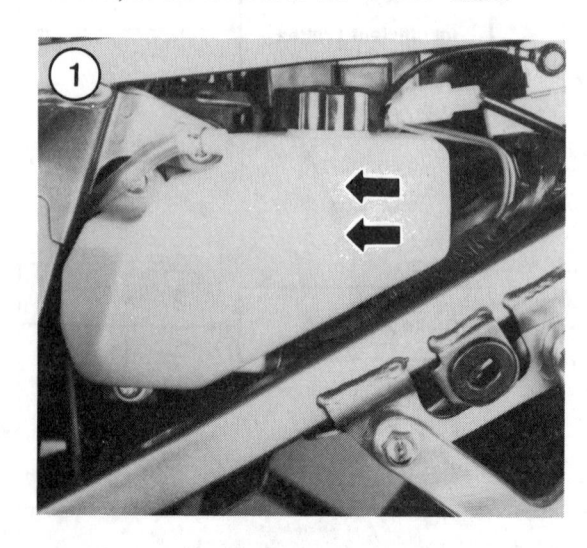

PERIODIC LUBRICATION, MAINTENANCE AND TUNE-UP

General Inspection

1. Examine the engine for signs of oil or fuel leakage.
2. Check the tires for embedded stones. Pry them out with your ignition key.
3. Make sure all lights work.

NOTE
At least check the brake light. It can burn out anytime. Motorists cannot stop as quickly as you and need all the warning you can give.

Tire Pressure

Tire pressure must be checked with the tires cold. Correct tire pressure depends on the load you are carrying. See **Table 2**.

Battery

The battery must be removed to check the electrolyte level. For complete details see *Battery Removal/Installation and Electrolyte Level Check* in this chapter.

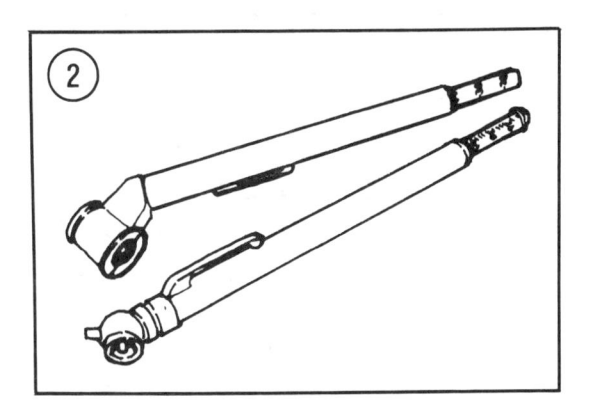

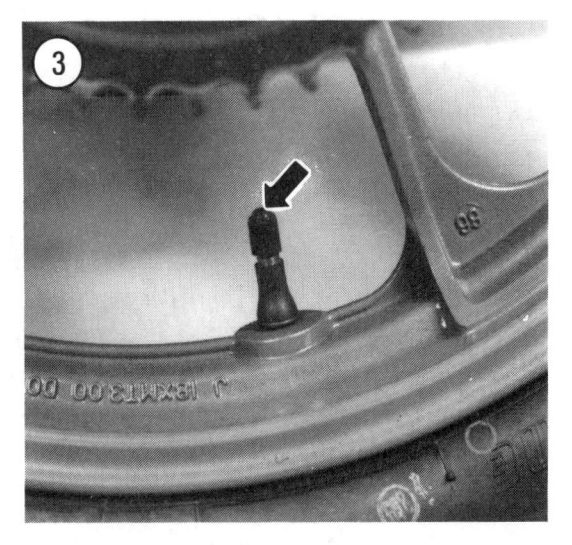

Lights and Horn

With the engine running, check the following.
1. Pull the front brake lever and check that the brake light comes on.
2. Push the rear brake pedal and check that the brake light comes on soon after you have begun depressing the pedal.
3. With the engine running, check to see that the headlight and taillight are on.
4. Move the dimmer switch up and down between the high and low positions and check to see that both headlight elements are working.
5. Push the turn signal switch to the left position and the right position and check that all 4 turn signal lights are working.
6. Push the horn button and note that the horn blows loudly.
7. If the horn or any light failed to work properly, refer to Chapter Eight.

MAINTENANCE INTERVALS

The services and intervals shown in **Table 1** are recommended by the factory. Strict adherence to these recommendations will insure long life from your Yamaha. If the bike is run in an area of high humidity, the lubrication services must be done more frequently to prevent possible rust damage.

For convenience when maintaining your motorcycle, most of the services shown in **Table 1** are described in this chapter. Those procedures which require more than minor disassembly or adjustment are covered elsewhere in the appropriate chapter. The *Table of Contents* and *Index* can help you locate a particular service procedure.

TIRES

Tire Pressure

Tire pressure should be checked and adjusted to accommodate rider and luggage weight. A simple, accurate gauge (**Figure 2**) can be purchased for a few dollars and should be carried in your motorcycle tool kit. The appropriate tire pressures are shown in **Table 2**.

NOTE
*After checking and adjusting the air pressure, make sure to reinstall the air valve cap (**Figure 3**). The cap prevents small pebbles and/or dirt from collecting in the valve stem; this could allow air leakage or result in incorrect tire pressure readings.*

Tire Inspection

The likelihood of tire failure increases with tread wear. It is estimated that the majority of all tire failures occur during the last 10% of usable tread wear. Check tire tread for excessive wear, deep cuts and embedded objects such as stones, nails, etc.

Check also for high spots that indicate internal tire damage. Replace tires that show high spots or swelling. If you find a nail in a tire, mark its location with a light crayon before pulling it out. This will help locate the hole for repair. Refer to *Tubeless Tires and Tubeless Tire Changing* in Chapter Ten.

Measure tread wear at the center of the tire with a tread depth gauge (**Figure 4**) or small ruler. Because tires sometimes wear unevenly, measure wear at several points. Minimum tread depth for front and rear tires is 1.0 mm (0.04 in.).

Rim Inspection

Frequently inspect the wheel rims (**Figure 5**). If a rim has been damaged it might have been knocked out of alignment. Improper wheel alignment can cause severe vibration and result in an unsafe riding condition. If any portion of an alloy wheel is damaged the wheel must be replaced as it cannot be repaired.

BATTERY

CAUTION
If it becomes necessary to remove the battery breather tube when performing any of the following procedures, make sure to route the tube correctly during installation to prevent electrolyte or gas from spewing onto the frame, chain or any other component. Incorrect breather tube routing can cause structural and/or cosmetic damage.

Removal/Installation and Electrolyte Level Check

The battery is the heart of the electrical system. It should be checked and serviced as indicated in **Table 1**. Most electrical system troubles can be attributed to neglect of this vital component.

In order to correctly service the electrolyte level it is necessary to remove the battery from the frame. The electrolyte level should be maintained between the two marks on the battery case (**Figure 6**). If the electrolyte level is low, it's a good idea to completely clean, service and check the battery.

1. Remove the seat.
2. Disconnect the battery hold-down strap.
3. Disconnect the negative battery cable (A, **Figure 7**) from the battery.
4. Disconnect the positive battery cable (B, **Figure 7**).
5. Lift the battery up slightly and disconnect the battery breather tube.
6. Lift the battery out of the battery box and remove it.

WARNING
Protect your eyes, skin and clothing. If electrolyte gets into your eyes, flush your eyes thoroughly with clean water and get prompt medical attention.

CAUTION
Be careful not to spill battery electrolyte on painted or polished surfaces. The liquid is highly corrosive and will damage the finish. If it is spilled, wash it off immediately with soapy water and thoroughly rinse with clean water.

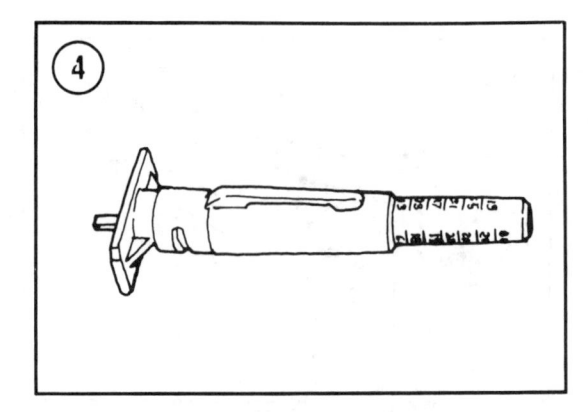

PERIODIC LUBRICATION, MAINTENANCE AND TUNE-UP

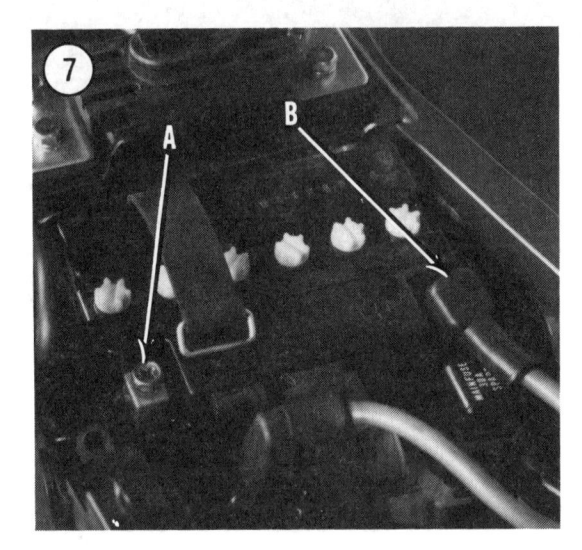

7. Rinse the battery off with clean water and wipe dry.

8. Remove the caps (**Figure 8**) from the battery cells and add distilled water. Never add electrolyte (acid) to correct the level. Fill only to the upper battery level mark (**Figure 6**).

9. After the level has been corrected and the battery allowed to stand for a few minutes, check the specific gravity of the electrolyte in each cell with a hydrometer (**Figure 9**). Follow the manufacturer's instructions for reading the instrument. See *Battery Testing* in this chapter.

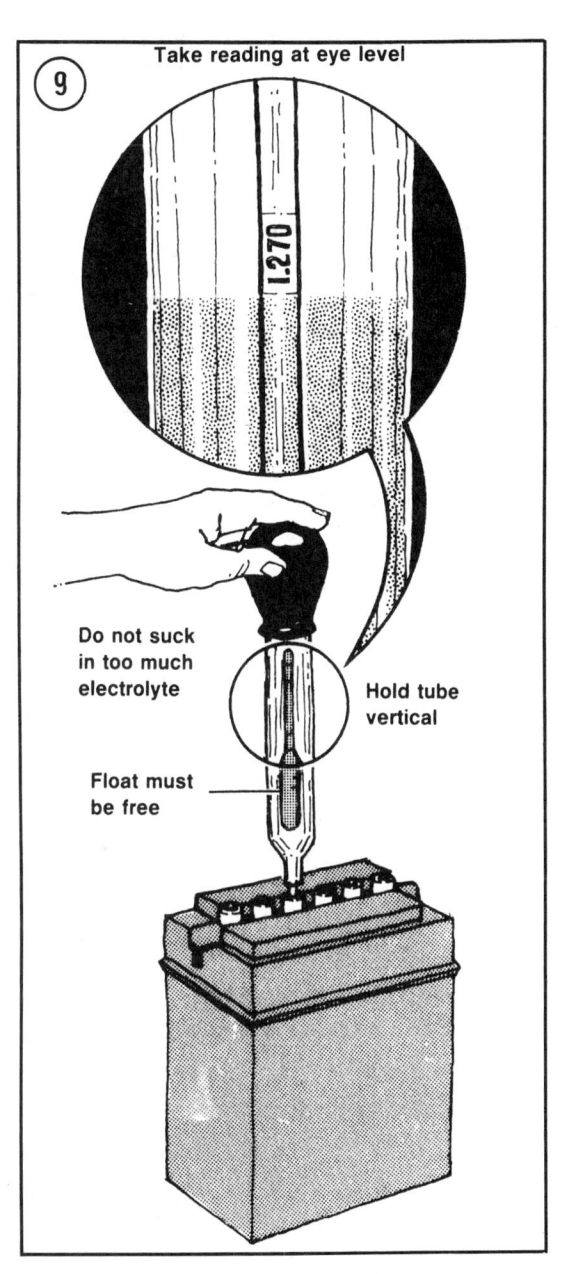

10. After the battery has been refilled, recharged or replaced, install it by reversing these removal steps.

CAUTION
Make sure to reconnect the battery breather tube to the battery. If the tube was removed with the battery, make sure to route it in its correct position.

CAUTION
*Make sure to reconnect the battery hold-down strap (**Figure 10**) to prevent the battery from vibrating during service. Vibration can damage the battery plates and short out the battery.*

Testing

Hydrometer testing is the best way to check battery condition. Use a hydrometer with numbered graduations from 1.100 to 1.300 rather than one with just color-coded bands. To use the hydrometer, squeeze the rubber ball, insert the tip into the cell and release the ball. Draw enough electrolyte to float the weighted float inside the hydrometer. Note the number in line with the electrolyte surface; this is the specific gravity for this cell. Return the electrolyte to the cell from which it came. See **Figure 9**.

The specific gravity of the electrolyte in each battery cell is an excellent indication of that cell's condition (**Table 3**). A fully charged cell will read 1.260-1.280.

NOTE
Specific gravity varies slightly with temperature. Make sure the battery is at room temperature before testing.

If the cells test in the poor range, the battery requires recharging. The hydrometer is useful for checking the progress of the charging operation. **Table 3** shows approximate state of charge.

Charging

CAUTION
Always remove the battery from the motorcycle before connecting charging equipment.

WARNING
During charging, highly explosive hydrogen gas is released from the battery. The battery should be charged only in a well-ventilated area, and open flames and cigarettes should be kept away. Never check the charge of the battery by arcing across the terminals; the resulting spark can ignite the hydrogen gas.

1. Remove the battery from the motorcycle as described in this chapter.
2. Connect the positive (+) charger lead to the positive battery terminal and the negative (-) charger lead to the negative battery terminal.

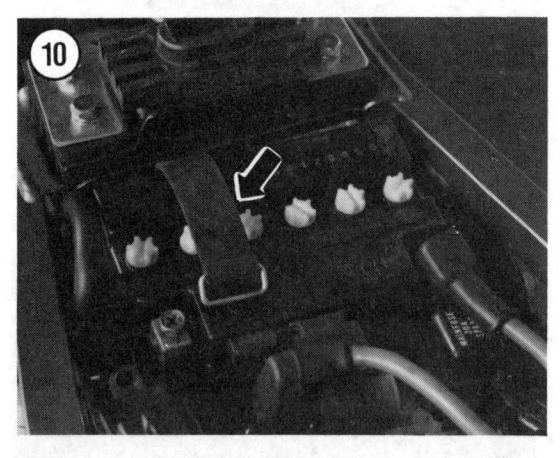

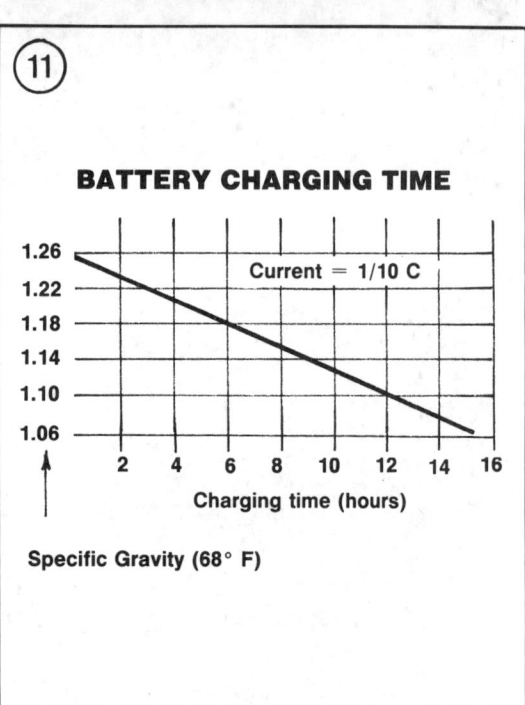

PERIODIC LUBRICATION, MAINTENANCE AND TUNE-UP

3. Remove all vent caps from the battery, set the charger at 12 volts, and switch it on. Normally, a battery should be charged at a slow charge rate of 1/10 its given capacity. The recommended charging rate for batteries in models covered in this manual is 1.4 amps.

CAUTION
The electrolyte level must be maintained at the upper level during the charging cycle; check and refill as necessary.

4. The charging time depends on the discharged condition of the battery. The chart in **Figure 11** can be used to determine approximate charging times at different specific gravity readings. For example, if the specific gravity of your battery is 1.180, the approximate charging time would be 6 hours.

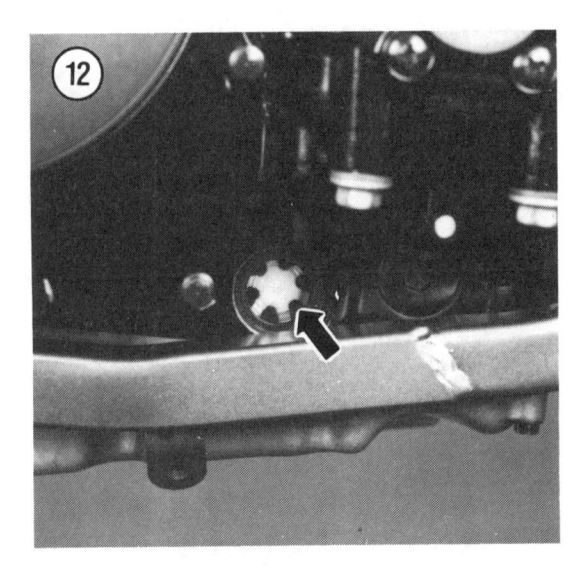

5. To ensure good electrical contact, cables must be clean and tight on the battery's terminals. If the cable terminals are badly corroded, even after performing the above cleaning procedures, the cables should be disconnected, removed from the bike and cleaned separately with a wire brush and a baking soda solution. After cleaning, apply a very thin coating of petroleum jelly (Vaseline) to the battery terminals before reattaching the cables. After connecting the cables, apply a light coating to the connections also—this will delay future corrosion.

New Battery Installation

When replacing the old battery with a new one, be sure to charge it completely (specific gravity, 1.260-1.280) before installing it in the bike. Failure to do so, or using the battery with a low electrolyte level, will permanently damage the battery. When purchasing a new battery, the correct battery capacity for models covered in this manual is 12 volts/14 amp hours.

PERIODIC LUBRICATION

Engine Oil Level Check

Engine oil level is checked through the inspection window located at the bottom of the clutch cover (**Figure 12**).

NOTE
*On FZ700 models, the oil inspection window can be observed by looking through the inspection hole in the fairing. See (**Figure 13**).*

1. Start the engine and let it reach normal operating temperature.
2. Stop the engine and allow the oil to settle.
3. On models with center stand, park the vehicle on the center stand. On models without center stand, have an assistant hold the bike so that it is *straight up and level*.

CAUTION
If the bike is not parked correctly, an incorrect oil level reading will be observed.

4. The oil level should be between the maximum and minimum window marks (**Figure 12** or **Figure 13**). If necessary, remove the oil fill cap (**Figure 14**) and add the recommended oil (**Table 4**) to raise the oil to the proper level. Do not overfill.

Engine Oil and Filter Change

The factory-recommended oil and filter change interval is specified in **Table 1**. This assumes that the motorcycle is operated in moderate climates. The time interval is more important than the mileage interval because combustion acids formed by gasoline and water vapor will contaminate the oil eve if the motorcycle is not run for several months. If a motorcycle is operated under dusty conditions, the oil will get dirty more quickly and should be changed more frequently than recommended.

Use only a detergent oil with an API classification of SF. The classification is printed on top of the can (**Figure 15**) or on the container label. Try always to use the same brand of oil. Use of oil additives is not recommended. Refer to **Table 4** for correct weight of oil to use under different temperatures.

To change the engine oil and filter you will need the following:

  a. Drain pan.
  b. Funnel.
  c. Can opener or pour spout.
  d. Wrench or socket to remove drain plug.
  e. Oil (see **Table 5**).
  f. Oil filter element.
  g. Heavy gloves to prevent burns.

There are a number of ways to discard the used oil safely. The easiest way is to pour it from the drain pan into a gallon plastic bleach, juice or milk container for disposal.

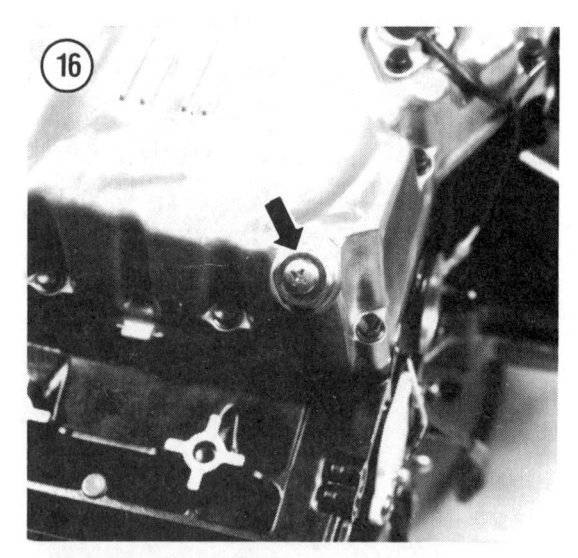

PERIODIC LUBRICATION, MAINTENANCE AND TUNE-UP

NOTE
Some service stations and oil retailers will accept your used oil for recycling. Do not discard oil in your household trash or pour it onto the ground.

1. Place the motorcycle on the center stand or secure it so that it is level.
2. *FZ700 and FZ750:* Remove the lower fairing as described in Chapter Thirteen.
3. Start the engine and run it until it is at normal operating temperature, then turn it off.
4. Place a drain pan under the crankcase and remove the drain plug (with a socket) from the oil pan. See **Figure 16** (typical).

NOTE
Figure 16 *shows the engine removed for clarity.*

5. Replace the oil filter as follows:

CAUTION
The oil filter mounting bolt is made of soft material. To prevent damaging the bolt head, always loosen the bolt with a socket or box-end wrench. Do not use an adjustable wrench.

WARNING
*The exhaust pipes will be **hot**. Wear thick work gloves when removing the oil filter.*

a. Unscrew the filter mounting bolt (**Figure 17**) at the front of the engine and remove the filter cover O-ring assembly.
b. Hold the mounting bolt (**Figure 18**) and turn the filter cover (**Figure 19**) then remove the oil filter element. Discard the oil filter.
c. Remove the washer (**Figure 20**) and spring (**Figure 21**).

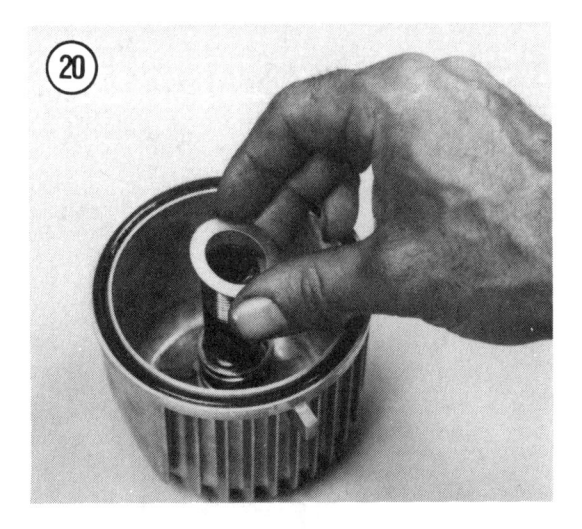

d. Pull the mounting bolt (**Figure 18**) out of the filter cover.
e. Inspect the filter cover O-ring (**Figure 22**) and mounting bolt O-ring (A, **Figure 23**). Replace the O-rings if deformed, cracked or if the filter cover leaked previously.
f. Clean the filter cover of all oil residue.
g. The oil filter bypass valve (B, **Figure 23**) is located in the mounting bolt. Clean the mounting bolt in solvent and check bypass valve assembly for damage. Check the mounting bolt hex head (C, **Figure 23**) for damage that could make further removal of the bolt difficult. Replace the bolt if necessary.
h. Wipe the crankcase gasket surface with a clean, lint-free cloth. Install the new oil filter as follows (**Figure 24**).
i. With the mounting bolt and filter cover O-rings installed, insert the bolt through the filter cover.
j. Slide the spring (**Figure 21**) and washer (**Figure 20**) over the mounting bolt.
k. Install the oil filter (**Figure 19**) by turning it onto the mounting bolt. Make sure the rubber grommets (**Figure 25**) on both sides of the oil filter do not dislodge or tear.
l. Install the oil filter assembly into the crankcase. Align the tab on the filter housing with the notch on the crankcase (**Figure 26**). Tighten the mounting bolt to 15 N•m (11 ft.-lb.).

CAUTION
The mounting bolt is made of soft material. To prevent damaging the hex head, always tighten the bolt with a socket or box-end wrench. Do not use an adjustable wrench.

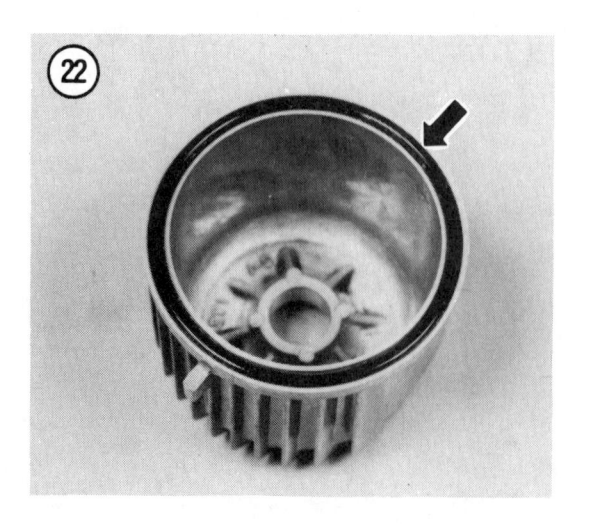

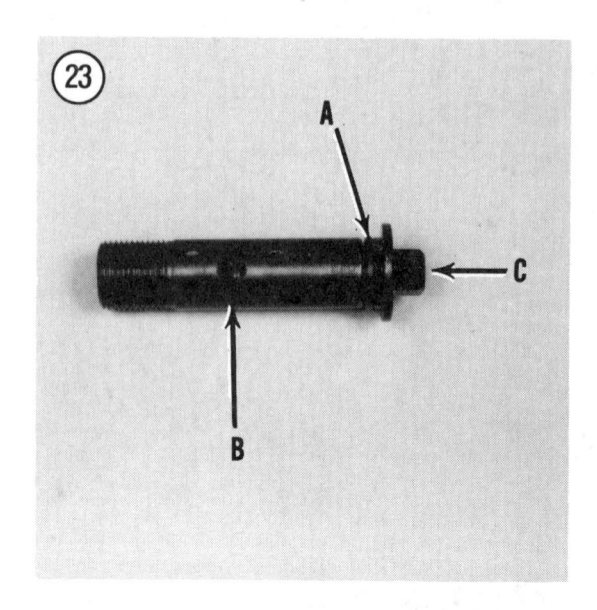

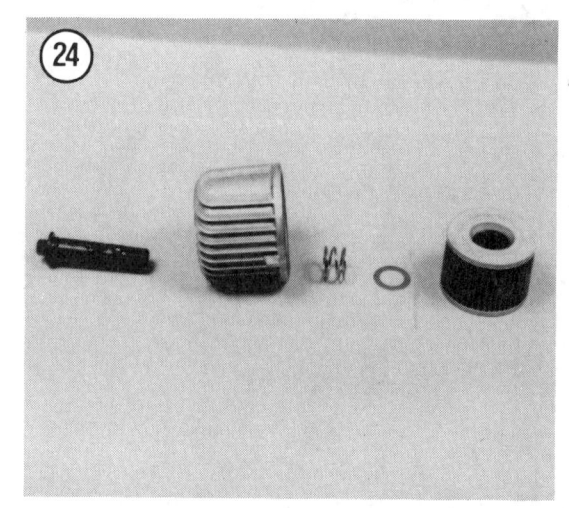

PERIODIC LUBRICATION, MAINTENANCE AND TUNE-UP

6. Replace the oil drain plug gasket if deformed.
7. Install the oil drain plug and gasket and tighten to 43 N•m (31 ft.-lb.).
8. Remove the oil filler cap (**Figure 14**) and fill the crankcase with the correct weight (**Table 4**) and quantity of oil (**Table 5**).
9. Screw in the oil fill plug securely.
10. After completing Step 9, check the oil pressure as follows:
   a. Slightly loosen the oil check bolt in the cylinder head (**Figure 27**).
   b. Start the engine and allow it to idle. Do not increase engine speed.
   c. Oil should seep out of the hole (**Figure 27**) within one minute. If oil seeps out of the hole, engine oil pressure is okay. If not, immediately stop the engine and check the lubrication system.

See *Oil Pump and Strainer, Service Notes* in Chapter Four.

11. Turn the engine off and allow the oil to settle. Then check for correct oil level as described under *Engine Oil Level Check* in this chapter. Adjust if necessary.
12. *FZ700 and FZ750:* Reinstall the lower fairing assembly as described in Chapter Thirteen.

Front Fork Oil Change

1. Support the front end so that the front tire is clear of the ground.
2A. *FZX700:* Remove the air valve cap from one of the fork tubes and depress the valve stem (**Figure 28**) with a screwdriver to release all air from the fork tube. Repeat for the opposite fork tube. Remove the valve stem(s) from the air valve.
2B. *FZ750:* Remove the air valve cap from the right-hand fork tube and depress the valve stem (**Figure 29**) with a screwdriver to release all air from both fork tubes. Remove the valve stem(s) from the air valve.

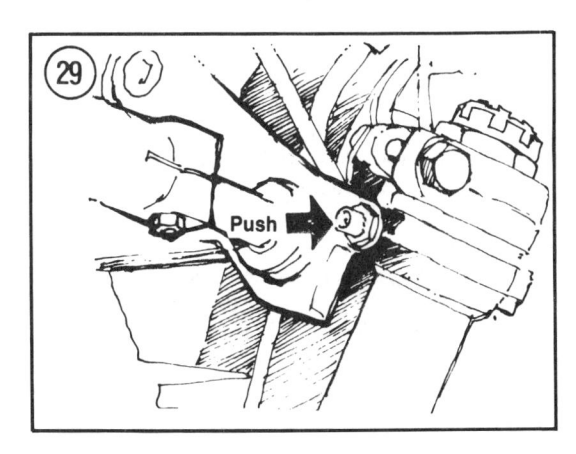

3. Place a drain pan beside one fork tube and remove the drain screw (**Figure 30**). Allow the oil to drain until it stops. Then with both of the bike's wheels on the ground, apply the front brake and push down on the front end and allow it to return. Repeat to remove as much oil as possible.

WARNING
Do not allow the fork oil to come in contact with any of the brake components.

4. Install the drain screw (**Figure 30**).
5. Repeat Steps 3 and 4 for the opposite side.
6. Raise the vehicle front end so that the front wheel clears the ground. Reinstall the valve stem(s) into the air valve.
7. Loosen the upper steering stem pinch bolts (A, **Figure 31**) and loosen the fork cap (B, **Figure 31**).
8. Working on one fork tube only, perform the following:
    a. *FZX700:* Remove the fork cap, spring seat and spring.
    b. *FZ700:* Remove the fork cap, spring seat and spring.
    c. *FZ750:* Remove the fork cap, spacer, spring seat and spring.
9. Fill the fork tube with the specified quantity of oil (**Table 5**). **Table 4** lists the recommended fork oil to use.

NOTE
In order to measure the correct amount of fluid, use a baby bottle. These bottles have measurements in cubic centimeters (cc) and fluid ounces (oz.) imprinted on the side.

10. After filling the fork tube, slowly pump the forks up and down to distribute the oil throughout the fork damper.

CAUTION
An excessive amount of oil can cause a hydraulic locking of the forks during compression.

11. Reverse Step 8 to reinstall the spring, spacer (FZ750), spring seat and fork cap. Install the fork spring so that the end with the coils closest together face to the *top*. Tighten the fork cap to 23 N•m (17 ft.-lb.). Tighten the steering stem pinch bolt to 20 N•m (14 ft.-lb.).
12. Repeat Steps 3-11 for the opposite side.
13. *FZX700 and FZ750:* Fill the forks with air as described under *Front Fork Air Adjustment* in this chapter.
14. Road test the bike and check for oil and air leaks.

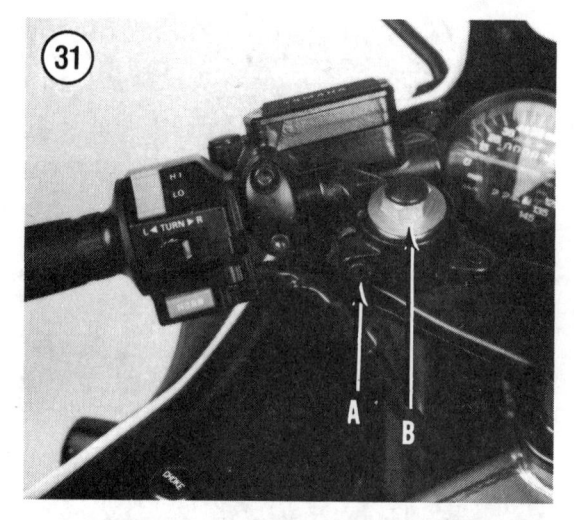

PERIODIC LUBRICATION, MAINTENANCE AND TUNE-UP

Throttle Cable Lubrication

The throttle cable should be lubricated at the intervals specified in **Table 1**. At this time, it should also be inspected for fraying, and the cable sheath should be checked for chafing. The throttle cable is relatively inexpensive and should be replaced when found to be faulty.

The throttle cable can be lubricated with cable lubricant and a cable lubricator available at most motorcycle dealers.

NOTE
The main cause of cable breakage or cable stiffness is improper lubrication. Maintaining the throttle cable as described in this section will assure long service life.

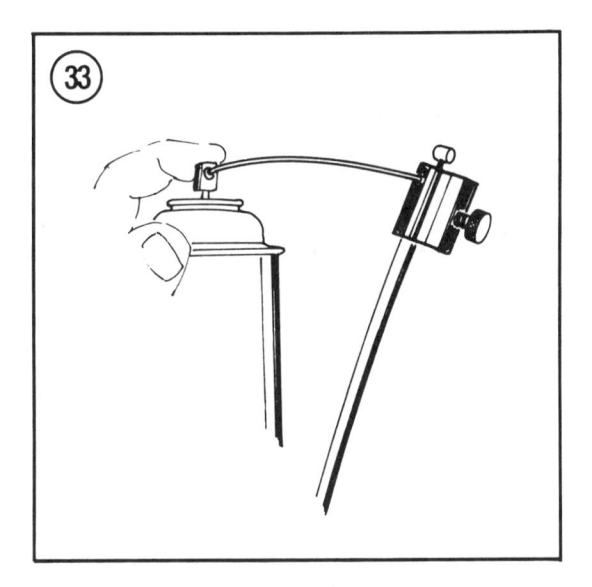

1. Remove the screws securing the throttle housing (**Figure 32**) and separate the throttle housing assembly. Disconnect the throttle cable from the twist grip and remove it from the throttle housing.
2. Attach a cable lubricator (**Figure 33**) to the cable following the manufacturer's instructions.
3. Insert the nozzle of the lubricant can into the lubricator, then press the button on the can and hold it down until the lubricant begins to flow out of the other end of the cable.

NOTE
Place a shop cloth at the end of the cable to catch all excess lubricant that will flow out.

NOTE
If lubricant does not flow out the end of the cable, check the entire cable for fraying, bending or other damage.

4. Remove the lubricator, reconnect and adjust the throttle cable as described under *Throttle Cable Adjustment* in this chapter.

Swing Arm Bearings Lubrication

The rear swing arm needle bearings should be cleaned in solvent and lubricated with a molybdenum disulfide grease at the intervals specified in **Table 1**. The swing arm must be removed to service the needle bearings. Refer to *Rear Swing Arm Removal/Installation* in Chapter Eleven.

Relay Arm and Connecting Arm Lubrication (FZ700 and FZ750)

The relay arm and connecting rod needle bearings should be cleaned in solvent and lubricated with molybdenum disulfide grease at the intervals specified in **Table 1**. The relay arm linkage must be removed to service the needle bearings. Refer to *Relay arm and Connecting Rod Removal/Installation* in Chapter Eleven.

Speedometer Cable Lubrication

Lubricate the speedometer cable every year or whenever needle operation is erratic.

1. Unscrew the end of the speedometer cable (**Figure 34**) at the instrument cluster and at the front wheel (**Figure 35**).

2. Pull the cable from the sheath.
3. If the grease is contaminated, thoroughly clean off all old grease.
4. Thoroughly coat the cable with a good grade of multi-purpose grease and reinstall into the sheath.
5. Make sure the cable is correctly seated into the speedometer drive unit (**Figure 36**).

Wheel Bearings
Inspection/Lubrication

Worn wheel bearings cause excessive wheel play that results in vibration and other steering troubles. At the intervals specified in **Table 1**, the bearings should be inspected and lubricated with wheel bearing grease. Refer to *Front Hub* in Chapter Ten and *Rear Hub* in Chapter Eleven.

Steering Stem Lubrication

Refer to *Steering Head* in Chapter Ten.

Drive Chain Lubrication

Yamaha recommends SAE 30 to SAE 50 motor oil or a chain lubricant *specified* for use on O-ring drive chains for lubrication; it is less likely to be thrown off the chain than lighter oils.

NOTE
*If the drive chain is obviously dirty, remove and clean it as described under **Drive Chain Cleaning** in Chapter Eleven before lubricating it as described in this procedure.*

CAUTION
*The factory drive chain is equipped with O-rings between the side plates (**Figure 37**) that seal lubricant between the pins and bushings. To prevent damaging these O-rings, use only kerosene for cleaning. Do not use gasoline or other solvents that will cause the O-rings to swell or deteriorate. Refer to cleaning procedures in Chapter Eleven.*

1. Place the bike on the center stand. On FZ700 models, support the bike so that the rear wheel clears the ground.
2. Oil the bottom chain run with SAE 30 to 50 motor oil or a commercial drive chain lubricant (approved for O-ring use). Concentrate on getting the oil down behind the side plates of the chain links (**Figure 37**).
3. Rotate the rear wheel and continue until the entire chain has been lubricated.

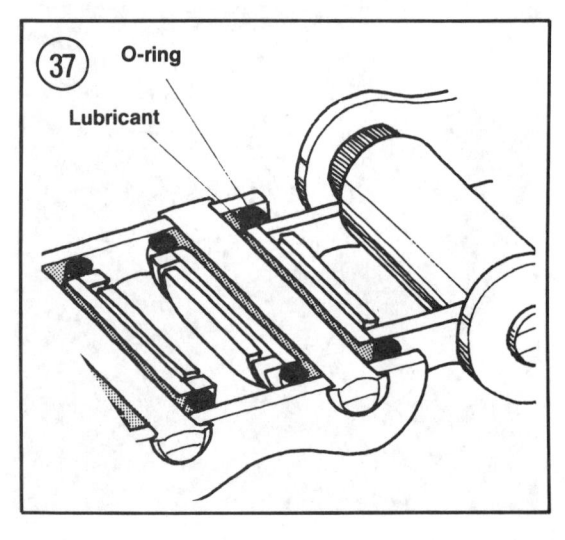

PERIODIC LUBRICATION, MAINTENANCE AND TUNE-UP

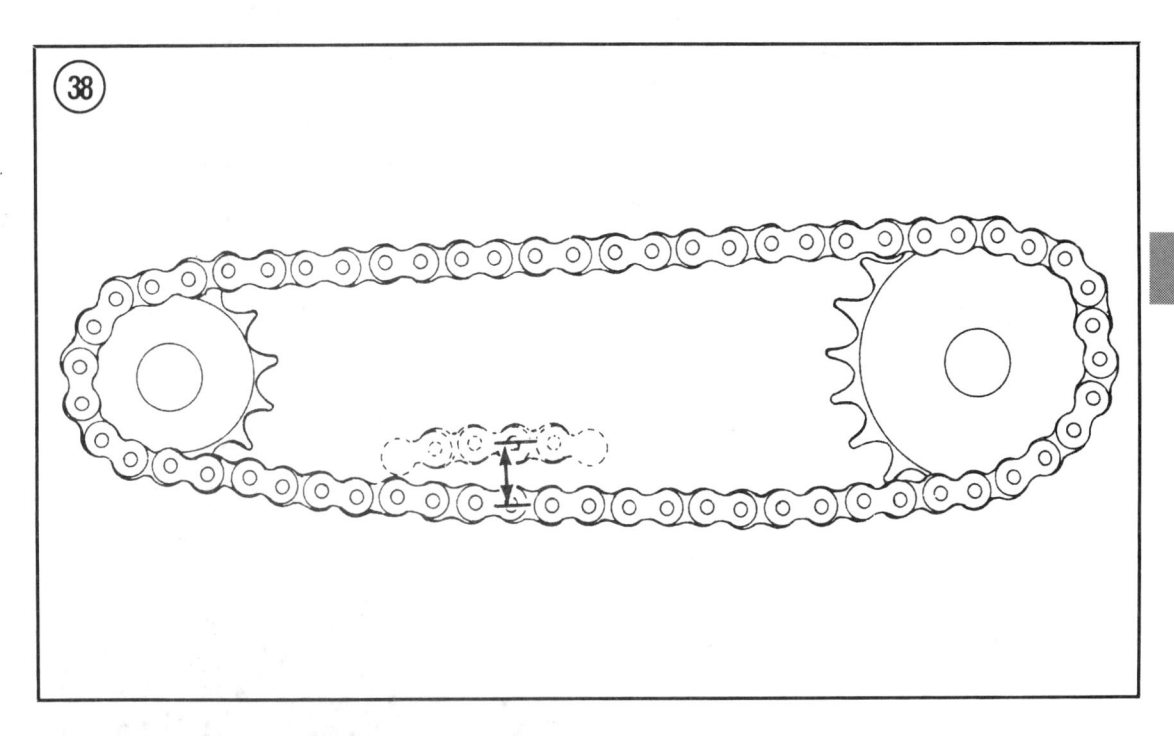

PERIODIC MAINTENANCE

Drive Chain Adjustment

NOTE
As drive chains stretch and wear in use, the chain will become tighter at one point. The chain must be checked and adjusted at this point.

1. Place the motorcycle on the center stand. On FZ700 models, support the bike so that the rear wheel clears the ground.
2. Turn the rear wheel and check the chain for its tightest point. Mark this spot and turn the wheel so that the mark is located on the chains lower run, midway between both drive sprockets. Check and adjust the drive chain as follows.
3. With thumb and forefinger, lift up and press down the chain at that point, measuring the distance the chain moves vertically.
4. The drive chain should have approximately 15-20 mm (19/32-25/32 in.) of vertical travel at midpoint (**Figure 38**). If necessary, adjust the chain as follows.
5. Remove the rear axle cotter pin and loosen the axle nut (**Figure 39**).
6. Loosen the axle adjuster locknut (A, **Figure 40**) on both sides of the wheel.
7. Turn each adjuster nut (B, **Figure 40**) clockwise to take up slack in the chain. To loosen the chain, turn each adjuster bolt counterclockwise. Be sure to turn each adjuster stud equally to maintain rear

wheel alignment. Alignment is checked by observing the swing arm marks (**Figure 41**) on both sides of the swing arm. Adjust the chain until the correct amount of free play is obtained (Step 4). See **Figure 38**.

8. Check rear wheel alignment by sighting along the chain as it runs over the rear sprocket. It should not appear to bend sideways. See **Figure 42**.
9. Tighten the rear axle nut to 107 N•m (77 ft.-lb.). Tighten the adjuster locknut (A, **Figure 40**) to 15 N•m (11 ft.-lb.).
10. Recheck chain play.
11. Install a new cotter pin through the rear axle and bend the ends over to lock it (**Figure 39**).
12. Perform the *Rear Brake Light Switch Adjustment* in this chapter.

Disc Brake Inspection

The hydraulic brake fluid in the disc brake master cylinders should be checked every month. The disc brake pads should be checked at the intervals specified in **Table 1**. Replacement is described under *Brake Pad Replacement* in Chapter Twelve.

Disc Brake Fluid Level Inspection

1. Place the bike on its center stand. On FZ700 models, support the bike so that it rests straight up.
2. Turn the handlebars so that the front master cylinder is level.
3. The brake fluid must be kept above the lower level lines. See **Figure 43** (front) or **Figure 44** (rear).

Adding Brake Fluid

1. Clean the outside of the reservoir cap thoroughly with a dry rag and remove the reservoir cap. See **Figure 45** (front) or **Figure 44** (rear). Remove the diaphragm under the cap.

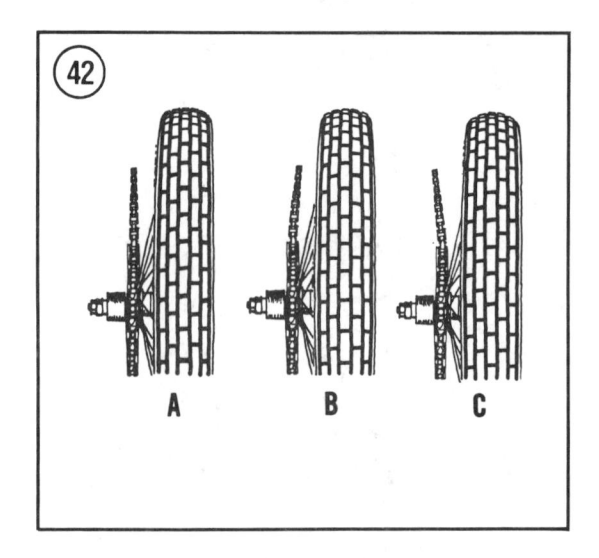

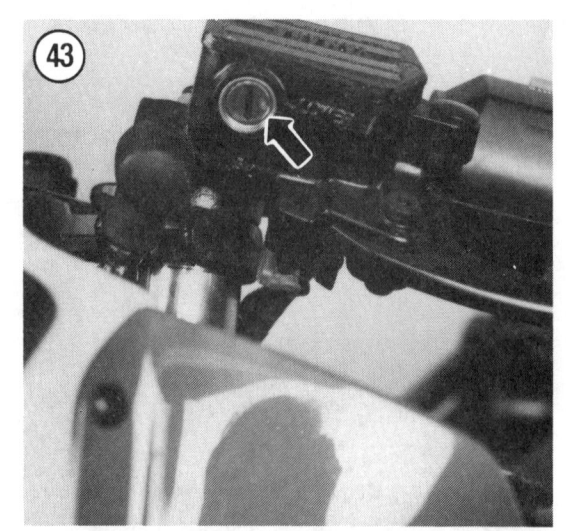

PERIODIC LUBRICATION, MAINTENANCE AND TUNE-UP

2. The fluid level in the reservoir should be up to the upper level line. Add fresh DOT 3 brake fluid as required.

WARNING
Use brake fluid clearly marked DOT 3 only and specified for disc brakes. Others may vaporize and cause brake failure.

CAUTION
Be careful not to spill brake fluid on painted or plated surfaces as it will destroy the surface. Wash immediately with soapy water and thoroughly rinse it off.

3. Reinstall all parts. Make sure the cap is tightly secured.

NOTE
*If the brake fluid was so low as to allow air in the hydraulic system, the brakes will have to be bled. Refer to **Bleeding The System** in Chapter Twelve.*

Disc Brake Hoses and Seals

Disc brake hoses should be replaced every 4 years; the brake piston seals should be replaced every 2 years.

Check brake hoses between the master cylinder and the brake caliper. If there is any leakage, tighten the connections and bleed the brakes as described in Chapter Twelve. If this does not stop the leak or if a line is obviously damaged, cracked, or chafed, replace the hose and seals and bleed the brake.

Disc Brake Pad Inspection

Inspect the disc brake pads for wear according to the maintenance schedule.
1. Apply the front or rear brake.
2. Shine a light between the caliper and the disc. See **Figure 46** (front) or **Figure 47** (rear).
3. If a pad's wear indicator (**Figure 48**) almost touches the brake disc, replace both pads as a set.

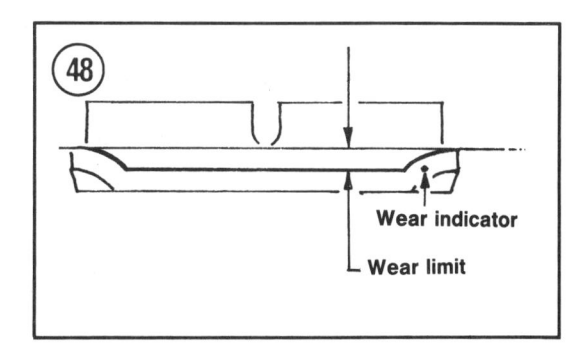

NOTE
On front brakes, replace both left- and right-hand brake pads at the same time.

4. Replace brake pads as described under *Brake Pad Replacement* in Chapter Twelve.

Disc Brake Fluid Change

Every time you remove the reservoir cap, a small amount of dirt and moisture enters the brake fluid. The same thing happens if a leak occurs or when any part of the hydraulic system is loosened or disconnected. Dirt can clog the system and cause unnecessary wear. Water in the fluid vaporizes at high temperatures, impairing the hydraulic action and reducing brake performance.

To change brake fluid, drain the master cylinders as described under *Front Master Cylinder Removal/Installation* or *Rear Master Cylinder Removal/Installation* in Chapter Twelve. Add new fluid to the master cylinder and bleed at the caliper until the fluid leaving the caliper is clean and free of contaminants and air bubbles. Refer to *Bleeding the System* in Chapter Twelve.

WARNING
Use brake fluid clearly marked DOT 3 only. Others may vaporize and cause brake failure.

Front Brake Lever Adjustment

The front brake lever free play must be maintained or the front brake may drag and overheat. An adjuster is provided to maintain the front brake lever free play.

NOTE
Free play is the distance the lever travels from the at-rest position to the applied position (the point at which the master cylinder is depressed by the lever adjuster).

1. Loosen the adjuster locknut (**Figure 49**) and turn the adjuster to obtain the free play measurement for your model:

  a. *FZX700:* 5-8 mm (3/16-5/16 in.).
  b. *FZ700 and FZ750:* 2-5 mm (3/32-3/16 in.).
2. Tighten the locknut.
3. Rotate the front wheel and check for brake drag. Also operate the brake lever several times to make sure it returns to the at-rest position immediately after release.

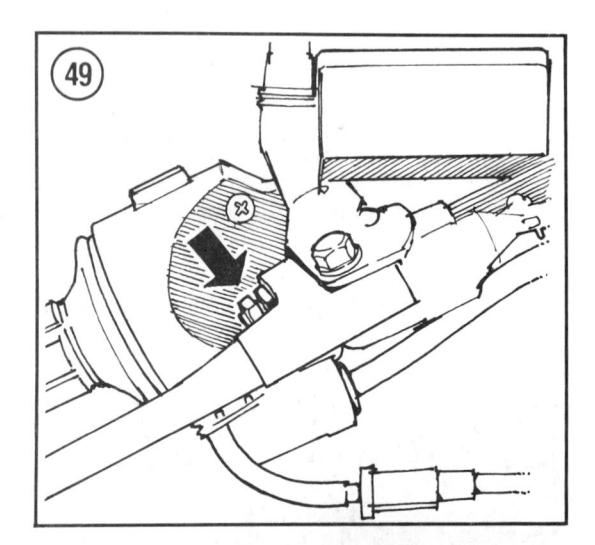

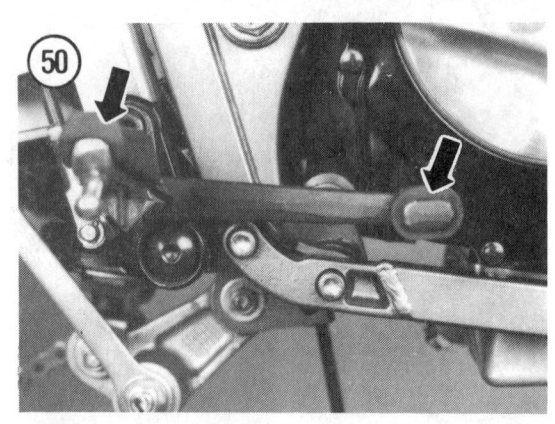

PERIODIC LUBRICATION, MAINTENANCE AND TUNE-UP

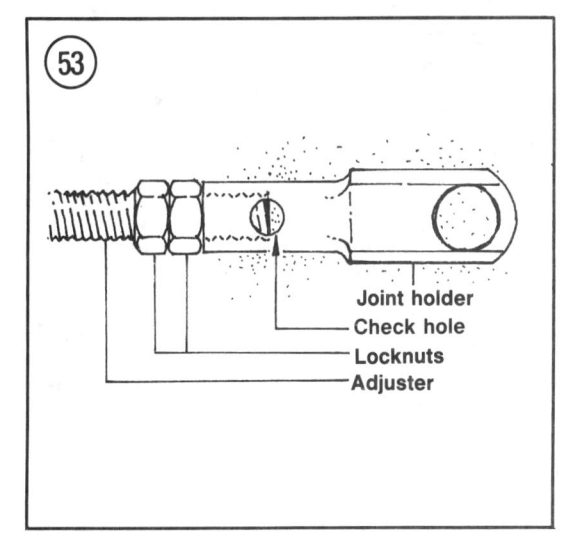

Rear Brake Pedal Height Adjustment

Rear brake pedal height is the distance from the top of the footpeg to the top of the brake pedal (**Figure 50**).

1. Place the motorcycle on the center stand. On FZ700 models, support the bike so that it sits straight up.
2. Check to be sure the brake pedal is in the at-rest position.
3. The correct height position from the top of the footpeg to the top of the brake pedal is as follows:
   a. *FZX700:* 20 mm (3/4 in.).
   b. *FZ700 and FZ750:* 35 mm (1 3/8 in.). To adjust, proceed to Step 4.
4A. *FZX700:* Remove the side cover.
4B. *FZ700 and FZ750:* Remove the footpeg and brake pedal assembly (**Figure 51**). On FZ750 models, remove the brake switch assembly from the brake pedal panel.
5. Loosen the locknuts (A, **Figure 52**) and turn the adjuster (B, **Figure 52**) until the brake pedal is at the correct position (see Step 3 for pedal height). On FZ700 and FZ750 models it will be necessary to reinstall the footpeg and brake pedal assembly and check the height measurement after making the adjustment. Tighten the locknuts.

WARNING
*After adjusting the brake pedal, check that the end of the adjuster is visible through the hole in the joint holder as shown in **Figure 53**. If the adjuster is not positioned correctly, check for worn or damaged brake pedal and adjuster components. Do not ride the motorcycle until the rear brake pedal is adjusted correctly.*

6A. *FZX700:* Install the side cover.
6B. *FZ700 and FZ750:* Tighten the foot peg/brake pedal assembly bolts securely.

Rear Brake Light Switch Adjustment

1. Turn the ignition switch ON.
2. Depress the brake pedal. The brake light should come on after the brake pedal is depressed. If necessary, adjust as follows.
3. *FZX700:* Remove the right-hand side cover.
4. To make the light come on earlier, hold the switch body (**Figure 54**) and turn the adjusting locknut to move the switch body *up*. Move the

5. Reinstall the side cover.
6. Perform Step 2 to check brake light operation.

WARNING
Do not ride the bike until the rear brake light operates properly.

Clutch Fluid Level Check

The clutch is hydraulically operated and requires no routine adjustment.

The hydraulic fluid in the clutch master cylinder should be checked weekly or whenever the level drops, whichever comes first. The same type of fluid is used for clutch and brakes. Bleeding the clutch system and servicing clutch components are covered in Chapter Five.

CAUTION
If the clutch operates correctly when the engine is cold or in cool weather, but operates erratically (or not at all) after the engine warms up or in hot weather, there is air in the hydraulic line and the clutch must be bled. Refer to Chapter Five.

The fluid level in the reservoir should be up above the lower mark on the reservoir window (A, **Figure 55**). The fluid level must be corrected by adding fresh DOT 3 hydraulic (brake) fluid.

1. Park the bike on level ground and turn the handlebars so the master cylinder reservoir is level.
2. Clean any dirt from the area around the top cover prior to removing the cover.
3. Remove the top cover (B, **Figure 55**) and diaphragm. Add clutch fluid until the level is above the lower line on the reservoir window. Use fresh hydraulic fluid from a sealed hydraulic fluid container.

WARNING
Only use hydraulic fluid from a sealed container clearly marked DOT 3. Do not intermix different brands or types of hydraulic fluid as they may not be compatible. Do not intermix a silicone based (DOT 5) hydraulic fluid as it can cause clutch component damage leading to clutch release system failure.

CAUTION
Be careful when handling hydraulic fluid. Do not spill it on painted or plated surfaces as it will destroy the surface. Wash the area immediately with soapy water and thoroughly rinse it off.

4. Reinstall the diaphragm and the top cover. Tighten the screws securely.

Clutch Hydraulic Lines

Check clutch lines between the master cylinder and the clutch slave cylinder. If there is any leakage, tighten the connections and bleed the clutch as described under *Bleeding the Clutch* in Chapter Five. If this does not stop the leak or if a clutch line is obviously damaged, cracked or chafed, replace the clutch line and bleed the system.

Throttle Cable Adjustment

Always check the throttle cable before you make any carburetor adjustments. Too much free play causes delayed throttle response; too little free play will cause unstable idling.

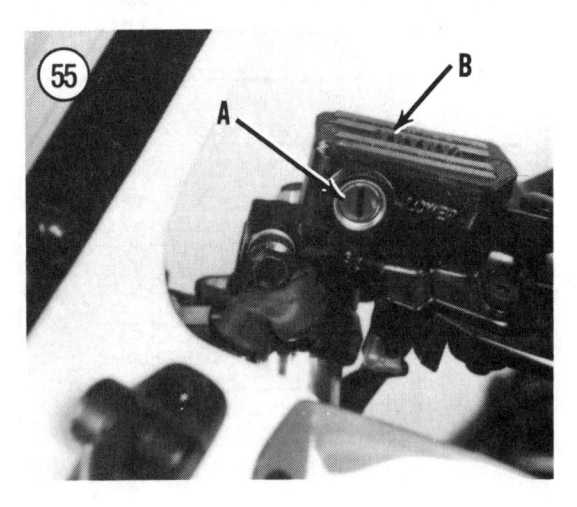

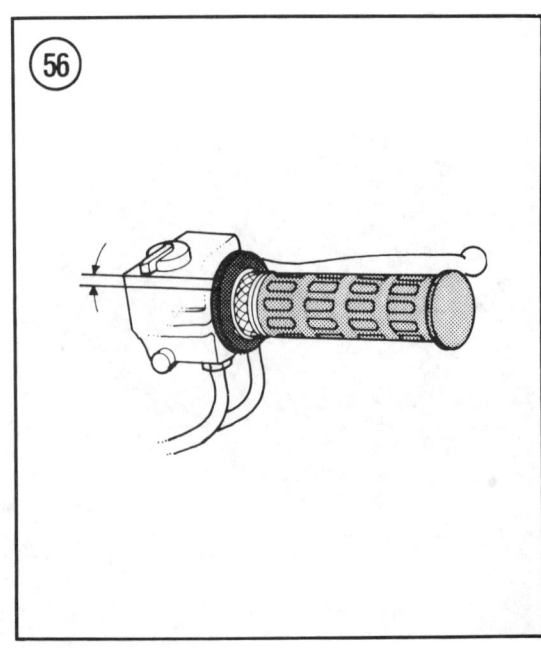

PERIODIC LUBRICATION, MAINTENANCE AND TUNE-UP

Check the throttle cable from grip to carburetors. Make sure it is not kinked or chafed. Replace the cable if necessary.

Make sure that the throttle grip rotates smoothly from fully closed to fully open. Check at center, full left, and full right position of steering. If necessary, remove the throttle grip and apply a lithium base grease to it.

Check free play at the throttle grip flange (**Figure 56**). It should be approximately 2-3 mm (1/8 in.). If adjustment is necessary, loosen the locknut and turn the adjuster (**Figure 57**) in or out to achieve proper free play rotation. Tighten the locknut.

> **WARNING**
> *If idle speed increases when the handlebar is turned to right or left, check throttle cable routing. Do not ride the motorcycle in this unsafe condition.*

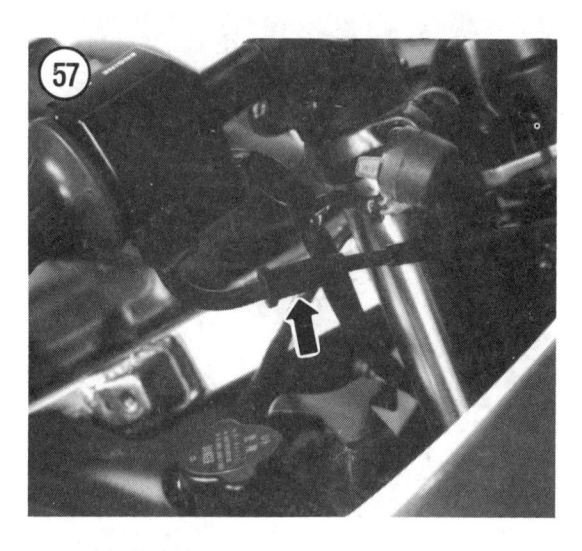

Choke Cable Adjustment (FZ700 and FZ750)

If the choke cable fails to pull the starter shaft completely open, loosen the choke cable bracket screw at the carburetor and reposition the choke cable (**Figure 58**). Tighten the screw and recheck the starter shaft operation.

Fuel Valve/Filter

At the intervals specified in **Table 1**, remove and drain the fuel tank. Remove the fuel shutoff valve and clean it of all dirt and debris. Replace worn or damaged O-rings and gaskets. Refer to *Fuel Valve* in Chapter Seven.

Fuel and Vacuum Line Inspection

Inspect the condition of all fuel and vacuum lines for cracks or deterioration; replace if necessary. Make sure the hose clamps are in place and holding securely.

Exhaust System

Check for leakage at all fittings. Tighten all bolts and nuts; replace any gaskets as necessary. Refer to *Exhaust System* in Chapter Seven.

Air Cleaner
Removal/Installation

A clogged air cleaner can decrease the efficiency and life of the engine. Never run the bike without the air cleaner installed; even minute particles of dust can cause severe internal engine wear.

The service intervals specified in **Table 1** should be followed with general use. However, the air cleaner should be serviced more often if the bike is ridden in dusty areas.

The stock air filter is a dry-element type; no oiling is required.

1. Remove the seat and fuel tank.

2. Remove the air filter cover screws and remove the cover. See **Figure 59** (FZX700) or **Figure 60** (FZ700 and FZ750).
3. Remove the air filter element (**Figure 61**).
4. Inspect the air filter element (**Figure 62**) for tears or other damage that would allow unfiltered air to pass into the engine. Check the sponge gasket (**Figure 63**) on the element for tears. Replace the element if necessary.
5. Clean the air filter element with compressed air from the outside of the element as shown in **Figure 64**.
6. Install by reversing these steps.

Steering Play

The steering head should be checked for looseness at the intervals specified in **Table 1** or whenever the following symptoms or conditions exist:
  a. The handlebars vibrate more than normal.
  b. The front forks make a clicking or clunking noise when the front brake is applied.
  c. The steering feels tight or slow.
  d. The motorcycle does not want to steer straight on level road surfaces ("hunting").

Inspection

1. Prop up the motorcycle so that the front tire clears the ground.
2. *FZ700 and FZ750:* Remove the upper and lower fairings. See Chapter Thirteen.

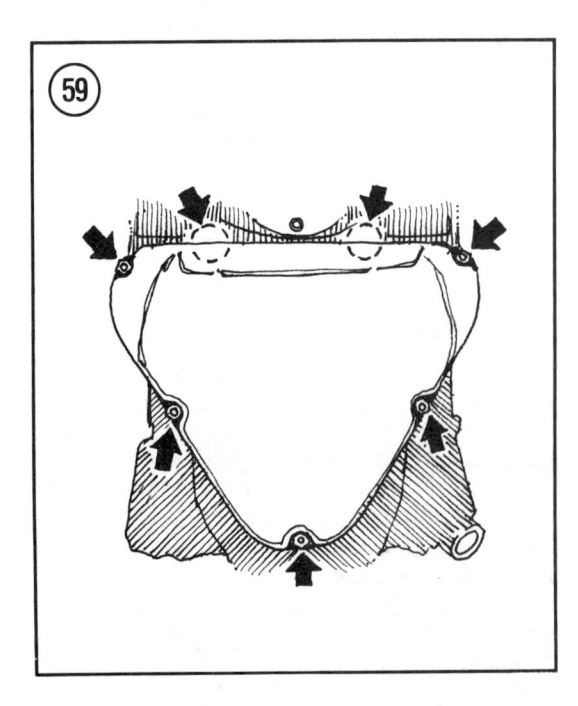

PERIODIC LUBRICATION, MAINTENANCE AND TUNE-UP

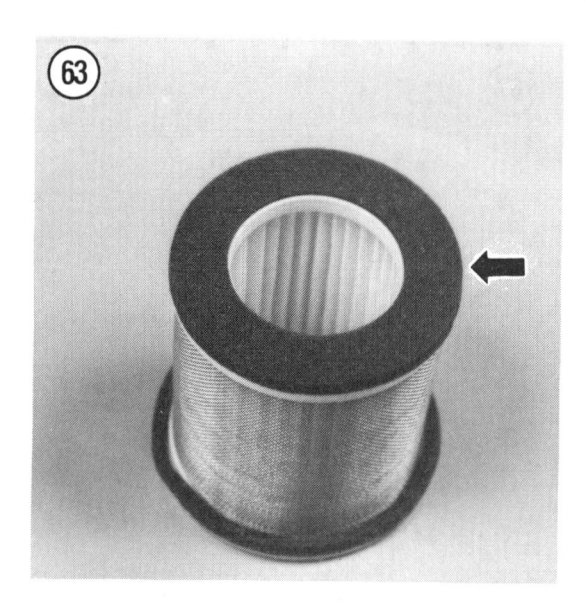

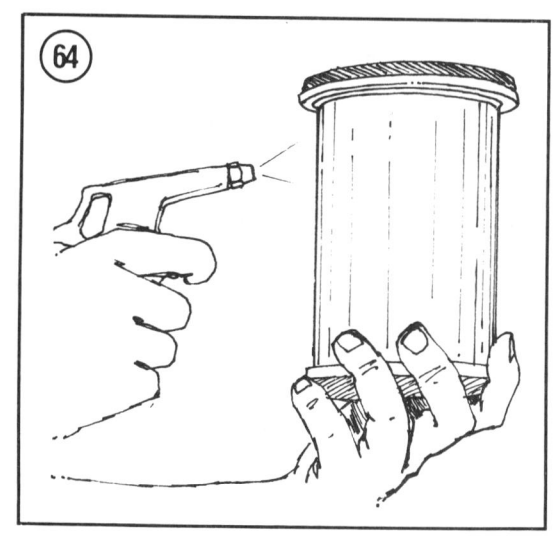

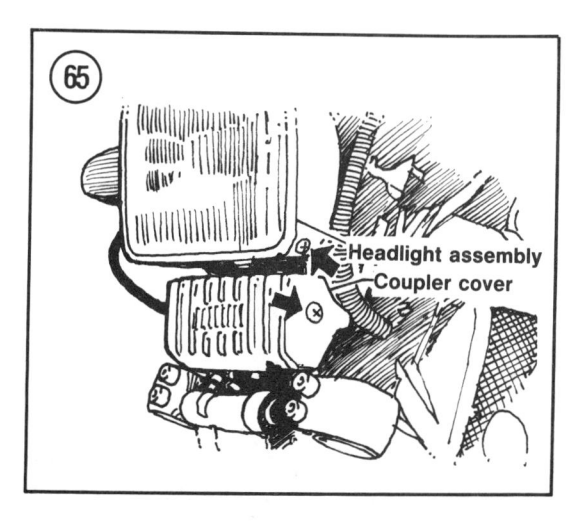

3. Center the front wheel. Push lightly against the left handlebar grip to start the wheel turning to the right, then let go. The wheel should continue turning under its own momentum until the forks hit their stop.

4. Center the wheel, and push lightly against the right handlebar grip.

5. If, with a light push in either direction, the front wheel will turn all the way to the stop, the steering adjustment is not too tight.

6. If the front wheel would not turn all the way to the stop, the steering is too tight. Adjust the steering as described in this chapter.

7. Center the front wheel and kneel in front of it. Grasp the bottoms of the 2 front fork slider legs. Try to pull the forks toward you, and then try to push them toward the engine. If no play is felt, the steering adjustment is not too loose.

8. If the steering adjustment is too tight or too loose, adjust it as described in this chapter.

Adjustment

1. Prop up the motorcycle so that the front tire clears the ground.
2. Remove the fuel tank as described in Chapter Seven.
3. *FZ700 and FZ750:* Remove the upper and lower fairings. See Chapter Thirteen.
4. Remove the handlebars as described in this chapter.
5. *FZX700:* Remove the coupler cover and the lower headlight stay bolt (**Figure 65**). Then remove the headlight assembly.
6. See **Figure 66**. Remove the steering stem nut (A) and lift the upper steering stem (B) off of the steering stem shaft.

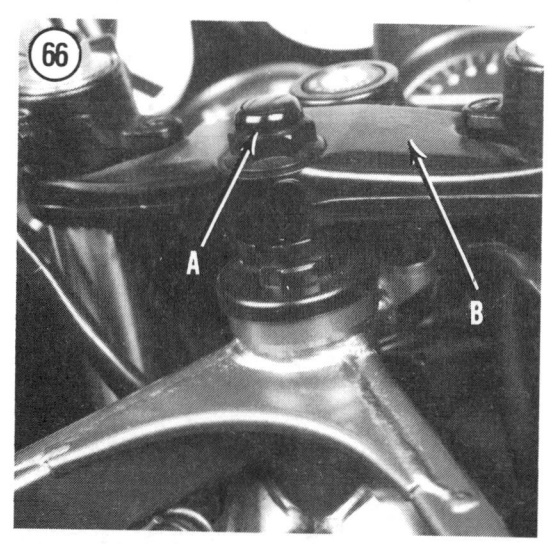

7. Remove the lockwasher.
8. Remove the upper ring nut (**Figure 67**).
9. Remove the washer.

NOTE
*Yamaha sells a special ring nut wrench (part no. YU-33975) that can be used with a torque wrench for accurate steering stem adjustment. See **Figure 68**.*

10. Tighten the lower ring nut (**Figure 68**) in the following order:
   a. Tighten the lower ring nut to 52 N•m (37 ft.-lb.).
   b. Loosen the lower ring nut completely.
   c. Retighten the lower ring nut to 3 N•m (2.2 ft.-lb.).
11. Install the washer and the upper ring nut. (**Figure 67**). Tighten the upper ring nut finger tight. Then check that the upper ring nut grooves line up with the lower ring nut grooves. If not, tighten the upper ring nut as required.
12. Install the lockwasher.
13. Install the upper steering stem and the steering stem nut (**Figure 66**).
14. Turn the steering stem again by hand to make sure it turns freely and does not bind. If the steering stem is too tight, the bearings can be damaged; if the steering stem is too loose, the steering will become unstable. Repeat Steps 6-13 if necessary.
15. Reverse Steps 1-5 to complete installation.
16. Recheck the steering adjustment. Repeat if necessary.

Cooling System Inspection

At the intervals indicated in **Table 1**, the following items should be checked. If you do not have the test equipment, the tests can be done by a Yamaha dealer, radiator shop or service station.

WARNING
Do not remove the radiator cap when the engine is hot.

1. Have the radiator cap pressure tested (**Figure 69**). The specified radiator cap relief pressure is 0.75-1.05 kg/cm2 (10.7-14.9 psi). The cap must be able to sustain this pressure for 6 seconds. Replace the radiator cap if it does not hold pressure or if the relief pressure is too high or too low.
2. Leave the radiator cap off and have the entire cooling system pressure tested (**Figure 70**). The entire cooling system should be pressurized up to, but not exceeding, 1.0 kg/cm2. (14 psi). The system

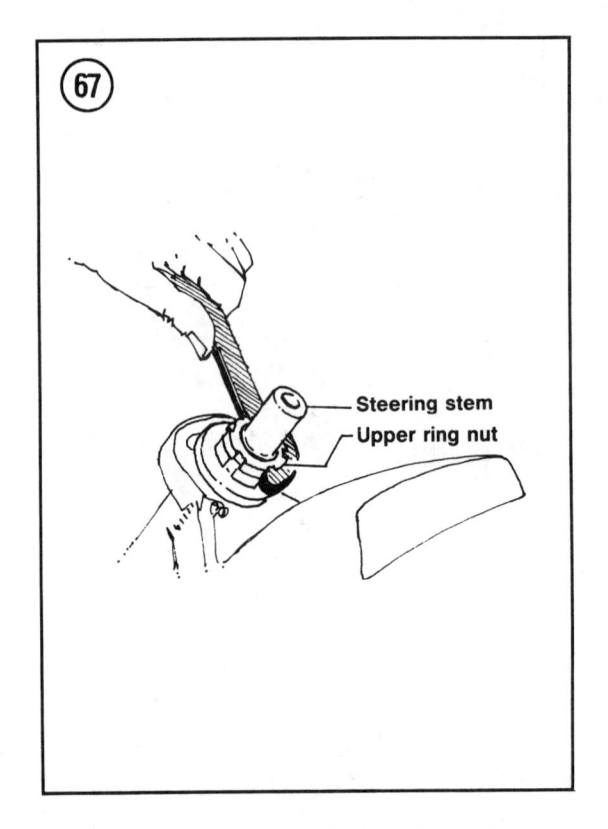

PERIODIC LUBRICATION, MAINTENANCE AND TUNE-UP

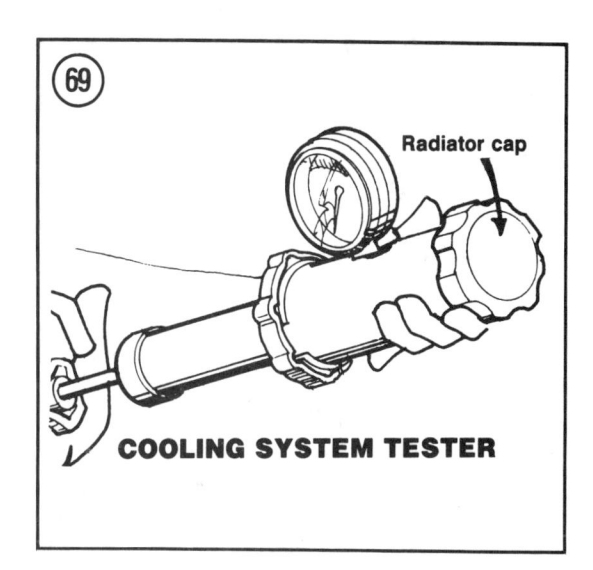

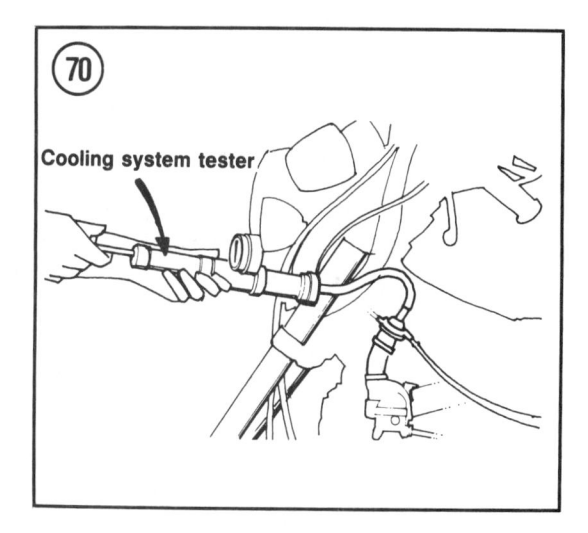

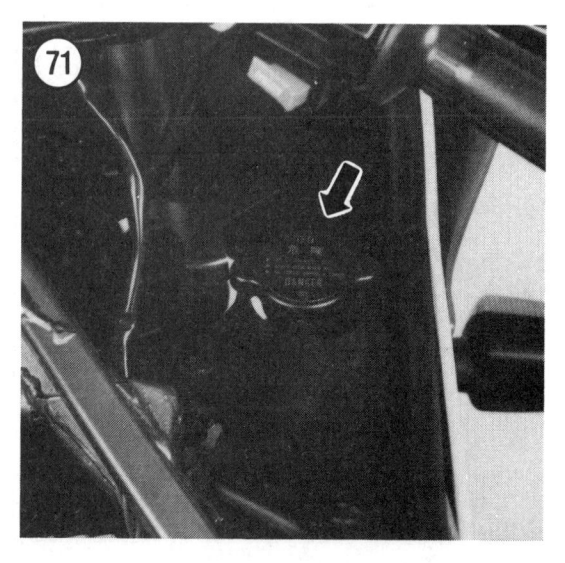

must be able to sustain this pressure for 6 seconds. Replace or repair any components that fail this test.

CAUTION
If test pressures exceed specifications, the radiator may be damaged.

3. Test the specific gravity of the coolant with an antifreeze tester to ensure adequate temperature and corrosion protection. Never let the mixture become less than 40 percent or more than 70 percent antifreeze or corrosion protection will be impaired.

4. Check all cooling system hoses for damage or deterioration. Replace any hose that is questionable. Make sure all hose clamps are tight.

5. Carefully clean any road dirt, bugs, mud, etc. from the radiator core. Use a whisk broom, compressed air or low-pressure water. If the radiator has been hit by a small rock or other item, *carefully* straighten out the fins with a screwdriver.

Coolant Change

The cooling system should be completely drained and refilled at the interval indicated in **Table 1**.

CAUTION
Use only a high quality ethylene glycol antifreeze specifically labeled for use with aluminum engines. Do not use an alcohol-based antifreeze.

In areas where freezing temperatures occur, add a higher percentage of antifreeze to protect the system to temperatures far below those likely to occur. Under normal conditions, use a 50/50 mixture of antifreeze and water. **Table 5** lists cooling system capacity. The following procedure must be performed when the engine is cool.

CAUTION
Be careful not to spill antifreeze on painted surfaces as it will destroy the surface. Wash immediately with soapy water and rinse thoroughly with clean water.

1. Place the bike on the center stand. On FZ700 models, support the bike so that it rests straight up.
2. *FZ700 and FZ750:* Remove the lower fairing. See Chapter Thirteen.

WARNING
Do not remove the radiator cap when the engine is hot.

3. Remove the radiator cap (**Figure 71**).

4A. *FZX700:* Place a drain pan under the frame on the left-hand side of the bike under the water pump and cylinder block. Remove the 4 drain screws:
  a. Cylinder drain bolt (**Figure 72**).
  b. Water pump drain bolt (A, **Figure 73**).
  c. Down tube train bolt (B, **Figure 73**).
  d. Radiator drain bolt (**Figure 74**).

4B. *FZ700 and FZ750:* Place a drain pan under the frame on the left-hand side of the bike. Remove the 2 drain screws.
  a. Cylinder drain bolt (**Figure 75**).
  b. Water pump drain bolt (**Figure 76**).

5. Reinstall the drain screws and washers after the coolant has drained.
6. Remove the reservoir tank (**Figure 77**) and drain it.
7. Refill the radiator. Add the coolant through the radiator filler neck (**Figure 71**). Use a 50/50 antifreeze to water mixture in the amount specified in **Table 5**. Fill to the radiator filler neck (just below the reservoir tank tube opening).
8. Install the radiator cap. Turn the radiator cap clockwise to the first stop. Then push the cap down and turn it clockwise until it stops. Reinstall the can cover.
9. Start the engine and let it run at idle speed until the engine reaches normal operating temperature. Make sure there are no air bubbles in the coolant and that the coolant level stabilizes at the correct level. Add coolant as necessary.
10. Add coolant to the reservoir tank (**Figure 77**) to correct the level.
11. Test ride the bike and readjust the coolant level in the reservoir tank if necessary.

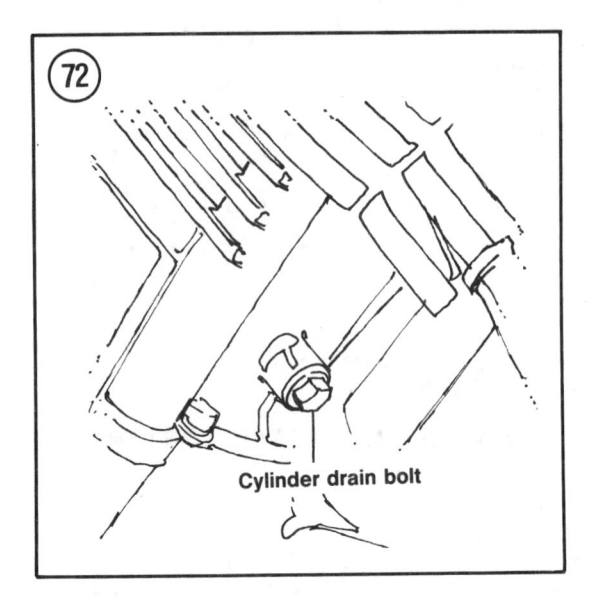

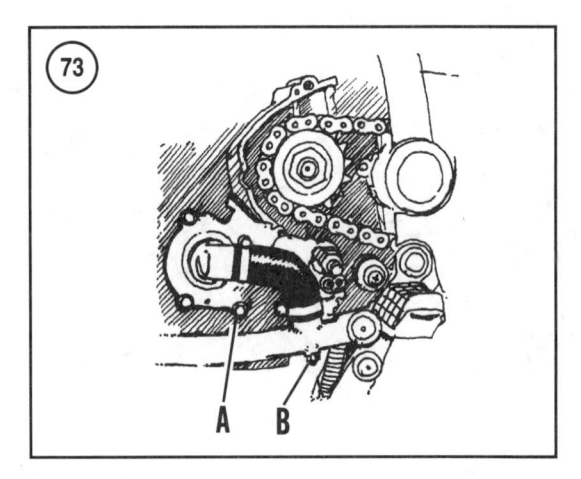

Front Suspension Check

1. Apply the front brake and pump the fork up and down as vigorously as possible. Check for smooth operation and check for any oil leaks.
2. Make sure the upper and lower steering stem pinch bolts are tight.
3. Check that the front axle pinch bolt is tight.
4. Check that the front axle nut cotter pin is in place and that the axle nut is tight.

WARNING
If any of the previously mentioned bolts and nuts are loose, refer to Chapter Ten for correct procedures and torque specifications.

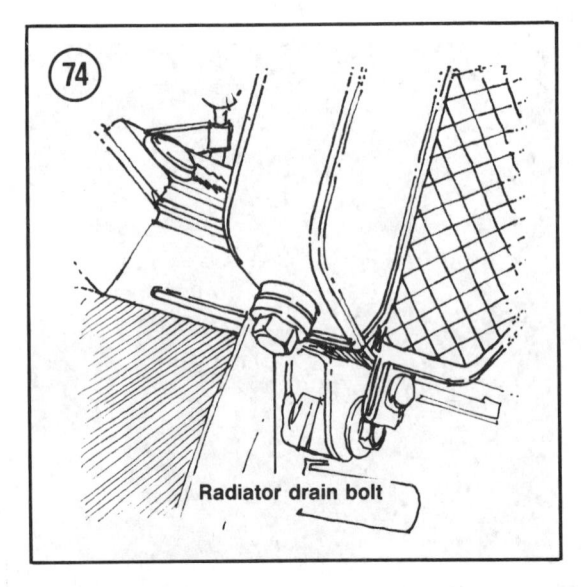

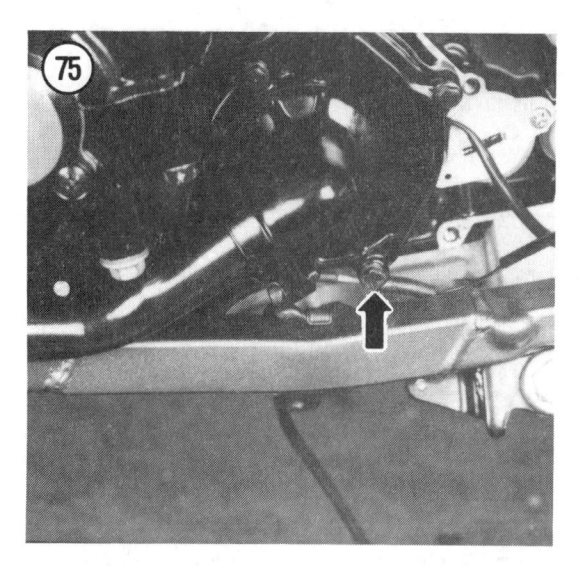

PERIODIC LUBRICATION, MAINTENANCE AND TUNE-UP

Rear Suspension Check

1. Place the bike on the center stand. On FZ700 models, jack up the vehicle so that the rear wheel clears the ground.
2. Push hard on the rear wheel sideways to check for side play in the rear swing arm bearings.
3. Check the tightness of the shock absorber mounting nuts and bolts.
4. Check the tightness of the rear brake torque arm bolts.
5. Make sure the rear axle nut is tight and the cotter pin is still in place.

WARNING
If any of the previously mentioned nuts or bolts are loose, refer to Chapter Eleven for correct procedures and torque specifications.

Nuts, Bolts, and Other Fasteners

Constant vibration can loosen many fasteners on a motorcycle. Check the tightness of all fasteners, especially those on:
   a. Engine mounting hardware.
   b. Engine crankcase covers.
   c. Handlebars and front forks.
   d. Gearshift lever.
   e. Sprocket bolts and nuts.
   f. Brake pedal and lever.
   g. Exhaust system.
   h. Lighting equipment.
   i. Fairing assembly.

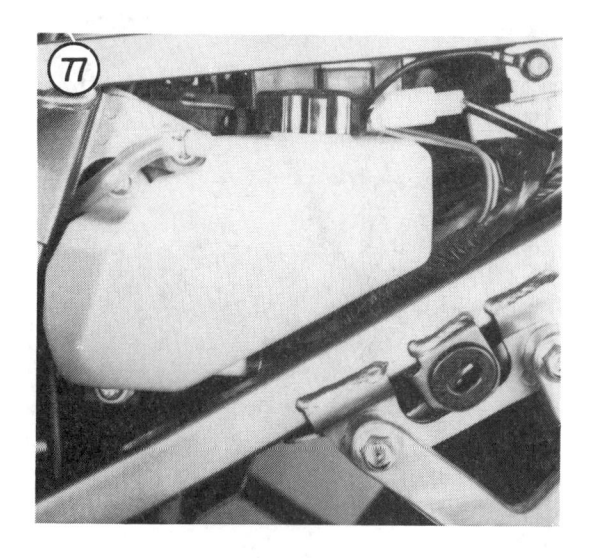

SUSPENSION ADJUSTMENT

The front forks must be adjusted to correspond to rear shock absorber adjustment and vehicle load. Refer to the following for your model:
   a. **Table 6** (FZX700).
   b. **Table 7** (FZ700).
   c. **Table 8** (FZ750).

Front Fork Air Adjustment (FZX700 and FZ750)

Both the fork springs and air pressure support the motorcycle and rider. Air pressure should be measured with the forks at normal room temperature.

The air pressure can be varied to suit the load and your ride preference. Don't use a high-pressure hose or bottle to pressurize the forks; a tire pump is a lot closer to the scale you need. Note the following when adjusting the front fork air pressure:
  a. Increase air pressure for heavy loads.
  b. If the suspension is too hard, reduce air pressure.
  c. If the suspension is too soft, increase air pressure.
1. Support the bike with the front wheel off the ground.
2. Remove the air valve cap. See **Figure 78** (FZX700) or **Figure 79** (FZ750).
3. Connect a pump to the valve and pump the fork(s) to the desired air pressure. See **Table 6** (FZX700) or **Table 8** (FZ750).

CAUTION
*Do not exceed the maximum air pressure listed in **Table 9** or the fork seals will be damaged.*

4. Slowly bleed off the pressure to reach the desired value. The standard pressure is listed in **Table 9**.

NOTE
Each application of a pressure gauge bleeds off some air pressure in the process of applying and removing the gauge.

5. Install the valve cap(s).

Front Fork Spring Preload Adjustment (FZ700)

The spring preload can be adjusted to 4 different positions to best suit riding, load and speed conditions. **Table 7** list adjuster positions in relation to various road and riding conditions. The different adjuster ranges are as follows:
  a. Hard: Turn the preload adjuster clockwise.
  b. Soft: Turn the preload adjuster counterclockwise.
1. Remove the rubber cap from the fork tube (**Figure 80**).

CAUTION
When adjusting the spring preload in Step 1, make adjustments in increments of 1. Test ride the motorcycle before further adjustment.

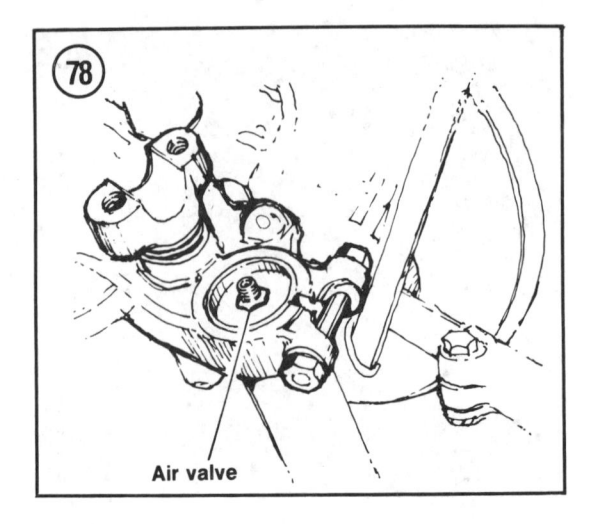

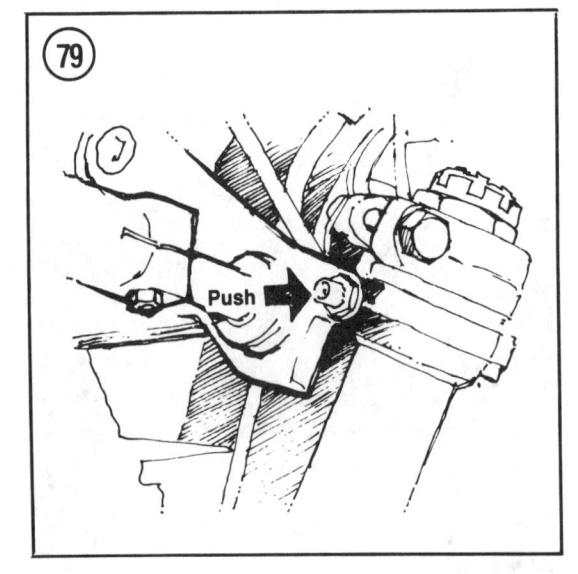

PERIODIC LUBRICATION, MAINTENANCE AND TUNE-UP

2. Insert a screwdriver into the spring preload adjuster. Then compress the adjuster and turn it clockwise (hard) or counterclockwise (soft) in increments of 1.
3. Repeat for the opposite fork tube.

WARNING
Always adjust each fork to the same setting. Different adjustment settings can cause unstable handling and loss of control.

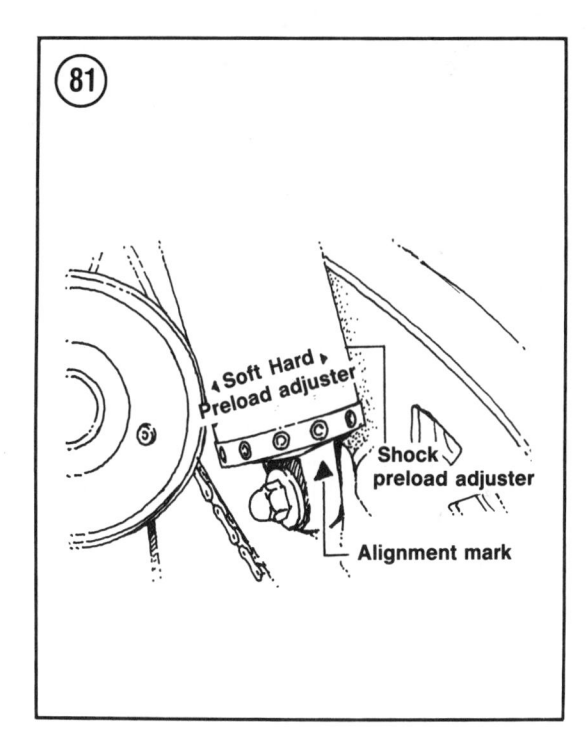

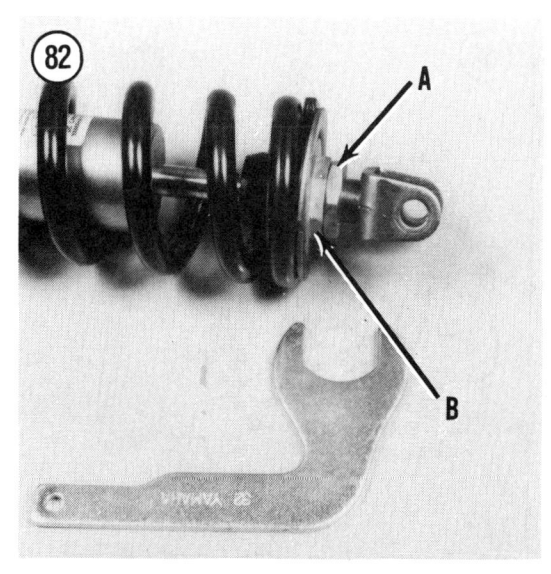

NOTE
The factory recommended setting for average riding with no accessories is adjuster position No. 1. See Table 7.

Rear Shock Absorber Adjustment

FZX700

The spring preload can be adjusted to 5 different positions to best suit riding, load and speed conditions. **Table 6** lists adjuster positions in relation to various road and riding conditions. The different adjuster ranges are as follows:
  a. Soft: No. 1.
  b. Standard: No. 2.
  c. Hard: No. 3, 4 and 5.
1. Place the bike on the center stand.

CAUTION
When adjusting the spring preload in Step 2, make adjustments in increments of 1. Test ride the motorcycle before further adjustment.

2. Turn the spring preload adjuster and align the adjuster number with the alignment mark (**Figure 81**).
3. Repeat for the opposite shock absorber.

WARNING
Always adjust each shock absorber to the same setting. Different adjustment settings can cause unstable handling and loss of control.

NOTE
The factory recommended setting for average riding with no accessories is adjuster position No. 2.

FZ700

The monoshock unit on these models is equipped with a spring preload adjuster. The spring preload must be set to correspond to front fork preload adjustment (see **Table 7**).
1. Using the 32 mm wrench provided in the owner's tool kit, loosen the locknut (A, **Figure 82**) and turn the adjuster (B, **Figure 82**). Tighten it to

increase spring preload or loosen it to decrease it. Turning the adjuster 1 turn changes spring length 1.0 mm (0.4 in.). See **Figure 83**.

NOTE
Adjustments should be made in increments of 2 mm each time; test ride the bike after each adjustment.

2. The installed spring length (**Figure 84**) must be maintained within the range specified in **Table 7**.
3. After the adjustment is correct, tighten the locknut (A, **Figure 82**) to 42 N•m (30 ft.-lb.).

FZ750

The monoshock unit on these models is equipped with spring preload and damping

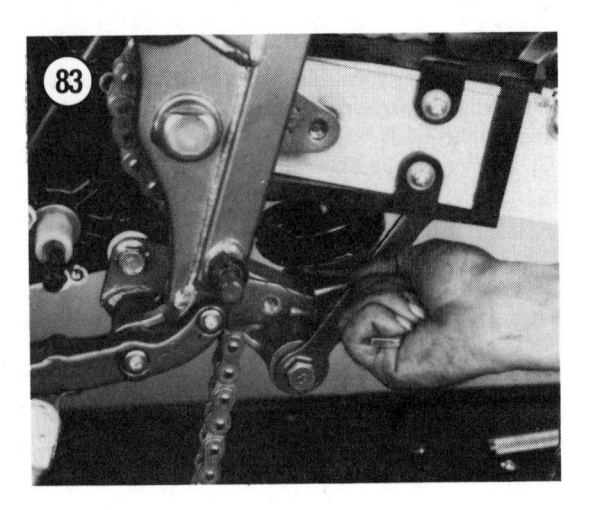

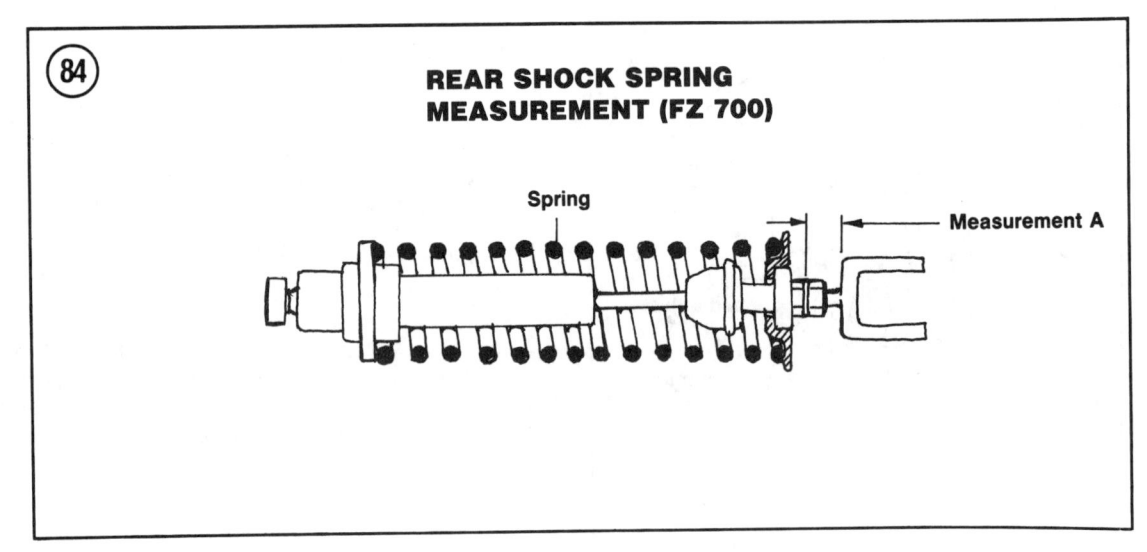

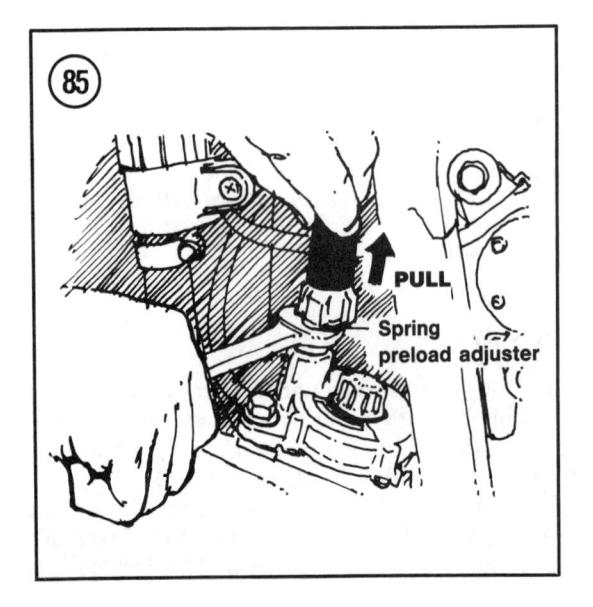

PERIODIC LUBRICATION, MAINTENANCE AND TUNE-UP

adjusters. The spring preload and damping adjustments must be set to correspond to front fork air pressure and vehicle load (see **Table 8**).

CAUTION
When performing the following adjustments, be adjustments in increments of 1.

1. Adjust spring preload as follows:
   a. Place the bike on the center stand.
   b. Pull the adjuster cover up with your hand and turn the spring preload adjuster. See **Figure 85**.
   c. Turning the adjuster counterclockwise softens the spring preload; turning the adjuster clockwise stiffens the spring preload.
2. Adjust rear shock damping as follows:
   a. Place the bike on the center stand.
   b. Turn the damping adjuster clockwise to soften the damping or counterclockwise to stiffen the damping. See **Figure 86**.

TUNE-UP

A complete tune-up restores performance and power that is lost due to normal wear and deterioration of engine parts. Because engine wear occurs over a combined period of time and mileage, the engine tune-up should be performed at the intervals specified in **Table 1**. More frequent tune-ups may be required if the bike is ridden primarily in stop-and-go traffic.

Table 10 lists tune-up specifications.

Before starting a tune-up procedure, make sure to have all the necessary new parts on hand.

Because different systems in an engine interact, the procedures should be done in the following order:
   a. Clean or replace the air cleaner element.
   b. Adjust valve clearances (at specified time or mileage interval). See **Table 1**.
   c. Check engine compression.
   d. Check or replace the spark plugs.
   e. Check the ignition timing.
   f. Synchronize carburetors and set idle speed.

Tools

To perform a tune-up on your Yamaha, you will need the following tools:
   a. Spark plug wrench.
   b. Socket wrench and assorted sockets.
   c. Flat feeler gauge.
   d. Compression gauge.
   e. Spark plug wire feeler gauge and gapper tool.
   f. Ignition timing light.
   g. Carburetor synchronization tool (to measure manifold vacuum).

Air Cleaner Element

The air cleaner element should be cleaned or replaced prior to doing other tune-up procedures. Refer to *Air Cleaner Removal/Installation* in this chapter.

Valve Clearance Measurement

CAUTION
Valve clearance check and adjustment must be performed with the engine cold.

1. Remove the cylinder head cover. Refer to *Cylinder Head Cover Removal/Installation* in Chapter Four.
2. Remove the spark plugs as described in this chapter. This will make it easier to turn the engine by hand.
3. Remove the left crankshaft end cover (A, **Figure 87**).

NOTE
To prevent damaging the plastic timing plug screw in Step 4, loosen it with a large straight-tipped screwdriver.

4. Unscrew and remove the timing plug screw (B, **Figure 87**).

5. Thread an 8 mm bolt and nut into the left crankshaft end (**Figure 88**). Lock the bolt with the nut.

6. Using the bolt installed in Step 5, rotate the countershaft counterclockwise until the top dead center (TDC) mark on the crankshaft web for the No. 1 and No. 4 cylinders aligns with the fixed pointer on the crankcase as viewed through the porthole (**Figure 89**). The No. 1 cylinder is now on either the compression stroke or the exhaust stroke. It must be on the compression stroke for the valve adjustment. Check to see if the cam lobes for cylinder No. 1 are pointing directly away from the lifters. If not, the engine is on TDC exhaust. Rotate the crankshaft one full turn until the "T" mark is again aligned with the fixed pointer on the crankcase, and the No. 1 cam lobes point away from the lifters.

NOTE
The pistons are numbered 1-4, starting with the left piston and reading left to right.

7. On No. 1 cylinder insert a feeler gauge between the cam and the lifter surface (**Figure 90**). In order to obtain a correct measurement, the lobe must be directly opposite the lifter surface (**Figure 91**). The clearance is correct if there is a slight drag on the feeler gauge when it is inserted and withdrawn. The correct valve clearance for intake and exhaust valves is listed in **Table 10**. Measure the valve clearance with a metric feeler gauge as it will be easier to calculate pad replacement.

8. Record valve clearances for the No. 1 cylinder intake and exhaust valves.

9. Rotate the crankshaft counterclockwise in the following order and measure the No. 2, 4 and 3 cylinder valves and record the clearances. Repeat Step 7 for each cylinder.

   a. No. 2 cylinder: Rotate crankshaft 180°.
   b. No. 4 cylinder: Rotate crankshaft additional 180°.
   c. No. 3 cylinder: Rotate crankshaft additional 180°.

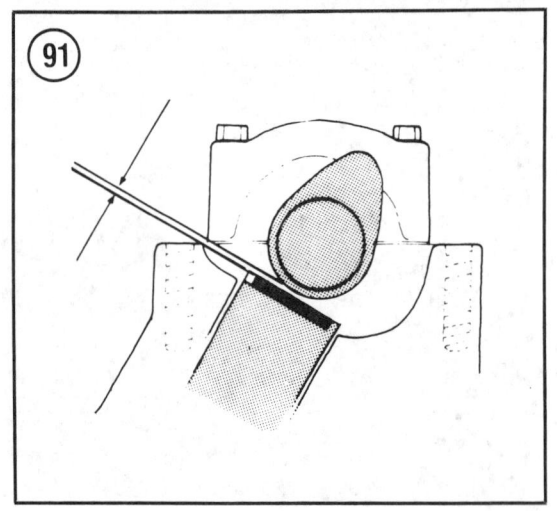

PERIODIC LUBRICATION, MAINTENANCE AND TUNE-UP

10. Measure all valves and record the clearance. They must be measured very accurately. If any are out of specification, correct the clearance as described under *Valve Clearance Adjustment*.

11. Reinstall the cylinder head cover as described in Chapter Four.

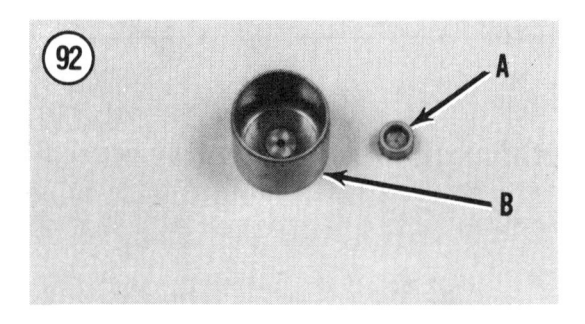

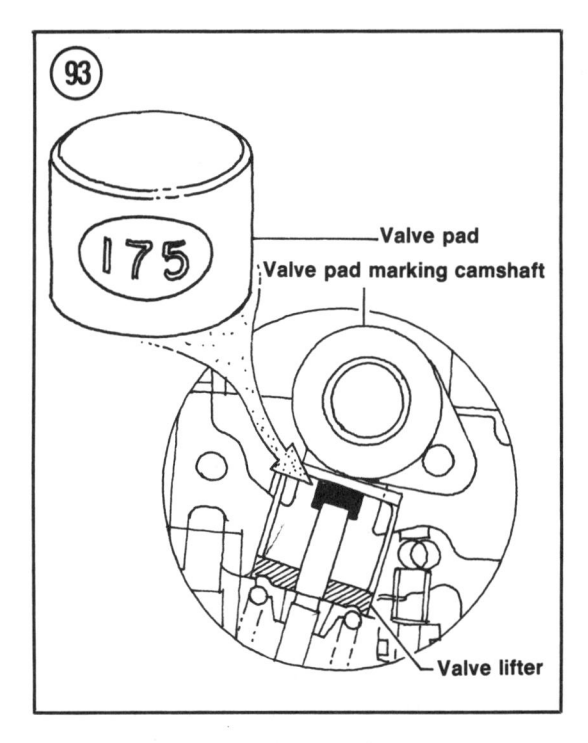

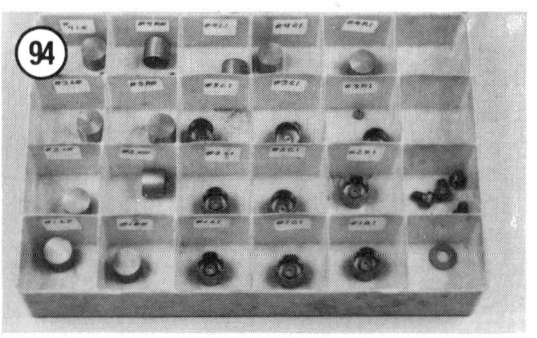

Valve Clearance Adjustment

To correct the valve clearance, the camshafts must be removed. Then the pad (A, **Figure 92**) installed under the valve lifter (B, **Figure 92**) must be replaced with one of the correct size. These pads are available in 25 different sizes from No. 120 (1.20 mm) to No. 240 (2.40 mm) in increments of 0.05 mm. They are available from Yamaha dealers. The thickness is marked on the side of the pad (**Figure 93**).

1. Remove the camshafts as described under *Camshaft Removal* in Chapter Four.

> *NOTE*
> *To prevent the intermixing of parts, a divided container should be used to store the lifters and pads until the components are installed. See **Figure 94**.*

2. Remove the valve lifter (**Figure 95**) and remove the pad (**Figure 96**).
3. Note the number on the pad (**Figure 93**).
4. For correct pad selection, proceed as follows:

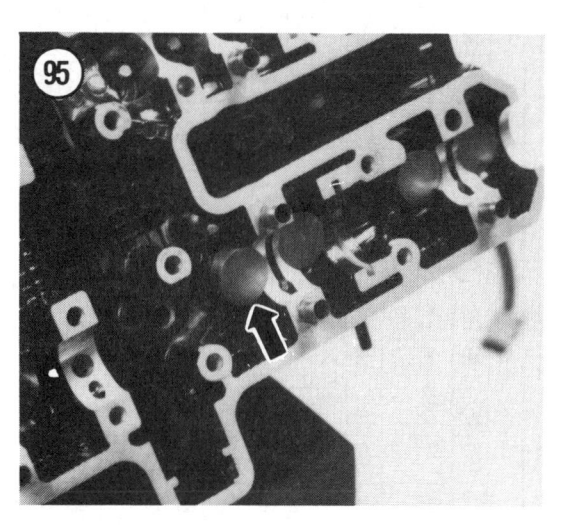

CHAPTER THREE

NOTE

The following numbers are examples only. Use the actual measured clearance, correct clearance specification and existing pad number from your engine.

For example, if the actual measured clearance is 0.28 mm (intake valve) and the existing pad number is 170, cross-reference the clearance (0.28 mm) and the pad number (170) with the chart in **Figure 97** (intake) or **Figure 98** (exhaust). Where these 2 figures intersect is the new pad. In our example, the new pad number would be 185.

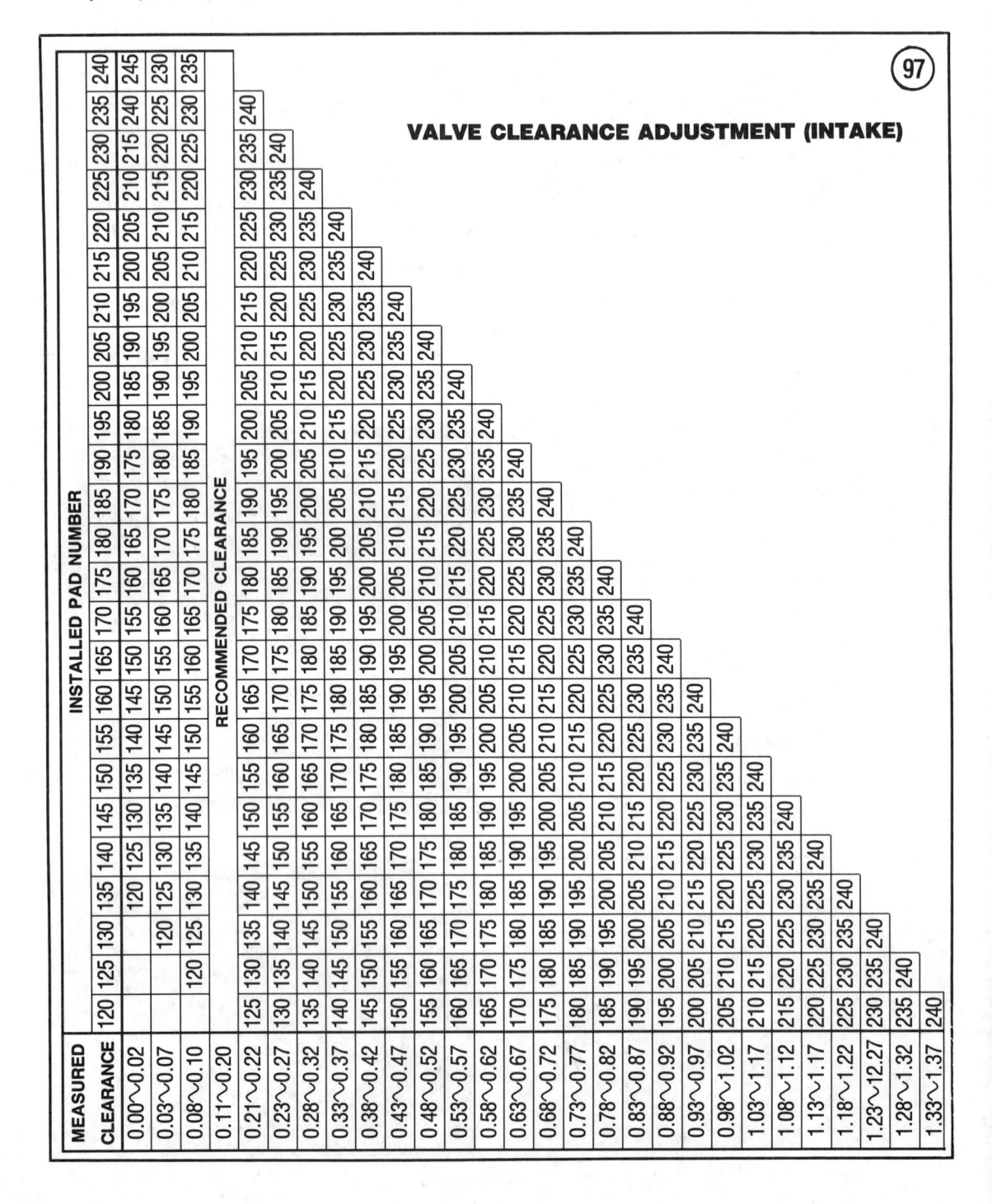

VALVE CLEARANCE ADJUSTMENT (INTAKE)

Figure 97

PERIODIC LUBRICATION, MAINTENANCE AND TUNE-UP

NOTE
Apply molybdenum disulfide grease to all pads before assembly.

5. Install the new pad onto the valve (**Figure 96**) and install the valve lifter (**Figure 95**).

6. Repeat for each valve that had excessive valve clearance outside the recommended range.

7. After replacing all valve pads and lifters, reinstall the camshaft as described in Chapter Four. Then recheck valve clearance as described under *Valve Clearance Measurement*. If clearance is incorrect, repeat these steps until proper clearance is obtained.

VALVE CLEARANCE ADJUSTMENT (EXHAUST)

Compression Test

At every tune-up, check cylinder compression. Record the results and compare them at the next check. A running record will show trends in deterioration so that corrective action can be taken before complete failure.

The results, when properly interpreted, can indicate general cylinder, piston ring and valve condition.

> *NOTE*
> *The valves must be properly adjusted to correctly interpret the results of this test.*

1. Warm the engine to normal operating temperature. Ensure that the choke is in the OFF position.
2. Remove the spark plugs as described in this chapter.

> *NOTE*
> *A screw-in type compression tester (**Figure 99**) will be required for this procedure.*

3. Connect the compression tester to one cylinder following manufacturer's instructions.
4. While holding the throttle wide open crank the engine over until there is no further rise in pressure.
5. Remove the tester and record the reading.
6. Repeat Steps 3-5 for the other cylinder.
7. When interpreting the results, actual readings are not as important as the difference between the readings. Standard compression pressure is specified in **Table 10**. Greater differences indicate worn or broken rings, leaky or sticky valves, blown head gasket or a combination of all.

If compression readings do not differ between cylinders by more than 10 psi, the rings and valves are in good condition.

If a low reading (10% or more) is obtained on one of the cylinders, it indicates valve or ring trouble. To determine which, pour about a teaspoon of engine oil through the spark plug hole onto the top of the piston. Turn the engine over once to distribute the oil, then take another compression test and record the reading. If the compression increases significantly, the valves are good but the rings are defective on that cylinder. If compression does not increase, the valves require servicing. A valve could be hanging open or burned or a piece of carbon could be on a valve seat.

> *NOTE*
> *If the compression is low, the engine cannot be tuned to maximum performance. The worn parts must be replaced and the engine rebuilt.*

Correct Spark Plug Heat Range

Spark plugs are available in various heat ranges that are hotter or colder than the spark plugs originally installed at the factory.

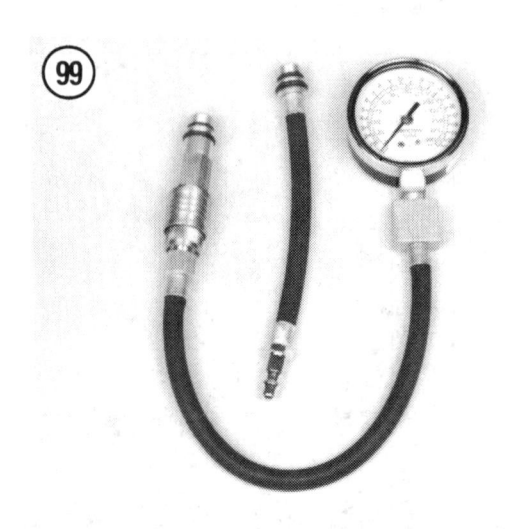

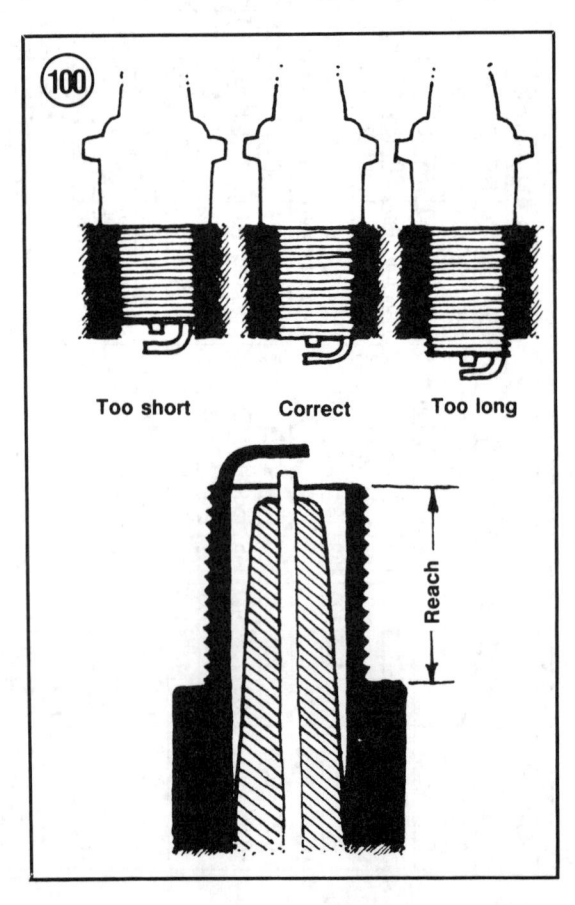

PERIODIC LUBRICATION, MAINTENANCE AND TUNE-UP

Select plugs in a heat range designed for the loads and temperature conditions under which the engine will operate. Using incorrect heat ranges, however, can cause fowled plugs, piston seizure, scored cylinder walls or damaged piston crowns.

In general, use a hotter plug for low speeds, low loads and low temperatures. Use a colder plug for high speeds, high engine loads and high air temperatures.

NOTE
In areas where seasonal temperature variations are great, the factory recommends a "two-plug system"—a cold plug for hard summer riding and a hot plug for slower winter operation. This may prevent spark plug and engine problems.

The reach (length) of a plug is also important. A longer than normal plug could interfere with the valves and pistons, causing permanent and severe damage (**Figure 100**). The standard heat range spark plugs are listed in **Table 10**.

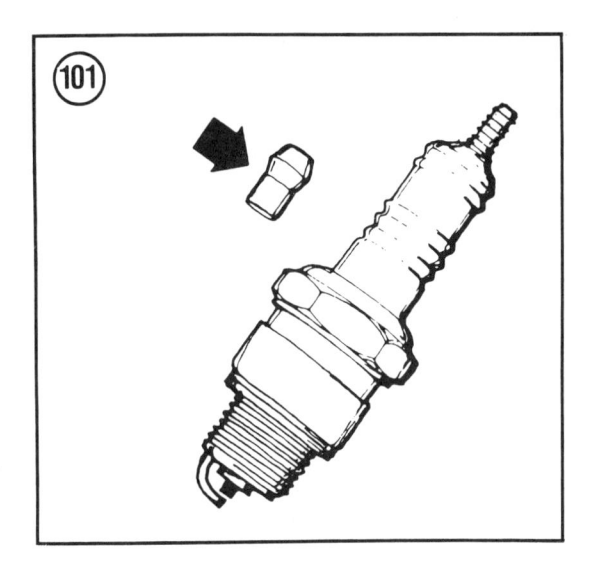

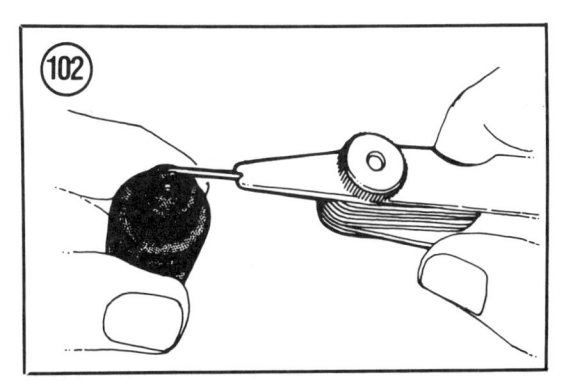

Spark Plug Removal

1. *FZ700 and FZ750:* Remove the lower fairing (see Chapter Thirteen).
2. Remove the fuel tank as described in Chapter Seven.
3. Grasp the spark plug leads as near to the plug as possible and pull them off the plugs.
4. Blow away any dirt that has accumulated in the spark plug wells.

CAUTION
The dirt could fall into the cylinders when the plugs are removed, causing serious engine damage.

5. *FZX700:* Remove the No. 3 spark plug as follows:
   a. Remove the No. 4 cylinder spark plug cap.
   b. Lay a wrench across the cylinder head cover. Then slip a 14 mm wrench over the top of the first wrench and engage it with the spark plug cap. Pry the 14 mm wrench up and lift the cap off of the spark plug.
   c. Remove the spark plug with the spark plug wrench installed in your bike's tool kit.
6. Remove the spark plugs with a spark plug wrench.

CAUTION
If plugs are difficult to remove, apply penetrating oil, like WD-40 or Liquid Wrench, around base of plugs and let it soak in (about 10-20 minutes).

7. Inspect spark plugs carefully. Look for plugs with broken center porcelain, excessively eroded electrodes and excessive carbon or oil fouling. Replace such plugs.

NOTE
Spark plug cleaning with the use of a sand-blast type device is not recommended. While this type of cleaning is thorough, the plug must be perfectly free of all abrasive cleaning material when done. If not, it is possible for the cleaning material to fall into the engine during operation and cause damage.

Gapping and Installing the Plugs

New plugs should be carefully gapped to ensure a reliable, consistent spark. You must use a special spark plug gapping tool with a wire gauge.

1. Remove the new plugs from the box. *Do not screw in the small pieces that are loose in each box* (**Figure 101**); they are not used.
2. Insert a wire gauge between the center and the side electrode of each plug (**Figure 102**). The

correct gap is found in **Table 10**. If the gap is correct, you will feel a slight drag as you pull the wire through. If there is no drag or the gauge won't pass through, bend the side electrode *with the gapping tool* (**Figure 103**) to set the proper gap (**Table 10**).

3. Put a small drop of oil on the threads of each spark plug.

4. Screw each spark plug in by hand until it seats. Very little effort is required. If force is necessary, you have the plug cross-threaded; unscrew it and try again.

NOTE
If a spark plug is difficult to install, the cylinder head threads may be dirty or slightly damaged. To clean the threads, apply grease to the threads of a spark plug tap and screw it carefully into the cylinder head. Turn the tap slowly until it is completely installed. If the tap cannot be installed, the threads are severely damaged.

5. Tighten the spark plugs to a torque of 17.5 N•m (12.5 ft.-lb.). If you don't have a torque wrench, an additional 1/4 to 1/3 turn is sufficient after the gasket has made contact with the head. If you are reinstalling old, regapped plugs and are reusing the old gasket, tighten only an additional 1/4 turn.

CAUTION
Do not overtighten. Besides making the plug difficult to remove, the excessive torque will squash the gasket and destroy its sealing ability.

6. Install each spark plug wire. Make sure it goes to the correct spark plug.

NOTE
*On FZX700 models, route the No. 3 cylinder spark plug behind the radiator fan motor with the spark plug cap tail facing toward the No. 2 cylinder spark plug as shown in **Figure 104**.*

Reading Spark Plugs

Much information about engine and spark plug performance can be determined by careful examination of the spark plugs. This information is more valid after performing the following steps.

1. Ride bike a short distance at full throttle in any gear.

2. Turn off kill switch before closing throttle, and simultaneously, pull in clutch and coast to a stop. *Do not* downshift transmission in stopping.

3. Remove spark plugs and examine them. Compare them to **Figure 105**.

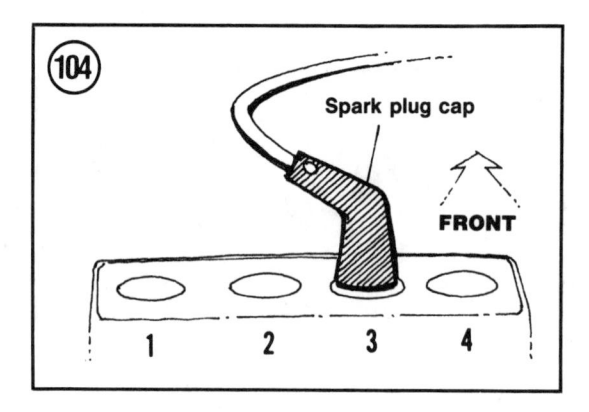

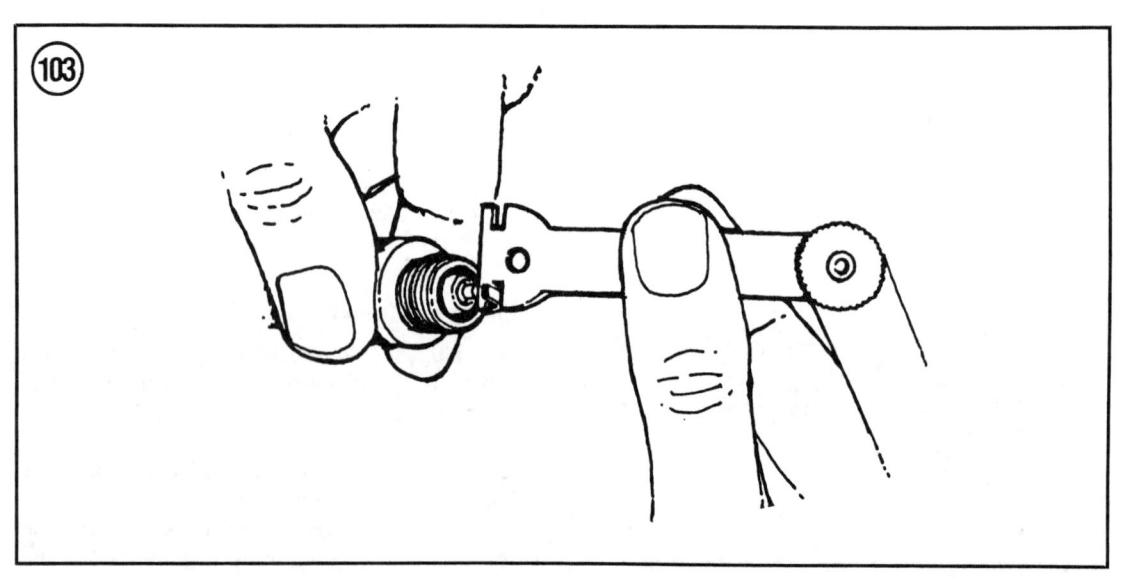

PERIODIC LUBRICATION, MAINTENANCE AND TUNE-UP

⑩ SPARK PLUG CONDITIONS

NORMAL USE

OIL FOULED

CARBON FOULED

OVERHEATED

GAP BRIDGED

SUSTAINED PREIGNITION

WORN OUT

If the insulator tip is white or burned, the plug is too hot and should be replaced with a colder one.

A too-cold plug will have sooty deposits ranging in color from dark brown to black. Replace with a hotter plug and check for too-rich carburetion or evidence of oil blow-by at the piston rings.

If any one plug is found unsatisfactory, replace all 4.

IGNITION TIMING

The models covered in this manual are equipped with a capacitor discharge ignition (CDI) system. This system uses no breaker points and is non-adjustable. The timing should be checked to make sure all ignition components are operating correctly.

1. Start the engine and let it reach normal operating temperature. Shut the engine off.
2. Remove the timing cover on the left-hand crankcase (B, **Figure 87**).
3. Connect a portable tachometer following the manufacturer's instructions. The bike's tachometer is not accurate enough in the low rpm range for this adjustment.
4. Connect a timing light to the No. 1 spark plug following the manufacturer's instructions.
5. Start the engine and let it idle at the idle speed listed in **Table 10**.
6. Aim the timing light at the timing hole in the crankcase and pull the trigger. If the timing mark (**Figure 106**) aligns with the stationary pointer on the crankcase cover (**Figure 106**), the timing is correct.
7. If the timing is incorrect, refer to *Ignition System Troubleshooting* in Chapter Eight. There is no method of adjusting ignition timing.
8. Shut off the engine and disconnect the timing light and portable tachometer. Install the timing cover.

CARBURETOR

Idle Speed

Proper idle speed is necessary to prevent stalling and to provide adequate engine compression braking, but you can't set it perfectly with the bike's tachometer—it's not accurate at the low rpm range. A portable tachometer is required for this procedure.

1. Attach a portable tachometer, following the manufacturer's instructions.
2. Start the engine and warm it to normal operating temperature.

3. Sit on the seat while the engine is idling and adjust your weight to raise the front wheel off the ground (models equipped with a centerstand). Turn the front wheel from side to side without touching the throttle grip. If the engine speed increases when the wheel is turned, the throttle cable may be damaged or incorrectly adjusted. Perform the *Throttle Cable Adjustment* as described in this chapter.

NOTE
Figure 107 *is shown with the carburetor assembly removed for clarity. Do not remove the carburetor assembly when performing this procedure.*

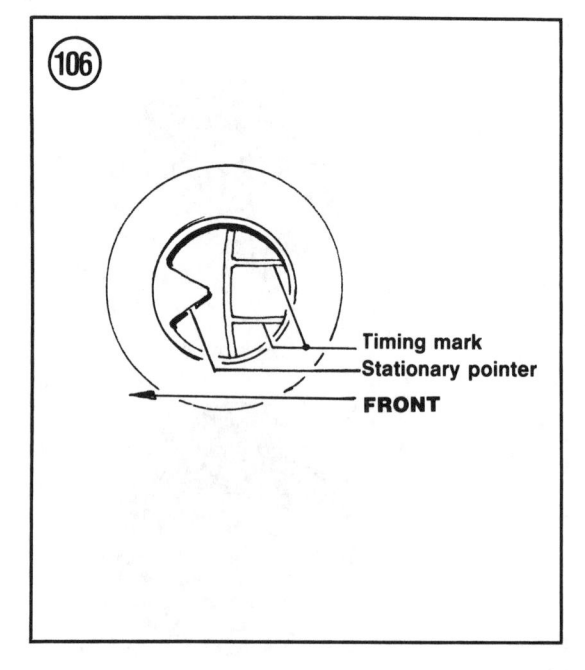

PERIODIC LUBRICATION, MAINTENANCE AND TUNE-UP

4. Turn the throttle stop screw (**Figure 107**) to set the idle speed as specified in **Table 10**.

5. Rev the engine a couple of times to see if it settles down to the set speed. Readjust, if necessary.

Carburetor Synchronization

Synchronizing the carburetors makes sure that one cylinder doesn't try to run faster than the others, cutting power and gas mileage. The only accurate way to synchronize the carburetors is to use a set of vacuum gauges that measure the intake vacuum of all 4 cylinders at the same time.

1. Start the engine and warm it up fully.
2. Adjust the idle speed as described in this chapter.
3. Remove the fuel tank as described in Chapter Seven.
4. Install an auxiliary fuel tank onto the motorcycle and attach its fuel hose the carburetor.

NOTE
Carburetor synchronization cannot be performed with the stock fuel tank in place because there isn't enough room to install the gauges and make adjustments. An auxiliary fuel tank is required to supply fuel to the carburetors during this procedure.

NOTE
Fuel tanks from small displacement motorcycles and ATV's make excellent auxiliary fuel tanks. Make sure the tank is mounted securely and positioned so that connecting fuel hose is not kinked or obstructed.

WARNING
When supplying fuel by temporary means, make sure the auxiliary fuel tank is secure and that all fuel lines are tight—no leaks.

5. Remove the 4 vacuum port plugs (**Figure 108**).

NOTE
Figure 108 *shows the vacuum port plugs used on FZ700 models. All other models use rubber plugs.*

6. Install the vacuum line adapters into the vacuum hole in each manifold.
7. Connect the vacuum lines from the carb-synch tool, following the manufacturer's instructions. Be sure to route the vacuum lines to the correct cylinder.
8. Start the engine and let it idle at the idle speed listed in **Table 10**.
9. If the difference in gauge readings is 10 mm Hg (0.4 in. Hg) or less between the 4 cylinders, the carburetors are considered synchronized. If not, proceed as follows.

NOTE
Figure 109 *is shown with the carburetor assembly removed for clarity. Do not remove the carburetor assembly for this procedure.*

  a. The carburetor adjusting screws are identified in **Figure 109**.
  b. With the engine at idle, synchronize the No. 1 and No. 2 carburetors by turning the left-hand adjusting screw (A, **Figure 109**).
  c. Then synchronize the No. 3 and No. 4 carburetors by turning the right-hand adjusting screw (C, **Figure 109**).
  d. Finally synchronize the No. 1 and No. 2 carburetors to the No. 3 and No. 4 carburetors

by turning the middle adjusting screw (B, **Figure 109**).

NOTE
To gain the utmost in performance and efficiency from the engine, adjust the carburetors so that the gauge readings are as close to each other as possible.

10. Reset the idle speed, stop the engine and install the vacuum plugs.

NOTE
Make sure the vacuum plugs are tight to prevent a vacuum leak.

11. Install the fuel tank.

Table 1 MAINTENANCE SCHEDULE *

Every 300 miles (500 km)	• Lubricate drive chain • Check drive chain tension; adjust if necessary
Initial 600 miles (1,000 km) or 1 month	• Change engine oil and filter • Check carburetor synchronization; adjust if necessary • Check front and rear brake free play; adjust if necessary • Check front brake pad and rear brake pad thickness • Lubricate all control cables
Initial 4,400 miles (7,000 km); thereafter every 3,800 miles (6,000 km)	• Check crankcase ventilation hose for cracks or damage • Check fuel and vacuum hoses for cracks or damage • Check exhaust system for leakage • Check carburetor synchronization; adjust if necessary • Check engine idle speed; adjust if necessary • Change engine oil and filter • Clean air filter; replace if damaged • Check cooling system hoses for cracks or damage • Check front and rear brake free play; adjust if necessary • Check front and rear brake pad thickness • Lubricate all control cables • Check drive chain freeplays; adjust if necessary • Lubricate brake and clutch lever pivot shafts • Lubricate brake pedal and shift shaft pedal pivot shafts • Lubricate center and sidestand pivot shafts • Check front fork operation and check for oil seal leakage • Check steering play; adjust if necessary

(continued)

PERIODIC LUBRICATION, MAINTENANCE AND TUNE-UP

Table 1 MAINTENANCE SCHEDULE * (cont.)

Interval	Item
Initial 4,400 miles (7,000 km); thereafter every 3,800 miles (6,000 km) (continued)	• Check wheel bearing operation • Check battery level and specific gravity • Check sidestand switch operation
Initial 4,400 miles (7,000 km) or 7 months; then every 7,600 miles (12,000 km) or 19 months	• Check spark plugs; adjust gap and clean
Initial 8,200 miles (13,000 km) or 13 months; then every 7,600 miles (12,000 km) or 12 months	• Replace spark plugs
Every 15,200 miles (24,000 km)	• Repack steering head bearings
Every 15,800 miles (25,000 km) or 25 months	• Lubricate swing arm pivot shaft • Lubricate rear suspension pivot shafts
Initial 19,600 miles (31,000 km); then every 19,000 miles (30,000 km)	• Replace fuel filter
Every 26,000 miles (42,000 km)	• Check and adjust valve clearance
Every 24 months	• Change engine coolant

* This Yamaha factory maintenance schedule should be used as a guide to general maintenance and lubrication intervals. Harder than normal use and exposure to mud, water, sand, high humidity, etc., will dictate more frequent attention to most maintenance items.

Table 2 TIRE INFLATION PRESSURE (COLD)

Load	Psi (kg/cm^2)
FZX700	
Up to 198 lb. (90 kg) load	
Front	32 (2.3)
Rear	32 (2.3)
198-500 lb. (90-227 kg) load	
Front	32 (2.3)
Rear	36 (2.5)
FZ700 & FZ750	
Up to 198 lb. (90 kg) load	
Front	28 (2.0)
Rear	32 (2.3)
198-470 lb. (90-213) load	
Front	32 (2.3)
Rear	42 (2.9)
High speed riding	
Front	32 (2.3)
Rear	36 (2.5)

Table 3 BATTERY STATE OF CHARGE

Specific gravity	State of charge
1.110-1.130	Discharged
1.140-1.160	Almost discharged
1.170-1.190	One-quarter charged
1.200-1.220	One-half charged
1.230-1.250	Three-quarters charged
1.260-1.280	Fully charged

Table 4 RECOMMENDED LUBRICANTS AND FLUIDS

Engine oil	
Temperatures 40° F and below	SAE 10W/30 SE/SF
Temperatures 40° F and up	SAE 20W/40 SE/SF
Brake fluid	DOT 3
Battery refilling	Distilled water
Fork oil	10 weight
Cables and pivot points	Yamaha chain and cable lube or SAE 10W/30 motor oil
Fuel	Regular
Drive chain	SAE 30-50 motor oil
Coolant	High-quality ethylene glycol antifreeze compounded for aluminum engines

Table 5 APPROXIMATE REFILL CAPACITIES

Engine oil	
With filter change	3,000 cc (3.1 qt.)
Without filter change	2,700 cc (2.7 qt.)
Engine rebuild	3,500 cc (3.7 qt.)
Front forks	
FZX700	294 cc (9.94 oz.)
FZ700	404 cc (13.7 oz.)
FZ750	408 cc (13.8 oz.)
Cooling system	
FZX700 and FZ750	2.3 L (2.4 qt.)
FZ700	2.6 L (2.7 qt.)
Fuel tank	
FZX700	3.4 gal. (13.0 l)
FZ700	5.6 gal. (21.0 l)
FZ750	5.8 gal. (22.0 l)

Table 6 RECOMMENDED FRONT FORK TO REAR SHOCK SETTINGS (FZX700)

Load	Front fork air pressure kg/cm^2 (psi)	Rear shock absorber spring seat setting
Rider	0.4-0.8 (5-7)	1-2
Rider plus passenger	0.4-0.8 (5-7)	3-5
Rider plus passenger and/or luggage	0.6-1.0 (8.5-14)	3-5
Maximum vehicle load	0.8-1.2 (12-18)	5

PERIODIC LUBRICATION, MAINTENANCE AND TUNE-UP

Table 7 RECOMMENDED FRONT FORK TO REAR SHOCK SETTINGS (FZ700)

Load	Front fork spring preload adjuster	Rear shock spring length
Rider	1, 2	12.5-16.5 mm (0.49-0.65 in.)
Rider plus passenger	2, 3	14.5-18.5 mm (0.57-0.73 in.)
Rider plus luggage	2, 3	14.5-18.5 mm (0.57-0.73 in.)
Maximum vehicle load	3, 4	16.5-20.5 mm (0.65-0.81 in.)

Table 8 RECOMMENDED FRONT FORK TO REAR SHOCK SETTINGS (FZ750)

Load	Front fork damper	Front fork air pressure Kg/cm² (psi)	Rear shock absorber Spring preload adjuster
Rider	1, 2	0-0.4 (0-5.7)	1, 2
Rider plus passenger	3, 4	0-0.4 (0-5.7)	3, 4
Rider plus luggage	2, 3	0-0.4 (0-5.7)	2, 3
Maximum vehicle load	4, 5	0-0.4 (0-5.7)	4, 5

Table 9 FRONT FORK AIR PRESSURE

Model	Standard kg/cm² (psi)	Maximum kg/cm² (psi)
FZX700	0.4 (5.7)	1.2 (17)
FZ750	0 (0)	0.4 (5.7)

Table 10 TUNE-UP SPECIFICATIONS

Air filter element	Dry element type
Firing order	1-2-4-3
Ignition timing	Fixed
Valve clearance (cold)	
Intake	0.11-0.20 mm (0.0043-0.0079 in.)
Exhaust	0.21-0.30 mm (0.0083-0.0118 in.)
Spark plug	
Type	NGK DP8EA-9 or ND X24EP-U9
Gap	0.8-0.9 mm (0.031-0.035 in.)
Tightening torque	17.5 N•m (12.5 ft.-lb.)
Idle speed	950-1,050 rpm
Compression pressure (cold @ sea level)	
Standard	11 kg/cm² (156 psi)
Minimum	9 kg/cm² (128 psi)
Maximum	12 kg/cm² (171 psi)
Maximum difference between cylinders: 14 psi (1.0 kg/cm²)	

CHAPTER FOUR

ENGINE

The engine is a liquid-cooled, double overhead cam, five-valve inline four. Valves are operated by chain-driven overhead camshafts.

This chapter provides complete service and overhaul procedures, including information for disassembly, removal, inspection, service and reassembly of the engine.

Before starting any work, read the service hints in Chapter One. You will do a better job with this information fresh in your mind.

Table 1 lists engine specifications. **Tables 1-3** are at the end of the chapter.

SERVICING ENGINE IN FRAME

Many components can be serviced while the engine is mounted in the frame:
  a. Cylinder head.
  b. Cylinders and pistons.
  c. Gearshift mechanism.
  d. Clutch.
  e. Carburetors.
  f. Starter motor.
  g. Generator and electrical systems.

ENGINE PRINCIPLES

Figure 1 explains how the engine works. This will be helpful when troubleshooting or repairing your engine.

ENGINE

Removal/Installation
(FZX700)

1. Place the motorcycle on its center stand.
2. Remove the seat.
3. Disconnect the negative battery terminal (**Figure 2**).
4. Remove the fuel tank as described in Chapter Seven.
5. Drain the engine oil as described in Chapter Three.
6. Drain the cooling system as described in Chapter Three.
7. Remove the air cleaner housing as follows:
   a. Remove the carburetor side covers (**Figure 3**).
   b. Disconnect the crankcase ventilation hose (**Figure 4**) at the housing.
   c. Loosen the hose clamps and lift the air cleaner housing (**Figure 4**) off of the carburetors.
8. Remove the carburetors as described in Chapter Seven.

CAUTION
*Stuff clean shop rags into the intake manifold openings (**Figure 5**). Objects dropped into the intake manifolds will fall into the cylinder head.*

ENGINE

① 4-STROKE PRINCIPLES

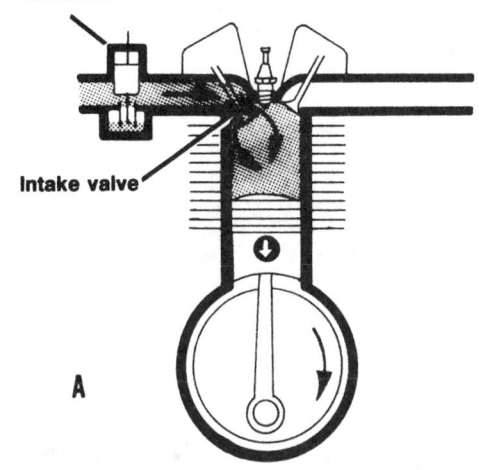

A

As the piston travels downward, the exhaust valve is closed and the intake valve opens, allowing the new air-fuel mixture from the carburetor to be drawn into the cylinder. After the piston passes the bottom of its travel (BDC), the intake valve closes and remains closed for the next 1 1/2 revolutions of the crankshaft.

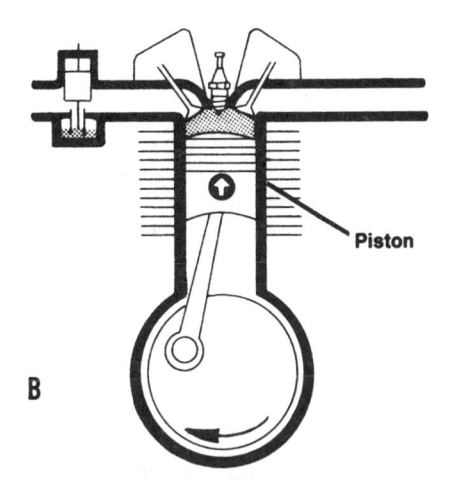

B

While the crankshaft continues to rotate, the piston moves upward, compressing the air-fuel mixture.

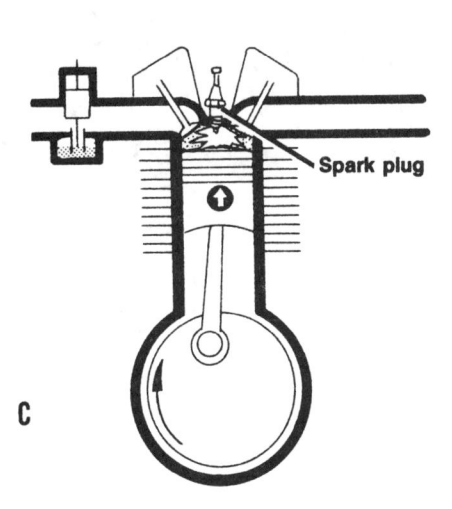

C

As the piston almost reaches the top of its travel, the spark plug fires, igniting the compressed air-fuel mixture. The piston continues to top dead center (TDC) and is pushed downward by the expanding gases.

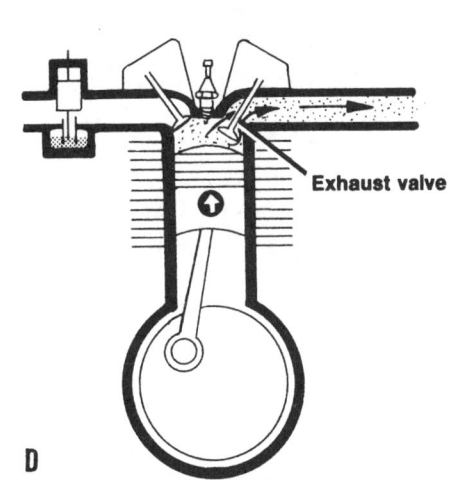

D

When the piston almost reaches BDC, the exhaust valve opens and remains open until the piston is near TDC. The upward travel of the piston forces the exhaust gases out of the cylinder. After the piston passes TDC, the exhaust valve closes and the cycle starts all over again.

CHAPTER FOUR

9. Remove the radiator as described under *Radiator and Fan Removal/Installation* in Chapter Nine.
10. Unscrew the front side reflectors, then remove the side covers. See **Figure 6**.
11. Remove the thermostat and housing as described in Chapter Nine.
12. Remove the exhaust system as described in Chapter Seven.
13. Remove the plug gaps as described in Chapter Three.
14. Disconnect the crankcase ventilation hose from the right-hand side of the engine (**Figure 7**).
15. Remove the pipe (**Figure 7**) and right-hand side panel (**Figure 7**).

CAUTION
The bolt securing the gearshift lever must be removed completely or damage to the shift lever splines will occur.

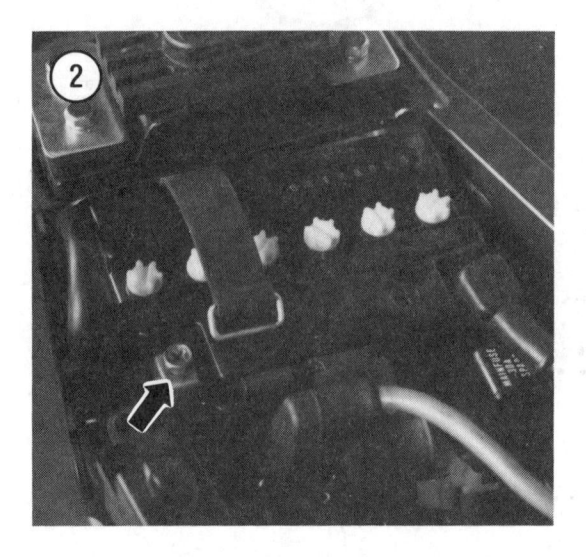

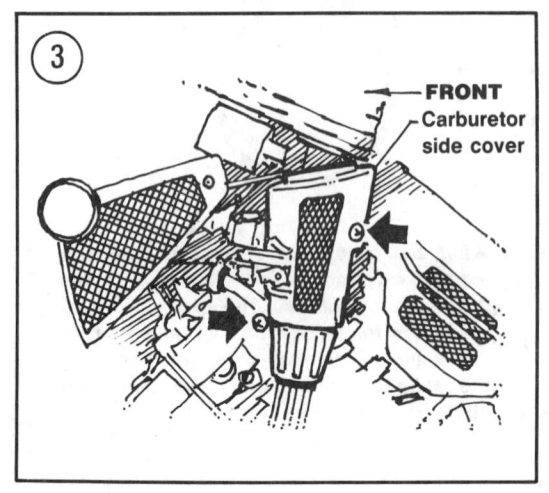

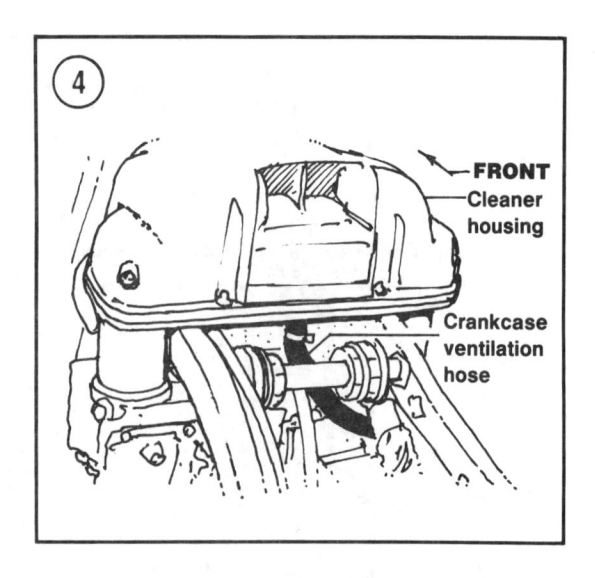

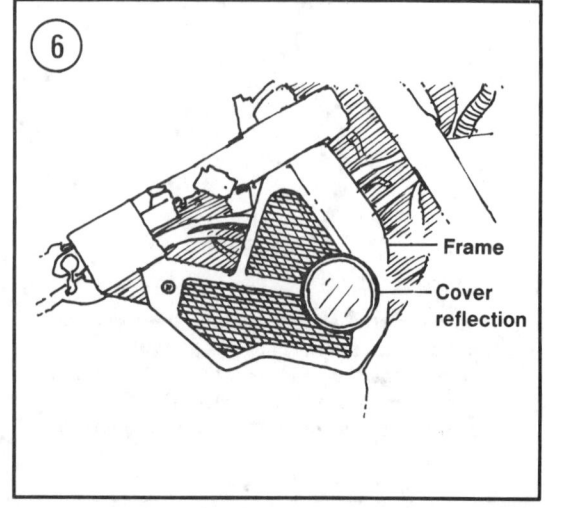

ENGINE

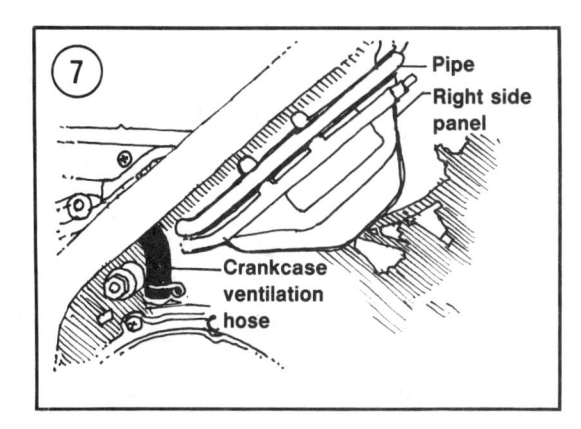

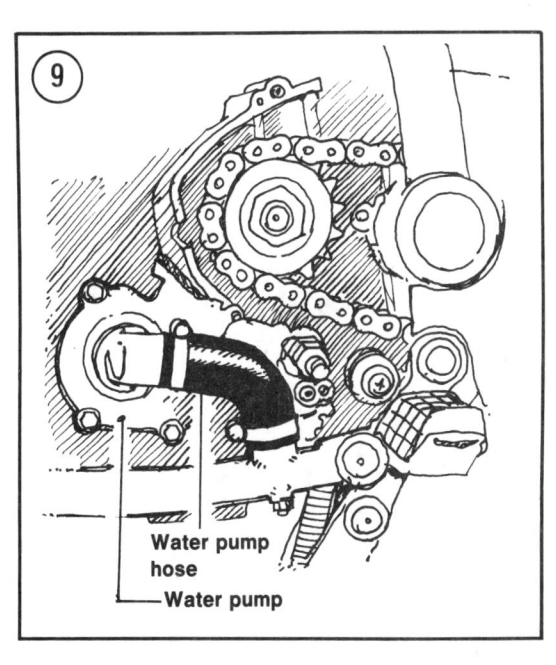

16. Scratch an alignment mark across the gearshift lever and the end of the shift shaft. Then remove the gearshift lever bolt and slide the lever (A, **Figure 8**) off of the shaft.

NOTE
If the gearshift lever is tight, insert a flat-tipped screwdriver into the shift lever slot and pry open the shift lever hole.

17. Remove the sprocket cover screws and slide the cover off the shift shaft (B, **Figure 8**). Secure the sprocket cover with a bungee cord to prevent damage to the clutch hydraulic hose.

NOTE
It is not necessary to remove the clutch release mechanism from the sprocket cover.

18. Remove the front sprocket as described under *Engine Sprocket* in Chapter Six.
19. Disconnect the water pump hose at the engine (**Figure 9**).
20. Disconnect the following electrical leads:
    a. Starter motor (**Figure 10**).
    b. Sidestand switch (**Figure 10**).
    c. Generator (**Figure 10**).
    d. Neutral/oil level switch connector (**Figure 10**).
21. Remove the igniter as described under *Igniter Removal/Installation* in Chapter Eight.
22. Remove the footrest and brake pedal assembly from the right-hand side.
23. *Engine disassembly:* If the engine requires disassembly, it will be easier to remove many of the large sub-assembles while the engine is

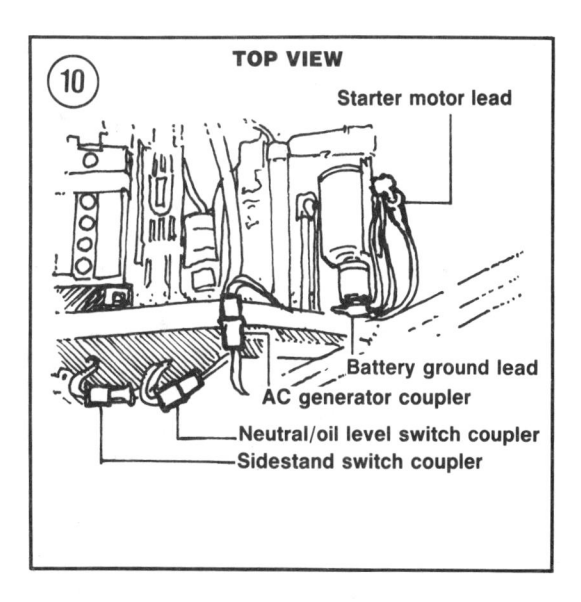

mounted in the frame. Remove the following as described in this chapter unless otherwise noted:
   a. Cylinder head.
   b. Cylinder block.
   c. Pistons.
   d. Generator (Chapter Eight).
   e. Starter (Chapter Eight).
   f. Clutch (Chapter Five).
   g. External shift mechanism (Chapter Six).
24. Place a jack under the crankcase to support the engine once the mounting bolts are removed.
25. Referring to **Figure 11**, remove the following in order:
   a. Front engine mounting bolts.
   b. Rear upper engine mounting bolt and spacer (**Figure 12**).
   c. Rear lower engine mounting bolt.
   d. Front down tube bolt.
   e. Middle down tube bolts.
   f. Rear down the tube bolt.

WARNING
The engine is very heavy and has many sharp edges. It may shift or drop suddenly when removing the mounting bolts. Never place your hands or any other part of your body where the engine could drop and crush your hands or arms. One or more assistants will be required to remove the engine from the frame. Do not attempt engine removal by yourself.

NOTE
Double check that all electrical leads have been disconnected.

26. Lower the jack and slide it and the engine out from the right-hand side. Then with an assistant, lift the engine off the jack and place it on the workbench.
27. While the engine is removed for service, check all of the frame engine mounts for cracks or other damage. If any cracks are detected, take the chassis assembly to a Yamaha dealer for further examination.
28. Install by reversing the removal steps. Note the following.
29. Install the engine mounting bolts and nuts, but do not tighten them yet. Install the spacer (**Figure 12**) onto the right rear upper engine mount.
30. Tighten the down tube bolts in the following order:
   a. Tighten the rear upper bolt to 28 N•m (20 ft.-lb.). See **Figure 11**.
   b. Tighten the rear down tube bolt to 28 N•m (20 ft.-lb.).

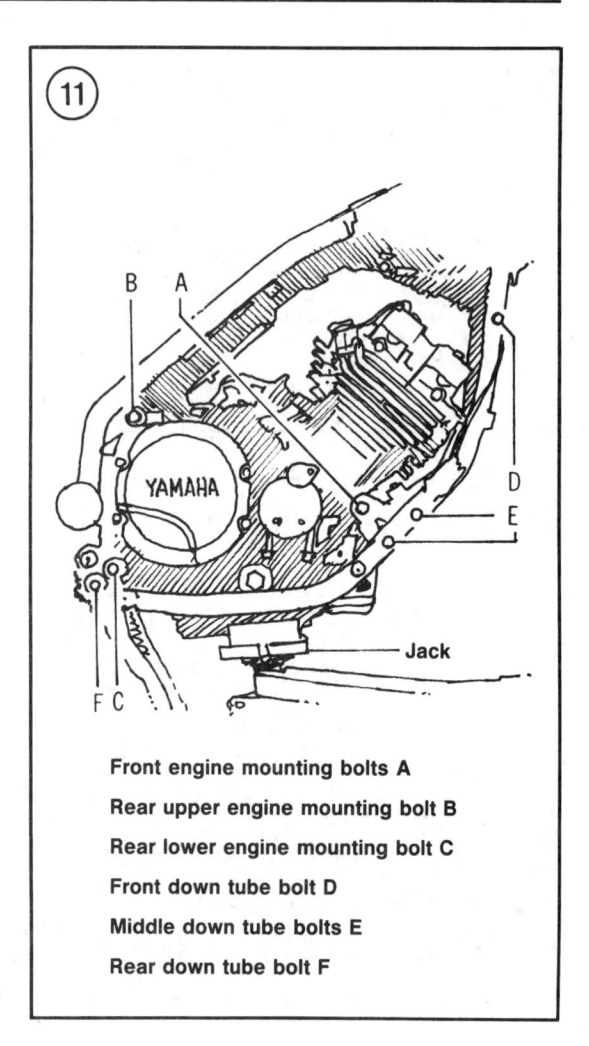

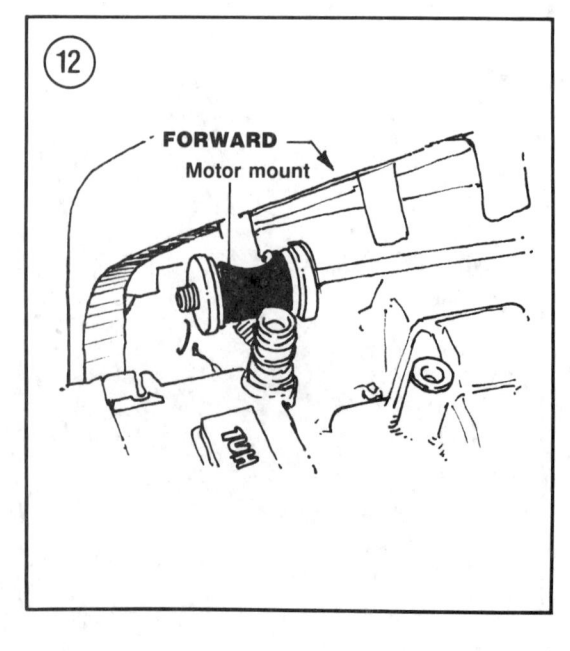

Front engine mounting bolts A
Rear upper engine mounting bolt B
Rear lower engine mounting bolt C
Front down tube bolt D
Middle down tube bolts E
Rear down tube bolt F

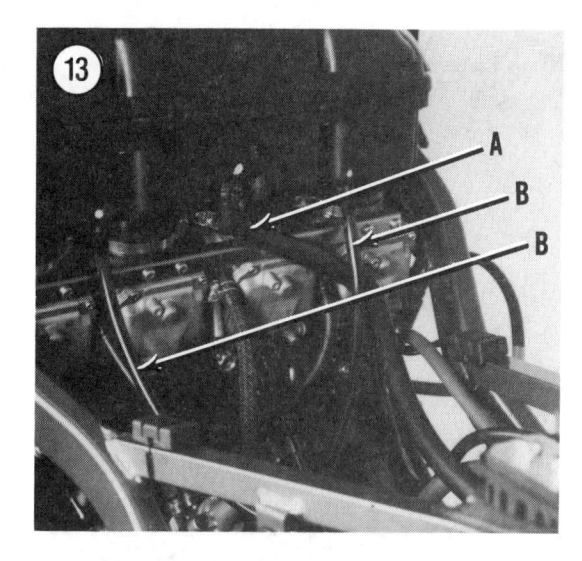

ENGINE

c. Tighten the down tube cross pipe nuts to 20 N•m (14 ft.-lb.).
d. Tighten the footrest bolt to 28 N•m (20 ft.-lb.).
e. Retighten the rear down tube bolt to 28 N•m (20 ft.-lb.).

31. Fill the crankcase with the recommended type and quantity of engine oil. Refer to *Engine Oil and Filter Change* in Chapter Three.
32. Refill the cooling system. See *Coolant Change* in Chapter Three.
33. Adjust the following as described in Chapter Three:
    a. Drive chain.
    b. Rear brake.
    c. Throttle cable.
34. If the hydraulic clutch line was opened, bleed the clutch as described under *Bleeding the Clutch* in Chapter Five.
35. Start the engine and check for leaks.

Removal/Installation (FZ700 and FZ750)

1. Place the motorcycle on its center stand. On FZ700 models, support the bike so that it is secure.
2. Remove the seat.
3. Remove the fairing assembly as described in Chapter Thirteen.
4. Disconnect the negative battery terminal (**Figure 2**).
5. Remove the fuel tank as described in Chapter Seven.
6. Drain the engine oil as described in Chapter Three.
7. Drain the cooling system as described in Chapter Three.
8. Remove the air cleaner housing as follows:
    a. Disconnect the crankcase ventilation hose (A, **Figure 13**) at the housing.
    b. Disconnect the 2 air vent hoses (B, **Figure 13**) at the housing.
    c. Loosen the hose clamps and lift the air cleaner housing (**Figure 14**) off of the carburetors.
9. Remove the carburetors as described in Chapter Seven.

CAUTION
*Stuff clean shop rags into the intake manifold openings (**Figure 5**). Objects dropped into the intake manifolds will fall into the cylinder head.*

10. Remove the air baffle plate bolts and remove the 3 air baffle plates. See **Figure 15** (side) and **Figure 16** (middle).

CHAPTER FOUR

11. Remove the radiator as described under *Radiator and Fan Removal/Installation* in Chapter Nine.

12. Remove the thermostat valve housing as described in Chapter Nine.

13. Remove the exhaust system as described in Chapter Seven.

NOTE
Before pulling the spark plug caps off of the spark plugs, twist the caps from side to side to break the mating seal.

14. Label and disconnect the spark plug wires.
15. Disconnect the crankcase ventilation hose from the right-hand side of the engine.

CAUTION
The bolt securing the gearshift lever must be removed completely or damage to the shift lever splines will occur.

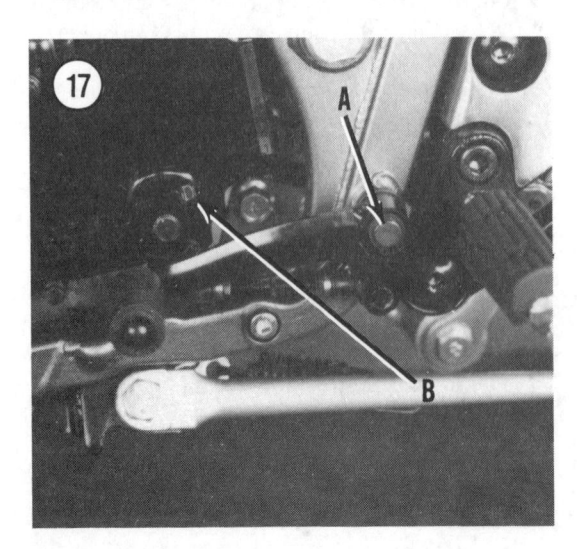

ENGINE

16. Remove the gearshift lever as follows:
    a. Remove the pivot shaft circlip (A, **Figure 17**).
    b. Scratch an alignment mark across the gearshift lever and the end of the shift shaft. Then remove the gearshift lever bolt (B, **Figure 17**) and slide the lever off of the shaft.

NOTE
If the gearshift lever is tight, insert a flat-tipped screwdriver into the shift lever slot and pry open the shift lever hole.

17. Remove the sprocket cover screws and slide the cover off the shift shaft (**Figure 18**). Secure the sprocket cover with a bungee cord to prevent damage to the clutch hydraulic hose.

NOTE
It is not necessary to remove the clutch release mechanism from the sprocket cover.

18. Disconnect the engine water pump hose at the front connection (A, **Figure 19**). Then pull the hose out of the water pump (B, **Figure 19**) and remove the hose.
19. Remove the front sprocket as described under *Engine Sprocket* in Chapter Six.
20. Disconnect the following electrical leads:
    a. Pick-up coil (**Figure 20**).
    b. Oil level switch (**Figure 21**).
    c. Neutral switch (**Figure 22**).
    d. Starter motor (**Figure 23**).
    e. Sidestand switch (**Figure 24**).
21. Remove the footrest and brake pedal assembly from the right-hand side.
22. *Engine disassembly:* If the engine requires disassembly, it will be easier to remove many of

the large sub-assemblies while the engine is mounted in the frame. Remove the following as described in this chapter unless otherwise noted:
 a. Cylinder head.
 b. Cylinder block.
 c. Pistons.
 d. Generator and pickup coil (Chapter Eight).
 e. Starter (Chapter Eight).
 f. Clutch (Chapter Five).
 g. External shift mechanism (Chapter Six).

23. Place a jack under the crankcase to support the engine once the mounting bolts are removed.

24. Remove the following in order:
 a. Front down tube bolts (**Figure 25**).
 b. Middle down tube bolts (A, **Figure 26**).
 c. Rear down tube bolts (**Figure 27**).
 d. Front upper mounting bolt (B, **Figure 26**).
 e. Front lower mounting bolt (C, **Figure 26**).
 f. Rear upper mounting bolt (**Figure 28**).
 g. Rear lower mounting bolt (**Figure 29**).
 h. Rear upper mounting spacer (**Figure 30**) from the right-hand side.
 i. Left- and right-hand down-tube assemblies (**Figure 31**).

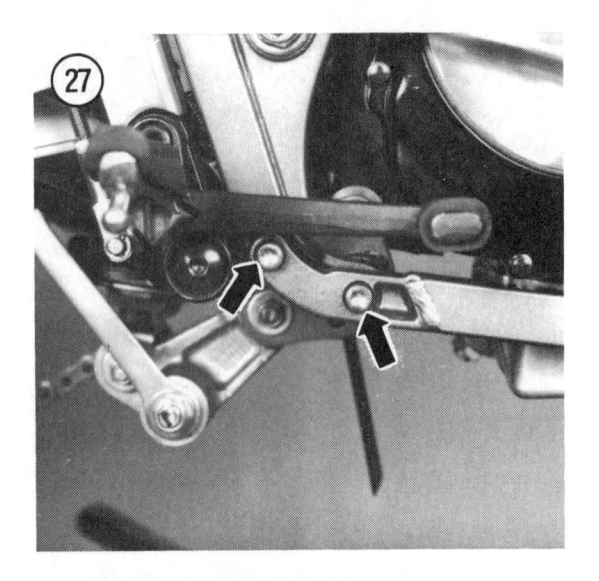

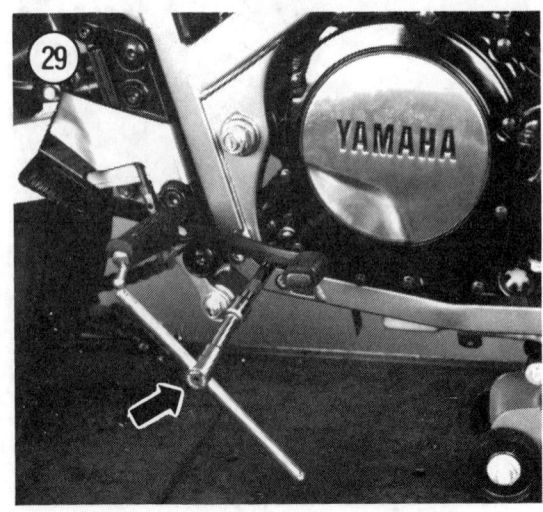

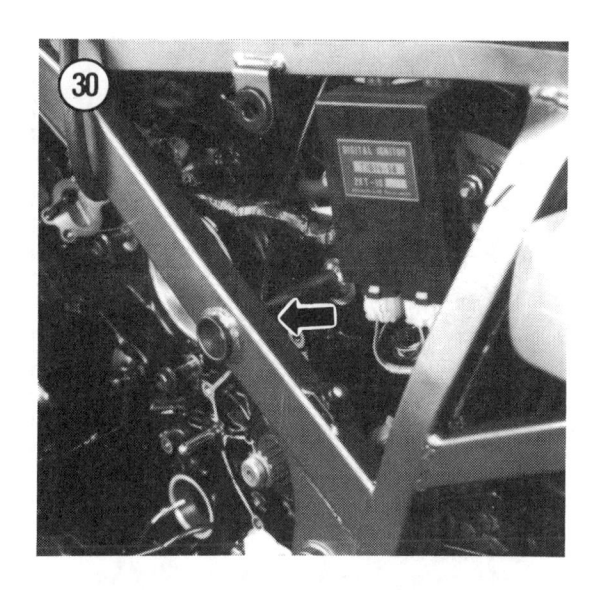

ENGINE

WARNING
The engine is very heavy and has many sharp edges. It may shift or drop suddenly when removing the mounting bolts. Never place your hands or any other part of your body where the engine could drop and crush your hands or arms. One or more assistants will be required to remove the engine from the frame. Do not attempt engine removal by yourself.

NOTE
Double check that all electrical leads have been disconnected.

25. Lower the jack (**Figure 32**) and slide it and the engine out from the right-hand side. Then with an assistant, lift the engine off the jack and place it on the workbench.
26. While the engine is removed for service, check all of the frame engine mounts for cracks or other damage. See **Figure 33**. If any cracks are detected, take the chassis assembly to a Yamaha dealer for further examination.
27. Install by reversing the removal steps. Note the following.
28. Install the spacer (**Figure 30**) onto the right rear upper engine mount.
29. Tighten the engine mounting bolts to the torque specifications in **Table 3**.
30. Fill the crankcase with the recommended type and quantity of engine oil. Refer to *Engine Oil and Filter Change* in Chapter Three.
31. Refill the cooling system. See *Coolant Change* in Chapter Three.

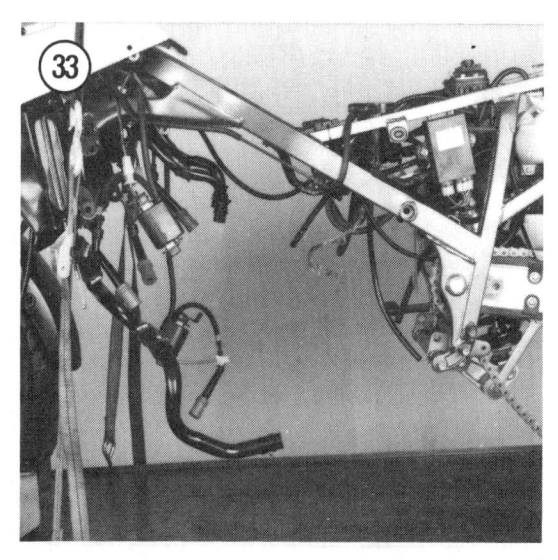

32. Adjust the following as described in Chapter Three:
   a. Drive chain.
   b. Rear brake.
   c. Throttle cable.
   d. Choke cable.

33. If the hydraulic clutch line was opened, bleed the clutch as described under *Bleeding the Clutch System* in Chapter Five.

34. Start the engine and check for leaks.

CYLINDER HEAD COVER AND CAMSHAFTS

This section describes removal, inspection and installation procedures for the camshaft components.

Cylinder Head Cover Removal/Installation

1. Park the bike on the center stand. On FZ700 models, support the bike so that it is stable.
2. Remove the seat.
3. Disconnect the negative battery terminal (**Figure 2**).

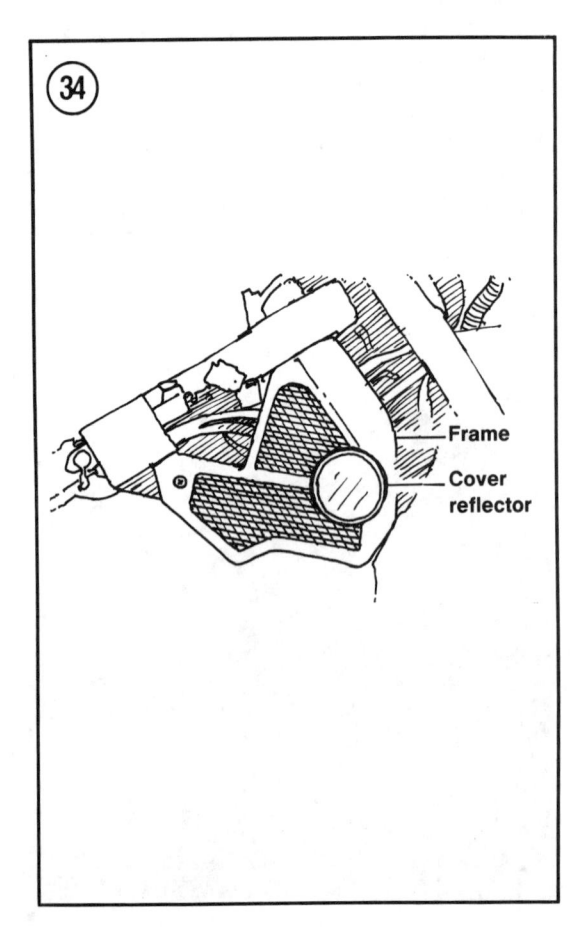

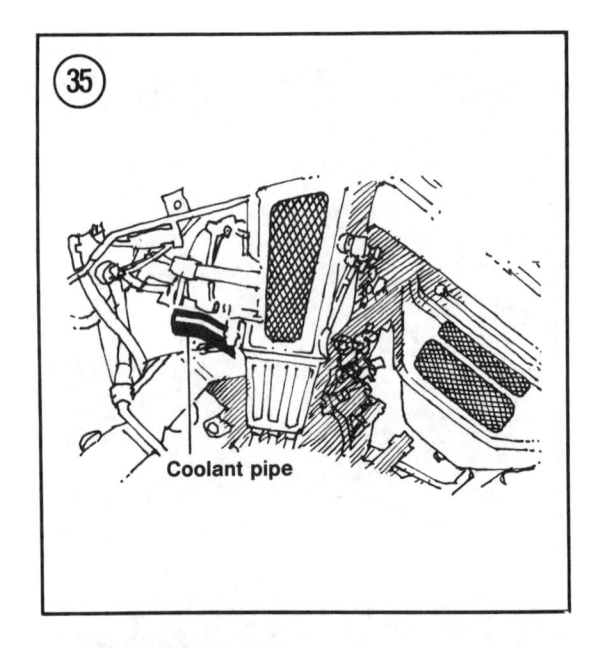

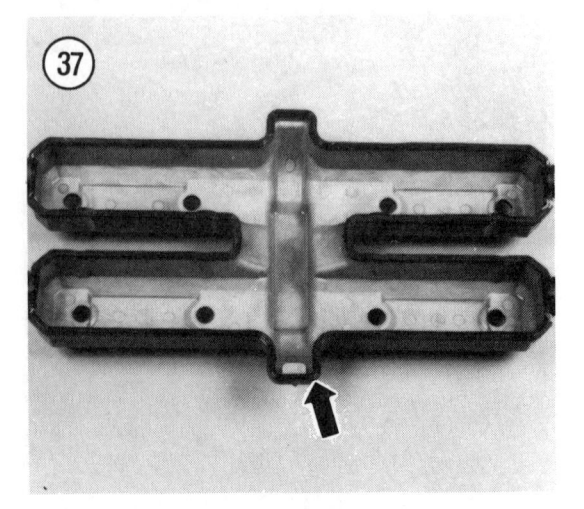

ENGINE

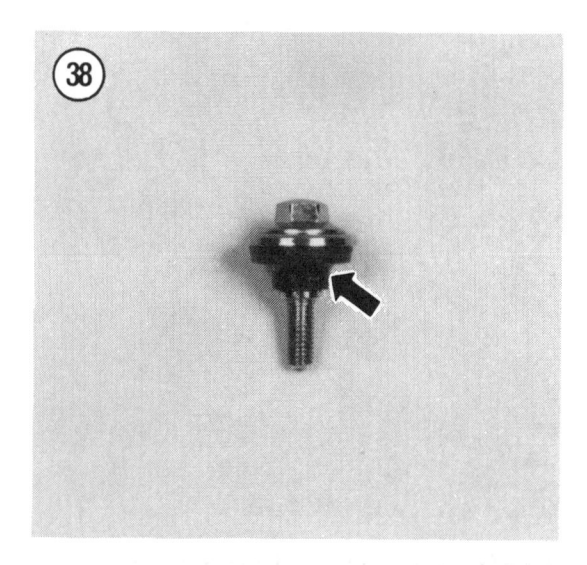

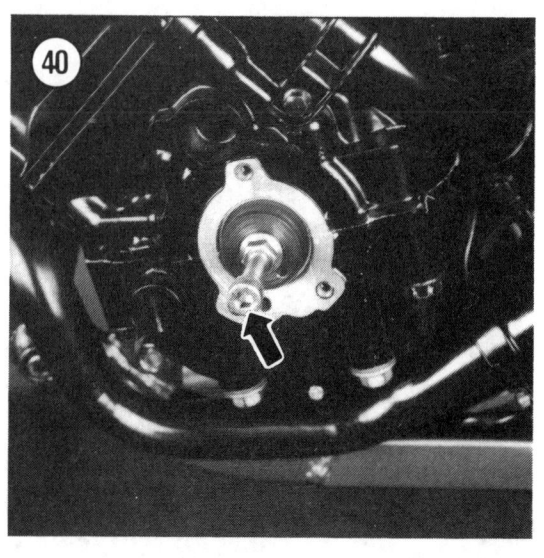

4. Remove the fuel tank as described in Chapter Seven.
5. *FZX700:* Unscrew the front side reflectors, then remove the side covers. See **Figure 34**.
6. *FZ700 and FZ750:* Remove the lower fairing as described in Chapter Thirteen.
7. Remove the radiator and fan assembly as described under *Radiator and Fan Removal/Installation* in Chapter Nine.
8. Remove the thermostat housing as described in Chapter Nine.
9. *FZX700:* Remove the rear coolant pipe (**Figure 35**).
10. Remove the cylinder head cover bolts and remove the cover (**Figure 36**).
11. Installation is the reverse of these steps, noting the following.
12. Replace the cylinder head cover gasket (**Figure 37**) and bolt seals (**Figure 38**) if worn, damaged or if there are signs of oil leakage.
13. Tighten the cylinder head cover bolts to 10 N•m (7.2 ft.-lb.).
14. Refill the engine coolant as described under *Coolant Change* in Chapter Three.

Camshaft Removal

1. Remove the cylinder head cover as described in this chapter.
2. Disconnect the battery ground cable.
3. Remove the spark plugs. This will make it easier to turn the engine by hand.
4. Remove the left crankshaft end cover (A, **Figure 39**).

NOTE
To prevent damaging the plastic timing plug screw in Step 5, loosen it with a large straight-tipped screwdriver.

5. Unscrew and remove the timing plug screw (B, **Figure 39**).
6. Thread an 8 mm bolt and nut into the left crankshaft end (**Figure 40**). Lock the bolt with the nut.

NOTE
*The factory specified valve clearance check is every 26,600 miles (42,000 km). Because valve adjustment requires camshaft removal to gain access to the pads and valve lifters, it is a good idea to first check valve clearance before the camshafts are removed. Record all valve clearances and purchase new pads so that they can be reinstalled during camshaft installation. Refer to **Valve Clearance Measurement** in Chapter Three.*

CHAPTER FOUR

7. Using the bolt installed in Step 6, rotate the crankshaft counterclockwise until the top dead center (TDC) "T" mark on the crankshaft web for the No. 1 and No. 4 cylinders aligns with the fixed pointer on the crankcase as viewed through the port hole (**Figure 41**). The cam lobes for No. 1 cylinder should also point upward. If not, rotate the crankshaft one full turn counterclockwise. The No. 1 cylinder is now at top dead center (TDC) on the compression stroke.

8. Remove the camshaft chain tensioner as described in this chapter.

9. Remove the upper chain guide bolts and lift the chain guide off the engine (A, **Figure 42**).

10. Lift the front chain guide out of the engine (A, **Figure 43**).

NOTE
*Each camshaft cap is marked with an arrow (pointing forward) and with a letter and number representing position. See **Figure 44**. If the camshaft cap markings on your bike differ from those in **Figure 44** or if there are no marks, label them for direction and position before performing Step 11.*

11. Remove the No. 3 exhaust camshaft cap (B, **Figure 42**) and intake camshaft cap (C, **Figure 42**).

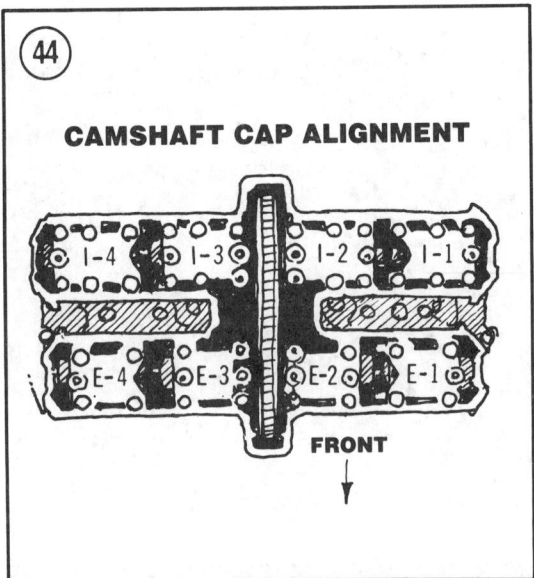

CAMSHAFT CAP ALIGNMENT

I-4 I-3 I-2 I-1

E-4 E-3 E-2 E-1

FRONT

ENGINE

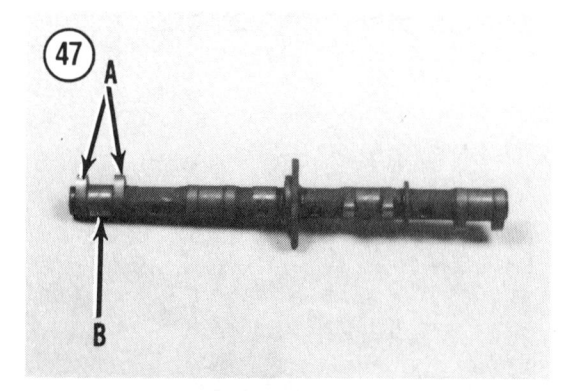

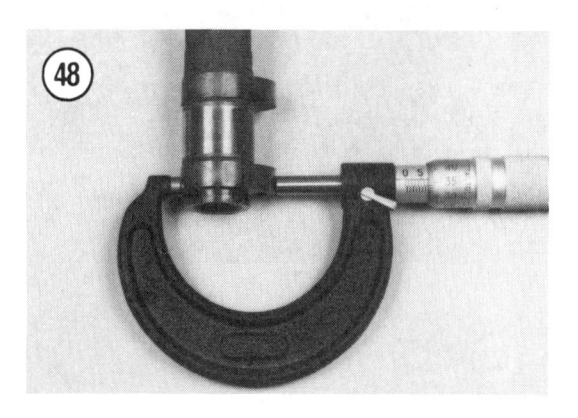

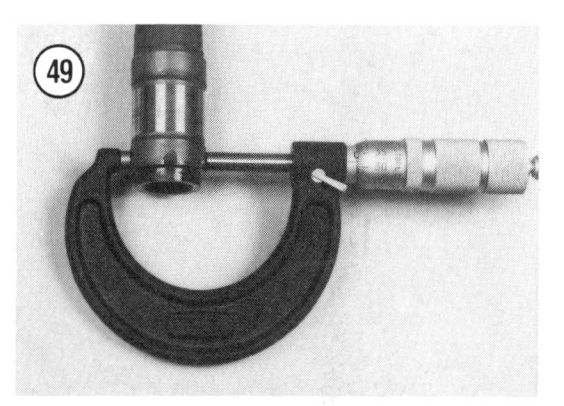

12. Remove the camshaft sprocket bolts (B, **Figure 43**).

NOTE
It will be necessary to turn the crankshaft counterclockwise to provide access to all camshaft sprocket bolts.

13. Remove the remaining camshaft caps (**Figure 45**).
14. Secure the camshaft chain with wire. Then remove both camshafts and their sprockets (**Figure 46**). Remove the camshafts slowly to prevent damaging any cam lobe or bearing surface.

CAUTION
If the crankshaft must be rotated while the camshafts are removed, lift up on the cam chain to prevent it from binding on the crankshaft sprocket.

Camshaft Inspection

1. Wash the camshafts thoroughly in solvent and blow dry.
2. Check cam lobes (A, **Figure 47**) for wear. The lobes should not be scored and the edges should be square. Slight damage may be removed with a silicon carbide oilstone. Use No. 100-120 grit initially, then polish with a No. 280-320 grit.
3. Even though the cam lobe surfaces appear to be satisfactory, with no visible signs of wear, they must be measured with a micrometer as shown in **Figure 48** and **Figure 49**. Replace the shaft(s) if worn beyond the service limits (measurements less than those given in **Table 1**).
4. Check the camshaft bearing journals (B, **Figure 47**) for wear and scoring.
5. Even though the camshaft bearing journal surface appears satisfactory, with no visible signs of wear, the camshaft bearing journals must be measured with a micrometer (**Figure 50**). Replace the shaft(s) if worn beyond the service limits (measurements less than those given in **Table 1**).

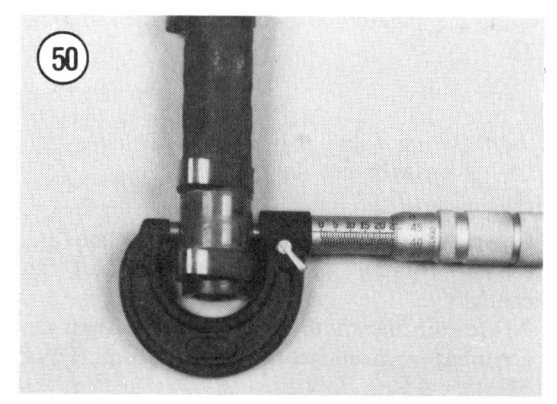

6. Place the camshaft on a set of V-blocks and check its runout with a dial indicator. Replace the camshaft if runout exceeds specifications in **Table 1**. Repeat for the opposite camshaft.
7. Inspect the camshaft sprockets (**Figure 51**) for wear; replace if necessary.

NOTE
If the camshaft sprockets are worn, also check the camshaft chain, chain guides and chain tensioner as described in this chapter.

8. Check the camshaft bearing journals in the cylinder head (**Figure 52**) and camshaft caps (**Figure 53**) for wear and scoring. They should not be scored or excessively worn. If necessary, replace the cam case and camshaft caps as a matched pair.

Camshaft Bearing Clearance Measurement

This procedure requires the use of a Plastigage set. The camshaft must be installed into the head. Prior to installation, wipe all oil residue from each cam journal and bearing.

1. Install all locating dowels into their camshaft caps.
2. Wipe all oil from the cam bearing journals prior to using the Plastigage. Install the camshaft (**Figure 46**).
3. Place a strip of Plastigage material on top of each cam bearing journal (**Figure 54**), parallel to the cam.
4. Place the camshaft caps into position.
5. Install all camshaft cap bolts. Install finger-tight at first, then tighten in a crisscross pattern (**Figure 44**) to the final torque specification listed in **Table 2**.

CAUTION
Do not rotate the camshaft with the Plastigage material in place.

6. Gradually remove the camshaft cap bolts in a crisscross pattern. Remove the camshaft caps carefully.
7. Measure the width of the flattened Plastigage according to manufacturer's instructions (**Figure 55**).

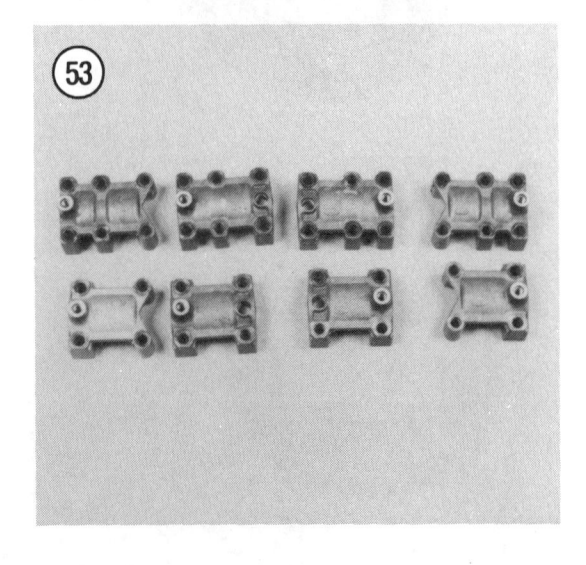

ENGINE

54

Plastigage strip

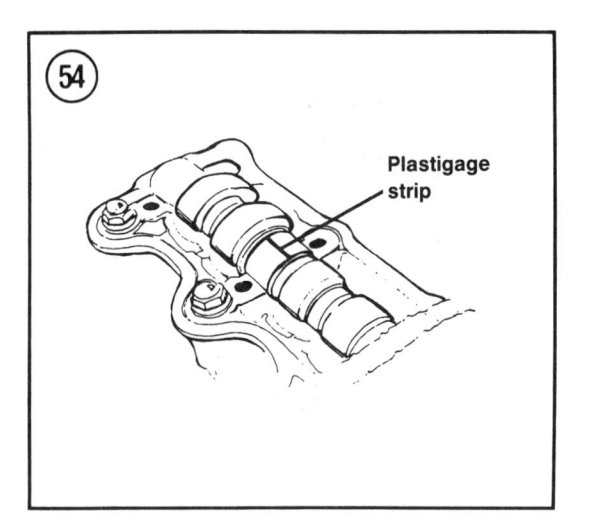

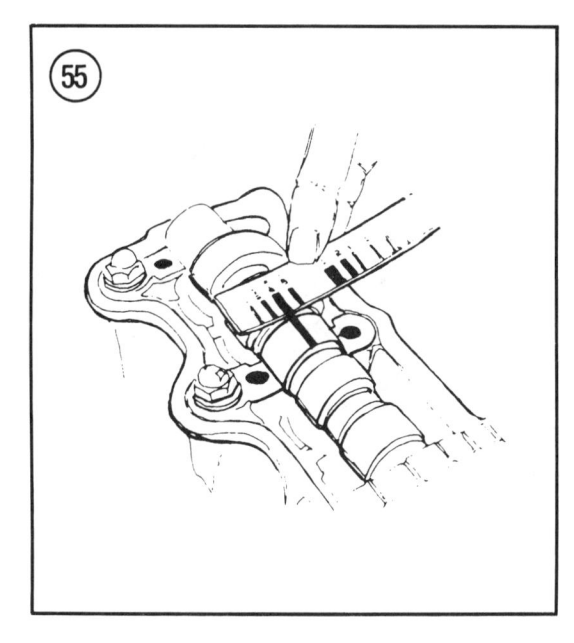

55

56

8. If the clearance exceeds the wear limits in **Table 1**, measure the camshaft bearing journals (**Figure 50**) with a micrometer and compare to the limits in **Table 1**. If the camshaft bearing journal is less than dimension specified, replace the cam. If the cam is within specifications, the cam case and camshaft caps must be replaced as a matched set.

CAUTION
Remove all particles of Plastigage from all camshaft bearing journals and the camshaft holder. Be sure to clean the camshaft holder groove. This material must not be left in the engine as it can plug up an oil control orifice and cause severe engine damage.

Camshaft Chain and Sprockets Inspection/Replacement

Examine the camshaft sprockets (**Figure 51**) for any signs of wear, cracks or tooth damage. If the camshaft sprockets are worn, also check the camshaft chain and the crankshaft drive sprocket for wear. See *Crankshaft Inspection* in this chapter. Severe wear of one component will require the replacement of both sprockets and chain.

Camshaft Chain Guides

Inspect the camshaft chain guides (**Figure 56**) for severe wear or damage. Replace if necessary.

Camshaft Installation

1. If camshaft bearing clearance was checked, make sure all Plastigage material has been removed from the camshaft and camshaft cap surfaces.

CAUTION
When rotating the crankshaft in Step 2, lift the cam chain tightly on the exhaust side (front) to prevent it from binding on the crankshaft sprocket.

2. Using the bolt installed in Step 6 of *Camshaft Removal*, rotate the crankshaft counterclockwise until the top dead center (TDC) "T" mark on the crankshaft web aligns with with fixed pointer on the crankcase as viewed through the port hole (**Figure 41**). The No. 1 cylinder is now at TDC.
3. Coat all camshaft lobes and bearing journals with molybdenum disulfide grease or assembly oil.
4. Also coat the bearing surfaces in the cylinder head and camshaft bearing caps.

NOTE
The exhaust camshaft is machined with a series of 2 lobes and the intake camshaft is machined with a series of 3 lobes. See **Figure 57**.

5. Slide the sprocket onto each camshaft. Do not seat the sprockets onto the camshaft sprocket shoulders at this time.

6. Lift the cam chain and slide the exhaust camshaft through and set it in the front bearing blocks (**Figure 46**). Install the intake camshaft through the cam chain and set it in the rear bearing blocks.

CAUTION
The camshaft caps were machined with the camshaft case at the time of manufacture. If the caps are not installed in their original position, camshaft seizure may result.

7. Referring to **Figure 58**, install the following camshaft caps with their dowel pins:
   a. No. 1 exhaust (E-1).
   b. No. 2 exhaust (E-2).
   c. No. 4 exhaust (E-4).
   d. No. 1 intake (I-1).
   e. No. 2 intake (I-2).
   f. No. 4 exhaust (I-4).

8. Apply engine oil onto the camshaft cap bolt threads and install the bolts. Tighten the camshaft cap bolts in a crisscross pattern to the torque specifications in **Table 2**.

9. Engage the exhaust sprocket with the cam chain and slide the sprocket onto the exhaust camshaft sprocket shoulder.

10. Install the exhaust sprocket as follows:
   a. Place the "E-3" camshaft cap onto the cylinder head (**Figure 59**).

CAUTION
Do not rotate the camshaft more than 1/2 turn in Step "b" or piston and/or valve damage may occur.

   b. Install a suitable size wrench on the camshaft as shown in **Figure 60**. Then turn the camshaft and align the camshaft timing mark with the "E-3" camshaft cap timing mark. See **Figure 61**.

CAUTION
Do not rotate the exhaust cam after aligning it in Step "b".

   c. Remove the "E-3" camshaft cap (**Figure 59**).
   d. Push the exhaust sprocket onto the camshaft sprocket shoulder.

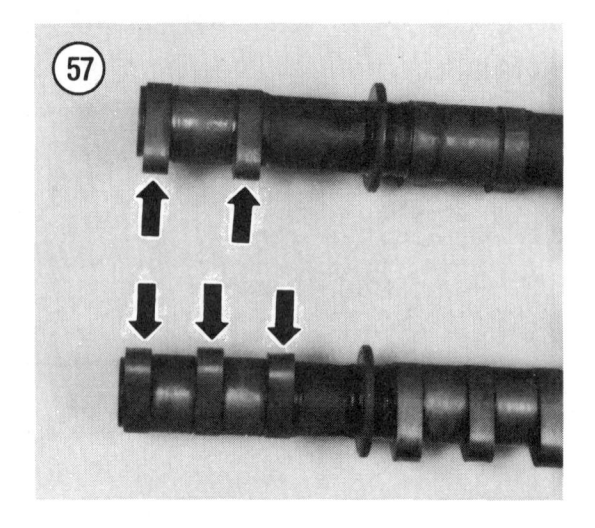

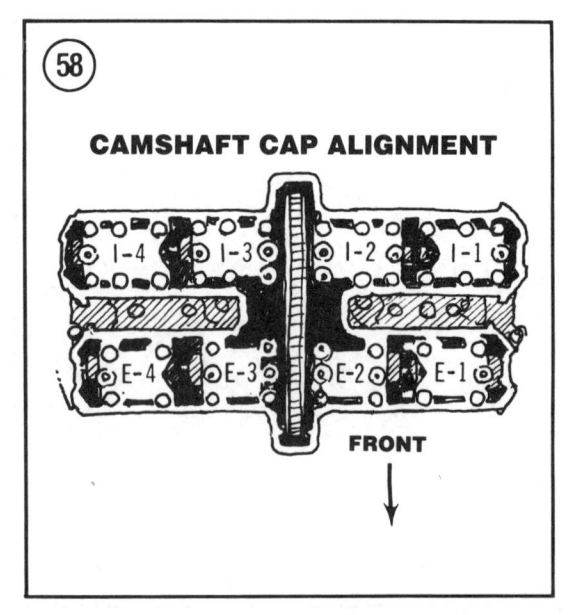

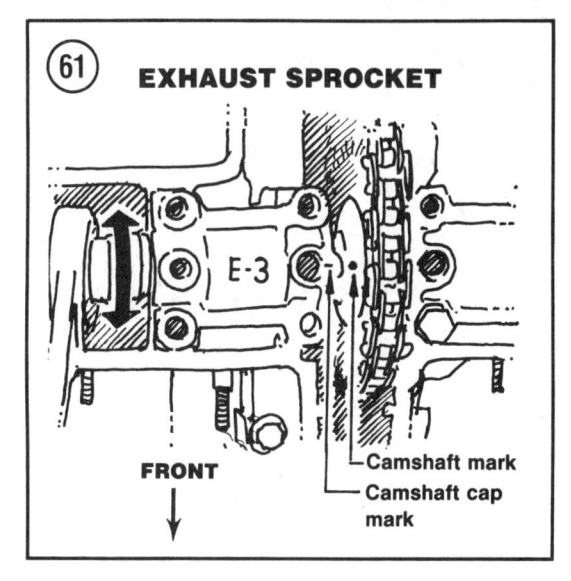

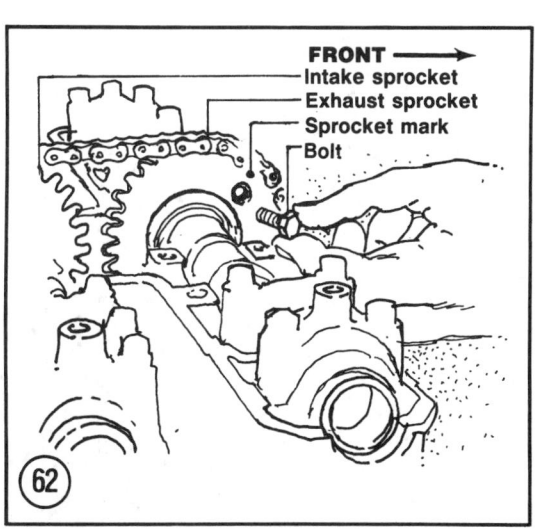

ENGINE

e. Working from the right-hand side of the engine, move the exhaust sprocket counterclockwise to remove all cam chain slack.

f. Align the marked sprocket bolt hole with the exhaust cam threaded hole and slide the sprocket onto the camshaft shoulder. See **Figure 62**.

CAUTION
*If the sprocket and camshaft holes do not align in Step "f," adjust the chain links between the exhaust cam and the crankshaft. **Do not** rotate the exhaust cam or the cam timing will be incorrect.*

g. When the exhaust sprocket and camshaft holes align, install one exhaust cam sprocket bolt and tighten securely.

11. Install the intake sprocket as follows:
   a. Place the "I-3" camshaft cap onto the cylinder head (**Figure 63**).

CAUTION
Do not rotate the camshaft more than 1/2 turn in Step "b" or piston and/or valve damage may occur.

   b. Install a suitable size wrench on the camshaft as shown in **Figure 63**. Then turn the camshaft and align the camshaft timing mark with the "I-3" camshaft cap timing mark. See **Figure 63**.

WARNING
Do not rotate the intake cam after aligning it in Step "b".

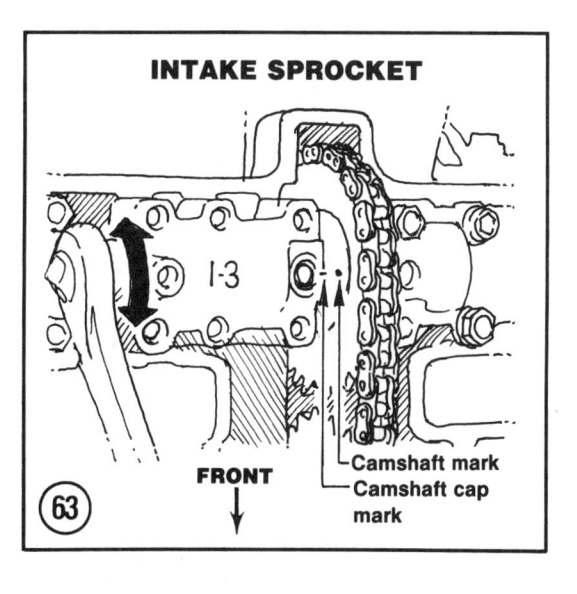

CHAPTER FOUR

c. Remove the "I-3" camshaft cap (**Figure 63**).
d. Working from the right-hand side of the engine, move the intake sprocket counterclockwise to remove all cam chain slack.
e. Align the marked sprocket bolt hole with the intake cam threaded hole and slide the sprocket onto the camshaft shoulder (**Figure 64**).

CAUTION
If the sprocket and cam holes do not align in Step "e," adjust the chain links between the intake cam and the crankshaft. ***Do not*** *rotate the intake cam or the cam timing will be incorrect.*

f. When the intake sprocket and camshaft holes align, install one intake cam sprocket bolt and tighten securely.

12. Install the cam chain tensioner as described in this chapter.
13. Rotate the crankshaft counterclockwise using the bolt installed on the end of the crankshaft (**Figure 65**) to provide access to the remaining cam sprocket bolt holes and install the bolts. Tighten all cam sprocket bolts (**Figure 66**) to 24 N•m (17 ft.-lb.).

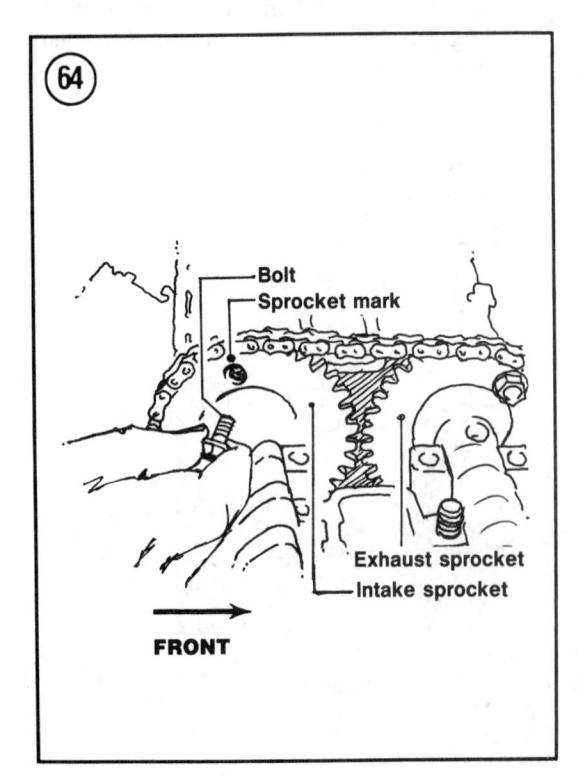

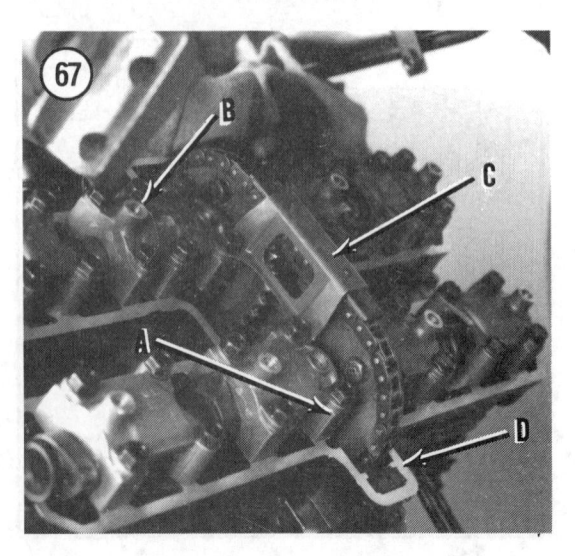

ENGINE

14. Install the No. 3 exhaust (A, **Figure 67**) and the No. 3 intake (B, **Figure 67**) camshaft caps and their dowel pins.
15. Rotate the crankshaft counterclockwise two full turns and align the "T" crankshaft web mark with the stationary pointer as viewed through the port hole (**Figure 68**). Then check that the exhaust and intake camshaft timing marks align with the camshaft cap marks. See **Figure 61** (exhaust) and **Figure 63** (intake). If all marks align as indicated, cam timing is correct.

CAUTION
*If there is any binding while turning the crankshaft, **stop**. Recheck the camshaft timing marks. Improper timing can cause valve and piston damage.*

16. If the cam timing is incorrect, remove the camshaft caps and reposition the camshafts as described in Steps 5-15.
17. Install the upper chain guide (C, **Figure 67**) and bolts. Tighten the bolts securely.
18. Insert the front exhaust chain guide through the camshaft case and cylinder head (D, **Figure 67**).
19. Check valve clearance as described under *Valve Clearance Measurement* in Chapter Three.
20. Install the cylinder head cover as described in this chapter.
21. Remove the 8 mm bolt and nut from the end of the crankshaft (**Figure 65**).
22. Install the left-end crankshaft end cover (A, **Figure 69**) and the port plug (B, **Figure 69**).

CAM CHAIN TENSIONER

The automatic tensioner is continually self-adjusting. The tensioner pushrod is free to move inward, but can't move out. Whenever the cam chain tensioner bolts are loosened, the tensioner assembly must be completely removed and reset as described in this section.

Removal/Inspection/Installation

1. Perform Steps 1-7 under *Camshaft Removal* in this chapter.
2. Loosen but do not remove the tensioner end cap bolt (B, **Figure 70**).
3. Remove the tensioner bolts (A, **Figure 70**) and lift the tensioner (**Figure 71**) off of the cylinder housing.

4. See **Figure 72**. Disassemble and inspect the tensioner assembly as follows:
   a. Remove the end cap bolt (F) and washer (E).
   b. Pull the spring (D) and rod out of the tensioner body (C).
   c. Inspect the tension rod (A) and one-way cam (B) for smooth movement. Replace the tensioner housing assembly if the cam movement is rough or if there is noticeable wear or damage.
   d. Inspect the spring (D) for breakage, sagging or other damage.
   e. Replace worn or damaged parts as required.
5. Install the tensioner assembly as follows.

NOTE
If the crankshaft has not been moved since removing the tensioner assembly, then tensioner is ready to install. If the crankshaft was moved, perform Step 2 under **Camshaft Installation**.

6. See **Figure 73.** Push the one-way cam (B, **Figure 72**) to release the cam. Then push the tension rod assembly into the housing.
7. Install the tensioner housing (**Figure 74**) so that the one-way cam (B, **Figure 72**) faces *downward*.

NOTE
On some models, the tensioner housing is marked with "UP" on the front of the housing. Install the housing so that the "UP" mark faces up.

8. Install the tensioner bolts and tighten to the torque specifications in **Table 2**.
9. Insert the spring and rod (**Figure 75**) into the tensioner housing.
10. Install the tensioner end cap bolt (**Figure 76**) and tighten to the torque specifications in **Table 2**.

CAM CASE AND CYLINDER HEAD

The cam case and cylinder head assembly can be removed with the engine in the frame. Some of the photos in this procedure show service with the engine removed. The engine has been removed for clarity.

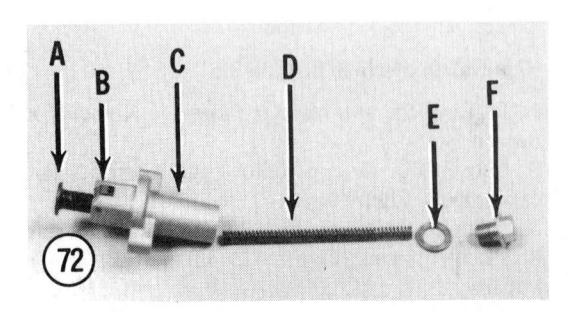

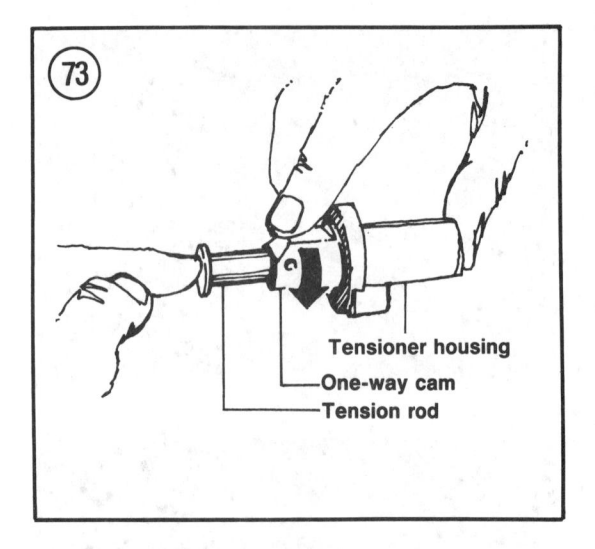

ENGINE

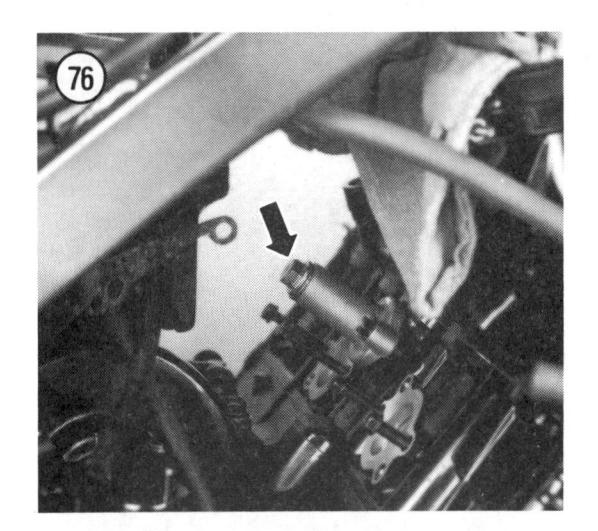

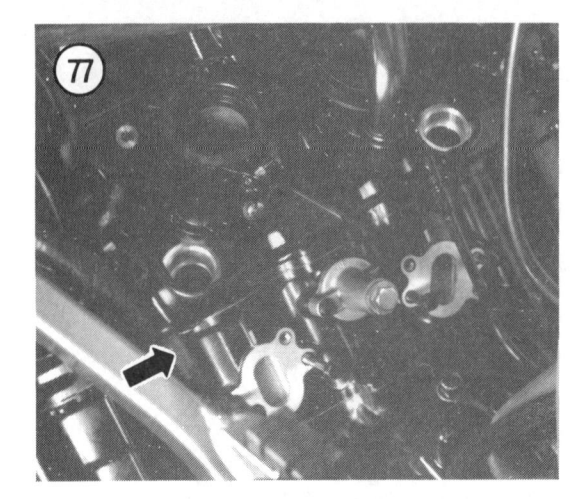

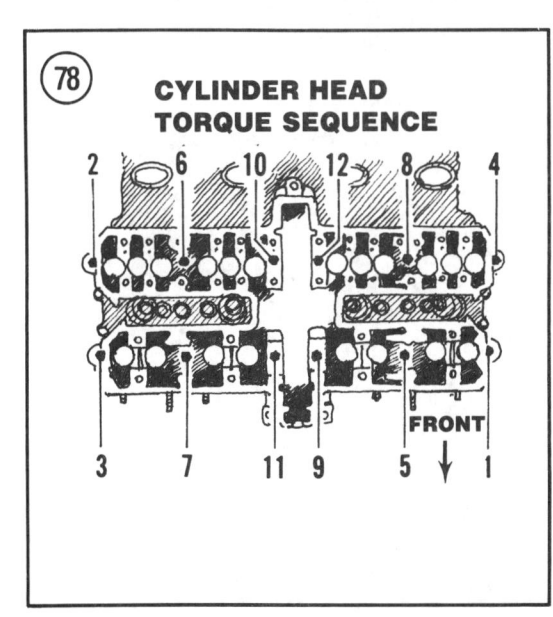

Removal

1. Remove the cylinder head cover as described under *Cylinder Head Cover Removal/Installation* in this chapter.
2. Remove the camshafts as described in this chapter.
3. Remove the carburetors as described in Chapter Seven.
4. Remove the cylinder head oil line (**Figure 77**) banjo bolts and brackets and lift the oil line away from the engine.
5. Remove the cylinder head nuts and bolts in a crisscross pattern as shown in **Figure 78**.

NOTE
*The cylinder head nuts in the camshaft case can be loosened with a long 6 mm Allen wrench as shown in **Figure 79**. Yamaha sells a hexagon wrench (part no. YM-3448) that can be used to remove the nuts.*

6. Loosen the cylinder head by tapping around the perimeter with a rubber or plastic mallet.
7. Remove the cylinder head/cam case assembly (**Figure 80**) by pulling it straight up and off the cylinder block. Place a clean shop rag into the cam chain tunnel in the cylinder to prevent the entry of foreign matter.

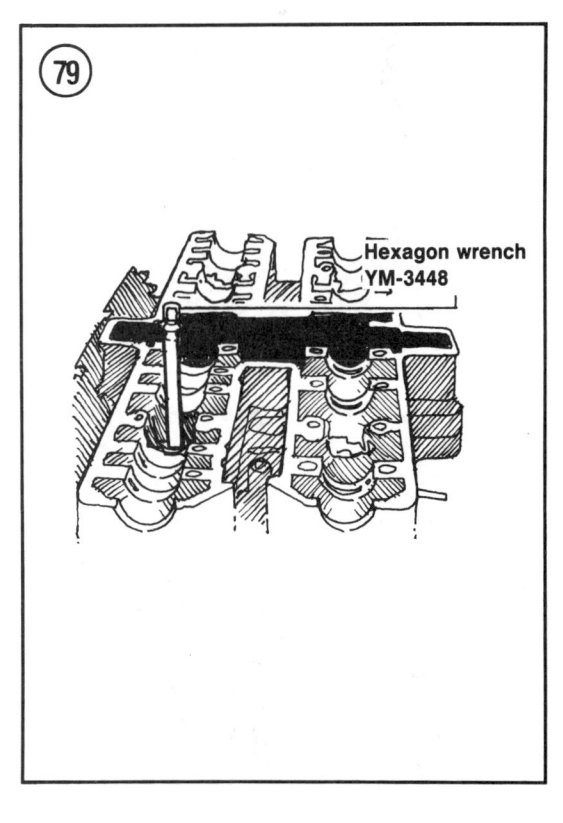

CHAPTER FOUR

NOTE
After removing the cylinder head, check the top and bottom mating surfaces for any indications of leakage. Also check the head and base gaskets for signs of leakage. A blown gasket could indicate possible cylinder head warpage or other damage.

8. Remove the 4 dowel pins (**Figure 81**) and the cylinder head gasket (**Figure 82**).

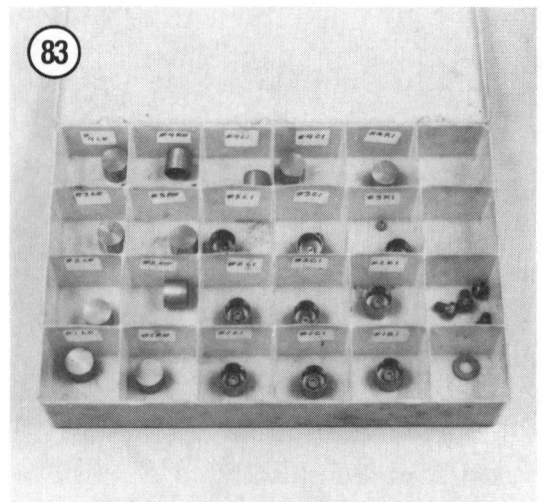

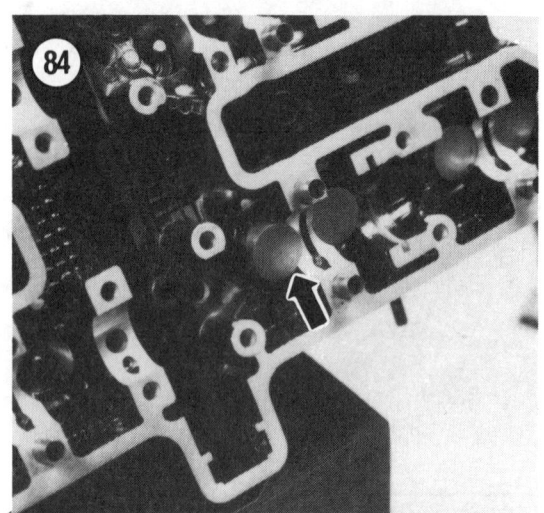

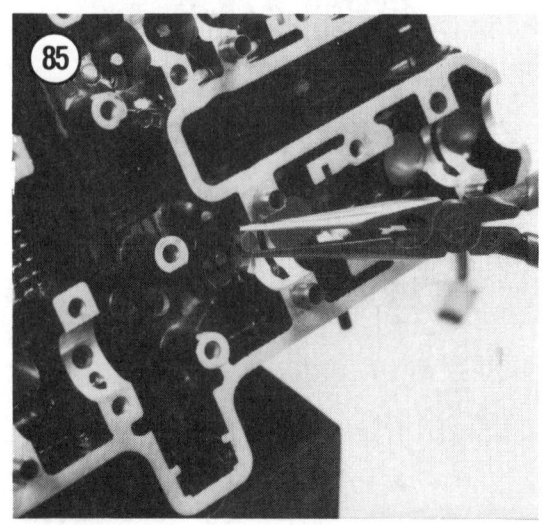

ENGINE

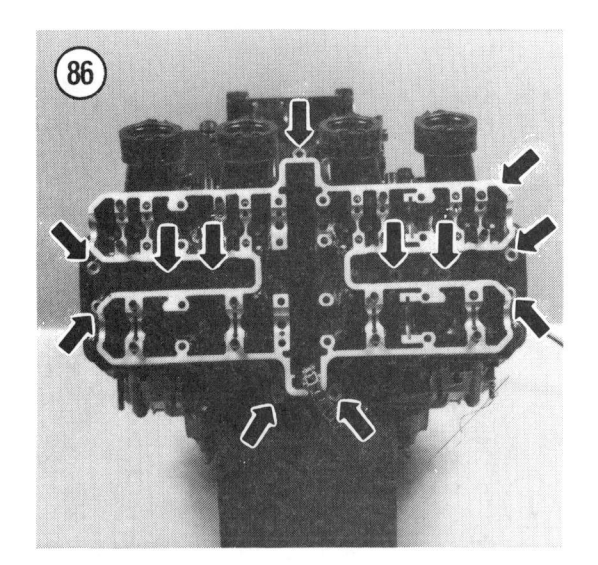

Camshaft Case Removal

This procedure requires separation of the camshaft case and cylinder head assemblies. The camshaft case can be removed from the cylinder head while mounted on the engine.

NOTE
*The valve lifters and pads must be reinstalled in their exact same positions as they determine valve clearance. Store all parts in order (**Figure 83**) so that they can be reinstalled in their original positions.*

NOTE
The valve lifters and pads must be removed from the camshaft case before separating the case from the cylinder head. If not, the lifters and pads will fly off when the camshaft case is removed.

1. Remove the valve lifters (**Figure 84**) and pads (**Figure 85**).
2. Remove the camshaft case-to-cylinder head bolts (**Figure 86**) and remove the camshaft case (**Figure 86**).
3. Remove the 2 dowel pins (**Figure 87**) and gasket (**Figure 88**).
4. Remove the oil line bracket bolt (A, **Figure 89**) and lift the oil pipes (B, **Figure 89**) from the camshaft case. See **Figure 90**.

Cylinder Head Inspection

1. Remove all traces of gasket residue from the head (A, **Figure 91**) and cylinder mating surfaces. Do not scratch the gasket surface.

2. Without removing valves, remove all carbon deposits from the combustion chambers (B, **Figure 91**) with a wire brush or wooden scraper. Take care not to damage the head, valves or spark plug threads.

> **CAUTION**
> *Do not attempt to clean the combustion chambers while the valves are removed. A damaged or even slightly scratched valve seat will cause poor valve sealing.*

3. Examine the spark plug threads in the cylinder head for damage. If damage is minor or if the threads are dirty or clogged with carbon, use a spark plug thread tap to clean the threads following the manufacturer's instructions. If thread damage is severe, refer further service to a Yamaha dealer or machine shop.

4. After all carbon is removed from combustion chambers, and valve ports and the spark plug threads are repaired, clean the entire head in solvent.

5. Check for cracks in the combustion chamber (B, **Figure 91**) and exhaust ports (A, **Figure 92**). A cracked head must be replaced.

> **CAUTION**
> *When cleaning coolant passages in Step 6, use care and do not damage the cylinder head gasket surface.*

6. Check the coolant passages (C, **Figure 91**) in the cylinder head for residue or sludge build-up. Remove residue and sludge with narrow rifle cleaning brushes.

7. Check the intake manifold boots (**Figure 93**) for cracks and damage that would allow unfiltered air to enter the engine. Also check the hose clamps for breakage or fatigue. Replace parts as necessary.

8. After the head has been thoroughly cleaned, place a straightedge across the gasket surface at several points (**Figure 94**). Measure warp by inserting a feeler gauge between the straightedge and cylinder head at each location. Maximum allowable warpage is 0.03 mm (0.0012 in.). Warpage or nicks in the cylinder head surface could cause an air leak and result in coolant leakage and overheating. If warpage exceeds this limit, the cylinder head must be replaced.

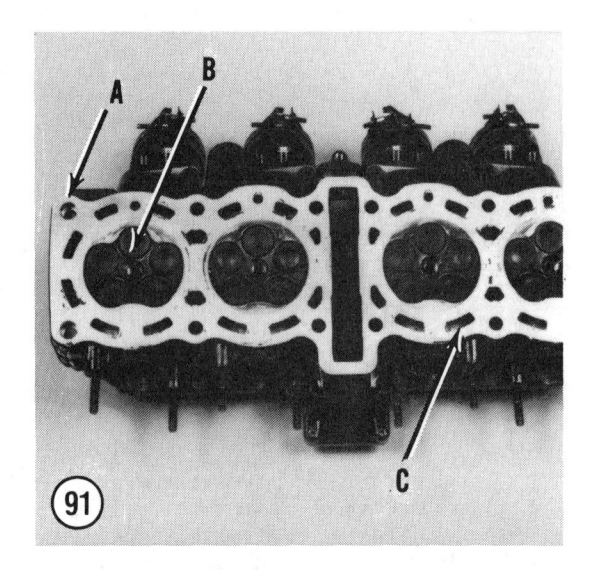

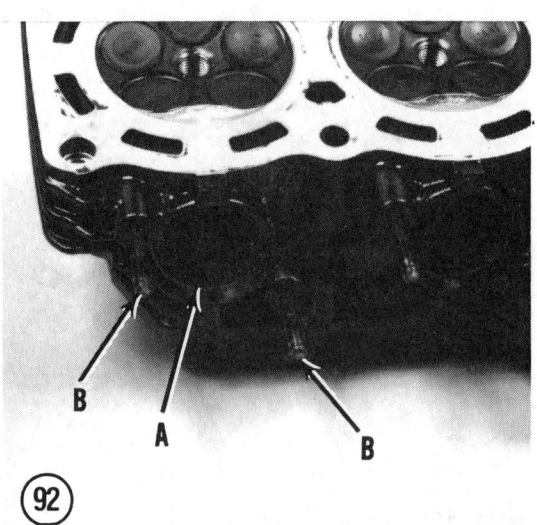

ENGINE

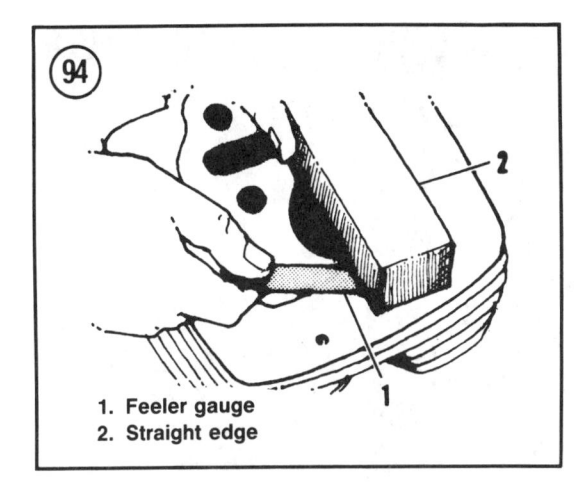

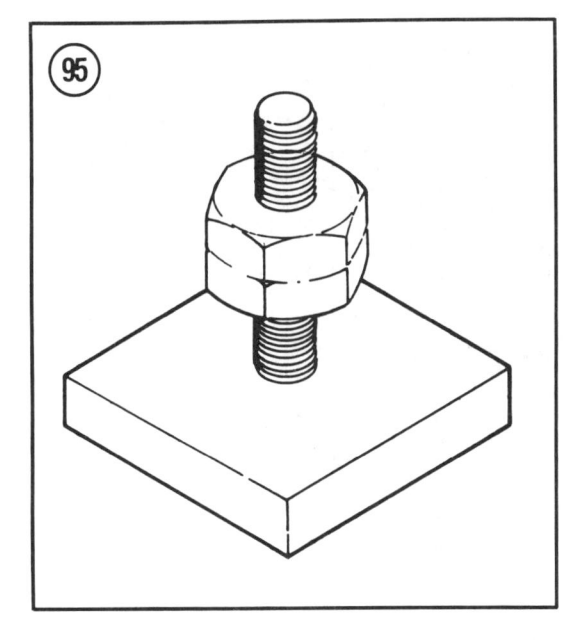

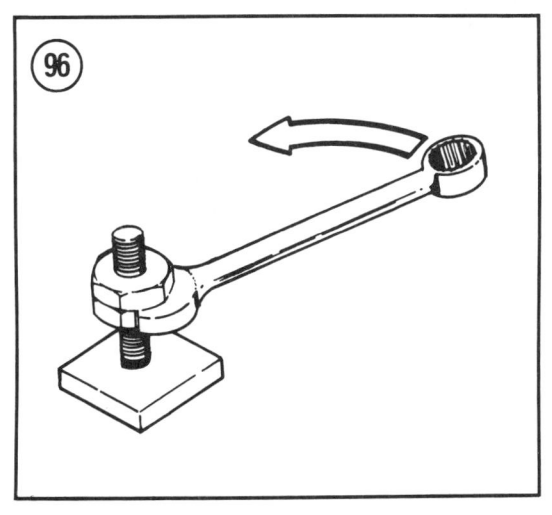

94

1. Feeler gauge
2. Straight edge

9. Check the exhaust pipe studs (B, **Figure 92**) for looseness or thread damage. Slight thread damage can be repaired with a thread file or die. If thread damage is severe, replace the damaged stud(s) as follows:
   a. Screw two 6 mm nuts onto the end of a stud as shown in **Figure 95**.
   b. With 2 wrenches, tighten the nuts against each other.
   c. Unscrew the stud with a wrench on the lower nut (**Figure 96**).
   d. Clean the tapped hole with solvent and check for thread damage or carbon build-up. If necessary, clean the threads with a 6×1.00 tap.
   e. Remove the nuts from the old stud and install them on the end of a new stud.
   f. Tighten the nuts against each other.
   g. Apply Loctite 242 (blue) to the threads of the new stud.
   h. Screw the stud into the cylinder head with a wrench on the upper nut. Tighten the stud securely.
   i. Remove the nuts from the new stud.

10. Clean the camshaft case (**Figure 97**) thoroughly in solvent. Remove any gasket residue from all machined surfaces. Inspect the case for cracks, breakage or other damage. Check the threads in the camshaft case to be sure they are clean. If dirty or damaged, use a tap to true up the threads and remove any deposits.

11. Clean the valves as described under *Valves and Valve Components* in this chapter.

Camshaft Case Assembly

1. Replace the camshaft case oil pipe O-rings.
2. Insert the oil pipes into the camshaft case (**Figure 90**). Secure the oil pipes with the oil pipe bracket bolt (A, **Figure 89**). Tighten the bolt securely.

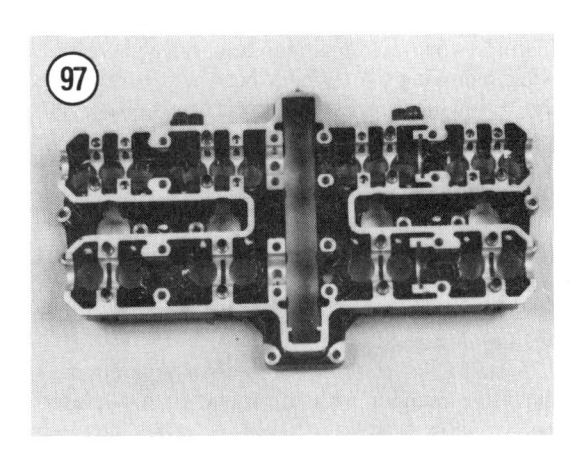

3. Install the 2 dowel pins (**Figure 87**) and a new camshaft case gasket (**Figure 88**). Install the gasket so that the word UP faces as shown in **Figure 98**.
4. Install the camshaft case (**Figure 86**) onto the cylinder head.
5. Install the camshaft case-to-cylinder head bolts (**Figure 86**) and tighten to the torque specifications in **Table 2**.
6. Install the pads (**Figure 85**) and valve lifters (**Figure 84**) into their original positions.

Installation

1. Clean the cylinder head and cylinder mating surfaces of all gasket residue.
2. Blow out the cylinder head oil passages before installing the head.

NOTE
*The cylinder head gasket is stamped with the word "HEAD" on one side (**Figure 99**). This side must face up.*

3. Install a new head gasket and the 4 dowel pins (**Figure 81**).
4. Install the cylinder head/camshaft case assembly (**Figure 80**).
5. Install the bolts securing the cylinder head. Tighten the bolts in a crisscross pattern (**Figure 78**) to the torque specifications listed in **Table 2**.
6. Install the main oil pipe banjo bolts, using new copper washers (**Figure 77**). Tighten the bolts to the specifications listed in **Table 2**.
7. Install the camshafts as described in this chapter.

VALVES AND VALVE COMPONENTS

Correct valve service requires a number of special tools. The following procedures describe how to check for valve component wear and to determine what type of service is required. In most cases, valve troubles are caused by poor valve seating, worn valve guides and burned valves. After removing the cylinder head and performing the following checks and procedures, have the valve guides, valves and guides serviced by a Yamaha dealer. A valve spring compressor (**Figure 100**) will be required to remove the valves.

Refer to **Figure 101** for this procedure.
1. Remove the cylinder head as described in this chapter.
2. Separate the camshaft case from the cylinder head as described in this chapter.
3. Install a valve spring compressor squarely over the valve retainer with other end of tool placed against valve head.

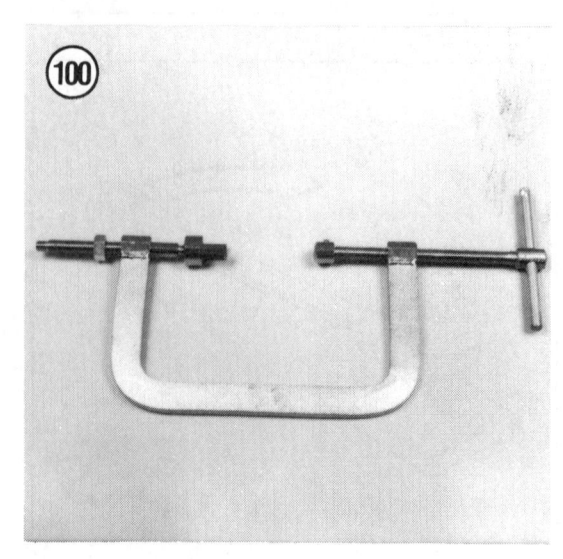

ENGINE

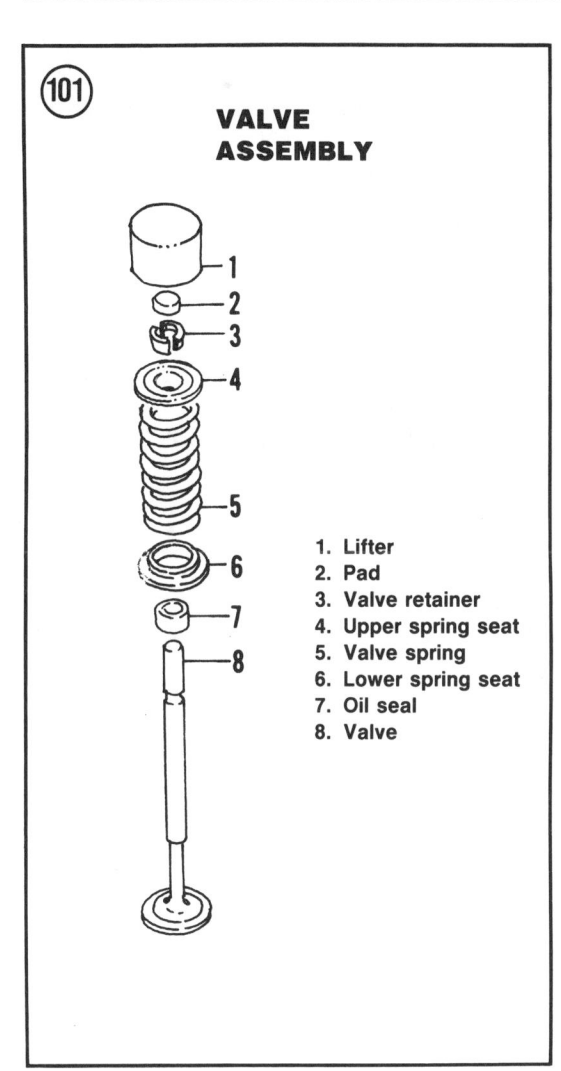

101 VALVE ASSEMBLY

1. Lifter
2. Pad
3. Valve retainer
4. Upper spring seat
5. Valve spring
6. Lower spring seat
7. Oil seal
8. Valve

102

Deburr
Valve stem

4. Tighten the valve spring compressor until the split valve retainers separate. Lift out split retainers with needle nose pliers.
5. Gradually loosen the valve spring compressor and remove from head. Remove the upper valve spring seat.
6. Remove the inner and outer valve springs.
7. Remove the lower valve spring seat.

CAUTION
*Remove any burrs from the valve stem grooves before removing the valve (**Figure 102**). Otherwise the valve guides will be damaged.*

NOTE
*Before removing the valves, note that there are 5 valves (3 intake and 2 exhaust) for each cylinder. See **Figure 103**. Also note that 2 different intake valves are used (different Yamaha part numbers). The center intake valve is different from the left- and right-hand intake valves (**Figure 104**). The center*

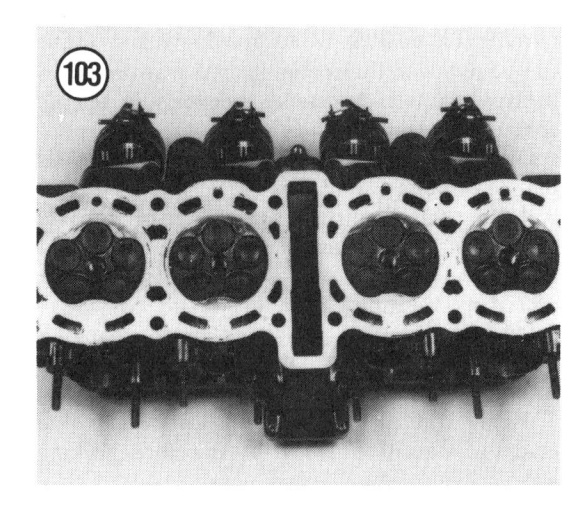

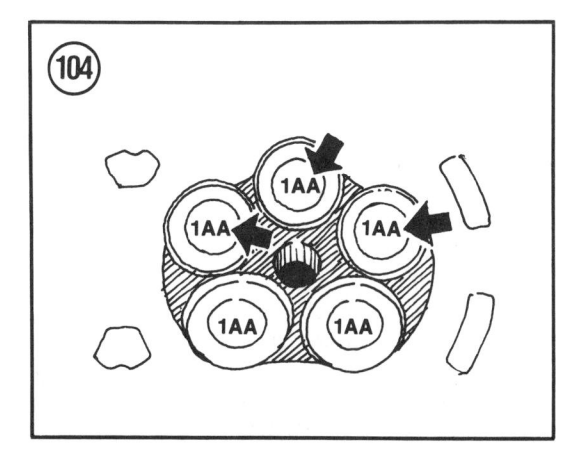

103

104

intake valve is marked "1AA." and the left- and right-hand intake valves are marked "1AA:". Make a valve holding fixture by drilling holes in a piece of plywood in a pattern similar to that in the cylinder head so that the valves can be stored in order and then returned to their original position.

8. Remove the valve.
9. Pull the oil seal off the end of the valve guide.

CAUTION
All parts of each valve assembly must be kept together. Do not mix with like components from other valves or excessive wear may result.

10. Repeat Steps 2-9 and remove remaining valve(s).

Inspection

1. Clean valves in solvent. Do not gouge or damage the valve seating surface.
2. Inspect the contact surface of each valve for burning (**Figure 105**). Minor roughness and pitting can be removed by lapping the valve as described in this chapter. Excessive unevenness to the contact surface is an indication that the valve is not serviceable. If the contact surface of a valve is burned or damaged, replace the valve.
3. Inspect the valve stems for wear and roughness and measure the vertical runout of the valve stem as shown in **Figure 106**. The runout should not exceed specifications (**Table 1**).
4. Measure valve stems for wear using a micrometer (**Figure 107**). Compare with specifications in **Table 1**.
5. Remove all carbon and varnish from the valve guides with a stiff spiral wire brush before checking wear.

NOTE
Step 6 and Step 7 require special measuring equipment. If you do not have the required measuring devices, proceed to Step 8.

6. Measure each valve guide at top, center and bottom with a small hole gauge. Compare measurements with specifications in **Table 1**.
7. Subtract the measurement made in Step 4 from the measurement made in Step 6 above. The difference is the valve guide-to-valve stem clearance. See specifications in **Table 1** for correct clearance. Replace any guide or valve that is not within tolerance. Valve guide replacement is described later in this chapter.

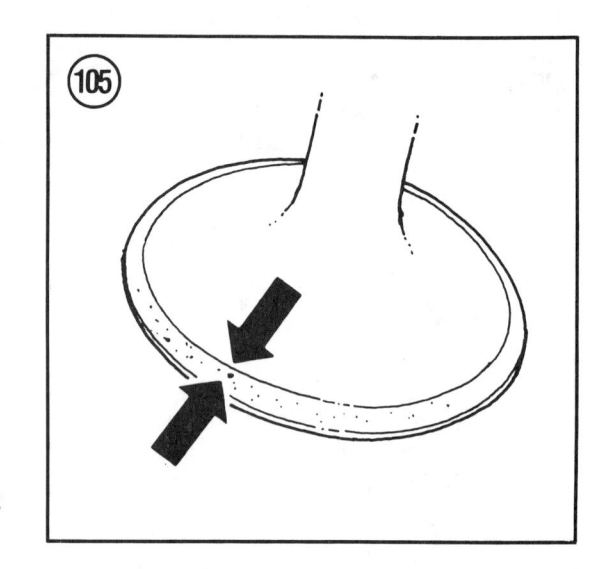

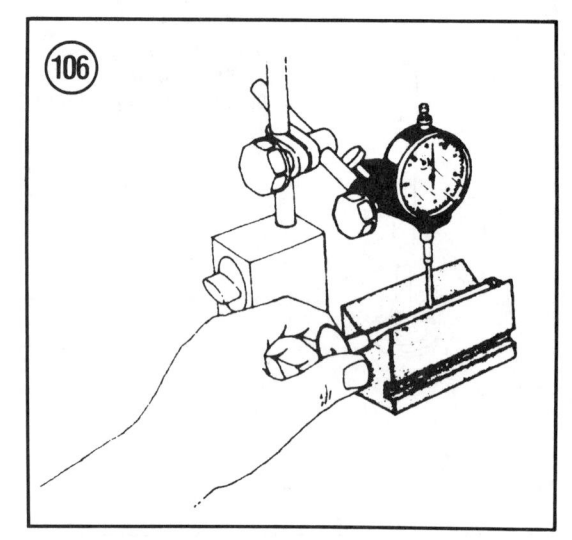

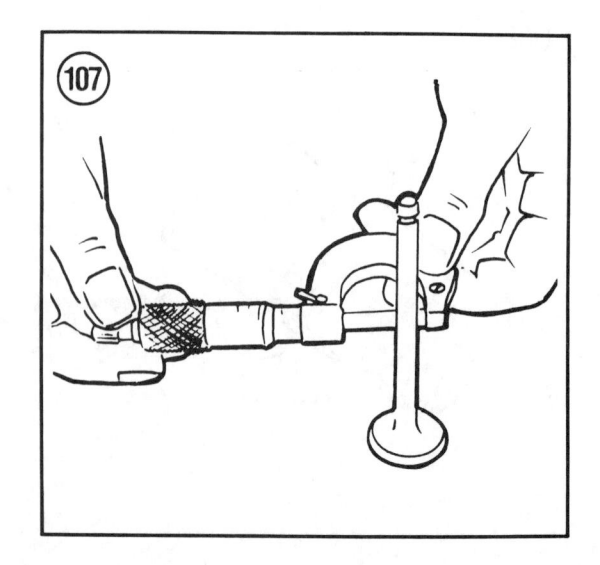

ENGINE

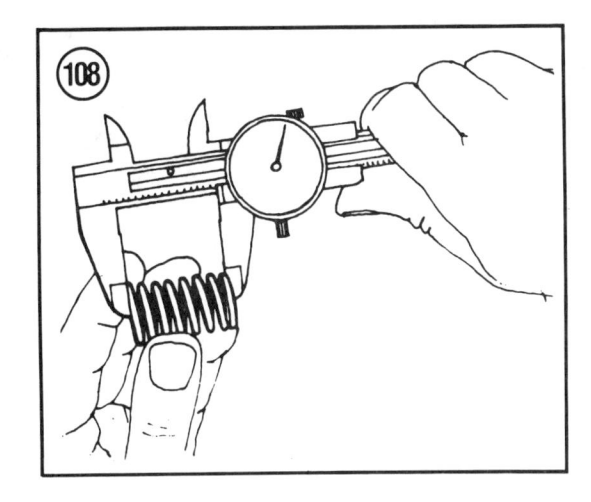

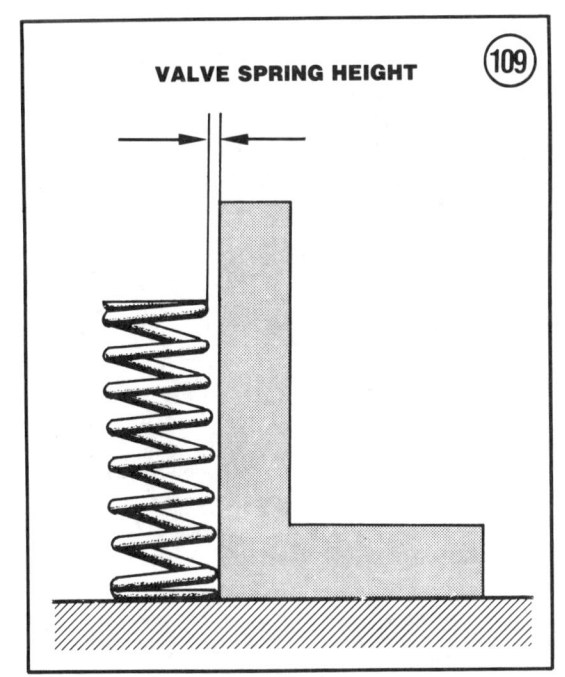

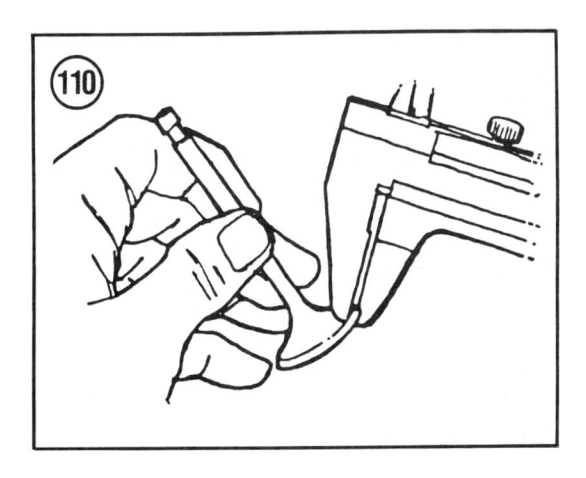

108

109 VALVE SPRING HEIGHT

110

NOTE
If you do not have the special measuring equipment for Step 7, perform Step 8. Step 8 assumes that all valve stems have been measured and are within specifications. Replace any valves that have worn stems before performing Step 8.

8. Insert each valve in its guide. Hold the valve just slightly off its seat and rock it sideways. If it rocks more than slightly, the guide is probably worn and should be replaced. As a final check, take the head to a dealer and have the valve guides measured.

9. Measure the valve spring length with a vernier caliper (**Figure 108**). All should be of length specified in **Table 1**. Replace defective springs.

10. Measure the tilt of all valve springs as shown in **Figure 109**. Replace if tilt exceeds 1.5 mm (0.059 in.).

11. Check the valve spring retainers and valve spring seats. If they are in good condition, they may be reused.

12. Inspect valve seats. If worn or burned, they may be reconditioned. This should be performed by your dealer or local machine shop. Seats and valves in near-perfect condition can be reconditioned by lapping with fine carborundum paste. Lapping, however, is always inferior to precision grinding. Check as follows:

   a. Clean the valve seat and valve mating areas with contact cleaner.

   b. Coat the valve face with machinist's blue or Dykem.

   c. Install the valve into its guide and rotate it against its seat with a valve lapping tool. See *Valve Lapping* in this chapter.

   d. Lift the valve out of the guide and measure the seat width with vernier calipers (**Figure 110**).

   e. The standard seat width for intake and exhaust is 9.9-1.1 mm (0.035-0.043 in.) all the way around the seat. The wear limit is 1.8 mm (0.07 in.).

   f. If the seat width is too narrow, too wide or is uneven, have the valve seats reground by a Yamaha dealer.

   g. Remove all machinist's blue residue from the seats and valves.

Installation

1. Coat a valve stem with molybdenum disulfide paste and install into its correct guide.

2. Carefully slide a new oil seal over the valve and seat it onto the end of the valve guide.

NOTE
Oil seals should be replaced whenever a valve is removed or replaced.

3. Install the lower valve spring seat.
4. Install valve springs with the narrow pitch end (end with coils closest together) facing the cylinder head.
5. Install the upper valve spring seat.
6. Push down on the upper valve spring seat with the valve spring compressor and install valve keepers. After releasing tension from compressor, examine valve keepers and make sure they are seated correctly (**Figure 111**).
7. Repeat Steps 1-6 for remaining valve(s).

Valve Guide Replacement

When guides are worn so that there is excessive stem-to-guide clearance or valve tipping, they must be replaced. This job should be done only by a Yamaha dealer or qualified specialist as special tools are required.

Valve Seat Reconditioning

This job is best left to a Yamaha dealer. They have the special equipment and knowledge for this exacting job. You can still save considerable money by removing the cylinder head and taking just the head to the shop.

Valve Lapping

Valve lapping is a simple operation which can restore the valve seal without machining if the amount of wear or distortion is not too great.

ENGINE

This procedure should be performed only after determining that valve seat width and outside diameter are within specifications.

CAUTION
Make sure to keep all valve grinding compound off of the valve stems and out of the valve guides or excessive valve stem-to-guide clearance will occur.

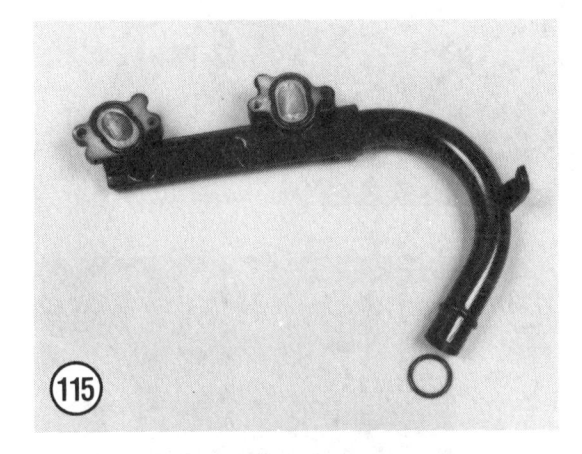

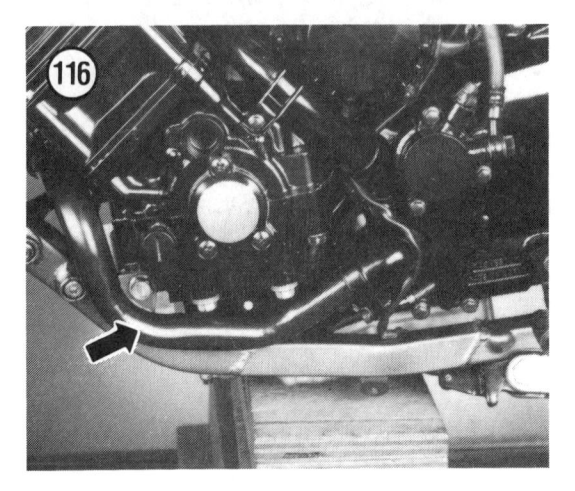

1. Smear a light coating of fine grade valve lapping compound on seating surface of valve.
2. Insert the valve into the head.
3. Wet the suction cup of the lapping stick (**Figure 112**) and stick it onto the head of the valve. Lap the valve to the seat by spinning the lapping stick in both directions. Every 5 to 10 seconds, rotate the valve 180° in the valve seat. Continue this action until the mating surfaces on the valve and seat are smooth and equal in size.
4. Closely examine valve seat in cylinder head. It should be smooth and even with a smooth, polished seating "ring."
5. Thoroughly clean the valves and cylinder head in solvent to remove all grinding compound. Any compound left on the valves or the cylinder head will cause excessive wear and damage.
6. After the lapping has been completed and the valve assemblies have been reinstalled into the head, the valve seal should be tested. Check the seal of each valve by pouring solvent into each of the intake and exhaust ports. There should be no leakage past the seat. If leakage occurs, the combustion chamber will appear wet. If fluid leaks past any of the seats, disassemble that valve assembly and repeat the lapping procedure until there is no leakage.

CYLINDER BLOCK

The aluminum cylinder block has cast-in iron cylinder sleeves, which can be bored to 0.5 mm (0.020 in.) oversize or 1 mm (0.040 in.) oversize to compensate for wear.

Removal

1. Remove the cylinder head cover as described under *Cylinder Head Cover Removal/Installation* in this chapter.
2. Remove the cylinder head as described in this chapter.
3. Remove the screws securing the water pipe (**Figure 113**) to the cylinder block and the water pipe clamp bolt (A, **Figure 114**). Then pull the water pipe (B, **Figure 114**) out of the water pump and remove it. See **Figure 115**.
4. Remove the front water pipe clamp bolts at the cylinder block (**Figure 116**), if so equipped.
5. Remove the 4 dowel pins (**Figure 117**) and head gasket.

6. Loosen the cylinder block (**Figure 118**) by tapping around the perimeter with a rubber or plastic mallet.
7. Pull the cylinder block (**Figure 118**) straight up and off the pistons and cylinder studs.

NOTE
Be sure to keep the cam chain wired up to prevent it from falling into the lower crankcase.

8. Stuff clean shop rags into the crankcase opening beneath each piston and cam chain to prevent objects from falling into the crankcase.
9. Remove the 2 dowel pins (**Figure 119**) and base gasket.

Inspection

1. Wash the cylinder block in solvent to remove any oil and carbon particles. The cylinder bores must be cleaned thoroughly before attempting any measurement as incorrect readings may be obtained.
2. Remove all gasket residue from the top (A, **Figure 120**) and bottom (**Figure 121**) gasket surfaces.
3. Clean the cylinder block water ports (B, **Figure 120**) of all coolant sludge build-up.
4. Measure the cylinder bores with a cylinder gauge or inside micrometer at the points shown in **Figure 122**.
5. Measure in 2 axes—in line with the piston pin and at 90° to the pin. If the taper or out-of-round is greater than specifications (**Table 1**), the cylinders must be rebored to the next oversize and new pistons and rings installed. Rebore all 4 cylinders even though only one may be worn.

NOTE
*The new pistons should be obtained first before the cylinders are bored so that the pistons can be measured; each cylinder must be bored to match one piston only. Piston-to-cylinder clearance is specified in **Table 1**.*

6. If the cylinder(s) are not worn past the service limits, check the bore carefully for scratches or gouges. The cylinder still may require boring and reconditioning.
7. If the cylinders require reboring, remove all dowel pins from the cylinder block (**Figure 119**) before taking the cylinder block to the dealer or machine shop.
8. After the cylinders have been serviced, wash each cylinder bore in hot soapy water. This is the only way to clean the cylinders of the fine grit material left from the bore or honing job. After

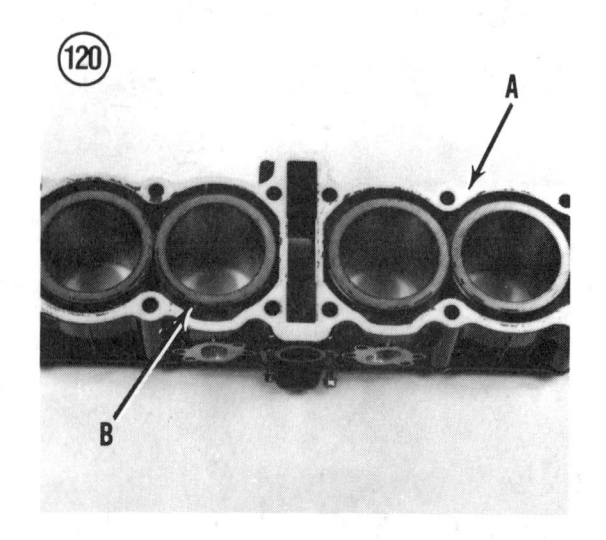

ENGINE

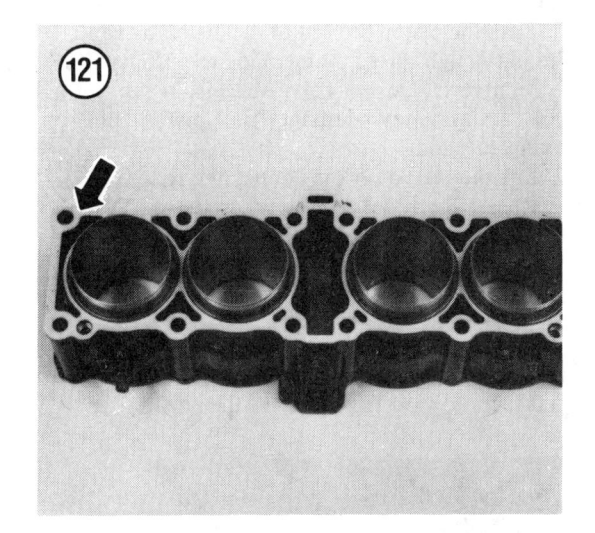

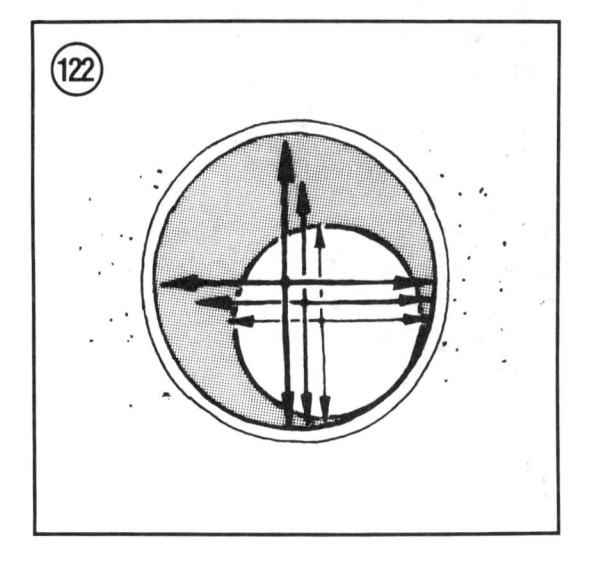

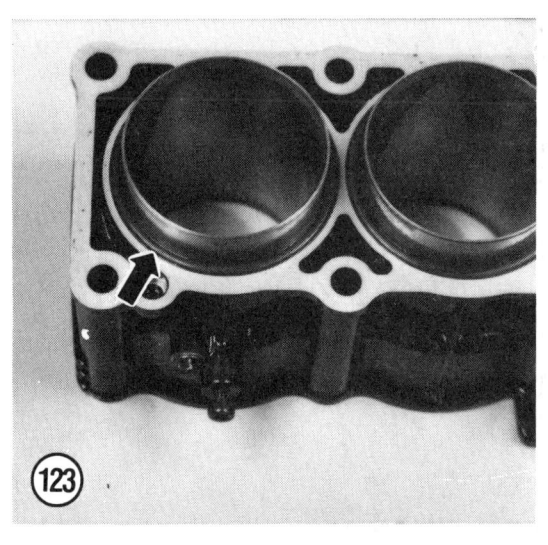

121

122

washing the cylinder walls, run a clean white cloth through each bore; it should show no traces of grit or other debris. If the rag is dirty, the wall is not thoroughly clean and must be rewashed. After the cylinder is cleaned, lubricate the cylinder walls with clean engine oil to prevent the cylinder liners from rusting.

CAUTION
A combination of soap and water is the only solution that will completely clean cylinder walls. Solvent and kerosene cannot wash fine grit out of cylinder crevices. Grit left in the cylinder will act as a grinding compound and cause premature wear to the new rings.

9. Check the cylinder O-rings (**Figure 123**) for deterioration, wear or other damage. Replace if necessary.

Installation

1. Check that the top and bottom cylinder surfaces are clean of all gasket residue.
2. Install the 2 dowel pins onto the crankcase (**Figure 119**).
3. Install a new cylinder base gasket. Make sure all holes align.
4. Install a piston holding fixture under the pistons.
5. Lubricate cylinders and pistons liberally with engine oil prior to installation.
6. Carefully align the cylinder with the pistons.

NOTE
*Once the cylinder is installed, run the chain and wire up through the cam chain tunnel (**Figure 124**).*

NOTE
Make sure to align the rear chain guide with the cylinder block cam chain tunnel.

123

124

7. Compress each ring as it enters the cylinder with your fingers or by using aircraft type hose clamps of appropriate diameter.

> *CAUTION*
> *Don't tighten the clamp any more than necessary to compress the rings. If the rings can't slip through easily, the clamp may gouge the rings.*

8. Remove the piston holding fixture and push the cylinder block all the way down.
9. Install the cylinder head as described in this chapter.
10. Apply engine oil to the water pipe O-rings (**Figure 115**).
11. Secure the front water pipe attaching bolts (**Figure 116**) at the cylinder, if so equipped.
12. Install the O-rings onto the rear water pipe (**Figure 115**). Then insert the end of the water pipe into the water pump (B, **Figure 114**) and align the opposite end with the cylinder block water ports (A, **Figure 114**). Install the water pipe to cylinder screws and the side bracket bolts (**Figure 114**) and tighten securely.
13. Install the cylinder head as described in this chapter.

PISTONS AND PISTON RINGS

Piston
Removal/Installation

1. Remove the cylinder block as described in this chapter.
2. Stuff the crankcase with clean shop rags to prevent objects from falling into the crankcase.
3. Lightly mark each piston crown with an identification number (1-4), starting with the No. 1 piston (left-hand side).
4. Remove the piston rings as described in this chapter.
5. Before removing the piston, hold the rod tightly and rock the piston. Any sideways rocking motion (do not confuse with the normal sliding motion or with the normal rocking motion around the piston pin axis) indicates wear on the piston pin, rod bushing, pin bore, or more likely, a combination of all three. Mark the piston and pin so that they will be reassembled into the same set.
6. Remove the circlips from the piston pin bores (**Figure 125**).

> *NOTE*
> *Discard the piston circlips. New circlips must be installed during reassembly.*

7. Push the piston pin out of the piston by hand. If the pin is tight, use a homemade tool (**Figure 126**) to remove it. Do not drive the piston pin out as this action may damage the piston pin or connecting rod.
8. Lift the piston off the connecting rod.
9. Repeat Steps 4-8 for the other pistons.
10. Inspect the piston as described in this chapter.

> *NOTE*
> *New piston circlips must be installed during assembly.*

11. Install one circlip in each piston on the side that faces toward the center of the engine.

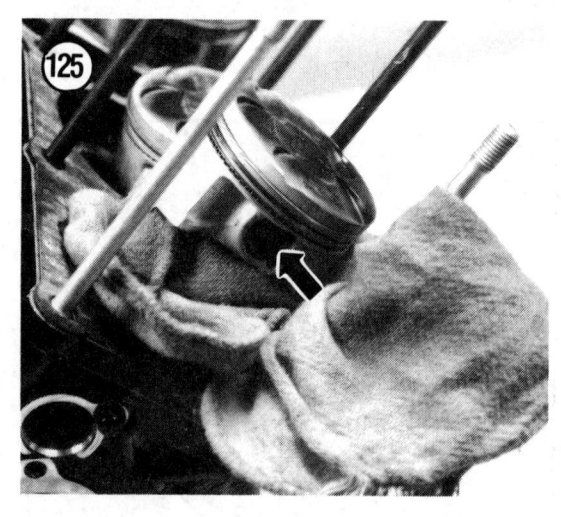

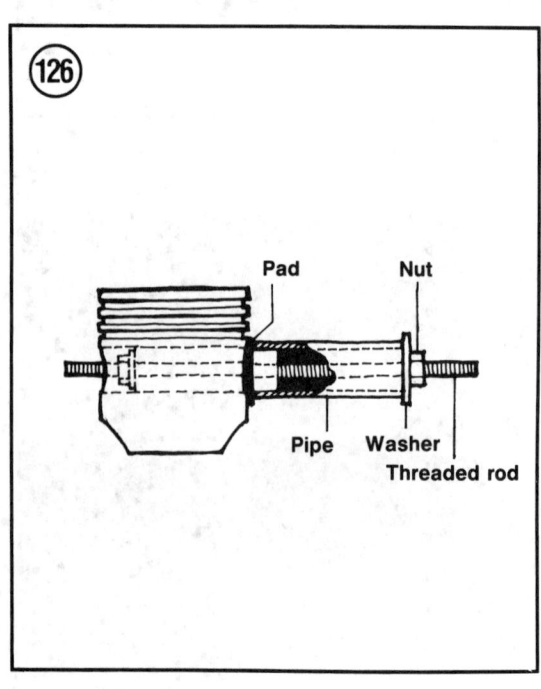

ENGINE

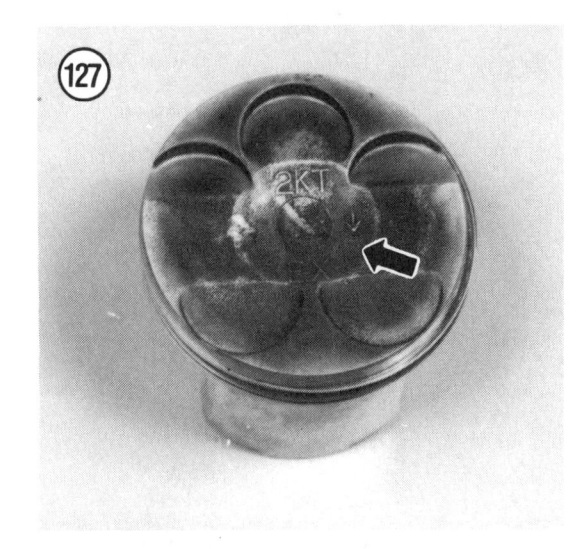

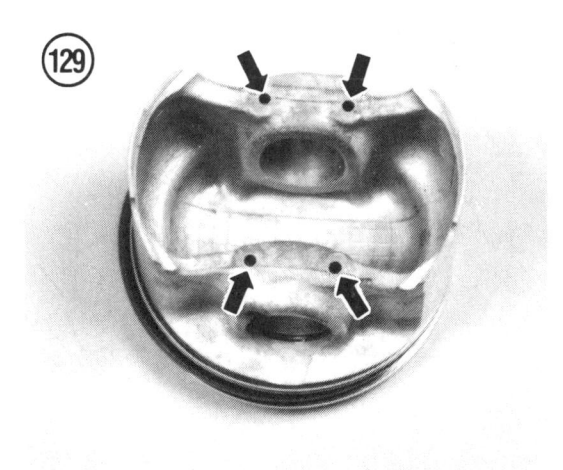

12. Coat the connecting rod bushing, piston pin and piston with assembly oil.
13. Place the piston over the connecting rod. If you are installing old parts, make sure the piston is installed on the correct rod as marked during removal. If the cylinders were bored, install the new pistons as marked by the machinist. The arrow on each piston crown (**Figure 127**) must face to the front of the engine. Install the pistons in the following order:
    a. No. 2 (**Figure 128**).
    b. No. 1.
    c. No. 3.
    d. No. 4.

CAUTION
When installing the piston pin in Step 14, do not push the pin too far, or the circlip installed in Step 11 will be forced into the piston metal, destroying the circlip groove and loosening the circlip.

14. Insert the piston pin through one side of the piston until it starts to enter the connecting rod. Then it may be necessary to move the piston around until the pin enters the connecting rod. Do not force installation or damage may occur. If the pin does not slide easily, use the homemade tool (**Figure 126**) but eliminate the piece of pipe. Push the pin in until it is centered in the piston.
15. Install the outer circlip (**Figure 125**) in the circlip groove.
16. Install piston rings as described in this chapter.
17. Repeat Steps 13-16 for the opposite pistons.

Piston Inspection

1. Carefully clean the carbon from the piston crown (**Figure 127**) with a soft scraper. Large carbon accumulations reduce piston cooling and causes detonation and piston damage. Do not remove or damage the carbon ridge around the circumference of the piston above the top ring. If the pistons, rings and cylinders are found to be dimensionally correct and can be reused, removal of the carbon ring from the top of the piston may promote excessive oil consumption.

CAUTION
Do not wire brush piston skirts.

2. Examine each ring groove for burrs, dented edges and wide wear. Pay particular attention to the top compression ring groove, as it usually wears more than the others.
3. Check the pin lubrication holes in the piston (**Figure 129**) for carbon or oil sludge buildup. Clean the holes with a small diameter drill bit.

4. Check the piston skirts for cracks or other damage. If a piston(s) shows signs of partial seizure (bits of aluminum build-up on the piston skirts), the pistons should be replaced and the cylinders bored (if necessary) to reduce the possibility of engine noise and further piston seizure.
5. Measure piston-to-cylinder clearance as described under *Piston Clearance* in this chapter.
6. If damage or wear indicate piston replacement, select a new piston as described under *Piston Clearance* in this chapter.
7. Inspect the piston pins for chrome flaking or cracks. Replace if necessary.

Piston Clearance

1. Make sure the piston and cylinder walls are clean and dry.
2. Measure the inside diameter of the cylinder at a point 13 mm (1/2 in.) from the upper edge with a bore gauge.
3. Measure the outside diameter of the piston at a point 5 mm (3/16 in.) from the lower edge of the piston 90° to piston pin axis (**Figure 130**).
4. Subtract the piston diameter from the bore diameter; the difference is piston-to-cylinder clearance. Compare to specifications in **Table 1**. If clearance is excessive, the pistons should be replaced and the cylinders rebored. Purchase the new pistons first; measure their diameters and add the specified clearance to determine the proper cylinder bore diameters.

NOTE
If one cylinder requires boring, the other cylinders must be bored also.

Piston Ring
Removal/Installation

WARNING
The edges of all piston rings are very sharp. Be careful when handling them to avoid cut fingers.

1. Measure the side clearance of each ring in its groove with a flat feeler gauge (**Figure 131**) and compare with the specifications in **Table 1**. If the clearance is greater than specified, the rings must be replaced. If the clearance is still excessive with the new rings, the piston must be replaced.
2. Remove the old rings with a ring expander tool or by spreading the ring ends with your thumbs and lifting the rings up evenly (**Figure 132**).
3. Using a broken piston ring, remove all carbon from the piston ring grooves.
4. Inspect grooves carefully for burrs, nicks or broken or cracked lands. Replace piston if necessary.

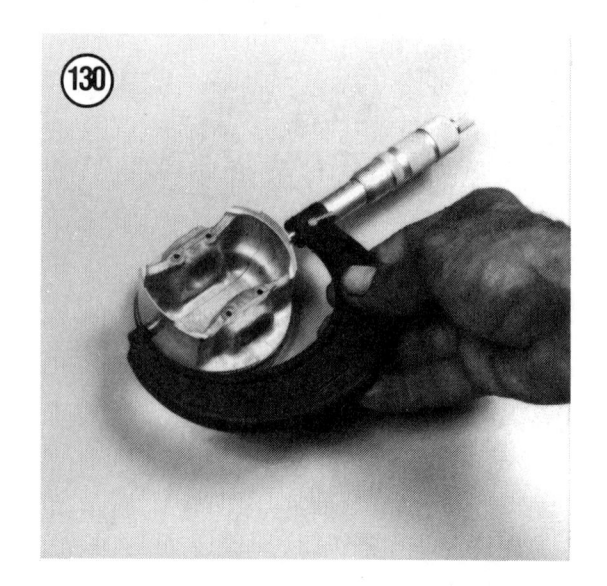

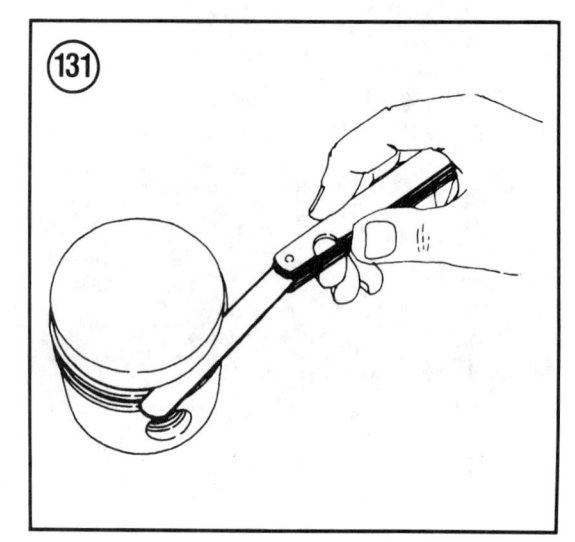

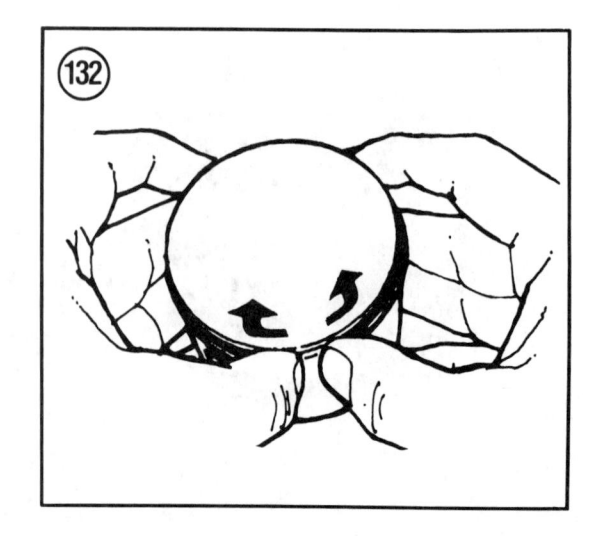

ENGINE

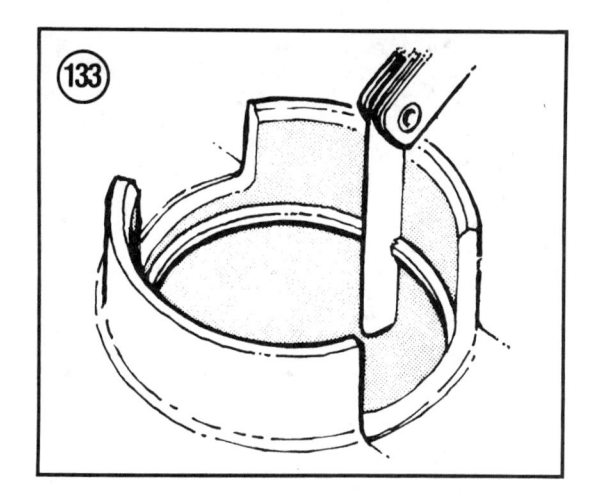

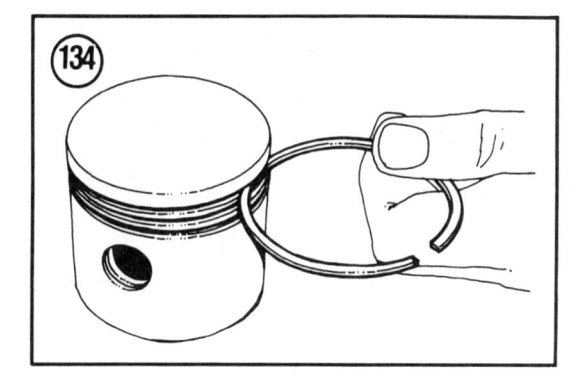

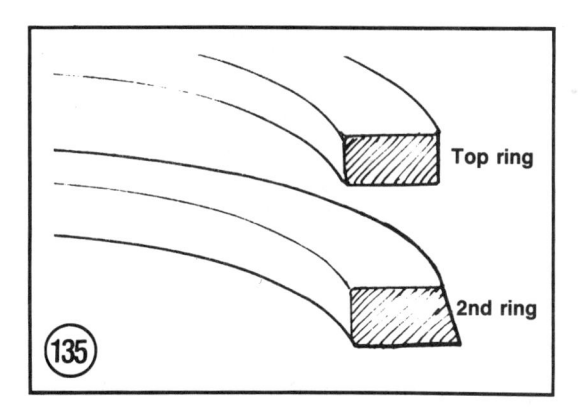

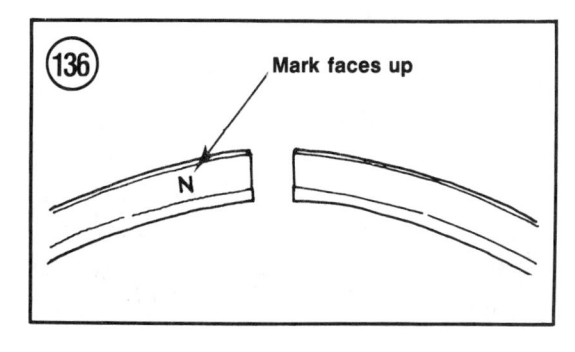

5. Check end gap of each ring. To check, insert the ring into the bottom of the cylinder bore and square it with the cylinder wall by tapping it with the piston. The ring should be pushed in about 15 mm (5/8 in.). Insert a feeler gauge as shown in **Figure 133**. Compare with **Table 1**. Replace ring if end gap is too large. If the gap on the new ring is smaller than specified, you may have the wrong size rings or the cylinder may not have been bored out far enough. Check both. If the rings and bore are the correct size, hold a small file in a vise, grip the ring with your fingers and file the ends of the ring to enlarge the gap.
6. Roll each ring around its piston groove as shown in **Figure 134** to check for binding. Minor binding may be cleaned up with a fine-cut file.
7. Install the piston rings in the order shown in **Figure 135**.

NOTE
*Install all rings with the manufacturer's markings facing up (**Figure 136**).*

NOTE
Oversize compression rings (top and second) are stamped with a .50 or 1.00 to indicate oversize. The oil control expander (bottom ring) is color-coded to indicate oversize. The colors are red (.50) and yellow (1.00).

8. Install the piston rings—first the bottom, then the middle, then the top ring—by carefully spreading the ends with your thumbs and slipping the rings over the top of the piston. Remember that the piston rings must be installed with the marks on them facing up toward the top of the piston or there is the possibility of oil pumping past the rings.
    a. Install the oil ring assembly into the bottom ring groove. The assembly is comprised of 2 steel rails and 1 expander. The expander is installed in the middle of the steel rails.
    b. The top and middle piston rings are different. The middle ring is slightly tapered and must be installed as shown in **Figure 135**. The top ring is symmetrical and must be installed as shown in **Figure 135**.
9. Make sure the rings are seated completely in their grooves all the way around the piston and that the end gaps are distributed around the piston as shown in **Figure 137**. It is important that the ring gaps are not aligned with each other when installed to prevent compression pressures from escaping past them.
10. If installing oversize compression rings, check the number to make sure the correct rings are being

110 CHAPTER FOUR

installed. The ring numbers should be the same as the piston oversize number.

11. If new rings are installed, the cylinders must be deglazed or honed. This will help the new rings to seat properly. Refer honing service to a Yamaha dealer. After honing, measure the end clearance of each ring (**Figure 133**) and compare to dimensions in **Table 1**.

NOTE
If the cylinders were deglazed or honed, clean the cylinders as described under **Cylinder Block Inspection** *in this chapter.*

OIL PUMP AND STRAINER

A wet sump system with a trochoid oil pump is used on all models. Two rotors are enclosed in a housing located behind the clutch. The inner rotor is shaft driven. The oil pump shaft is driven by the water pump impeller shaft. The oil pan and oil pump can be removed with the engine mounted in the frame.

Service Notes

Because the lubrication system is a vital key to engine reliability, note the following during service and inspection:
  a. Was the engine oil level correct?
  b. Was the engine oil contaminated with sludge or coolant?
  c. Was the oil pump properly mounted?
  d. Were external oil lines damaged or their fittings loose?
  e. Were banjo bolts loose or clogged?
  f. Was the oil filter element clogged?

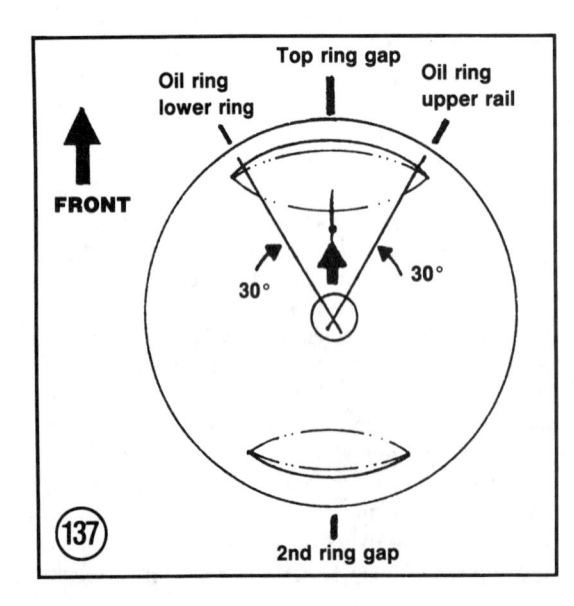

ENGINE

g. Was the oil pump screen clogged?
h. Was the relief valve working properly, clogged or damaged?
i. Were all O-rings properly installed or were they damaged?
j. Were the oil passages partially restricted or clogged?

Oil Pump
Removal/Installation

1. Remove the clutch as described in Chapter Five.
2. Insert an Allen wrench through the oil pump gear and remove the 3 oil pump mounting screws (**Figure 138**).
3. Pull the oil pump assembly (**Figure 139**) out of the crankcase.
4. Remove the dowel pin (**Figure 140**) and gasket.
5. Installation is the reverse of these steps. Note the following:
   a. Install the dowel pin (**Figure 140**) and a new oil pump gasket.
   b. Align the notch on the end of the oil pump shaft (**Figure 141**) with the impeller shaft notch and install the oil pump.
   c. Tighten the oil pump screws to the torque specifications in **Table 2**.
   d. Refill the engine oil as described under *Engine Oil and Filter Change* in Chapter Three.

Disassembly/Inspection/Assembly

The oil pump is sold as a complete assembly. If any one part is worn or damaged, the entire pump must be replaced.

The work area should be clean when disassembling and reassembling the oil pump.

CAUTION
If compressed air is not available to dry parts after cleaning, place the oil pump parts on newspaper or lint-free towels and allow to air dry. Do not dry with towels as lint may be picked up on a part. The oil pump operates with very close tolerances. Small dirt or lint particles left in a pump can score the pump's rotors and reduce pressure output.

1. Remove the oil pump as described in this chapter.
2. Remove the screw (**Figure 142**) and pull the cover (**Figure 143**) off of the oil pump.
3. Remove the outer (**Figure 144**) and inner (**Figure 145**) rotors.

4. Slide the pin (**Figure 146**) out of the oil pump shaft.
5. Remove the washer (**Figure 147**).
6. Slide the oil pump gear/shaft assembly (**Figure 148**) out of the housing.
7. Remove the 2 pins (**Figure 149**) from the pump cover.
8. Clean the oil pump parts (**Figure 150**) in solvent and blow dry.
9. Inspect the rotors (**Figure 150**) for wear, cracks or other damage.
10. Inspect the pump gear (**Figure 150**).
11. Inspect the oil pump housing and cover (**Figure 150**) for cracks or bore damage.
12. Check the pump shaft (**Figure 150**) for scoring, pin hole damage or seizure.
13. Install the outer rotor and check the clearance between the housing and the rotor (**Figure 151**) with a flat feeler gauge. The side clearance should be within the specifications listed in **Table 1**. If the clearance is greater, replace the oil pump.

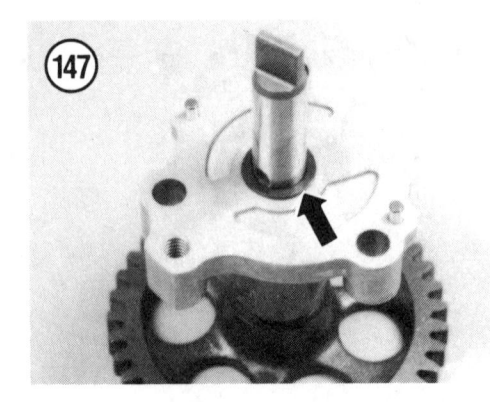

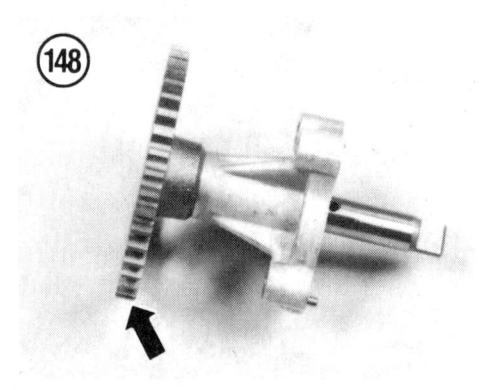

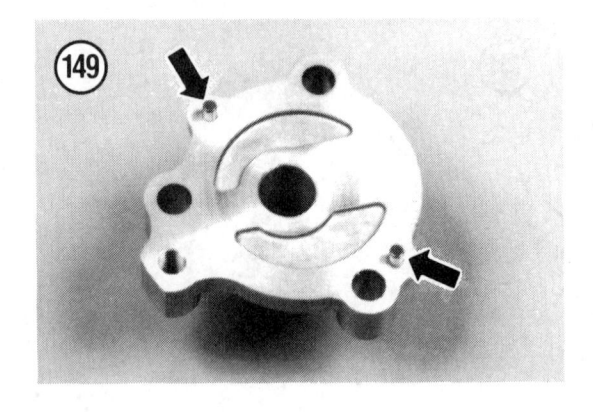

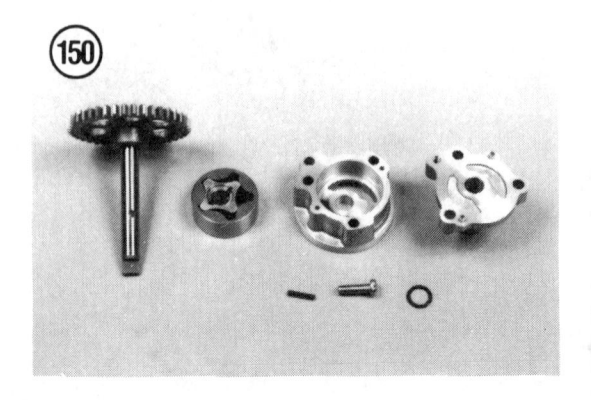

NOTE
Install the pump shaft when performing Step 14. The pump shaft is removed in the photo for clarity.

14. Install the inner rotor and pump shaft and check the side clearance between the inner and outer rotor (**Figure 152**) with a flat feeler gauge. The clearance should be within the specifications listed in **Table 1**. If the clearance is greater, replace the oil pump.
15. Install both rotors and check the end clearance between the pump housing and rotors with a flat feeler gauge and straightedge as shown in **Figure 153**. The clearance should be within the specifications listed in **Table 1**. If the clearance is greater, replace the oil pump.

ENGINE

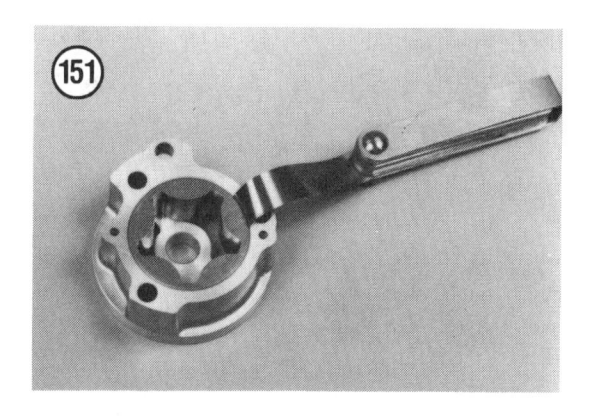

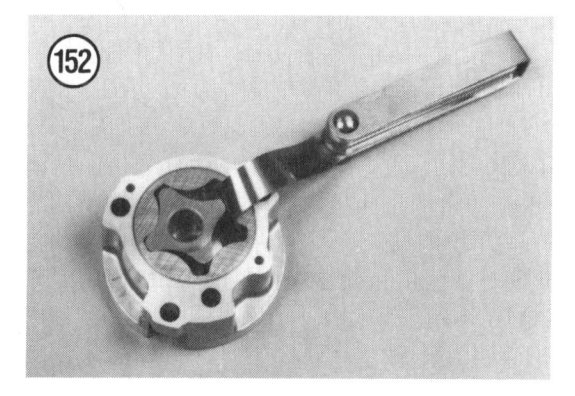

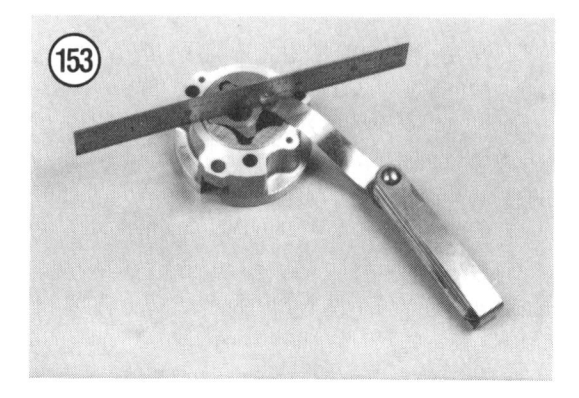

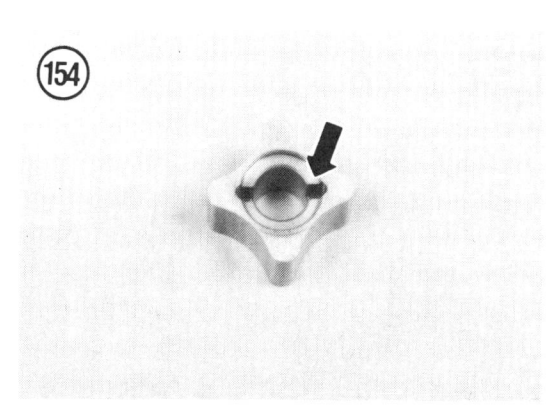

NOTE
Proceed with Step 16 only when the above inspection and measurement steps indicate the parts are in good condition.

16. Coat all parts with fresh engine oil prior to assembly.

17. Reverse Steps 2-7 to reassemble the oil pump. When installing the inner rotor, align the slot in the rotor (**Figure 154**) with the pin (**Figure 146**). Tighten the oil pump screw securely.

Oil Pan and Strainer Removal/Installation

1. Remove the mufflers as described under *Exhaust System Removal/Installation* in Chapter Seven.

2. Drain the engine oil and remove the oil filter as described under *Engine Oil and Filter Change* in Chapter Three.

3. Disconnect the oil level switch connector (**Figure 155**).

4. *FZX700:* Disconnect the sidestand switch connector.

NOTE
On FZX700 models, the sidestand switch is mounted onto the oil pan. Trace the connector from that point.

5. Keep the oil drain pan underneath the engine. Then loosen the oil pan mounting bolts all the way around the pan and allow more oil to drain into the pan.

NOTE
The photographs used in the following procedure are shown with the engine removed for clarity. The engine need not be removed for this procedure.

6. Completely remove the oil pan mounting bolts and lower the pan (**Figure 156**) away from the crankcase and remove it.

7. Remove the 2 dowel pins (**Figure 157**) and gasket.

8. Remove the 2 oil strainer bolts and lower the oil strainer assembly (**Figure 158**) away from the engine.

9. If necessary, remove the 3 oil pipe bolts and lower the oil pipe (**Figure 159**) out of the engine.

10. If necessary, remove or replace the oil level switch or relief valve as described in this chapter.

11. Before cleaning the oil pan, check the inside for signs of excessive aluminum or metal debris that may indicate engine, clutch or transmission problems.

12. Inspect the strainer screen (**Figure 160**) for aluminum build-up or damage. If necessary, replace the strainer screen. Pull the strainer screen off of the housing. Install the strainer so that the element screen (window) faces against the housing arrow as shown in **Figure 161**.

13. Inspect the oil pipe for breakage or damage. Replace the 3 O-rings (**Figure 162**) before installation.

14. Installation is the reverse of these steps, noting the following:
   a. Apply clean engine oil to all O-rings.
   b. Install the 3 O-rings onto the oil pipe (**Figure 162**).
   c. Remove all gasket residue from the oil pan and crankcase. Then install a new gasket. Make sure the bolt holes align properly.
   d. Install the relief valve and/or oil level switch if removed.
   e. Tighten the oil pipe bolts to the torque specifications in **Table 2**.
   f. Tighten the oil strainer bolts to the torque specifications in **Table 2**.

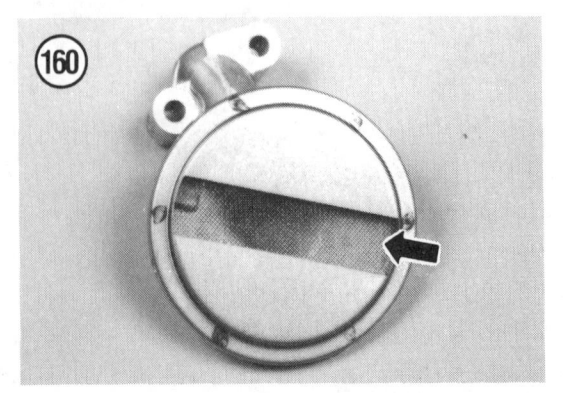

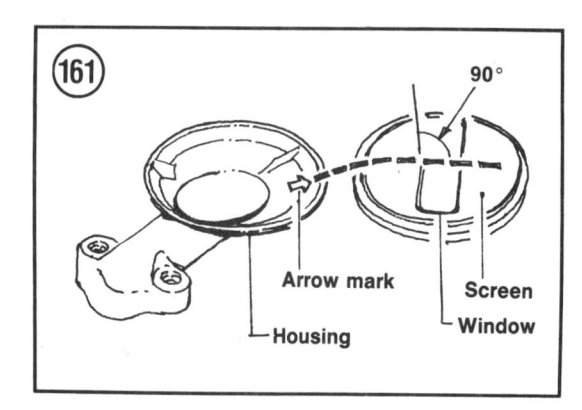

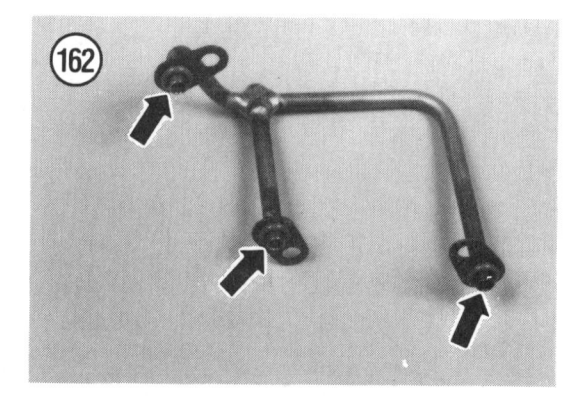

ENGINE

g. Tighten the oil pan mounting bolts to the specifications in **Table 2**.
h. Install a new oil filter and refill the engine oil as described in Chapter Three.

OIL PRESSURE RELIEF VALVE

Removal/Installation

1. Remove the oil pan as described in this chapter.
2A. *Removal only:* Pull the relief valve out of the crankcase (A, **Figure 163**) and remove it.
2B. *Disassembly:* Perform the following:

> *WARNING*
> *The relief valve cap is held under spring pressure. When the cotter pin is removed in Step "a," the cap will fly off. Take precautions to protect your face and to prevent the loss of parts during disassembly.*

a. Remove the cotter pin (B, **Figure 163**).
b. Remove the cap (**Figure 164**).
c. Remove the spring (**Figure 165**).
d. Remove the plunger (**Figure 166**).

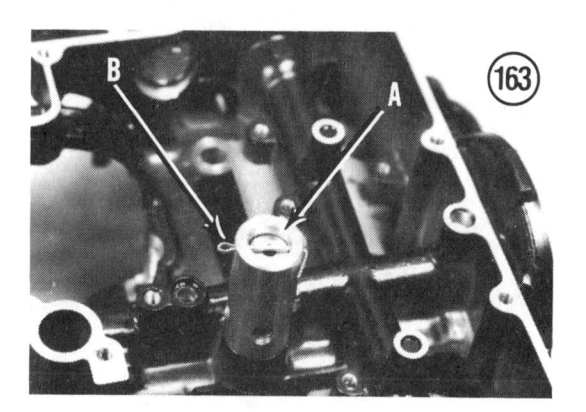

e. Lift the housing (**Figure 167**) off of the crankcase.

f. Inspect the relief valve assembly (**Figure 168**) for excessive wear or damage. Replace the relief valve housing O-ring.

3. Install or reassemble the relief valve by reversing these steps. If the relief valve was disassembled, install a new cotter pin (**Figure 169**). Bend the ends of the cotter pin to lock it (B, **Figure 163**).

4. Install the oil pan as described in this chapter.

OIL LEVEL SWITCH

Removal/Installation

1. Drain the engine oil as described under *Engine Oil and Filter Change* in Chapter Three.

2. Disconnect the oil level switch connector (**Figure 155**).

3. Remove the oil level switch screws and remove the switch (**Figure 170**).

4. Installation is the reverse of these steps. Note the following.

   a. Make sure the area around the switch mounting position is clean of all dirt and debris.
   b. Replace the oil level switch O-ring if deformed or if there are signs of oil leakage.
   c. Tighten the oil level switch screws to the torque specifications in **Table 2**.
   d. Refill the engine oil as described in Chapter Three.

CRANKCASE

Service to the lower end requires that the crankcase assembly be removed from the motorcycle frame and disassembled (split).

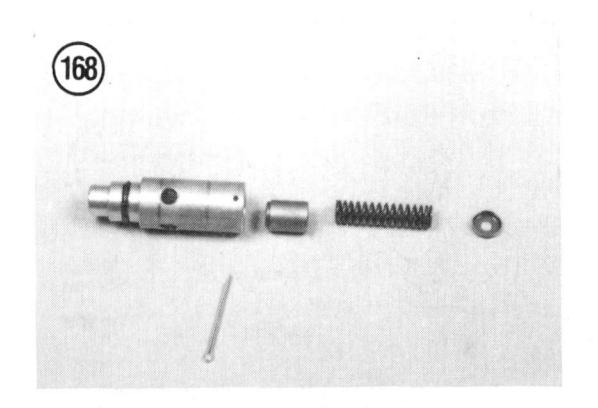

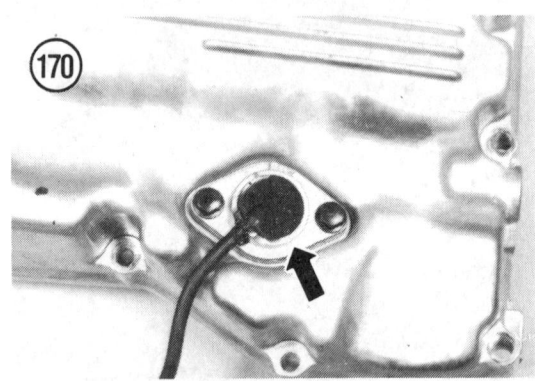

ENGINE

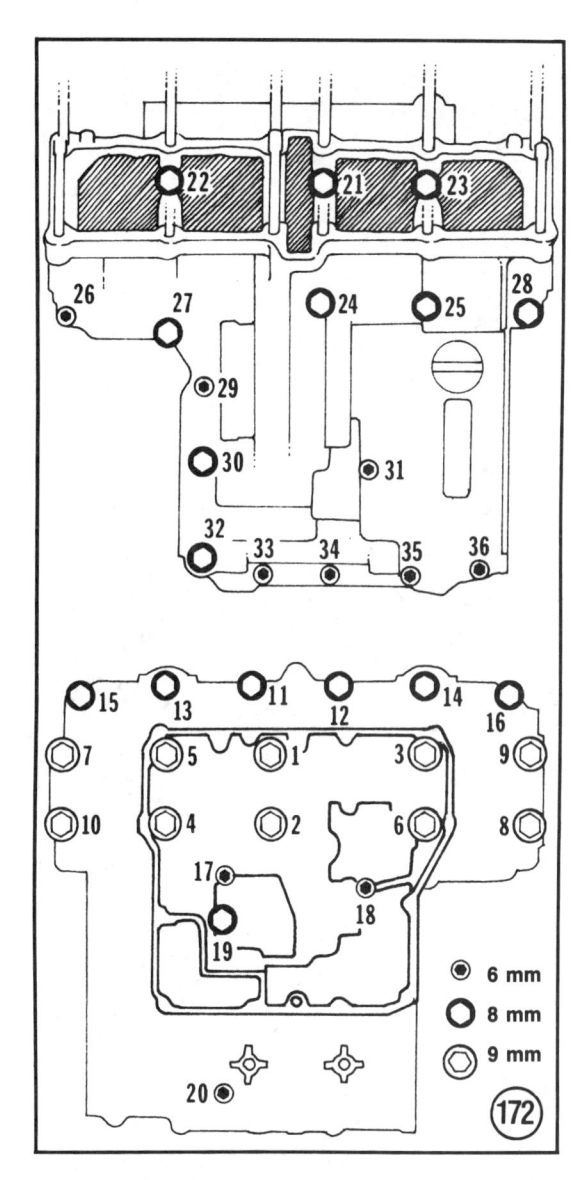

Disassembly

NOTE
On all models, the cylinders must be removed before removing the lower crankcase half.

1. Remove the engine as described in this chapter. Remove all exterior assemblies from the crankcase as described in this chapter and other related chapters.
2. Remove the oil pan, strainer and oil pipe as described under *Oil Pump and Strainer* in this chapter.

NOTE
A No. 30 Torx driver socket will be required to remove the retainer bolts in Step 3.

3. Remove the screws securing the transmission main shaft retainer (**Figure 171**) and remove the retainer.

NOTE
When removing the crankcase bolts, start with the higher number bolts and work to the lowest number. Crankcase bolt numbers are cast into the upper and lower crankcase halves next to the bolt holes.

4. Remove the upper crankcase bolts by reversing the bolt tightening sequence in **Figure 172**.
5. Turn the engine so that the bottom end faces up.
6. Loosen the lower crankcase bolts by reversing the bolt tightening sequence in **Figure 172**.

CAUTION
The crankcase halves are made of thin-walled aluminum. To avoid damage to the cases, do not hammer projected walls. These areas are easily damaged.

7. Tap around the perimeter of the crankcase halves with a plastic mallet—do not use a metal hammer as it will damage the crankcase.
8. Lift the lower crankcase (**Figure 173**) half way up and remove it.

CAUTION
Do not pry the crankcase between any gasket surfaces. The crankcases are machined as a set and damage to one will necessitate replacement of both.

9. After separating the crankcase halves, the transmission and crankshaft will stay in the upper crankcase half.

10. Remove the 2 dowel pins and O-rings (**Figure 174**) from the lower crankcase.
11. Remove the transmission, shift forks and shift drum assemblies as described in Chapter Six.
12. Remove the oil plug plate bolt and remove the plug (A, **Figure 175**) and gasket.
13. Remove the oil pipe stop bolt (B, **Figure 175**) and remove the stop. Then withdraw the oil pipe (A, **Figure 176**) out of the crankcase.
14. Remove the idler gear shaft (C, **Figure 175**) and lift the idler gear (B, **Figure 176**) out of the crankcase.
15. Remove the secondary shaft and starter clutch as described under *Starter Clutch Assembly* in this chapter.
16. Pull the oil spray nozzle (**Figure 177**) out of the upper crankcase.
17. Remove the crankshaft and the crankshaft bearing inserts as described under *Crankshaft* in this chapter.
18. Remove the rear chain guide bolt and remove the guide (**Figure 178**) from the lower crankcase.
19. Remove the primary chain guide bolt and remove the guide (**Figure 179**) from the upper crankcase.
20. Remove the oil baffle plate bolts and remove the baffles (**Figure 180**) from the lower crankcase.

Inspection

1. Thoroughly clean the inside and outside of both crankcase halves with cleaning solvent. Dry with compressed air. Make sure there is no solvent residue left in the cases as it will contaminate the engine oil.
2. Make sure all oil passages are clean; blow them out with compressed air.
3. Check the crankcases for cracks or other damage. Inspect the mating surfaces of both halves. They must be free of gouges, burrs or any damage that could cause an oil leak.
4. Inspect the crankshaft bearing inserts as described in this chapter.

Crankcase Ball Bearings
Inspection/Replacement

1. Turn the starter clutch bearing (**Figure 181**) in the upper crankcase and check for damaged races, balls or rollers. Replace the bearing if it has excessive side or radial side play. If the bearing is okay, oil the races or rollers with clean engine oil. If necessary, replace the bearing as follows.

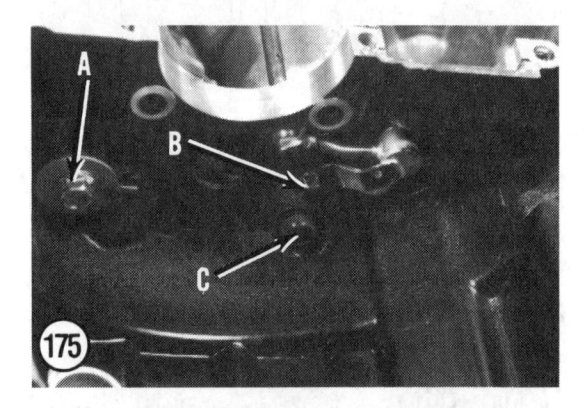

ENGINE

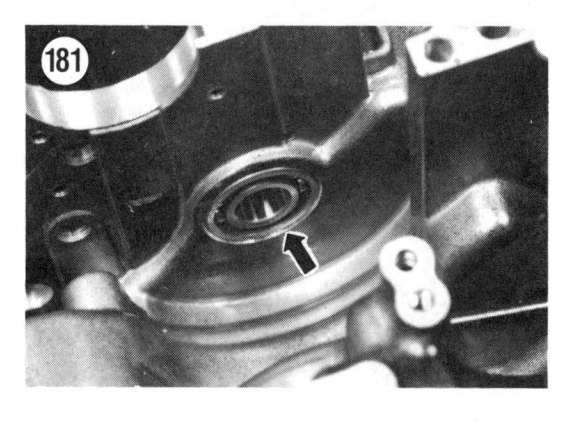

NOTE
If bearing replacement is required, purchase the new bearing and place it in a freezer for approximately 2 hours before installation. Chilling the bearing will reduce its overall diameter while the hot crankcase is slightly larger due to heat expansion. This will make installation much easier.

WARNING
Before heating the crankcase as described in Step 2, wash the crankcase thoroughly in soap and water. Make sure there are no gasoline or solvent fumes present.

2. The bearing is installed with a slight interference fit. The upper crankcase must be heated to a temperature of about 212° F (100° C) in a shop oven or on a hot plate.

CAUTION
Do not heat the case with a torch (propane or acetylene)—never bring a flame into contact with the bearing or case. The direct heat may warp the case.

NOTE
Wear insulated gloves when handling heated parts.

3. Remove the case from the oven and place onto wooden blocks.
4. Pull the bearing out of the crankcase with a blind bearing puller.
5. Reheat the crankcase.
6. Remove the crankcase and place it on wood blocks as before.
7. Press the new bearing into the crankcase by hand until it seats completely. If necessary, tap the bearing with a socket on the *outer* race. Do not hammer it in. If the bearing will not seat, remove it and freeze it again. Reheat the crankcase and install the bearing again. Install the bearing so that the outside bearing surface is even with the crankcase.

Assembly

1. Prior to assembly, coat all parts with assembly lube or engine oil.
2. Insert the oil baffle plates into the lower crankcase (**Figure 180**). Apply Loctite 242 (blue) to the baffle plate screws and tighten the screws to the torque specifications in **Table 2**.
3. Install the primary chain guide (**Figure 179**) into the upper crankcase. Apply Loctite 242 (blue) to the tensioner bolts and tighten to 10 N•m (7.2 ft.-lb.).

4. Install the rear chain guide (**Figure 178**) into the lower crankcase. Apply Loctite 242 (blue) to the tensioner bolts and tighten to 10 N•m (7.2 ft.-lb.).

5. Insert the oil spray nozzle (**Figure 177**) into the upper crankcase. **Figure 182** shows the oil spray nozzle installed.

6. Install the crankshaft bearing inserts as described under *Crankshaft Removal/Installation* in this chapter. If reusing old bearings, make sure that they are installed in the same location. Refer to marks made during crankshaft removal. Make sure they are locked in place.

7. Install the crankshaft as described in this chapter.

8. Install the secondary shaft and starter clutch as described under *Starter Clutch Assembly* in this chapter.

9. Insert the idler gear into the crankcase (B, **Figure 176**) and engage it with the starter clutch gear. Insert the idler gear shaft (C, **Figure 175**) through the crankcase and engage the idler gear.

10. Insert the oil pipe (A, **Figure 176**) partway into the crankcase. Then install the 2 O-rings onto the pipe and insert it all the way into the crankcase. See **Figure 183** and **Figure 184**.

11. Apply Loctite 242 (blue) onto the oil pipe stop bolt and install the stop and bolt (B, **Figure 175**). Tighten the bolt securely.

12. Install the oil plug plate (A, **Figure 175**), gasket and bolt. Tighten the bolt securely.

13. Install the shift drum, shift forks and transmission as described in Chapter Six.

NOTE
*Before installing the transmission, make sure both set rings (**Figure 185**) are installed in the upper crankcase.*

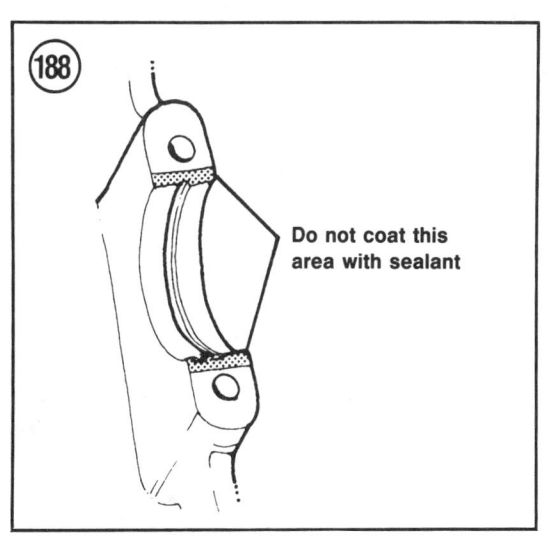

ENGINE

Figure 186

NOTE
Before assembling the crankcase halves, shift the transmission through all 6 gears to make sure the transmission operates correctly.

14. Install the 2 dowel pins and O-rings (**Figure 174**) into the lower crankcase.
15. Shift the transmission into NEUTRAL.

NOTE
*Make sure the main shaft bearing pin (A, **Figure 186**) faces to the front and the countershaft bearing pins (B, **Figure 186**) face to the rear. See **Figure 187**.*

Figure 187

16. Make sure the case half sealing surfaces are perfectly clean and dry.
17. Apply a light coat of gasket sealer to the lower crankcase half sealing surface. Cover only flat surfaces, not curved bearing surfaces. Make the coating as thin as possible. Do not apply sealant close to the edge of the bearing inserts (**Figure 188**) as it would restrict oil flow and cause damage.

NOTE
Use Gasgacinch Gasket Sealer, Three Bond or equivalent. A black colored silicone sealant (RTV) works well and blends with the black crankcases.

18. In the upper crankcase, position the shift drum into NEUTRAL. The shift forks should be located in the approximate positions shown in **Figure 189**.

Figure 188 — Do not coat this area with sealant

Figure 189

NOTE
*When assembling the crankcase halves Step 19, make sure to insert the chain guide through the tunnel in the upper crankcase. See **Figure 190**.*

19. Position the lower crankcase onto the upper crankcase. Set the front portion down first and lower the rear while making sure the shift forks (**Figure 189**) engage properly into the transmission assemblies (**Figure 191**).
20. Lower the crankcase completely.

CAUTION
Do not install any crankcase bolts until the sealing surface around the entire crankcase perimeter has seated completely.

21. Prior to installing the bolts, slowly spin the transmission shafts and shift the transmission through all 6 gears. This is done to check that the shift forks are properly engaged.
22. Apply oil to the threads of all crankcase bolts and install them finger-tight.

NOTE
*Copper washers are installed on bolts 7, 8, 9 and 10. See **Figure 172**.*

23. Tighten the lower crankcase bolts (**Figure 172**) to the following torque specifications:
    a. 6 mm bolts: 12 N•m (8.7 ft.-lb.).
    b. 8 mm bolts: 24 N•m (17 ft.-lb.).
    c. 9 mm bolts: 32 N•m (23 ft.-lb.).
24. Turn the crankcase assembly over and install all upper crankcase bolts finger-tight (**Figure 172**). Tighten the bolts to the following torque specifications:
    a. 6 mm bolts: 12 N•m (8.7 ft.-lb.).
    b. 8 mm bolts: 24 N•m (17 ft.-lb.).

NOTE
A No. 30 Torx driver socket will be required to tighten the retainer bolts in Step 25.

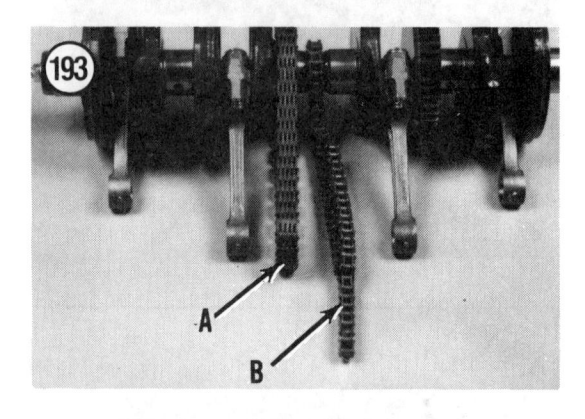

ENGINE

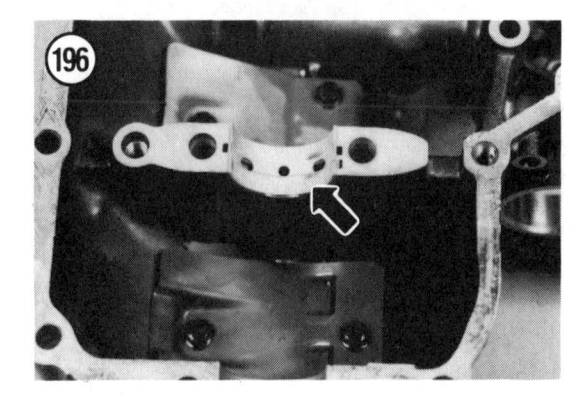

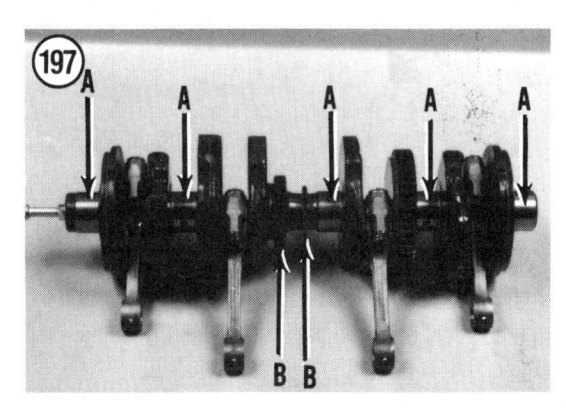

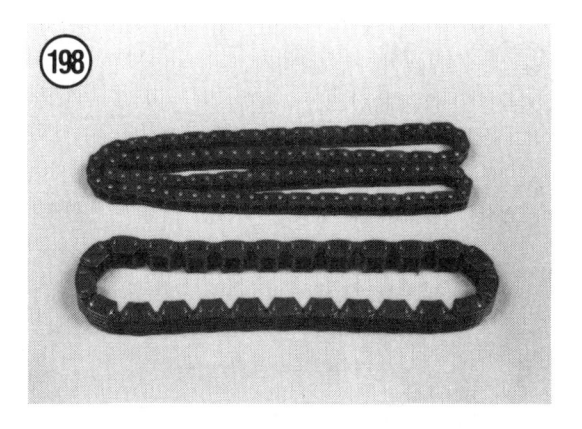

25. Install the transmission main shaft retainer (**Figure 171**). Apply Loctite 242 (blue) to the retainer bolts and tighten the bolts securely.
26. Reverse Steps 1 and 2 and install all engine assemblies that were removed.
27. Install the engine as described in this chapter.

CRANKSHAFT

Removal/Installation

1. Split the crankcase as described under *Crankcase Disassembly* in this chapter.
2. Remove the secondary shaft and starter motor clutch as described under *Starter Clutch* in this chapter.
3. Lift the crankshaft out of the crankcase (**Figure 192**). Then slip the primary chain (A, **Figure 193**) and camshaft chain (B, **Figure 193**) off the crankshaft.
4. Remove the crankshaft oil seal (**Figure 194**).
5. Remove the crankcase main bearing inserts (**Figure 195**) from the upper and lower crankcase halves. Mark the backsides of the inserts with a 1, 2, 3, 4 or 5 and U (upper) or L (lower) starting from the left-hand side, so they can be reinstalled into the same positions.
6. Installation is the reverse of these steps. Note the following:
   a. Install the primary chain and camshaft drive chain over the crankshaft (**Figure 193**).
   b. Install a new crankshaft oil seal (**Figure 194**).
   c. Algin the tab on the bearing inserts with the notch in the case and install the inserts. See **Figure 196**.

Crankshaft Inspection

1. Clean crankshaft thoroughly with solvent. Clean oil holes with rifle cleaning brushes; flush thoroughly and dry with compressed air. Lightly oil all oil journal surfaces immediately to prevent rust.
2. Inspect each journal (A, **Figure 197**) for scratches, ridges, scoring, nicks, etc.
3. If the surface on all journals is satisfactory, measure the journals with a micrometer and check out-of-roundness, taper and wear on the journals. Check against measurements given in **Table 1**.
4. Inspect the camshaft and primary chain drive sprockets (B, **Figure 197**). If they are worn or damaged, the crankshaft will have to be replaced.
5. Inspect both drive chains (**Figure 198**) for visible wear or damage. If necessary, replace the chain(s) as required.

6. Measure the connecting rod side clearance with a feeler gauge at the point shown in **Figure 199** and compare to the specifications in **Table 1**. If the clearance is excessive, replace the connecting rod and remeasure. If the clearance is still excessive, replace the crankshaft.

Crankshaft Main Bearing Clearance Measurement

1. Check the inside and outside surfaces of the bearing inserts for wear, bluish tint (burned), flaking abrasion and scoring. If the bearings are good, they may be reused. If any insert is questionable, replace the entire set.
2. Clean the bearing surfaces of the crankshaft and the main bearing inserts.
3. Measure the main bearing clearance by performing the following steps.
4. Set the upper crankcase upside down on the workbench on wood blocks.
5. Install the existing main bearing inserts into the upper and lower crankcase in their original positions. See **Figure 195**.
6. Install the crankshaft (**Figure 192**) into the upper crankcase.
7. Place a piece of Plastigage over each main bearing journal parallel to the crankshaft (**Figure 200**).

CAUTION
Do not rotate crankshaft while Plastigage is in place.

8. Install the lower crankcase over the upper crankcase.
9. Apply oil to the bolt threads and install bolts No. 1-10 (**Figure 201**); be sure to place copper washers under No. 7, 8, 9 and 10.
10. Tighten the bolts to 32 N•m (23 ft.-lb.). The torque pattern is indicated by the bolt number adjacent to the bolt hole (**Figure 201**).

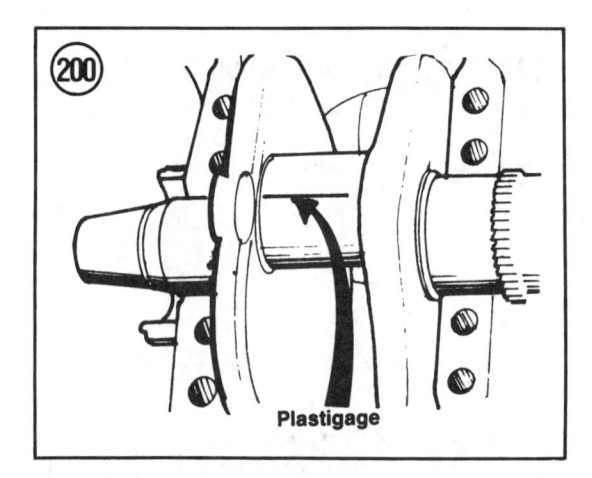

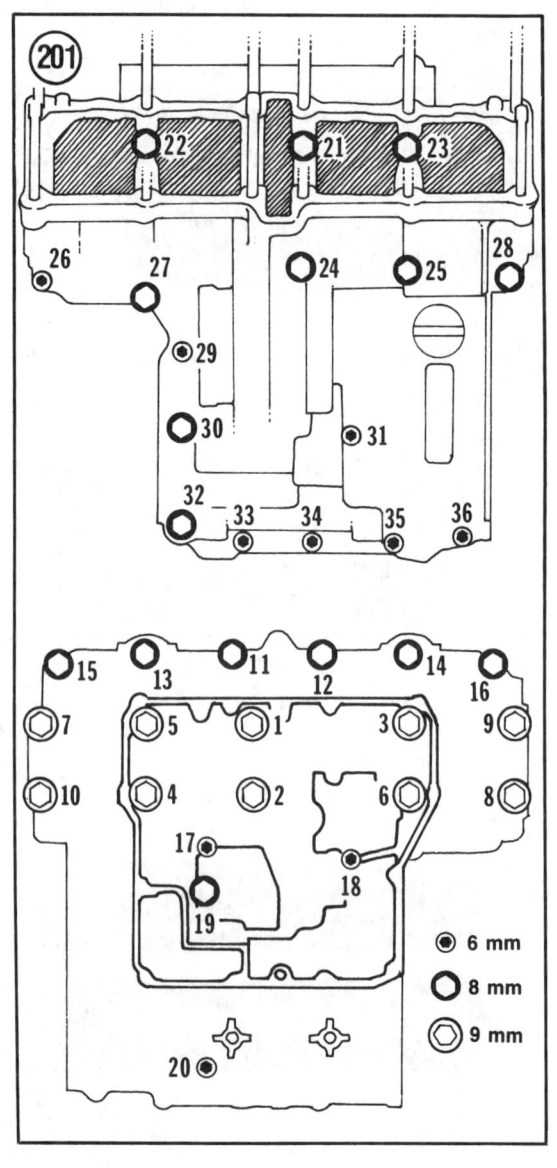

ENGINE

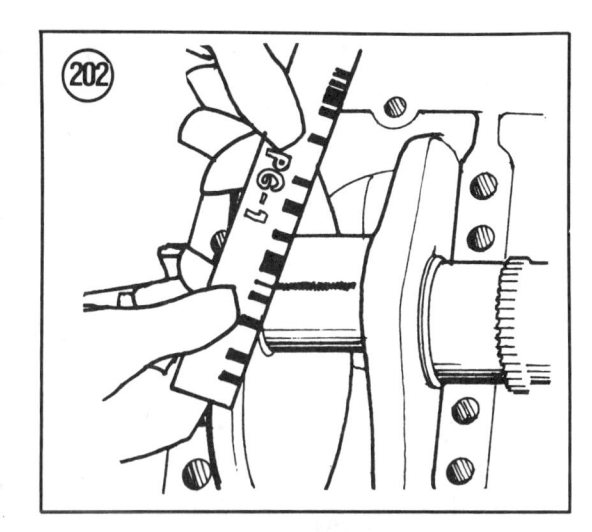

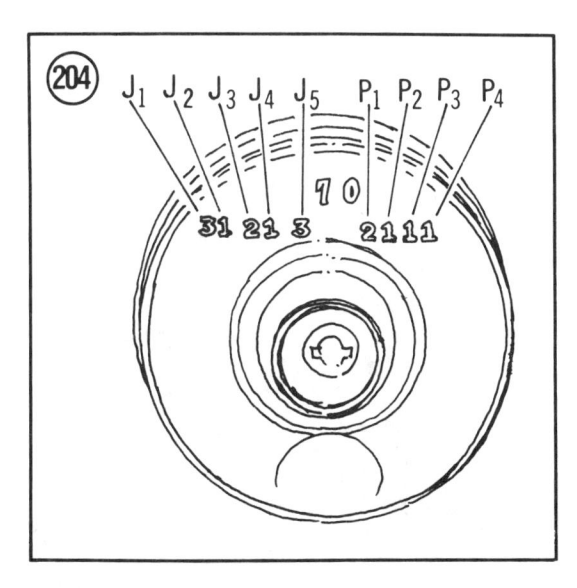

11. Remove bolts No. 1-10 in the reverse order of installation.

12. Carefully remove the lower crankcase. Do not move the crankshaft.

13. Measure the width of the flattened Plastigage according to the manufacturer's instructions (**Figure 202**). Measure at both ends of the strip. A difference of 0.025 mm (0.001 in.) or more indicates a tapered crankpin. Confirm with a micrometer. Remove the Plastigage strips from all bearing journals.

14. New bearing clearance should be 0.020-0.044 mm (0.0008-0.0017 in.). Remove the Plastigage strips from all bearing journals.

15. If the bearing clearance is greater than specified, use the following steps for new bearing selection.

16. The crankshaft is marked on the left-hand counterbalancer with 5 numbers as shown in **Figure 203** that relate to the crankshaft main bearing journals. See **Figure 204**.

NOTE
*The group of 4 numbers on the left-hand counterbalancer relates to the crankshaft connecting rod journals—**do not** refer to these 4 numbers.*

17. The 5 numbers stamped on the upper crankcase half (**Figure 205**) relate to the crankcase bearing journals. The numbers read from left to right (with the top crankcase half facing up as it sits

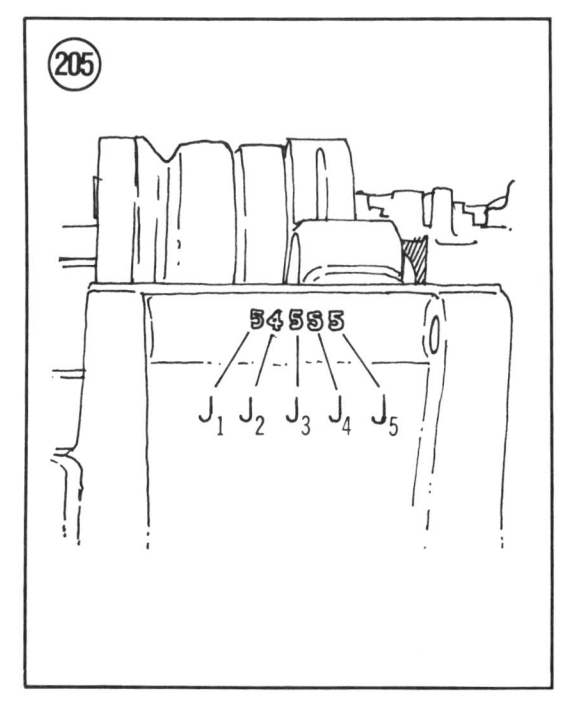

on the bike). The first number on the left is for the No. 1 crankcase journal; the numbers continue from left to right for journals No. 2-5. See **Figure 206**.

18. To select the proper main bearing insert number, subtract the crankshaft bearing journal number from the crankcase bearing journal number. For example, if the crankcase journal is a No. 5 and the crankshaft journal is a No. 2, 5 - 2 = 3. The new bearing insert is a No. 3. The bearings are then identified by number and color as follows:
   a. No. 1 (blue).
   b. No. 2 (black).
   c. No. 3 (brown).
   d. No. 4 (green).
   e. No. 5 (yellow).

NOTE
Determine the bearing insert number for all main bearing journals, then take the insert numbers to a Yamaha dealer for bearing purchase.

19. Repeat steps 13-18 for all bearing journals.
20. After new bearings have been selected, recheck the clearance as described in steps 13-18. If the clearance is out of specification, the crankshaft bearing journals are worn. Refer to *Crankshaft* in this chapter.
21. Clean all Plastigage from the crankshaft and bearing inserts. Assemble the crankcase as described in this chapter.

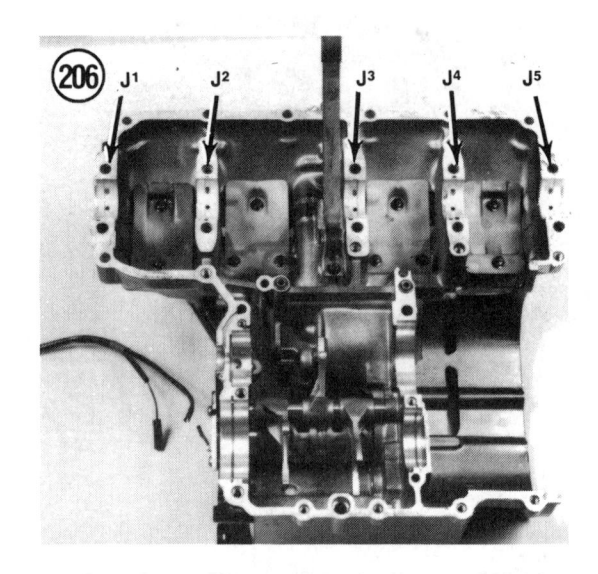

CONNECTING RODS

Removal/Installation

1. Remove the engine as described in this chapter.
2. Split the crankcase and remove the crankshaft as described in this chapter.
3. Measure the connecting rod big end side clearance. Insert a feeler gauge between a connecting rod big end and either crankshaft machined web (**Figure 199**). Record the clearance for each connecting rod and compare to the specifications in **Table 1**. If the clearance is excessive, replace the connecting rod(s) and recheck clearance. If clearance is still excessive, replace the crankshaft.

NOTE
Prior to disassembly, mark the rods and caps with a "1", "2", "3" and "4" starting from the left-hand side.

4. Remove the connecting rod cap nuts (A, **Figure 207**) and separate the rods from the crankshaft. Keep each cap with its original rod, with the weight mark on the end of the cap matching the mark on the rod (B, **Figure 207**).

NOTE
Keep each bearing insert in its original place in the crankcase, rod or rod cap. If you are going to assemble the engine with the original inserts, they must be installed exactly as removed in order to prevent rapid wear.

5. Install by reversing these removal steps. Note the following procedures.
6. Install the bearing inserts into each connecting rod and cap. Make sure they are locked in place correctly. See **Figure 208**.

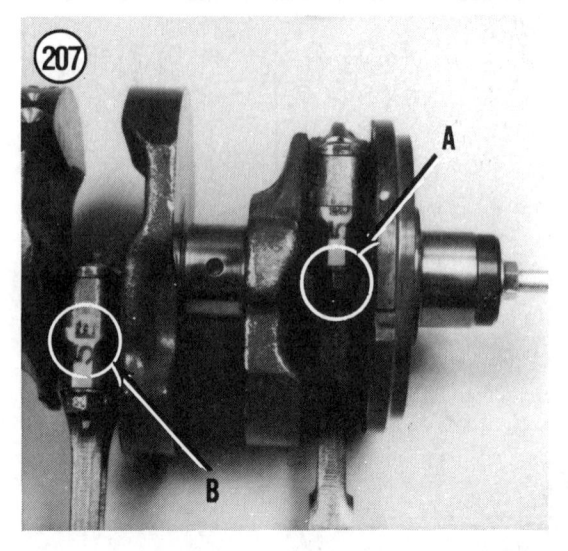

ENGINE

NOTE
*Each connecting rod is embossed with a "Y" on one side (**Figure 209**). The connecting rod must be installed so that the "Y" mark faces toward the left crankshaft end.*

7. Apply assembly lube to the bearing inserts.
8. If new bearing inserts are going to be installed, check the bearing clearance as described in this chapter.

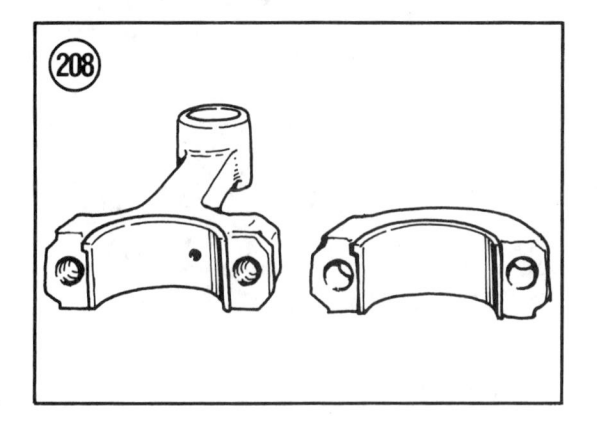

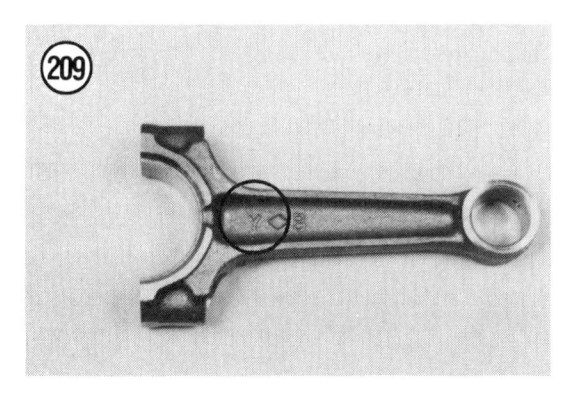

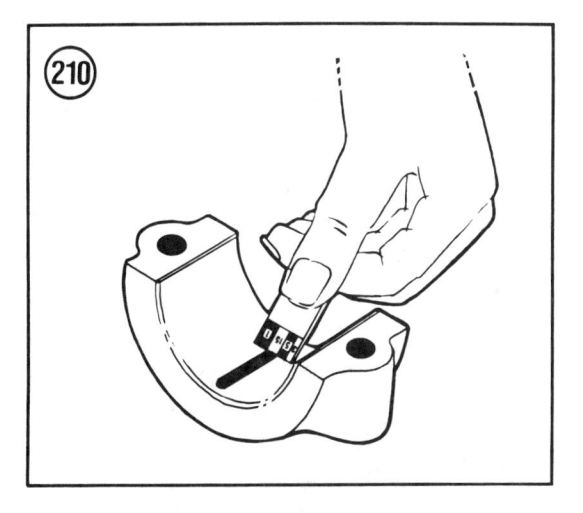

9. Install the bearing caps so that the number on the rod and cap align with each other. See B, **Figure 207**.
10. Tighten the connecting rod nuts (A, **Figure 207**) to the torque specifications in **Table 2**.

Connecting Rod Inspection

1. Check each rod for obvious damage such as cracks and scoring.
2. Check the piston pin bushing for wear or scoring.
3. Take the rods to a machine shop and have them checked for twisting and bending.
4. Examine the bearing inserts (**Figure 208**) for wear, scoring or burning. They are reusable if in good condition. Make a note of the bearing size or color (if any) on the back of the insert if the bearing is to be discarded; a previous owner may have used undersize bearings.
5. Remove the connecting rod bearing bolts and check them for cracks or twisting. Replace any bolts as required.
6. Check bearing clearance as described in this chapter.

Connecting Rod Bearing Clearance Measurement

CAUTION
If the old bearings are to be reused, be sure that they are installed in their exact original locations.

1. Wipe bearing inserts and crankpins clean. Install bearing inserts in rod and cap (**Figure 208**).
2. Place a piece of Plastigage on one crankpin parallel to the crankshaft.
3. Install rod and cap. Tighten nuts to torque specifications in **Table 2**.

NOTE
*Each connecting rod is embossed with a "Y" on one side (**Figure 209**). The connecting rod must be installed so that the "Y" mark faces toward the left crankshaft end.*

CAUTION
Do not rotate crankshaft while Plastigage is in place.

4. Remove the rod cap.
5. Measure width of flattened Plastigage according to the manufacturer's instructions (**Figure 210**). Measure at both ends of the strip. A difference of 0.025 mm (0.001 in.) or more indicates a tapered crankpin; the crankshaft must be replaced. Confirm with a micrometer measurement of the journal OD.

6. If the crankpin taper is within tolerance, measure the bearing clearance with the same strip of Plastigage. Correct bearing clearance is specified in **Table 1**. Remove Plastigage strips.

7. If the bearing clearance is greater than specified, use the following steps for new bearing selection.

8. Bearing clearance should be within the specifications in **Table 1**. Remove the Plastigage strips from all bearing journals.

9. If the bearing clearance is greater than specified, use the following steps for new bearing selection.

10. The connecting rods and caps are marked with a No. 4 or No. 5 (B, **Figure 207**). The crankshaft is marked on the left-hand counterbalancer with 4 numbers that relate to the crankshaft connecting rod journals as shown in **Figure 204**.

NOTE
*The group of 5 numbers on the left-hand counterbalancer relates to the crankshaft main bearing journals; **do not** refer to these 5 numbers.*

11. To select the proper bearing insert number, subtract the crankshaft connecting rod journal number from the connecting rod and cap number. For example, if the connecting rod is marked with a No. 4 and the matching crankshaft journal is a No. 2, 4 - 2 = 2. The new bearing insert is a No. 2. The bearings are then identified by number and color as follows:
   a. No. 1 (blue).
   b. No. 2 (black).
   c. No. 3 (brown).
   d. No. 4 (green).

NOTE
Determine the bearing insert number for all 4 connecting rods. Then take insert numbers and colors to a Yamaha dealer for bearing purchase.

12. Repeat Steps 1-11 for the other 3 connecting rods.

13. After new bearings have been selected, recheck clearances as described in Step 6. If clearance is still out of specification, take the crankshaft and connecting rods to a Yamaha dealer for further service. Yamaha does not provide connecting rod or crankpin journal wear specifications.

14. Clean all Plastigage from crankshaft and bearing inserts. Install the connecting rods as described under *Connecting Rods Removal/Installation* in this chapter.

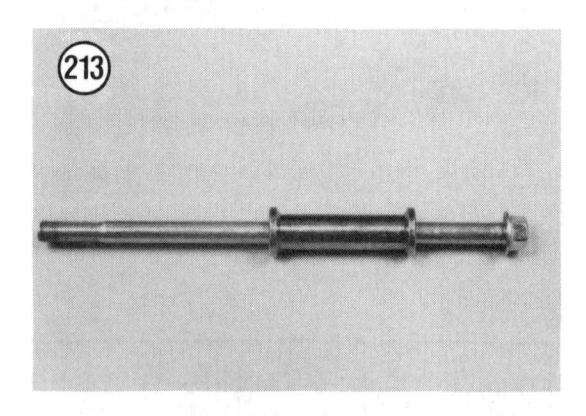

ENGINE

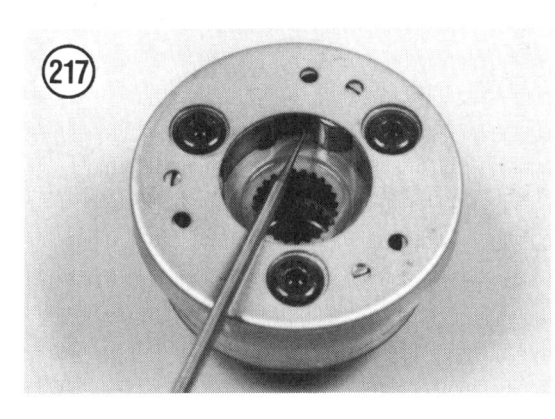

STARTER CLUTCH ASSEMBLY

Removal

1. Disassemble the crankcase as described in this chapter.
2. Remove the transmission components as described in Chapter Six.
3. Remove the oil pipe and the starter idler gear from the upper crankcase as described under *Crankcase Disassembly* in this chapter.
4. Remove the starter clutch shaft bearing plate bolts (**Figure 211**) and remove the plate.
5. Thread the end of a knock puller (**Figure 212**) into the starter clutch shaft and pull the shaft out of the crankcase.

> *NOTE*
> *A knock puller can be assembled from existing parts. Use a rear motor mount bolt and engine spacer as shown in* **Figure 212** *and* **Figure 213**. *If the engine spacer is not heavy enough to remove the shaft, drill a hole through a larger piece of scrap metal to accept the motor mount bolt.*

6. Lift the primary chain (A, **Figure 214**) and remove the starter clutch assembly (B, **Figure 214**).

Starter Motor Clutch Disassembly/Inspection/Reassembly

1. Remove the bushing (**Figure 215**) from the idler gear.
2. Pull the idler gear (**Figure 216**) off the starter clutch assembly.
3. Remove the 3 rollers (**Figure 217**), spring and cap (**Figure 218**) assemblies.
4. Inspect the teeth on the starter clutch gear for chipped or missing teeth. Check the bushing for scoring or other damage. Inspect the teeth on the starter clutch gear for chipped or missing teeth.
5. Check the rollers, springs and caps in the starter clutch for uneven or excessive wear; replace as a set if any are bad.
6. Check the starter clutch Allen bolts (**Figure 219**) for tightness. If the bolts are loose, remove them

and apply Loctite 242 (blue) to the threads. Then install the bolts and tighten to 25 N•m (18 ft.-lb.).
7. Inspect the idler gear (A, **Figure 220**) for chipped or missing teeth. Check the idler gear shaft (B, **Figure 220**) for scoring or damage.
8. Pull the bearing (**Figure 221**) off the starter clutch shaft. Spin the bearing by hand and check it for roughness, excessive noise or damage. Replace the bearing if questionable. If the bearing is okay, oil the races and balls with clean engine oil.
9. Check the starter clutch shaft (**Figure 222**) for pitting, seizure or other damage. Check the shaft splines for wear or cracking. Replace the shaft if necessary.
10. Assembly of the starter motor clutch is the reverse of Steps 1-3. Note the following:
    a. Install the spring, cap and roller into each receptacle in the starter clutch. See **Figure 218** and **Figure 217**.
    b. Insert the starter clutch gear (**Figure 216**) into the starter clutch assembly.
    c. Insert the bushing into the starter clutch gear (**Figure 215**).
11. Test the starter clutch operation as follows:
    a. Turn the starter gear one way and then the other.
    b. The starter gear should turn freely one way but not the other.
    c. If the starter clutch does not operate correctly, disassemble and check for worn spring, caps, rollers or gear.

Installation

1. Assemble the starter clutch assembly as described in this chapter.
2. Lift the primary chain and engage the secondary sprocket with the chain (**Figure 214**).
3. Slide the bearing onto the starter clutch shaft (**Figure 221**). Then insert the starter clutch shaft into the crankcase and through the starter clutch assembly.
4. Tap the secondary shaft until the bearing seats into the crankcase.
5. Install the starter clutch shaft bearing plate. Apply Loctite 242 (blue) to the bolts and tighten to 10 N•m (7.2 ft.-lb.).
6. Assemble the crankcase and install the engine as described in this chapter.

BREAK-IN

Following cylinder servicing (boring, honing, new rings, etc.) or major lower end work, the engine should be broken in just as if it were new. The performance and service life of the engine depends on a careful and sensible break-in.

500-mile Service

It is essential that oil and filter be changed after the first 500 miles. In addition, it is a good idea to change the oil and filter at the completion of break-in (about 1,500 miles) to ensure that all of the particles produced during break-in are removed from the lubrication system. The small added expense may be considered a smart investment that will pay off in increased engine life.

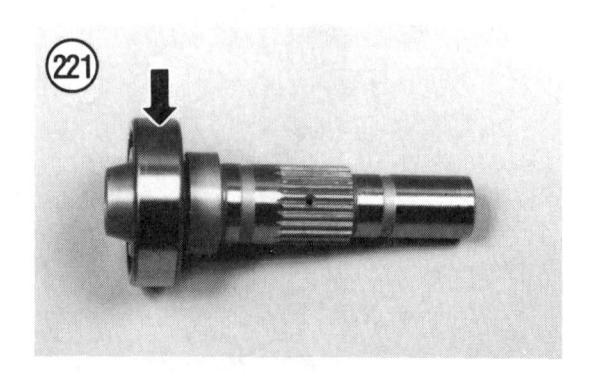

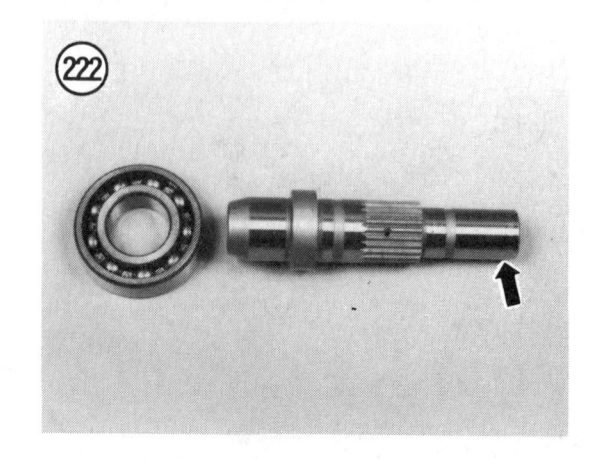

ENGINE

Table 1 ENGINE SPECIFICATIONS

Item	Specifications mm (in.)	Wear limit mm (in.)
General		
Type	4-stroke, liquid-cooled, inline four	
Number of cylinders	4	
Bore and stroke		
FZX700 & FZ700	68.0×48.0 mm (6.68×1.89 in.)	
FZ750	68.0×51.6 mm (6.68×2.03 in.)	
Displacement		
FZX700 & FZ700	697 cc (42.52 cu. in.)	
FZ750	749 cc (45.64 cu. in.)	
Compression ratio	11.2:1	
Cylinders		
Cylinder liner	Aluminum alloy with cast iron sleeve	
Cylinder head		
Warp limit		0.03 (0.0012)
Bore	68.000-68.005 (2.67717-2.67736)	
Taper		0.05 (0.002)
Out-of-round		0.05 (0.002)
Piston/cylinder clearance	0.06-0.08 (0.0024-0.0031)	0.10 (0.0039)
Pistons		
Diameter	67.925-67.940 (2.6742-2.6748)	
Measuring point		
FZX700 & FZ750	5.0 (0.197)	
FX700	3 (0.12)	
Piston rings		
Number per piston		
Compression	2	
Oil control	1	
Ring end gap		
Top	0.30-0.45 (0.0118-0.0177)	
Second	0.20-0.35 (0.0079-0.0138)	
Oil (side rail)	0.2-0.7 (0.0079-0.0276)	
Ring side clearance	0.03-0.07 (0.0012-0.0028)	
Crankshaft (FZX700 & FZ750)		
Runout		0.03 (0.0012)
Connecting rod oil clearance	0.032-0.056 (0.00126-0.00220)	
Journal oil clearance	0.020-0.044 (0.0008-0.0017)	
Big end side clearance	0.160-0.262 (0.0063-0.0103)	

(continued)

Table 1 ENGINE SPECIFICATIONS (cont.)

Item	Specifications mm (in.)	Wear limit mm (in.)
Crankshaft (FZ700)		
Runout		0.03 (0.0012)
Connecting rod oil clearance	0.032-0.056 (0.00126-0.0017)	
Journal oil clearance	0.040-0.064 (0.002-0.003)	
Camshaft		
Runout		0.03 (0.0012)
Lobe height		
FZX700 Lobe height		
Intake	31.95-32.05 (1.2578-1.2618)	31.85 (1.253)
Exhaust	32.4-32.5 (1.2756-1.2795)	32.3 (1.27)
FZ700 & FZ700 Lobe height		
Intake	32.55-32.65 (1.2815-1.2854)	32.45 (32.45
Exhaust	32.4-32.5 (1.2756-1.2795)	32.3 (1.27)
Lobe width (all)	24.95-25.05 (0.9823-0.9862)	24.85 (0.978)
Camshaft outside diameter	24.437-24.450 (0.9621-0.9626)	
Cam cap inside diameter		
I-2, I-3, E-2, E-3	24.500-24.521 (0.9646-0.9654)	
I-1, I-4, E-1, E-4	24.470-24.491 (0.9634-0.9642)	
Camshaft clearance		
I-2, I-3, E-2, E-3	0.050-0.084 (0.00197-0.00331)	
I-1, I-4, E-1, E-4	0.020-0.054 (0.00079-0.00213)	
Valves		
Head diameter		
Intake	20.9-21.1 (0.8228-0.8307)	
Exhaust	22.9-23.1 (0.9016-0.9094)	
Face width		
Intake and exhaust	1.98-2.55 (0.0779-0.1004)	
Seat width		
Intake and exhaust	0.9-1.1 (0.0354-0.0433)	
Margin thickness		
Intake and exhaust	0.6-0.8 (0.0236-0.0315)	

(continued)

Table 1 ENGINE SPECIFICATIONS (cont.)

Item	Specifications mm (in.)	Wear limit mm (in.)
Stem diameter		
Intake	4.975-4.990 (0.1959-0.1965)	4.945 (0.1947)
Exhaust	4.960-4.975 (0.1953-0.1959)	4.930 (0.1941)
Runout		0.01 (0.0004)
Valve guide inside diameter		
Intake and exhaust	5.000-5.012 (0.1969-0.1973)	5.05 (0.1988)
Valve stem to guide clearance		
Intake	0.010-0.037 (0.0004-0.0015)	0.08 (0.0031)
Exhaust	0.025-0.052 (0.0010-0.0020)	0.10 (0.0039)
Valve springs free length		
Intake	39.76 (1.565)	
Exhaust	39.96 (1.573)	
Valve spring tilt limit		1.7 (0.067)
Oil pump		
End clearance	0.09-0.15 (0.00354-0.00591)	
Side clearance	0.03-0.08 (0.0012-0.0031)	

Table 2 ENGINE TIGHTENING TORQUES

	N·m	ft.-lb.
Spark plug	17.5	12.5
Cylinder head cover bolts	10	7.2
Camshaft cap bolts	10	7.2
Camshaft case bolts	10	7.2
Cylinder head nuts	37	27
Exhaust stud nuts	5	3.6
Connecting rod nuts	36	25
Cam chain sprocket bolt	24	17
Cam chain tensioner bolt	10	7.2
Cam chain tensioner end cap bolt	20	14
Chain guide (intake side)	10	7.2
Oil pump		
Housing screws	10	7.2
Mount bolt	10	7.2
Oil filter housing	15	11
Oil pan bolts	10	7.2

(continued)

Table 2 ENGINE TIGHTENING TORQUES (cont.)

	N·m	ft.-lb.
Engine drain pan	43	31
Oil pipe union bolt	21	15
Oil plug plate bolt	10	7.2
Oil level switch	10	7.2
Exhaust pipe flange nut	10	7.2
Muffler clamp bolt	20	14
Exhaust pipe blind plug	10	7.2
Crankcase stud bolts	10	7.2
Main shaft bearing stopper	10	7.2
Crankshaft end cover screws	7	5.1
Crankcase bolts		
M6×1.0	12	8.7
M8×1.25	24	17
M9×1.25	32	23
Starter clutch bolt	25	18
Starter chain guide	10	7.2
Clutch boss nut	70	50
Drive sprocket nut	70	50
Baffle plate screws	10	7.2
Banjo bolts	21	15

Table 3 ENGINE MOUNT TIGHTENING TORQUES (FZ700 & FZ750)

	N·m	ft.-lb.
Down tube bolts/nuts	28	20
All other bolts/nuts	55	40

CHAPTER FIVE

CLUTCH

The clutch is a wet-multi-plate type which operates immersed in engine oil. It is mounted on the right-hand side of the transmission mainshaft. The clutch can be serviced with the engine in the frame.

The clutch release mechanism is hydraulic and requires no routine adjustment. The mechanism consists of a clutch master cylinder on the left-hand handlebar, a slave cylinder mounted on the sprocket cover on the left-hand side of the engine and a pushrod that rides within the transmission mainshaft.

Table 1 (end of chapter) lists clutch specifications.

CLUTCH COVER

Clutch Cover
Removal/Installation

1. *FZ700 and FZ750:* Remove the lower fairing. See Chapter Thirteen.

NOTE
If the clutch or transmission are going to be serviced because of suspected wear or damage, drain the engine oil into a clean container so that it can be checked for broken gear teeth or other debris.

2. Drain the engine oil as described under *Engine Oil and Filter Change* in Chapter Three.
3. Remove the bolts securing the clutch cover in place and remove the clutch cover. See **Figure 1**.
4. Remove the dowel pins (A, **Figure 2**) and gasket (B, **Figure 2**).
5. Installation is the reverse of these steps. Note the following:
   a. Replace the clutch cover gasket if damaged or if it leaked previously.
   b. Remove all gasket residue from the clutch cover and crankcase mating surfaces.

CAUTION
When installing the cover screws, check that each one sticks up the same amount before you screw them all in. A long scew in the wrong hole can damage the crankcase threads.

   c. Refill the engine oil as described in Chapter Three.

Clutch Cover Breather
Removal/Installation

1. Remove the clutch cover as described in this chapter.

2. Remove the breather cover screws (A, **Figure 3**) and remove the breather (B, **Figure 3**).
3. Remove the screws (A, **Figure 4**) and remove the washers and grommets (B, **Figure 4**).
4. Check the grommets for wear or damage; replace if necessary.
5. Installation is the reverse of these steps. Note the following:
   a. Apply Loctite 242 (blue) to the washer screws. Then tighten the screws securely.
   b. Replace the breather cover gasket if necessary.
   c. Install the clutch cover as described in this chapter.

CLUTCH

Refer to **Figure 5** (FZ750N and NC) or **Figure 6** (FZ750S, FZ700 and FZX700).

Removal

1. Remove the clutch cover as described in this chapter.

> *NOTE*
> *Do not operate the clutch lever after the clutch assembly or slave cylinder are removed from the engine. If the lever is applied it will force the slave cylinder piston out of the body and make slave cylinder installation difficult.*

2. Place a block of wood between the clutch lever and the hand grip to hold the lever in the released position. Secure the wood with a rubber band or tape. This will prevent the clutch lever from being applied accidentally after the clutch slave cylinder is removed from the crankcase.

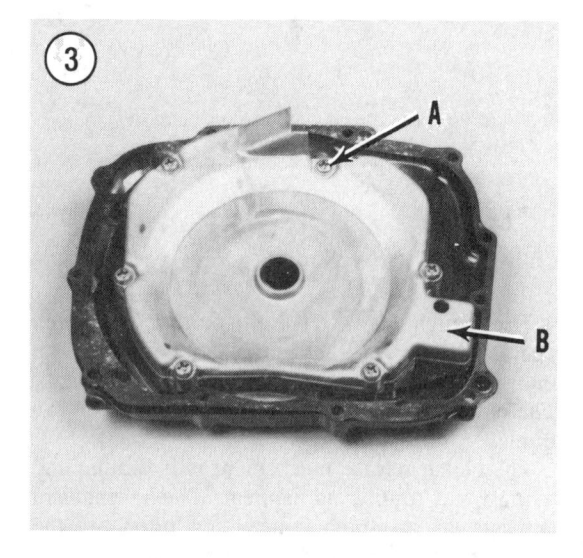

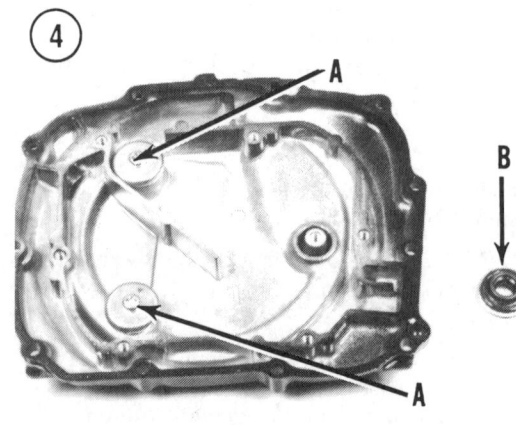

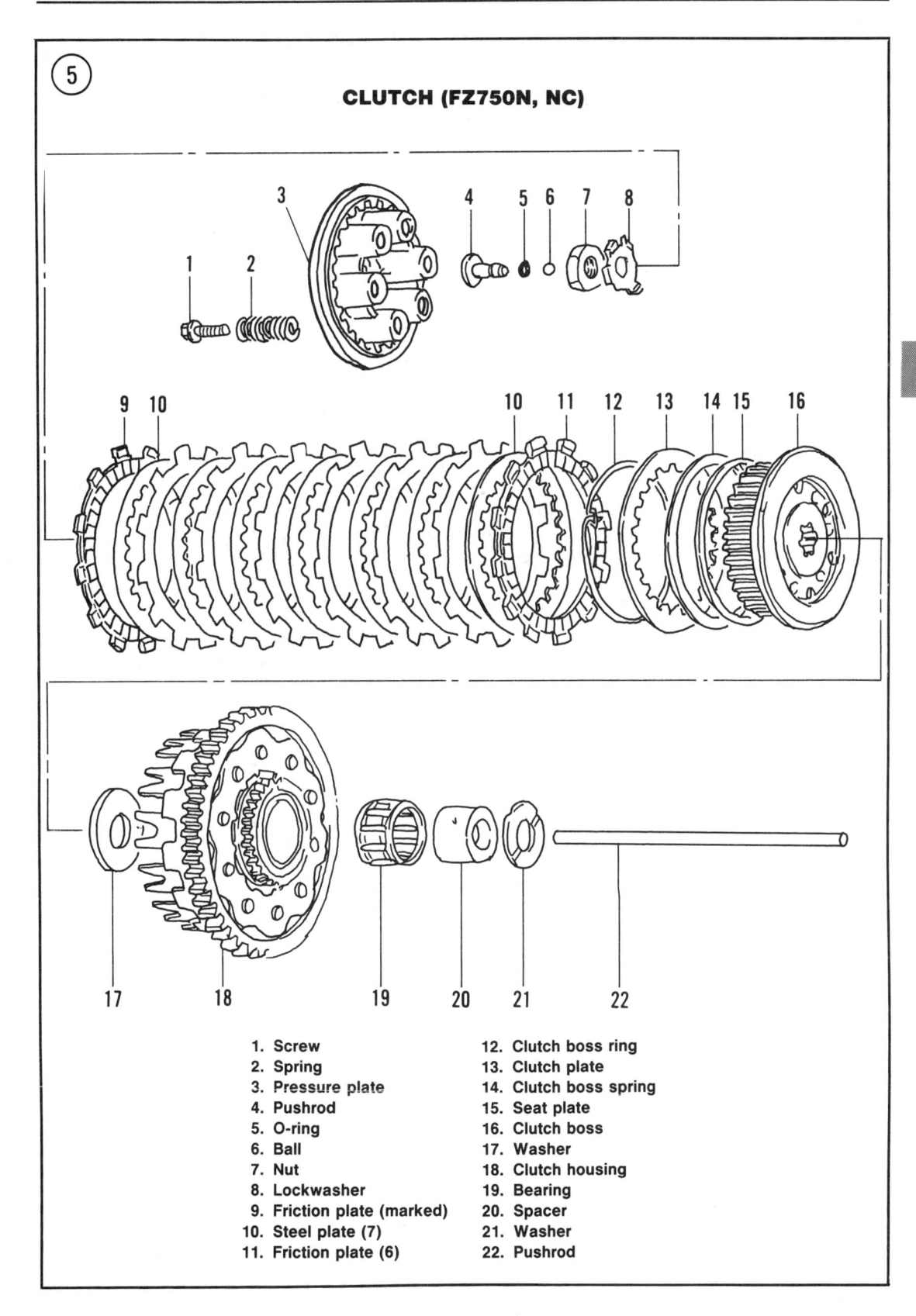

CLUTCH

CLUTCH (FZ750N, NC)

1. Screw
2. Spring
3. Pressure plate
4. Pushrod
5. O-ring
6. Ball
7. Nut
8. Lockwasher
9. Friction plate (marked)
10. Steel plate (7)
11. Friction plate (6)
12. Clutch boss ring
13. Clutch plate
14. Clutch boss spring
15. Seat plate
16. Clutch boss
17. Washer
18. Clutch housing
19. Bearing
20. Spacer
21. Washer
22. Pushrod

CHAPTER FIVE

CLUTCH
(FZX700, FZ700 and FZ750S)

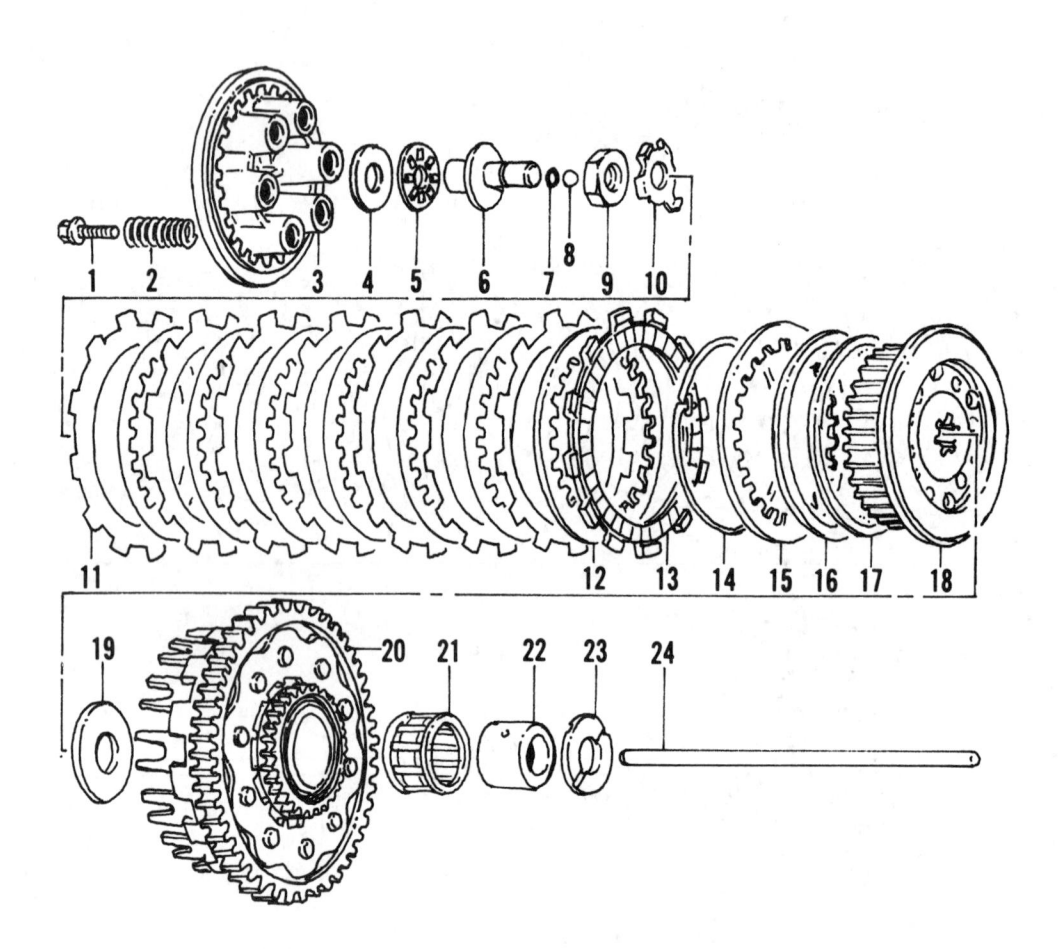

1. Screw
2. Spring
3. Pressure plate
4. Washer
5. Bearing
6. Pushrod
7. O-ring
8. Ball
9. Nut
10. Lockwasher
11. Friction plate (marked)
12. Steel plate (7)
13. Friction plate (6)
14. Clutch boss ring
15. Clutch plate
16. Clutch boss spring
17. Seat plate
18. Clutch boss
19. Washer
20. Clutch housing
21. Bearing
22. Spacer
23. Washer
24. Pushrod

CLUTCH

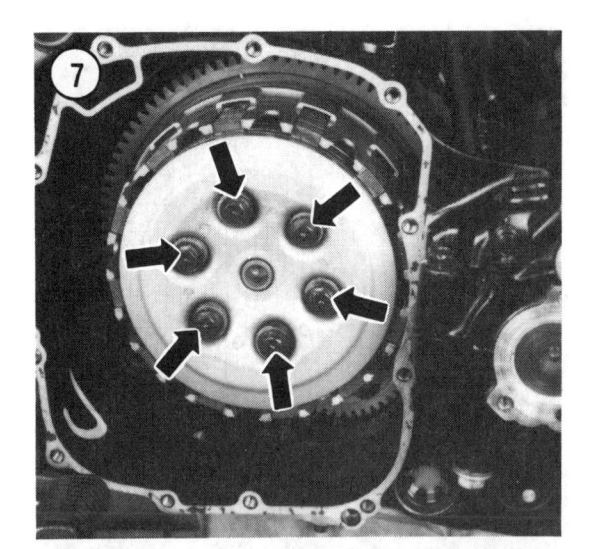

3. Loosen the 6 pressure plate screws (**Figure 7**) in a crisscross pattern. Then remove the screws and springs (**Figure 8**).
4. Remove the pressure plate (**Figure 9**).
5. Referring to **Figure 5** or **Figure 6**, remove the clutch plates in order. Stack plates in order of removal.
6. *All 1986-on:* Remove the flat washer and bearing (**Figure 10**).
7. Remove the short pushrod (**Figure 11**).
8. Using a magnet, pull the ball (**Figure 12**) out of the transmission mainshaft.

140 CHAPTER FIVE

NOTE
To keep the clutch housing from turning when removing the clutch hub nut in Step 9, use the "Grabbit" special tool available from motorcycle dealers.

9. Straighten out the locking tab on the clutch nut and remove the clutch nut (**Figure 13**).
10. Remove the washer (**Figure 14**).
11. Remove the large washer (**Figure 15**).
12. Thread a 5 mm screw (A, **Figure 16**) into the spacer and pull the spacer (B, **Figure 16**) out of the clutch housing and remove it.
13. Remove the bearing (**Figure 17**).

NOTE
*The crankshaft counterbalancer must be positioned away from the crankcase hole opening at the point shown in A, **Figure 18** for clutch housing removal. If the clutch housing hits the counterbalancer, perform Step 14 to reposition the crankshaft.*

14. Perform the following:
   a. Disconnect the battery ground cable.
   b. Remove the spark plugs. This will make it easier to turn the engine by hand.
   c. Remove the left crankshaft end cover (**Figure 19**).

CLUTCH

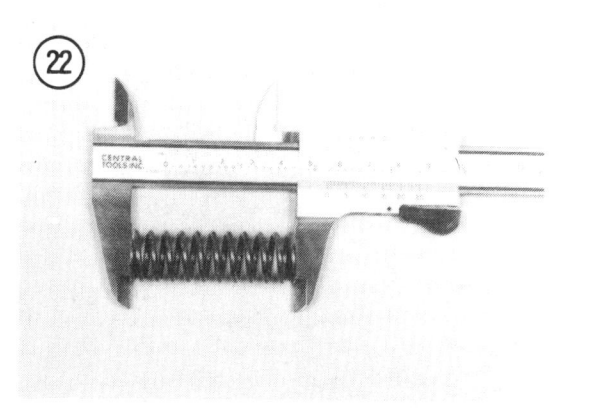

d. Thread an 8 mm bolt and nut into the left crankshaft end (**Figure 20**). Lock the bolt with the nut.

e. Using the bolt installed in step d, rotate the crankshaft counterclockwise until the counterbalancer clears the crankcase hole.

15. Remove the clutch housing (B, **Figure 18**).
16. Remove the spacer (**Figure 21**).
17. Pull the pushrod out of the transmission mainshaft.

Inspection

1. Clean all clutch parts in a petroleum-based solvent such as kerosene, and thoroughly dry with compressed air.
2. Measure the free length of each clutch spring as shown in **Figure 22**. Replace any springs that are too short (**Table 1**).
3. Check the friction discs (**Figure 23**) for tab breakage or other damage. Measure the thickness of each friction disc at several places around the disc as shown in **Figure 24**. See **Table 1** for specifications. Replace all friction discs if any one is found too thin. Do not replace only 1 or 2 discs.

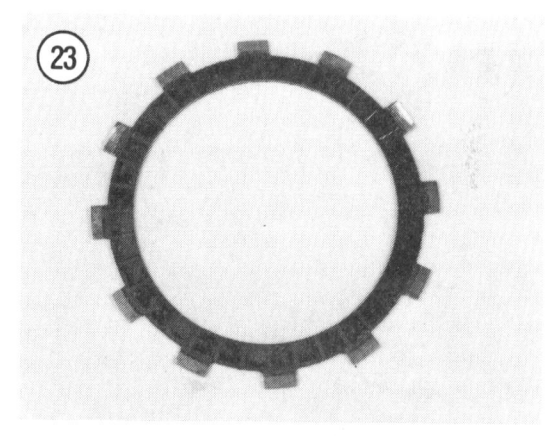

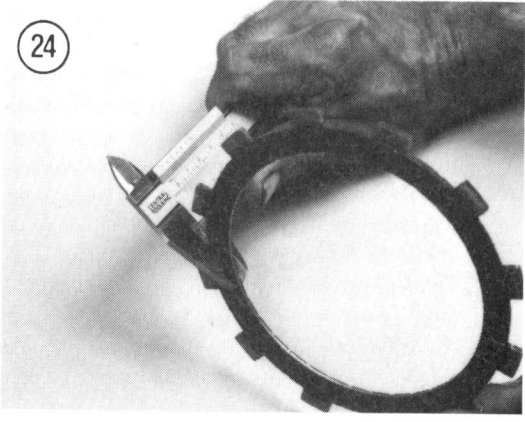

4. Check the clutch metal plates (**Figure 25**) for excessive bluing or cracks. Then check the plates for warpage as shown in **Figure 26**. If any plate is warped more than specified (**Table 1**), replace the entire set of plates. Do not replace only 1 or 2 plates.

5. Inspect the clutch boss assembly for cracks or galling in the grooves (A, **Figure 27**) where the clutch plate teeth slide. They must be smooth for chatter-free clutch operation.

6. Inspect the shaft splines (B, **Figure 27**) in the clutch boss assembly. If damage is only a slight amount, remove any small burrs with a fine cut file; if damage is severe, replace the assembly.

NOTE
*The clutch boss is equipped with a built-up clutch damper (C, **Figure 27**) that is secured with a wire ring. See **Figure 5** and **Figure 6**. Disassembly of the clutch damper is required only if the bike experiences severe clutch chatter. Disassemble by removing the wire ring and removing the plates in order. Install a new wire ring during installation.*

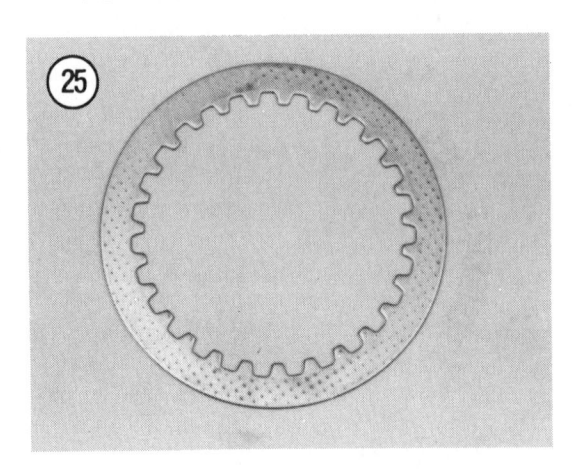

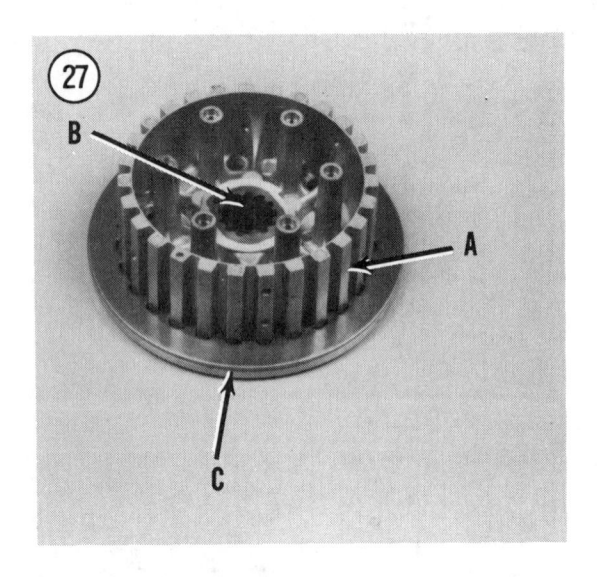

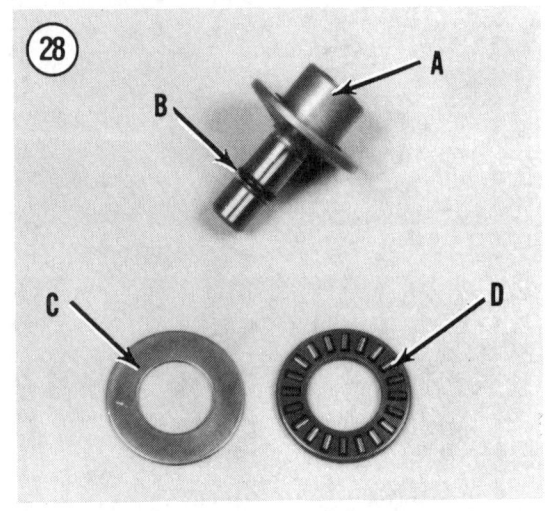

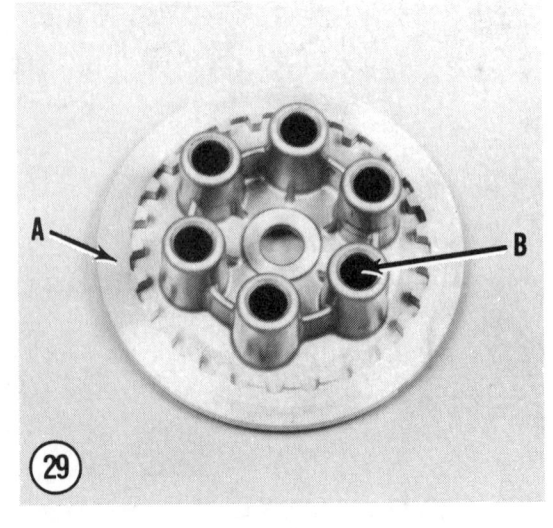

CLUTCH

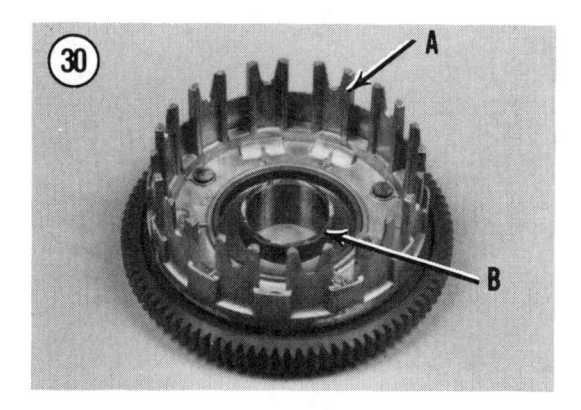

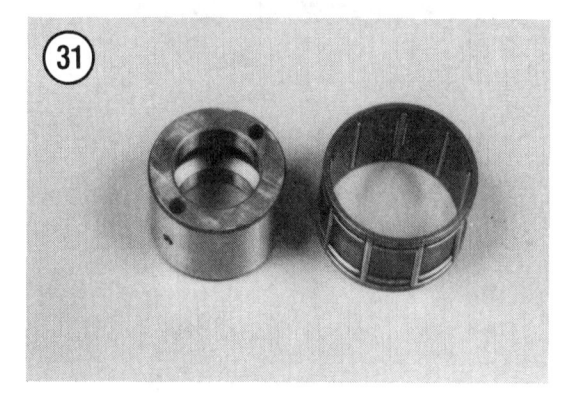

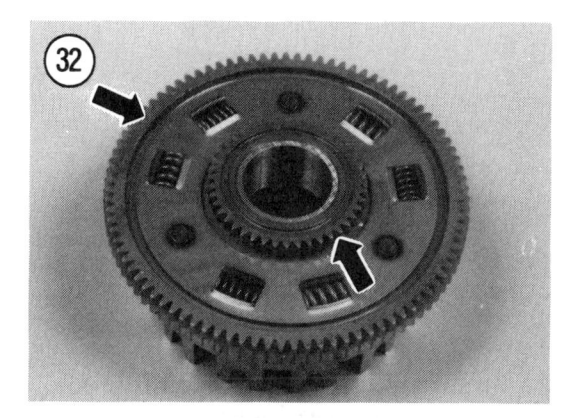

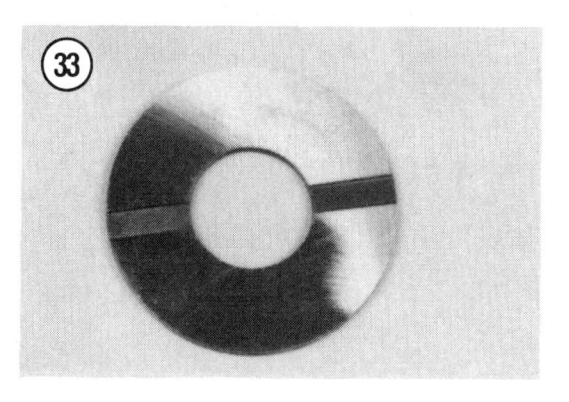

7. See **Figure 28**. Inspect the short pushrod (A) for galling or other damage. Also check the pushrod O-ring (B) and replace it if necessary. On 1986 and later models, inspect the flat (C) and thrust washers (D) for galling or damage.

8. Inspect the pressure plate for signs of damage or warpage (A, **Figure 29**). Check the spring towers (B, **Figure 29**) for cracks or damage. Replace the pressure plate if necessary.

9. Inspect the clutch housing for cracks or galling in the grooves (A, **Figure 30**) where the clutch friction disc tabs slide. They must be smooth for chatter-free clutch operation.

10. Check clutch housing bearing bore (B, **Figure 30**) for cracks, deep scoring, excessive wear or heat discoloration. If the bearing bore is damaged, also check the clutch bearing and bearing sleeve (**Figure 31**) for damage. Replace worn or damaged parts.

11. Check the clutch housing gears (**Figure 32**) for tooth wear, damage or cracks. Replace the clutch housing if necessary.

12. Check the large washer (**Figure 33**) for galling or damage.

13. Check the ends of the pushrod for wear or damage. Replace if necessary.

Installation

Refer to **Figure 5** or **Figure 6**.

1. Apply clean engine oil to all spacers, washers and bearing surfaces before installation.
2. Insert the long pushrod into the transmission mainshaft.
3. Install the washer (**Figure 34**).

NOTE
When installing the spacer in Step 4, install it so that the end with the tapped threads faces out.

CHAPTER FIVE

4. Slide the clutch housing (A, **Figure 35**) over the transmission mainshaft. Then install the spacer (B, **Figure 35**). See **Figure 36**.

   NOTE
   *If the clutch housing will not slide onto the transmission mainshaft because it hits the engine crankshaft counterweight, reposition the crankshaft as described in Step 14 under **Clutch Removal** in this chapter.*

5. Install the large washer (**Figure 37**).
6. Install the clutch boss (**Figure 38**).
7. Install a new clutch lockwasher (**Figure 39**).

   NOTE
   *Use the same tool as during removal to prevent the clutch boss from turning when tightening the clutch nut (**Figure 40**).*

8. Install the clutch nut and tighten to 70 N•m (50 ft.-lb.).

   NOTE
   If you are installing new dry plates, first wet them with oil to prevent clutch plate seizure.

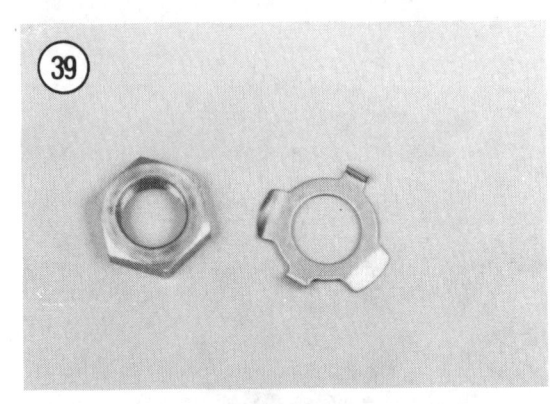

CLUTCH

8A. *FZ750N and NC:* Install the clutch plates. The sequence is friction plate (**Figure 41**) and then metal plate (**Figure 42**) and ending with a friction plate. Take care to align the plate tabs carefully with the clutch housing and clutch boss splines.

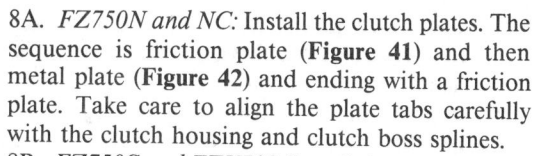

8B. *FZ750S and FZX700:* Install the clutch plates. The sequence is friction plate (**Figure 41**) and then metal plate (**Figure 42**) and ending with a friction plate. The last friction plate installed should be the plate with the one circular mark (**Figure 43**). Align the circular mark with the clutch housing match mark (**Figure 44**).

8C. *FZ700:* Install the clutch plates in the following order:

   a. Install 3 friction plates (**Figure 41**) and 3 steel plates (**Figure 42**) in alternate order.
   b. Install the cushion spring (**Figure 45**) and the 1 small friction plate.

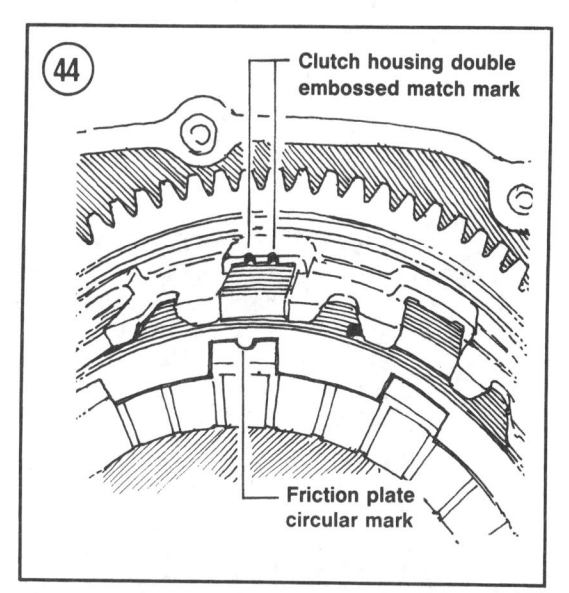

c. Install 4 steel plates (**Figure 42**) and 3 friction plates (**Figure 41**) in alternate order.

d. The last plate installed should be the friction plate with the one circular mark (**Figure 43**). Align the circular mark with the clutch housing match mark (**Figure 44**).

9. Insert the clutch ball into the transmission mainshaft (**Figure 46**).

10. Insert the short pushrod (**Figure 47**) into the transmission mainshaft.

11. *1986-on models:* Install the bearing (**Figure 48**) and washer onto the short pushrod.

12. See **Figure 49**. Align the mark on the pressure plate with the mark on the clutch boss and install the pressure plate (**Figure 50**).

13. Install the 6 clutch springs and bolts (**Figure 51**). Tighten the bolts gradually in a crisscross pattern.

14. Install the clutch cover as described in this chapter.

CLUTCH HYDRAULIC SYSTEM

The clutch is actuated by hydraulic fluid pressure and is controlled by the hand lever on the clutch

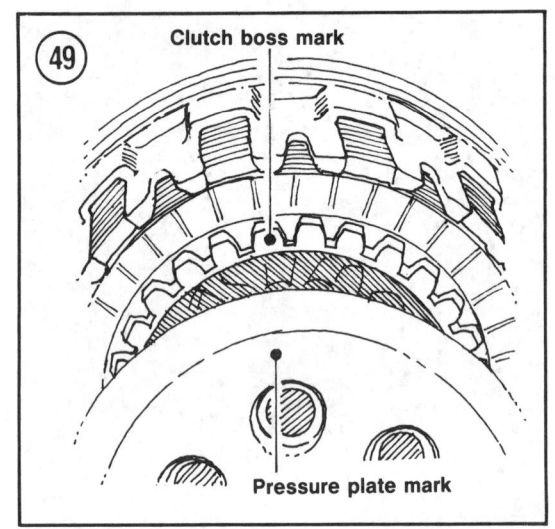

CLUTCH

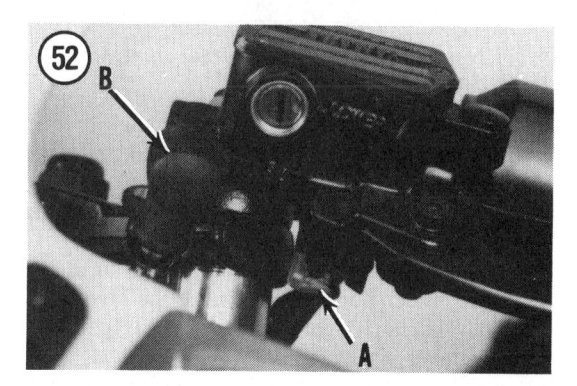

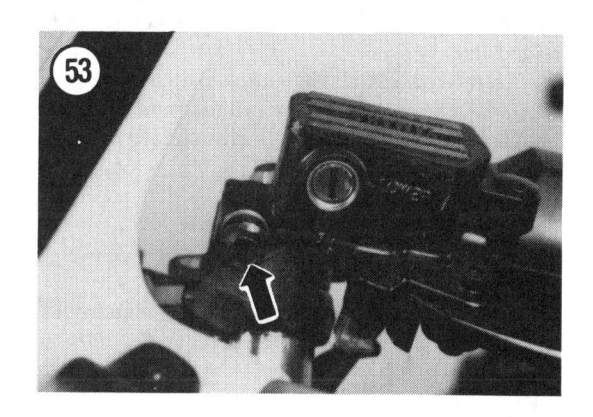

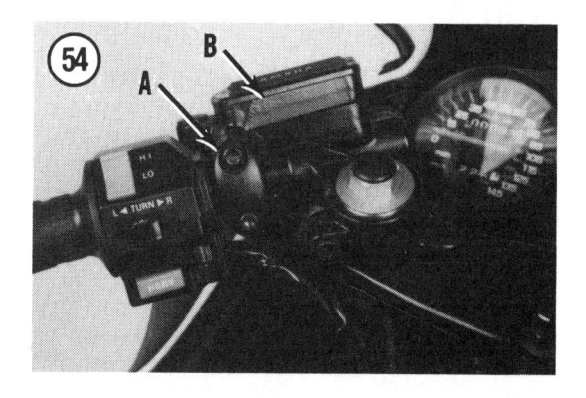

master cylinder. As clutch components wear, the slave cylinder piston moves out to automatically adjust for wear. There is no routine adjustment necessary or possible.

When working on the clutch hydraulic system, it is necessary that the work area and all tools be absolutely clean. Any tiny particles of foreign matter and grit in the clutch slave cylinder or the clutch master cylinder can damage the components. Also, sharp tools must not be used inside the slave cylinder or on the piston. If there is any doubt about your ability to correctly and safely carry out major service on the clutch hydraulic system, take the job to a dealer.

CAUTION
*Throughout the text, reference is made to hydraulic fluid. Hydraulic fluid is the same as DOT 3 brake fluid. Use only DOT 3 brake fluid; do **not** use other types of fluids as they are not compatible. Do not intermix silicone-based (DOT 5) brake fluid as it can cause clutch component damage leading to clutch system failure.*

CLUTCH MASTER CYLINDER

Removal/Installation

1. *FZX700:* Remove the left-hand rear view mirror.

CAUTION
Cover the fuel tank and instrument cluster with a heavy cloth or plastic tarp to protect them from accidental hydraulic fluid spills. Wash fluid off any painted or plated surfaces immediately as it will destroy the finish. Use soapy water and rinse completely.

2. Disconnect the electrical connector to the clutch switch (A, **Figure 52**).
3. Pull back the rubber boot (B, **Figure 52**) and remove the union bolt (**Figure 53**) securing the clutch hose to the clutch master cylinder. Remove the clutch hose; tie the hose up and cover the end to prevent entry of foreign matter.
4. Remove the clamping bolts and clamp (A, **Figure 54**) securing the clutch master cylinder to the handlebar and remove the clutch master cylinder (B, **Figure 54**).
5. Install by reversing these removal steps. Note the following:
   a. Install the clamp (A, **Figure 54**) so that the arrow faces up.
   b. Install the clamp screws and tighten securely.

c. Install the clutch hose (**Figure 53**) onto the clutch master cylinder. Be sure to place a new sealing washer on each side of the fitting and install the union bolt (**Figure 55**). Tighten the union bolt to 26 N•m (19 ft.-lb.).
d. Attach the electrical connector (A, **Figure 52**) to the clutch switch.
e. Bleed the clutch as described in this chapter.

Disassembly

Refer to **Figure 56** for this procedure.
1. Remove the clutch master cylinder as described in this chapter.
2. Remove the pivot bolt and nut securing the clutch lever and remove the lever and spring.
3. Remove the pushrod.
4. Remove the screws securing the cover and remove the cover and diaphragm; pour out the hydraulic fluid and discard it. *Never* reuse hydraulic fluid.
5. Remove the rubber boot.
6. Using circlip pliers, remove the internal circlip and washer from the body.
7. Remove the piston assembly in the order shown in **Figure 56**.
8. Remove the clutch switch if necessary.

Inspection

1. Clean all parts in denatured alcohol or fresh hydraulic fluid. Inspect the cylinder bore and piston contact surfaces for signs of wear and damage. If either part is less than perfect, replace it.
2. Check the end of the piston for wear caused by the hand lever pushrod. Replace the piston if necessary.
3. Check both the cups for damage. Replace as necessary. Yamaha recommends replacement of the piston cups every 2 years.
4. Check the hand lever pivot bore in the clutch master cylinder. If worn or elongated, the master cylinder must be replaced.
5. Inspect the pivot bore in the hand lever. If worn or elongated it must be replaced.
6. Make sure the passages in the bottom of the fluid reservoir are clear. Check the reservoir cap and diaphragm for damage and deterioration and replace as necessary.

Assembly

1. Soak the new cups in fresh hydraulic fluid for at least 15 minutes to make them pliable. Coat the inside of the cylinder with fresh fluid prior to assembly of parts.

CAUTION
When installing the piston assembly, do not allow the cups to turn inside out as they will be damaged and allow clutch fluid leakage within the cylinder bore.

2. Install the piston assembly in the order shown in **Figure 56**.

NOTE
Install the cups with the larger diameter end inward.

3. Compress the piston assembly slightly and install the circlip with circlip pliers. Make sure the circlip seats in the housing groove completely.
4. Slide in the rubber boot. Then install the spring and pushrod and the pushrod end piece.
5. Install the spring and clutch lever onto the master cylinder body. Then secure the lever with the bolt and nut. Tighten the nut securely. Check that the lever pivots easily.
6. Install the diaphragm and cover. Do not tighten the cover screws at this time as fluid will have to be added later.
7. If removed, install the clutch switch.
8. Install the clutch master cylinder and bleed the clutch system as described in this chapter.

SLAVE CYLINDER

Removal/Installation

1. Place a piece of wood between the clutch lever and the hand grip to hold the lever in the released

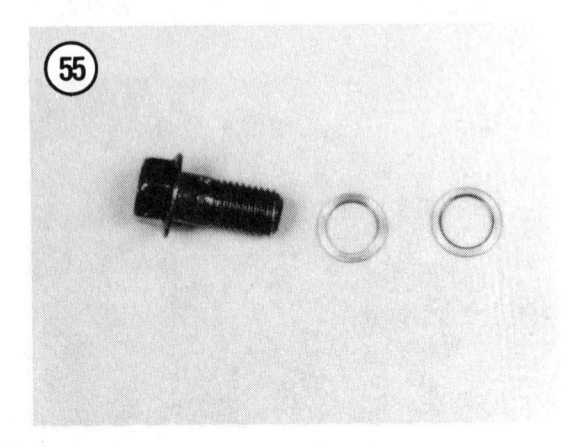

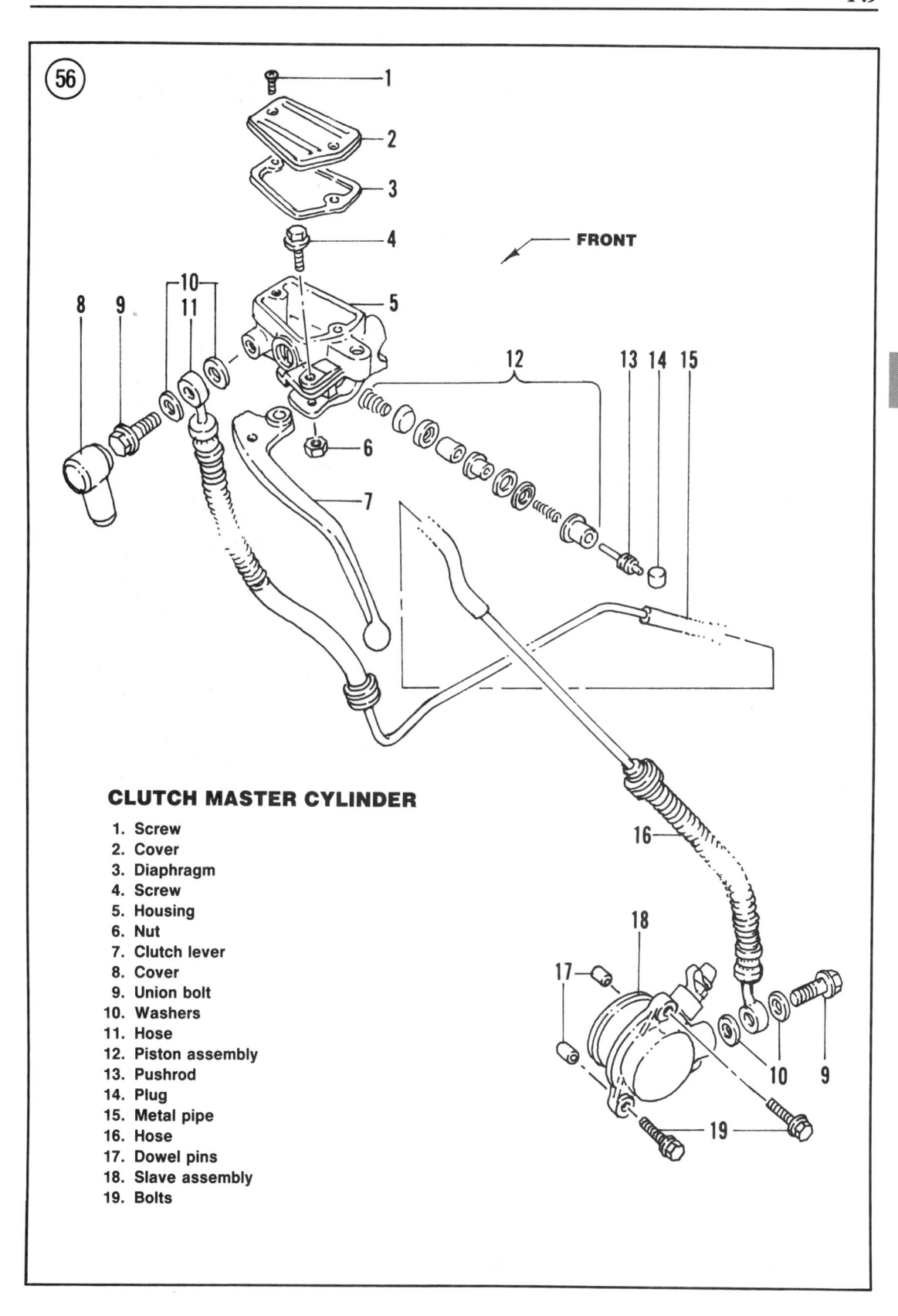

CLUTCH

149

(56)

FRONT

CLUTCH MASTER CYLINDER

1. Screw
2. Cover
3. Diaphragm
4. Screw
5. Housing
6. Nut
7. Clutch lever
8. Cover
9. Union bolt
10. Washers
11. Hose
12. Piston assembly
13. Pushrod
14. Plug
15. Metal pipe
16. Hose
17. Dowel pins
18. Slave assembly
19. Bolts

position. Secure the piece of wood with a rubber band or tape. This will prevent the clutch lever from being applied accidentally after the clutch slave cylinder is removed from the crankcase.

> *NOTE*
> *Do not operate the clutch lever after the slave cylinder is removed from the crankcase. If the clutch lever is applied, it will force the piston out of the slave cylinder body and make installation difficult.*

2. Attach a hose to the bleed valve on the clutch slave cylinder (C, **Figure 57**).
3. Place the loose end of the hose into a container and open the bleed valve. Operate the clutch lever until all fluid is pumped out of the system. Close the bleed valve and remove the hose.

> *WARNING*
> *Dispose of this fluid—never reuse hydraulic fluid. Contaminated fluid can cause clutch failure.*

4. Place a container under the clutch hose at the clutch slave cylinder to catch any remaining fluid. Remove the union bolt and sealing washers (A, **Figure 57**) securing the clutch hose to the clutch slave cylinder. Remove the clutch hose and let any remaining fluid drain out into the container.
5. Remove the bolts (B, **Figure 57**) securing the clutch slave cylinder to the sprocket cover and withdraw the unit from the cover.
6. Remove the 2 dowel pins.
7. Installation is the reverse of these steps. Note the following:
   a. Install the 2 dowel pins.
   b. Tighten the 3 slave cylinder bolts to 10 N•m (7.2 ft.-lb.).
   c. Install the union bolt and new sealing washers onto the slave cylinder. Tighten the union bolts to 26 N•m (19 ft.-lb.).
   d. Turn the handlebar to level the clutch master cylinder. Clean the top of the clutch master cylinder of all dirt and foreign matter. Remove the cap and diaphragm. Fill the reservoir almost to the top line; insert the diaphragm and install the cap loosely.
   e. Bleed the clutch as described in this chapter.

Disassembly/Inspection/Assembly

Refer to **Figure 58** for this procedure.
1. To remove the piston, perform the following:
   a. Remove the union bolt (A, **Figure 57**) from the slave cylinder.
   b. Hold the slave cylinder body in your hand with the piston facing away from you. Place a clean shop cloth behind the piston.

> *WARNING*
> *Do not use your hand to catch the piston as it is removed from the slave cylinder body.*

c. Apply compressed air in the hole where the union bolt was attached. The air pressure will force the piston out of the body.

> *CAUTION*
> *Be sure to catch the piston when it is pushed out of the body. Failure to do so will result in damage to the piston.*

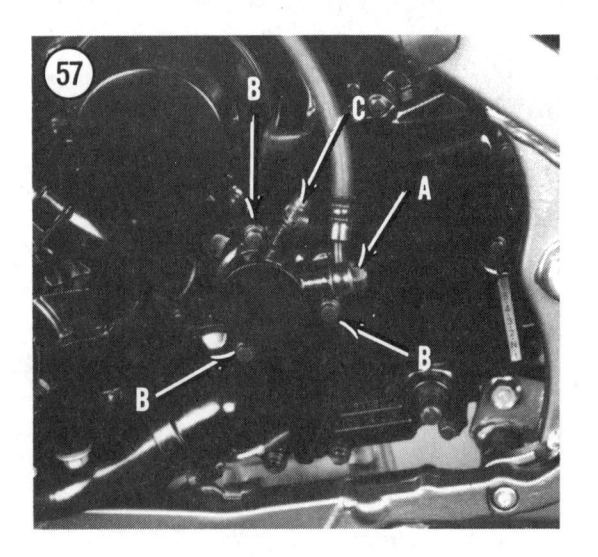

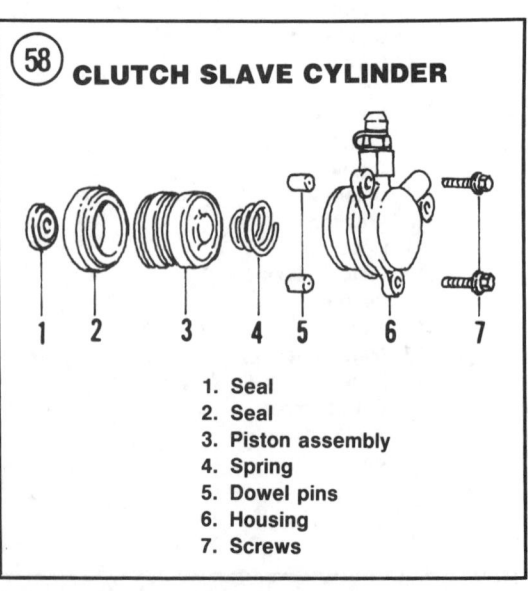

CLUTCH SLAVE CYLINDER

1. Seal
2. Seal
3. Piston assembly
4. Spring
5. Dowel pins
6. Housing
7. Screws

CLUTCH

2. Remove the spring from the piston.
3. Check the spring for damage or sagging. Replace the spring if its condition is doubtful.
4. Remove the oil seal from the piston and replace it.
5. Check the piston and cylinder body for scratches, severe wear or damage. Replace questionable parts.
6. Apply a light coat of hydraulic fluid to the piston and new piston seal prior to installation.
7. Install the seal on the piston.
8. Insert the piston into the slave cylinder.

BLEEDING THE CLUTCH

This procedure is not necessary unless the clutch feels spongy (air in the line), there has been a leak in the system, a component has been replaced or the hydraulic fluid is being replaced. If the clutch operates when the engine is cold or in cool weather but operates erratically (or not at all) after the engine warms up or in hot weather, there is air in the hydraulic line and the clutch must be bled.

CAUTION
*Throughout the text, reference is made to hydraulic fluid. Hydraulic fluid is the same as DOT 3 brake fluid. Use only DOT 3 brake fluid; do **not** use other types of fluids as they are not compatible. Do not intermix silicone-based (DOT 5) brake fluid as it can cause clutch component damage leading to clutch system failure.*

1. Remove the dust cap from the bleed valve on the clutch slave cylinder (C, **Figure 57**).
2. Connect a length of clear tubing to the bleed valve.
3. Place the other end of the tube into a clean container. Fill the container with enough fresh hydraulic fluid to keep the end submerged. The tube should be long enough so that a loop can be made higher than the bleed valve to prevent air from being drawn into the clutch slave cylinder during bleeding.

CAUTION
Cover the clutch slave cylinder and lower frame with heavy cloth or plastic tarp to protect them from accidental fluid spill. Wash any fluid off of any painted or plated surface immediately, as it will destroy the finish. Use soapy water and rinse completely.

4. Clean the top of the clutch master cylinder of all dirt and foreign matter. Remove the cap and diaphragm. Fill the reservoir to almost to the top. Insert the diaphragm and install the cap loosely.

CAUTION
Failure to install the diaphragm on the master cylinder will allow fluid to spurt out when the clutch lever is applied.

CAUTION
Use hydraulic fluid clearly marked DOT 3 only. Others may vaporize and cause clutch failure. Always use the same brand name; do not intermix as many brands are not compatible. Do not intermix silicone based (DOT 5) brake fluid as it can cause clutch component damage leading to clutch system failure.

5. Slowly apply the clutch lever several times. Hold the lever in the applied position. Open the bleed valve about one-half turn. Allow the lever to travel to its limit. When the limit is reached, tighten the bleed valve. Occasionally tap or jiggle the clutch flexible hoses to loosen any trapped air bubbles that won't come out the normal way. As the fluid enters the system, the level will drop in the reservoir. Maintain the level at the top of the reservoir to prevent air from being drawn into the system.
6. Repeat Step 5 until fluid emerging from the hose is completely free of bubbles.

NOTE
Do not allow the reservoir to empty during the bleeding operation or air will enter the system. If this occurs, the entire procedure must be repeated.

7. Hold the lever in, tighten the bleed valve, remove the bleed tube and install the bleed valve dust cap.

8. If necessary, add fluid to correct the level in the reservoir. It should be above the lower level line (**Figure 59**).
9. Install the diaphragm and reservoir cap.
10. Test the feel of the clutch lever. It should be firm and should offer the same resistance each time it's operated. If it feels spongy, it is likely that there still is air in the system and it must be bled again. When all air has been bled from the system and the fluid level is correct in the reservoir, double-check for leaks and tighten all the fittings and connections.

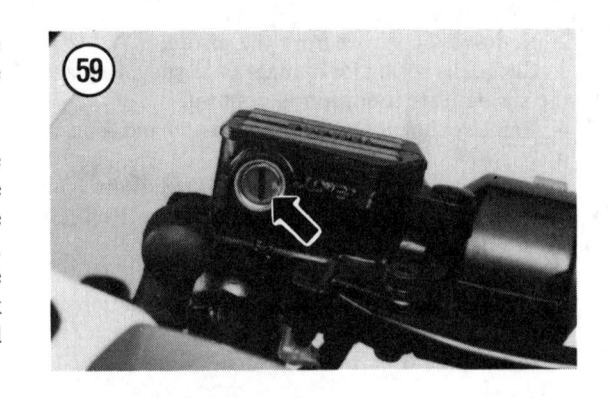

Table 1 CLUTCH SPECIFICATIONS

Item	Standard mm (in.)	Minimum mm (in.)
Friction plate (8)		
Thickness	2.9-3.1 (0.1142-0.1220)	2.8 (0.11)
Clutch plate (7)		
Thickness	1.9-2.1 (0.0748-0.0827)	
Warp limit		0.1 (0.0039)
Clutch springs		
Free length	55.5 (2.185)	54.0 (2.126)
Push rod out of round	0.3 (0.012)	
Clutch fluid	DOT 3	

CHAPTER SIX

TRANSMISSION

This chapter covers all the parts that transmit power from the clutch to the drive chain: engine sprocket, transmission gears, shift drum and forks and shift linkage.

SPROCKET COVER

Removal/Installation

1. Remove the shift linkage (**Figure 1**); remove the pivot circlip (A) and the pinch screw (B) securing the shift linkage and pull the shift linkage off. If the pivot boss is tight on the shaft shaft, spread the slot open with a screwdriver. On FZX700 models, remove the pinch screw.

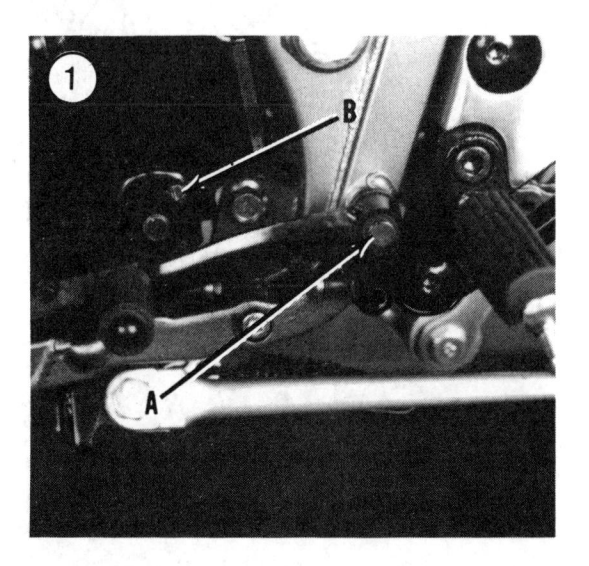

NOTE
It is not necessary to remove the clutch slave cylinder from the sprocket cover when removing the sprocket cover from the engine.

2. Remove the screws securing the engine sprocket cover and remove the cover (**Figure 2**).
3. Remove the spacer (A, **Figure 3**) if necessary.
4. To install the sprocket cover, reverse the removal steps.
5. If the clutch slave cylinder was removed, install it as described under *Clutch Slave Cylinder Removal/Installation* in Chapter Five. Bleed the clutch as described in Chapter Five.

NEUTRAL SWITCH

Removal/Installation

The neutral switch is activated by a switch mounted under the sprocket cover (B, **Figure 3**). The switch is turned on when the shift drum end plate is at its NEUTRAL positon.

1. Disconnect the electrical connector at the neutral switch.

2. Remove the neutral switch screws and remove the switch (B, **Figure 3**).
3. If necessary, test the switch as described under *Switches* in Chapter Eight.
4. If there are signs of oil leakage around the neutral switch, replace the O-ring (**Figure 4**) on the back of the switch housing.
5. Reverse to install.

ENGINE SPROCKET

The engine sprocket is on the left-hand end of the transmission countershaft, behind the sprocket cover. The drive chain is endless—it has no master link. To remove the drive chain, remove the engine sprocket from the countershaft and remove the swing arm; see *Swing Arm Removal/Installation* in Chapter Eleven.

Removal

1. Remove the engine sprocket cover as described in this chapter.
2. Remove the rear axle cotter pin and loosen the rear axle nut (**Figure 5**). Then loosen the drive chain adjusters (**Figure 6**) at the swing arm.
3. Pry the lockwasher tab away from the sprocket nut and loosen the sprocket nut (C, **Figure 3**). If necessary, apply the rear brake to prevent the sprocket from turning when loosening the nut.
4. Slide the sprocket and chain off the countershaft (**Figure 7**).
5. Installation is the reverse of these steps. Note the following:
   a. Position the drive chain on the sprocket, then slide the sprocket onto the countershaft (**Figure 7**).
   b. Install a new sprocket lockwasher.
   c. Install the sprocket nut and tighten to 70 N•m (50 ft.-lb.). Bend the lockwasher tab over the sprocket to lock the nut.
   d. Adjust the drive chain. See *Drive Chain Adjustment* in Chapter Three.

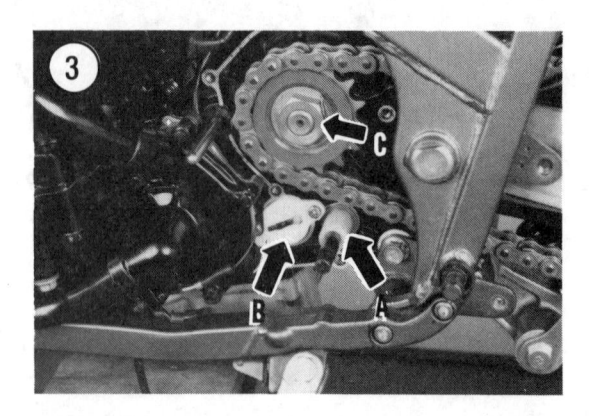

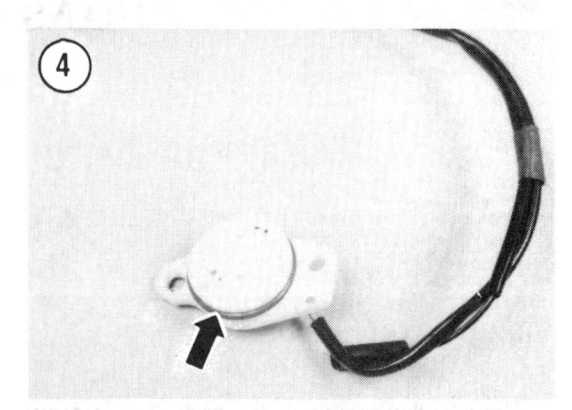

TRANSMISSION

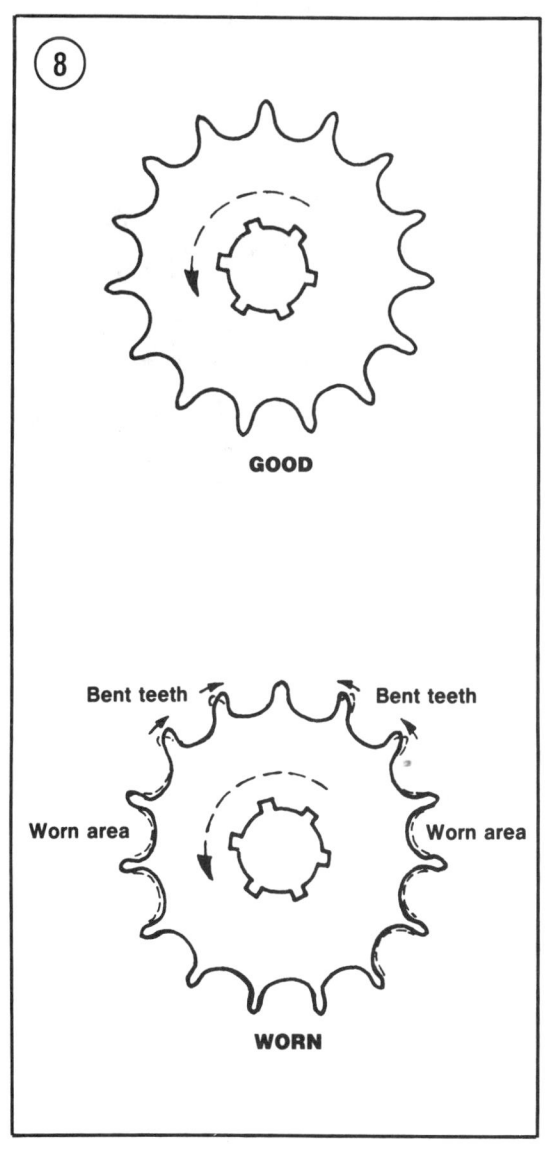

Inspection

Inspect the engine sprocket for wear. If the teeth are undercut as shown in **Figure 8**, install a new sprocket.

EXTERNAL SHIFT MECHANISM

The external shift mechanism can be removed with the engine in the frame.

Removal/Installation

1. Remove the engine sprocket as described in this chapter.
2. Drain the engine oil as described under *Engine Oil and Filter Change* in Chapter Three.
3. Remove the clutch as described under *Clutch Removal/Installation* in Chapter Five.
4. Slide the spacer (**Figure 9**) off of the shift shaft.
5. Using circlip pliers, remove the circlip and washer (**Figure 10**) from the shift shaft.
6. Move the shift linkage arms out of engagement with the shift drum (A, **Figure 11**) and pull the shift linkage/shift shaft assembly (B, **Figure 11**) out of the crankcase.

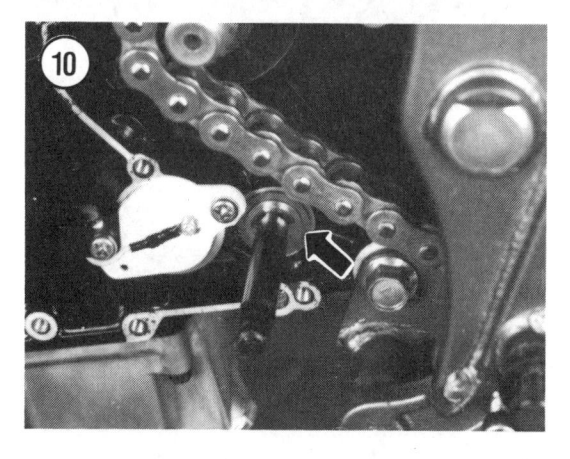

7. Remove the 2 bolts (A, **Figure 12**) and remove the stopper lever (B, **Figure 12**), spring and shift fork guide bar stopper assembly.

Inspection

1. If the transmission fails to shift gears, check for a weak pawl spring; bent, worn or binding pawls (A, **Figure 13**); a broken return spring (B, **Figure 13**); a broken return spring pin; or worn shift drum pins (**Figure 14**).
2. If the transmission undershifts or overshifts, check for bent or worn pawls; worn shift drum pins; a loose return spring pin; a bent or weak return spring; or worn stopper lever spring or roller (**Figure 15**).
3. Replace any other broken, bent, binding or worn parts, including the shift drum pin assembly.

NOTE
*If the shift drum pins (**Figure 14**) are worn or damaged, it will be necessary to replace the shift drum assembly as described in this chapter.*

Installation

1. Assemble the stopper lever assembly as shown in **Figure 16** and install it into the crankcase (**Figure 12**). Apply Loctite 242 (blue) onto the stopper lever bolts and tighten the bolts to 10 N•m (7.2 ft.-lb.). Engage the stopper lever roller with the shift cam (A, **Figure 17**) and hook the return spring with the crankcase boss (B, **Figure 17**). Make sure the shift fork shaft stopper (C, **Figure 17**) aligns with the shift fork shaft.
2. See **Figure 11**. Insert the shift shaft (B) partway through the crankcase. Then engage the shift pawls

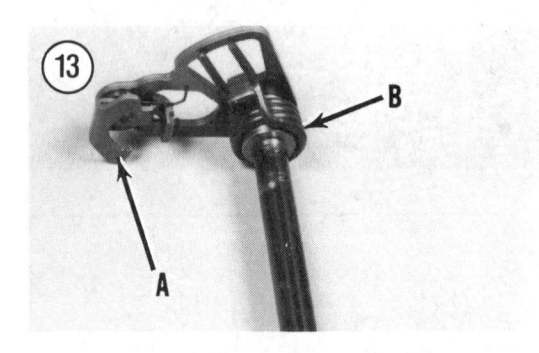

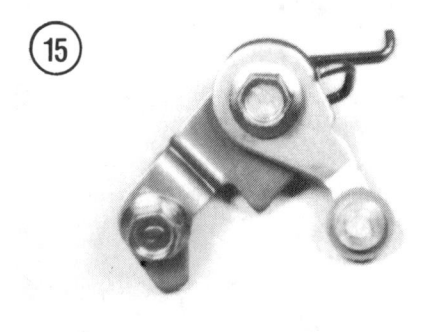

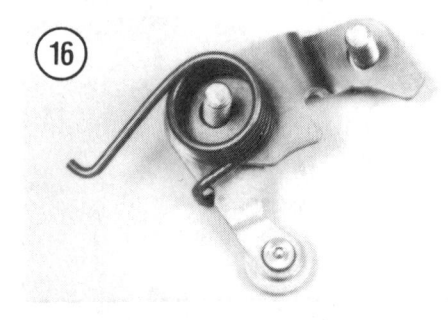

TRANSMISSION

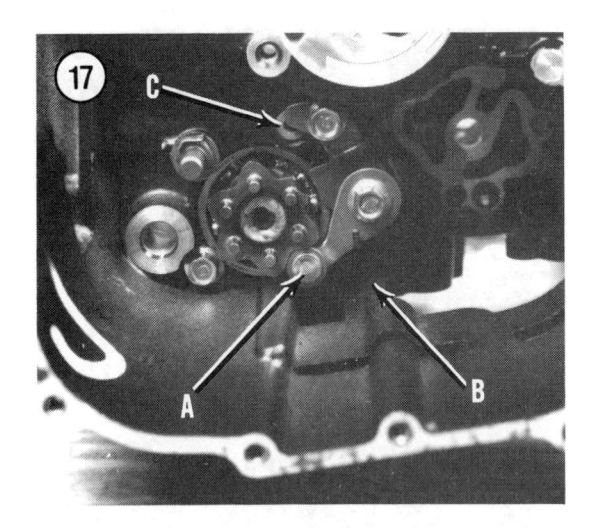

(A) with the shift cam pins and the return spring with the crankcase pin (C) and push the shift shaft all the way in.

3. Install the washer and circlip (**Figure 10**).
4. Slide the spacer (**Figure 9**) onto the shift shaft.
5. Install the clutch as described in Chapter Five.
6. Install the engine sprocket as described in this chapter.
7. Install the engine sprocket cover as described in this chapter.
8. Refill the engine oil as described in Chapter Three.

TRANSMISSION GEARS

Removal/Installation

Refer to **Figure 18** for this procedure.

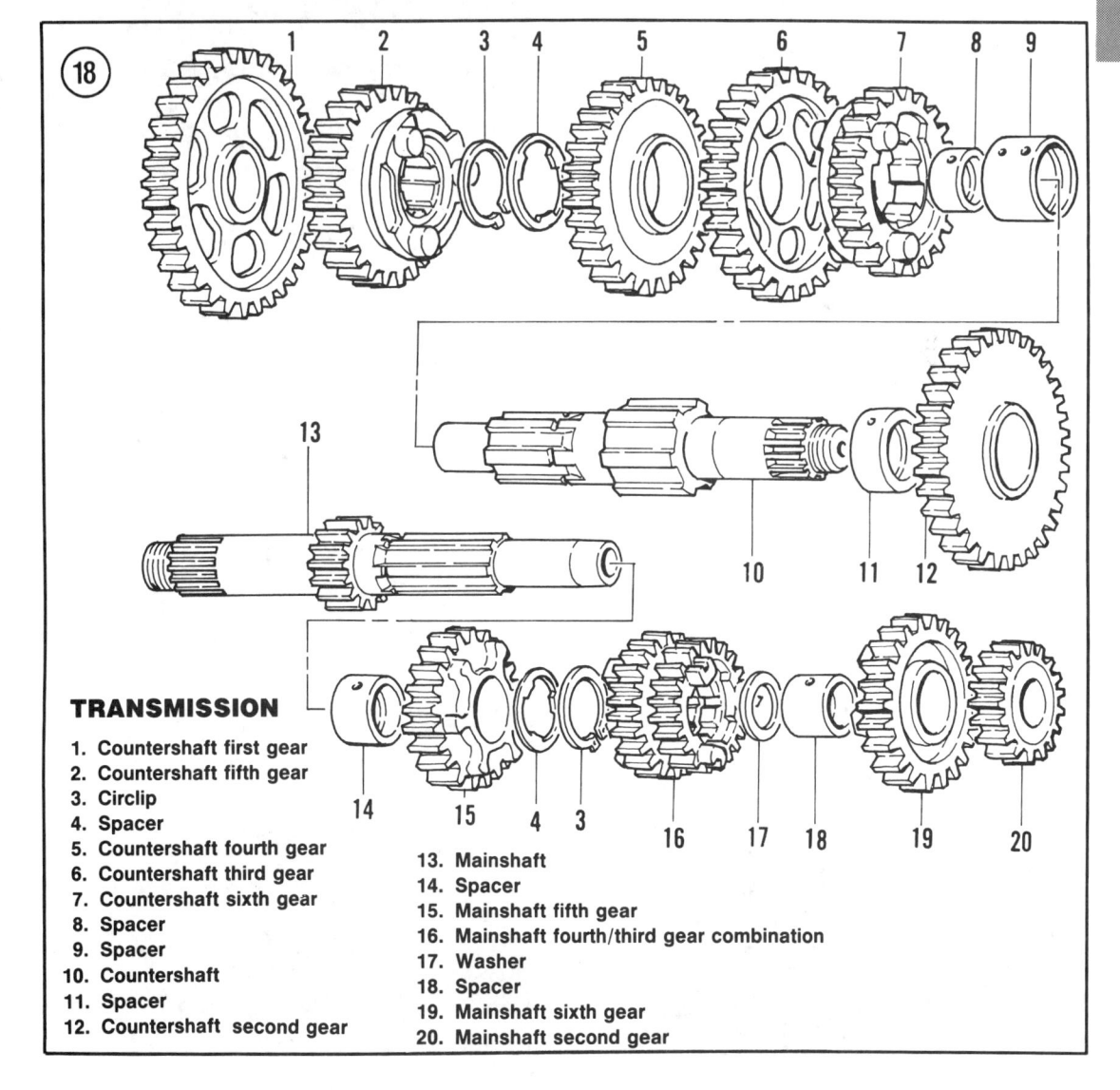

TRANSMISSION

1. Countershaft first gear
2. Countershaft fifth gear
3. Circlip
4. Spacer
5. Countershaft fourth gear
6. Countershaft third gear
7. Countershaft sixth gear
8. Spacer
9. Spacer
10. Countershaft
11. Spacer
12. Countershaft second gear
13. Mainshaft
14. Spacer
15. Mainshaft fifth gear
16. Mainshaft fourth/third gear combination
17. Washer
18. Spacer
19. Mainshaft sixth gear
20. Mainshaft second gear

CHAPTER SIX

1. Remove the engine and split the crankcase as described under *Crankcase Disassembly* in Chapter Four.

> *NOTE*
> *It is not necessary to remove crankshaft (Figure 19), primary chain or starter clutch when removing the transmission shafts.*

2. See **Figure 20**. Carefully lift the mainshaft (A) and then the countershaft (B) out of the upper crankcase.
3. Remove the 2 transmission bearing circlips from the upper crankcase (**Figure 21**).
4. Install by reversing these steps. Note the following:
   a. Prior to installing any components, coat all bearing surfaces with assembly oil.
   b. When installing the transmission shaft assemblies, make sure the transmission bearing circlips (**Figure 21**) are in place in the upper crankcase prior to installing the transmission assemblies.

> *CAUTION*
> *If the mainshaft and countershaft bearings do not engage the transmission bearing circlips correctly, there will be excessive clearance between the crankcase and the outer bearing races.*

> *CAUTION*
> *If a transmission bearing circlip (Figure 21) is left out, the transmission could lock up during riding.*

   c. See **Figure 20**. Install the mainshaft (A) and countershaft (B) assemblies.
   d. See **Figure 22**. Replace the countershaft (A) and mainshaft (B) oil seals.

> *NOTE*
> *Make sure the mainshaft bearing pin (A, Figure 23) faces to the front and the countershaft bearing pins (B Figure 23) face to the rear. See Figure 24.*

TRANSMISSION

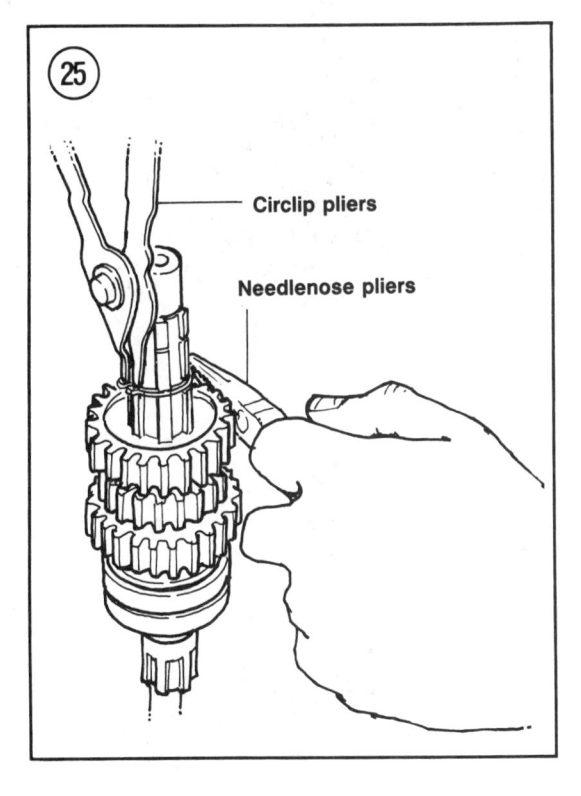

e. Assemble and install the engine as described in Chapter Four.

Transmission Service Notes

1. A divided container such as an egg carton can be used to help maintain correct alignment and positioning of the parts as they are removed from the transmission shaft.
2. The circlips are a tight fit on the transmission shafts. Replace all circlips during reassembly.
3. Circlips will turn and fold over making removal and installation difficult. To ease replacement, open the circlips with a pair of circlip pliers while at the same time holding the back of the circlip with a pair of pliers and remove them. See **Figure 25**. Repeat for installation.

Countershaft Disassembly/Assembly

Refer to **Figure 18** for this procedure.
1. Remove the bearing (**Figure 26**).
2. Slide off first gear (**Figure 27**).
3. Slide off fifth gear (**Figure 28**).

4. Remove the circlip and washer (**Figure 29**).
5. Slide off fourth gear (**Figure 30**).
6. Slide off third gear (**Figure 31**).
7. Slide off sixth gear (**Figure 32**).
8. See **Figure 33**. Press off the bearing (A) and slide off second gear (B).
9. Inspect the countershaft assembly as described in this chapter.
10. Assemble by reversing these disassembly steps. Note the following:
    a. Refer to **Figure 34** for correct placement of the gears.
    b. Make sure the shifting dogs or slots in each gear engages properly to the adjoining gear where applicable.

Mainshaft
Disassembly/Assembly

Refer to **Figure 18**.

NOTE
A press is required to disassemble the countershaft assembly.

1. Slide off the right-hand bearing (**Figure 35**).
2. Using a press, remove the left-hand bearing (A, **Figure 36**).

NOTE
Removal of the left-hand bearing is not necessary unless it must be replaced. If the bearing is ok, leave it on the mainshaft.

3. Measure the width of the assembled gear cluster with a vernier caliper and record the measurement (G, **Figure 36**). This measurement will be used when assembling the countershaft.
4. Press off second gear (F, **Figure 36**).
5. Slide off sixth gear (E, **Figure 36**).
6. Remove the washer and a spacer.
7. Slide off the third/fourth gear combination (D, **Figure 36**).
8. Remove the circlip and washer.
9. Slide off fifth gear (C, **Figure 36**).

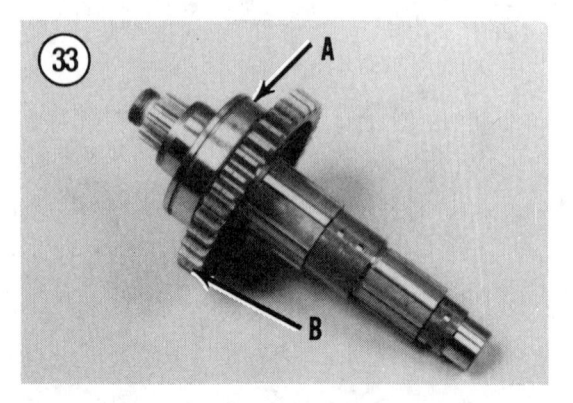

TRANSMISSION

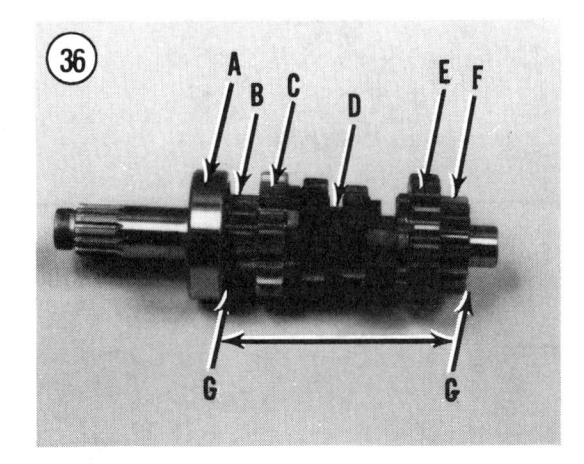

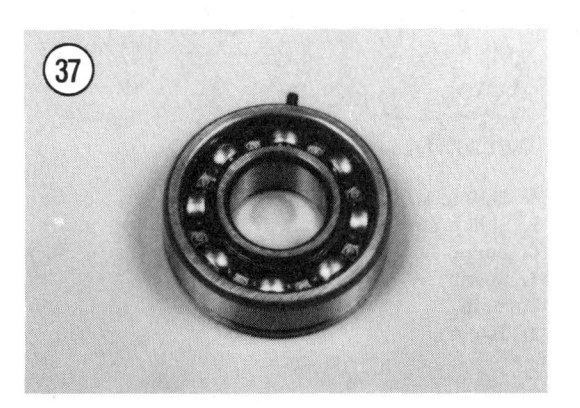

10. Inspect the countershaft assembly as described in this chapter.

11. Assemble by reversing these disassembly steps. Note the following:
   a. Refer to **Figure 36** for correct placement of the gears.
   b. Make sure the shifting dogs or slots in each gear engages properly to the adjoining gear where applicable.
   c. When pressing on second gear (F, **Figure 36**), install it so that the overall length of the assembled gear cluster is the same as that recorded during Step 3 (G, **Figure 36**).
   d. Install sealed bearings with the sealed side facing outward (away from the gears).

Inspection

1. Clean all parts in cleaning solvent and thoroughly dry.

2. Rotate the bearings (**Figure 37**) by hand and check for roughness or damage. Also check the bearing seal (**Figure 38**) for damage. Replace the bearing if necessary.

3. Inspect the gears visually for cracks, chips, broken teeth and burnt teeth. Check the gear dogs (**Figure 39**) to make sure they are not rounded off.

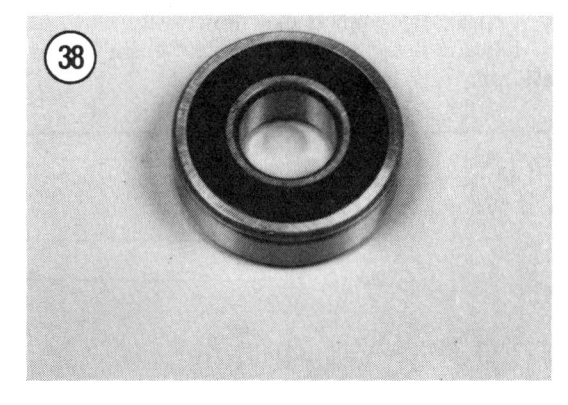

If dogs are rounded off, check the shift forks as described later in this chapter. More than likely, one or more of the shift forks is bent or worn.

NOTE
Defective gears should be replaced, and it is a good idea to replace the mating gear (Figure 40) even though it may not show as much wear or damage. Remember that accelerated wear to new parts is normally caused by contact from worn parts.

4. Inspect all freewheeling gear bearing surfaces (**Figure 41**) for wear, discoloration and galling. Inspect the mating shaft bearing surface also. If there is any metal flaking or visible damage, replace both parts.

5. Inspect the mainshaft and countershaft splines for wear or discoloration. Check the mating gear internal splines also. If no visual damage is apparent, install each sliding gear on its respective shaft and slide the gear back and forth to make sure it moves smoothly.

6. Replace any washers that show wear.

7. Discard the circlips and replace them during assembly.

Shift Drum and Forks
Removal/Installation

Refer to **Figure 42**.

1. Remove the shift fork shaft stopper assembly (**Figure 43**).

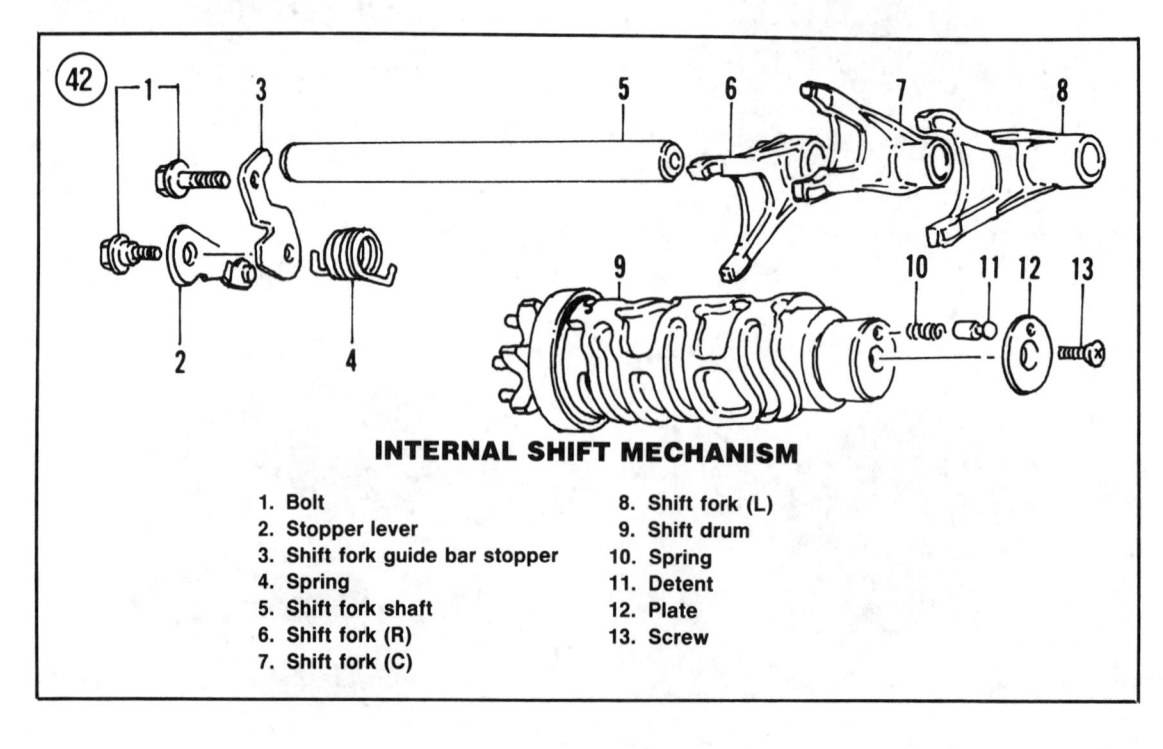

INTERNAL SHIFT MECHANISM

1. Bolt
2. Stopper lever
3. Shift fork guide bar stopper
4. Spring
5. Shift fork shaft
6. Shift fork (R)
7. Shift fork (C)
8. Shift fork (L)
9. Shift drum
10. Spring
11. Detent
12. Plate
13. Screw

TRANSMISSION

NOTE
Label the shift forks so that they can be reinstalled in their original positions.

2. Remove the shift fork shaft and remove the 3 shift forks from the lower crankcase. See **Figure 44**.
3. Remove the shift drum locating bolt (**Figure 45**) and pull the shift drum (**Figure 46**) out of the crankcase.
4. Inspect the shift drum and forks as described in this chapter.
5. Assemble the shift drum and forks as follows.
6. Apply engine oil to all bearing surfaces.
7. Insert the shift drum (**Figure 46**) through the crankcase.
8. Apply Loctite 242 (blue) to the shift drum locating bolt (**Figure 45**) and tighten it to 10 N•m (7.2 ft.-lb.).
9. Install the shift forks as follows:

NOTE
The shift forks are marked with identification letters: "L" (left), "C" (center) and "R" (right).

a. Insert the shift shaft (**Figure 47**) partway through the crankcase and install the shift fork labeled "L" (**Figure 48**). Engage the shift pin on the shift fork with the shift drum groove.

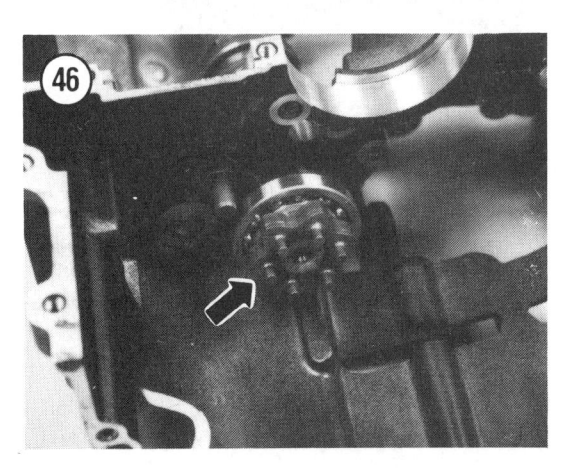

164 CHAPTER SIX

    b. Install the shift fork labeled "C" (**Figure 49**). Engage the shift pin on the shift fork with the shift drum groove.
    c. Install the shift fork labeled "R" (**Figure 50**). Engage the shift pin on the shift fork with the shift drum groove.

10. Install the transmission shafts as described in this chapter.

11. Install the stopper lever as described under *External Shift Mechanism Installation* in this chapter.

Inspection

1. Inspect each shift fork for signs of wear or cracking. See **Figure 51**. Examine the shift forks at

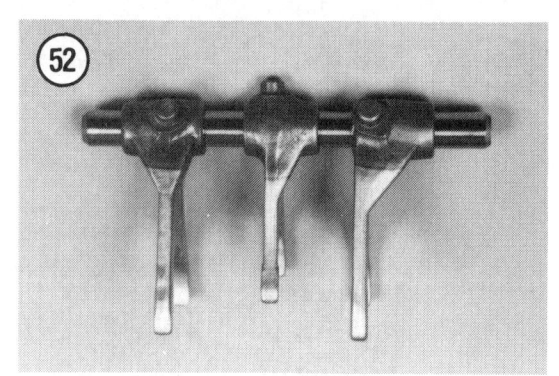

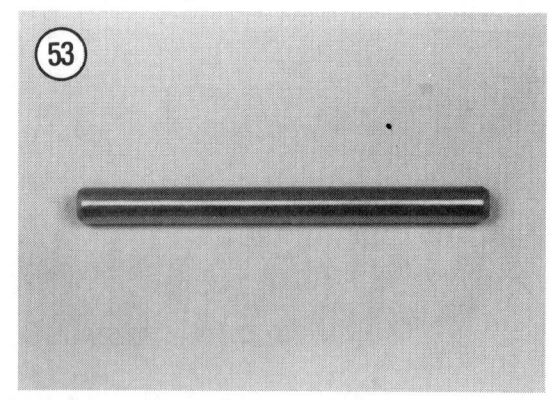

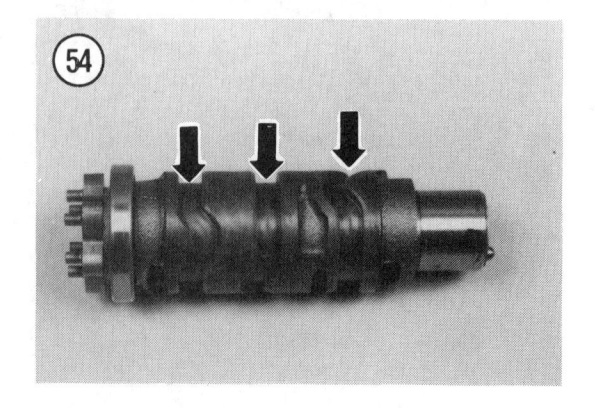

TRANSMISSION

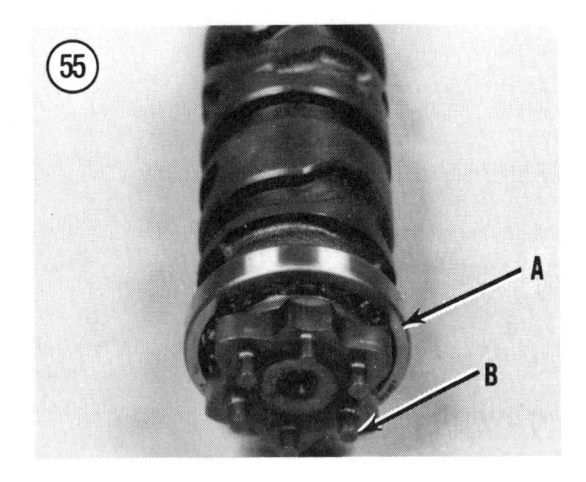

the points where they contact the slider gear. This surface should be smooth with no signs of wear or damage. Make sure the forks slide smoothly on the shaft (**Figure 52**). Make sure the shaft is not bent. This can be checked by removing the shift forks from the shaft (**Figure 53**) and rolling the shaft on a piece of glass. Any clicking noise detected indicates a bent shaft.

2. Check grooves in the shift drum (**Figure 54**) for wear or roughness. Replace the shift drum if any groove is worn or damaged.

3. Spin the shift drum bearing (A, **Figure 55**) and check for excessive play or roughness. Check the shift drum pins (B, **Figure 55**) for wear, damage or looseness. Replace the shift drum if necessary.

CHAPTER SEVEN

FUEL, EMISSION CONTROL AND EXHAUST SYSTEMS

This chapter describes complete procedures for servicing the fuel, emission control and exhaust systems. Carburetor specifications are listed in **Table 1**. **Table 1** and **Table 2** are at the end of the chapter.

CARBURETOR

Removal/Installation

Remove all 4 carburetors as an assembled unit.
1. Park the motorcycle on the center stand. On FZ700 models, part the bike so that it is secure.
2. *FZ700 and FZ750:* Remove the lower fairing assembly. See Chapter Thirteen.
3. Remove the fuel tank as described in this chapter.
4. Remove the battery as described under *Battery Removal/Installation and Electrolyte Level Check* in Chapter Three.
5A. *FZX700:* Perform the following:
   a. Remove the carburetor side covers (**Figure 1**).
   b. Disconnect the crankcase ventilation hose (**Figure 2**) at the air cleaner housing.
   c. Loosen the hose clamps and lift the air cleaner housing (**Figure 2**) off of the carburetors.

5B. *FZ700 and FZ750:* Perform the following:
   a. Disconnect the crankcase ventilation hose (A, **Figure 3**) at the air cleaner housing.
   b. Disconnect the 2 air vent hoses (B, **Figure 3**) at the air cleaner housing.

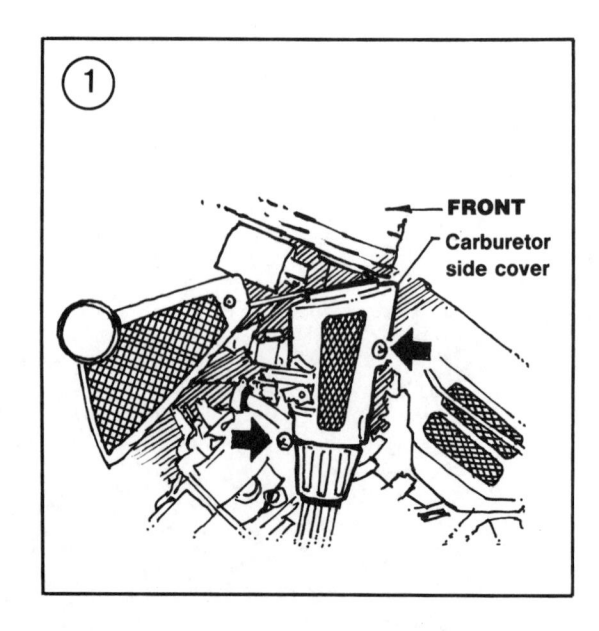

①
FRONT
Carburetor side cover

FUEL, EMISSION CONTROL AND EXHAUST SYSTEMS

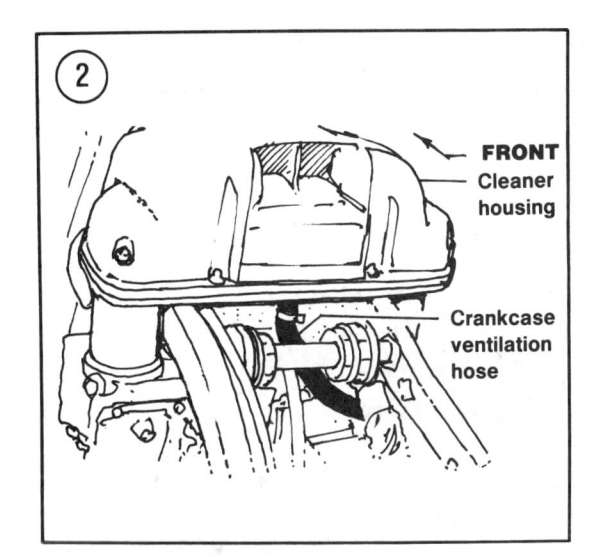

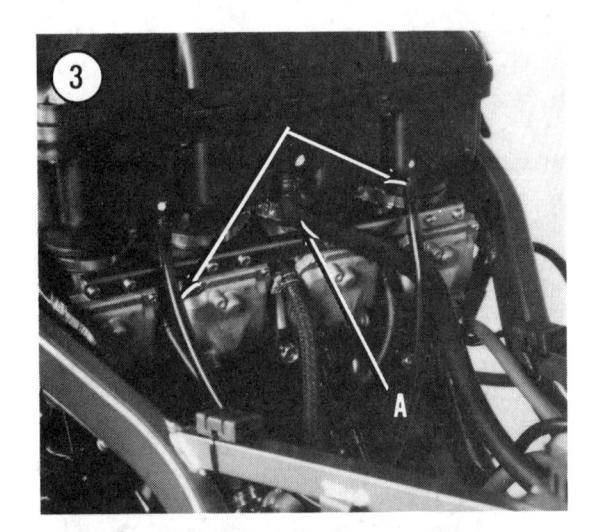

c. Loosen the hose clamps and lift the air cleaner housing (**Figure 4**) off of the carburetors.

d. Loosen the choke cable bracket screw and disconnect the cable at the carburetor (**Figure 5**).

6. Disconnect the throttle cable (**Figure 6**) at the carburetor.

7. Remove the carburetor-to-intake manifold boot clamps (**Figure 7**).

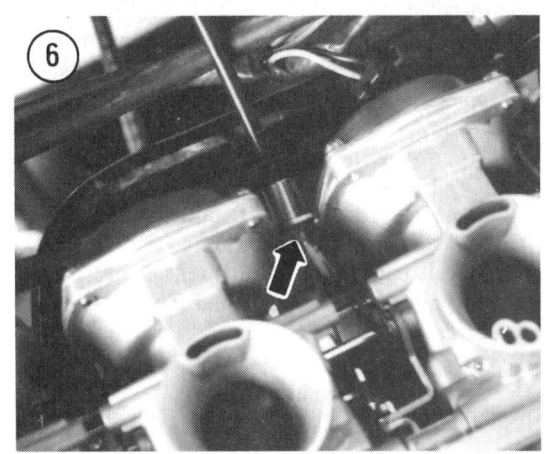

8. Grasp the carburetors on both ends. Work them up and down and remove them from the intake manifold boots (**Figure 8**).

CAUTION
*Stuff clean shops rags into the intake manifold openings (**Figure 9**). Objects dropped into the intake manifolds will fall into the cylinder head.*

9. Installation is the reverse of these steps. Note the following:
   a. Make sure the carburetors are fully seated forward in the rubber carburetor holders. You should feel a solid "bottoming out" when they're correctly installed. Tighten the boot clamps securely.

CAUTION
Make sure the carburetor boots are air tight. Air leaks can cause severe engine damage because of a lean mixture or the intake of dirt.

   b. Tighten the air cleaner housing mounting screws after the carburetors have been installed.
   c. Check throttle cable routing after installation. The cable must not be twisted, kinked or pinched.
   d. Adjust the throttle cable as described under *Throttle Cable Adjustment* in Chapter Three.
   e. On FZ700 and FZ750 models, adjust the choke cable as described under *Choke Cable Adjustment* in Chapter Three.
   f. Check carburetor adjustment as described under *Carburetor* in Chapter Three. Adjust if necessary.

Disassembly/Reassembly

Refer to **Figure 10** (FZX700) or **Figure 11** (FZ700 and FZ750). Disassemble and reassemble only one carburetor at a time to prevent accidental interchange of parts.

1. The carburetors can be cleaned without separating the individual body assemblies; proceed to Step 2. If necessary to separate the carburetor bodies, proceed as follows:
   a. *FZX700:* Remove the choke lever screws and remove the choke lever (**Figure 10**).
   b. Loosen the 4 starter lever bracket screws (**Figure 12**) and remove the starter lever.

NOTE
An impact driver with a Philips bit (described in Chapter One) will be necessary to loosen the screws securing the upper and lower brackets onto the carburetor housings. Attempting to loosen the screws with a Phillips screwdriver may ruin the screw heads.

   c. Remove the upper bracket screws and remove the upper bracket (**Figure 13**).

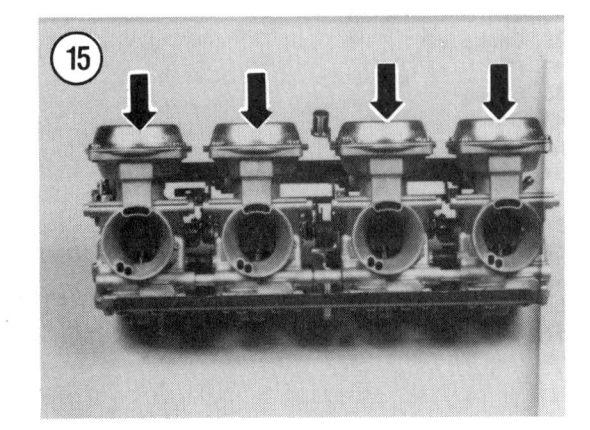

FUEL, EMISSION CONTROL AND EXHAUST SYSTEMS 169

NOTE
To avoid spilling gas, drain each float bowl before removing the lower bracket.

    d. Remove the lower bracket screws and remove the lower bracket (**Figure 14**).
    e. Separate the carburetor bodies (**Figure 15**).
2. Remove the vacuum chamber cover (**Figure 16**).
3. Remove the spring (**Figure 17**).
4. Lift the vacuum piston assembly (**Figure 18**) out of the carburetor.
5. Remove the plug (**Figure 19**), spring and washer. Then remove the vacuum piston assembly (**Figure 20**).

CARBURETOR
(FZX700)

1. Screw
2. Plate
3. Upper bracket
4. No. 4 carburetor housing
5. O-ring
6. Fuel pipe
7. Tube
8. Fuel hose
9. Hose clip
10. No. 3 carburetor housing
11. Throttle adjust screw
12. Spring
13. Fuel pipe
14. Stop screw assembly
15. Spring
16. Stop screw
17. Bracket
18. Lower bracket
19. Cable guide
20. Screw
21. Cover
22. Spring
23. Vacuum piston assembly
24. Pilot screw assembly
25. No. 2 carburetor housing
26. Float
27. Float pin
28. Main air jet
29. O-ring
30. Float bowl
31. Washer
32. Screw
33. Float needle assembly
34. Pilot jet
35. Fuel drain screw
36. Screw
37. Main jet assembly
38. Starter assembly
39. No. 1 carburetor housing
40. Hose
41. Hose guide
42. Clip
43. Tube
44. Bracket
45. Starter lever shaft
46. Choke lever
47. Pin
48. Circlip
49. Spacer
50. Starter assembly
51. Starter lever
52. Screw
53. Washers
54. Spring
55. Washer
56. Screw
57. Jet needle
58. Fuel pipe

FUEL, EMISSION CONTROL AND EXHAUST SYSTEMS 171

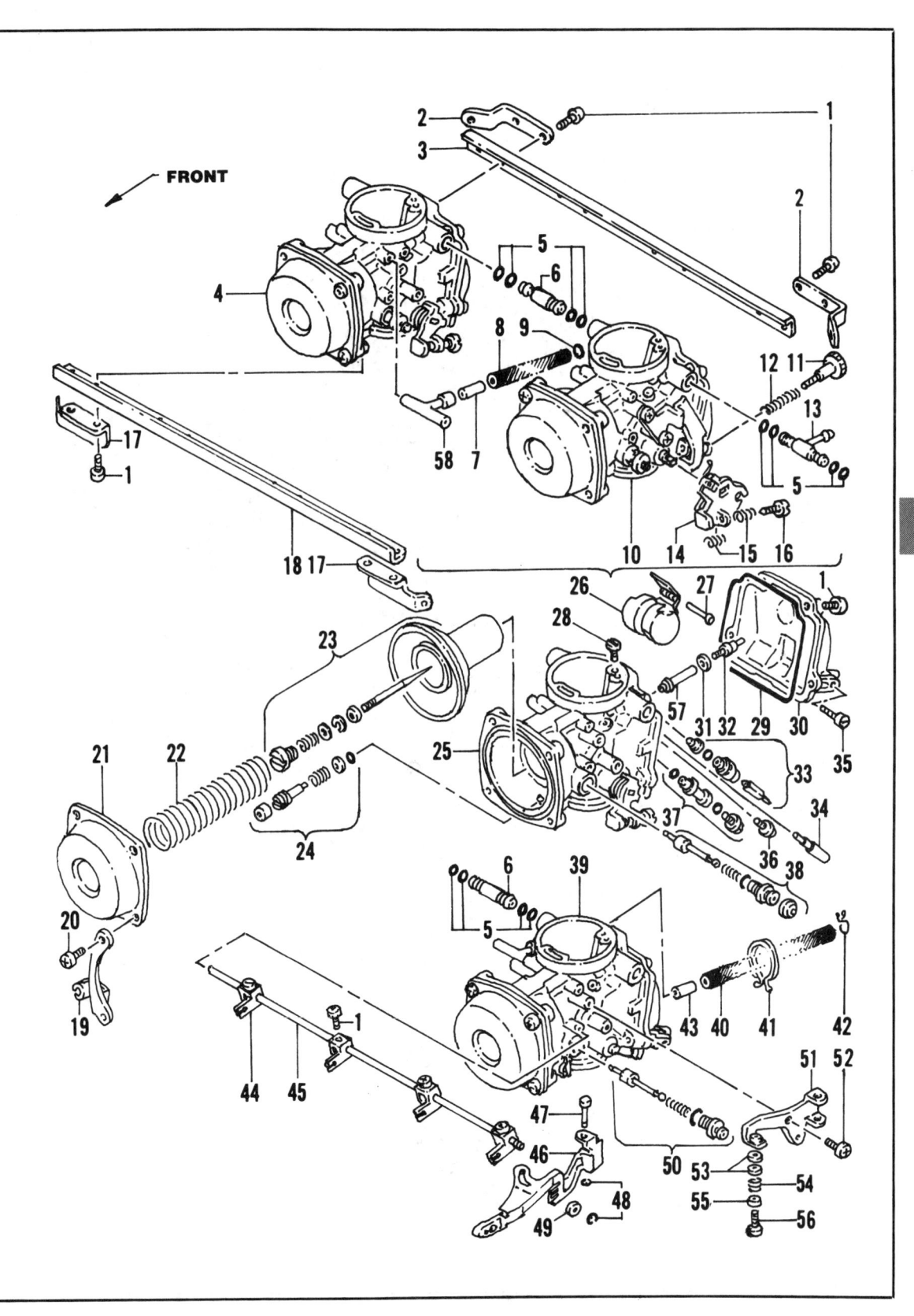

172   CHAPTER SEVEN

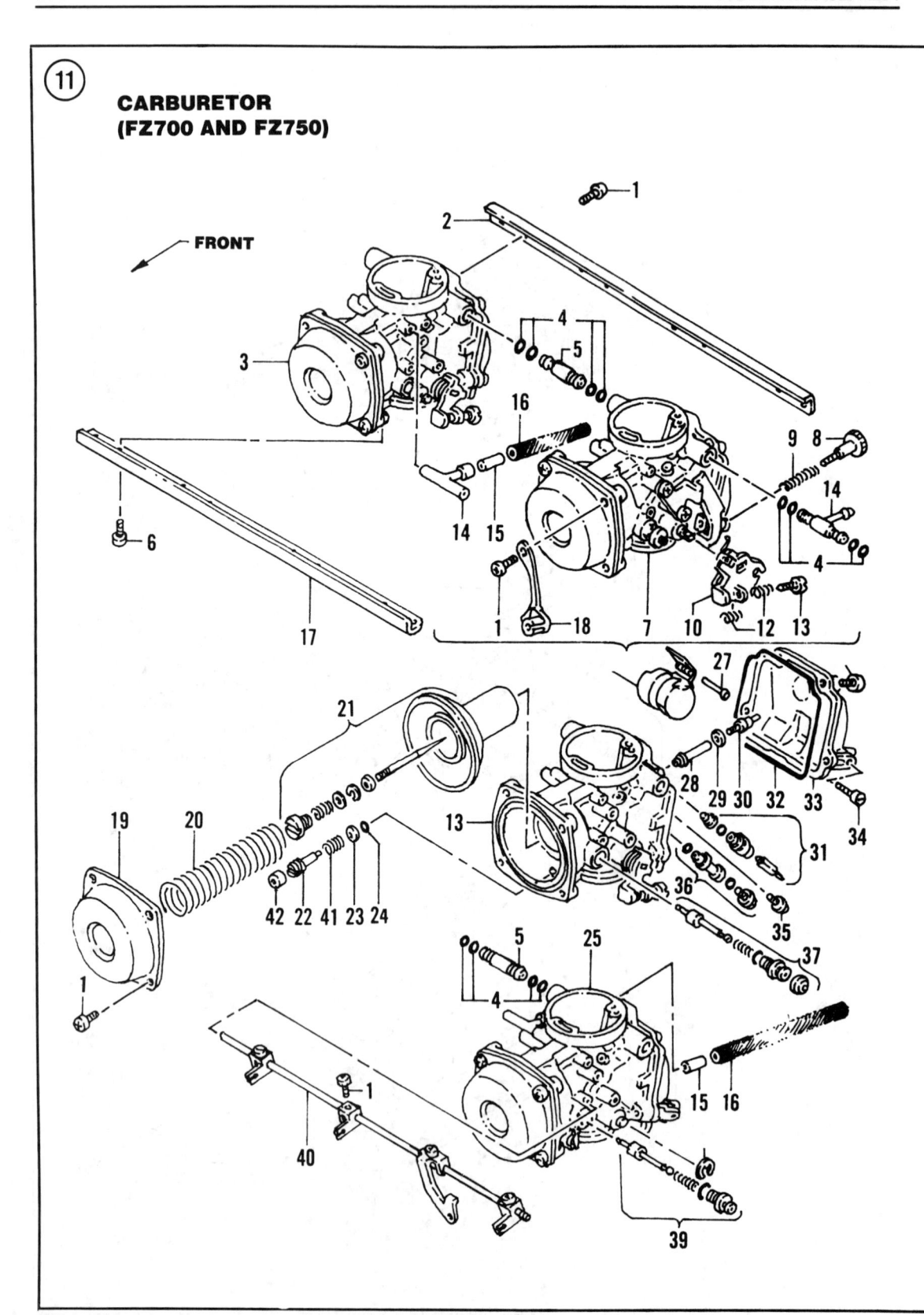

⑪ **CARBURETOR
(FZ700 AND FZ750)**

1. Screw
2. Upper bracket
3. No. 4 carburetor housing
4. O-rings
5. Fuel pipe
6. Screw
7. No. 3 carburetor housing
8. Throttle adjust screw
9. Spring
10. Stop screw assembly
11. Stop screw
12. Spring
13. No. 2 carburetor housing
14. Fuel pipe
15. Tube
16. Fuel hose
17. Lower bracket
18. Cable guide
19. Cover
20. Spring
21. Vacuum piston
22. Pilot screw
23. Plug
24. O-ring
25. No. 1 carburetor
26. Float
27. Float pin
28. Needle jet
29. Washer
30. Screw
31. Float needle assembly
32. O-ring
33. Float bowl
34. Fuel drain screw
35. Pilot jet
36. Main jet assembly
37. Starter assembly
38. Clip
39. Starter assembly
40. Starter lever shaft
41. Spring
42. Plug (FZ700)

6. Remove the float bowl (**Figure 21**).
7. Remove the float pin (**Figure 22**) and float (**Figure 23**).
8. Pull the float needle (**Figure 24**) off of the float.
9. Remove the plug (**Figure 25**) and washer. Then remove the needle jet through the top of the carburetor.
10. Remove the main jet (**Figure 26**).

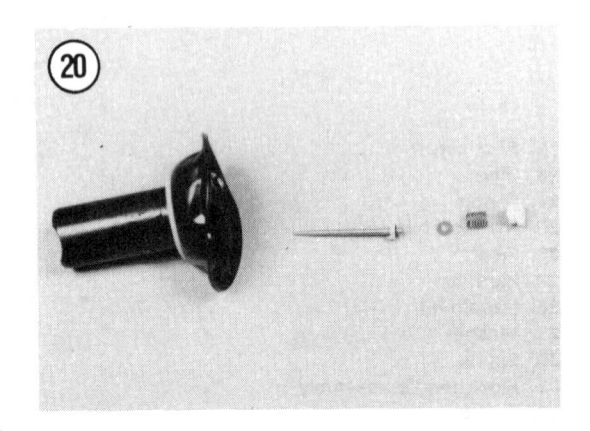

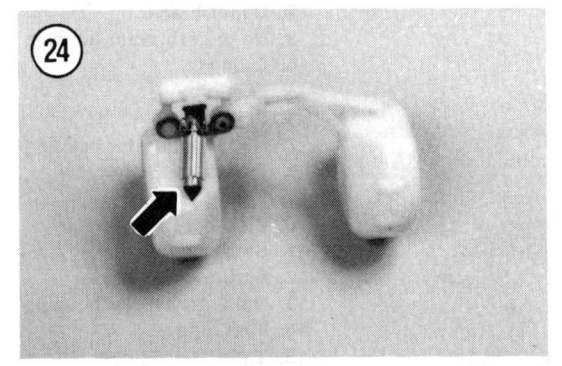

FUEL, EMISSION CONTROL AND EXHAUST SYSTEMS

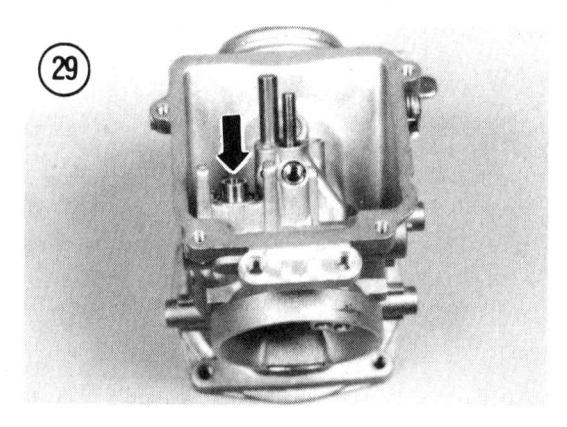

11. Remove the pilot jet (**Figure 27**).
12. Remove the screw (**Figure 28**) and remove the needle seat (**Figure 29**).
13. Remove the starter assembly (**Figure 30**).
14. Remove the pilot air jet. See **Figure 10** or **Figure 11**.
15. Clean and inspect the carburetor as described in this chapter.
16. Installation is the reverse of these steps. Note the following.
17. Check the throttle shaft and throttle plate (**Figure 31**) for excessive play or damage. Check the throttle plate screws for looseness. If the throttle shaft and/or plate is damaged, the carburetor body must be replaced as an assembly.
18. Replace the float bowl O-ring (**Figure 32**) if deformed, cracked or if the bowl leaked.

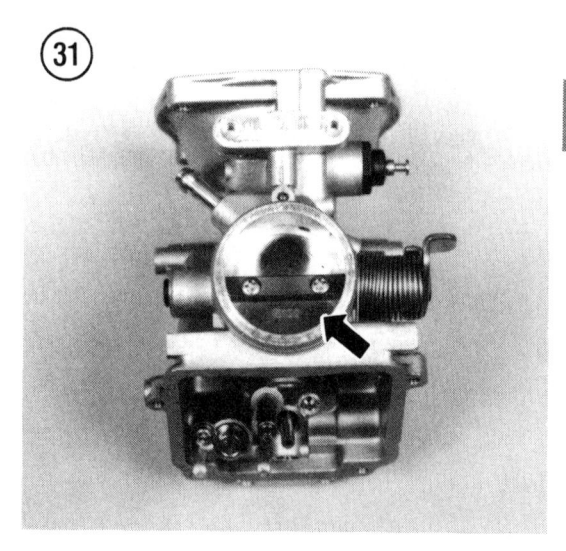

CHAPTER SEVEN

19. Install the jet needle through the center hole in the vacuum piston (**Figure 33**). Then install the washer, spring and plug (**Figure 20**).

20. Align the tab on the diaphragm with the notch in the carburetor body (**Figure 34**) and install the vacuum piston assembly. Then align the notch in the vacuum chamber cover (**Figure 35**) with the diaphragm tab (**Figure 34**) and install the cover. See **Figure 36**.

21. Repeat Steps 2-20 for the remaining carburetors.

22. If the carburetors were separated in Step 1, note the following:
   a. Assemble the fuel hoses (**Figure 37**). Install new O-rings if necessary.
   b. Tighten the upper and lower bracket screws securely.
   c. When assembling the starter shaft, align the end of the bracket screw (A, **Figure 38**) with the notch in the shaft (B, **Figure 38**). Then align the notch in the bracket with the choke lever and tighten the bracket screw securely.
   d. *FZX700:* Install the choke lever assembly.

23. Check the fuel level. See *Fuel Level Inspection/Adjustment* in this chapter.

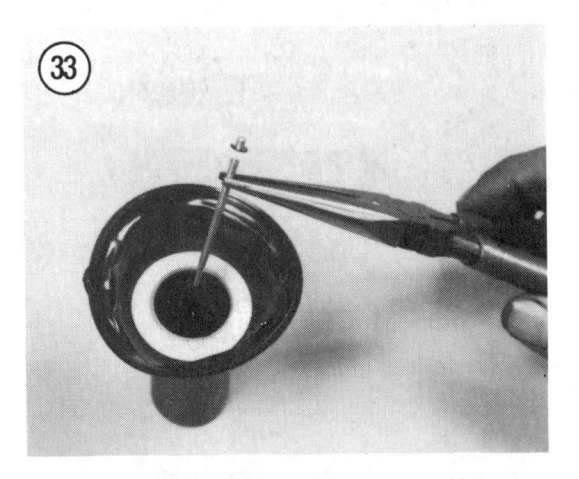

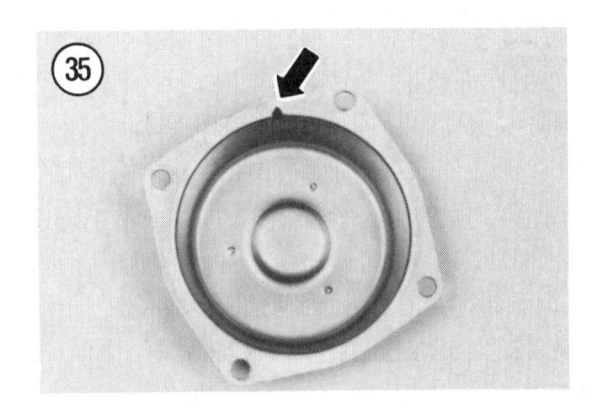

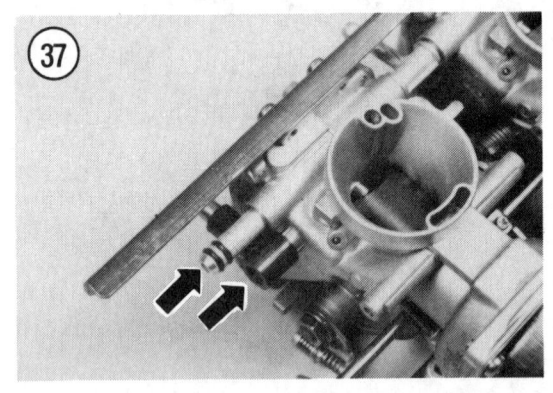

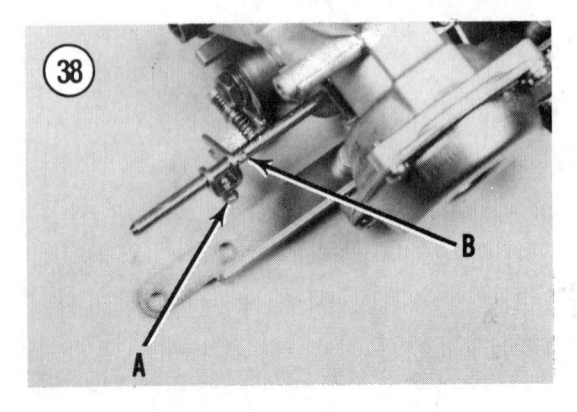

FUEL, EMISSION CONTROL AND EXHAUST SYSTEMS

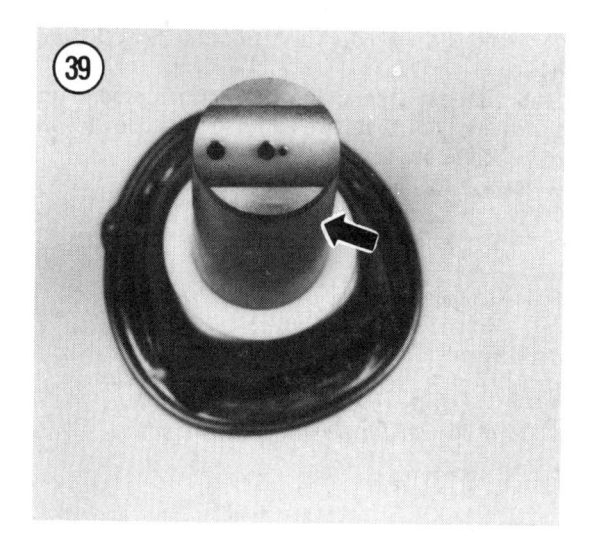

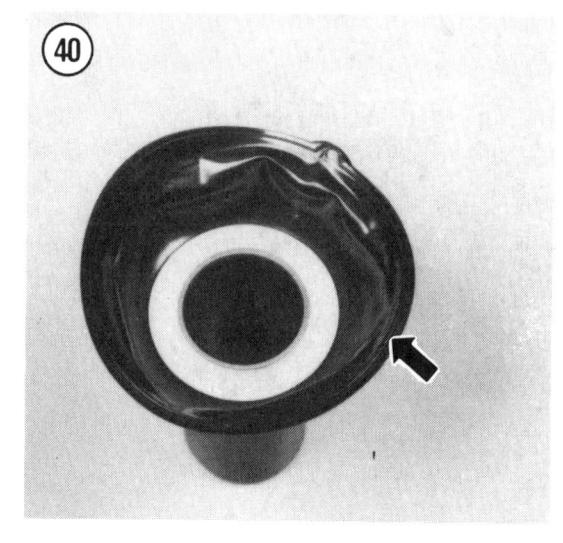

Cleaning and Inspection

1. Thoroughly clean and dry all parts. Yamaha does not recommend the use of a caustic carburetor cleaning solvent. Instead, clean metal carburetor parts in a petroleum-based solvent, then rinse in clean water. Do not use solvent on the O-rings or the vacuum piston diaphragm. Allow the carburetor to dry thoroughly before assembly.
2. Blow out all the passages and jets with compressed air. Don't use wire to clean any of the orifices; wire will enlarge or gouge them and change the air/fuel ratio.
3. Inspect the vacuum piston (**Figure 39**) for scoring and wear. Replace if necessary.
4. Inspect the diaphragm (**Figure 40**) for tears, cracks or other damage. Replace the vacuum piston assembly if the diaphragm is damaged.
5. Check the cone of the float needle (**Figure 41**) and replace it if scored or pitted.

FUEL LEVEL

The fuel level in the carburetor float bowls is critical to proper performance. The fuel flow rate from the bowl up to the carburetor bore depends not only on the vacuum in the throttle bore and the size of the jets, but also on the fuel level. Yamaha gives a specification of actual fuel level, measured from the top edge of the float bowl with the carburetors mounted on the motorcycle (**Figure 42**).

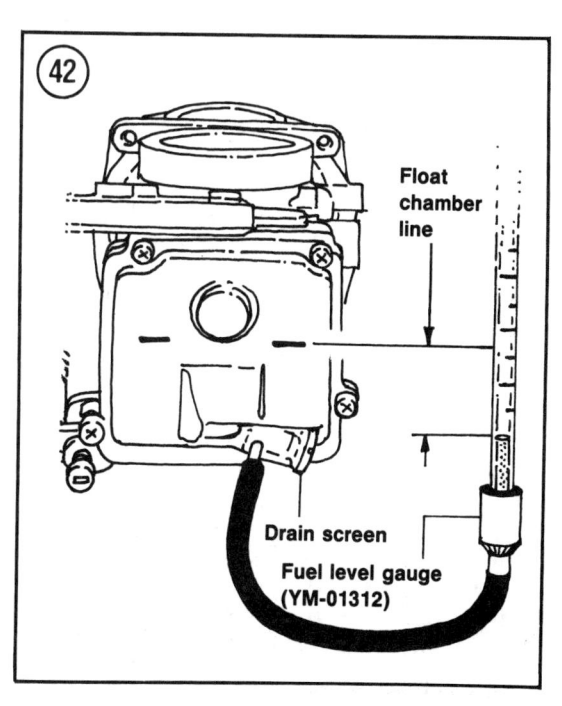

This measurement is more useful than a simple float height measurement because the actual fuel level can vary from bike to bike, even when their floats are set at the same height. Fuel level inspection requires a special fuel level gauge (Yamaha part No. YM-01312) or a vinyl tube with an inside diameter of 6 mm (0.24 in.). See **Figure 42**.

The fuel level is adjusted by bending the float arm tang.

Inspection/Adjustment

Carburetors leave the factory with float levels properly adjusted. Rough riding, a worn needle valve or bent float arm can cause the float level to change. To adjust the float level on these carburetors, perform the following.

WARNING
Some gasoline will drain from the carburetors during this procedure. Work in a well-ventilated area, at least 50 feet from any open flame including the pilot lights on water heaters and clothes driers. Do not smoke. Wipe up spills immediately.

1. Remove the air cleaner housing as described under *Carburetor Removal/Installation* in this chapter.

CAUTION
The following steps will be performed with the carburetors' vacuum piston openings exposed. Do not place tools or other objects where they could fall into the carburetors.

2. Connect the fuel level gauge (Yamaha part No. YM-01312) or a vinyl tube (with a 6 mm/0.24 in. inside diameter) to the float chamber cover on the left-hand carburetor (left side) as shown in **Figure 42**. Secure the gauge so that it aligns vertically with the float bowl line (**Figure 42**) and so the "0" level gauge is aligned with the float bowl as shown in **Figure 42**.
3. Turn the petcock to ON and loosen the carburetor drain screw (**Figure 42**).
4. Start the engine and allow it to idle for a few minutes. Turn the engine off.
5. Wait until the fuel in the gauge settles. Then slowly lower the gauge until the "0" line is even with the bottom edge of the carburetor body (**Figure 42**). The fuel level should be 8.3 ±1 mm (**Table 2**) above the edge of the carburetor body.
6. If the fuel level is incorrect, adjust the float height. Remove the float bowl from the carburetor and remove the float pin and float (**Figure 43**).
7. Remove the needle valve from the float (**Figure 44**).
8. Bend the float tang (**Figure 45**) as required to get the right float level. Install the float bowl and recheck the fuel level.
9. Repeat for the remaining carburetors.

FUEL TANK

WARNING
Some fuel may spill in the following procedure. Work in a well-ventilated area at least 50 feet from any sparks or flames, including gas appliance pilot lights. Do not smoke in the area. Keep a BC rated fire extinguisher handy.

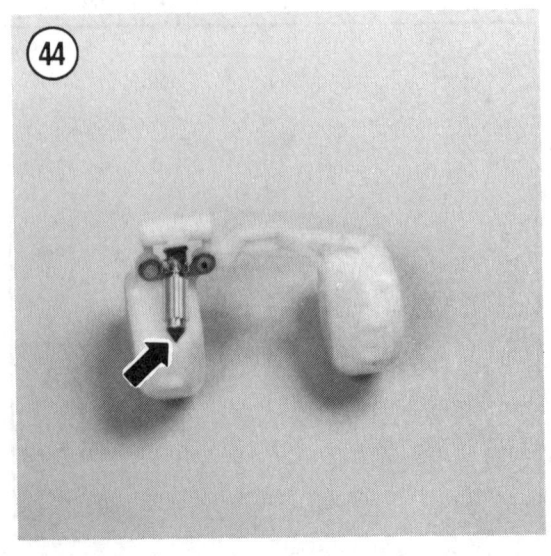

FUEL, EMISSION CONTROL AND EXHAUST SYSTEMS

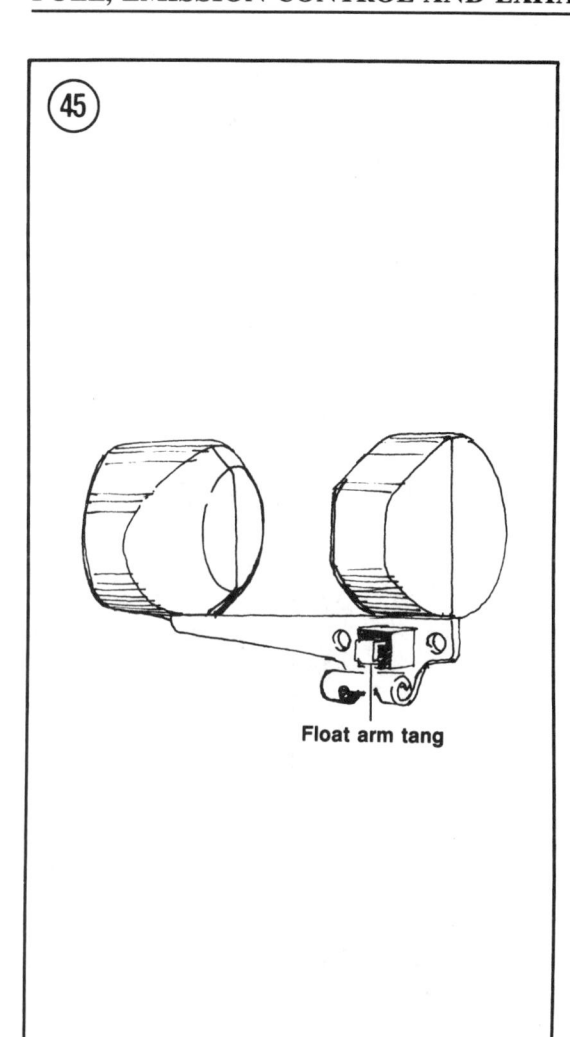

Figure 45 — Float arm tang

Removal/Installation

1. Check that the ignition switch is off.
2. Place the bike on its center stand. On FZ700 models, support the bike so that it is secure.
3. Remove the seat and both side covers.
4. Remove the battery cover and disconnect the negative battery terminal (**Figure 46**).
5A. *FZX700:* Perform the following:
   a. Turn the petcock to OFF.
   b. Remove the meter panel cover screws and remove the meter panel cover (**Figure 47**).
   c. Open the fuel tank cap. Then remove the stopper plate screw (**Figure 48**) and remove the stopper plate.

CAUTION
Do not drop the screw into the fuel tank when removing it.

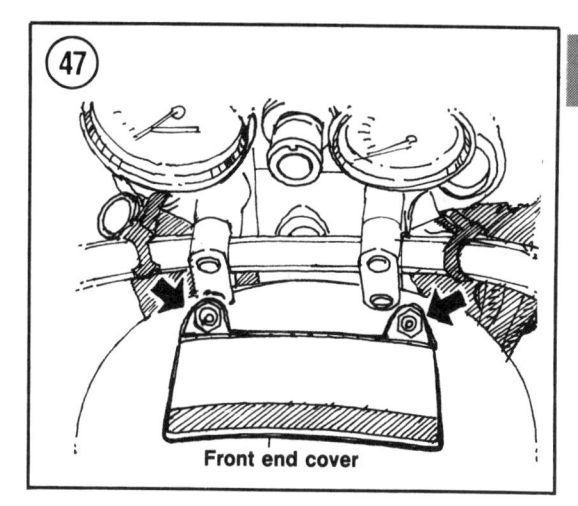

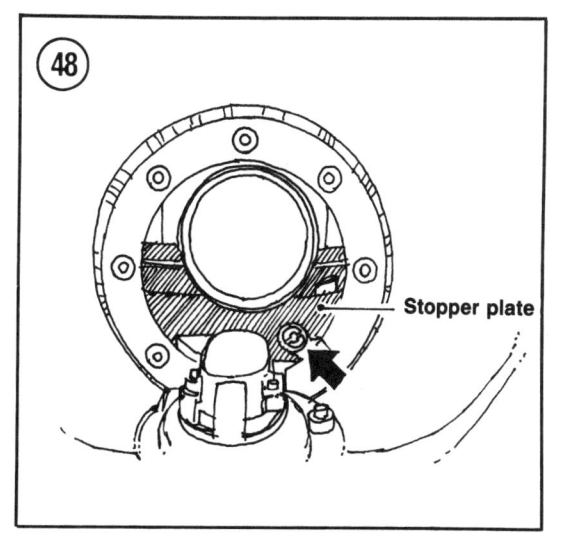

Figure 47 — Front end cover

Figure 46

Figure 48 — Stopper plate

CHAPTER SEVEN

d. Turn the levers backward and lift the top cover up and remove it. See **Figure 49**.
e. Close the fuel tank cap.
f. Remove the rear fuel tank mounting bolt.
g. Disconnect all electrical connectors leading from the fuel tank.
h. Disconnect all fuel hoses (fuel valve, fuel filter and fuel pump) at the fuel tank.
i. On California models, disconnect the evaporative hose from underneath the fuel tank.
j. Remove the fuel tank.

5B. *FZ700 and FZ750:* Perform the following:
a. Turn the petcock to OFF.
b. Disconnect the fuel sender lead connector (leading from the fuel tank) on the left-hand side.
c. Disconnect the hose (A, **Figure 50**) at the rear of the fuel tank.
d. Remove the front (**Figure 51**) and rear (B, **Figure 50**) mounting bolts.
e. On California models, disconnect the evaporative hose from underneath the fuel tank.
f. Remove the fuel tank.

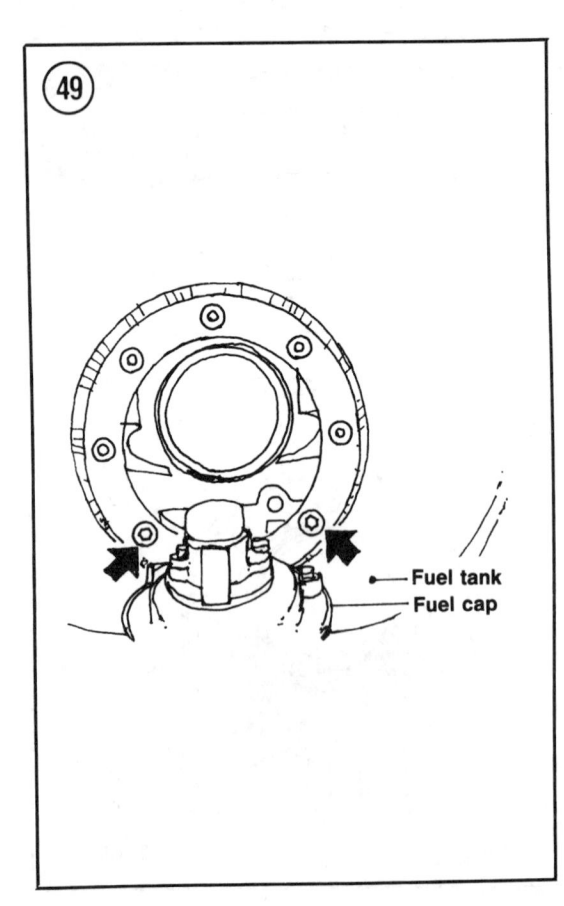

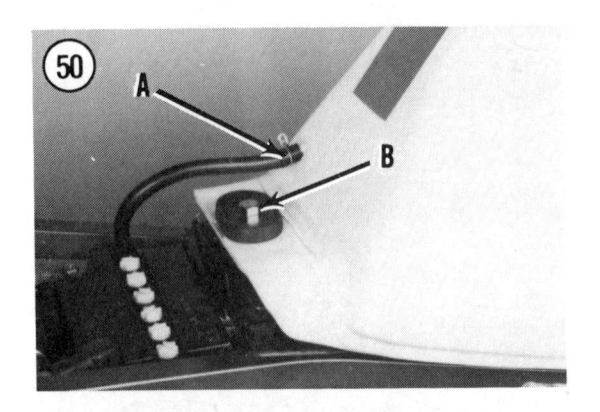

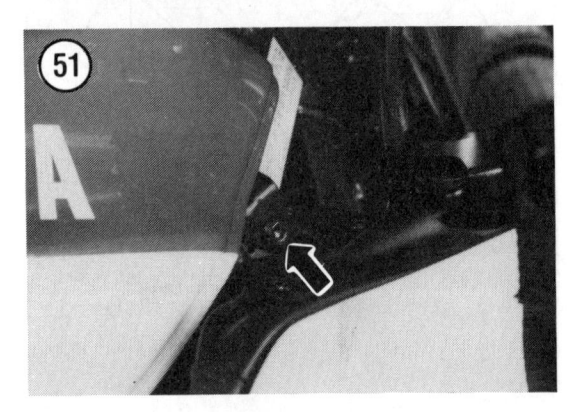

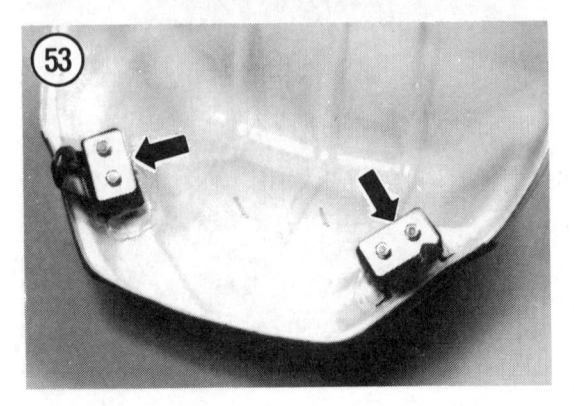

FUEL, EMISSION CONTROL AND EXHAUST SYSTEMS

6. If necessary, pour the fuel into a container
7. Inspect the fuel tank dampers (**Figure 52**) for damage and replace if necessary.
8. Check any fuel tank mounting brackets (**Figure 53**) for looseness. Tighten if necessary.
9. To install the fuel tank, reverse the removal steps. Note the following:

   a. Don't pinch any wires or control cables during installation.
   b. Reconnect all hoses and connectors.

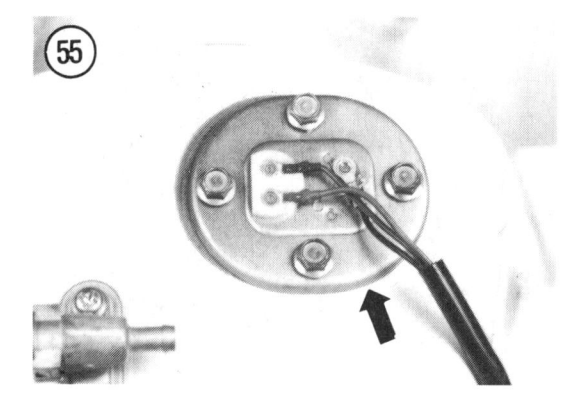

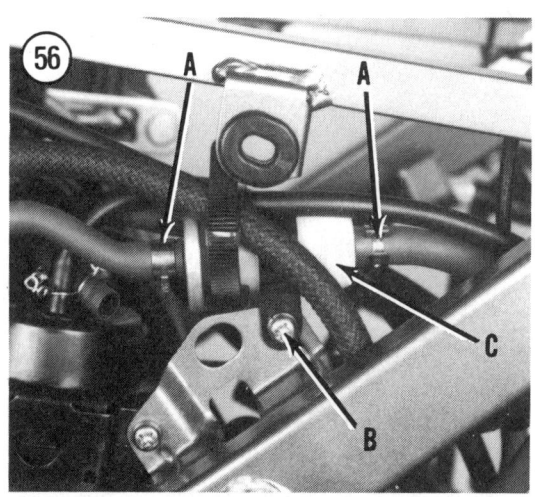

FUEL VALVE

Removal/Installation

WARNING
Some fuel may spill in the following procedure. Work in a well-ventilated area at least 50 feet from any sparks or flames, including gas appliance pilot lights. Do not smoke in the area. Keep a BC rated fire extinguisher handy.

1. Remove the fuel tank as described in this chapter.
2. Remove the 2 fuel valve mounting bolts, the valve and O-ring. See **Figure 54**.
3. Inspect the fuel valve mounting O-ring; replace if necessary.
4. Install the fuel valve by reversing these steps. Note the following.
5. Pour a small amount of gasoline into the tank after installing the fuel valve and check for leaks.

FUEL LEVEL SENDER

A fuel level sender is mounted in the bottom of the fuel tank (**Figure 55**). When installing a sender, make sure the O-ring is in good condition.

FUEL FILTER

All models are equipped with a separate fuel filter that cannot be cleaned. If dirty, a new filter must be installed. The filter must be periodically replaced (no replacement intervals are specified by Yamaha).

Removal/Installation

1. Remove the right-hand side cover.
2. Remove the seat and disconnect the negative battery cable (**Figure 46**).
3. *FZX700:* Remove the fuel tank as described in this chapter.

NOTE
Figure 56 shows the fuel filter on FZ700 models; the fuel filter on other models is similar.

4. Disconnect the flexible fuel lines from the fuel filter (A, **Figure 56**). Plug the ends of the fuel lines with golf tees.
5. Remove the fuel filter clamp screw (B, **Figure 56**) and remove the filter (C, **Figure 56**).

6. Install by reversing these removal steps, noting the following:
   a. Install the fuel filter so that the small end faces forward.
   b. Check the fuel line clamps for damage; replace if necessary.
   c. After installation is complete, thoroughly check for leaks.

FUEL PUMP

Removal/Installation

1. Remove the right-hand side cover.
2. Remove the seat and disconnect the negative battery cable (**Figure 46**).
3. *FZX700:* Remove the fuel tank as described in this chapter.

NOTE
Figure 57 shows the fuel pump on FZ700 models; the fuel pump on other models is similar.

4. See **Figure 57**. Disconnect the fuel inlet (A) and outlet (B) fuel lines from the fuel pump. Plug the ends of the fuel lines with golf tees to prevent fuel leakage.
5. Remove the fuel pump mounting bolts and remove the fuel pump (C, **Figure 57**).
6. Install by reversing these removal steps.
7. After installation is complete, thoroughly check for fuel leaks.

EMISSION CONTROL

All 1985-on models sold in California are equipped with an evaporative emission control system to reduce the amount of fuel vapors released into the atmosphere. The system consists of a charcoal canister, roll-over valve, assorted vacuum lines and a modified carburetor and fuel tank. A schematic of the emission control system is on a special decal on one of the side covers (**Figure 58**).

During engine operation, fuel vapors formed in the fuel tank exit the tank though a roll-over valve and enter the charcoal canister through a connecting hose. The vapors are stored in the charcoal canister (**Figure 59**) until the bike is ridden at high speed, when the vapors are then passed through a hose to the carburetor and mixed and burned with the incoming fuel and fresh air. During low-speed engine operation or when the bike is parked, the fuel vapors are stored in the charcoal canister.

The roll-over valve is installed in line with the fuel tank and charcoal canister. Air and fuel vapor passing through the valve is controlled by an internal weight (**Figure 60**). During normal riding (or when the fuel tank is properly positioned), the weight is at the bottom of the valve. In this position, the breather passage is open to allow the fuel vapors to flow to the charcoal canister at the correct engine speed. When the bike is rolled or turned over, the weight moves to block off the passage.

In this position it is impossible for stored fuel vapors to flow to the charcoal canister.

Service to the emission control system is limited to replacement of damaged parts. No attempt should be made to modify or remove the emission control system.

Parts Replacements

When purchasing replacement parts (carburetor and fuel tank), always make sure the parts are for

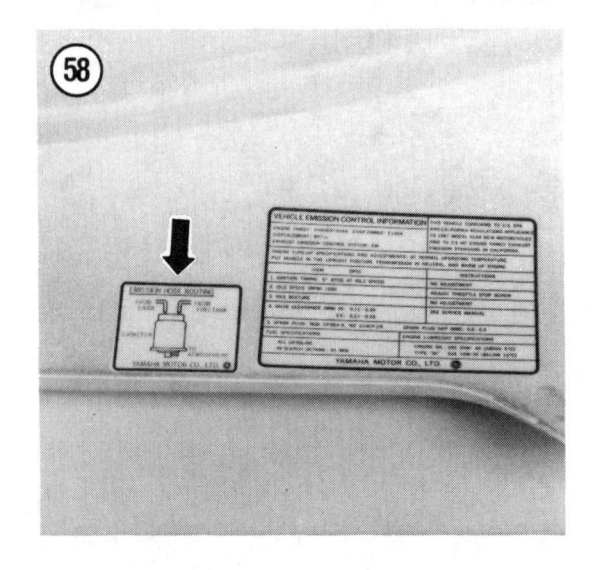

FUEL, EMISSION CONTROL AND EXHAUST SYSTEMS

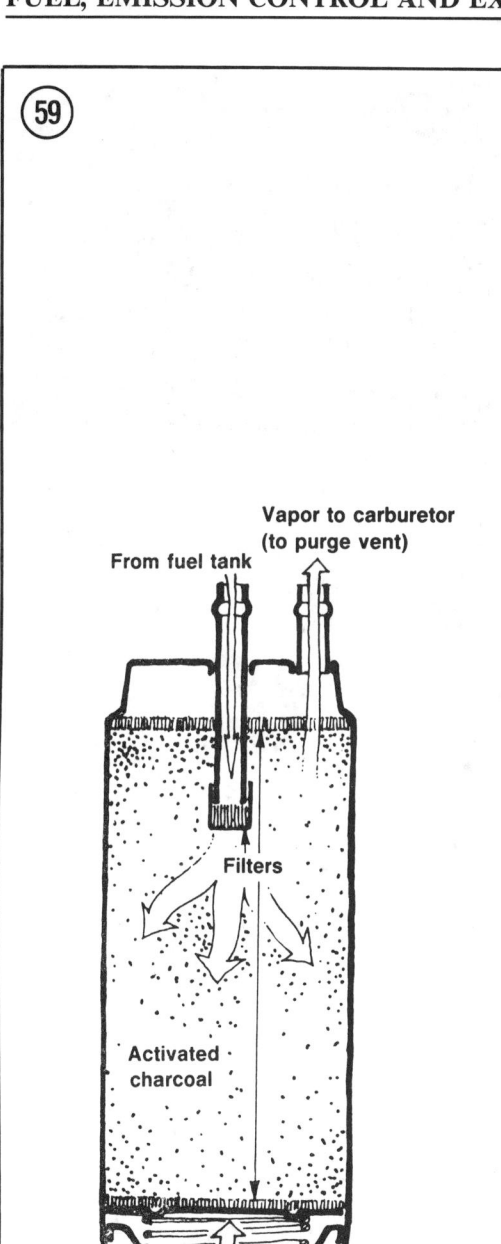

California emission control bikes. Parts sold for non-emission control bikes will not work with the emission control system.

Inspection/Replacement

Maintenance to the evaporative emission control system consists of periodic inspection of the hoses for proper routing and a check of the canister mounting brackets.

WARNING
Because the evaporative emission control system stores fuel vapors, make sure the work area is free of all flames or sparks before working on the emission system.

1. Whenever servicing the evaporative system, make sure the ignition switch is turned off.
2. Make sure all hoses are attached as indicated in **Figure 58** and that they are not damaged or pinched.
3. Replace any worn or damaged parts immediately.
4. The canister (**Figure 61**) is capable of working through the motorcycle's life without maintenance, provided that it is not damaged or contaminated.

Roll-over Valve Replacement

FZX700

The roll-over valve on these models is located between the hose that connects the carbon canister to the fuel tank. Remove the roll-over valve bracket screw and disconnect the valve from the hose. Reverse to install.

FZ700 and FZ750

The roll-over valve is mounted underneath the fuel tank.

1. Remove the fuel tank as described in this chapter.
2. Drain the fuel tank of all gasoline. Store the gasoline in a safety approved canister.
3. Remove the roll-over valve (**Figure 62**) with a socket or wrench. Remove the O-ring.
4. Installation is the reverse of these steps. Install a new O-ring.

EXHAUST SYSTEM

Removal/Installation (FZX700)

1. Place the bike on the center stand.
2. Loosen the cross-over pipe bracket pinch bolts.
3. Loosen the header pipe clamp nuts at the cylinder head.
4. Remove the muffler mounting bolts and nuts.
5. Remove the header pipe clamp nuts and remove the exhaust system.
6. To install, reverse the removal steps. Note the following:
   a. Use new gaskets in the cylinder head exhaust ports.
   b. Replace muffler gaskets as required.
   c. Tighten the header pipe clamp nuts at the cylinder head first, gradually and evenly. Then tighten the rear bolts and nuts.
   d. Start the engine and check for leakage. Tighten the clamps again after the engine has cooled down.

Removal/Installation (FZ750)

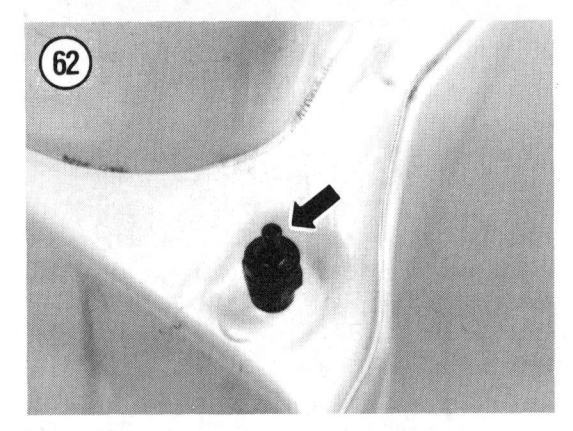

1. Place the bike on the center stand.
2. Loosen the cross-over pipe bracket pinch bolts.

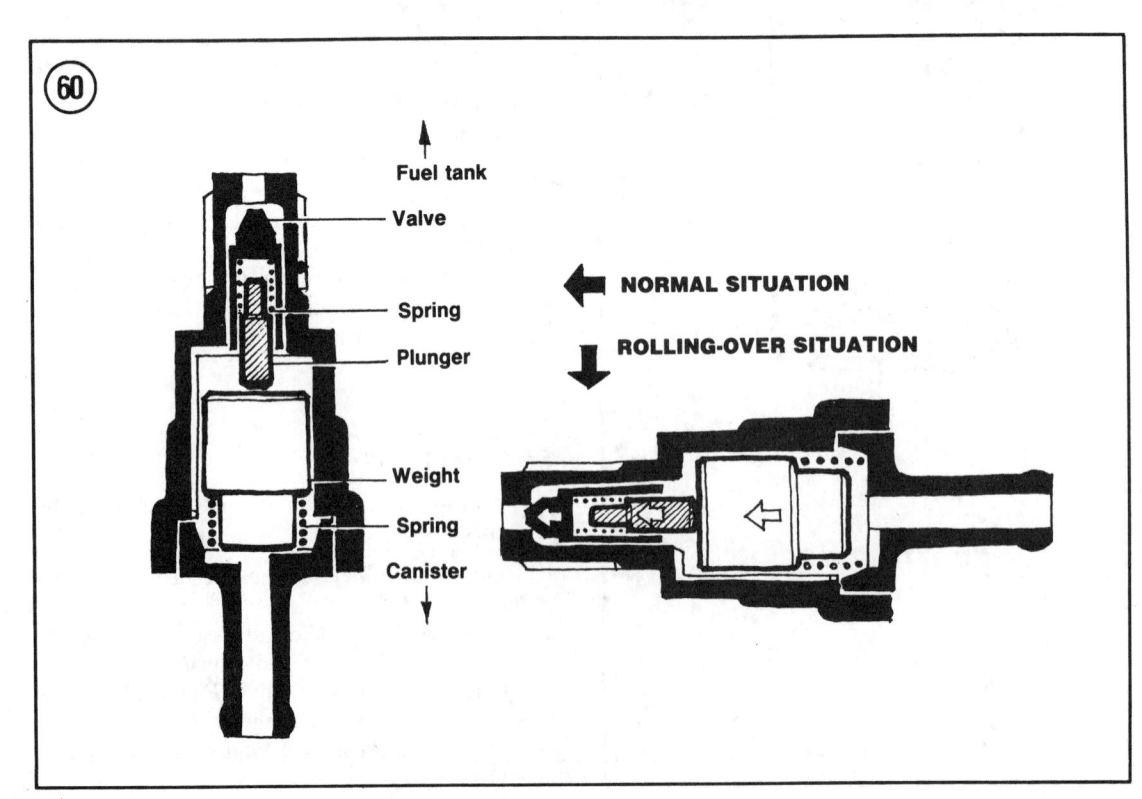

FUEL, EMISSION CONTROL AND EXHAUST SYSTEMS

3. Loosen the header pipe clamp nuts at the cylinder head.
4. Remove the muffler mounting bolts and nuts.
5. Remove the header pipe clamp nuts and remove the exhaust system.
6. To install, reverse the removal steps. Note the following:

   a. Use new gaskets in the cylinder head exhaust ports.
   b. Replace muffler gaskets as required.
   c. Tighten the header pipe clamp nuts at the cylinder head first, gradually and evenly. Then tighten the rear bolts and nuts.
   d. Start the engine and check for leakage. Tighten the clamps again after the engine has cooled down.

Removal/Installation (FZ700)

1. Remove the lower fairing. See Chapter Thirteen.
2. Remove the muffler mounting bolt and nut (**Figure 63**).
3. Loosen the header pipe clamp nuts (**Figure 64**) at the cylinder head.
4. Remove the mounting bolt underneath the exhaust system and remove the exhaust assembly (**Figure 65**).
5. To install, reverse the removal steps. Note the following:

   a. Use new gaskets in the cylinder head exhaust ports.
   b. Replace muffler gaskets as required.
   c. Tighten the header pipe clamp nuts at the cylinder head first, gradually and evenly. Then tighten the rear bolts and nuts.
   d. Start the engine and check for leakage. Tighten the clamps again after the engine has cooled down.

Maintenance

The exhaust system is a vital key to the motorcycle's operation and performance, You should periodically inspect, clean and polish (if required) the exhaust system. Special chemical cleaners and preservatives compounded for exhaust systems are available at most motorcycle shops.

Severe dents which cause flow restrictions require replacement of the damaged part.

To prevent internal rust buildup, remove the pipes and turn them on end to drain any trapped moisture.

Tables are on the following page.

Table 1 CARBURETOR SPECIFICATIONS

Item	FZX700	FZ700 & FZ750
Main jet		
Cylinders 1 & 4	102.5	105
Cylinders 2 & 3	105	100
Main air jet	65	65
Jet needle		
All carbs	5CEZ04	—
Cylinders 1 & 4	—	5CDZ4
Cylinders 2 & 3	—	5CEZ2
Needle jet	Y-0	Y-0
Pilot air jet		
All carbs	—	120
Cylinders 1 & 4	135	—
Cylinders 2 & 3	130	—
Pilot jet	15	15
Pilot screw	2 turns out	Preset
Starter jet		
GS.1 jet	30	35
GS.2 jet	0.4	0.7
Idle speed (rpm)	950-1,050	950-1,050

Table 2 FUEL LEVEL SPECIFICATIONS

All models	8.3 ±1.0 mm (0.326 ±0.04 in.)

CHAPTER EIGHT

ELECTRICAL SYSTEM

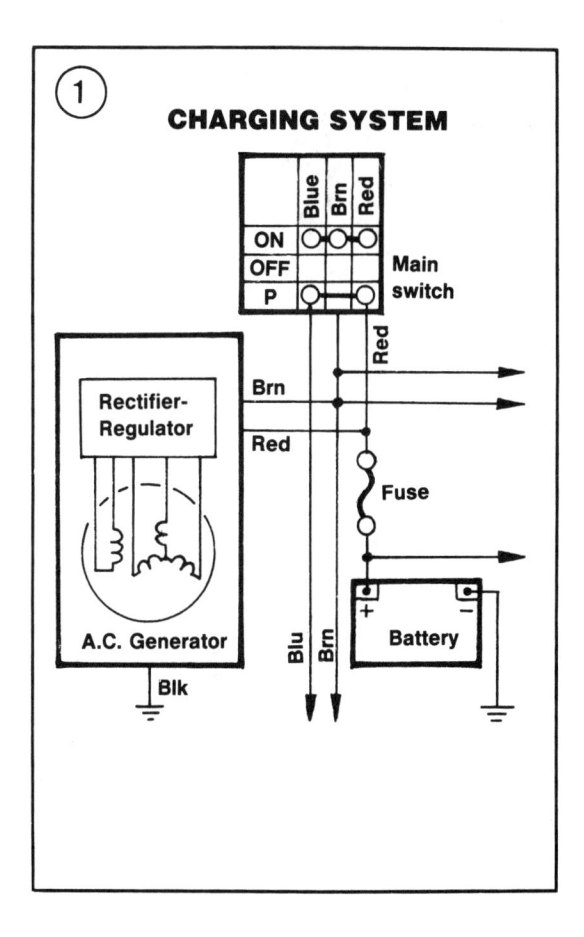

This chapter describes service procedures for the electrical system. **Tables 1-3** are at the end of the chapter.

CHARGING SYSTEM

The charging system consists of the battery, main fuse, main switch, generator and the rectifier/regulator assembly (**Figure 1**).

Charging System Test

Whenever the charging system is suspected of trouble, make sure the battery is fully charged before testing further. Clean and test the battery as described under *Battery* in Chapter Three. If the battery is in good condition, test the charging system as follows:
1. Remove the seat.
2. Refer to the charging system schematic in **Figure 1** and check all connections to make sure they are clean and tight. Check the wiring for fraying or other damage. Electrical connections should be cleaned with electrical contact cleaner and reconnected.

NOTE
Do not disconnect either the positive or negative battery cables; they are to remain in the circuit as is.

CHAPTER EIGHT

2. Test the battery as described in Chapter Three under *Battery*. Once the battery charge is correct, proceed to Step 3.

3. Connect a voltmeter to the battery terminals as shown in **Figure 2**. Start the engine and accelerate to approximately 5,000 rpm. Voltage should read 13.5-15.3 volts. Interpret results in Step 4.

4A. *Charging voltage lower than 13.5 volts:* First check the main fuse (**Figure 3**). Pull the fuse out of its holder and visually inspect it. If the fuse is blown, refer to *Fuses* in this chapter. If the main fuse is okay, test the following components in order as described in this chapter:
   a. Rectifier (see *Rectifier Testing/Replacement*).
   b. Stator coil resistance (see *Stator Coil Testing/Replacement*).
   c. Field coil resistance (see *Field Coil Resistance Check*).

4B. *Charging voltage higher than 15.3 volts:* Remove the generator cover (**Figure 4**). Then check the regulator assembly mounted on the generator (A, **Figure 5**) for loose connections. If the regulator mounting and electrical connections appear okay, replace the regulator.

Rectifier
Testing/Replacement

The rectifier is mounted on the generator assembly. An ohmmeter is required for this procedure.

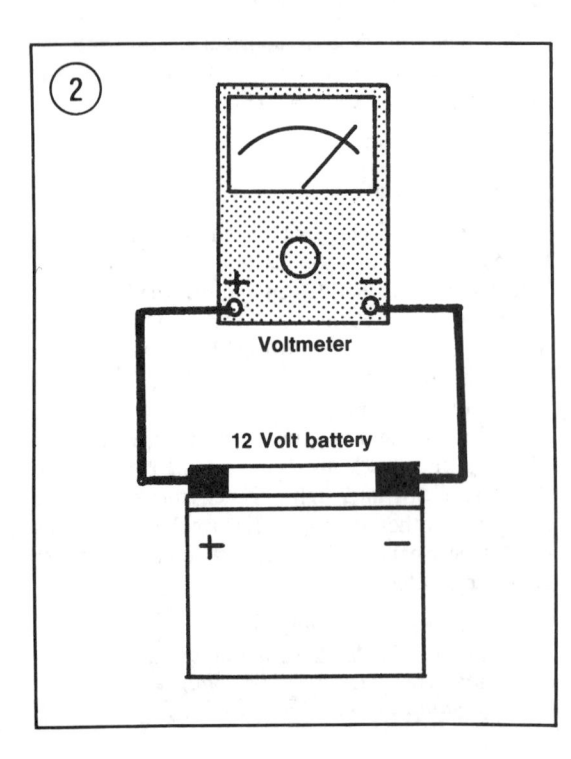

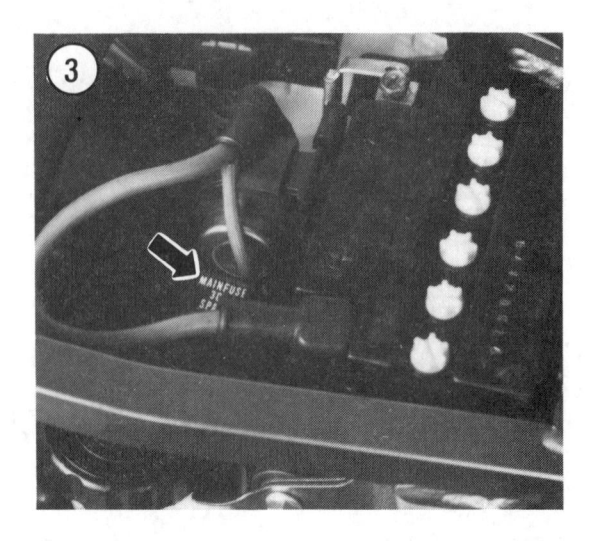

ELECTRICAL SYSTEM

1. Remove the generator cover (**Figure 4**).

> *CAUTION*
> *If the rectifier is subjected to overcharging it can be damaged. Be careful not to short-circuit or incorrectly connect the battery positive and negative leads. Never directly connect the rectifier to the battery for a continuity check.*

2. Measure the resistance between each of the following terminals with an ohmmeter (**Figure 6**). Record each of the measurements:
   a. D and A.
   b. D and B.
   c. D and C.
   d. A and E.
   e. B and E.
   f. C and E.

3. Reverse the ohmmeter leads, then repeat Step 3. Compare results with **Figure 7**. Each set of measurements must be high with the ohmmeter connected one way and low with the ohmmeter leads reversed. It is not possible to specify exact ohmmeter readings.

4. Even if only one of the elements is defective, replace the rectifier assembly. Remove the generator as described in this chapter and have the rectifier assembly replaced by a Yamaha dealer.

Stator Coil
Testing/Replacement

The stator coil is mounted on the generator assembly. An ohmmeter is required for this test procedure.

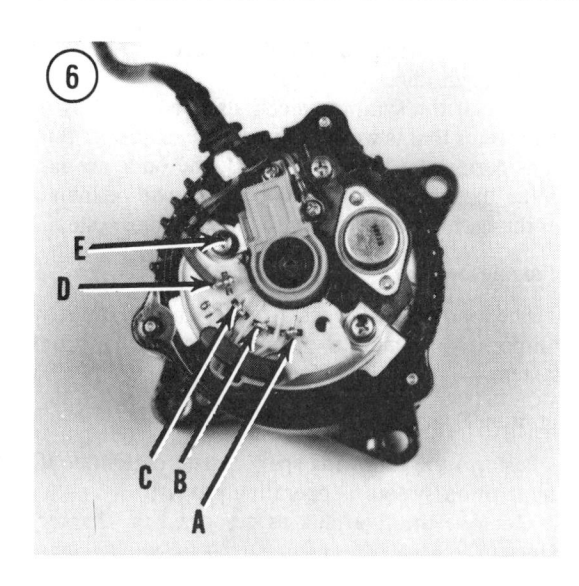

1. Remove the generator cover (**Figure 4**).

> *NOTE*
> *The test in Step 2 should be made with the engine at room temperature (68° F/20° C).*

2. Measure the resistance between each of the following terminals with an ohmmeter (**Figure 8**).

Checking Element	Pocket Tester Connecting Point Red (+)	Pocket Tester Connecting Point Blk (−)	Good
D_1	D	A	O
	A	D	X
D_2	D	B	O
	B	D	X
D_3	D	C	O
	C	D	X
D_4	A	E	O
	E	A	X
D_5	B	E	O
	E	B	X
D_6	C	E	O
	E	C	X

O: Continuity
X: No continuity (∞)

Record each of the measurements:
  a. A and B.
  b. A and C.
  c. B and C.
3. The correct reading is 0.2 ohms.
4. Even if only one of the elements is defective, replace the stator coil assembly. Remove the generator as described in this chapter and have a Yamaha dealer replace the stator coil assembly.

Field Coil Resistance Check

Because the field coil resistance check requires complete disassembly of the generator, refer service to a Yamaha dealer. Remove the generator as described in this chapter.

Generator Brush Length

1. Remove the generator cover (**Figure 4**).
2. Remove the brush holder (B, **Figure 5**) and remove the brushes and springs.
3. Measure the brushes with a vernier caliper. Replace the brush holder assembly if the brushes measure 4.5 mm (0.180 in.) or less.
4. Install by reversing these steps.

Generator
Removal/Installation

1. Park the bike on its center stand. On FZ700 models, support the bike securely.
2. *FZ700 and FZ750*: Remove the lower fairing. See Chapter Thirteen.
3. Disconnect the generator electrical connector.
4. Remove the generator mounting bolts and remove the generator (**Figure 9**).
5. Install by reversing these steps. Note the following:
  a. Check the generator O-ring (A, **Figure 10**) for flat spots or wear; replace if necessary.
  b. Align the generator shaft (B, **Figure 10**) with the starter clutch and install the generator assembly.
  c. Tighten the generator mounting bolts to 20 N•m (14 ft.-lb.).

IGNITION SYSTEM

The ignition system is a breakerless type. Most problems involving failure to start, poor driveability or rough running are caused by trouble in the ignition system.

Note the following symptoms:
  a. Engine misses.
  b. Stumbles on acceleration (misfiring).
  c. Loss of power at high speed (misfiring).
  d. Hard starting (or failure to start).
  e. Rough idle.

Most of the symptoms can also be caused by a carburetor that is worn or improperly adjusted. But considering the law of averages, the odds are far better that the source of the problem will be found in the ignition system rather than the fuel system.

Troubleshooting

The following basic tests are designed to quickly pinpoint and isolate problems in the ignition system.

Ignition Spark Test

Perform the following spark test to determine if the ignition system is operating properly.
1. Remove the fuel tank as described in Chapter Seven.
2. Remove one of the spark plugs.

ELECTRICAL SYSTEM

3. Connect the spark plug wire and connector to the spark plug and touch the spark plug base to a good ground like the engine cylinder head. Position the spark plug so you can see the electrodes.

WARNING
During the next step, do not hold the spark plug, wire or connector or a serious electrical shock may result. If necessary, use a pair of insulated pliers to hold the spark plug or wire. The high voltage generated by the ignition system could produce serious or fatal shocks.

4. Crank the engine over with the starter. A fat blue spark should be evident across the spark plug electrodes.

5A. If a spark is obtained in Step 4, the problem is not in the breakerless ignition or coil. Check the fuel system and spark plugs.

5B. If no spark is obtained, proceed with the following tests.

Testing

Test procedures for troubleshooting the ignition system for are found in the diagnostic chart in **Figure 11**. A multimeter, as described in Chapter One, is required to perform the test procedures.

Before beginning actual troubleshooting, read the entire test procedure (**Figure 11**). When required, the diagnostic chart will refer you to a certain procedure in this chapter for testing.

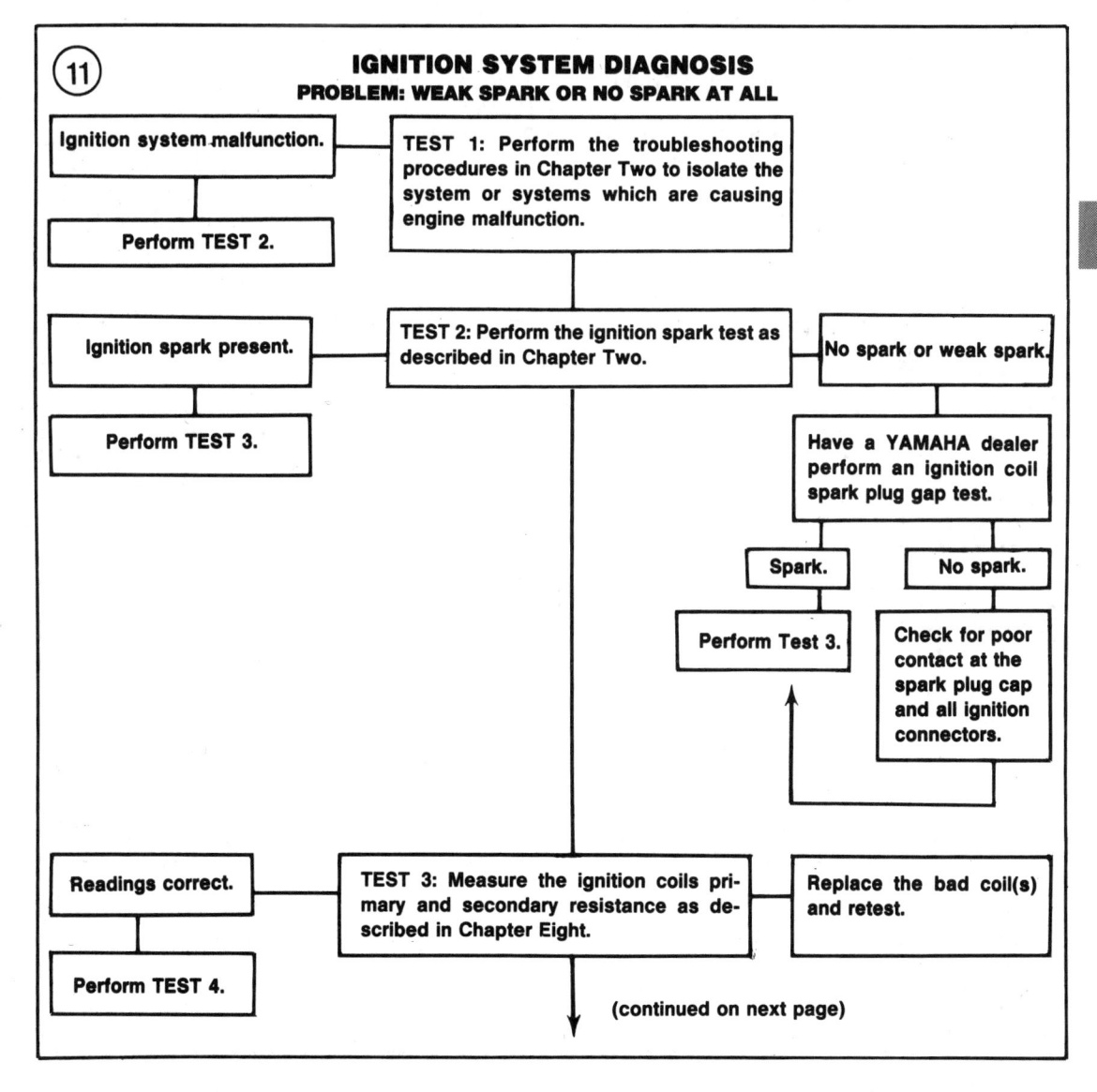

11. IGNITION SYSTEM DIAGNOSIS
PROBLEM: WEAK SPARK OR NO SPARK AT ALL

- Ignition system malfunction. → Perform TEST 2.
- TEST 1: Perform the troubleshooting procedures in Chapter Two to isolate the system or systems which are causing engine malfunction.
- Ignition spark present. → Perform TEST 3.
- TEST 2: Perform the ignition spark test as described in Chapter Two.
- No spark or weak spark. → Have a YAMAHA dealer perform an ignition coil spark plug gap test.
  - Spark. → Perform Test 3.
  - No spark. → Check for poor contact at the spark plug cap and all ignition connectors.
- Readings correct. → Perform TEST 4.
- TEST 3: Measure the ignition coils primary and secondary resistance as described in Chapter Eight.
- Replace the bad coil(s) and retest.

(continued on next page)

Pick-Up Coil
Testing

1. Remove the seat and the left-hand side cover.

NOTE
FZX750 and FZ750 models use 2 pick-up coils; FZ700 models use 1 pick-up coil.

2. Disconnect the pick-up coil connector at the igniter (A, **Figure 12**). The connector wire colors used are:
   a. FZX700 and FZ750: 3 wires (gray, orange and black).
   b. FZ700: 2 wires (gray and black).

3A. *FZX700 and FZ700*: Use an ohmmeter set on R×100 to measure the pick-up coil resistance between the following terminals:
   a. Pick-up coil for No. 1 and No. 4 cylinders: Black to orange.
   b. Pick-up coil for No. 2 and No. 3 cylinders: Black to gray.

3B. *FZ700*: Use an ohmmeter set on R×100 and measure the pick-up coil resistance between the gray and black terminals.

4. Compare the pick-up coil readings to the specifications in **Table 1**. Replace the pick-up coil(s) if it does not meet the test specifications.

Pick-up Coil
Removal/Installation

1. Remove the seat and the left-hand side cover.
2. Disconnect the pick-up coil connector (A, **Figure 12**) at the igniter.
3. Remove the screw and pull the pick-up coil assembly out of the upper crankcase (**Figure 13**). On FZ700 models, the pick-up coil is mounted on the right-hand side (**Figure 13**). On FZX700 and FZ750 models, pick-up coils are installed on both sides of the crankcase.
4. Install by reversing these steps. Check the pick-up coil O-ring and replace it if worn or damaged.

Ignition Coil
Testing

Refer to **Figure 14** for this procedure.

1. Remove the ignition coils as described in this chapter.
2. Measure the coil primary resistance using an ohmmeter set at R×1. Measure between the coil's primary terminals as shown in **Figure 15**. The correct primary resistance is listed in **Table 1**.
3. Measure the secondary resistance using an ohmmeter set at R×100. Connect the ohmmeter

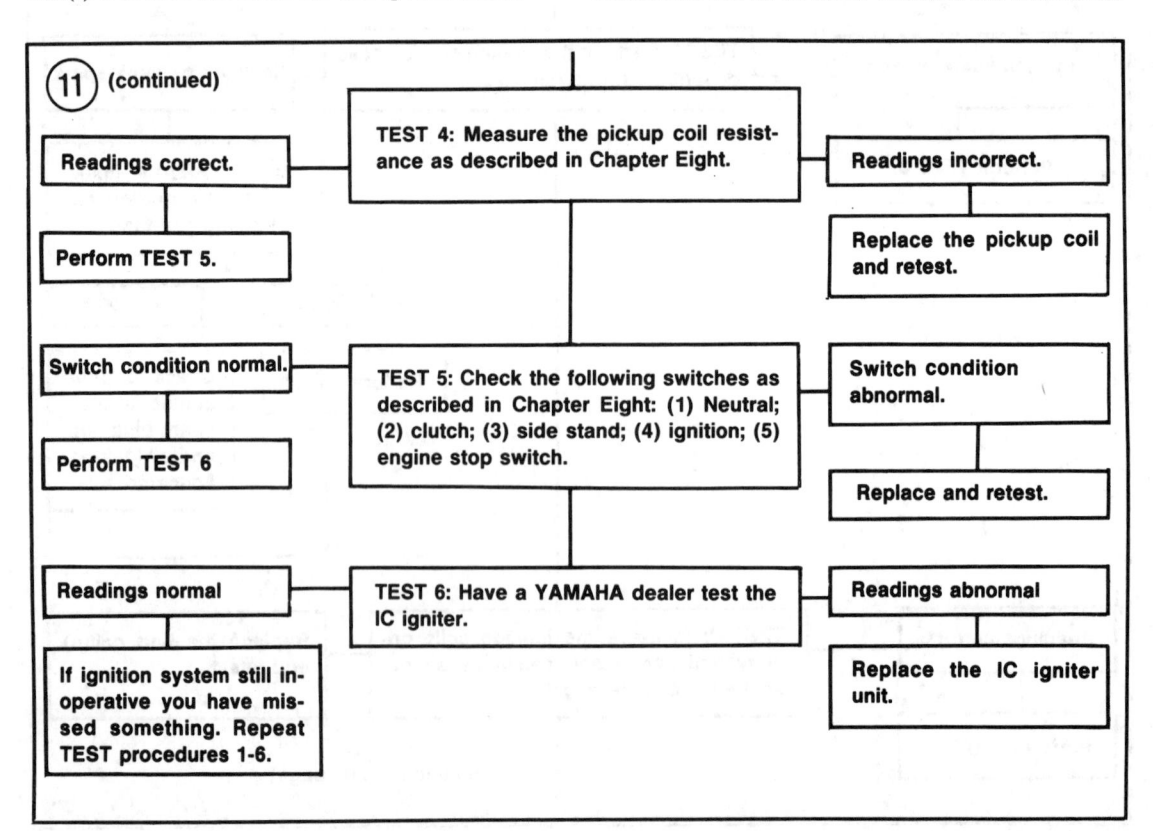

---

(11) (continued)

- Readings correct. → **TEST 4:** Measure the pickup coil resistance as described in Chapter Eight. → Readings incorrect. → Replace the pickup coil and retest.
- Perform TEST 5.
- Switch condition normal. → **TEST 5:** Check the following switches as described in Chapter Eight: (1) Neutral; (2) clutch; (3) side stand; (4) ignition; (5) engine stop switch. → Switch condition abnormal. → Replace and retest.
- Perform TEST 6
- Readings normal → **TEST 6:** Have a YAMAHA dealer test the IC igniter. → Readings abnormal → Replace the IC igniter unit.
- If ignition system still inoperative you have missed something. Repeat TEST procedures 1-6.

ELECTRICAL SYSTEM

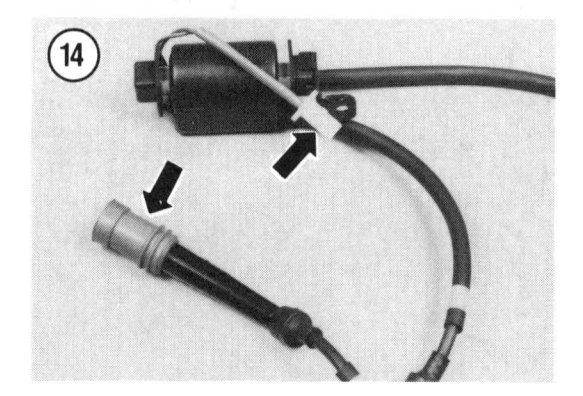

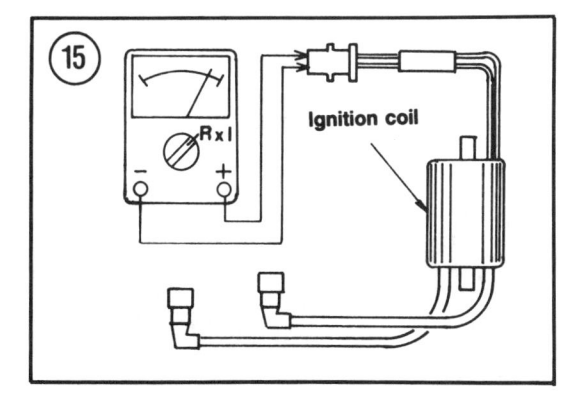

as shown in **Figure 16**. The correct secondary resistance is listed in **Table 1**.

4. Replace the ignition coil(s) if it doesn't test within the specifications in Step 2 or Step 3.

Spark Plug Cap
Testing

1. Disconnect the spark plug cap at the spark plug(s).
2. Pull the spark plug cap off of the ignition coil high tension wire.
3. Check the spark plug resistance with an ohmmeter. Attach the ohmmeter leads to both ends of the spark plug cap (**Figure 17**).
4. Replace the spark plug cap if the resistance exceeds the specification in **Table 1**.
5. Repeat for each spark plug cap.

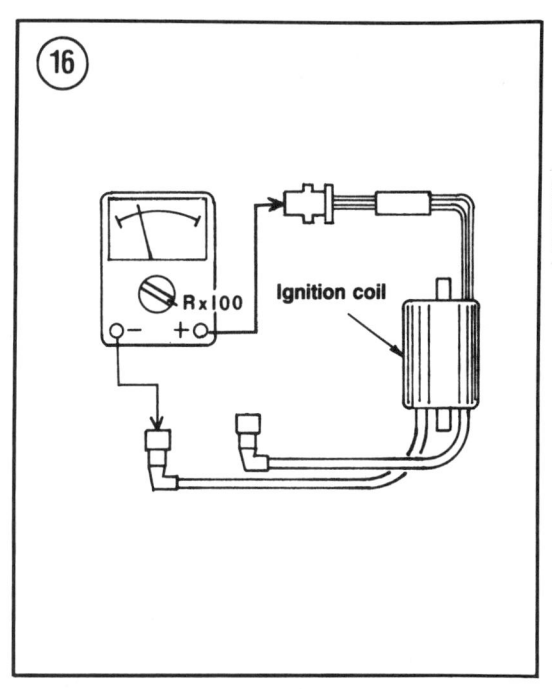

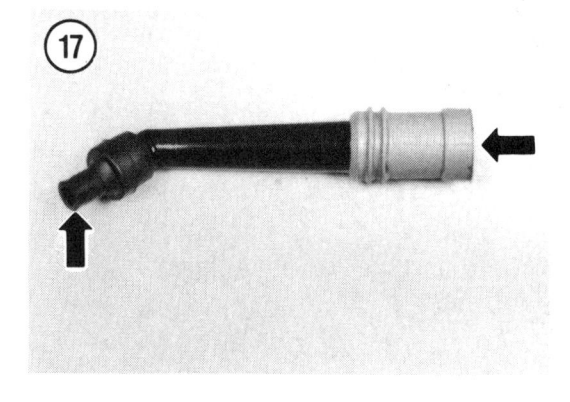

Ignition Coil
Removal/Installation

1. *FZ700 and FZ750*: Remove the lower fairing assembly. See Chapter Thirteen.
2. Remove the seat and fuel tank.
3. Disconnect the spark plug leads and the primary electrical connectors (A, **Figure 18**).
4. Remove the ignition coil mounting screws (**Figure 19**) and remove the ignition coil (B, **Figure 18**).

NOTE
On FZ700 models, don't lose the 2 rubber insulators on each end of the coil.

5. Repeat for the opposite coil.
6. Install by reversing these steps. On FZ700 models, make sure the rubber insulators are installed as shown in **Figure 20**.

Switches

Test the following switches as described under *Switches* in this chapter.
   a. Neutral switch.
   b. Side stand switch.
   c. Main switch.
   d. Left handlebar switch.

Sidestand Relay

Test the sidestand relay as described under *Electrical Components* in this chapter.

Igniter Check

A special Yamaha tester is necessary to check out the igniter (B, **Figure 12**). Refer the igniter to your Yamaha dealer or a qualified specialist for this test.

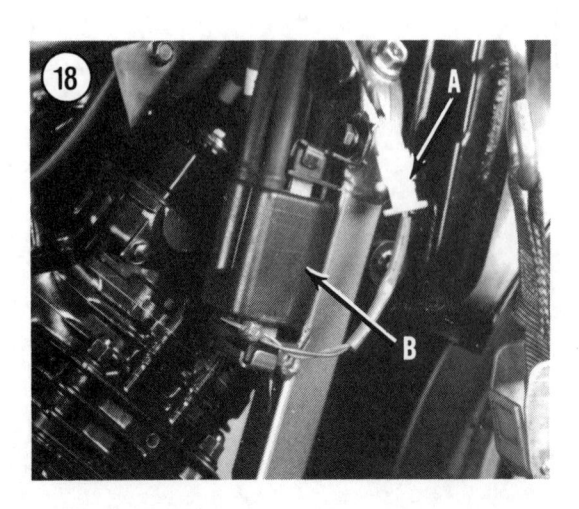

ELECTRICAL SYSTEM

Igniter
Removal/Installation

1. Remove the left-hand side cover.
2. Unplug the 2 connectors at the igniter.
3. Remove the igniter mounting bolts and remove the igniter (B, **Figure 12**).
4. Installation is the reverse of these steps. Note the following:
   a. Check the rubber igniter mount for cracks or damage. Replace the mount if necessary.
   b. Clean the connector with electrical contact cleaner before assembly.

ELECTRIC STARTER

The starter circuit includes the starter button, starter relay, battery and starter motor.

Removal/Installation

1. *FZ700*: Remove the lower fairing as described in Chapter Thirteen.
2. Remove the fuel tank as described in Chapter Seven.
3. Remove the sprocket cover as described under *Sprocket Cover Removal/Installation* in Chapter Six.
4. Remove the generator as described in this chapter.
5. Disconnect the cable at the starter.
6. Remove the starter mounting bolts and pull the starter (**Figure 21**) away from the crankcase.
7. Install by reversing these removal steps. Note the following.
8. Apply engine oil to the starter O-ring (**Figure 22**) before assembly.

Disassembly/Reassembly

Starter motor repair is generally a job for an electrical shop or a Yamaha dealer. The following procedure describes how to check overall starter condition. Refer to **Figure 23**.

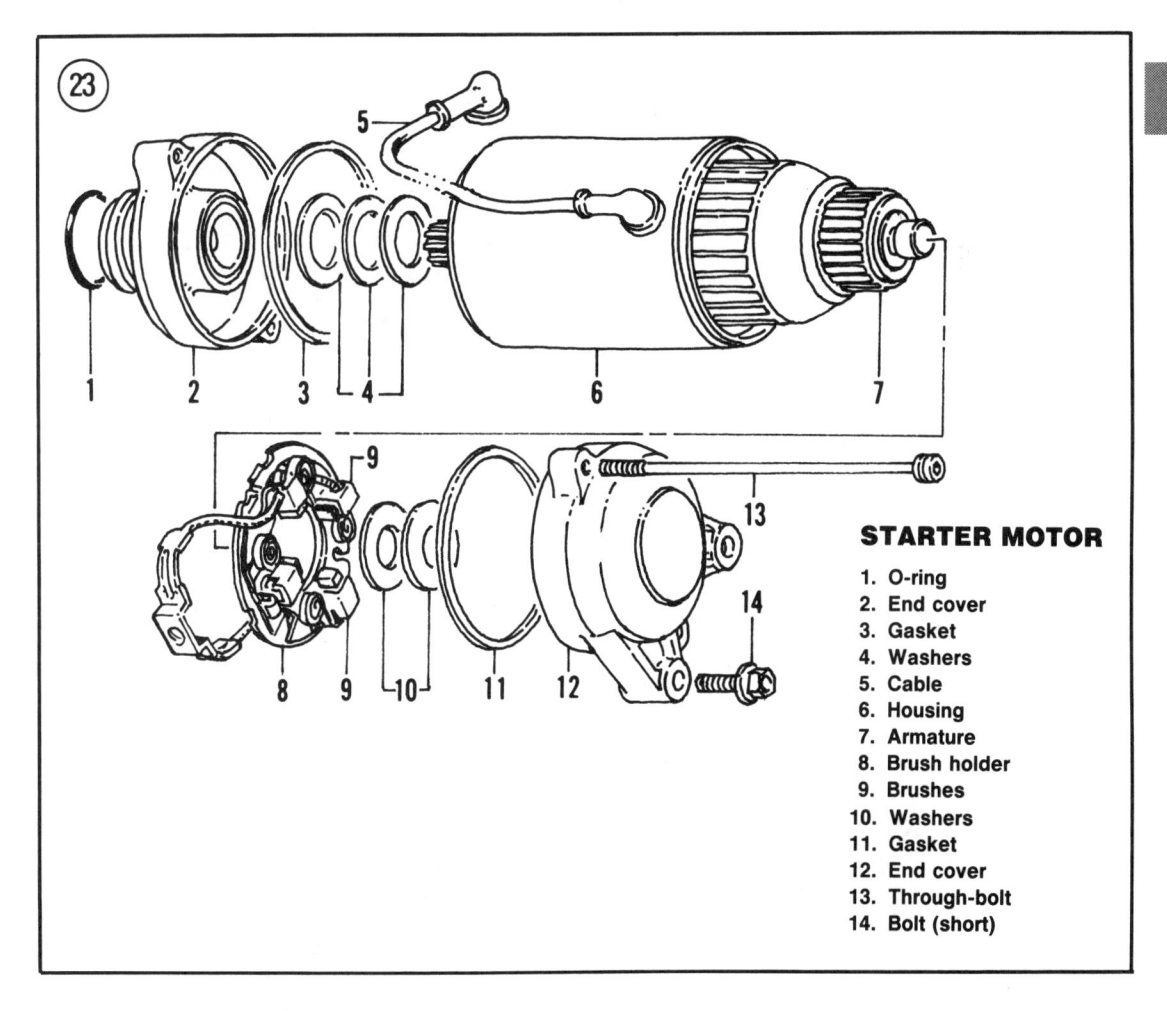

STARTER MOTOR

1. O-ring
2. End cover
3. Gasket
4. Washers
5. Cable
6. Housing
7. Armature
8. Brush holder
9. Brushes
10. Washers
11. Gasket
12. End cover
13. Through-bolt
14. Bolt (short)

1. Remove the 2 starter bolts (**Figure 24**) and remove the 2 end covers (2 and 12, **Figure 23**).
2. Slide the armature (7) out of the housing (6).
3. Measure the length of each brush with a vernier caliper (**Figure 25**). If the length is less than specified in **Table 1**, it must be replaced. Replace the brushes as a set even though only one may be worn to this dimension.
4. Inspect the condition of the commutator. The mica in a good commutator is below the surface of the copper bars. On a worn commutator the mica and copper bars may be worn to the same level. See **Figure 26**. If necessary, have the commutator serviced by a dealer or electrical repair shop.
5. Use an ohmmeter and check for continuity between the commutator bars (**Figure 27**); there should be continuity between pairs of bars. Also check continuity between the commutator bars and the shaft (**Figure 28**); there should be no continuity. If the unit fails either of these tests the armature is faulty and must be replaced.
6. Use an ohmmeter and inspect the field coil by checking continuity between the starter cable terminal and the starter case; there should be no continuity. Also check continuity between the starter cable terminal and each brush wire terminal; there should be continuity. If the unit fails either of these tests, the case/field coil assembly must be replaced.
7. Connect one probe of an ohmmeter to the brush holder plate and the other probe to each of the positive (insulated) brush holders; there should be no continuity. If the unit fails at either brush holder, the brush holder assembly should be replaced.
8. Assemble the starter as follows:
   a. Slide the brushes (9) out of their holders.
   b. Slide the armature (7) into the housing.

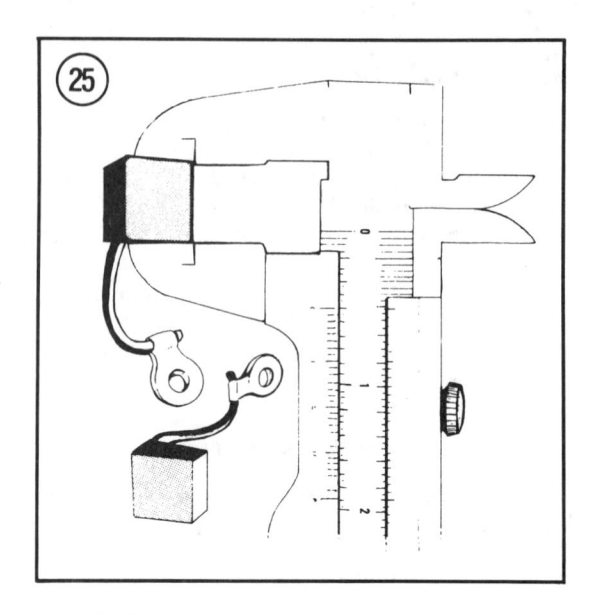

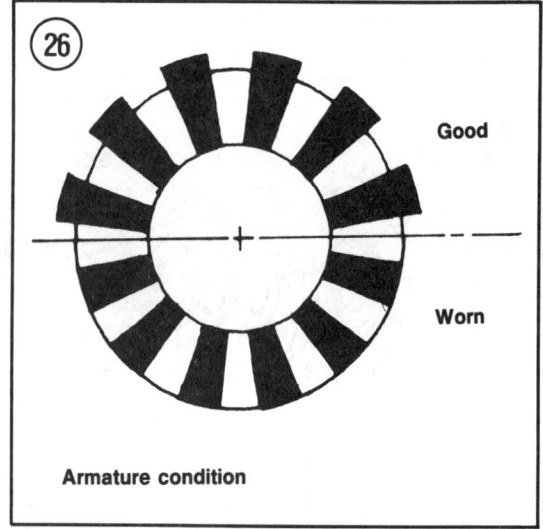

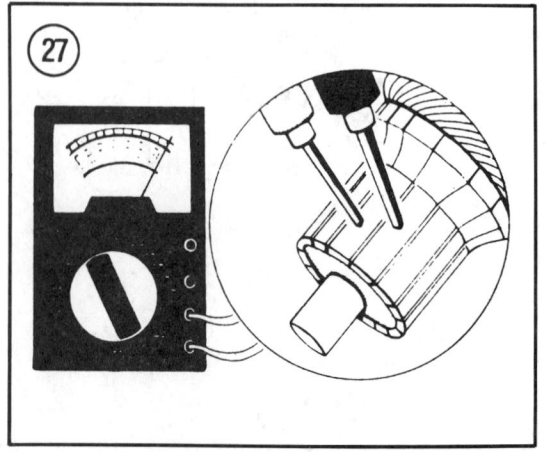

ELECTRICAL SYSTEM

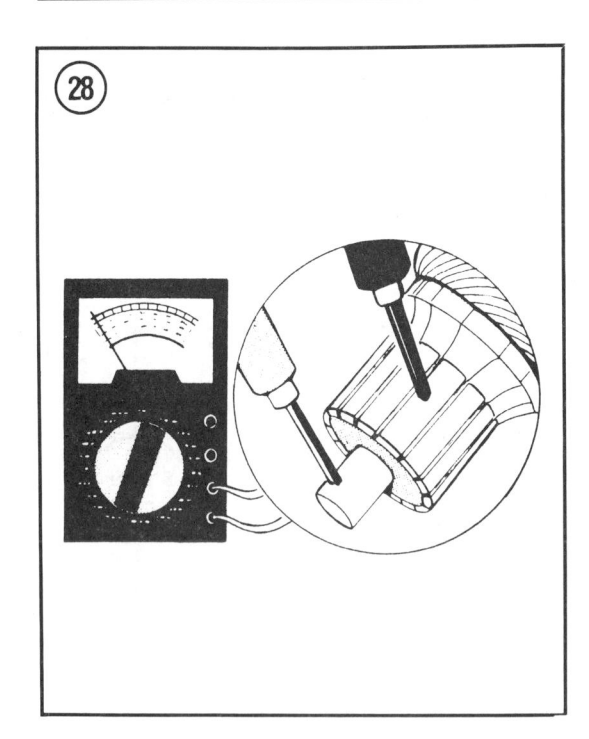

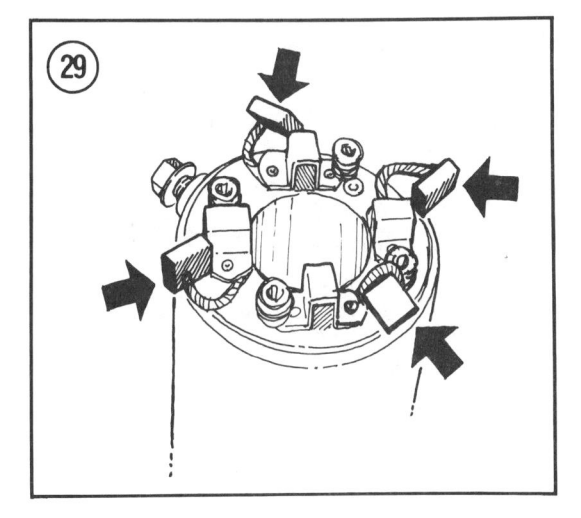

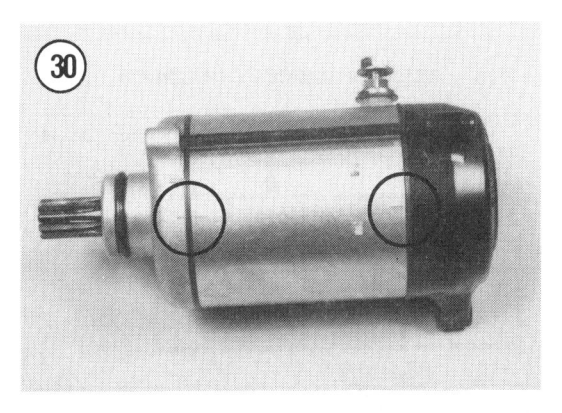

c. Align the brush plate with the housing and fit the brushes into their holders (**Figure 29**).

d. Install the end covers; align the marks on the end covers with the marks on the housing (**Figure 30**). Install the 2 bolts (**Figure 24**) and tighten securely.

Starter Troubleshooting

If the starter does not operate, check the main fuse. If it is good, perform the following.

1. Remove the seat and fuel tank.

WARNING
The jumper cable installed in Step 2 must be the same gauge as that of the battery leads or the jumper cable may burn.

2. Connect a jumper wire across the starter relay terminals as shown in **Figure 31**. The starter relay is shown in **Figure 32**.

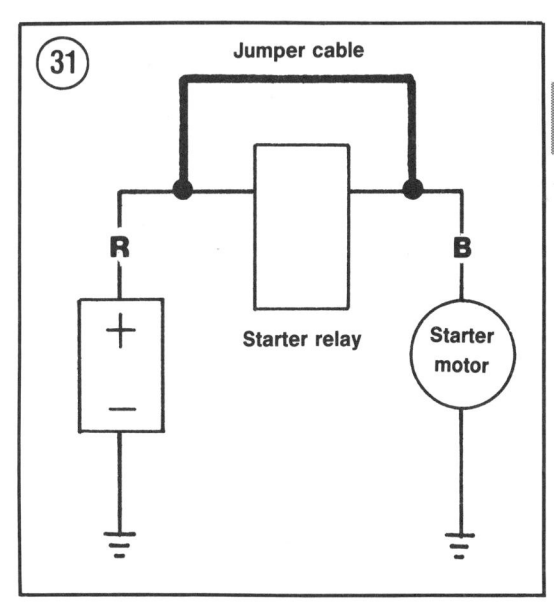

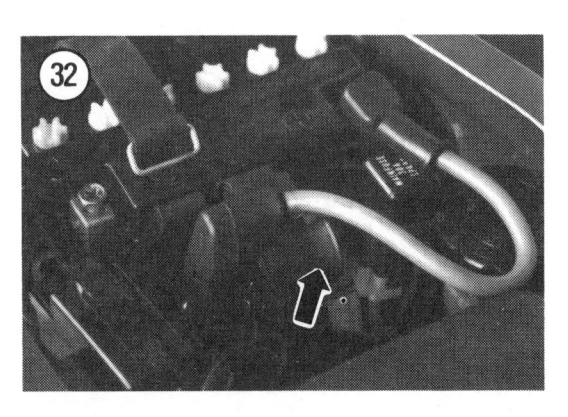

NOTE
When it is required to operate the starter in the following procedures, turn the main switch to ON and the engine stop switch to RUN. Shift the transmission into NEUTRAL and push the starter button. Turn the main switch off after performing each test.

3. Operate the starter. Interpret results as follows:
   a. Starter does not turn: Check the battery as described in Chapter Three. Recharge the battery if necessary. If the battery is okay, remove the starter and check the brushes and armature as described in this chapter.
   b. Starter turns: Perform Step 4.
4. Disconnect the starter relay blue/white connector and connect a jumper wire from the connector to ground as shown in **Figure 33**. Operate the starter. Interpret results as follows:
   a. Starter turns: Replace the starter relay.
   b. Starter does not turn: Perform Step 5.
5A. *FZX700*: Disconnect the flasher relay electrical connector. The flasher relay is located underneath the starter.
5B. *FZ700 and FZ750*: Disconnect the flasher relay assembly electrical connector. The relay assembly is located in the front fairing assembly (**Figure 34**).
6. Connect a jumper wire between the 2 blue/white coupler terminals on the wire harness side (**Figure 35**). Operate the starter. Interpret results as follows:
   a. Starter does not turn: Check the starter safety unit as described in this chapter. If the starter switch is okay, there is a faulty wire connection between the starter switch and the starter relay. Repair the connection and retest.
   b. Starter turns: Perform Step 7.
7. Refer to **Figure 36**. Perform the following:
   a. Disconnect the connector at the igniter (**Figure 37**).
   b. Disconnect the sidestand switch connector (**Figure 38**).
   c. Connect an ohmmeter to the igniter black and black/white terminals on the wire harness side (**Figure 36**).
   d. Connect a jumper wire to the sidestand switch black and blue/yellow terminals on the wire harness side (**Figure 36**).
   e. Check the resistance on the ohmmeter. It should read infinity. If the reading is incorrect, replace the sidestand relay. If the reading is correct, perform Step 8.
   f. Remove the ohmmeter and reconnect the igniter connector (**Figure 37**).

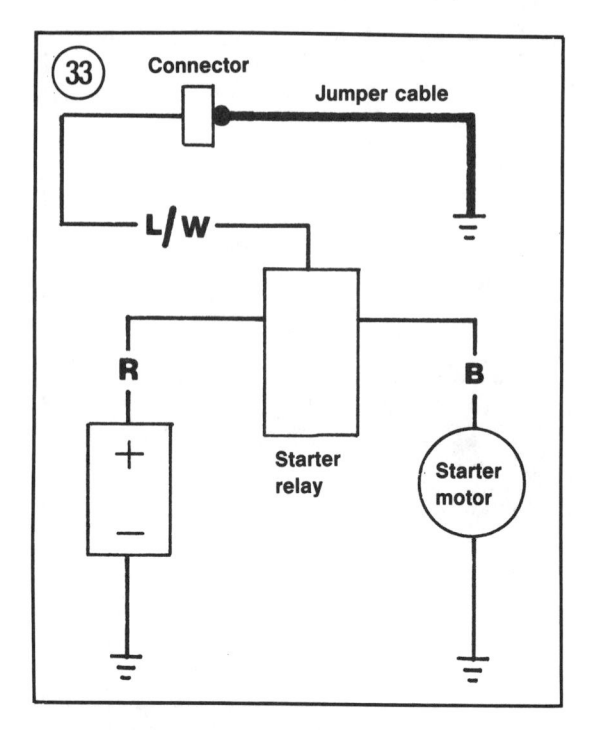

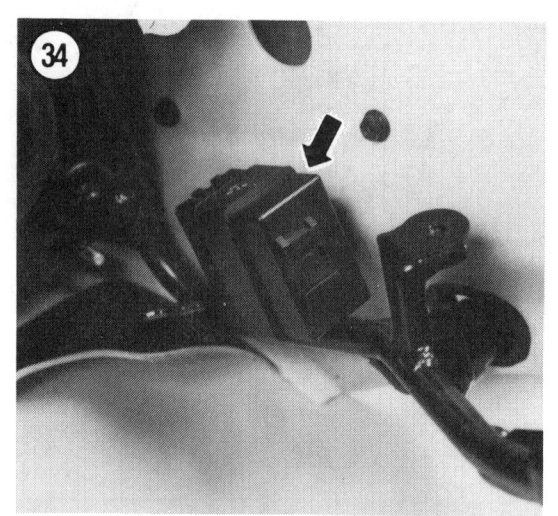

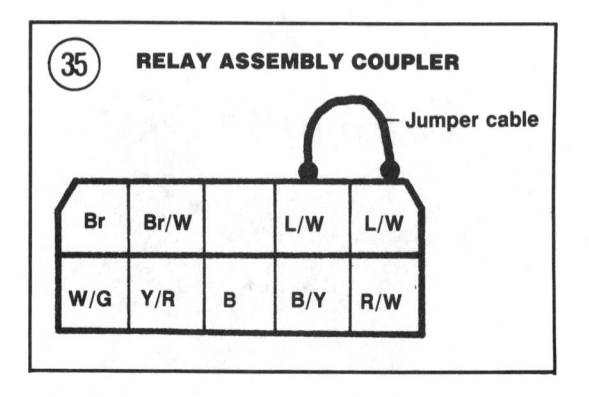

ELECTRICAL SYSTEM

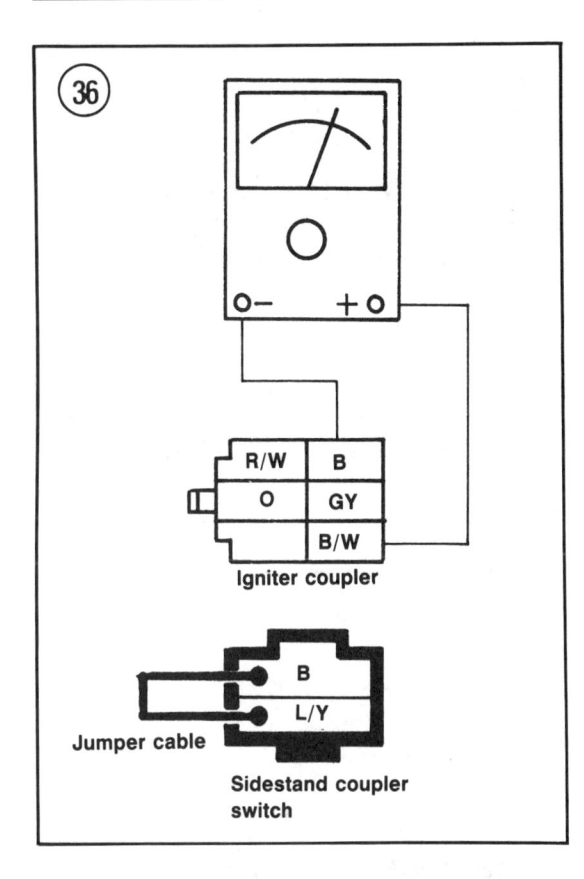

8. Connect a jumper wire from the sidestand switch blue/yellow terminal (on the wire harness side) to ground (**Figure 39**). Then perform the following:
   a. Turn the main switch ON.
   b. Turn the engine stop switch to RUN.
   c. Pull the clutch lever in and shift the transmission into gear.
9. Push the starter button. Interpret results as follows:
   a. Starter turns: Check the sidestand switch, neutral switch and diode as described in this chapter.
   b. Starter does not turn: Check the clutch switch as described in this chapter; replace if necessary. If the clutch switch is okay, replace the flasher relay assembly disconnected in Step 5.
10. Reconnect all connectors disassembled in this procedure.

Starter Relay
Removal/Installation

The starter relay (**Figure 32**) is installed underneath the seat.
1. Remove the seat.
2. Make sure the ignition switch is turned off.
3. Label and disconnect the wires at the starter relay (**Figure 32**) and pull it out of its holder.
4. Install by reversing these steps.

LIGHTING SYSTEM

The lighting system consists of the headlight, taillight/brakelight combination, directional signals, warning lights and speedometer and tachometer illumination lights. In the event of trouble with any light, the first thing to check is the affected bulb itself. If the bulb is good, check all wiring and connections with a test light. Replacement bulbs are listed in **Table 2**.

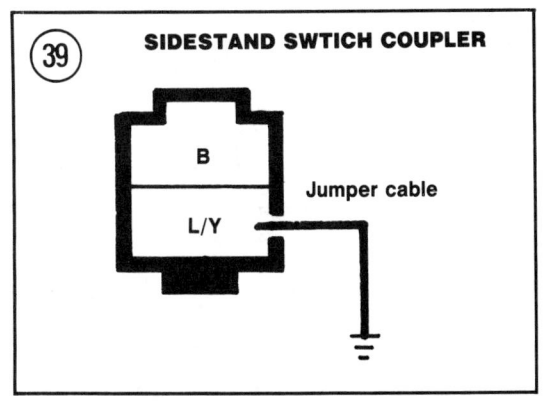

Headlight Replacement

> *CAUTION*
> *All models are equipped with quartz-halogen bulbs. Do not touch the bulb glass with your fingers because traces of oil on the bulb will drastically reduce the life of the bulb. Clean any traces of oil from the bulb with a cloth moistened in alcohol or lacquer thinner.*

> *WARNING*
> *If the headlight has just burned out or turned off it will be **hot**. Don't touch the bulb until it cools off.*

FZX700

1. Remove the 2 screws securing the headlight assembly (**Figure 40**).
2. Unplug the connector at the headlight assembly.
3. Turn the bulb holder counterclockwise (**Figure 41**) and lift the bulb out of the headlight assembly.
4. Install by reversing these steps.

FZ700 and FZ750

1. Remove the upper fairing as described in Chapter Thirteen.

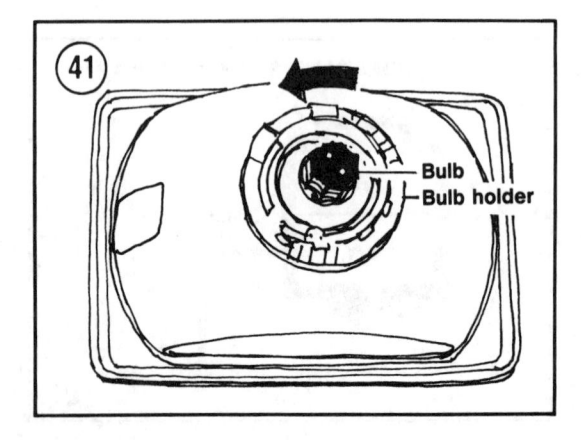

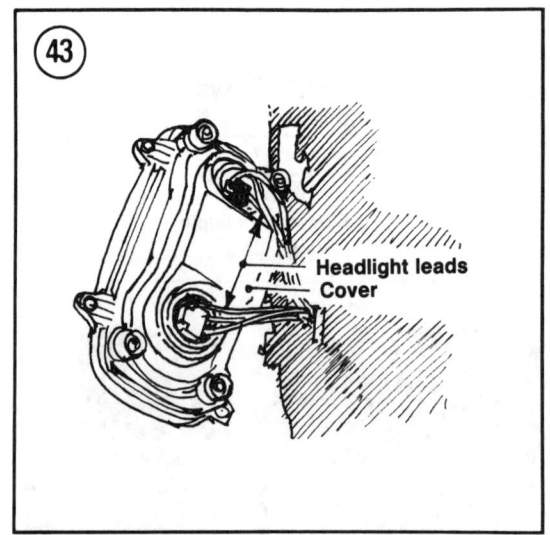

ELECTRICAL SYSTEM

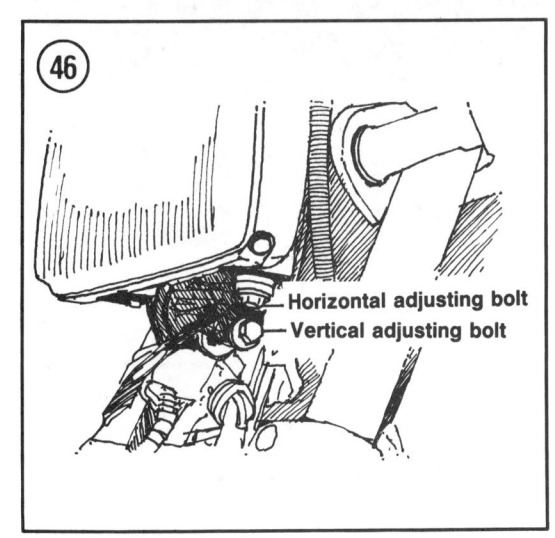

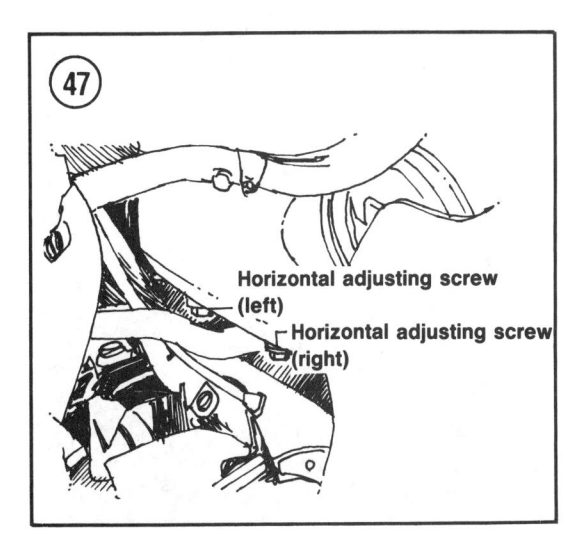

2. Remove the screws securing the headlight housing (**Figure 42**) and pull the housing away from the frame.
3. Unplug the connectors (**Figure 43**) at the headlight bulbs.
4. Remove the rear headlight housing cover (**Figure 43**).
5. Remove the bulb springs and lift the bulb(s) out of the housing. See **Figure 44** and **Figure 45**.
6. Install by reversing these steps.

Headlight Adjustment

Adjust the headlight horizontally and vertically according to the Department of Motor Vehicles regulations in your area.

When performing this procedure, make sure the tire pressure is correct and that the fuel tank is approximately 1/2 full to full. Have an assistant sit on the seat.

FZX700

1. Remove the cover below the headlight.
2. There are 2 adjustments: horizontal and vertical. The adjusters are identified in **Figure 46**; horizontal and vertical. Turn the adjusters as required.
3. Reinstall the cover.

FZ700 and FZ750

These models are equipped with dual headlights. Each headlight must be adjusted individually.

1. *Horizontal adjustment*: To adjust the beam to the right, turn the adjusting screw clockwise. To adjust the beam to the left, turn the screw counterclockwise. See **Figure 47**.
2. *Vertical adjustment*: To lower the beam, turn the screw counterclockwise. To raise the beam, turn the screw clockwise. See **Figure 48**.

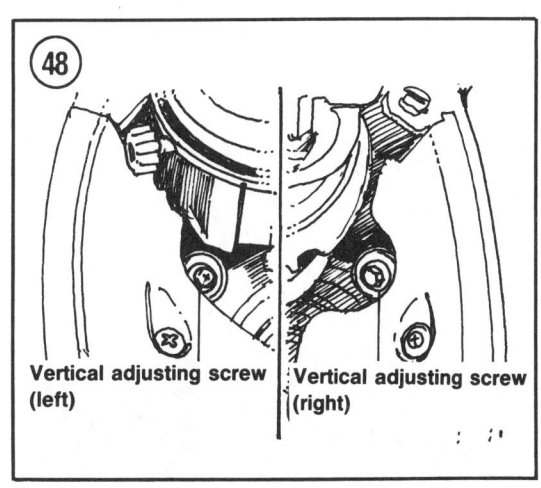

CHAPTER EIGHT

Taillight Replacement

1. Remove the seat.

NOTE
The rear tail panel is shown removed in the following procedure for clarity only; it is not necessary to remove the panel for taillight bulb replacement.

2. Remove the tool kit (**Figure 49**).
3. Turn the bulb holder counterclockwise (**Figure 50**) and remove it from the housing.
4. Turn the bulb (**Figure 51**) counterclockwise and remove it.
5. Push the new bulb into the socket and turn it clockwise to lock it in position.
6. Align the bulb holder and turn it clockwise to lock it in the housing.
7. Reverse Step 1 and Step 2 to complete installation.
8. Check bulb operation.

Directional Signal Light Replacement

Remove the lens securing screws and the lens (**Figure 52**). Wash the inside and outside of it with a mild detergent. Replace the bulb (**Figure 53**). Install the lens; do not overtighten the screws as that will crack the lens.

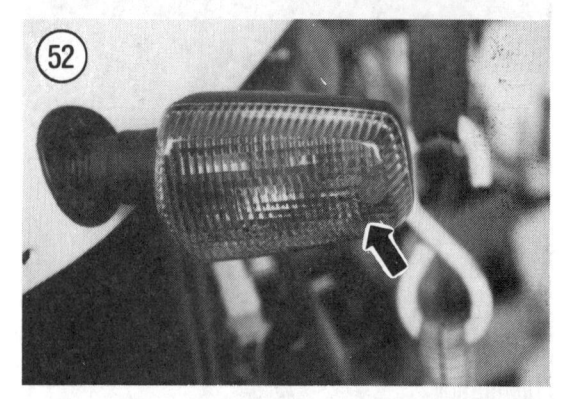

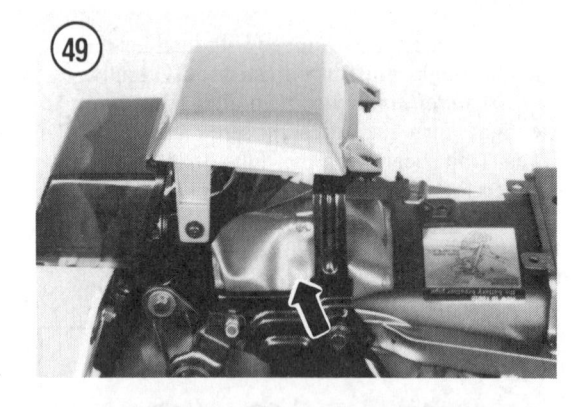

ELECTRICAL SYSTEM

55 HORN BUTTON

	Blk	Pink
FREE		
PUSH ON	O—————O	

56 MAIN SWITCH

	Red	Br	Blue
P	O———————O		
OFF			
ON	O———O———O		

57 ENGINE STOP SWITCH

	R/B	R/W
OFF		
RUN	O—————O	

58 DIMMER SWITCH

	Yel	Blu/Blk	Grn
HI	O———O		
LO		O———O	

59 TURN SWITCH

		Ch	Brn/White	Dk. Grn	Yel/Red	Blk
N	L	O———O			O———O	
	L	O———O				
	N					
	R		O———O			
	R		O———O		O———O	

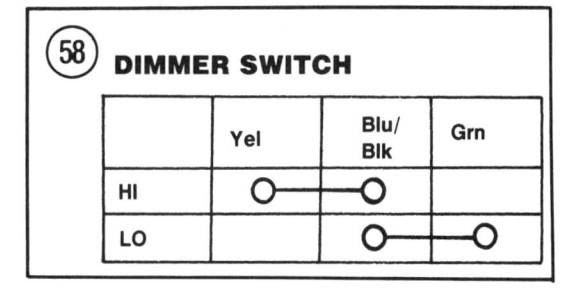

Speedometer and Tachometer Illumination Bulb Replacement

1A. *FZX700*: Remove the speedometer and tachometer covers.
1B. *FZ700 and FZ750*: Remove the upper fairing assembly as described in Chapter Thirteen.
2. Remove the socket from the meter assembly and remove the bulb. See **Figure 54**, typical.
3. Install a new bulb and push the socket into the meter.
4. Installation is the reverse of these steps.

SWITCHES

Switches can be tested for continuity with an ohmmeter (see Chapter One) or a test light at the switch connector plug by operating the switch in each of its operating positions and comparing results with the switch operation. For example, **Figure 55** shows a continuity diagram for a typical horn button. It shows which terminals should show continuity when the horn button is in a given position.

When the horn button is pushed, there should be continuity between terminals black and pink. This is indicated by the line on the continuity diagram. An ohmmeter connected between these 2 terminals should indicate little or no resistance and a test lamp should light. When the horn button is free, there should be no continuity between the same terminals.

If the switch or button doesn't perform properly, replace it. Refer to the following figures when testing the switches:
 a. Main switch: **Figure 56**.
 b. Engine stop switch: **Figure 57**.
 c. Dimmer switch: **Figure 58**.
 d. Turn switch: **Figure 59**.

e. Brake switch: **Figure 60**.
f. Starter switch: **Figure 61**.
g. Clutch switch: **Figure 62**.

When testing switches, note the following:
a. First check the fuses as described under *Fuses* in this chapter.
b. Check the battery as described under *Battery* in Chapter Three; bring the battery to the correct state of charge, if required.
c. Disconnect the negative cable from the battery if the switch connectors are not disconnected in the circuit.

CAUTION
Do not attempt to start the engine with the battery negative cable disconnected or you will damage the wiring.

d. When separating 2 connectors, pull on the connector housings and not the wires.
e. After locating a defective circuit, check the connectors to make sure they are clean and properly connected. Check all wires going into a connector housing to make sure each wire is properly positioned and that the wire end is not loose.
f. To properly connect connectors, push them together until they click into place.
g. When replacing handlebar switch assemblies, make sure the cables are routed correctly so that they are not crimped when the handlebar is turned from side to side.

Neutral Switch Test

Test the neutral switch as follows:
1. Remove the seat and the left-hand side cover.
2. Remove the sprocket cover as described in Chapter Six.
3. Disconnect the neutral switch electrical connector (**Figure 63**).
4. Connect an ohmmeter red lead to the neutral switch sky blue terminal and the ohmmeter black lead to ground. Switch the ohmmeter to the R×1 scale. Interpret results as follows:
   a. Transmission in NEUTRAL: Ohmmeter should read 0 ohms.
   b. Transmission in gear: Ohmmeter should read infinity.
5. If the neutral switch failed either test in Step 4, replace it as described in Chapter Six.

Sidestand Switch

Test the sidestand switch as follows:
1. Disconnect the sidestand switch electrical connector (**Figure 64**).

(60) BRAKE SWITCH

	Br	G/Y
Brake lever or Pedal Free		
Brake Lever or Pedal Depressed		O—O

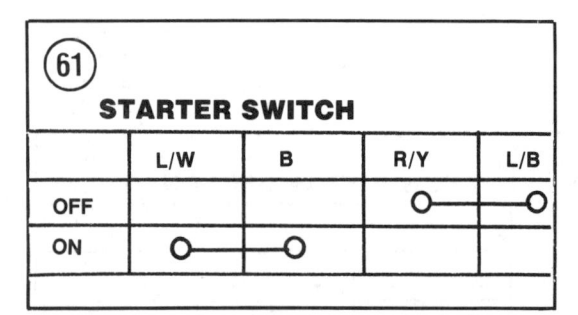

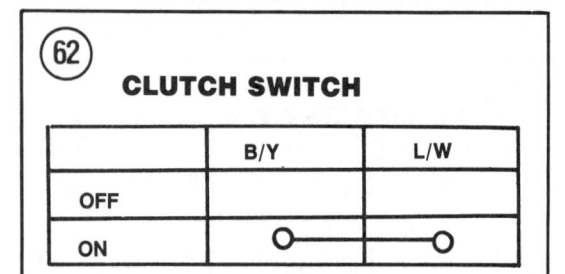

(61) STARTER SWITCH

	L/W	B	R/Y	L/B
OFF			O—O	
ON	O—O			

(62) CLUTCH SWITCH

	B/Y	L/W
OFF		
ON	O—O	

ELECTRICAL SYSTEM

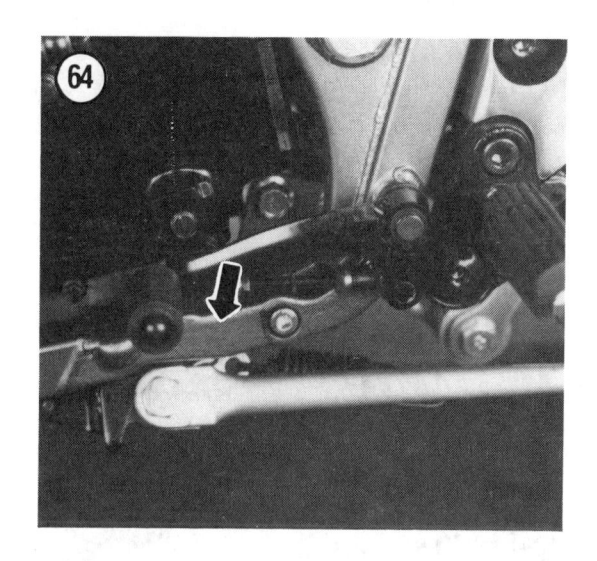

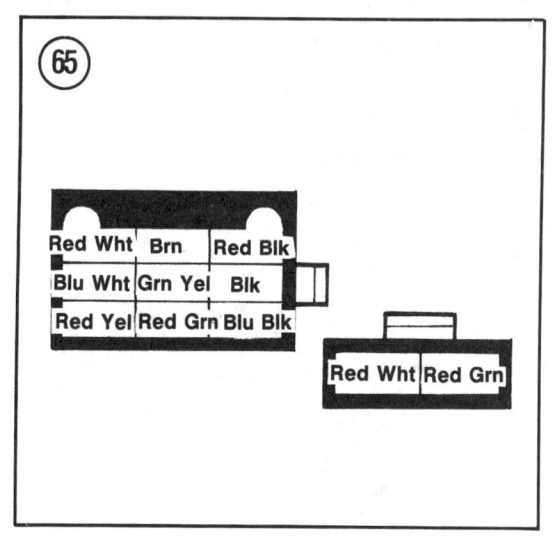

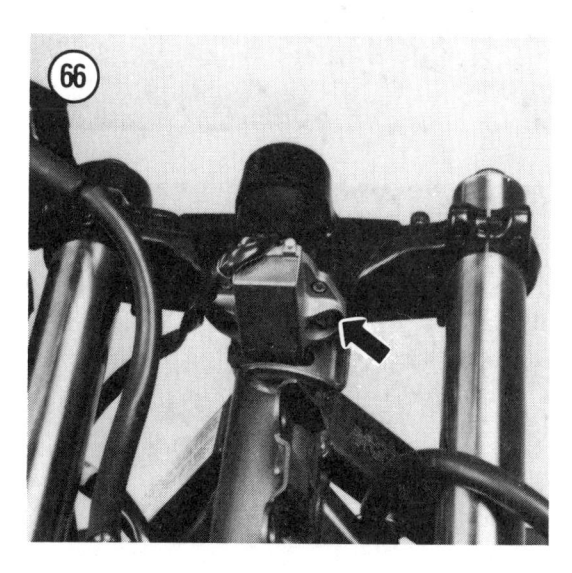

2. Connect an ohmmeter red lead to the sidestand switch blue/yellow terminal and the ohmmeter black lead to ground. Switch the ohmmeter to the R×1 scale. Interpret results as follows:
   a. Sidestand up: Ohmmeter should read 0 ohms.
   b. Sidestand down: Ohmmeter should read infinity.
3. If the sidestand switch failed either test in Step 2, replace it as described in this chapter.

Fuel Reserve Switch Test

Test the fuel reserve switch as follows:
1A. *FZX700*: Remove the right reflector and the right frame cover.
1B. *FZ700 and FZ750*: Remove the left front fairing panel.
2. Disconnect the fuel reserve switch (**Figure 65**).
3. Connect an ohmmeter red lead to the fuel reserve switch red/white terminal and the ohmmeter black lead to the red/green terminal. Switch the ohmmeter to the R×1 scale. Interpret results as follows:
   a. Fuel reserve switch in the RES position: Ohmmeter should read 0 ohms.
   b. Fuel reserve switch in the ON position: Ohmmeter should read infinity.
4. If the fuel reserve switch failed either test in Step 3, replace it as described in this chapter.

Main Switch Replacement

1A. *FZX700*: Remove the speedometer and tachometer assembly.
1B. *FZ700 and FZ750*: Remove the upper fairing assembly as described in Chapter Thirteen.
2. Disconnect the ignition switch electrical connector.
3. Remove the bolt securing the ignition switch to the steering stem and remove the switch (**Figure 66**).
4. Installation is the reverse of these steps.

Left Handlebar Switch Replacement

1. The left handlebar switch housing is equipped with the following switches:
   a. Dimmer.
   b. Turn signal.
   c. Horn.
2A. *FZX700*: Remove the headlight.
2B. *FZ700 and FZ750*: Remove the upper fairing as described in Chapter Thirteen.
3. Disconnect the switch connector(s).

4. Remove the switch housing screws and separate the housings.
5. Remove the switch housing and wiring harness. See **Figure 67**.
6. Installation is the reverse of these steps.

Right Handlebar Switch Replacement

1. The right handlebar switch housing is equipped with the following switches:
   a. Engine stop.
   b. Starter.
   c. Fuel reserve (FZX700).
2A. *FZX700*: Remove the headlight.
2B. *FZ700 and FZ750*: Remove the upper fairing as described in Chapter Thirteen.
3. Remove the switch housing screws and separate the housings. Disconnect the throttle cable.
4. Remove the switch housing and wiring harness.
5. Installation is the reverse of these steps. Adjust the throttle cable as described under *Throttle Cable Adjustment* in Chapter Three.

Fuel Reserve Switch (FZ700 and FZ750)

1. Pull the choke knob up (**Figure 68**). Then remove the choke knob screw and pull the knob off of the choke rod.
2. Remove the 2 screws and remove the panel cover (**Figure 69**).
3. Remove the side panel (**Figure 70**).
4. Unplug the fuel reserve switch connector.
5. Remove the fuel reserve switch mounting screw and lower the switch (**Figure 71**) out of the fairing assembly.
6. Install by reversing these steps.

Neutral Switch Replacement

Refer to *Neutral Switch Removal/Installation* in Chapter Six.

Oil Pressure Switch Replacement

Refer to *Oil Level Switch Removal/Installation* in Chapter Four.

ELECTRICAL SYSTEM

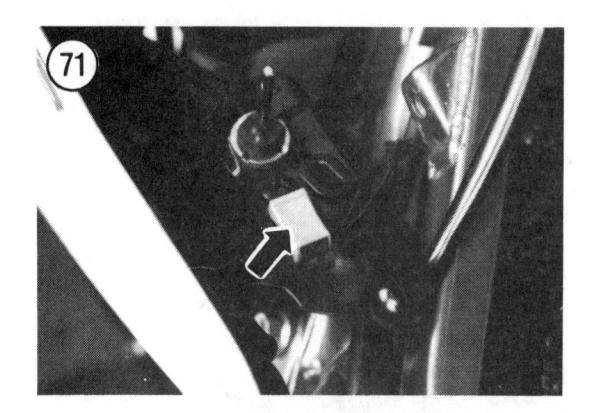

Front Brake Light Switch Replacement

The front brake switch is mounted underneath the front brake master cylinder (**Figure 72**). Disconnect the connector and remove the switch screw. Reverse to install. Check switch operation. The rear brake light should come on when applying the front brake lever.

NOTE
*The master cylinder is shown removed in **Figure 72** for clarity only. It is not necessary to disassemble or remove the master cylinder to remove the front brake light switch. If the master cylinder is removed, bleed the brake as described in Chapter Twelve.*

Rear Brake Light Switch Replacement

The rear brake switch is mounted on the right-hand side on the rear brake pedal mount (**Figure 73**).

1. *FZ700 and FZ750*: Remove the rear brake pedal mount (**Figure 74**).
2. Disconnect the electrical connector at the switch.
3. Disconnect the spring at the switch.
4. Unscrew the switch and remove it.
5. Screw a new switch into the switch mount. Attach the spring and plug-in the connector.
6. Adjust the rear brake switch as described under *Rear Brake Light Switch Adjustment* in Chapter Three.

Clutch Switch Replacement

The clutch switch is mounted underneath the front clutch master cylinder (**Figure 75**). Disconnect the connector and remove the switch screw. Reverse to install.

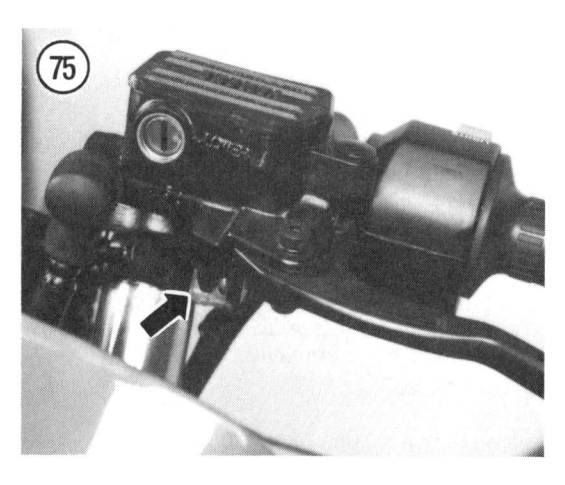

Sidestand Switch Replacement

The side stand switch is mounted on the kickstand (**Figure 76**).
1. Place the bike on its center stand. On FZ700 models, secure the bike without the use of the kickstand.
2. Pull the side stand down to gain access to the switch.
3. Disconnect the connector and remove the switch screws.
4. Install by reversing these steps.

WIRING CONNECTORS

Many electrical troubles can be traced to damaged wiring or connectors that are contaminated with dirt and oil. Connectors can be serviced by disconnecting them and cleaning with electrical contact cleaner. Multiple pin connectors should be packed with a dielectric silicone grease (available at most automotive supply stores).

ELECTRICAL COMPONENTS

This section contains information on electrical components other than switches covered under *Switches* in this chapter.

Instrument Cluster Removal/Installation

CAUTION
Whenever the instrument cluster is removed from the bike, it must be placed so that the gauges face up. If the meter is left in any other position it will become damaged.

FZX700

1. Place the bike on the center stand.
2. Remove the seat. Remove the fuel tank (see Chapter Seven).
3. Disconnect the cables at the gauges.
4. Remove the headlight assembly.
5. Disconnect the instrument cluster wiring harness connectors.
6. Remove the screws securing the instrument cluster bracket and remove the instrument cluster.

CAUTION
Do not turn or store the instrument cluster on its side or back as this would damage the instruments.

7. Install by reversing these steps.

FZ700 and FZ750

1. Disconnect the speedometer cable (**Figure 77**).
2. Remove the upper fairing assembly as described in Chapter Thirteen.
3. Disconnect the instrument cluster wiring harness connectors.

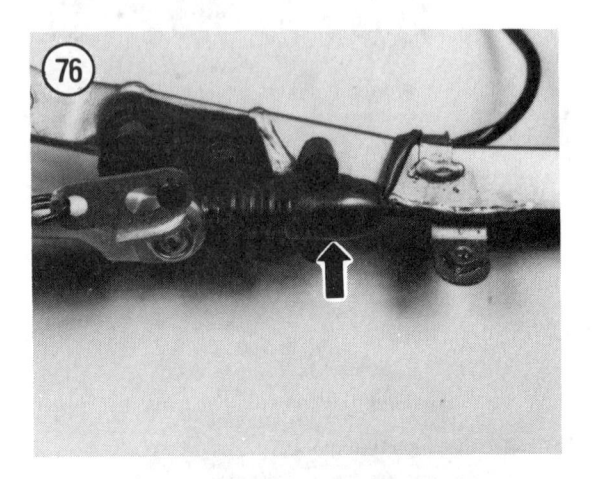

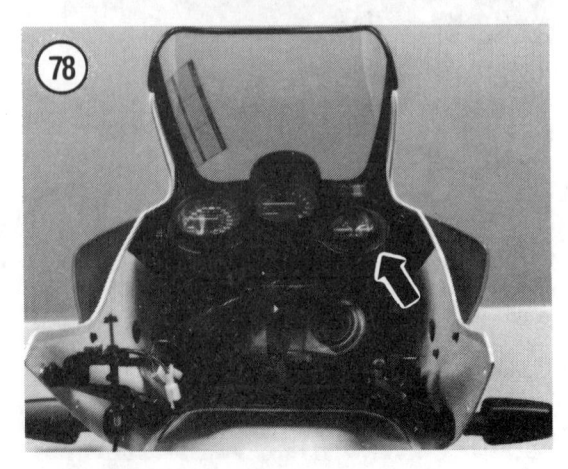

ELECTRICAL SYSTEM

4. Remove the screws securing the instrument cluster bracket and remove the instrument cluster (**Figure 78**).

> *CAUTION*
> *Do not turn or store the instrument cluster on its side or back as this would damage the instruments.*

5. Install by reversing these steps.

Water Temperature Sensor

1. Remove the water temperature sensor as described in Chapter Nine.
2. Fill a beaker or pan with water and place on a stove.
3. Mount the water temperature sensor so that the temperature sensing tip is submerged as shown in **Figure 79**.
4. Place a thermometer in the pan of water (use a cooking or candy thermometer that is rated higher than the test temperature).
5. Attach one ohmmeter lead to the fan switch terminal and the other lead to the body as shown in **Figure 79**. Check resistance as follows:
   a. Gradually heat the water.
   b. When the temperature rises to 122° F (50° C), the resistance should be 153.9 ohms.
   c. When the temperature rises to 176° F (80° C), the resistance should be 47.5-56.8 ohms.
   d. When the temperature rises to 212° F (100° C), the resistance should be 126.2-129.3 ohms.
6. Replace the temperature sensor if it failed to operate as described in Step 5.

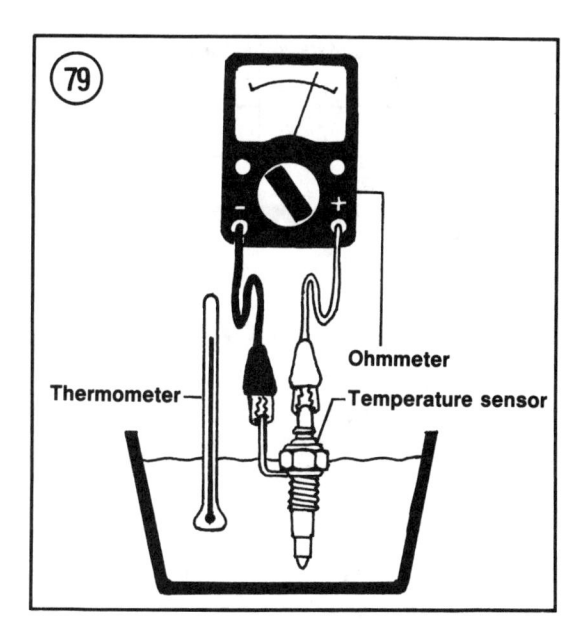

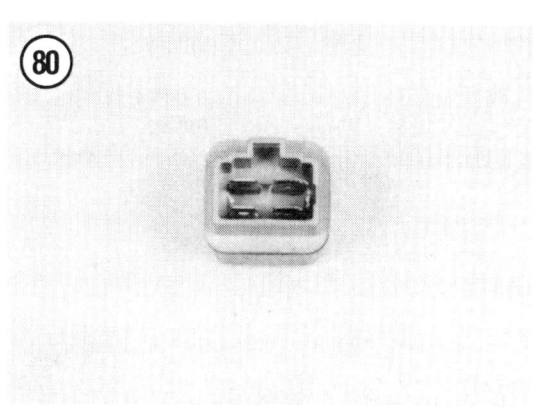

Thermostatic Switch
Testing

1. Remove the thermostatic switch as described in Chapter Nine.
2. Fill a beaker or pan with water and place on a stove.
3. Mount the thermostatic switch so that the temperature sensing tip is submerged as shown in **Figure 79**.
4. Place a thermometer in the pan of water (use a cooking or candy thermometer that is rated higher than the test temperature).
5. Attach one ohmmeter lead to the fan switch terminal and the other lead to the body as shown in **Figure 79**. Check resistance as follows:
   a. Gradually heat the water.
   b. When the temperature is below 208.4° F (98° C), the ohmmeter should show infinity.
   c. When the temperature exceeds 221° F (105° C), the ohmmeter should show continuity.
   d. Gradually cool the water.
   e. When the temperature drops from 221 to 208.4° F (105 to 98° C), the ohmmeter should show continuity.
   f. When the temperature drops to less then 208.4° F (98° C), the ohmmeter should show infinity.
6. Replace the thermostatic switch if it failed to operate as described in Step 5.

Sidestand Relay
Testing/Replacement

1A. *FZX700*: Remove the seat. Remove the fuel tank (Chapter Seven).
1B. *FZ700 and FZ750*: Remove the seat and the right-hand side cover.
2. Remove the sidestand relay (**Figure 80**).

3. Connect a 12-volt battery and ohmmeter to the sidestand relay as shown in **Figure 81**. Interpret results as follows:
   a. Battery connected: Ohmmeter should read infinity.
   b. Battery disconnected: Ohmmeter should read 0 ohms.
4. If the sidestand relay failed either test in Step 3, replace it with a new unit.

Diode Testing

1A. *FZX700*: Remove the right-hand side cover.
1B. *FZ700 and FZ750*: Remove the left front panel (**Figure 82**).
2. Disconnect the diode block from the wiring harness.
3. Check each diode and resistor in the diode block with an ohmmeter. Referring to **Figure 83**, check the diode between the indicated wires. Replace the diode if it fails any test.

Starter Safety Unit

This procedure describes how to test the starter safety unit that is incorporated in the relay assembly.

1A. *FZX700*: Remove the seat and fuel tank (Chapter Seven).
1B. *FZ700 and FZ750*: Remove the right front panel (**Figure 84**).
2. Remove the relay assembly (**Figure 85**).
3. Connect a 12-volt battery and ohmmeter to the relay assembly as shown in **Figure 86**. Interpret results as follows:
   a. Battery connected: Ohmmeter should read 0 ohms.
   b. Battery disconnected: Ohmmeter should read infinity.
4. If the starter safety unit failed either test in Step 3, replace the relay assembly with a new unit.

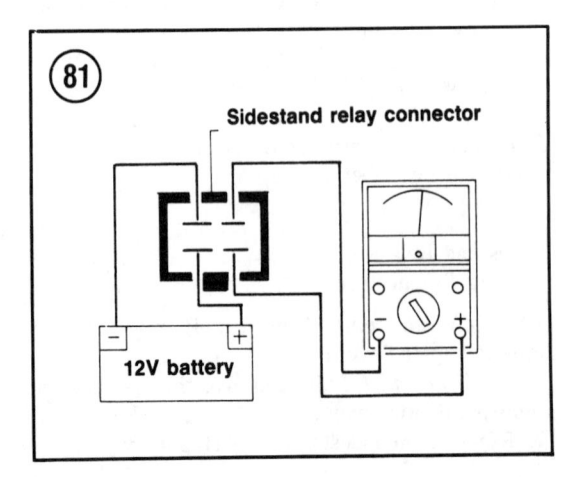

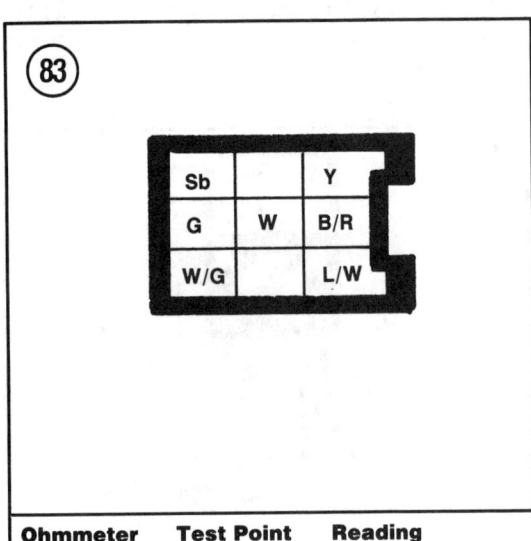

Ohmmeter (+ red)	Test Point (- black)	Reading
B/R	G	8.2 ohms
W	W/G	0 ohms
W/G	W	Infinity
L/W	G	0 ohms
G	L/W	Infinity
Sb	Y	0 ohms
Y	Sb	Infinity

ELECTRICAL SYSTEM

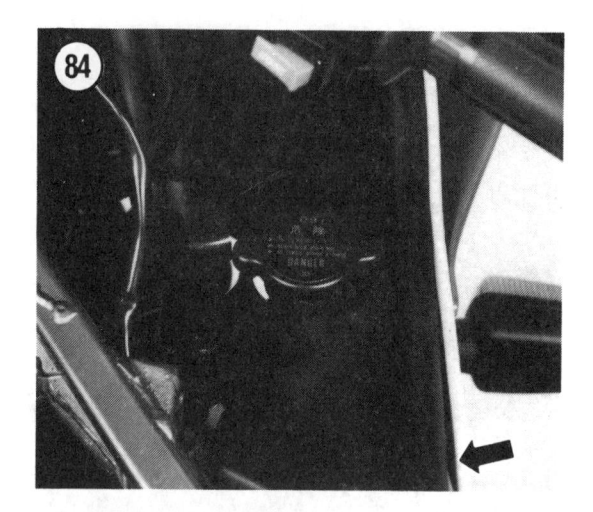

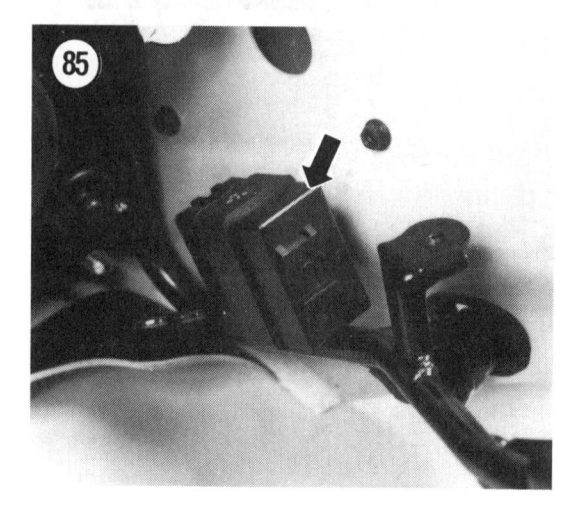

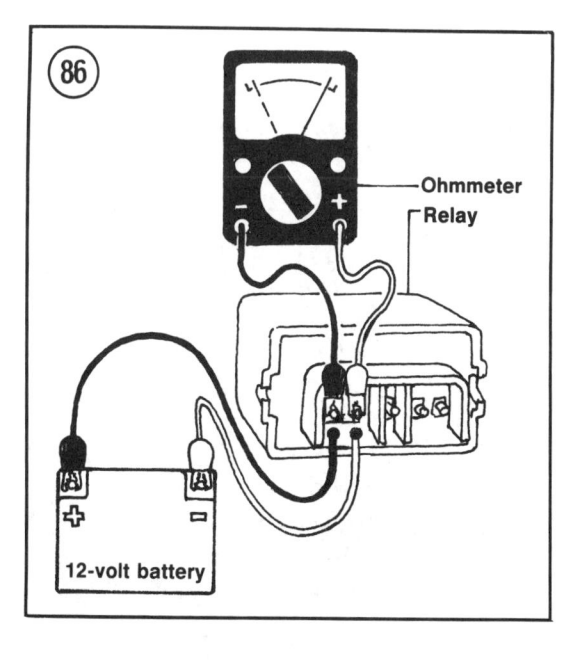

Electric Fan Testing

1. Check the battery as described in Chapter Three. If the battery, specific gravity and charge are okay, proceed with the following tests.
2A. *FZX700:* Remove the right-hand reflector and the right frame cover.
2B. *FZ700 and FZ750:* Remove the lower fairing.
3. Disconnect the thermostatic switch coupler (**Figure 87**).
4. See **Figure 88**; connect a voltmeter red lead to the thermostatic switch red connector wire and the black ohmmeter lead to ground. Turn the main switch on. Interpret results as follows:
   a. Less than 12 volts: Check the fan fuse and the main fuse. If these are okay, check the main switch as described in this chapter under *Switches*.
   b. 12-volt reading: Perform Step 5.

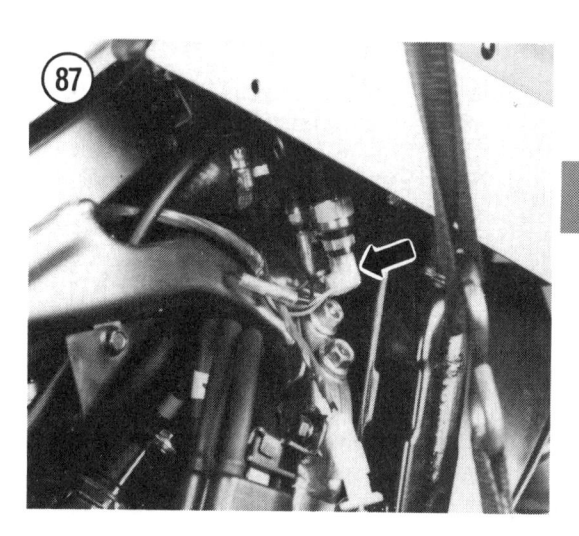

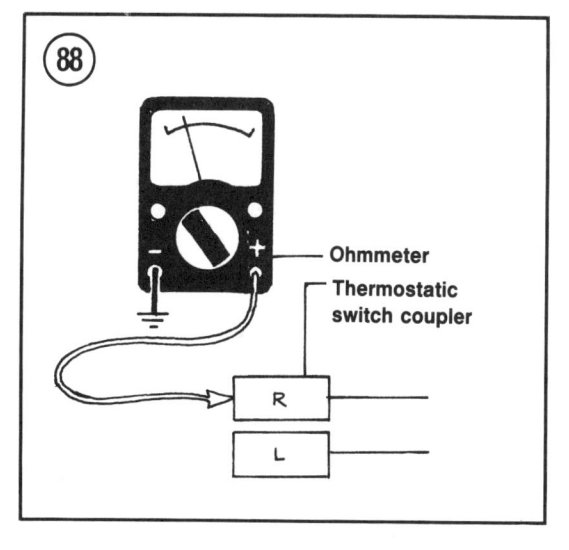

5. Connect a jumper wire between the thermostatic switch connector's red and blue wires (**Figure 88**). Turn the main switch on and check to see if the fan motor operates. Interpret results as follows:
   a. Fan operates: Check the thermostatic switch as described under *Thermostatic Switch Testing* in this chapter; replace the switch if necessary.
   b. Fan does not operate: Check all fan electrical connections; repair connections if necessary. If connections are okay, the fan motor may be damaged. Disconnect the fan electrical connector, then turn the fan blade by hand. The fan should turn smoothly. If the fan turns roughly, the fan is damaged and must be replaced.

Horn

Testing

1. Connect a red voltmeter lead to the horn brown wire and the black voltmeter lead to ground. Turn the main switch ON. Interpret results as follows:
   a. No voltage reading: There is an open or short in the horn brown wire. Locate the damaged area and repair it.
   b. 12-volt reading: Power is reaching the horn. The horn may be damaged; perform Step 2.
2. Disconnect the horn connector. Connect an ohmmeter red lead to the horn's brown lead and the ohmmeter black lead to the pink lead. Switch the ohmmeter on R×1. The resistance reading should be 1.05 ohms ±10 percent. If the resistance reading is out of specifications, replace the horn.

Adjustment

If you have noticed a drop-off in horn noise, adjust the horn as follows.
1. Remove the horn (**Figure 89**) from the motorcycle.
2. Connect a 12-volt battery and an ammeter to the horn as shown in **Figure 90**.
3. Turn the horn adjuster (**Figure 90**) so that maximum volume is reached at 2.5 amps.
4. Install the horn.

FUEL PUMP TESTING

Fuel pump removal and installation are described in Chapter Seven. Observe the following conditions when troubleshooting the fuel pump system.

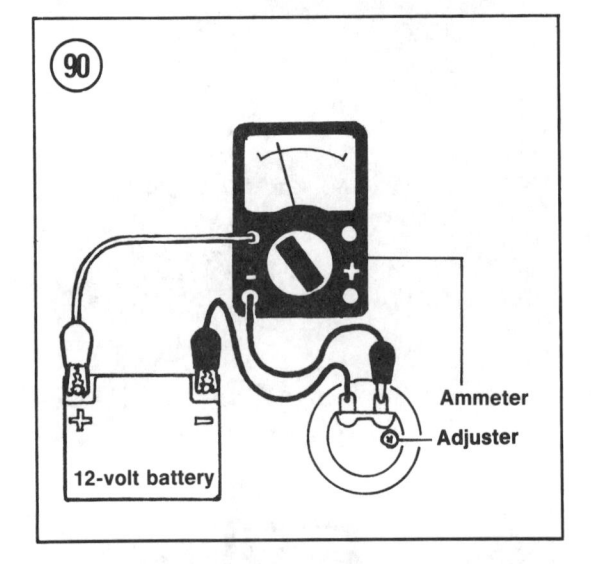

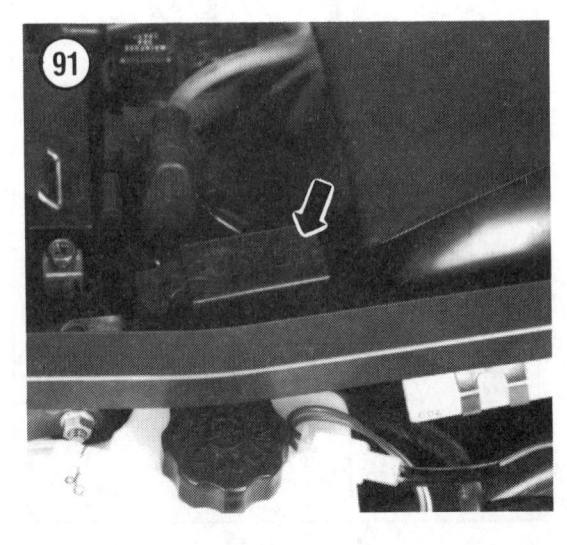

ELECTRICAL SYSTEM

1. Check all connections to make sure they are tight and free of corrosion.
2. Check the battery to make sure it is fully charged.
3. If the fuel pump does not operate properly, refer service to a Yamaha dealer as special tools and procedures are required.

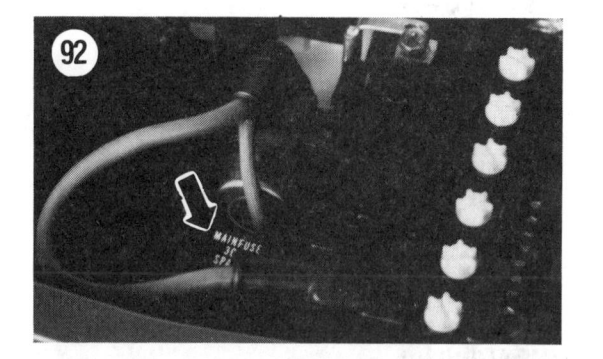

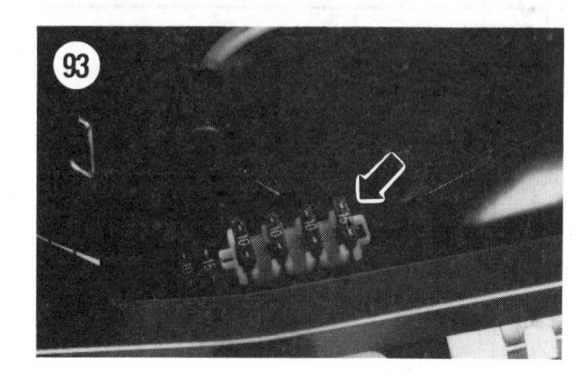

FUSES

Whenever a fuse blows, find out the reason for the failure before replacing the fuse. Usually, the trouble is a short circuit in the wiring. This may be caused by worn-through insulation or a disconnected wire shorting to ground. Fuse ratings are listed in **Table 3**.

CAUTION
Never substitute metal foil or wire for a fuse. Never use a higher amperage fuse than specified. An overload could result in fire and complete loss of the bike.

There are 4 fuses located in the fuse holder (**Figure 91**) mounted underneath the seat. The main fuse (**Figure 92**) is located in a separate holder underneath the seat. The fuse functions are:
  a. Main fuse: 30 amp.
  b. Headlight: 15 amp.
  c. Signal: 10 amp.
  d. Ignition: 10 amp.
  e. Fan: 10 amp.

If a fuse blows, remove the seat and remove the fuse cover. Remove the fuse (**Figure 92** or **Figure 93**) by pulling it out of its holder with needle nose pliers. Install a new fuse with the same amperage rating.

NOTE
*The fuse holder (**Figure 93**) is equipped with one 10 amp and one 30 amp replacement fuse. Always carry extra fuses.*

Table 1 ELECTRICAL SPECIFICATIONS

System voltage	12 volts
Ignition system	
Pickup coil resistance	
FZX700 & FZ700	135-165 ohms*
FZ750	171-209 ohms*
Ignition coil resistance	
FZX700 & FZ750	
Secondary	6.8-9.8 K ohms*
Primary	2.16-3.24 ohms*
FZ700	
Secondary	9.6-14.4 K ohms*
Primary	1.8-2.2 ohms*
Charging system	
Charging voltage	12 volts, 25 amps @ 5,000 rpm
Generator (FZX700 & FZ750)	
Stator coil resistance	0.19-0.21 ohms*
Field (rotor) coil resistance	3.8-4.2 ohms*
Brush length (new)	10.5 mm (0.41 in.)
Wear limit	4.5 mm (0.18 in.)
(continued)	

Table 1 ELECTRICAL SPECIFICATIONS (cont.)

Generator (FZ700)	
Stator coil resistance	0.17-08 ohms*
Field (rotor) coil resistance	3.8-4.2*
Brush length (new)	13.7 mm (0.54 in.)
Wear limit (minimum length)	4.7 mm (0.19 in.)
Electric starter	
Brush length (new)	12.5 mm (0.49 in.)
Wear limit (minimum length)	5.0 mm (0.2 in.)
Commutator diameter (new)	28 mm (1.1 in.)
Wear limit	27 mm (1.06 in.)
Mica undercut	0.8 mm (0.03 in.)
Coil winding resistance	4.3 ohms ±10%*
Spark plug cap resistance	10k ohms

* Test performed with unit @ a temperature of 68° (20° C).

Table 2 REPLACEMENT BULBS

Item	Wattage
Headlight	
FZX700 and FZ700	60/55W
FZ700	35/35W
Tail/brakelight	8/27W
Flasher light	27W
Meter light	
FZX700	3.0W
FZ700 & FZ750	3.4W
License light	
FZX700	3.0W
FZ700 & FZ750	8W
Indicator lights	
FZX700	3.0W
FZ700 & FZ750	3.4W

Table 3 FUSES

	Amperage
Main	30 amp
Headlight	15 amp
Signal	10 amp
Ignition	10 amp
Fan	10 amp

CHAPTER NINE

COOLING SYSTEM

The pressurized cooling system consists of the radiator, water pump, radiator cap, thermostat, electric cooling fan and a coolant reservoir tank.

It is important to keep the coolant level to the FULL mark on the coolant reservoir tank (**Figure 1**). Always add coolant to the reservoir tank, not to the radiator.

CAUTION
Drain and flush the cooling system at least every 2 years. Refill with a mixture of ethylene glycol antifreeze (formulated for aluminum engines) and distilled water. Do not reuse the old coolant as it deteriorates with use. ***Do not*** *operate the cooling system with only distilled water (even in climates where antifreeze protection is not required). This is important because the engine is all aluminum; it will not rust but it will oxidize internally and have to be replaced. Refer to* **Coolant Change** *in Chapter Three.*

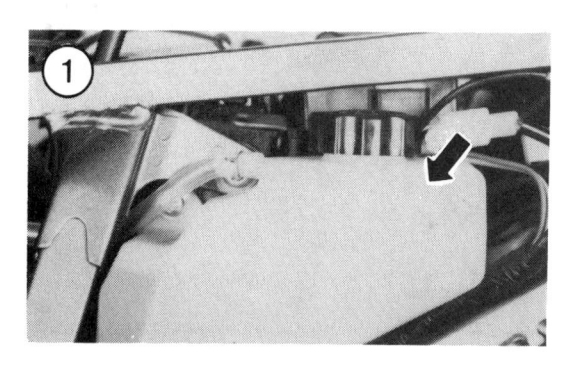

This chapter describes repair and replacement of cooling system components. **Table 1** at the end of the chapter lists all of the cooling system specifications. For routine maintenance of the system, refer to *Cooling System Inspection* in Chapter Three.

WARNING
Do not remove the radiator cap when the engine is hot. The coolant is very hot and is under pressure. Severe scalding could result if the coolant comes in contact with your skin.

WARNING
The radiator fan and fan switch are connected to the battery. Whenever the engine is warm or hot, the fan may start even with the ignition switch turned off. Never work around the fan or touch the fan until the engine is completely cool.

The cooling system must be cooled prior to removing any component of the system.

COOLING SYSTEM INSPECTION

1. If a substantial coolant loss is noted, the head gasket may be blown. In extreme cases sufficient coolant will leak into a cylinder(s) when the bike is left standing for several hours so the engine cannot

be turned over with the starter. White smoke (steam) might also be observed at the muffler(s) when the engine is running. Coolant may also find its way into the oil. To check, observe the oil level window on the clutch cover (**Figure 2**). On FZ700 models, the oil level window is visible through the hole in the fairing. If the oil is milky or foamy there is coolant in the oil system. If so, correct the probelm immediately.

> *CAUTION*
> *After the problem is corrected, drain and thoroughly flush out the engine oil system to eliminate all coolant residue. Refill with fresh engine oil; refer to **Engine Oil and Filter Change** in Chapter Three.*

2. Check the radiator for clogged or damaged fins. If more than 15% of the radiator fin area is damaged, repair or replace the radiator.
3. Check all coolant hoses for cracks or damage. Replace all questionable parts. Make sure the hose clamps are tight, but not so tight that they cut the hoses.
4. Pressure test the cooling system as described under *Cooling System Inspection* in Chapter Three.

COOLANT RESERVOIR

The coolant reservoir tank (**Figure 1**) is located on the left-hand side (FZX700) or right-hand side (FZ700 and FZ750). Replace the reservoir tank if cracked or otherwise damaged.

RADIATOR AND FAN

> *WARNING*
> *The radiator fan and fan switch are connected to the battery. Whenever the engine is warm or hot, the fan may start with the ignition switch turned off. Never work around the fan or touch the fan until the engine is completely cool.*

Fan Test

Test procedures for the cooling fan are included in Chapter Eight.

Removal/Installation (FZX700)

The radiator and fan are removed as an assembly.
1. Place the bike on the center stand.
2. Remove the side reflectors.
3. Remove the frame reflectors.
4. Drain the cooling system as described under *Coolant Change* in Chapter Three.

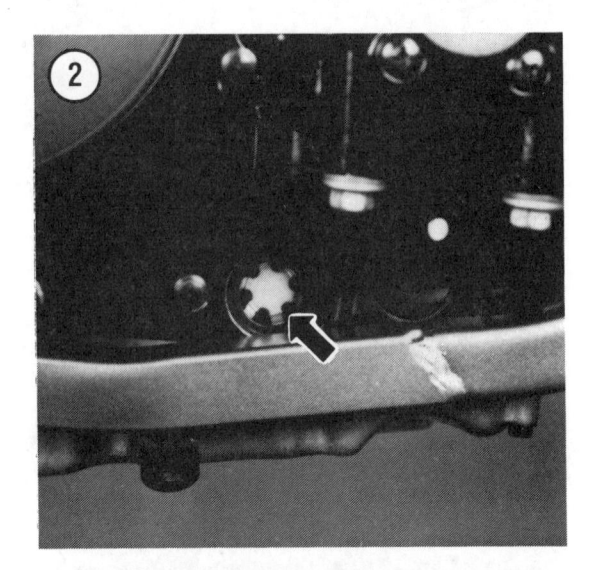

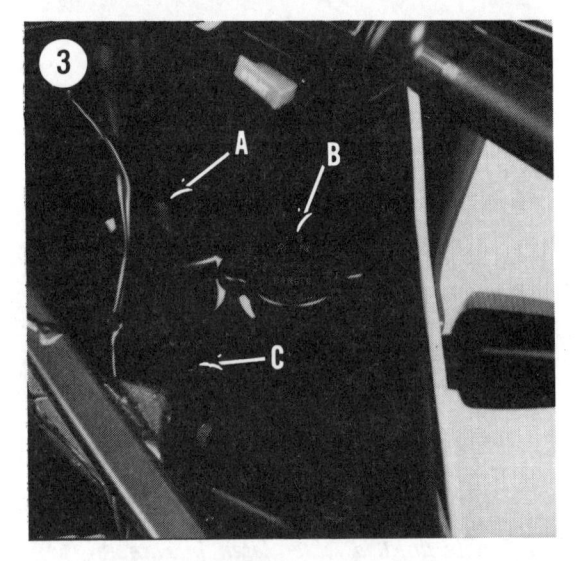

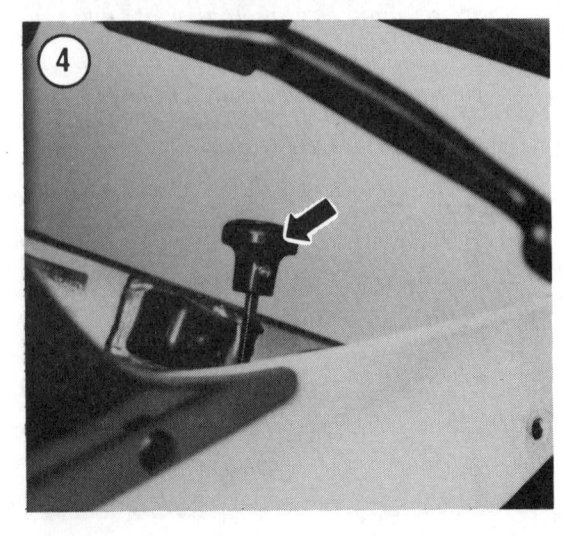

COOLING SYSTEM

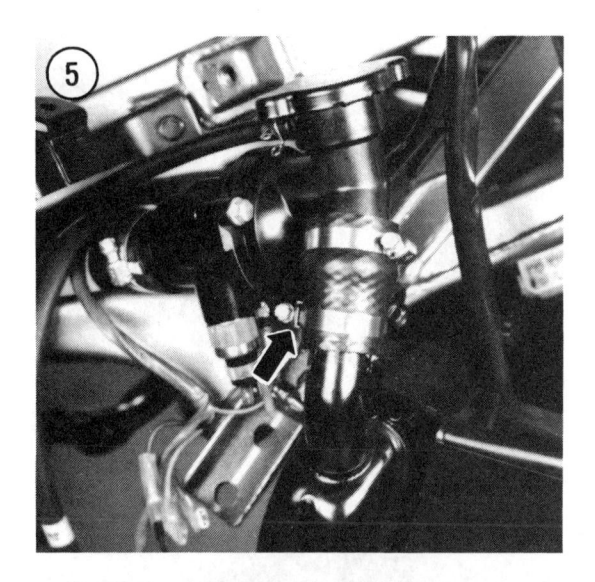

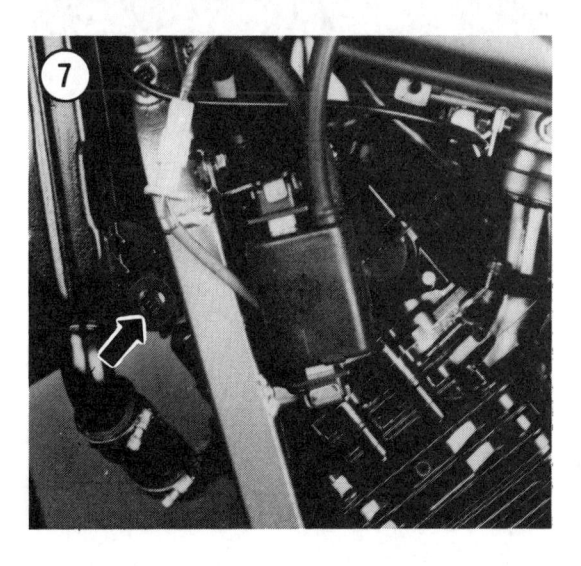

5. Loosen the clamping screws on the upper and lower radiator hose bands. Move the bands back onto the hoses and off of the necks of the radiator.
6. Disconnect the upper and lower hoses at the radiator.
7. Disconnect the overflow hose at the radiator.
8. Disconnect the electric fan switch connector.
9. Remove the upper and lower radiator bolts and remove the radiator.
10. Replace the radiator hose if deterioration or damage is noted.
11. Installation is the reverse of these steps. Note the following:
   a. Make sure the fan switch connector is reconnected.
   b. Refill the coolant as described under *Coolant Change* in Chapter Three.

Removal/Installation
(FZ700 and FZ750)

1. Drain the cooling system as described under *Coolant Change* in Chapter Three.
2. See **Figure 3**. Remove the following:
   a. Radiator cap cover (A).
   b. Radiator cap (B).
   c. Right front panel (C).
3. *FZ750*: Remove the choke knob (**Figure 4**) and the left front panel.
4. Remove the lower fairing. See Chapter Thirteen.
5. Loosen the clamping screws on the upper (**Figure 5**) and lower (**Figure 6**) radiator hose bands. Move the bands back onto the hoses and off of the necks of the radiator.
6. Remove the upper radiator mounting bolts.
7. Remove the lower radiator mounting bolts (**Figure 7**).
8. Remove the air baffle plates (**Figure 8**).

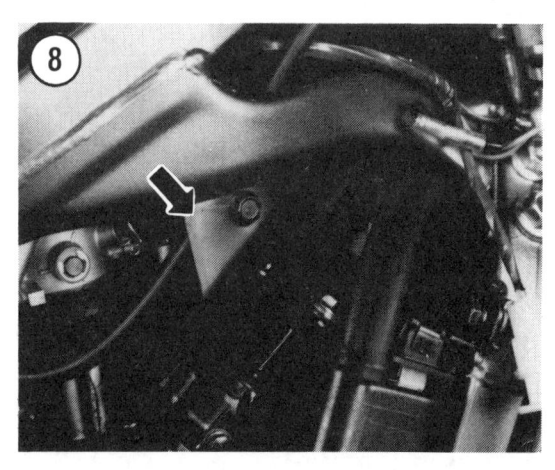

218 CHAPTER NINE

9. Disconnect the fan switch connector.
10. Remove the radiator.
11. Replace the radiator hoses if deterioration or damage is noted.
12. Installation is the reverse of these steps. Note the following:
    a. Make sure the fan switch connector is reconnected.
    b. Refill the coolant as described under *Coolant Change* in Chapter Three.

Inspection

CAUTION
When flushing the radiator fins with a hose, always point the hose perpendicular to the radiator and at a distance of 20 in. Never point a water or air hose at an angle to the radiator fins.

1. Flush off the exterior of the radiator with a garden hose on low pressure. Spray both the front and the back to remove all road dirt and bugs. Carefully use a whisk broom or stiff paint brush to remove any stubborn dirt.

CAUTION
Do not press too hard or the cooling fins and tubes may be damaged causing a leak.

2. Remove the cover (**Figure 9**) if so equipped.
3. Carefully straighten out any bent cooling fins with a broad-tipped screwdriver.
4. See **Figure 10**. Check for cracks or leakage (usually a moss-green colored residue) at the filler neck, the inlet and outlet hoses fittings and the upper and lower tank seams.
5. Refer to **Figure 11**. Inspect the radiator cap top seal (A) and bottom seal (B) for deterioration or damage. Check the spring for damage. Pressure test the radiator cap as described under *Cooling System*

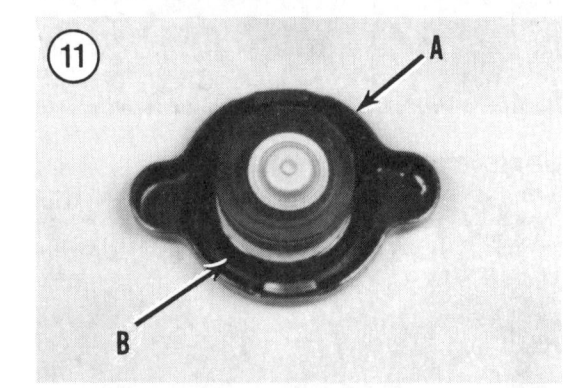

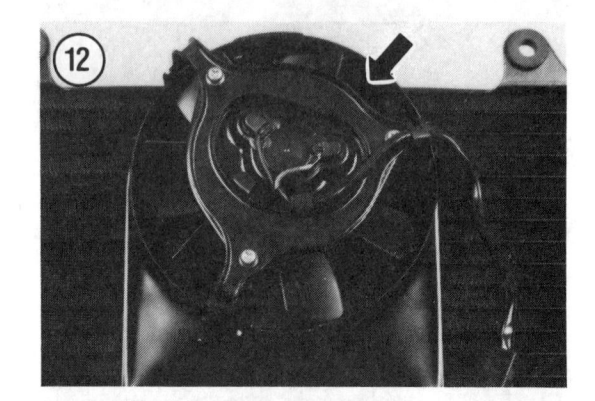

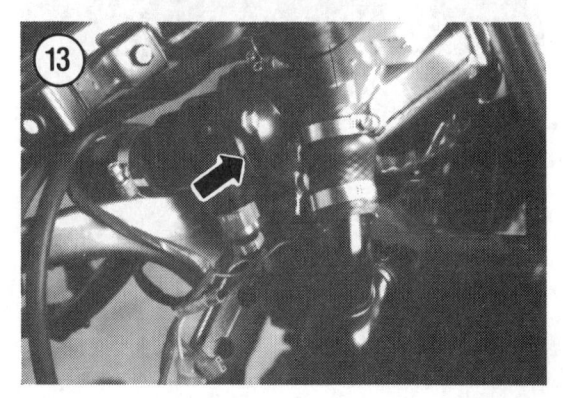

COOLING SYSTEM

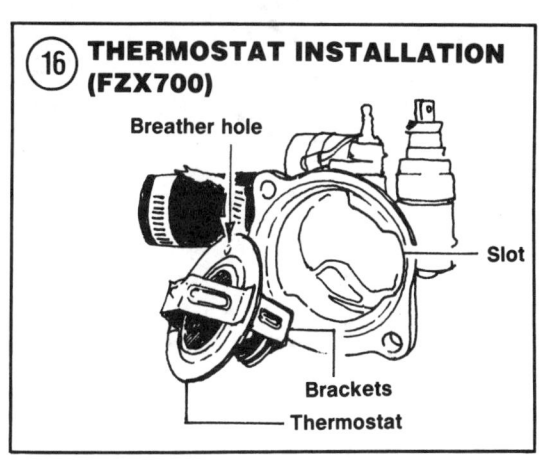

Inspection in Chapter Three. Replace the radiator cap if necessary.

Cooling Fan
Removal/Installation

1. Remove the radiator as described in this chapter.
2. See **Figure 12**. Remove the bolts securing the fan shroud and fan assembly and remove the assembly.
3. Installation is the reverse of these steps. Apply Loctite 242 (blue) to the fan mounting bolts and tighten securely.

THERMOSTAT

Removal/Installation

1. *FZ700 and FZ750*: Remove the upper fairing assembly. See Chapter Thirteen.
2. Drain the cooling system as described under *Coolant Change* in Chapter Three.

NOTE
When removing the thermostat cover in Step 3, hold a rag underneath the thermostat housing to absorb coolant left in the housing.

3. Remove the thermostat cover bolts and lift the cover off the housing. See **Figure 13**.
4. Lift the thermostat (**Figure 14**) out of the housing.
5. Test the thermostat as described in this chapter.
6. Install by reversing these steps. Note the following.
7. Replace the cover O-ring (**Figure 15**) if necessary.
8A. *FZX700*: Install the thermostat so that the valve bracket fits into the housing slot and with the breather hole facing up (at the twelve o'clock position). See **Figure 16**.
8B. *FZ700 and FZ750*: Install the thermostat so that the breather hole aligns with the housing slot. See **Figure 17**.
9. Tighten the cover bolts to 10 N•m (7.2 ft.-lb.).

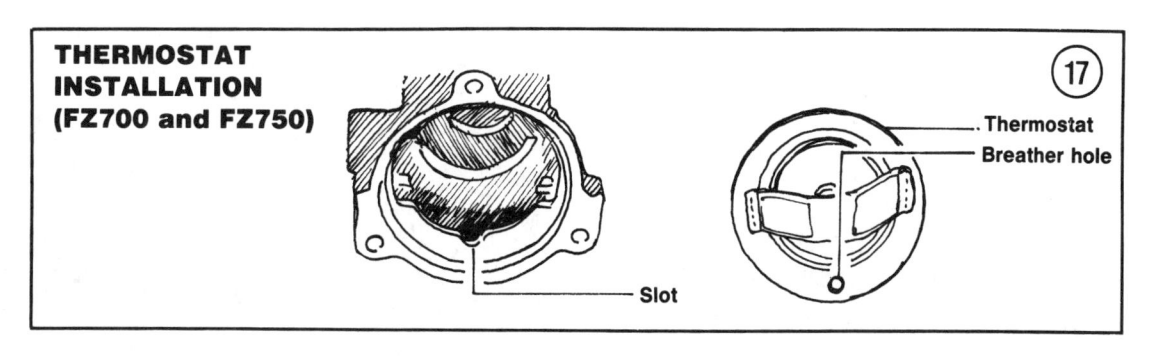

10. Refill the cooling system with the recommended type and quantity of coolant as described under *Coolant Change* in Chapter Three.

Inspection

Test the thermostat to ensure proper operation. The thermostat should be replaced if it remains open at normal room temperature or stays closed after the specified temperature has been reached during the test procedure.

Place the thermostat on a small piece of wood in a pan of water (**Figure 18**). Place a thermometer in the pan of water (use a cooking or candy thermometer that is rated higher than the test temperature). Gradually heat the water and continue to gently stir the water until it reaches 176.9-182.3° F (80.5-83.5° C). At this temperature the thermostat should start to open. At 203° F (95° C), the thermostat should be fully open.

NOTE
Valve operation is sometimes sluggish; it usually takes 3-5 minutes for the valve to operate properly.

If the valve fails to open, the thermostat should be replaced (it cannot be serviced). Be sure to replace it with one of the same temperature rating.

WATER PUMP

Removal

1. Drain the engine oil as described under *Engine Oil and Filter Change* in Chapter Three.

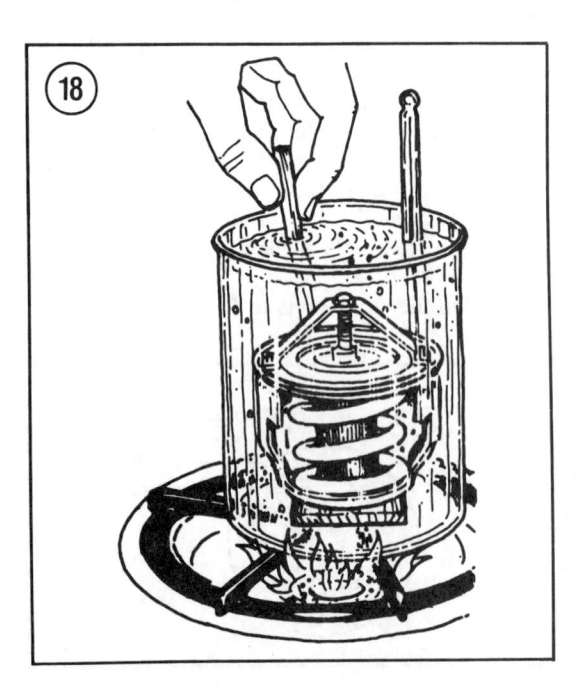

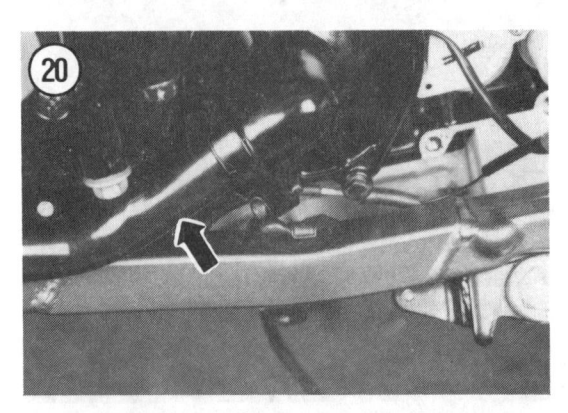

COOLING SYSTEM

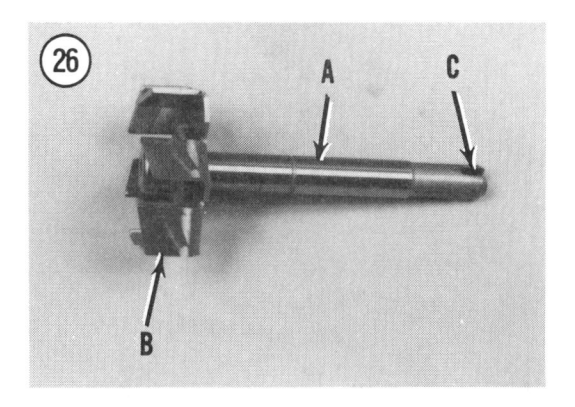

2. Drain the cooling system as described under *Coolant Change* in Chapter Three.
3. Remove the sprocket cover as described under *Sprocket Cover Removal/Installation* in Chapter Six.
4. Remove the lower water pump hose attaching bolts (**Figure 19**) and pull the hose out of the water pump (**Figure 20**).
5. Remove the upper water pump hose attaching bolts and pull the hose out of the water pump (**Figure 21**).
6. Remove the water pump mounting bolts and pull the cover (**Figure 22**) off of the pump housing.
7. Remove the O-ring (**Figure 23**).
8. Pull the pump housing (**Figure 24**) out of the crankcase.

Disassembly/Inspection

1. Pull the impeller shaft (**Figure 25**) out of the housing.
2. See **Figure 26**. Check the impeller shaft (A) for scoring, wear or damage. Check the oil pump engagement notch on the end of the impeller shaft (C) for rounding, cracks or damage. Replace the impeller shaft if necessary.
3. Check the impeller blades (B, **Figure 26**) for corrosion or damage. If corrosion is minor, clean the blades. If corrosion is severe or if the blades are cracked or broken, replace the water pump unit.
4. Inspect the seal (**Figure 27**) in the housing for wear or damage. If necessary, have the seal replaced by a Yamaha dealer as a press and special tools are required.

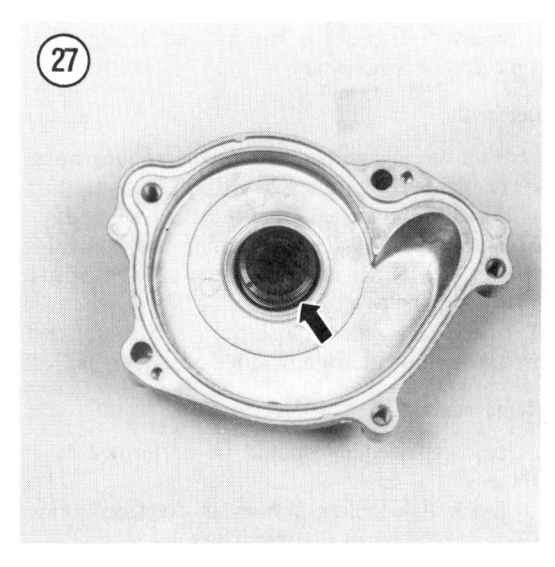

5. Turn the water pump housing bearing (**Figure 28**) by hand and check for excessive noise or roughness. If necessary, have the bearing replaced by a Yamaha dealer as a press is required.

6. Inspect the water pump coolant passage (**Figure 29**) for corrosion or sludge buildup. If corrosion is minor, clean the passage. If corrosion is severe or if the water passage is pitted, replace the water pump unit.

7. Replace the water pump O-rings if deformed or cracked or if there are indications of coolant leakage. See **Figure 30** and **Figure 31**.

8. Reverse Step 1 to install the impeller shaft.

Assembly/Installation

1. Align the notch on the end of the impeller shaft (**Figure 32**) with the oil pump drive shaft and install the water pump housing onto the crankcase (**Figure 24**).
2. Install the O-ring (**Figure 23**).
3. Install the water pump cover and bolts and tighten the bolts to 10 N•m (7.2 ft.-lb.).
4. Attach the upper (**Figure 21**) and lower (**Figure 20**) water pump hoses.
5. Install the sprocket cover. Refill the cooling system with the recommended type and quantity of coolant as described under *Coolant Change* in Chapter Three.

HOSES

Hoses deteriorate with age and should be replaced periodically or whenever they show signs of cracking or leakage. To be safe, replace the hoses every 2 years. The spray of hot coolant from a cracked hose can injure the rider and passenger. Loss of coolant can also cause the engine to overheat causing damage.

Whenever any component of the cooling system is removed, inspect the hoses(s) and determine if replacement is necessary.

Inspection

1. With the engine cool, check the cooling hoses for brittleness or hardness. A hose in this condition will usually show cracks and must be replaced.
2. With the engine hot, examine the hoses for swelling along the entire hose length. Eventually a hose will rupture at this point.
3. Check area around hose clamps. Signs of rust around clamps indicate possible hose leakage.

Replacement

Hose replacement should be performed when the engine is cool.

1. Drain the cooling system as described under *Coolant Change* in Chapter Three.

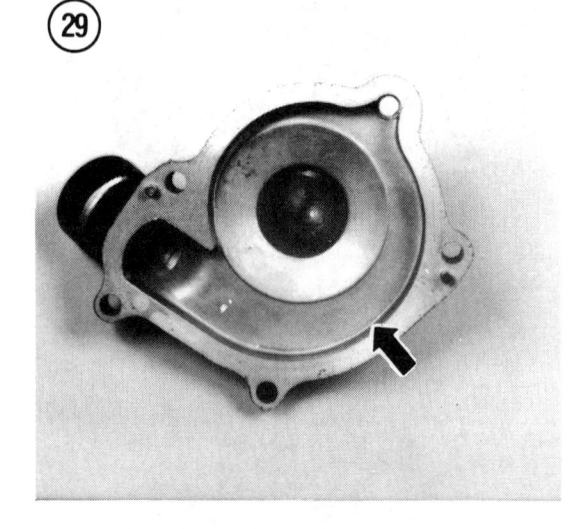

COOLING SYSTEM

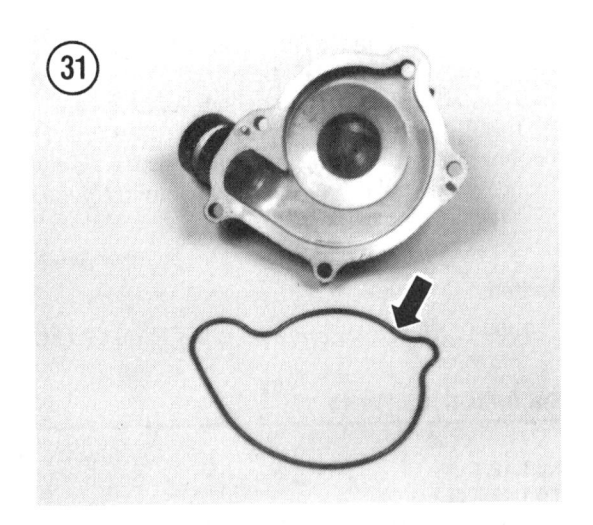

2. Loosen the hose clamps from the hose to be replaced. Slide the clamps along the hose and out of the way.
3. Twist the hose end to break the seal and remove from the connecting joint. If the hose has been on for some time, it may have become fused to the joint. If so, cut the hose parallel to the joint connections with a knife or razor. The hose then can be carefully pried loose with a screwdriver.

CAUTION
Excessive force applied to the hose during removal could damage the connecting joint.

4. Examine the connecting joint for cracks or other damage. Repair or replace parts as required. If the joint is okay, clean it of any rust with sandpaper.
5. Inspect hose clamps and replace as necessary.
6. Slide hose clamps over outside of hose and install hose to inlet and outlet connecting joint. Make sure hose clears all obstructions and is routed properly.

NOTE
If it is difficult to install a hose on a joint, soak the end of the hose in hot water for approximately 2 minutes. This will soften the hose and ease installation.

7. With the hose positioned correctly on joint, position clamps back away from end of hose slightly. Tighten clamps securely, but not so much that hose is damaged.
8. Refill cooling system as described under *Coolant Change* in Chapter Three. Start the engine and check for leaks. Retighten hose clamps as necessary.

THERMOSTATIC SWITCH AND WATER TEMPERATURE SENSOR

Removal/Installation

1. Drain the cooling system as described under *Coolant Change* in Chapter Three.
2. *FZ700 and FZ750*: Remove the lower fairing as described in Chapter Thirteen.
3. *Thermostatic switch*: Perform the following:
   a. Disconnect the connector at the unit (A, **Figure 33**).

b. Unscrew the thermostatic switch from the thermostat housing and remove it.
c. Apply a liquid gasket sealer to the fan switch threads before installation.
d. Install the switch and tighten securely.

4. *Water temperature sensor*: Perform the following:
   a. Disconnect the connector at the unit (B, **Figure 33**).
   b. Unscrew the water temperature sensor from the thermostat housing and remove it.
   c. Apply a liquid gasket sealer to the sensor threads before installation.
   d. Install the sensor and tighten securely.

5. Install the liner fairing (if removed). Refill the cooling system with the recommended type and quantity of coolant as described under *Coolant Change* in Chapter Three.

Testing

Refer to *Electrical Components* in Chapter Eight.

Table 1 COOLING SYSTEM SPECIFICATIONS

Coolant capacity	
FZX700 & FZ750	2.3 L (2.4 qt.)
FZ700	2.6 L (2.7 qt.)
Coolant type	High-quality ethylene glycol antifreeze compounded for aluminum engines
Coolant mix ratio	50/50
Radiator cap opening pressure	0.75-1.05 kg/cm^2 (10.7-14.9 psi)
Thermostat	
Begins to open	80.5-83.5° C (144.9-182.3° F)
Full open	95° C (203° F)

CHAPTER TEN

FRONT SUSPENSION AND STEERING

This chapter discusses service operations on suspension components, steering, wheels and related items. **Table 1** lists service specifications. **Table 1** and **Table 2** are at the end of the chapter.

FRONT WHEEL

Removal/Installation

1. Support the motorcycle with a jack so that the front wheel is clear of the ground. On FZ700 and FZ750 models, it will be necessary to remove the lower fairing assembly. See Chapter Thirteen.
2. Loosen the speedometer cable nut (**Figure 1**) and pull the cable out of the speedometer drive unit.
3. Remove the brake caliper mounting bolts (**Figure 2**) and lift the caliper off of the brake disc. Support the caliper with a bungee cord to prevent stress buildup on the brake hose.
4. Loosen the left-hand side axle clamp bolt (A, **Figure 3**). Then loosen the axle on the left-hand side (B, **Figure 3**).
5. Remove the axle and washer (FZ700 and FZ750) from the left hand side. See **Figure 4**.
6. Pull the wheel forward (**Figure 5**).
7. Remove the speedometer drive gear (A, **Figure 6**) from the left-hand side.
8. Remove the spacer (**Figure 7**) from the right-hand side.

CAUTION
Do not set the wheel down on the disc surface as it may be scratched or warped. Either lean the wheel against a wall or place it on a couple of wood blocks.

NOTE
*Insert a piece of wood in the calipers (**Figure 8**) in place of the disc. That way, if the brake lever is inadvertently squeezed, the piston will not be forced out of the cylinder. If this does happen, the calipers might have to be disassembled to reseat the piston and the system will have to be bled.*

9. When servicing the wheel assembly, install the spacer, speedometer drive gear and washer (FZ700 and FZ750) on the axle to prevent their loss.

10. Installation is the reverse of these steps. Note the following:
   a. To prevent axle seizure, coat the axle with an anti-seize compound such as Bostik Never-Seez Lubricating & Anti-Seize Compound (part no. 49501).
   b. Tighten the axle nut to specifications in **Table 2**.

FRONT SUSPENSION AND STEERING

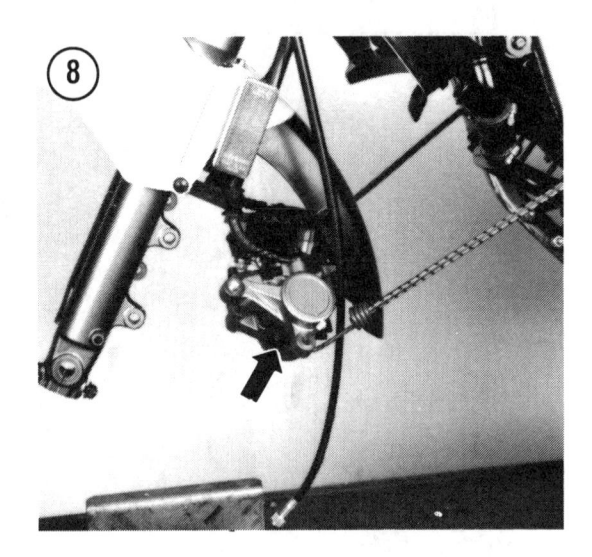

c. Align the 2 slots in the speedometer gear housing (**Figure 9**) with the 2 speedometer drive tabs (**Figure 10**) in the front wheel and install the gear housing. See A, **Figure 6**.

d. When installing the front wheel, align the notch on the speedometer gear housing (B, **Figure 6**) with the tab on the back of the left-hand fork tube. This locates the speedometer drive gear and prevents it from rotating when the wheel turns.

e. Make sure that the speedometer gear housing does not move as the axle nut is tightened.

f. Remove the brake caliper from the bungee cord and carefully align it with the brake disc and install it. Install the 2 caliper bolts (**Figure 2**) and tighten to the specifications in **Table 2**. Repeat for the opposite caliper.

g. Apply the front brake and compress the front forks several times to make sure the axle is installed correctly without binding the forks. Then tighten the axle pinch bolts to specifications (**Tables 2**).

Inspection

1. Remove any corrosion on the front axle with a piece of fine emery cloth.

2. Check axle runout. Place the axle on V-blocks and place the tip of a dial indicator in the middle of the axle (**Figure 11**). Rotate the axle and check runout. If the runout exceeds 0.2 mm (0.008 in.) but does not exceed 0.7 mm (0.027 in.), have it straightened by a dealer or machine shop to read

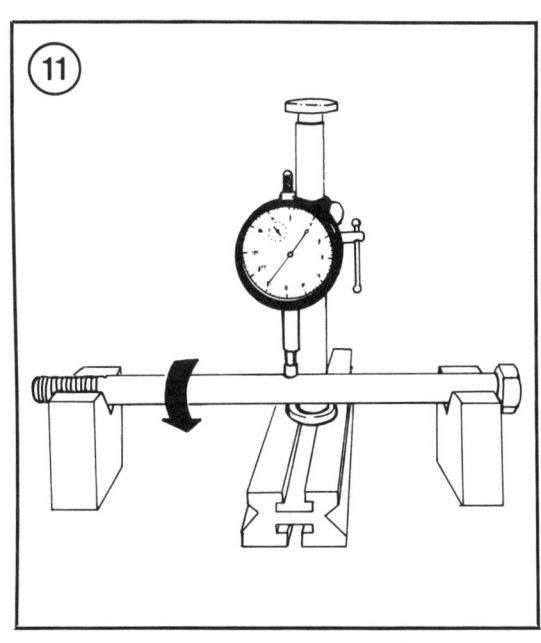

less than 0.2 mm (0.008 in.) runout. If the runout exceeds 0.7 mm (0.027 in.), replace the axle; do not attempt to straighten it.

3. Check rim runout as follows:

   a. Remove the tire from the rim as described in this chapter.
   b. Measure the radial (up and down) runout of the wheel rim with a dial indicator as shown in **Figure 12**. If runout exceeds 2.0 mm (0.08 in.), check the wheel bearings.
   c. Measure the axial (side to side) runout of the wheel rim with a dial indicator as shown in **Figure 12**. If runout exceeds 2.0 mm (0.08 in.), check the wheel bearings.
   d. If the wheel bearings are okay, the wheel cannot be serviced, but must be replaced.
   e. Replace the front wheel bearings as described under *Front Hub* in this chapter.

4. Inspect the wheel rim for dents, bending or cracks. Check the rim and rim sealing surface for scratches that are deeper than 0.5 mm (0.02 in.). If any of these conditions are present, replace the wheel.

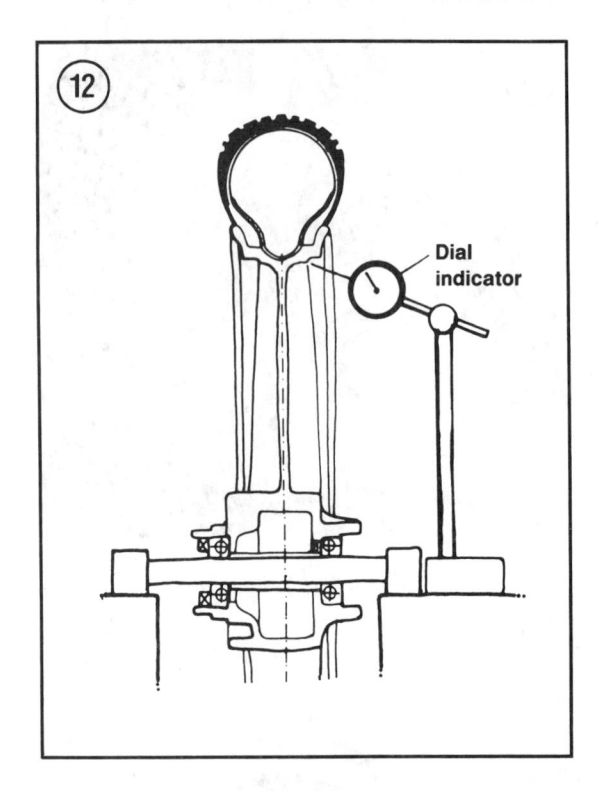

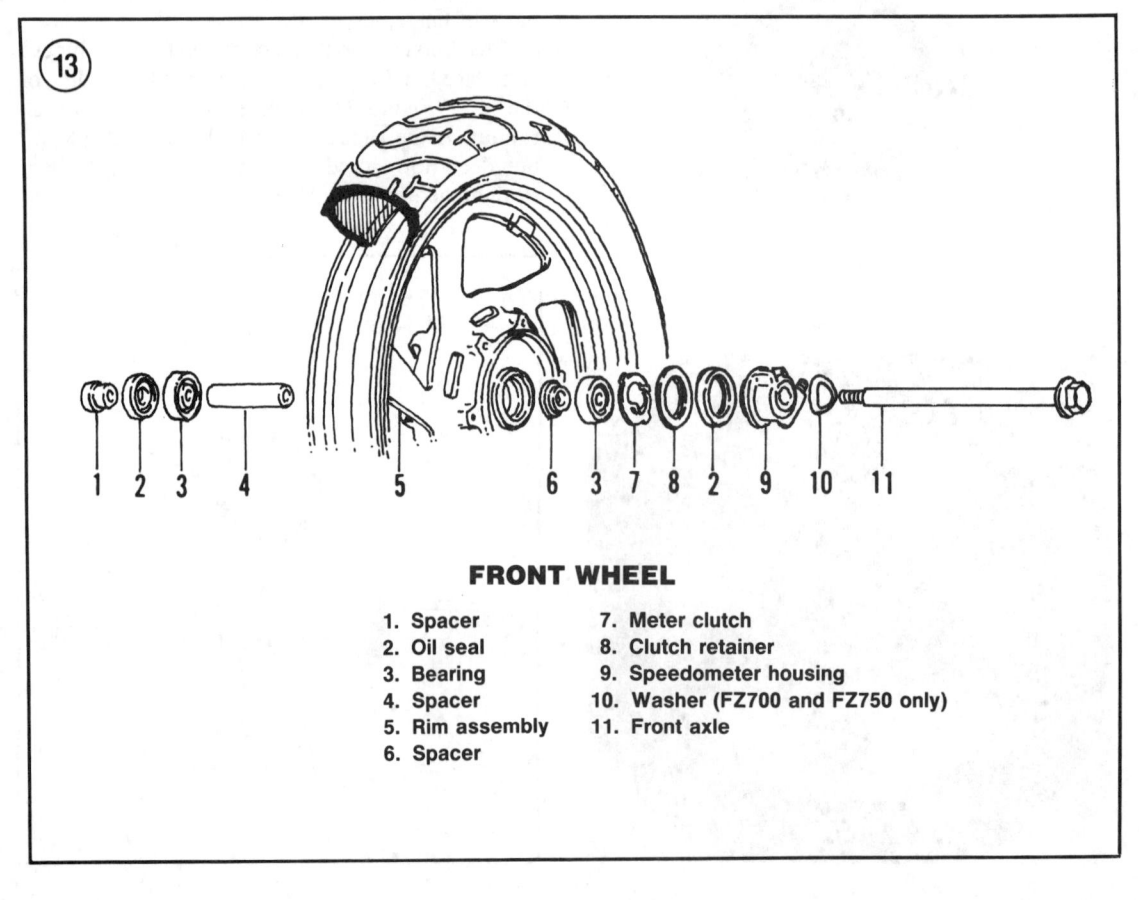

FRONT WHEEL

1. Spacer
2. Oil seal
3. Bearing
4. Spacer
5. Rim assembly
6. Spacer
7. Meter clutch
8. Clutch retainer
9. Speedometer housing
10. Washer (FZ700 and FZ750 only)
11. Front axle

FRONT SUSPENSION AND STEERING

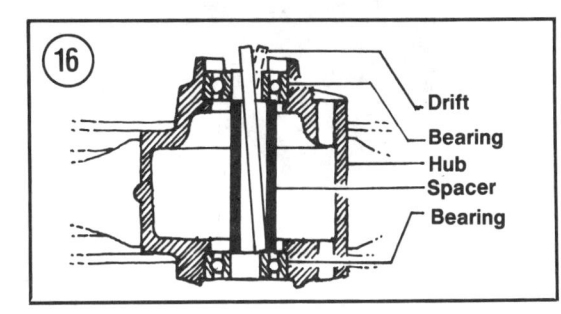

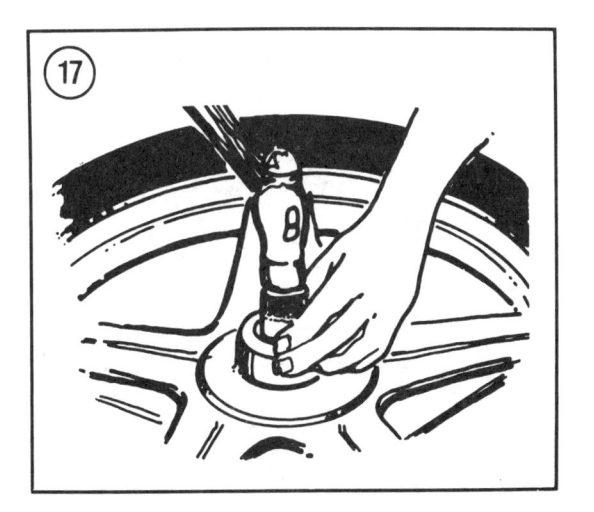

FRONT HUB

Disassembly/Inspection/Reassembly

Refer to **Figure 13** for this procedure.

1. Check the wheel bearings by rotating the inner race (**Figure 14**). Check for bearing roughness, excessive noise or damage. If necessary, replace the bearings as follows. Always replace bearings in a set.
2. Check the right-hand oil seal (**Figure 15**) for damage.
3. Replace the oil seal and bearings as follows.
4. Pry the oil seal from the left-hand side (**Figure 15**) and remove the speedometer housing and clutch retainer (**Figure 13**).
5. Using a long drift or screwdriver, pry the oil seal from the right-hand side.
6. Using a long drift and hammer, tilt the center spacer away from one side of the left-hand bearing (**Figure 16**). Then drive the left-hand bearing out of the hub. See **Figure 16**.
7. Remove the center spacer and remove the right-hand bearing.
8. Clean the axle spacer and hub thoroughly in solvent.
9. Tap the right-hand bearing into place carefully using a suitable size socket placed on the outer bearing race (**Figure 17**).
10. Install the center spacer and install the left-hand bearing as described in Step 9.
11. Install the clutch retainer and speedometer housing (**Figure 13**).
12. Install a new left-hand grease seal (**Figure 15**). Drive the seal in squarely with a large diameter socket on the outer portion of the seal (**Figure 18**). Drive the seal until it seats against the circlip.

13. Install a new right-hand grease seal (**Figure 14**). Drive the seal in squarely with a large diameter socket placed on the outer portion of the seal (**Figure 18**). Drive the seal in until it seats against the bearing or until the outer surface is flush with the hub.

WHEEL BALANCE

An unbalanced wheel results in unsafe riding conditions. Depending on the degree of unbalance and the speed of the motorcycle, the rider may experience anything from a mild vibration to a violent shimmy and loss of control.

Weights are attached to the rim (**Figure 19**). Weight kits are available from motorcycle dealers. These contain test weights and strips of adhesive-backed weights that can be cut to the desired length and attached directly to the rim.

NOTE
Be sure to balance the wheel with the brake disc(s) attached as it also affects the balance.

Before attempting to balance the wheels, check to be sure that the wheel bearings are in good condition and properly lubricated. The wheel must rotate freely.

1. Remove the wheel as described in this chapter or in Chapter Eleven.
2. Mount the wheel on a fixture such as the one in **Figure 20** so it can rotate freely.
3. Give the wheel a spin and let it coast to a stop. Mark the tire at the lowest point.
4. Spin the wheel several more times. If the wheel keeps coming to rest at the same point, it is out of balance.
5. Tape a test weight to the upper (or light) side of the wheel.
6. Experiment with different weights until the wheel, when spun, comes to rest at a different position each time.
7. Remove the test weight and install the correct size weight.

TUBELESS TIRES

WARNING
Do not install an inner tube inside a tubeless tire. The tube will cause an abnormal heat buildup in the tire.

Tubeless tires have the word "TUBELESS" molded in the tire sidewall (**Figure 21**) and the rims have "TUBELESS" cast on them.

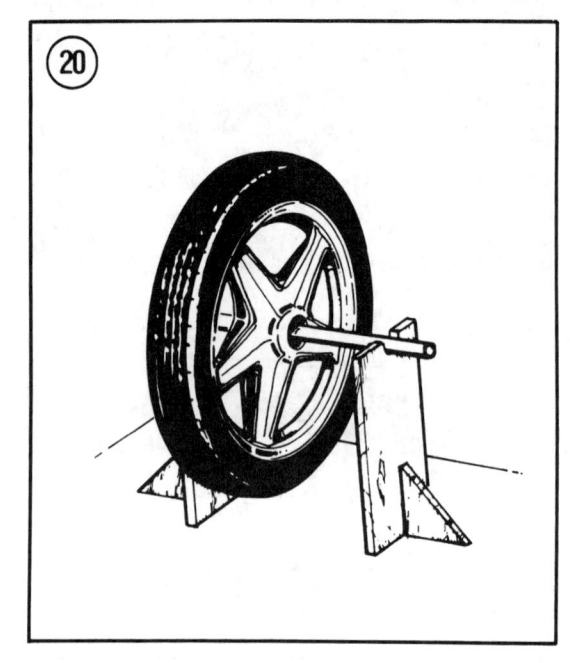

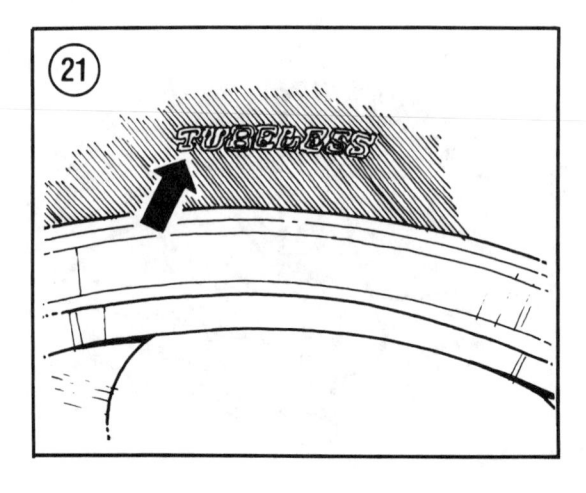

FRONT SUSPENSION AND STEERING

When a tubeless tire is flat, it is best to take it to a motorcycle dealer for repair. Punctured tubeless tires should be removed from the rim to inspect the inside of the tire and to apply a combination plug/patch from the inside. Don't rely on a plug or cord repair applied from outside the tire. They might be okay on a car, but they're too dangerous on a motorcycle.

After repairing a tubeless tire, don't exceed 50 mph (80 kph) for the first 24 hours. After 24 hours you must never exceed 80 mph (128 kph) on a tubeless tire which has been repaired with a plug/patch. Never race on a repaired tubeless tire. The patch could work loose from tire flexing and heat.

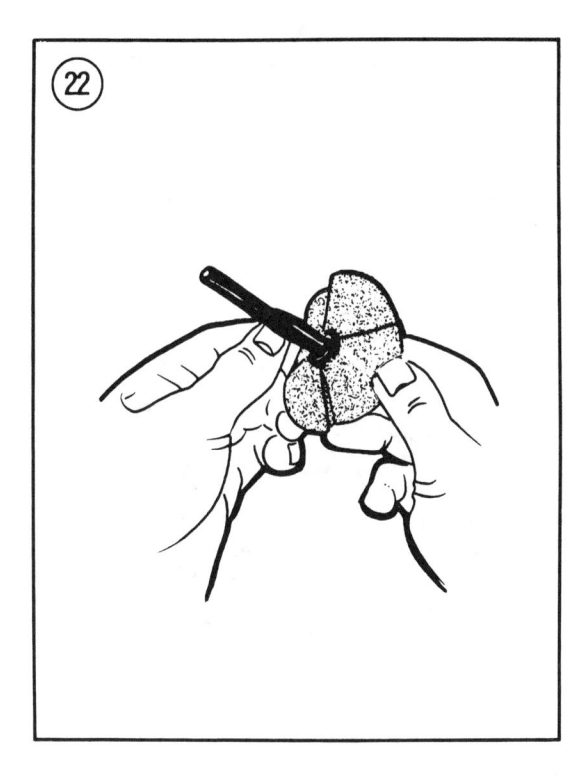

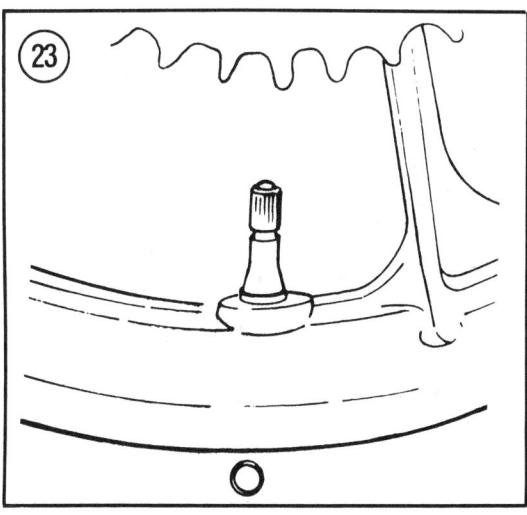

Repair

Do not rely on a plug or cord patch applied from outside the tire. Use a combination plug/patch applied from inside the tire (**Figure 22**).

1. Remove the tire from the rim as described in this chapter.
2. Inspect the rim inner flange. Smooth any scratches on the sealing surface with emery cloth. If a scratch is deeper than 0.5 mm (0.020 in.), the wheel should be replaced.
3. Inspect the tire inside and out. Replace a tire if any of the following are found:
    a. A puncture larger than 1/8 in. (3 mm) diameter.
    b. A punctured or damaged sidewall.
    c. More than 2 punctures in the tire.
4. Apply the plug/patch, following the instructions supplied with the patch.

TUBELESS TIRE CHANGING

The wheels can easily be damaged during tire removal. Special care must be taken with tire irons when changing a tire to avoid scratches and gouges to the outer rim surface. Insert scraps of leather between the tire iron and the rim to protect the rim from damage.

The stock cast wheels are designed for use with tubeless tires.

Tire repair is different and is covered under *Tubeless Tires* in this chapter.

When removing a tubeless tire, take care not to damage the tire beads, inner liner of the tire or the wheel rim flange. Use tire levers or flat-handled tire irons with rounded ends.

Removal

NOTE
While removing a tire, support the wheel on 2 blocks of wood, so the brake disc doesn't contact the floor.

1. Mark the valve stem location on the tire, so the tire can be installed in the same position for easier balancing. See **Figure 23**.
2. Remove the valve core to deflate the tire.

NOTE
Removal of tubeless tires from their rims can be very difficult because of the exceptionally tight bead/rim seal. Breaking the bead seal may require the

use of a special tool (**Figure 24**). If you have trouble breaking the seal, take the tire to a motorcycle dealer.

CAUTION
The inner rim and tire bead area are sealing surfaces on a tubeless tire. Do not scratch the inside of the rim or damage the tire bead.

3. Press the entire bead on both sides of the tire into the center of the rim.
4. Lubricate the beads with soapy water.

CAUTION
*Use rim protectors (**Figure 25**) or insert scraps of leather between the tire irons and the rim to protect the rim from damage.*

5. Insert the tire iron under the bead next to the valve (**Figure 26**). Force the bead on the opposite side of the tire into the center of the rim and pry the bead over the rim with the tire iron.
6. Insert a second tire iron next to the first to hold the bead over the rim. Then work around the tire with the first tool, prying the bead over the rim (**Figure 27**).

NOTE
Step 7 is required only if it is necessary to completely remove the tire from the rim.

7. Turn the wheel over. Insert a tire tool between the second bead and the same side of the rim that the first bead was pried over (**Figure 28**). Force the bead on the opposite side from the tool into the center of the rim. Pry the second bead off the rim, working around the wheel with 2 tire irons as with the first.
8. Inspect the valve stem seal. Because rubber deteriorates with age, it is advisable to replace the valve stem (**Figure 23**) when replacing a tire.

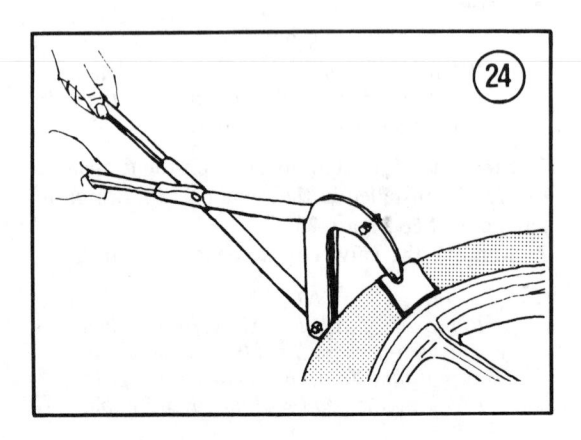

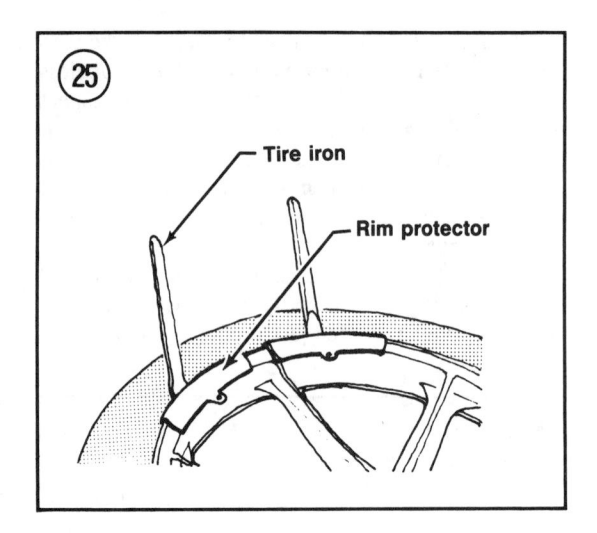

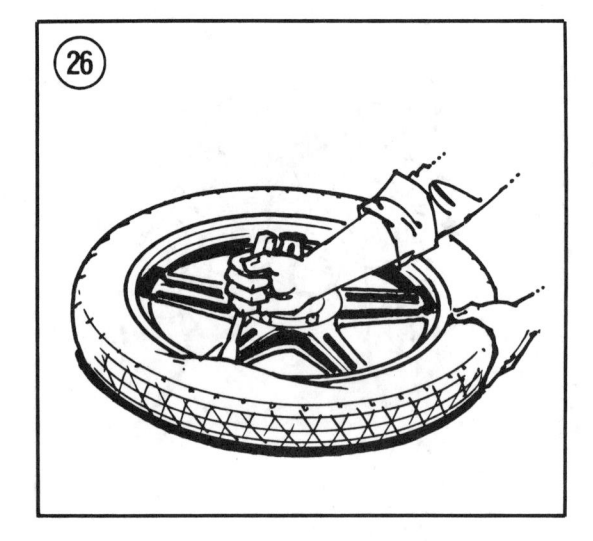

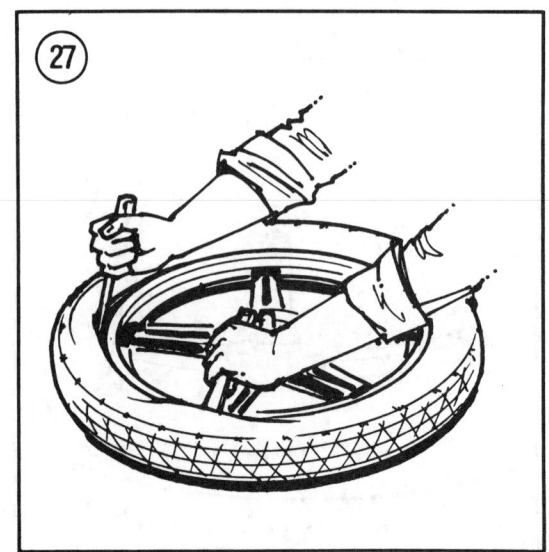

FRONT SUSPENSION AND STEERING

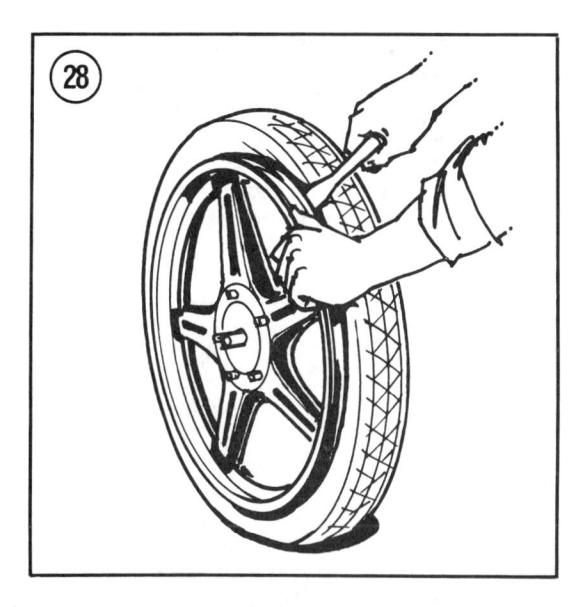

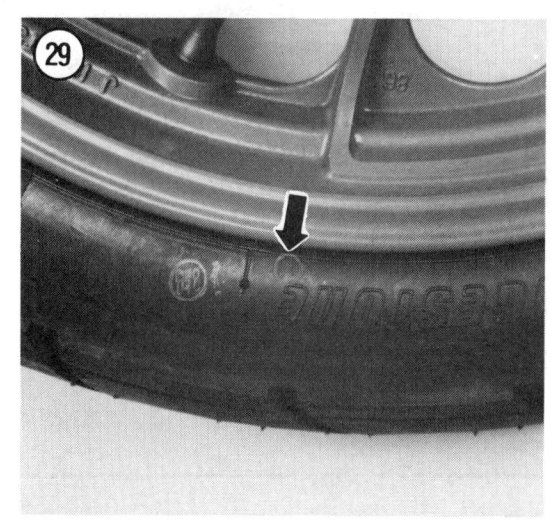

Installation

1. Carefully inspect the tire for any damage, especially inside.
2. A new tire may have balancing rubbers inside. These are not patches and should not be disturbed. A colored spot near the bead indicates a lighter point on the tire. This spot should be placed next to the valve stem (**Figure 29**). In addition, most tires have directional arrows labeled on the side of the tire that indicates the direction in which the tire should rotate (A, **Figure 30**). Make sure to install the tire accordingly.
3. Lubricate both beads of the tire with soapy water.
4. Place the backside of the tire into the center of the rim. The lower bead should go into the center of the rim and the upper bead outside. Work around the tire in both directions (**Figure 31**). Use a tire iron for the last few inches of bead (**Figure 32**).

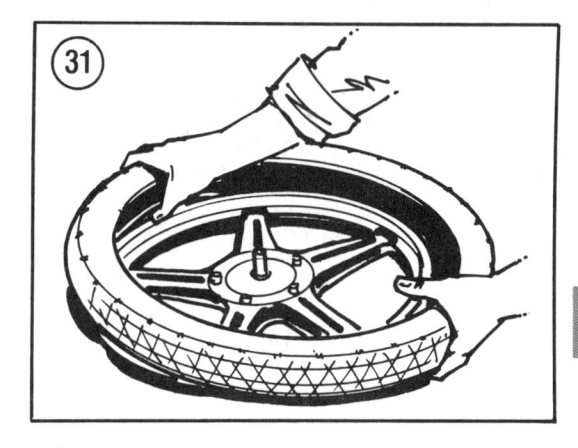

5. Press the upper bead into the rim opposite the valve (**Figure 33**). Pry the bead into the rim on both sides of the initial point with a tire tool, working around the rim to the valve.

6. Check the bead on both sides of the tire for an even fit around the rim. Check that the balance mark is still aligned with the valve stem (**Figure 29**).

7. Place an inflatable band around the circumference of the tire. Slowly inflate the band until the tire beads are pressed against the rim. Inflate the tire enough to seat it, deflate the band and remove it.

WARNING
Never exceed 56 psi (4.0 k/cm²) inflation pressure as the tire could burst, causing severe injury. Never stand directly over the tire while inflating it.

8. After inflating the tire, check to see that the beads are fully seated and that the tire rim lines (B, **Figure 30**) are the same distance from the rim all the way around the tire. If the beads won't seat, deflate the tire, relubricate the rim and beads with soapy water and reinflate the tire.

9. Inflate the tire to the required pressure. See *Tire Pressure* in Chapter Three. Screw on the valve stem cap.

10. Balance the wheel assembly as described in this chapter.

HANDLEBARS

Removal/Installation
(FZX700)

1. Remove the mirrors.

NOTE
If handlebar replacement is not required, proceed to Step 5.

CAUTION
Cover the frame and fuel tank with a heavy cloth or plastic tarp to protect it from accidental spilling of brake fluid. Wash spilled brake fluid off any painted or plated surface immediately, as it will destroy the finish. Use soapy water and rinse thoroughly.

2. Remove the 2 bolts securing the master cylinder and move it away from the handlebar. Secure the master cylinder with a bungee cord.

3. Remove the 2 bolts securing the clutch master cylinder and move it away from the handlebar. Secure the master cylinder with a bungee cord.

4. Remove the clamps securing the electrical cables to the handlebar.

5. Separate the 2 halves of the starter switch assembly. Disconnect the throttle cable from the twist grip. Separate the 2 halves of the directional signal switch assembly on the left-hand side.

6. Remove the 4 plugs and 4 Allen bolts.

7. Lift off the handlebar.

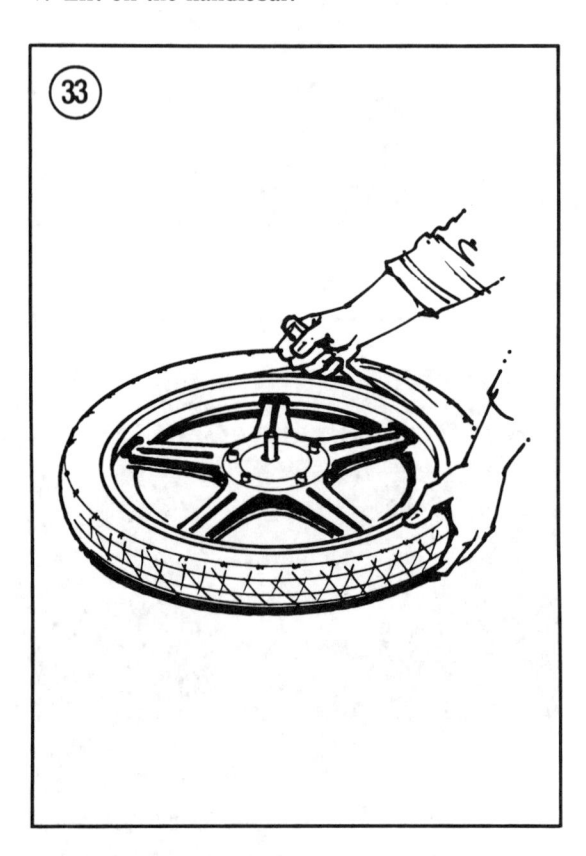

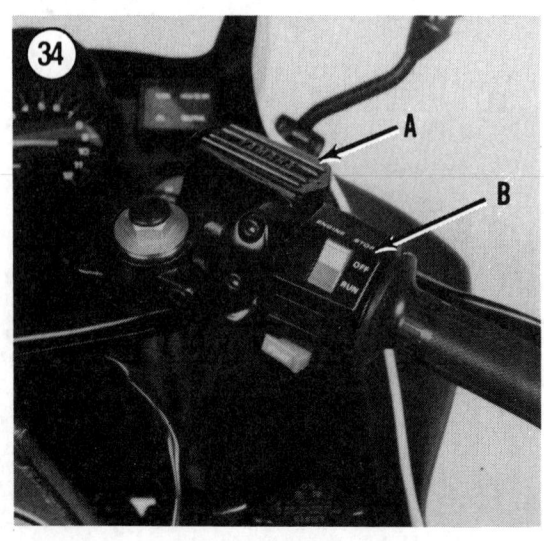

FRONT SUSPENSION AND STEERING

8. If necessary, replace the hand grips as follows:
   a. Insert a thin-bladed screwdriver under the hand grip.
   b. Squirt electrical contact cleaner under the hand grip and twist it quickly to break its seal and remove it.
   c. Squirt electrical contact cleaner into the new hand grip, then quickly install it by turning it onto the handlebar or twist grip.
   d. Check the hand grip(s) after 10 minutes to make sure they are tight.

WARNING
Do not ride with loose hand grips. Loss of control is sure to result.

9. Install by reversing these steps. Note the following:
   a. Replace the handlebar if bent.

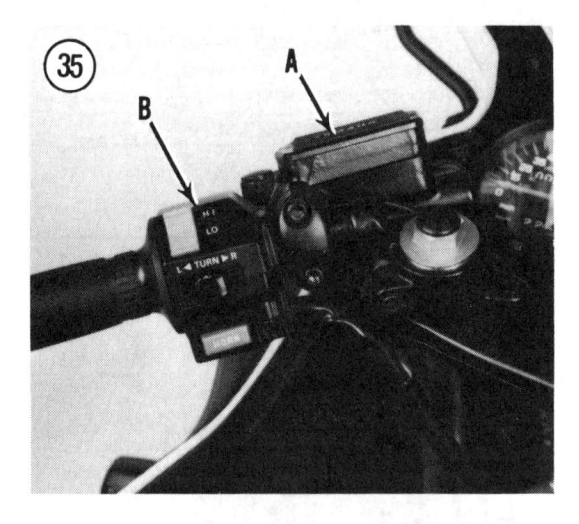

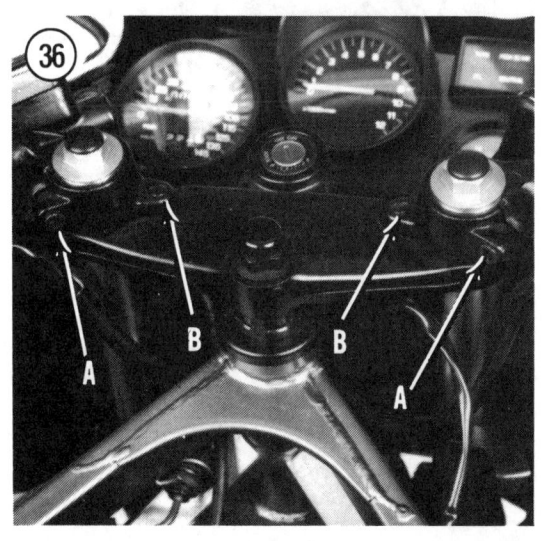

   b. Clean the handlebar knurled areas with contact cleaner or any non-oil based cleaner.
   c. Tighten the handlebar Allen bolts to the specifications in **Table 2**.
   d. When installing the throttle assembly, do not push the end of the hand grip against the end of the handlebar as this will cause grip drag when rotated. Leave a slight clearance between both parts.

Removal/Installation (FZ700 and FZ750)

These models use separate handlebar assemblies that slip over the top of the fork tubes and bolt directly to the upper steering stem.

NOTE
If handlebar replacement is not required, proceed to Step 4.

CAUTION
Cover the frame and fuel tank with a heavy cloth or plastic tarp to protect it from accidental spilling of brake fluid. Wash spilled brake fluid off any painted or plated surface immediately, as it will destroy the finish. Use soapy water and rinse thoroughly.

1. Remove the 2 bolts securing the brake master cylinder (A, **Figure 34**) and move it away from the handlebar. Secure the master cylinder with a bungee cord.
2. Remove the 2 bolts securing the clutch master cylinder (A, **Figure 35**) and move it away from the handlebar. Secure the master cylinder with a bungee cord.
3. Separate the 2 halves of the starter switch assembly (B, **Figure 34**). Disconnect the throttle cable from the twist grip. Separate the 2 halves of the directional signal switch assembly on the left-hand side (B, **Figure 35**).
4. Loosen the handlebar pinch bolt (A, **Figure 36**). Then remove the handlebar mounting bolt (B, **Figure 36**) and lift the handlebar off of the fork tube.
5. If necessary, replace the hand grips as follows:
   a. Remove the metal end grip.
   b. Insert a thin-bladed screwdriver under the hand grip.
   c. Squirt electrical contact cleaner under the hand grip and twist it quickly to break its seal and remove it.
   d. Squirt electrical contact cleaner into the new hand grip, then quickly install it by turning it onto the handlebar or twist grip.

e. Check the hand grip(s) after 10 minutes to make sure they are tight.

WARNING
Do not ride with loose hand grips. Loss of control is sure to result.

6. Install by reversing these steps. Note the following:
   a. Replace the handlebar if damaged.
   b. Clean the handlebar mounting area with contact cleaner or any non-oil based cleaner.
   c. Tighten the handlebar Allen bolts to the specifications in **Table 2**.

Inspection

Check the handlebars at their bolt holes and along the entire mounting area for cracks or damage. Replace a bent or damaged handlebar immediately. If the bike is involved in a crash, examine the handlebars, steering stem and front forks carefully.

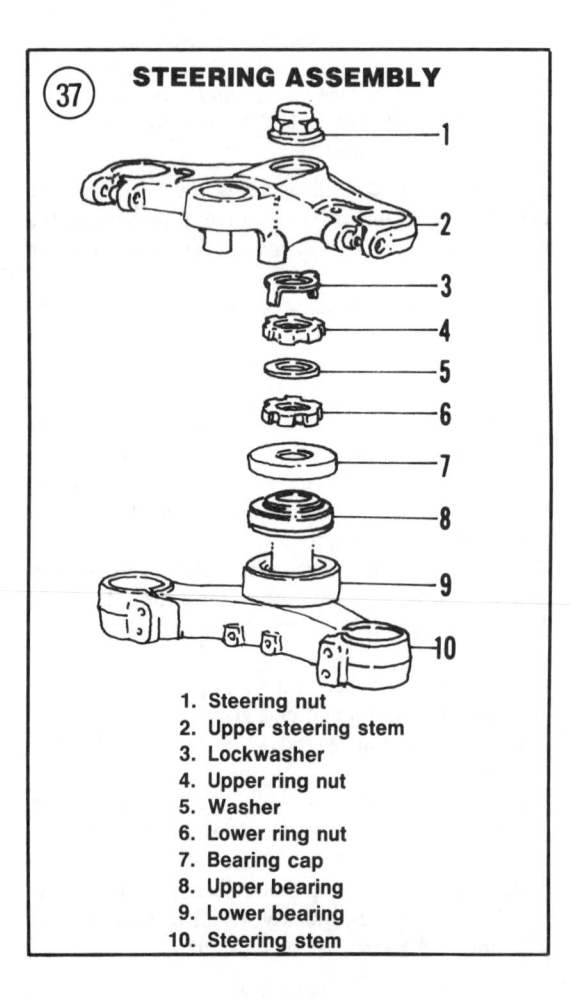

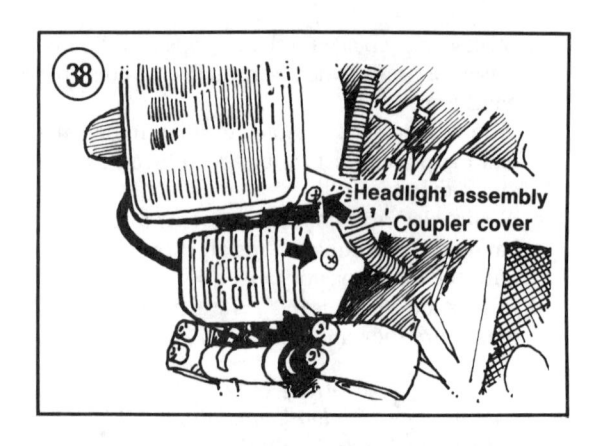

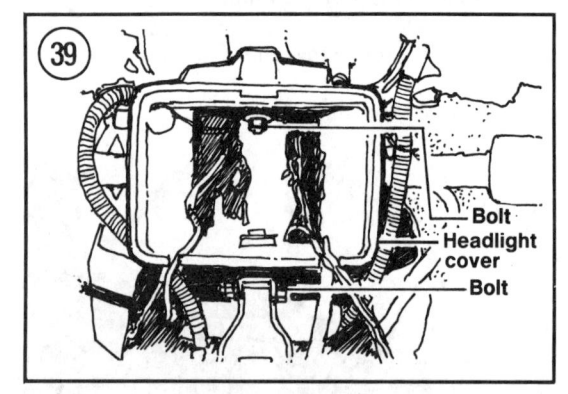

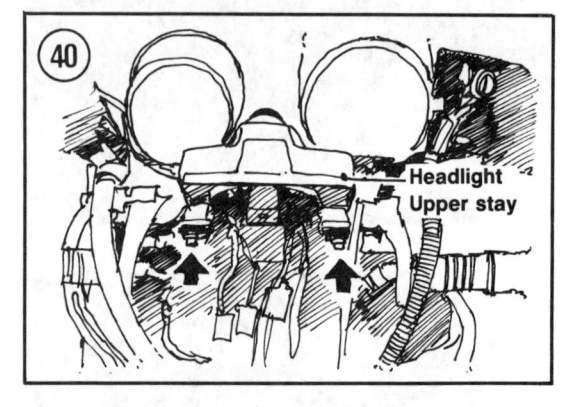

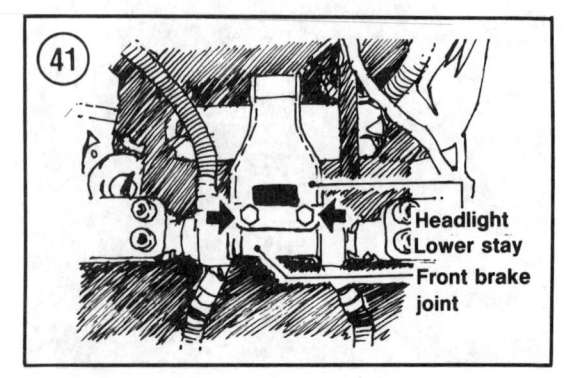

STEERING ASSEMBLY

1. Steering nut
2. Upper steering stem
3. Lockwasher
4. Upper ring nut
5. Washer
6. Lower ring nut
7. Bearing cap
8. Upper bearing
9. Lower bearing
10. Steering stem

FRONT SUSPENSION AND STEERING

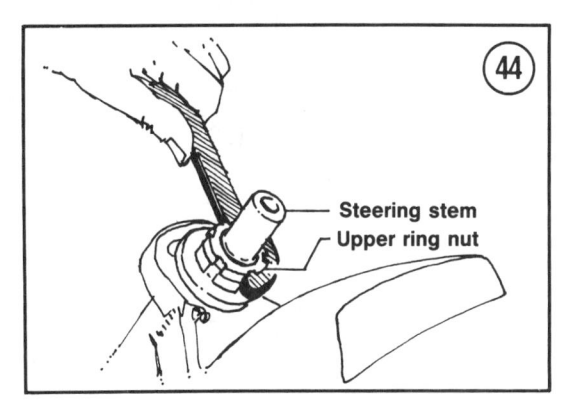

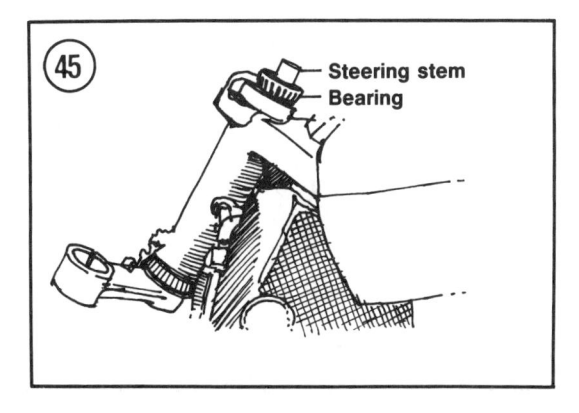

STEERING HEAD

The steering assembly for all models is shown in **Figure 37**.

Removal/Disassembly

1. Support the bike on the centerstand. On FZ700 models, support the bike securely.
2. Remove the front wheel as described in this chapter.
3. Remove the fuel tank as described in Chapter Seven.
4. Remove the handlebars as described in this chapter.
5. Remove the front forks as described in this chapter.
6A. *FZX700*: Perform the following:

   a. Remove the coupler cover and the headlight mounting screws (**Figure 38**).
   b. Disconnect the headlight connector and remove the headlight.
   c. Label and disconnect all wire harness connectors in the headlight cover. Then remove the headlight cover mounting bolts and remove the cover (**Figure 39**).
   d. Remove the upper headlight stay bolts and remove the upper headlight stay (**Figure 40**).
   e. Remove the bolts securing the front brake joint to the steering stem (**Figure 41**). Do not disconnect any hydraulic brake hose.
   f. Remove the lower headlight stay mounting bolts (**Figure 41**) and remove the lower headlight stay.

6B. *FZ700 and FZ750*: Perform the following:

   a. On FZ750 models, remove the cowling stay, headlight and instrument panel assembly.
   b. Remove the bolts securing the front brake joint (**Figure 42**) to the steering stem. Do not disconnect any hydraulic brake hose.

7. See **Figure 43**. Remove the steering stem nut (A) and lift the upper steering stem (B) off of the steering stem shaft.
8. Remove the lockwasher (3, **Figure 37**).
9. Loosen the upper ring nut (**Figure 44**) and remove it. Then remove the washer (5, **Figure 37**) and the lower ring nut (6, **Figure 37**).
10. Remove the bearing cap (7, **Figure 37**) and pull the steering stem out of the frame. See **Figure 45**.
11. Lift the upper bearing (**Figure 45**) from the frame tube.

12. If necessary, remove the lower bearing (**Figure 46**) as follows:
   a. Install a bearing puller (**Figure 47**) onto the steering stem and bearing.
   b. Pull the bearing and seal (**Figure 46**) off of the steering stem.

Assembly/Installation

Refer to **Figure 37**.

1. If the lower bearing was removed from the steering stem, install a new bearing as follows:
   a. Clean the steering stem thoroughly in solvent.
   b. Slide a new seal onto the steering stem.
   c. Slide the new bearing onto the steering stem until it stops.
   d. Align the bearing with the machined portion of the shaft and slide a long hollow pipe over the steering stem (**Figure 48**). Drive the bearing until it rests against the seal.
2. Apply a coat of wheel bearing grease to both bearings.
3. Apply a coat of wheel bearing grease to both bearing races.
4. Carefully slide the steering stem up through the frame neck.
5. Install the upper bearing (**Figure 45**) and the bearing cap (7, **Figure 37**).

NOTE
*Yamaha sells a special ring nut wrench (part No. YU-33975) that can be used with a torque wrench for accurate steering stem installation and adjustment. See **Figure 49**.*

6. Install the lower ring nut (6, **Figure 37**) and tighten in the following order:
   a. Tighten the lower ring nut to 52 N•m (37 ft.-lb.).
   b. Loosen the lower ring nut completely.
   c. Retighten the lower ring nut to 3 N•m (2.2 ft.-lb.).

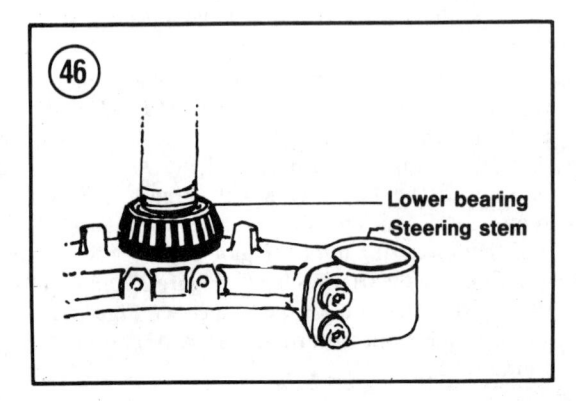

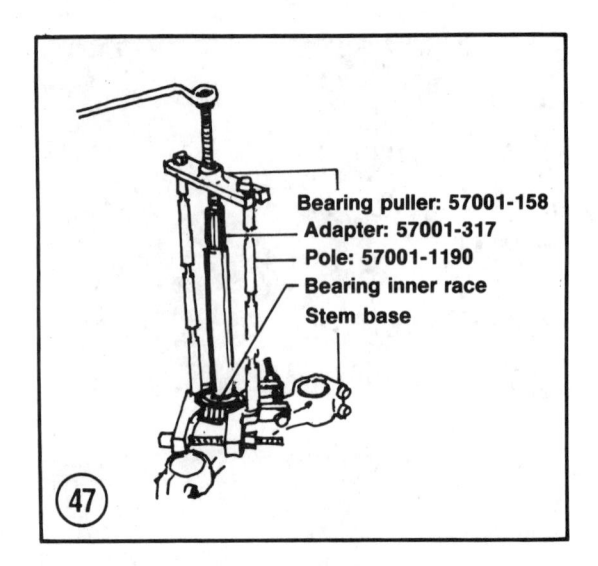

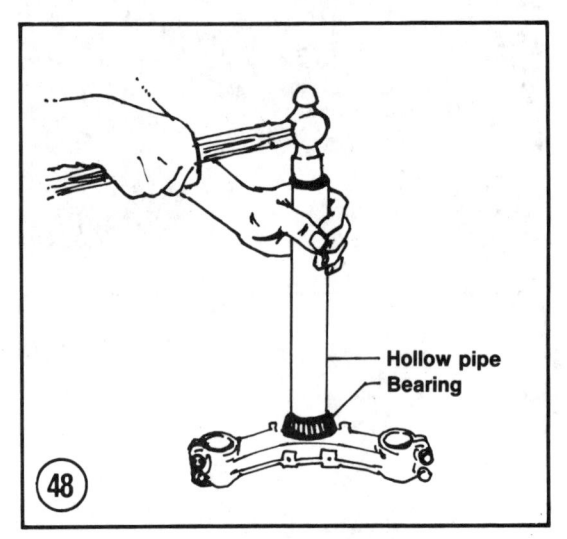

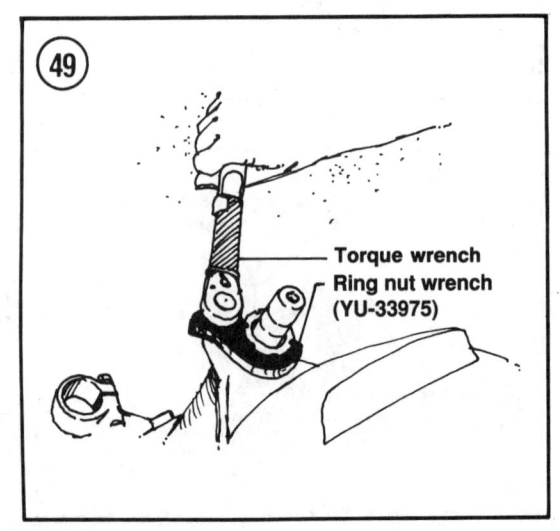

FRONT SUSPENSION AND STEERING

50

Steering nut
Fork tube

51

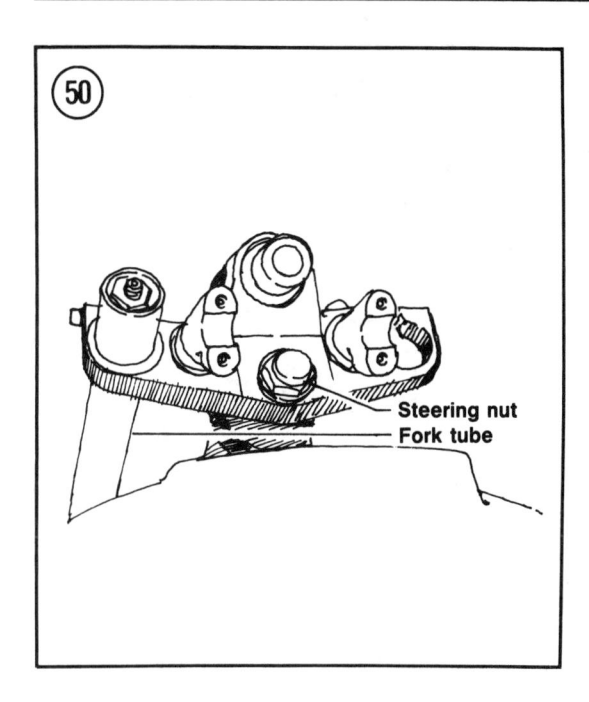

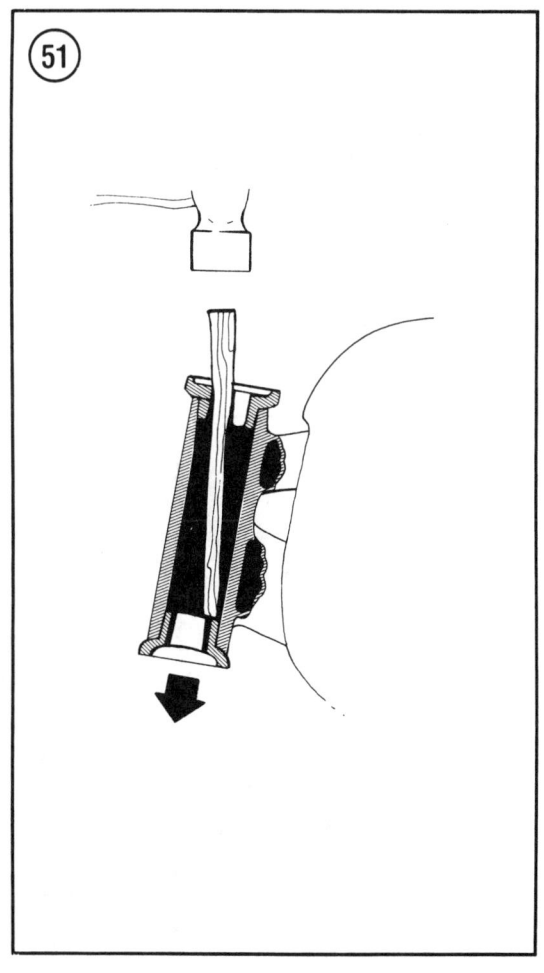

7. Install the washer (5, **Figure 37**) and the upper ring nut (**Figure 44**). Tighten the upper ring nut. Then check that the upper ring nut grooves line up with the lower ring nut grooves. If not, tighten the upper ring nut as required.

8. Install the lockwasher (3, **Figure 37**).

9. Install the upper steering stem and the steering stem nut (**Figure 37**).

10. Insert one fork tube through the steering stem as shown in **Figure 50**. Tighten the steering stem pinch bolts to hold the fork tube in position. Then tighten the steering stem nut to 110 N•m (80 ft.-lb.).

11. Turn the steering stem again by hand to make sure it turns freely and does not bind. If the steering stem is too tight, the bearings can be damaged and the bike will "hunt" at highway speeds; if the steering stem is too loose, the steering will become unstable. Repeat Steps 6-10 if necessary.

12. Reverse Steps 1-6 under *Disassembly* to complete installation.

13. Recheck the steering adjustment. Repeat if necessary.

14. If a brake line was disconnected, bleed the brake system as described under *Bleeding the System* in Chapter Twelve.

Inspection

1. Clean the bearing races in the steering head and both bearings with solvent.

2. Check for broken welds on the frame around the steering stem. If any are found, have them repaired by a competent frame shop or welding service familiar with motorcycle frame repair.

3. Check the bearings for pitting, scratches, or discoloration indicating wear or corrosion. Replace them in sets if any are bad.

4. Check the upper and lower races in the steering head for pitting, galling and corrosion. If any of these conditions exist, replace them as described under *Bearing Race Replacement* in this chapter.

5. Check steering stem for cracks and check its race for damage or wear. Replace if necessary.

Bearing Race Replacement

The headset and steering stem bearing races are pressed into place. Because they are easily bent, do not remove them unless they are worn and require replacement.

To remove a headset race, insert a brass drift into the head tube and carefully tap the race out from the inside (**Figure 51**). Tap all around the race so that neither the race nor the head tube is bent. To install a race, fit it into the end of the head tube. Tap it slowly and squarely with a block of wood (**Figure 52**).

FRONT FORK

Removal/Installation

1. Remove the front wheel as described in this chapter.
2. Remove the brake caliper(s) as described under *Front Caliper Removal/Installation* in Chapter Twelve.

NOTE
Insert a piece of wood in the calipers in place of the disc. That way, if the brake lever is inadvertently squeezed, the pistons will not be forced out of the calipers. If it does happen, the calipers might have to be disassembled to reseat the pistons. By using the wood, bleeding the brake is not necessary when installing the wheel.

3. *Air assist fork:* Remove the air valve cap and depress the valve (**Figure 53**) to release fork air pressure. See **Figure 53** or **Figure 54**.
4. Remove the front fender bolts and remove the front fender (**Figure 55**).

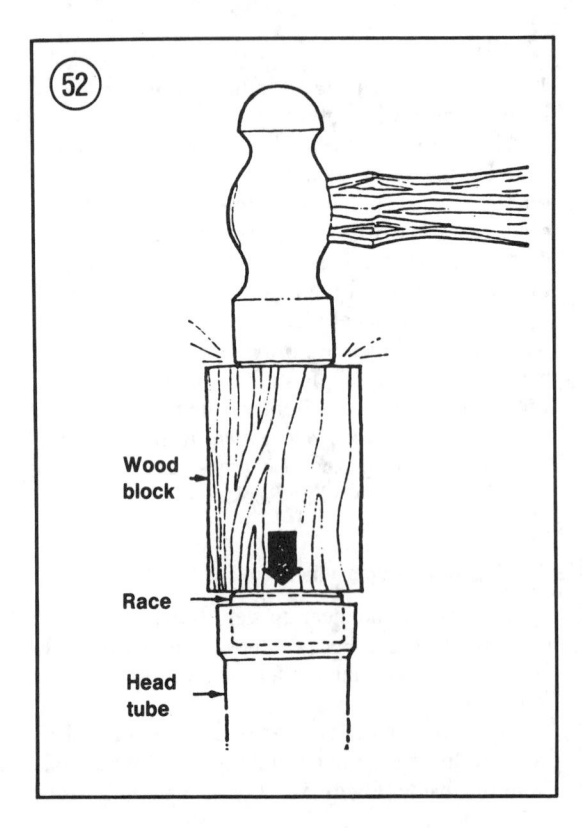

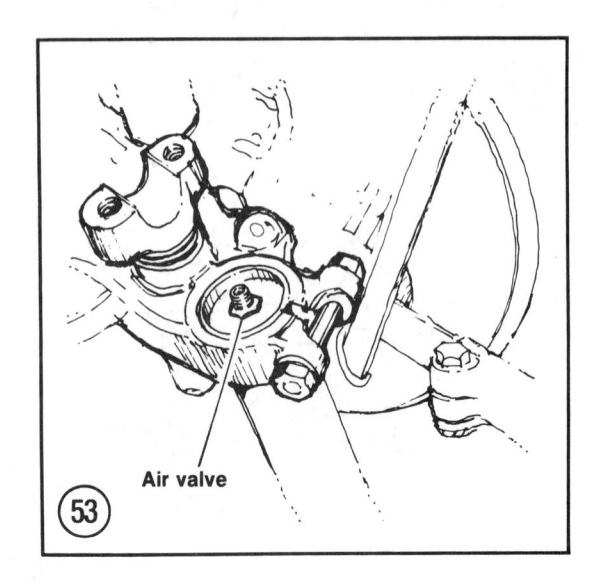

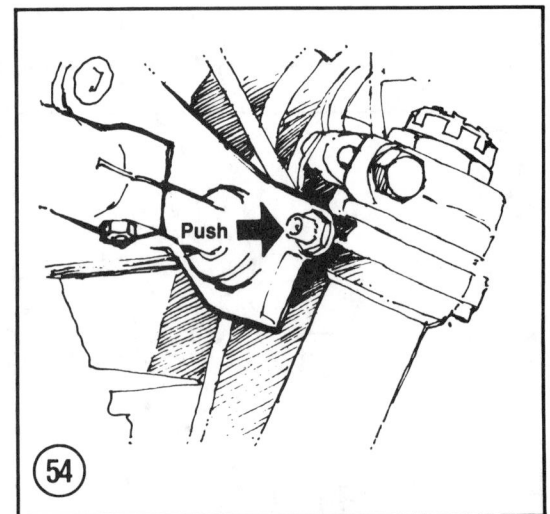

FRONT SUSPENSION AND STEERING

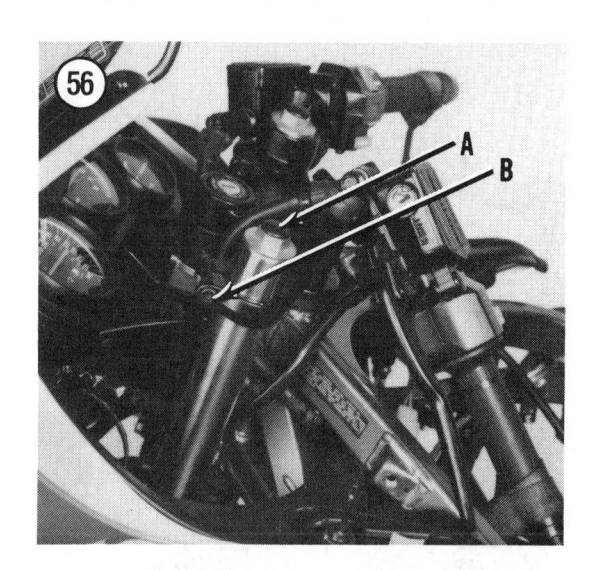

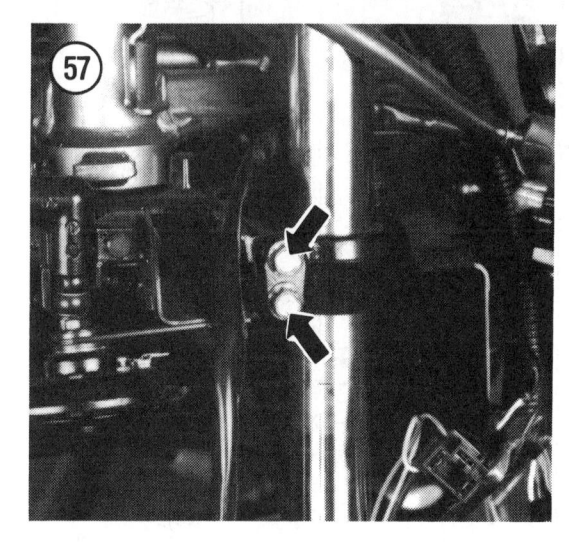

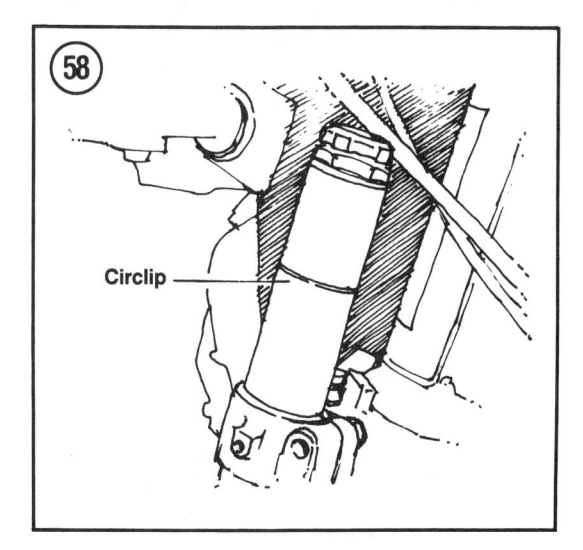

NOTE
Step 5 describes how to loosen the fork caps while the forks are held in the steering stem.

WARNING
The fork caps are held under spring pressure. Take precautions to prevent the caps from flying into your face during removal. Furthermore, if the fork tubes are bent, the fork caps will be under considerable pressure; have them removed by a Yamaha dealer.

5. If the front fork tubes will be disassembled, remove the handlebars (if necessary) as described in this chapter. Then loosen the fork caps (but do not remove them) with a socket. See A, **Figure 56**.

6. Loosen the upper (B, **Figure 56**) and lower (**Figure 57**) fork tube pinch bolts.

7A. *FZ750:* Remove the fork tubes as follows:
   a. Twist the fork tube and pull it down until the fork tube circlip (**Figure 58**) is accessible. Tighten the lower fork tube pinch bolt (**Figure 57**).
   b. Slide off the rubber spacer (**Figure 59**).
   c. Using a small-tipped screwdriver, pry the circlip out of its groove and slide it off of the fork tube (**Figure 58**).
   d. Loosen the lower fork tube pinch bolt (**Figure 57**) and slide the fork tube out of the lower steering stem.

7B. *FZX700:* Twist the fork tube and remove it.

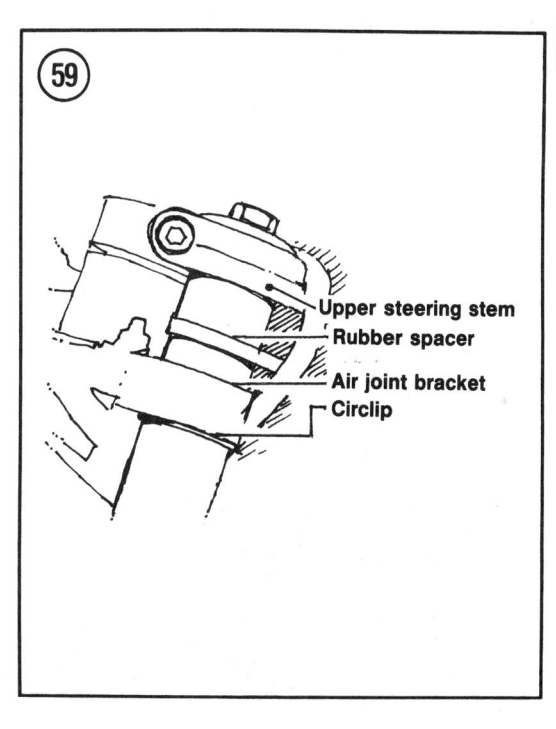

7C. *FZ700:* Remove the fork tube as follows:
   a. Measure the height of the fork tube in the upper steering stem (**Figure 60**). Record this measurement so that the fork tube can be reinstalled in the same position.
   b. Twist the fork tube (**Figure 61**) and remove it.
8. Repeat for the opposite side.
9. Install by reversing these removal steps. Note the following:
   a. Apply a coat of light machine oil to the fork cap threads before installation.
   b. *FZ750:* After installing the fork tube through the lower steering stem, slide the circlip over the top of the fork tube (**Figure 58**) and seat it in the fork tube groove. Then install the rubber spacer so that it is positioned between the air joint bracket and the upper steering stem (**Figure 59**). Then push the fork tube upward until the circlip seats against the air joint bracket.
   c. *FZ700:* Slide the fork tubes into the steering stem so that the distance from the upper steering step to the top of the fork tube is the same as that recorded in Step 7C. See **Figure 60**.
   d. Tighten the upper and lower fork tube pinch bolts to the specifications in **Table 2**.
   e. Apply Loctite 242 (blue) to the front fender bolts and tighten securely.
   f. After installing the front wheel, squeeze the front brake lever. If the brake lever feels spongy, bleed the brake(s) as described under *Bleeding the System* in Chapter Twelve.
   g. Refill the front fork air pressure as described under *Suspension Adjustment* in Chapter Three.

Disassembly

Refer to **Figure 62** (FZX700), **Figure 63** (FZ700) or **Figure 64** (FZ750).

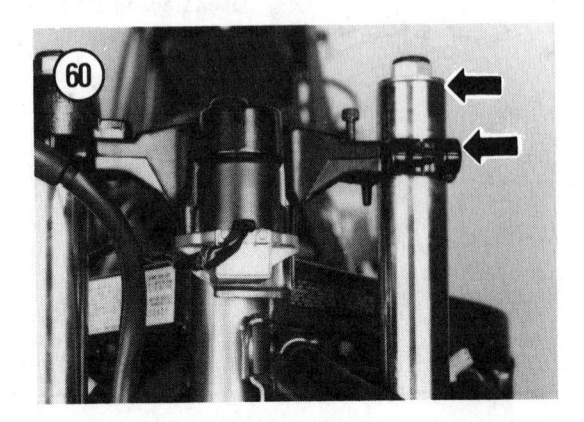

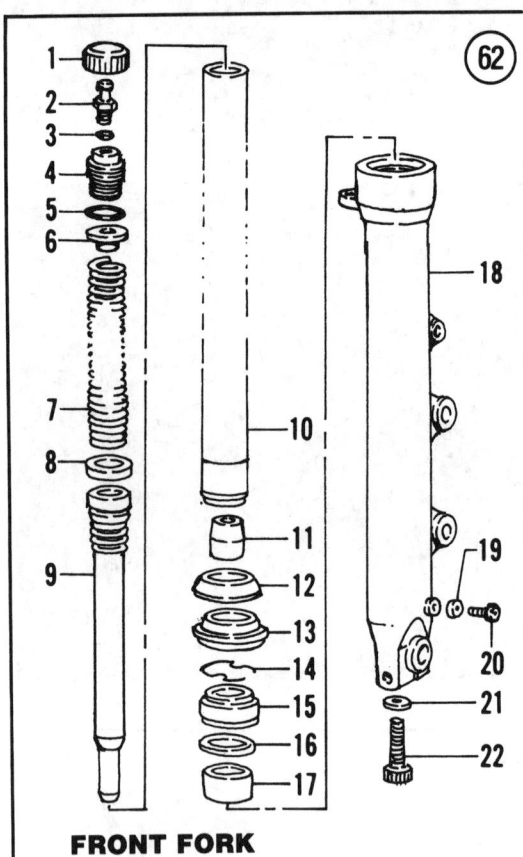

FRONT FORK (FZX700)

1. Cover
2. Air valve
3. O-ring
4. Fork cap
5. O-ring
6. Spring seat
7. Fork spring
8. Piston ring
9. Damper rod
10. Upper fork tube
11. Oil lock piece
12. Dust seal cover
13. Dust seal
14. Circlip
15. Oil seal
16. Washer
17. Bushing
18. Lower fork tube
19. O-ring
20. Screw
21. Washer
22. Allen bolt

FRONT SUSPENSION AND STEERING

63 FRONT FORK (FZ700)

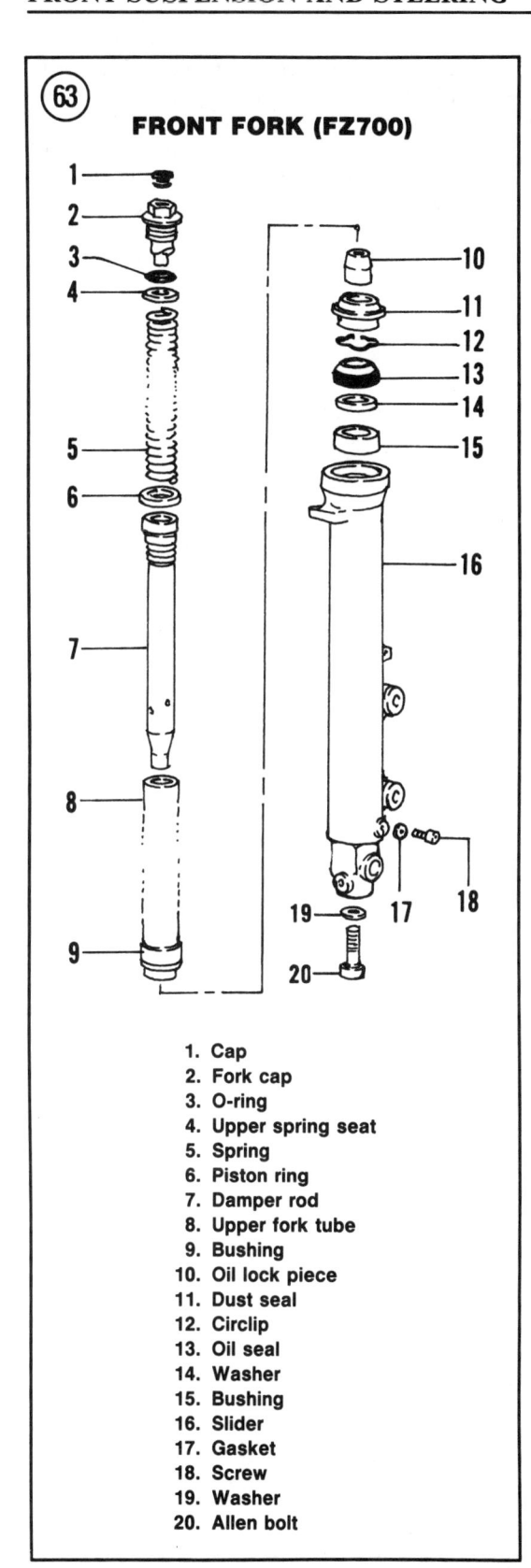

1. Cap
2. Fork cap
3. O-ring
4. Upper spring seat
5. Spring
6. Piston ring
7. Damper rod
8. Upper fork tube
9. Bushing
10. Oil lock piece
11. Dust seal
12. Circlip
13. Oil seal
14. Washer
15. Bushing
16. Slider
17. Gasket
18. Screw
19. Washer
20. Allen bolt

64

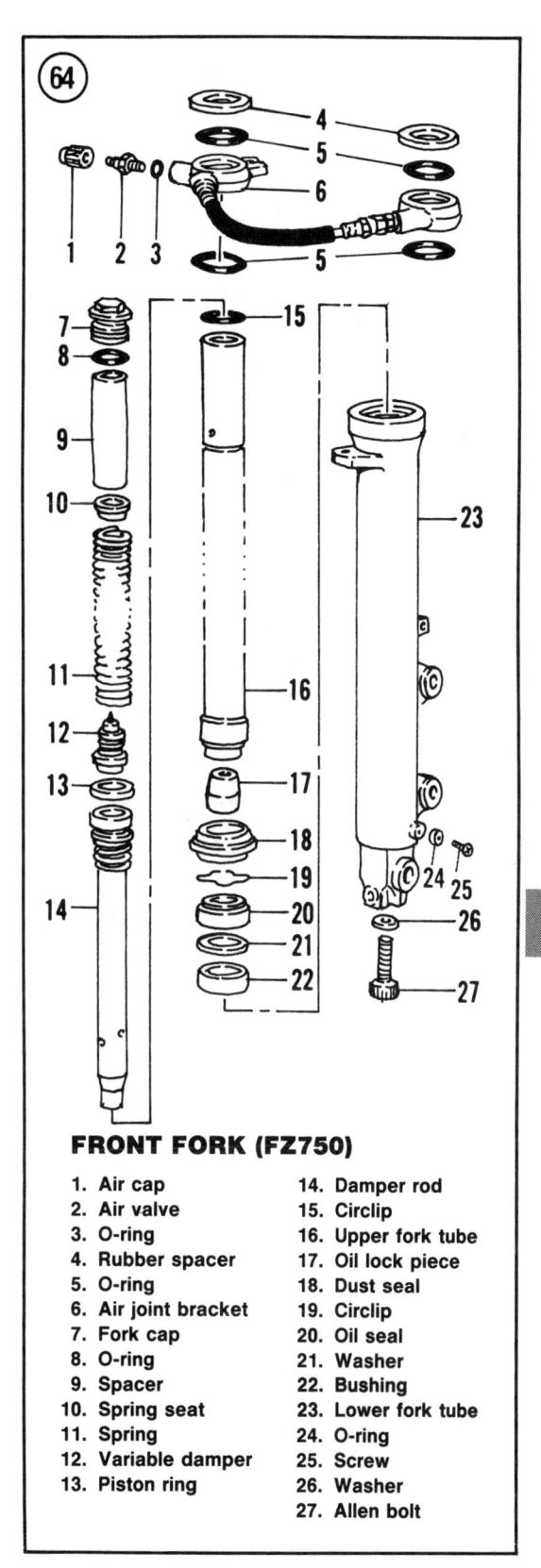

FRONT FORK (FZ750)

1. Air cap
2. Air valve
3. O-ring
4. Rubber spacer
5. O-ring
6. Air joint bracket
7. Fork cap
8. O-ring
9. Spacer
10. Spring seat
11. Spring
12. Variable damper
13. Piston ring
14. Damper rod
15. Circlip
16. Upper fork tube
17. Oil lock piece
18. Dust seal
19. Circlip
20. Oil seal
21. Washer
22. Bushing
23. Lower fork tube
24. O-ring
25. Screw
26. Washer
27. Allen bolt

1. Secure the fork tube in a vise with soft jaws.
2. The fork cap was loosened during removal. Remove the fork cap and the upper spring seat.
3. Remove the fork spring.
4. *FZ750:* Remove the variable damper (**Figure 64**).
5. Hold the fork tube over a drain pan. Pour the oil out and discard it. Pump the fork several times by hand to expel most of the remaining oil.
6. Remove the following parts in order:
   a. Dust seal cover (FZX700). See **Figure 65**.
   b. Dust seal.
   c. Circlip.

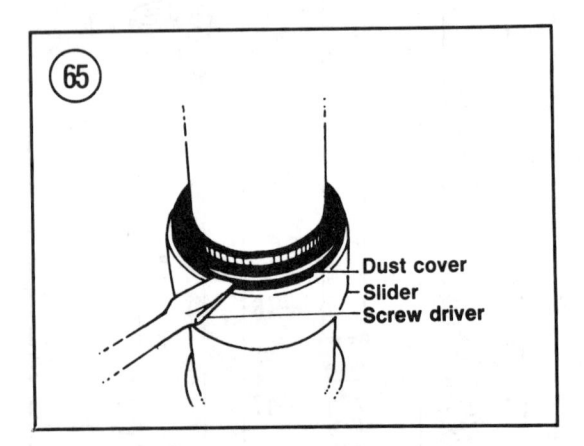

7. Remove the Allen bolt and gasket (**Figure 66**) from the bottom of the outer tube. Prevent the damper rod from turning with a long 3/8 in. drive T-handle and the Yamaha damper rod holder (YM-01300-1). Install the damper rod holder onto the T-handle (**Figure 67**) and insert the T-handle into the fork tube so that the damper rod holder locks the damper rod (**Figure 68**). Turn the Allen bolt and remove it.

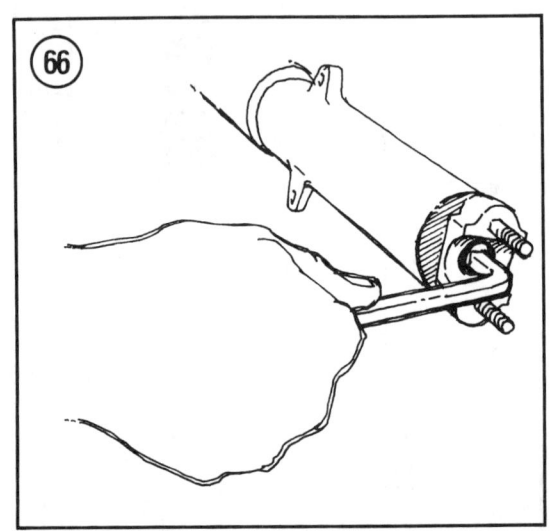

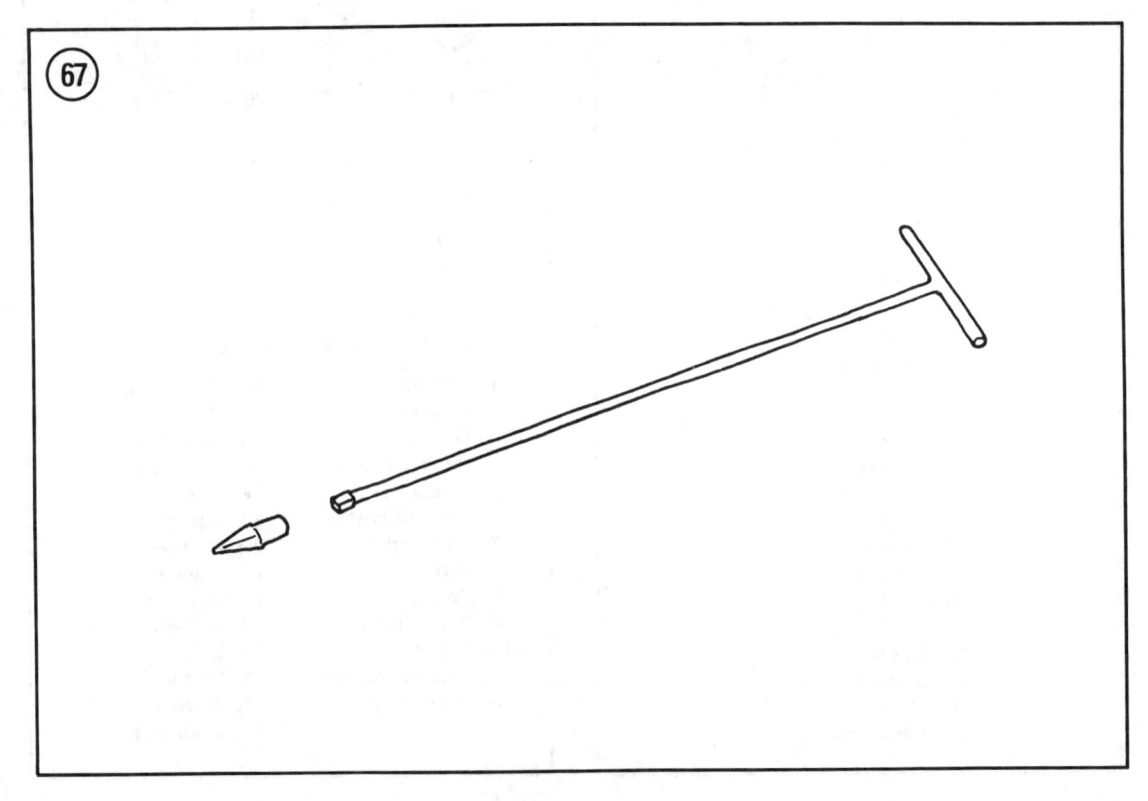

FRONT SUSPENSION AND STEERING

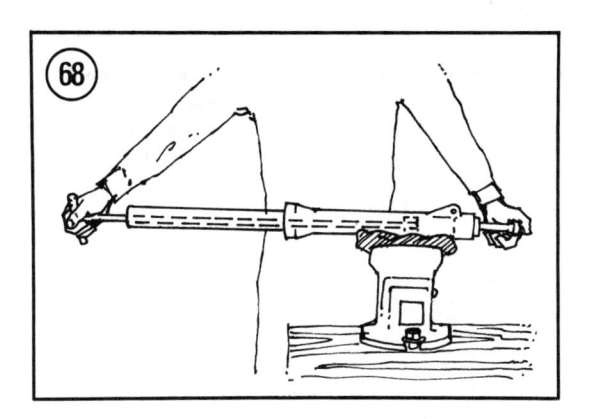

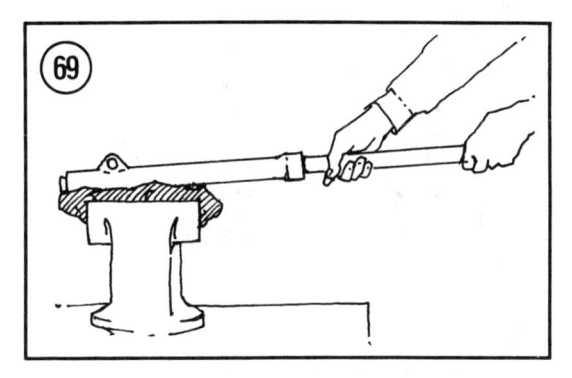

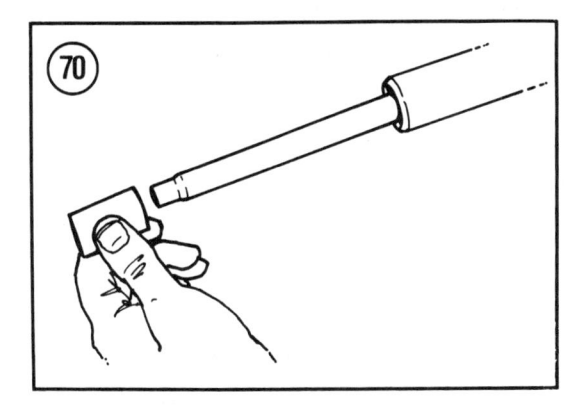

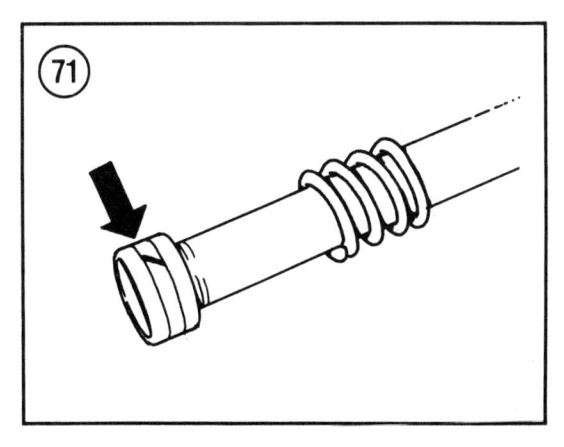

NOTE
The Allen bolt may be removed without holding the cylinder if an air impact driver is used.

8. Grasp the upper fork tube in one hand and the lower fork tube in the other. Work the lower fork tube back and forth and separate the fork tube assemblies. See **Figure 69**.
9. Remove the oil lock piece (**Figure 70**) and slide the damper rod and spring out of the upper fork tube.

Inspection

1. Thoroughly clean all parts in solvent and dry them.
2. Check both fork tubes for wear or scratches. Check the upper fork tube for straightness. If bent, refer service to a Yamaha dealer.
3. Check the upper fork tube for chrome flaking or creasing; this condition will damage oil seals. Replace the fork tube if necessary.
4. Check the lower fork tube oil seal area for dents or other damage that would allow oil leakage or impair movement. Replace the fork tube if necessary.
5. Check the damper rod for straightness.
6. Check the damper rod piston ring (**Figure 71**) for tearing, cracks or damage.
7. Check the guide bushings for scoring, nicks or damage. Replace if necessary by pulling off the fork tube.
8. Measure the uncompressed length of the fork springs with a tape measure and compare to specifications in **Table 1**. Replace the fork spring(s) if too short.

NOTE
If one fork spring is replaced, it is best to replace both springs to keep the forks balanced for steering stability.

9. Replace the fork cap O-ring if deformed or damaged.

10. *FZ750:* Check the variable damper as follows:
   a. Measure the height of the variable damper with a vernier caliper between the points indicated in **Figure 72**.
   b. The correct height measurement is 42 mm (1.65 in.). If the height measurement is incorrect, loosen the locknut (**Figure 72**) and turn the adjuster in or out as required. Tighten the locknut and recheck the measurement.
   c. Visually inspect the variable damper springs, spring seat and spool for cracks, breakage or other damage; replace the variable damper if necessary.

Assembly

1. Slide the damper rod into the upper fork tube.
2. *FZ750:* Install the variable damper into the upper fork tube so that the locknut end faces up (**Figure 72**).
3. Slide the oil lock piece (**Figure 70**) onto the damper rod.
4. Insert the damper rod/upper fork tube into the lower fork tube (**Figure 73**).
5. Apply Loctite 242 (blue) onto the fork tube Allen bolt (**Figure 74**). Install the Allen bolt and tighten to 40 N•m (29 ft.-lb.). Use the same tool to prevent the damper rod from turning as during disassembly.
6. Slide the bushing down the upper fork tube. Then drive the bushing into the lower fork tube with the Yamaha front fork seal driver (YM-33963) and adapter (YM-34482). See **Figure 75**.

NOTE
A piece of pipe can also work as a tool. If both ends of the pipe are threaded, wrap one end with duct tape to prevent the threads from damaging the interior of the slider.

7. Slide the washer down the upper fork tube until it rests against the bushing.
8. Position the oil seal with the marking facing slide down onto the fork tube. Drive the seal into the lower fork tube with the Yamaha Front fork seal driver (YM-33963) and adapter (YM-34482). See **Figure 75**. Drive the oil seal in until the circlip grove in the lower fork tube can be seen above the top surface of the oil seal.

NOTE
The oil seal can be driven in with a homemade tool as described in the NOTE following Step 6.

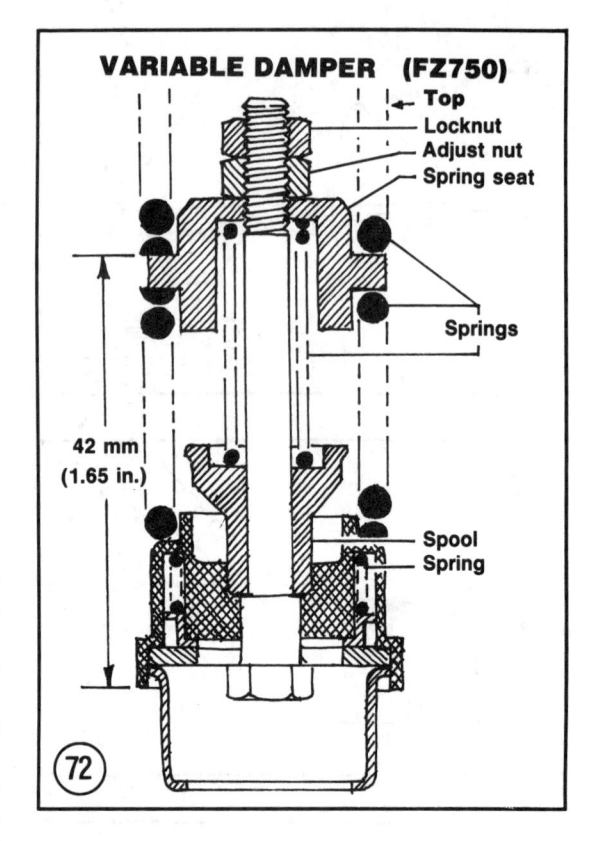

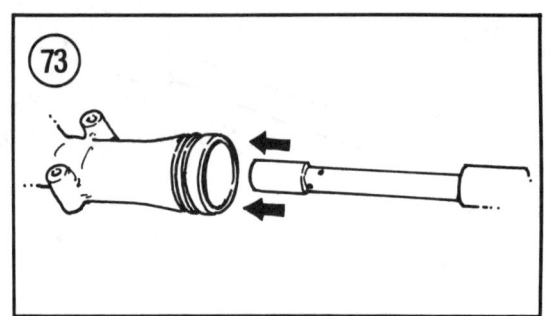

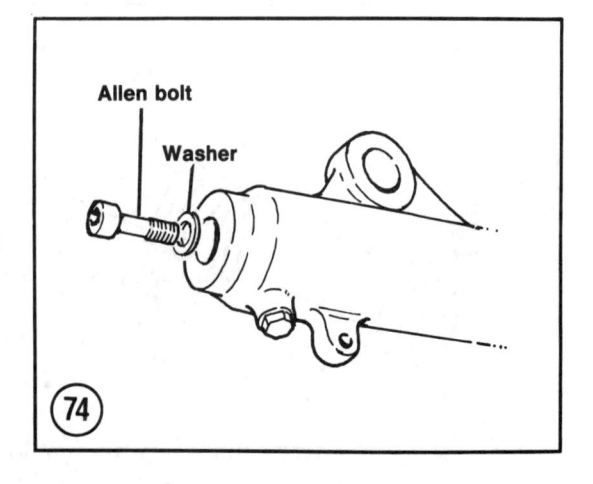

FRONT SUSPENSION AND STEERING

⑦⑤

- Lower fork tube
- Guide bushing
- Driver

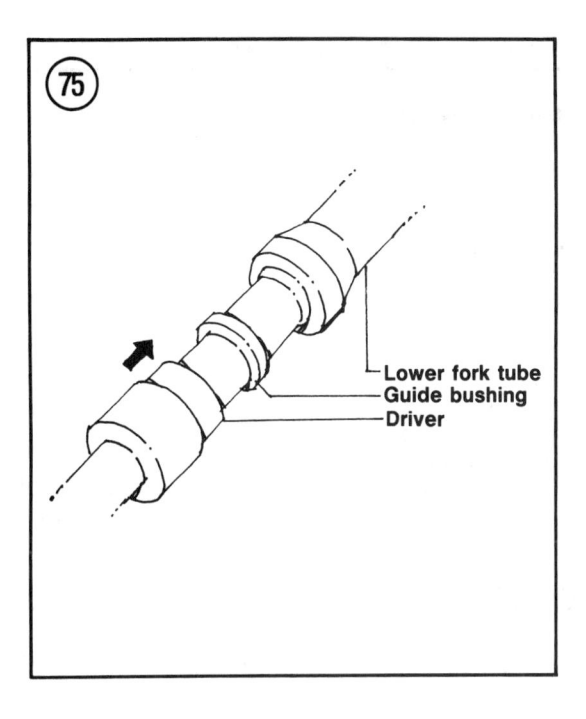

9. Slide the circlip down the inner fork tube and seat it in the lower fork tube groove. Make sure the circlip is completely seated in the groove.
10. Slide the dust seal down the inner fork tube and seat it in the lower fork tube.
11. *FZX700:* Slide the dust seal cover down the inner fork tube and seat it in the lower fork tube.
12. Fill the fork tube with the correct quantity of 10W fork oil as specified in **Table 1**.
13. Install the fork spring with the closer wound coils toward the top of the fork.
14. Install the spacer (if so equipped) and spring seat.
15. Pull the upper and lower fork tubes as far as apart as possible. Apply a light coat of oil to the fork cap and install it by slightly compressing the fork spring. Once the fork cap is installed, it can be tightened after installing the fork tube onto the motorcycle. See *Front Fork Removal/Installation* in this chapter.
16. Refill the front fork air pressure. See Chapter Three.

Tables are on the following page.

Table 1 FRONT SUSPENSION AND STEERING SPECIFICATIONS

Steering head	
Type	Tapered roller bearing
Front fork	
Front fork travel	140 mm (5.51 in.)
Spring free length wear limit	
FZX700	570.6 mm (22.46 in.)
FZ700	552.9 mm (21.77 in.)
FZ750	425 mm (16.73 in.)
Oil viscosity	10 weight
Air pressure	See Chapter Three
Front fork oil capacity	
FZX700	294 cc (9.94 oz.)
FZ700	404 cc (13.7 oz.)
FZ750	408 cc (13.8 oz.)
Front wheel runout	2.0 mm (0.079 in.)

Table 2 FRONT SUSPENSION TIGHTENING TORQUES

Item	N-m	ft.-lb.
Front axle	58	42
Front axle pinch bolt	20	14
Steering stem		
Steering stem nut	110	80
Upper pinch bolt	20	14
Lower pinch bolt	23	17
Handlebar holder (FTZ700)		
Upper bolt	20	14
Lower nut	30	22
Handlebar (FZ700 & FZ750)		
Handlebar to fork bolt	20	14
Handlebar to steering stem bolt	9	6.5
Handlebar end grip	26	19
Front fender bolts	9	6.5

CHAPTER ELEVEN

REAR SUSPENSION

This chapter includes repair and replacement procedures for the rear wheel, drive chain and rear suspension components.

Tables 1-6 (end of chapter) list rear suspension specifications and tightening torques.

REAR WHEEL

Removal/Installation

1. Support the bike so that the rear wheel clears the ground.

2. Remove the torque link nut (A, **Figure 1**) and disconnect the torque link at the brake caliper.

3. Remove the 2 brake caliper bolts (B, **Figure 1**) and lift the brake caliper off of the brake disc. Secure the caliper with a bungee cord.

NOTE
Insert a piece of wood in the caliper in place of the disc. That way, if the brake pedal is inadvertently pressed, the pistons will not be forced out of the cylinders. If this does happen, the caliper might have to be disassembled to reseat the pistons and the system will have to be bled.

4. Loosen the drive chain adjusting locknuts and adjuster bolts (**Figure 2**).

5. Remove the cotter pin and remove the rear axle nut (**Figure 3**) from the left-hand side.

6. Slide the axle (**Figure 4**) out of the wheel and allow the wheel to drop to the ground.

7. Lift the drive chain off the sprocket and pull the wheel away from the swing arm (**Figure 5**).

8. Remove the left- (**Figure 6**) and right-hand (**Figure 7**) axle spacers.

CAUTION
Do not set the wheel down on the disc surface as it may be scratched or bent. Either lean the wheel against a wall or place it on a couple of wood blocks.

9. If the wheel is going to be off for any length of time, or if it is to be taken to a shop for repair, install the chain adjusters and axle spacers on the axle along with the axle nut to prevent losing any parts.

10. If necessary, service the rear sprocket as described under *Rear Sprocket and Coupling* in this chapter.

11. Installation is the reverse of these steps. Note the following:
   a. To prevent axle seizure, coat the axle with an anti-seize compound such as Bostik Never-Seez Lubricating & Anti-Seize Compound (part no. 49501).
   b. Insert the rear sprocket/coupling assembly into the rear hub if removed. See **Figure 8**.
   c. Adjust the drive chain as described under drive chain adjustment in Chapter Three.

REAR SUSPENSION

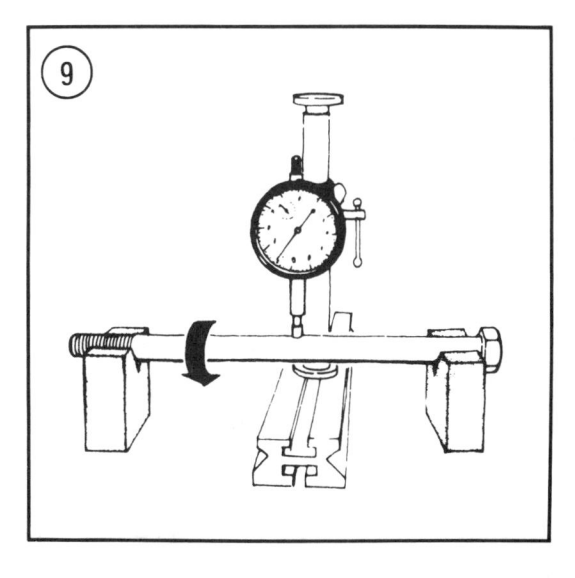

d. Tighten the torque link nut securely.
e. Tighten the axle nut to specifications in **Table 1**. Secure the nut with a new cotter pin.
f. Adjust the rear brake as described under *Rear Brake Pedal Height Adjustment* and *Rear Brake Light Switch Adjustment* in Chapter Three.
g. Spin the wheel several times to make sure it rotates freely and that the brake works properly.

Inspection

1. Remove any corrosion on the rear axle with a piece of fine emery cloth.
2. Check axle runout. Place the axle on V-blocks (**Figure 9**). Place the tip of a dial indicator in the middle of the axle. Rotate the axle and check runout. If the runout exceeds 0.2 mm (0.008 in.) but does not exceed 0.7 mm (0.027 in.), have it straightened by a dealer or machine shop to read less than 0.2 mm (0.008 in.) runout. If the runout exceeds 0.7 mm (0.027 in.), replace the axle; do not attempt to straighten it.
3. Check rim runout as follows:
   a. Remove the tire from the wheel as described under *Tubeless Tire Changing* in Chapter Ten.
   b. Measure the radial (up and down) runout of the wheel rim with a dial indicator as shown in **Figure 10**. If runout exceeds 2.0 mm (0.08 in.), check the wheel bearings as described under *Rear Hub* in this chapter.

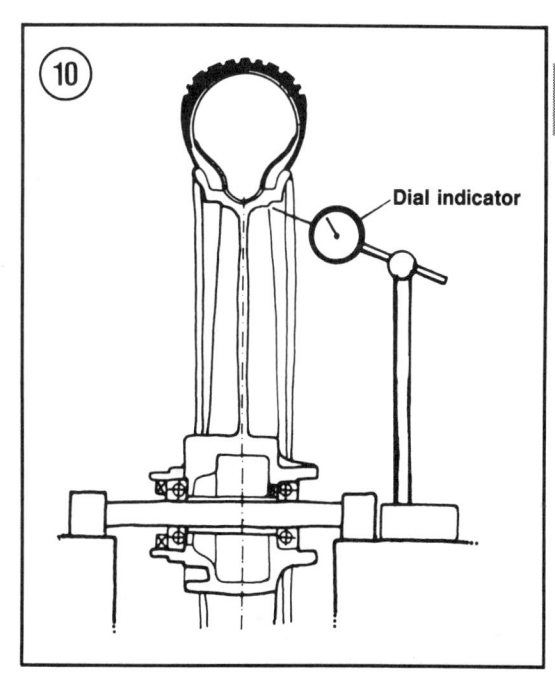

CHAPTER ELEVEN

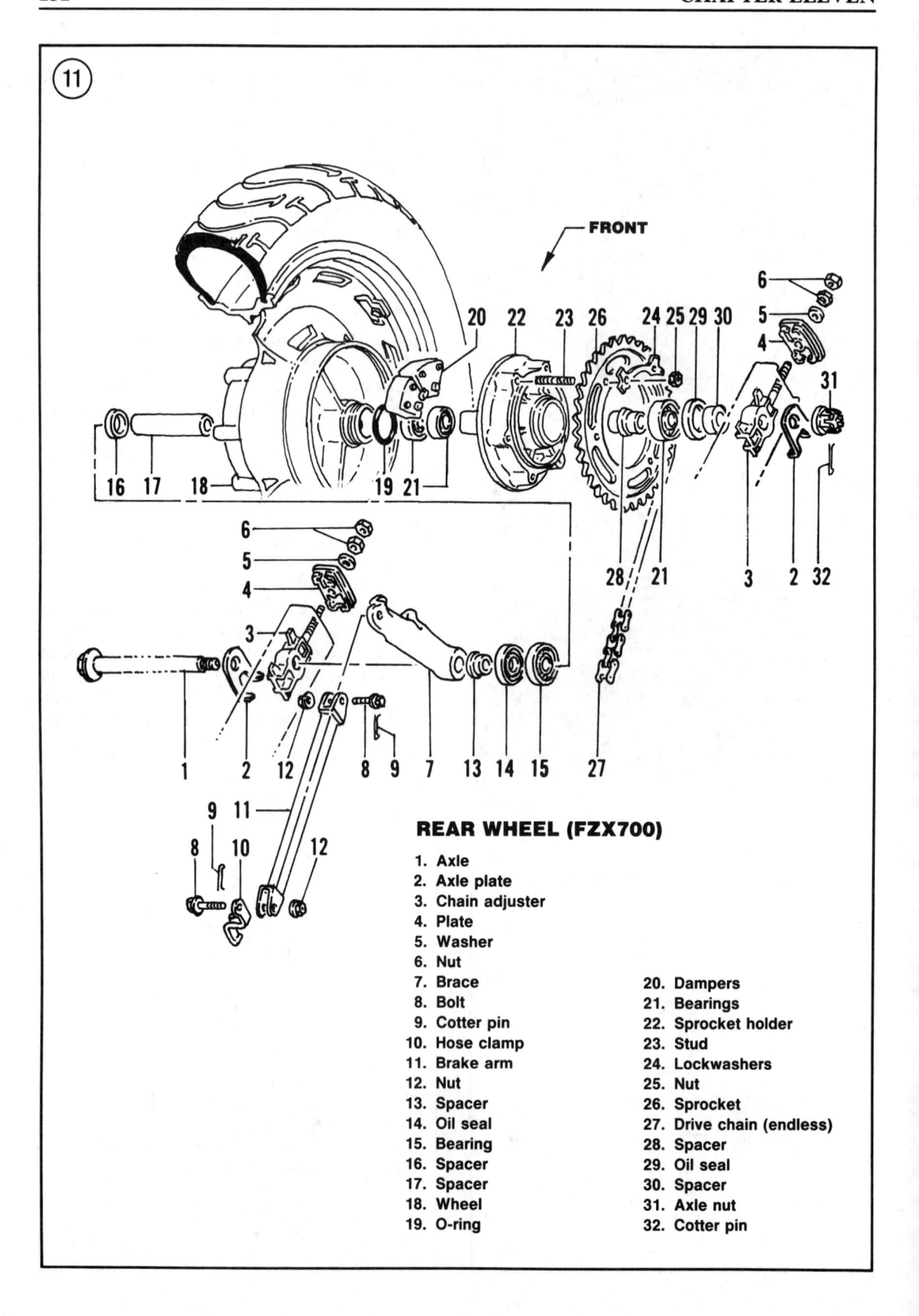

REAR WHEEL (FZX700)

1. Axle
2. Axle plate
3. Chain adjuster
4. Plate
5. Washer
6. Nut
7. Brace
8. Bolt
9. Cotter pin
10. Hose clamp
11. Brake arm
12. Nut
13. Spacer
14. Oil seal
15. Bearing
16. Spacer
17. Spacer
18. Wheel
19. O-ring
20. Dampers
21. Bearings
22. Sprocket holder
23. Stud
24. Lockwashers
25. Nut
26. Sprocket
27. Drive chain (endless)
28. Spacer
29. Oil seal
30. Spacer
31. Axle nut
32. Cotter pin

REAR SUSPENSION

c. Measure the axial (side to side) runout of the wheel rim with a dial indicator as shown in **Figure 10**. If runout exceeds 2.0 mm (0.08 in.), check the wheel bearings as described under *Rear Hub* in this chapter.
d. If the wheel bearings are okay, the wheel cannot be serviced, but must be replaced.
e. Replace the rear wheel bearings as described under *Rear Hub* in this chapter.

4. Inspect the wheel rim for dents, bending or cracks. Check the rim and rim sealing surface for scratches that are deeper than 0.5 mm (0.02 in.). If any of these conditions are present, replace the wheel.

REAR HUB

Disassembly/Inspection/Reassembly

Refer to **Figure 11** (FZX700) or **Figure 12** (FZ700 and FZ750) for this procedure.

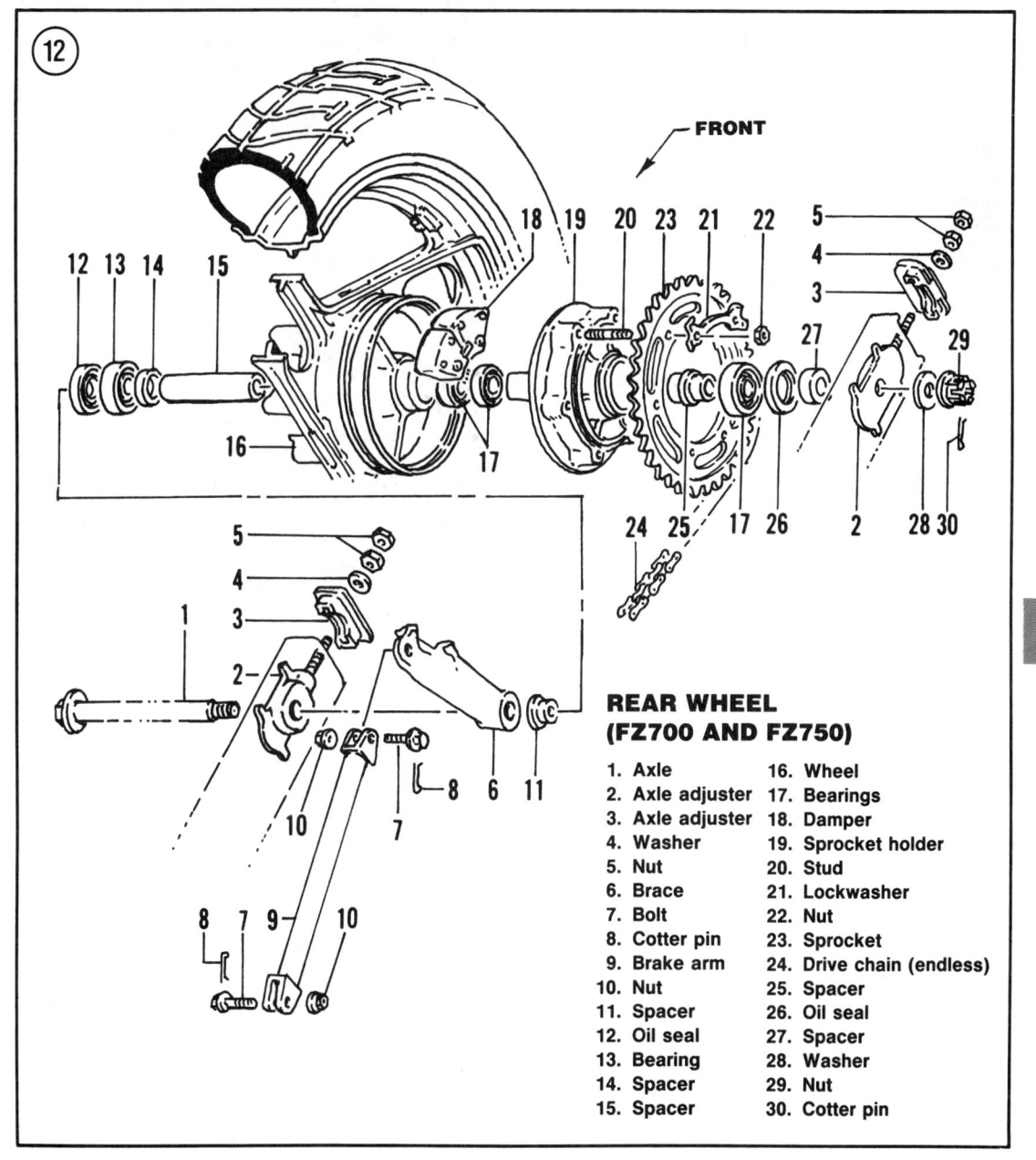

REAR WHEEL (FZ700 AND FZ750)

1. Axle
2. Axle adjuster
3. Axle adjuster
4. Washer
5. Nut
6. Brace
7. Bolt
8. Cotter pin
9. Brake arm
10. Nut
11. Spacer
12. Oil seal
13. Bearing
14. Spacer
15. Spacer
16. Wheel
17. Bearings
18. Damper
19. Sprocket holder
20. Stud
21. Lockwasher
22. Nut
23. Sprocket
24. Drive chain (endless)
25. Spacer
26. Oil seal
27. Spacer
28. Washer
29. Nut
30. Cotter pin

1. Check the wheel bearings (**Figure 13**) by rotating the inner race. Check for bearing roughness, excessive noise or damage. If necessary, replace the bearings as follows. Always replace bearings in a set.
2. Lift the rear sprocket/coupling assembly (**Figure 8**) out of the rear hub.
3. Using a long drift or screwdriver, pry the oil seal from the left- (**Figure 14**) and right-hand (**Figure 15**) sides.
4. Using a long drift and hammer, tilt the center spacer away from one side of the right-hand bearing (**Figure 16**). Then drive the right-hand bearing out of the hub. See **Figure 16**.
5. Remove the short and long spacers and remove the right-hand bearing.
6. Clean the spacers and hub thoroughly in solvent.
7. Tap the right-hand bearing into place carefully using a suitable size socket placed on the outer bearing race (**Figure 17**).
8. Install the short and long spacers and install the left-hand bearing as described in Step 7.
9. Install new left- and right-hand grease seals. Drive the seal in squarely with a large diameter socket on the outer portion of the seal (**Figure 18**). Drive the seal until it is flush with the side of the hub.

REAR SPROCKET AND COUPLING

The rear wheel coupling (**Figure 8**) connects the rear sprocket to the rear wheel. The coupling housing is equipped with an oil seal, ball bearing and spacer. Rubber shock dampers installed in the coupling absorb some of the shock that results from torque changes during acceleration or braking.

Removal/Installation

Refer to **Figure 11** (FZX700) or **Figure 12** (FZ700 and FZ750) for this procedure.
1. Remove the rear wheel as described in this chapter.
2. Pull the rear wheel sprocket holder assembly (**Figure 8**) up and out of the wheel hub.
3. Pull the dampers (**Figure 11** or **Figure 12**) out of the hub.
4. Remove the spacer.
5. To remove the sprocket, bend down the lockwasher tabs, loosen and remove the nuts (A, **Figure 19**) and lift the sprocket (B, **Figure 19**) off of the housing.
6. Perform *Inspection/Disassembly/Reassembly* as described in this chapter.

REAR SUSPENSION

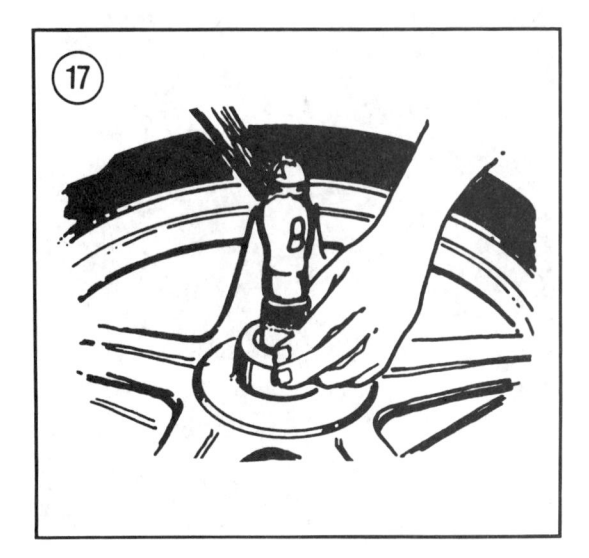

7. Install by reversing these steps. Note the following:
   a. Apply Loctite 242 (blue) to the sprocket nuts and tighten them to the specifications in **Tables 4-6** for your model.
   b. Bend the new lockwasher tabs over the sprocket nuts to lock them.

Inspection/Disassembly/Reassembly

1. Visually inspect the rubber dampers for damage or deterioration. Replace, if necessary, as a complete set.
2. Inspect the damper separators for cracks or damage. Replace the sprocket holder if necessary.
3. If necessary, replace the sprocket holder bearing as follows:
   a. Pry the seal from the housing (**Figure 14**).
   b. Using a large diameter socket or drift on the bearing, drive it out of the housing (from the inside out).
   c. Discard the bearing.
   d. Clean the sprocket holder thoroughly in solvent and check for cracks or damage in the bearing area.
   e. Blow any dirt or foreign matter out of the sprocket holder prior to installing the bearing.
   f. Pack non-sealed bearings with grease before installation. Sealed bearings do not require packing.
   g. Tap the bearing into position with a socket placed on the outer bearing race.
   h. Install a new seal by driving it in squarely with a socket and hammer.

Sprocket Inspection

Inspect the teeth of the sprocket. If the teeth are visibly worn, replace both sprockets and the drive chain. Never replace any one sprocket or chain as a separate item; worn parts will cause rapid wear of the new component.

Front sprocket replacement is described under *Engine Sprocket* in Chapter Six.

DRIVE CHAIN

Because the drive chain is endless (has no master link), the swing arm must be removed to remove the drive chain.

> **WARNING**
> *Yamaha uses an endless chain on all models for strength and reliability. Do not cut the chain with a chain cutter or install a chain with a master link. The chain may fail and rear wheel lockup and an accident could result.*

Removal/Installation

1. Remove the rear wheel as described in this chapter.
2. Remove the shift linkage (**Figure 20**); remove the pivot circlip (A) and the pinch bolt (B) securing the shift linkage and pull the shift linkage off. If the pivot boss is tight on the shaft, spread the slot open with a screwdriver. On FZX700 models, remove the pinch bolt.

> **NOTE**
> *It is not necessary to remove the clutch slave cylinder from the sprocket cover when removing the sprocket cover from the engine.*

3. Remove the screws securing the engine sprocket cover and remove the cover (**Figure 21**).
4. Remove the swing arm as described in this chapter.
5. Slip the drive chain off of the swing arm.
6. Install by reversing the removal steps. Note the following:
   a. If the clutch slave cylinder was removed, install it as described under *Clutch Slave Cylinder Removal/Installation* in Chapter Five. Bleed the clutch as described in Chapter Five.
   b. Adjust the drive chain as described under *Drive Chain Adjustment* in Chapter Three.
   c. Tighten the axle nut to the torque values in **Tables 4-6** for your model.
   d. Rotate the wheel several times to make sure it rotates smoothly. Apply the brake several times to make sure it operates correctly.
   e. Adjust the rear brake as described under *Rear Brake Pedal Height Adjustment* and *Rear Brake Light Switch Adjustment* in Chapter Three.

Cleaning

> **CAUTION**
> *The factory drive chain is equipped with O-rings between the side plates that seal lubricant between the pins and bushings. To prevent damaging these O-rings, use only kerosene for cleaning. Do not use gasoline or other solvents that will cause the O-rings to swell or deteriorate.*

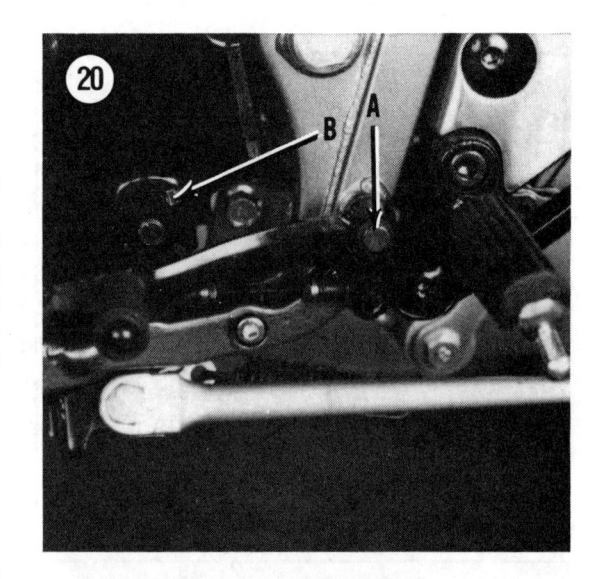

REAR SUSPENSION

Occasionally, the drive chain should be removed from the bike for a thorough cleaning and soak lubrication. Perform the following:
 a. Brush off excess dirt and grit.
 b. Remove the drive chain as described in this chapter.
 c. Soak the chain in kerosene for about half an hour and clean it thoroughly. Then hang the chain from a piece of wire and allow it to dry.
 d. Install the chain on the motorcycle as described in this chapter.

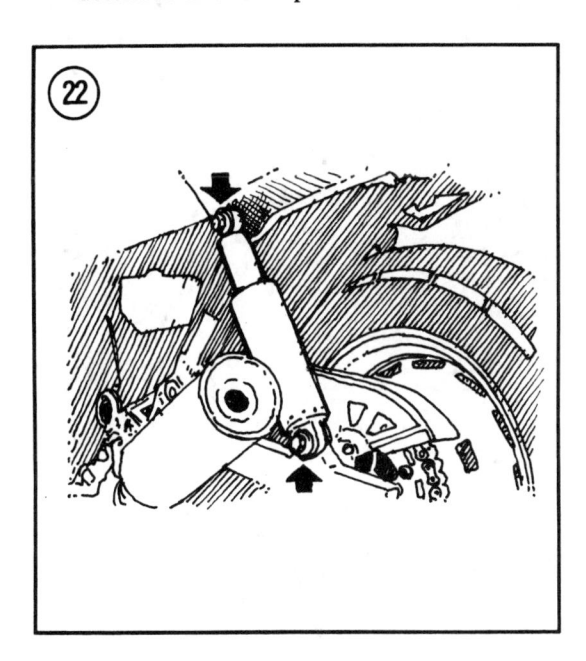

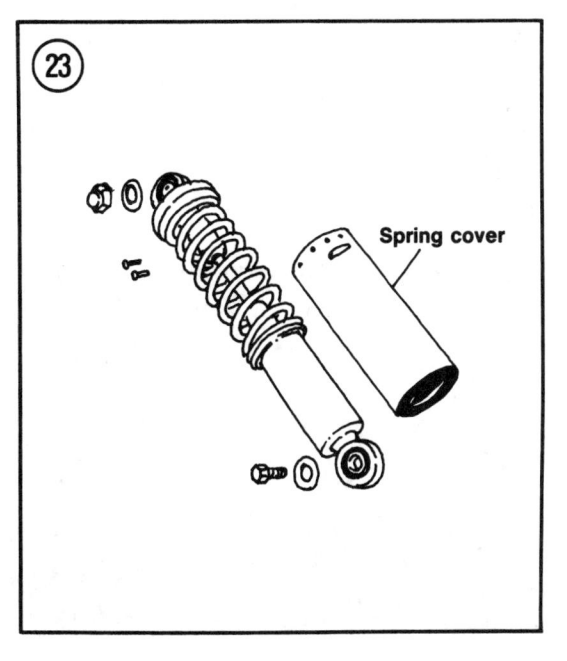

Lubrication

For lubrication of the drive chain, refer to *Drive Chain Lubrication* in Chapter Three.

WHEEL BALANCING

For complete information refer to *Wheel Balance* in Chapter Ten.

TIRE CHANGING AND REPAIR

Refer to *Tubeless Tires* and *Tubeless Tire Changing* in Chapter Ten.

REAR SHOCK ABSORBER

Removal/Installation (FZX700)

Removal and installation of the rear shocks is easier if they are done separately. The remaining unit will support the rear of the bike and maintain the correct relationship between the top and bottom mounts. If both shock absorbers must be removed at the same time, cut a piece of hardwood the same length as the shock absorber. Drill two holes in the wood the same distance apart as the bolt holes. Install the wood support after one shock absorber is removed. This will allow the bike to be easily moved around (not ridden) until the shock absorbers are reinstalled or replaced.

1. Place the bike on the center stand.
2. Remove the seat and side covers.
3. Remove the rear fender bolts and remove the rear fender.
4. Remove the upper and lower shock nuts and bolts (**Figure 22**).
5. Pull the shock off.
6. Remove the spring cover (**Figure 23**).
7. Check the shock absorber body for any signs of oil leakage. Replace the shock if necessary.
8. Check the bushings for wear, deterioration or damage. If replacement is necessary, drive the old bushings out and drive new ones in.
9. Install by reversing these removal steps. Torque the shock nut and bolts to the torque specifications in **Table 4**.

Removal/Installation (FZ700)

1. Remove the lower fairing assembly. See Chapter Thirteen.
2. Support the bike so that the rear wheel clears the ground.
3. Remove the seat and side covers.
4. Remove the exhaust system (Chapter Seven).

5. Remove the left-hand footrest bracket bolts and remove the bracket (**Figure 24**).

> *NOTE*
> *It is not necessary to remove the rear wheel to remove the rear shock absorber. The following procedure is shown with the rear wheel removed for clarity.*

6. Remove the left- and right-hand arm bolt (**Figure 25**) at the shock absorber and pull the arms away from the shock (A, **Figure 26**).
7. Remove the lower shock absorber bolt (B, **Figure 26**) at the relay arm.

> *NOTE*
> *Install the lower shock absorber bolt and nut through the relay arm to prevent losing the relay arm spacers (**Figure 27**).*

8. Remove the upper shock absorber bolt and nut (**Figure 28**) and lower the shock absorber out of the frame. See **Figure 29**.

> *WARNING*
> *The shock absorber contains highly compressed nitrogen gas. Do not tamper with or attempt to open the cylinder (**Figure 30**). Do not place it near an open flame or other extreme heat. Do not weld on the frame near it. Do not dispose of the shock absorber yourself. Take it to a Yamaha dealer where it can be deactivated and disposed of properly.*

9. Remove the spacer (**Figure 31**) from the upper shock absorber mount.
10. Check the shock absorber bushings (A, **Figure 32**) for galling, cracks or other damage. If

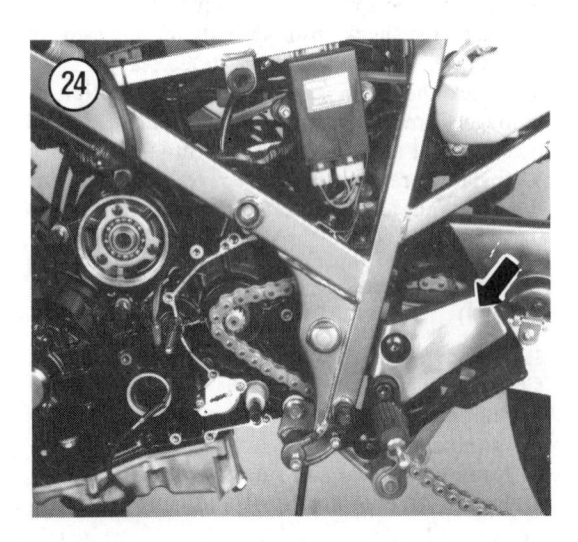

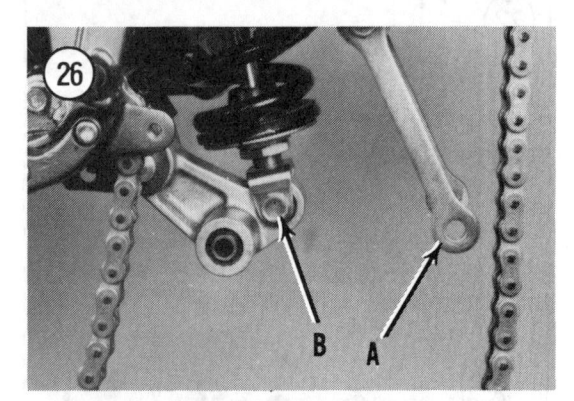

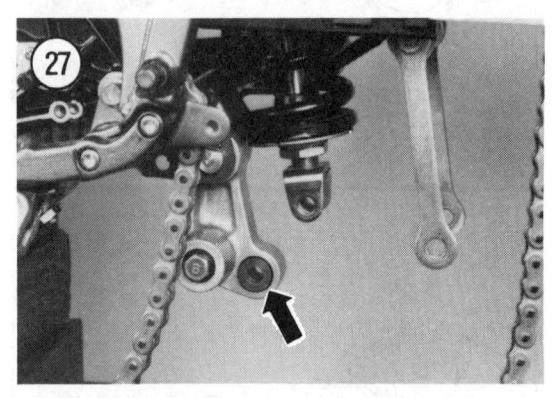

REAR SUSPENSION

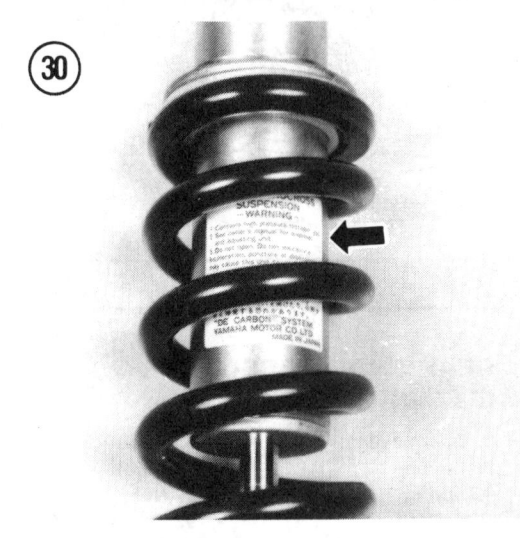

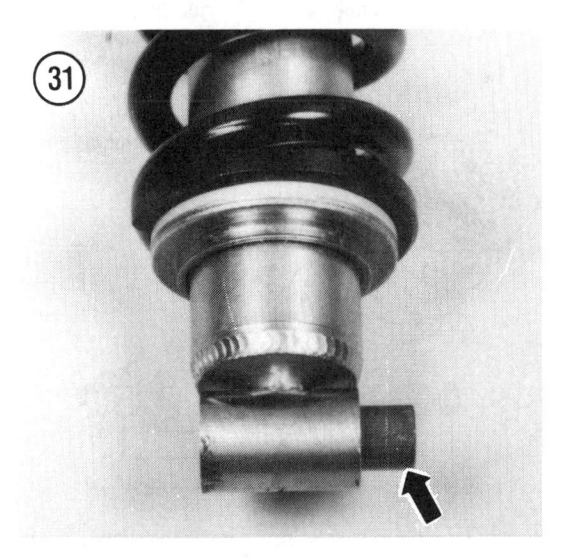

necessary, have the bushings pressed out and new ones installed by a dealer or machine shop.

11. Check the spacer (B, **Figure 32**) for galling, cracks or other damage; replace the spacer if necessary.

12. Check the spring (C, **Figure 32**) for cracks or damage or sagging; replace if necessary.

13. Check the upper and lower spring seats (D, **Figure 32**) for cracks or looseness. Also check the shock absorber body for oil leakage. Replace the shock absorber if any defects are noticed.

NOTE
The shock absorber cannot be disassembled and rebuilt; it must be replaced.

14. Install by reversing these steps. Note the following:
   a. Apply molybdenum grease to all bearings, spacers and dust seals.
   b. Tighten the upper shock absorber bolt to the specifications in **Table 5**.
   c. Don't forget to install the 2 lower shock absorber-to-relay arm spacers (**Figure 27**).
   d. Tighten the lower shock absorber bolt to the specifications in **Table 5**.
   e. Tighten the arm-to-relay arm bolt to the specifications in **Table 5**.

Removal/Installation (FZ750)

1. Place the bike on the center stand.
2. Remove the seat and side covers.
3. Remove the exhaust system (Chapter Seven).
4. Remove the battery as described in Chapter Three.
5. Remove the battery case and the starter relay switch.

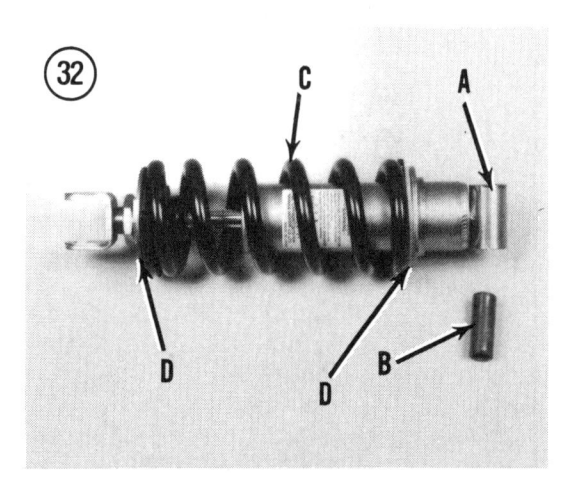

NOTE
It is not necessary to remove the rear wheel to remove the rear shock absorber.

6. Remove the relay arm pinch bolts (**Figure 33**).
7. See **Figure 33**. Remove the circlip, washer and lower pivot shaft.
8. Remove the shock absorber remote control unit mounting bolt (**Figure 34**) and lift the remote control unit away from adjusting chain and the connecting cable. See **Figure 35**.
9. Remove the upper shock absorber bolt and nut and lower the shock absorber and adjusting chain out of the frame.

WARNING
The shock absorber contains highly compressed nitrogen gas. Do not tamper with or attempt to open the cylinder. Do not place it near an open flame or other extreme heat. Do not weld on the frame near it. Do not dispose of the shock absorber yourself. Take it to a Yamaha dealer where it can be deactivated and disposed of properly.

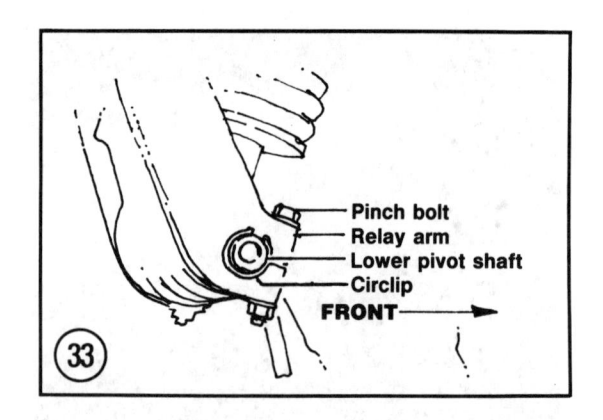

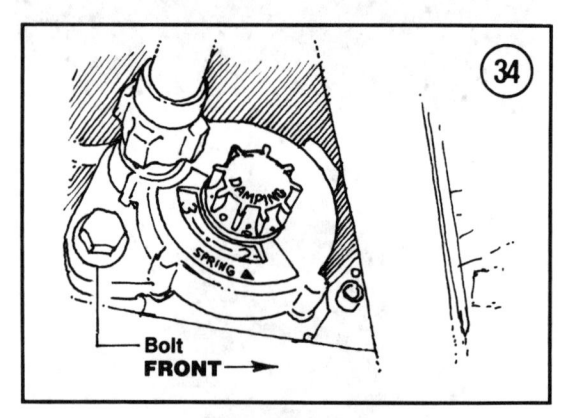

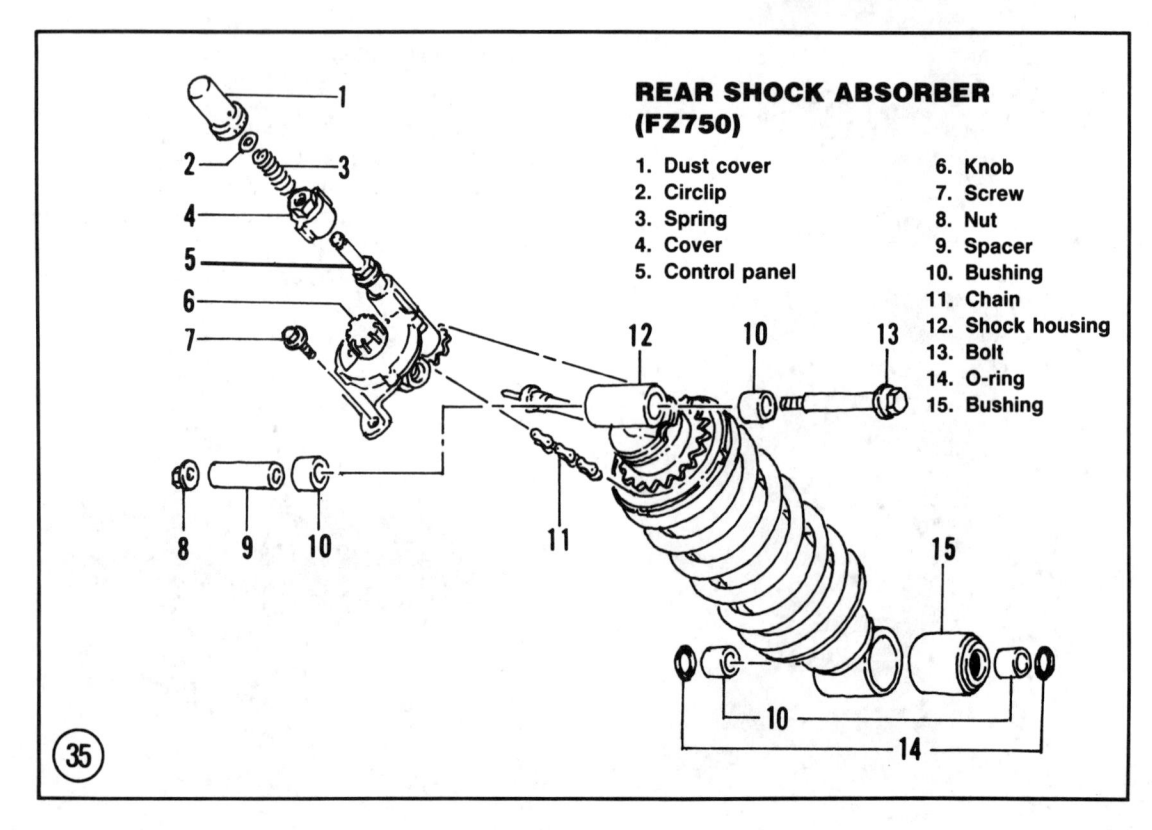

REAR SHOCK ABSORBER (FZ750)

1. Dust cover
2. Circlip
3. Spring
4. Cover
5. Control panel
6. Knob
7. Screw
8. Nut
9. Spacer
10. Bushing
11. Chain
12. Shock housing
13. Bolt
14. O-ring
15. Bushing

REAR SUSPENSION

10. Remove the spacer (**Figure 35**) from the upper shock absorber mount.

11. Remove the spacers and O-rings from the lower shock absorber mount (**Figure 35**).

12. Check the shock absorber bushings (**Figure 35**) for galling, cracks or other damage. If necessary, have the bushings pressed out and new ones installed by a dealer or machine shop.

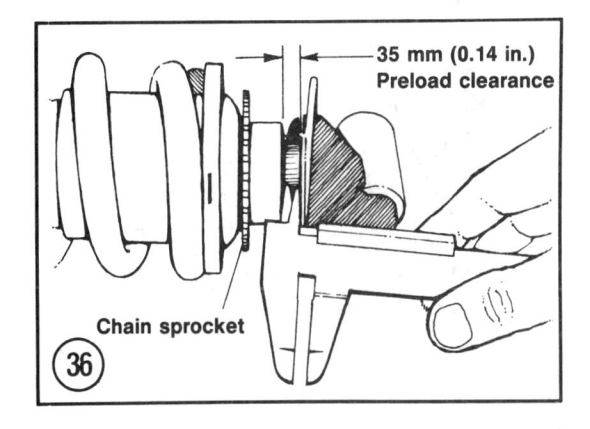

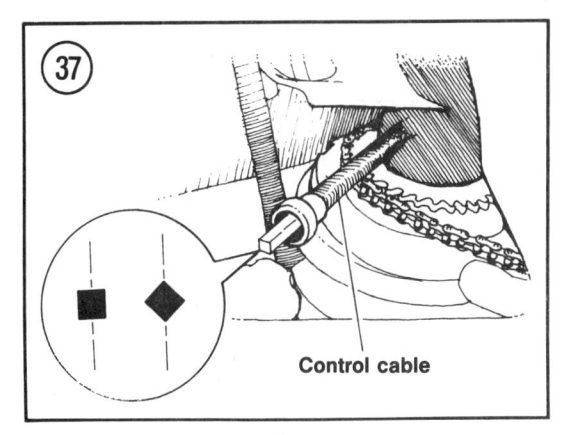

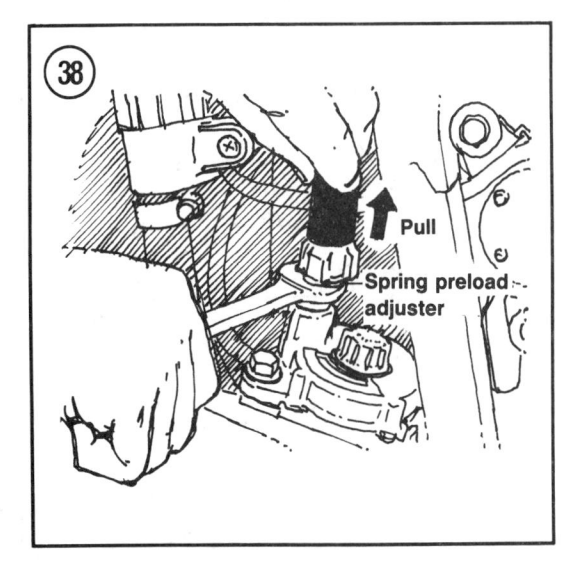

13. Check the spacers for galling, cracks or other damage; replace the spacer(s) if necessary.

14. Replace the lower shock absorber mount O-rings if necessary.

15. Turn the remote control unit (**Figure 34**) and check for smooth operation.

16. Inspect the adjust chain and both sprockets (**Figure 35**) for wear; replace worn or damaged parts as required.

17. Check the spring for cracks or damage; replace if necessary.

18. Check the upper and lower spring seats for cracks or looseness. Also check the shock absorber body for oil leakage. Replace the shock absorber if any defects are noticed.

NOTE
The shock absorber cannot be disassembled and rebuilt; it must be replaced.

19. Measure the swing arm preload clearance with a vernier caliper as shown in **Figure 36**. The correct clearance is 3.5 mm (0.14 in.). If necessary, adjust by turning the chain sprocket in or out.

20. Install by reversing these steps. Note the following.

21. Apply molybdenum grease to all bearings, spacers and dust seals.

22. Tighten the upper shock absorber bolt to the specifications in **Table 6**.

23. Tighten the shock absorber pivot shaft bolt to the specifications in **Table 6**.

24. Install and adjust the remote control unit as follows:

   a. Turn the control cable counterclockwise (**Figure 37**) so that the end of the cable is in one of the positions shown in **Figure 37** in relation to the center of the shock absorber.

   b. Turn the damping adjuster (**Figure 34**) to the No. 2 position.

   c. Lift the adjuster cover and turn the spring preload adjuster to the second preload position. See **Figure 38**.

WARNING
The spring preload and damping adjusters must be turned to compatible positions or poor handling will result.

   d. Connect the control cable to the remote control unit.

e. Connect the adjust chain to the remote control unit and the sprocket on the shock absorber (**Figure 39**).
f. Hook a spring scale onto the remote control and pull it until the scale reads 5-10 kg (11-22 lbs.). Then hold the remote control unit in this position and install the remote control unit bolt. Tighten the bolt securely.
g. Adjust the rear shock absorber to best suit riding conditions as described under *Suspension Adjustment* in Chapter Three.

SWING ARM

Removal/Installation (FZX700)

Refer to **Figure 40**.
1. Park the motorcycle on its center stand.
2. Remove the mufflers.
3. Remove the rear wheel as described in this chapter.
4. Remove the lower shock absorber bolts at the swing arm (**Figure 41**).

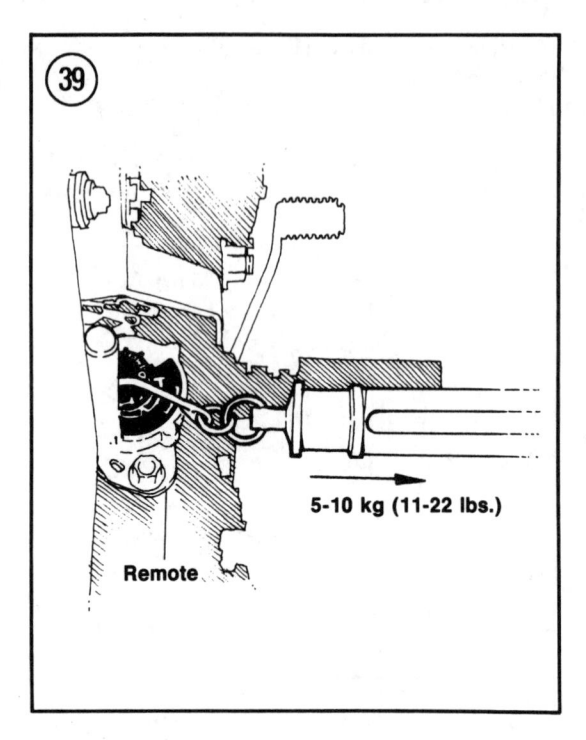

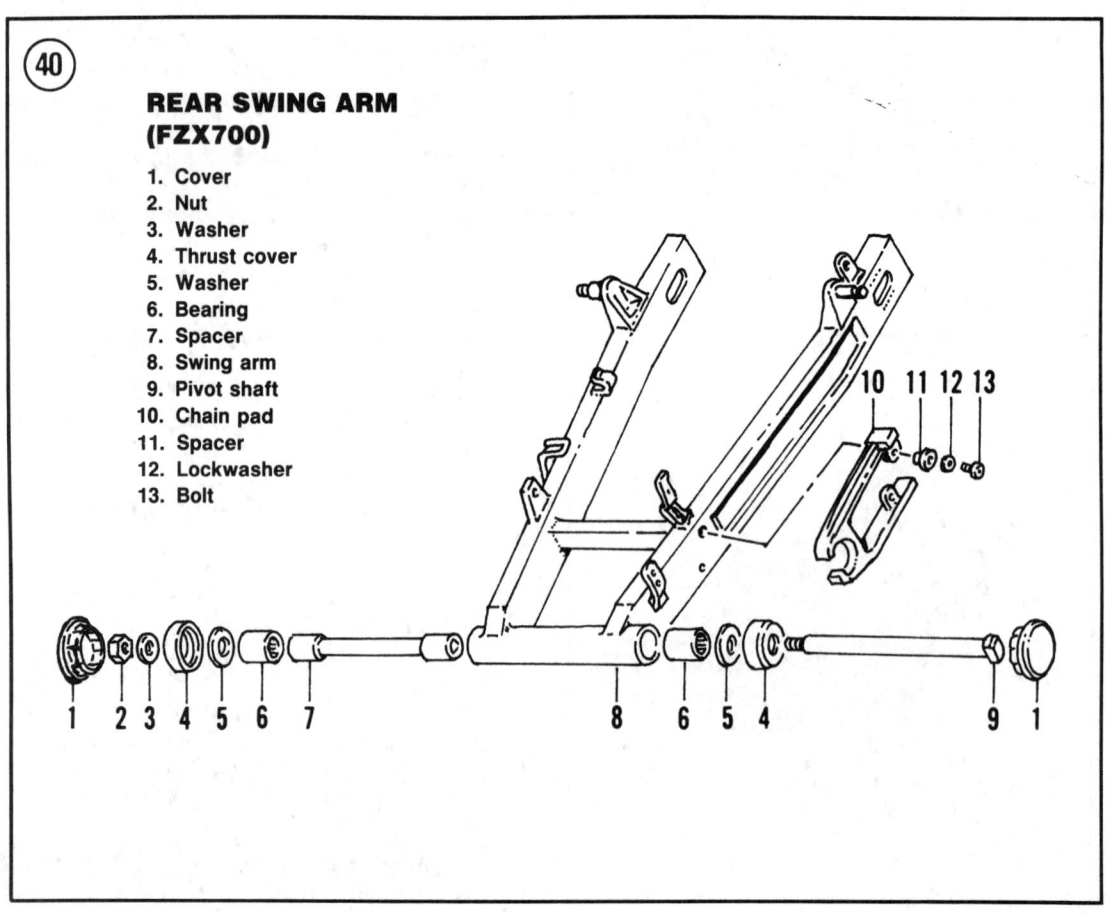

REAR SWING ARM (FZX700)

1. Cover
2. Nut
3. Washer
4. Thrust cover
5. Washer
6. Bearing
7. Spacer
8. Swing arm
9. Pivot shaft
10. Chain pad
11. Spacer
12. Lockwasher
13. Bolt

REAR SUSPENSION

5. Disconnect the brake hose from the clips on the swing arm.
6. *California models:* Label and disconnect the carbon canister hoses from the canister at the swing arm.
7. Remove the pinch screw and remove the shift shaft; if the pivot boss is tight on the shaft, spread the slot open with a screwdriver.

NOTE
It is not necessary to remove the clutch slave cylinder from the sprocket cover when removing the sprocket cover from the engine.

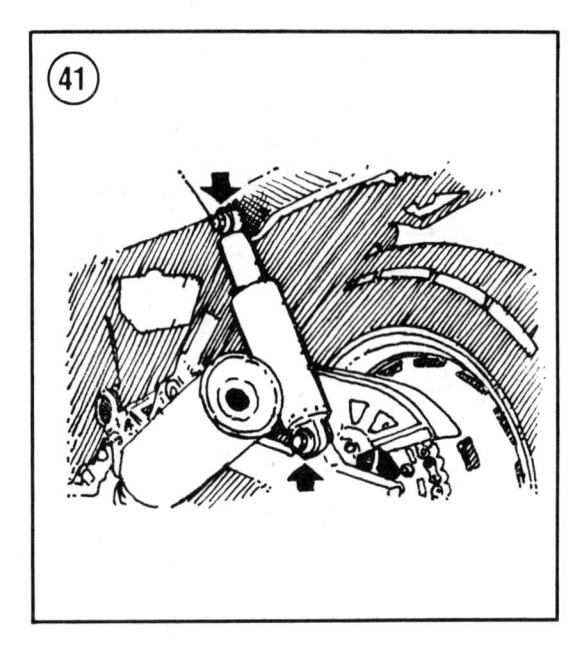

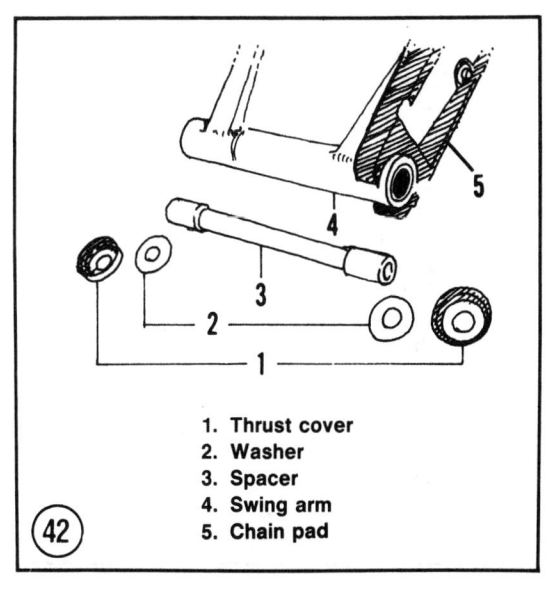

8. Remove the screws securing the engine sprocket cover and remove the cover (**Figure 21**).
9. Before removing the pivot shaft nut, check swing arm side play as follows.
    a. Grasp the swing arm at the rear and hold it in a horizontal position.
    b. Check swing arm side play by moving the swing arm from side to side. There should be no noticeable side play.
    c. Check swing arm movement by moving it up and down. The swing arm should move smoothly with no tightness or binding.
    d. If the swing arm moved abnormally during this test, replace the swing arm bearings as described in this chapter.
10. Remove the pivot shaft cap and remove the pivot shaft nut and washer.
11. Push the pivot shaft out from the right-hand side. If the pivot shaft is tight, use an aluminum or brass drift and tap the pivot shaft out.

NOTE
If the pivot shaft is very tight, try to push it out far enough so that its left end is clear of the frame. Then use an adjustable wrench on the end of the pivot shaft and turn the shaft back and forth to help break it loose. Continue to remove the pivot shaft with the brass or aluminum drift.

12. Pull the swing arm around the drive chain and away from the frame and remove it. Don't lose the thrust covers and washers, which may fall off during removal (**Figure 42**).
13. Remove the drive chain, if necessary.
14. Slide the spacer (**Figure 42**) out of the swing arm.
15. Inspect the swing arm, bearings and spacer as described in this chapter.
16. Installation is the reverse of these steps. Note the following:
    a. Replace the chain pad (**Figure 42**) if it is worn severely or damaged.
    b. Apply wheel bearing grease onto the spacer and pivot shaft.
    c. Tighten the swing arm pivot shaft to specifications (**Table 4**).
    d. Tighten the lower shock absorber bolts to the specifications in **Table 4**.
    e. Tighten the brake torque link nut securely.
    f. Adjust the drive chain as described under *Drive Chain Adjustment* in Chapter Three.

42

1. Thrust cover
2. Washer
3. Spacer
4. Swing arm
5. Chain pad

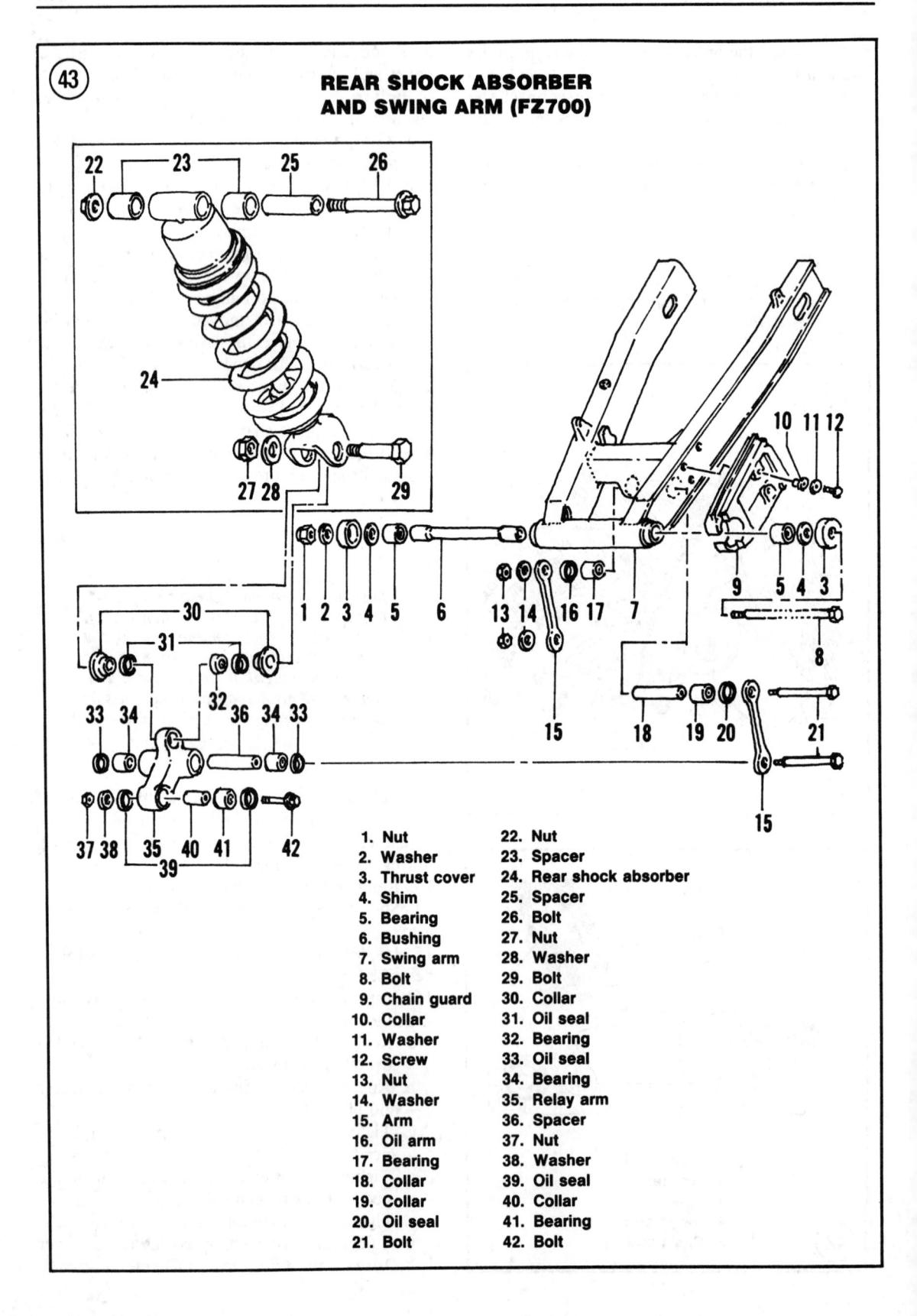

REAR SHOCK ABSORBER AND SWING ARM (FZ700)

1. Nut
2. Washer
3. Thrust cover
4. Shim
5. Bearing
6. Bushing
7. Swing arm
8. Bolt
9. Chain guard
10. Collar
11. Washer
12. Screw
13. Nut
14. Washer
15. Arm
16. Oil arm
17. Bearing
18. Collar
19. Collar
20. Oil seal
21. Bolt
22. Nut
23. Spacer
24. Rear shock absorber
25. Spacer
26. Bolt
27. Nut
28. Washer
29. Bolt
30. Collar
31. Oil seal
32. Bearing
33. Oil seal
34. Bearing
35. Relay arm
36. Spacer
37. Nut
38. Washer
39. Oil seal
40. Collar
41. Bearing
42. Bolt

REAR SUSPENSION

Removal/Installation (FZ700 and FZ750)

Refer to **Figure 43** (FZ700) and **Figure 44A** and **Figure 44B** (FZ750) for this procedure.

1A. *FZ700:* Jack up the rear end so that the rear wheel clears the ground.

1B. *FZ750:* Park the motorcycle on its center stand.

2. Remove the mufflers (FZ750) or exhaust system (FZ700). See Chapter Seven.

3. Remove the rear wheel as described in this chapter.

4A. *FZ700:* Perform the following:

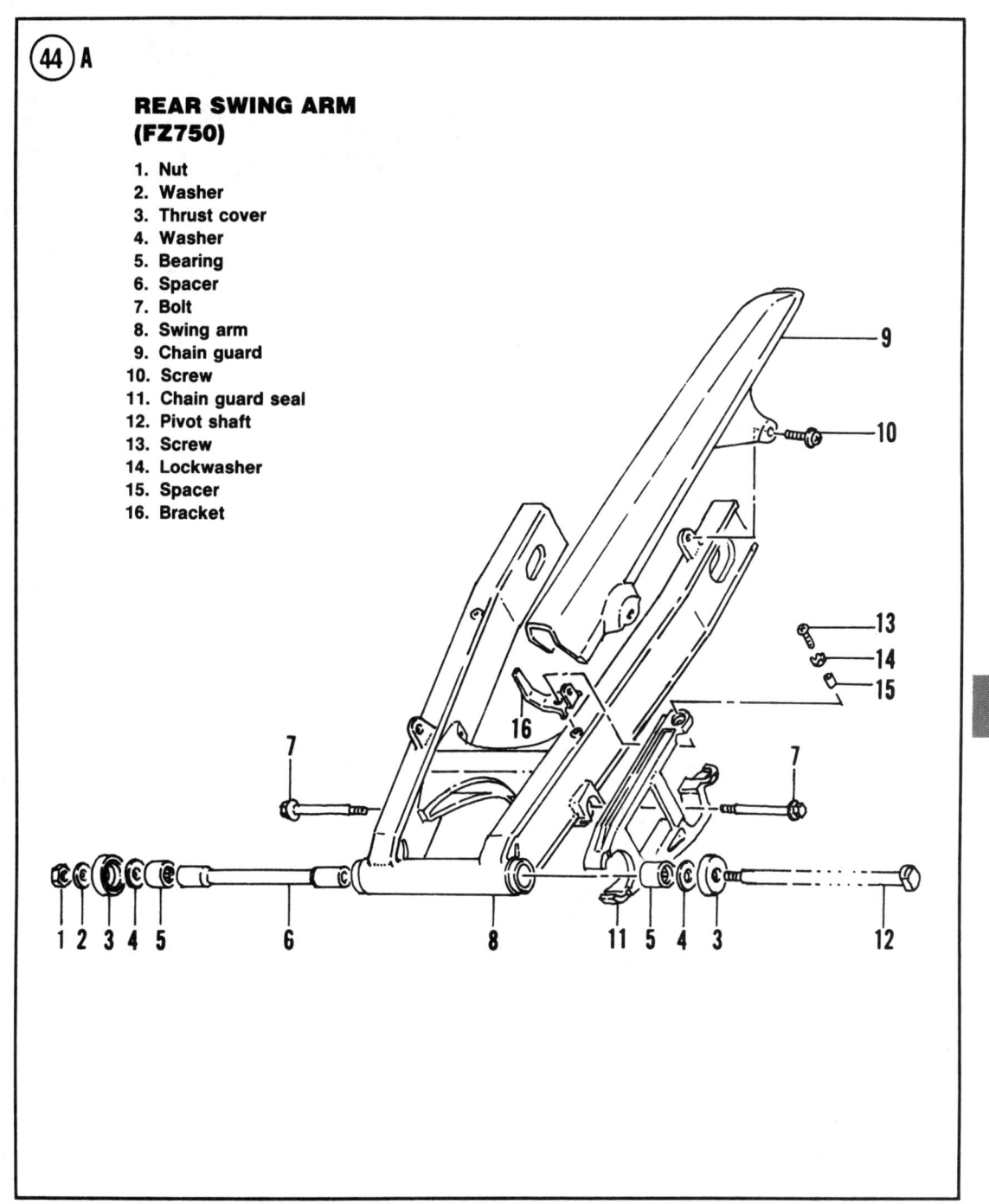

44 A

REAR SWING ARM (FZ750)

1. Nut
2. Washer
3. Thrust cover
4. Washer
5. Bearing
6. Spacer
7. Bolt
8. Swing arm
9. Chain guard
10. Screw
11. Chain guard seal
12. Pivot shaft
13. Screw
14. Lockwasher
15. Spacer
16. Bracket

a. Remove the left- and right-hand arm bolt (**Figure 45**) at the shock absorber and pull the arms away from the shock (A, **Figure 46**).
b. Remove the lower shock absorber bolt and spacers (B, **Figure 46**) at the relay arm.

4B. *FZ750:* Perform the following:
  a. Remove the relay arm pinch bolts (**Figure 47**).
  b. Remove the circlip, washer and lower pivot shaft (**Figure 47**).

5. Before removing the swing arm, grasp the swing arm as shown in **Figure 48** and move the swing arm from side to side and up and down. If you feel any more than a very slight movement of the swing arm and the pivot bolt is correctly tightened, remove the swing arm and check the bearings as described in this chapter.

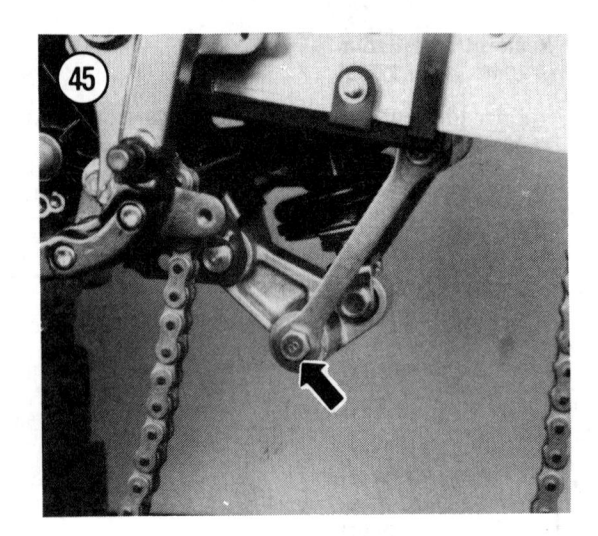

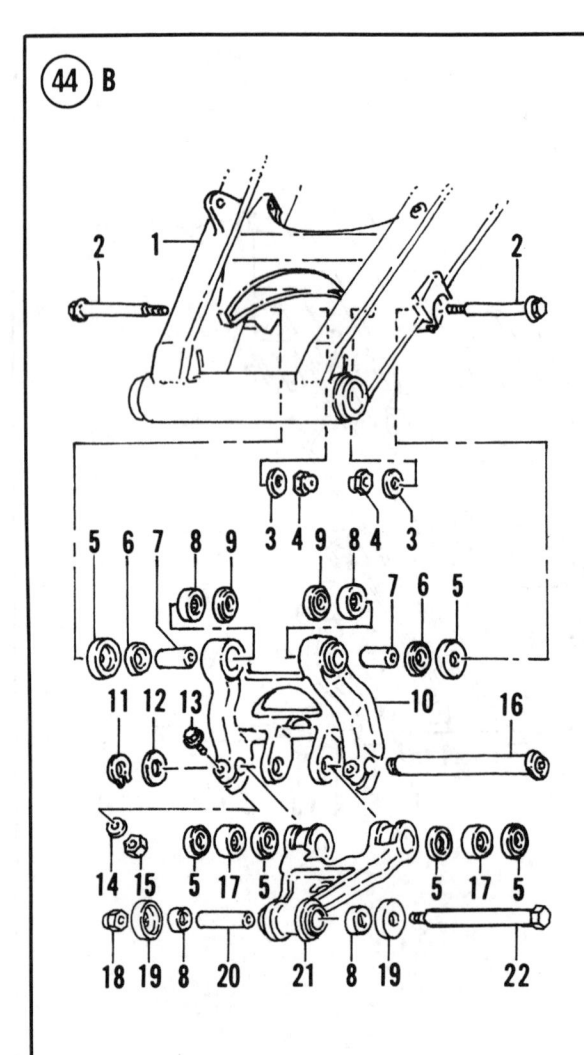

RELAY ARM ASSEMBLY (FZ750)

1. Swing arm
2. Bolt
3. Washer
4. Nut
5. Thrust cover
6. Oil seal
7. Spacer
8. Bearing
9. Oil seal
10. Relay arm
11. Circlip
12. Washer
13. Bolt
14. Washer
15. Nut
16. Lower pivot shaft
17. Bearing
18. Nut
19. Thrust cover
20. Pivot spacer
21. Relay arm
22. Pivot shaft

REAR SUSPENSION

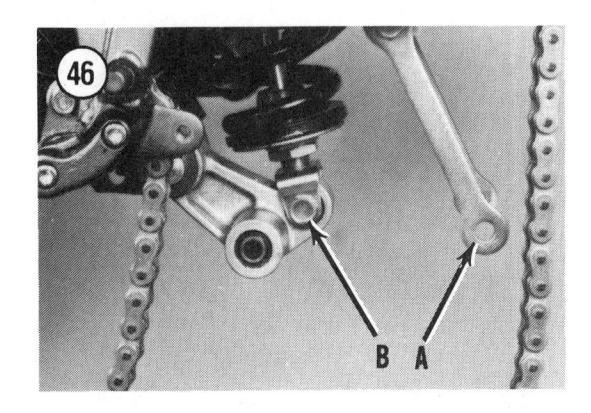

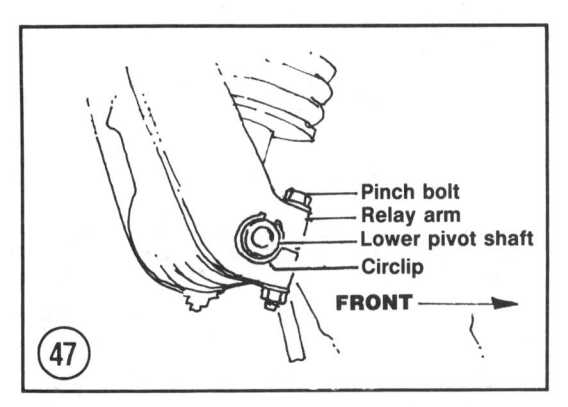

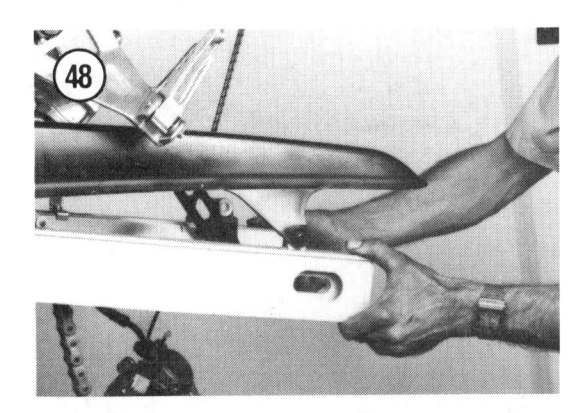

6. Loosen and remove the swing arm pivot shaft nut (**Figure 49**).
7. Remove the swing arm pivot shaft (**Figure 50**) and pull the swing arm toward the rear.
8. Pull the swing arm (**Figure 51**) away from the motorcycle.
9. Remove the bearing caps (**Figure 52**) from the swing arm.

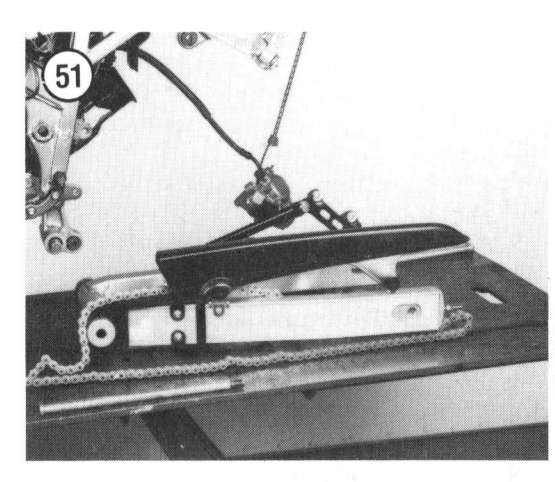

10. Remove the drive chain, if necessary.
11. Remove the relay arm and connecting rod as described in this chapter.
12. Installation is the reverse of these steps. Note the following.
13. Replace the swing arm chain pad (**Figure 53**) if it is worn severely or damaged.
14A. *FZ700:* Perform the following:
   a. Apply molybdenum grease to all bearings, spacers and dust seals.
   b. Tighten the swing arm pivot shaft to the specifications in **Table 5**.
   c. Install the lower shock absorber-to-relay arm spacers (**Figure 54**).
   d. Tighten the lower shock absorber bolt to the specifications in **Table 5**.
   e. Tighten the left- and right-hand arm-to-relay arm bolts to the torque specifications in **Table 5**.
   f. Install the rear wheel as described in this chapter.
14B. *FZ750:* Perform the following:
   a. Apply molybdenum disulfide grease to all bearings, spacers and dust seals.
   b. Tighten the swing arm pivot shaft to the specifications **Table 6**.
   c. Tighten the lower shock absorber pivot shaft pinch bolt to the torque specifications in **Table 6**.
   d. Install the rear wheel as described in this chapter.
15. Adjust the drive chain as described under *Drive Chain Adjustment* in Chapter Three.

Inspection and Bearing Replacement (All Models)

Refer to **Figure 40** (FZX700), **Figure 43** (FZ700) or **Figure 44A** and **Figure 44B** (FZ750).
1. Check the swing arm (**Figure 55**) for cracks, twisting, weld breakage or other damage. Refer repair to a competent welding shop.

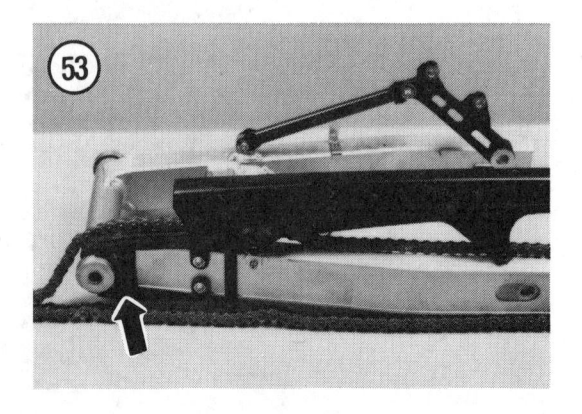

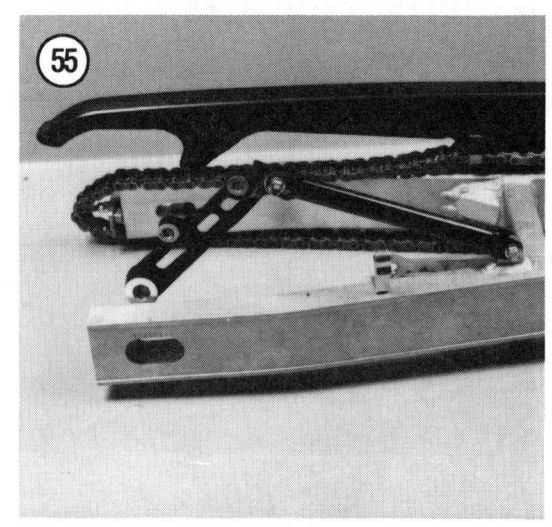

REAR SUSPENSION

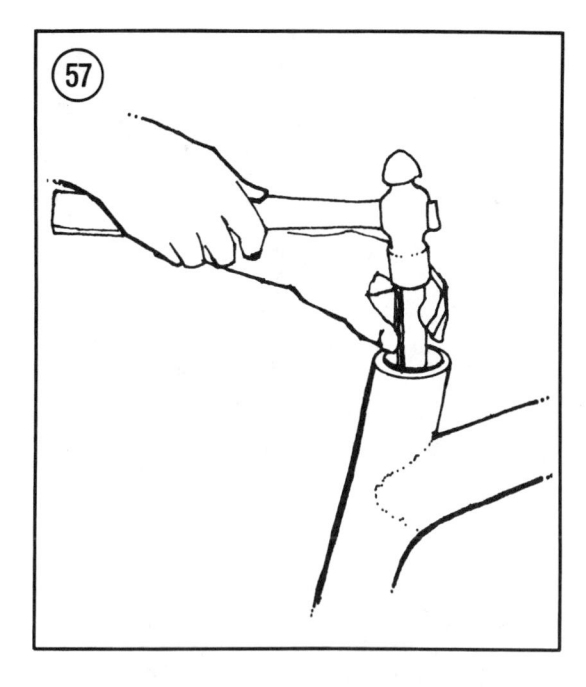

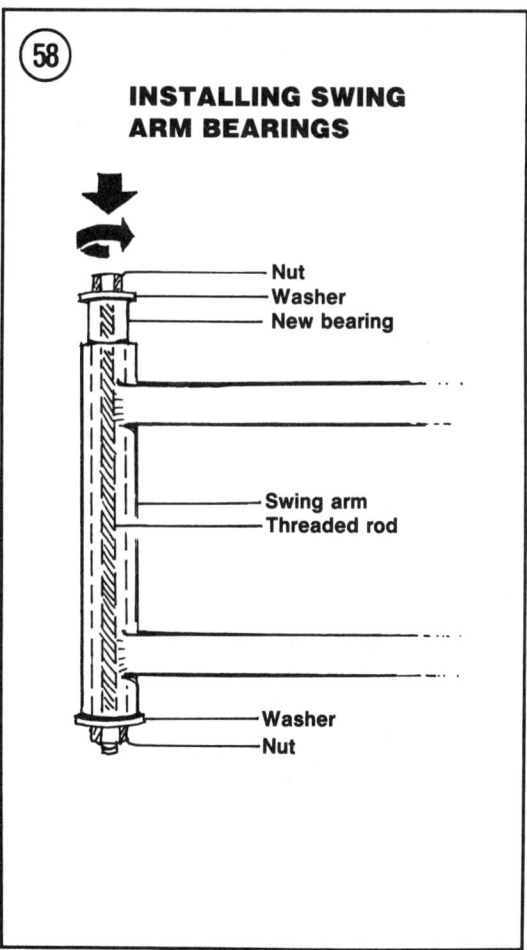

2. Pry the bearing caps (**Figure 52**) off the end of the swing arm.
3. Slide the spacer (**Figure 56**) out of the swing arm.
4. The roller bearings (**Figure 56**) wear very slowly and the wear is difficult to measure. Turn the bearings by hand. Make sure they rotate smoothly. Check the rollers for evidence of wear, pitting, or color change indicating heat from lack of lubrication. In severe instances, the needles will fall out of the bearing cage.
5. Replace the bearings as follows:
    a. Using a long metal rod or drift punch, tap one of the bearings out of the swing arm (**Figure 57**).
    b. Remove the opposite bearing in the same manner.
    c. Clean the swing arm bearing bore with solvent and allow to dry.
    d. Lubricate the bearings with oil before installation.
    e. Install the new bearings with a hydraulic press. If a press is not available, a bearing installer can be fabricated with a socket, 3 large washers, a long threaded rod and 2 nuts. Assemble the washers, threaded rod, bearing and nuts as shown in **Figure 58**. Hold the lower nut with a wrench and turn the upper nut to push the bearing into the swing arm. Turn the nut slowly and watch the bearing carefully. Make sure the bearing does not turn sideways. Install the bearing so that it is flush with the end of the swing arm. Repeat for the opposite bearing.

WARNING
Never reinstall a needle bearing that has been removed. During removal it is damaged and no longer true to alignment. If installed it will damage the sleeve and create an unsafe riding condition.

CAUTION
Do not drive the needle bearings into the swing arm or damage to the bearing will result.

   f. Apply a coat of molybdenum disulfide grease to the inner needle bearing surfaces.
6. Check the bearing caps for wear or damage. Check the seal inside each bearing cap for wear, tearing or deterioration. Replace the cap(s) if necessary.

7. Replace the chain guide (**Figure 59**) if damaged.

Relay Arm Assembly Removal/Installation (FZ700)

Refer to **Figure 43** for this procedure.

1. Support the bike so that the rear wheel clears the ground.
2. Remove the left-hand footrest bracket bolts and remove the bracket (**Figure 60**).
3. Remove the left- and right-hand arm bolt (**Figure 45**) at the relay arm and pull the arms away from the relay arm (A, **Figure 46**).
4. Remove the pivot bolt and nut (A, **Figure 61**) and remove the left- and right-hand arms (B, **Figure 61**) from the swing arm.
5. Remove the lower shock absorber bolt (B, **Figure 46**) at the relay arm.
6. Remove the spacers (**Figure 54**) from the relay arm.
7. Remove the pivot bolt (A, **Figure 62**) and remove the relay arm (B, **Figure 62**).
8. Installation is the reverse of these steps. Perform the following:
    a. Apply molybdenum disulfide grease to all pivot bolts, spacers and dust seals.
    b. Tighten the relay arm pivot bolts to the torque specifications in **Table 5**.

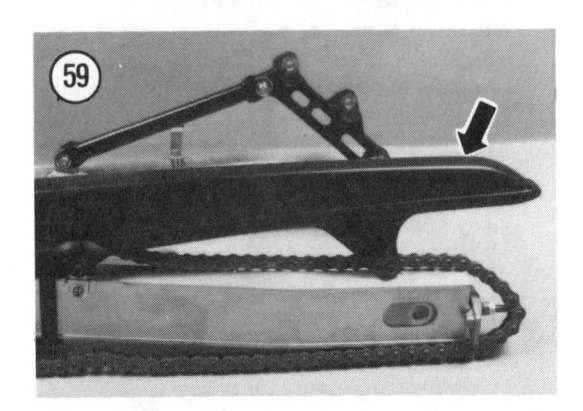

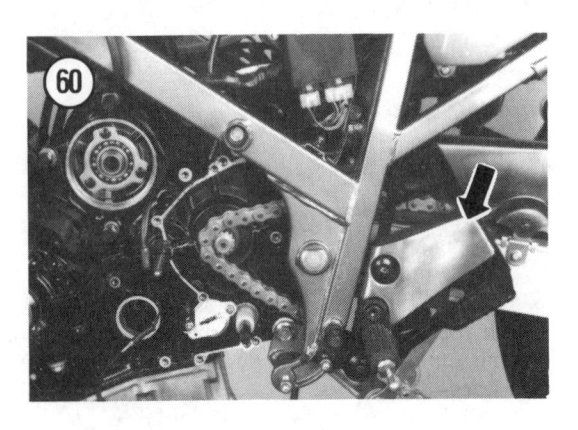

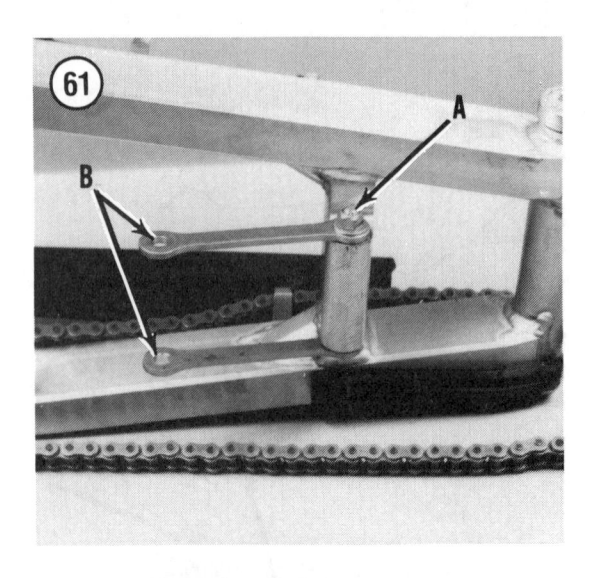

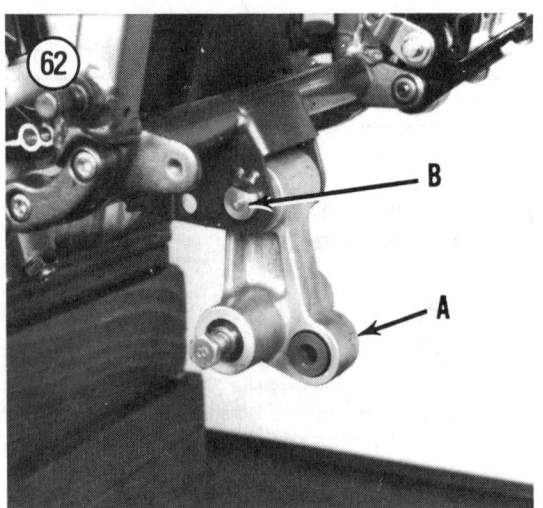

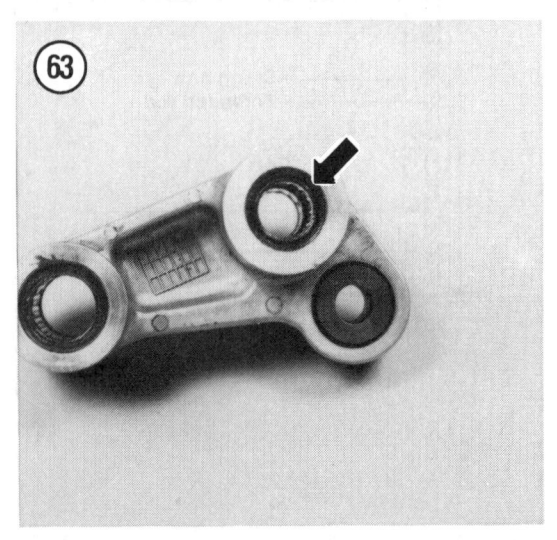

REAR SUSPENSION

c. Tighten the left- and right-hand arm to relay arm bolt to the torque specifications in **Table 5**.

d. Tighten the lower shock absorber pivot bolt to the torque specifications in **Table 5**.

Relay Arm Assembly Removal/Installation (FZ750)

Refer to **Figure 44B** for this procedure.
1. Support the bike on the center stand.
2. Remove the relay arm pinch bolts (**Figure 47**).
3. Remove the circlip, washer and lower pivot shaft (**Figure 47**).

4. Remove the connecting rod pivot bolt and remove the connecting rod.
5. Remove the relay arm pivot bolts and remove the relay arm.
6. Installation is the reverse of these steps. Perform the following:
   a. Apply molybdenum disulfide grease to all pivot bolts, spacers and dust seals.
   b. Tighten the relay arm pivot bolts to the torque specifications in **Table 6**.
   c. Tighten the connecting rod pivot bolts to the torque specifications in **Table 6**.
   d. Tighten the lower shock absorber pivot shaft pinch bolt to the torque specifications in **Table 6**.

Relay Arm and Connecting Rod Bearing Replacement

The relay arm and connecting rods are equipped with needle bearings. The bearings (**Figure 63**) wear very slowly and the wear is difficult to measure. First, remove the seals with a screwdriver as shown in **Figure 64**. Turn the bearings by hand. Make sure they rotate smoothly. Check the rollers for evidence of wear, pitting or color change indicating heat from lack of lubrication. In severe instances, the needles will fall out of the bearing cage.

If necessary, have the bearing replaced by a machine shop or dealer as a press is required.

Table 1 REAR SUSPENSION SPECIFICATIONS (FZX700)

Shock travel	15 mm (2.95 in.)
Shock spring free length	
New	167 mm (6.57 in.)
Wear limit	165 mm (6.50 in.)
Swing arm free play limit	
End play	1 mm (0.04 in.)
Side play	0.8 mm (0.03 in.)
Rear wheel runout limit	2.0 mm (0.079 in.)
Drive chain	
Type	50VA
No. of links	108

Table 2 REAR SUSPENSION SPECIFICATIONS (FZ700)

Shock travel	50 mm (1.97 in.)
Shock spring free length	
New	202 mm (7.95 in.)
Installed length	190 mm (7.48 in.)
Swing arm free play limit	
End play	1 mm (0.04 in.)
Side play	1 mm (0.04 in.)
Rear wheel runout limit	2.0 mm (0.079 in.)
Drive chain	
Type	50VA/DID
No. of links	112

Table 3 REAR SUSPENSION SPECIFICATIONS (FZ750)

Shock travel	40 mm (1.57 in.)
Shock spring free length	
New	174.5 mm (6.87 in.)
Wear limit	170 mm (6.70 in.)
Installed length	156.5 mm (6.16 in.)
Swing arm free play limit	
End play	1 mm (0.04 in.)
Side play	1 mm (0.04 in.)
Rear wheel runout limit	2.0 mm (0.079 in.)
Drive chain	
Type	50VA/DID
No. of links	110

Table 4 REAR SUSPENSION TIGHTENING TORQUES (FZX700)

Item	N-m	ft.-lb.
Rear axle	107	77.4
Pivot shaft	90	65
Shock absorber		
Upper bolt	20	14
Lower nut	30	22
Footpeg bolt	28	20
Drive chain sprocket	55	40

Table 5 REAR SUSPENSION TIGHTENING TORQUES (FZ700)

Item	N-m	ft.-lb.
Rear axle	107	77.4
Pivot shaft	90	65
Relay arm to frame pivot bolt	48	35
Arm to relay arm	74	53
Shock absorber		
Upper	42	30
Lower	40	29
Drive chain sprocket	55	40
Tension bar	28	20

REAR SUSPENSION

Table 6 REAR SUSPENSION TIGHTENING TORQUES (FZ750)

Item	N-m	ft.-lb.
Rear axle	107	77.4
Pivot shaft	90	65
Connecting rod to frame	90	65
Relay arm to swing arm	90	65
Shock absorber		
Pivot shaft pinch bolt	9	6.5
Upper bolt/nut	42	30
Footpeg	42	30
Drive chain sprocket	55	40
Tension bar	28	20

CHAPTER TWELVE

BRAKES

All models are equipped with front and rear disc brakes. This chapter describes repair and replacement procedures for all brake components.

Refer to **Table 1** for brake specifications. **Tables 1** and **2** are found at the end of the chapter.

DISC BRAKES

The disc brake units are actuated by hydraulic fluid controlled by the hand lever (front brake) or brake pedal (rear brake). As the front brake pads wear, the caliper pistons move out slightly to automatically adjust for pad wear. Rear disc brake pad wear is also automatically compensated but other parts of the system will need periodic adjustment; see *Rear Brake Pedal Height Adjustment* and *Rear Brake Light Switch Adjustment* in Chapter Three.

When working on a hydraulic brake system, it is necessary that the work area and all tools be absolutely clean. Any tiny particles of foreign matter or grit on the caliper assembly or the master cylinder can damage the components. Also, sharp tools must not be used inside a caliper or on a caliper piston. If there is any doubt about your ability to correctly and safely carry out major service on the brake components, take the job to a Yamaha dealer or brake specialist.

When adding brake fluid use only a type clearly marked DOT 3 and use it from a sealed container. Brake fluid will draw moisture from the air which greatly reduces its ability to perform correctly, so it is a good idea to purchase brake fluid in small containers.

Whenever *any* component has been removed from the brake system the system is considered "opened" and must be bled to remove air bubbles. Also, if the brake feels "spongy," this usually means there are air bubbles in the system and it must be bled. For safe brake operation, refer to *Bleeding the System* in this chapter for complete details.

CAUTION
Disc brake components rarely require disassembly, so do not disassemble unless necessary. Do not use solvents of any kind on the brake system's internal components. Solvents will cause the seals to swell and distort. When disassembling and cleaning brake components (except brake pads) use new brake fluid.

BRAKES

BRAKE PAD REPLACEMENT

There is no recommended mileage interval for changing the friction pads on the disc brakes. Pad wear depends greatly on riding habits and conditions. The pads should be checked for wear at specified intervals. See Chapter Three (**Table 1**).

Service Notes

Observe the following service notes before replacing brake pads.
1. Brake pads should be replaced only as a set.
2. Disconnecting the hydraulic brake hose is not required for brake pad replacement. Disconnect the hose only if caliper removal is required.

WARNING
Use brake fluid clearly marked DOT 3 from a sealed container. Other types may vaporize and cause brake failure. Always use the same brand name; do not intermix brake fluids, as many brands are not compatible.

WARNING
*Do not ride the motorcycle until you are sure the brake is operating correctly. If necessary, bleed the brake as described under **Bleeding the System** in this chapter.*

Front and Rear Pad Replacement

Brake pad replacement is the same for the front and rear calipers. Refer to **Figure 1** (front) or **Figure 2** (rear) for this procedure.

NOTE
It is not necessary to completely remove the caliper from the front fork when

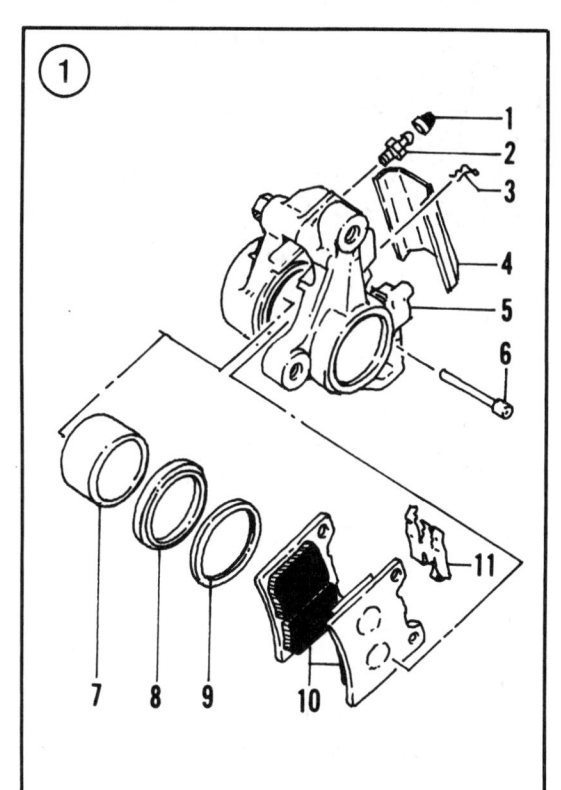

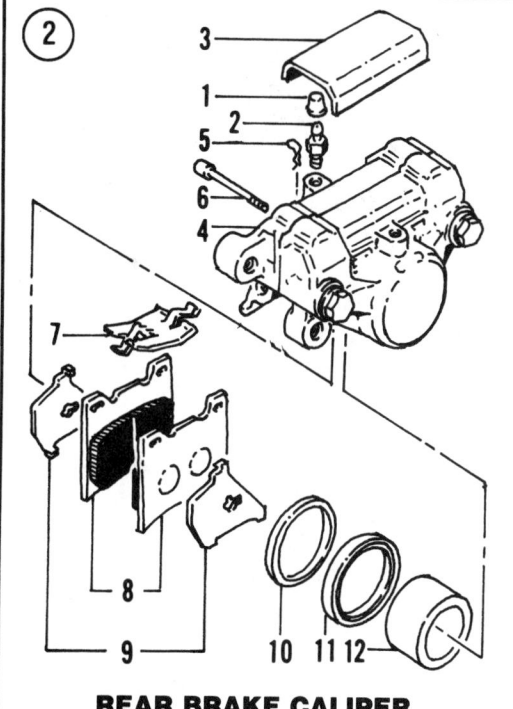

FRONT BRAKE CALIPER
1. Cap
2. Bleed screw
3. Retaining clip
4. Cover
5. Caliper housing
6. Retaining pin
7. Piston
8. Seal
9. Seal
10. Brake pads
11. Pad spring

REAR BRAKE CALIPER
1. Cap
2. Bleed screw
3. Cover
4. Caliper housing
5. Retaining clip
6. Retaining pin
7. Pad spring
8. Brake pads
9. Shim
10. Seal
11. Seal
12. Piston

servicing the brake pads. The caliper is shown removed in this procedure for clarity.

1. Remove the brake caliper bolts and lift the caliper off of the brake disc.
2. Pry the brake pad cover off of the caliper housing. See **Figure 3** (front) or **Figure 4** (rear).
3. See **Figure 5**. Pull the 2 retaining clips (**Figure 6**) out of the retaining pins.
4. Pull the upper (**Figure 7**) and lower (**Figure 8**) retaining pins out of the caliper.
5. Lift the pad spring (**Figure 9**) out of the caliper.
6. Lower the outer (**Figure 10**) and inner (**Figure 11**) brake pads out of the caliper.
7. *Rear brake caliper:* Remove the shim from the back of each brake pad.
8. Check the retaining pins and clips (**Figure 12**) for fatigue. Check the retaining pin clip holes for enlargement, cracks or other damage.

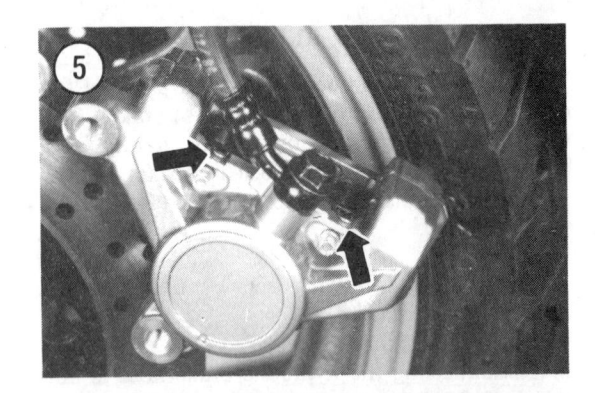

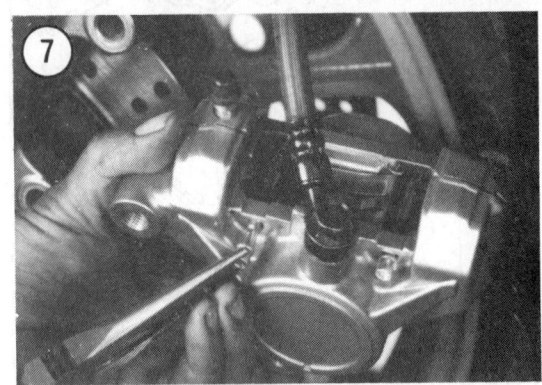

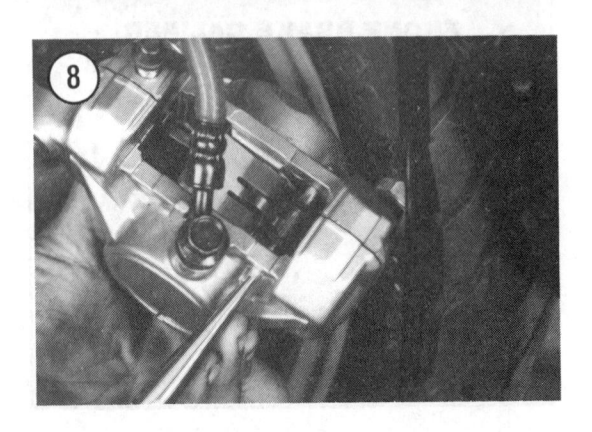

BRAKES

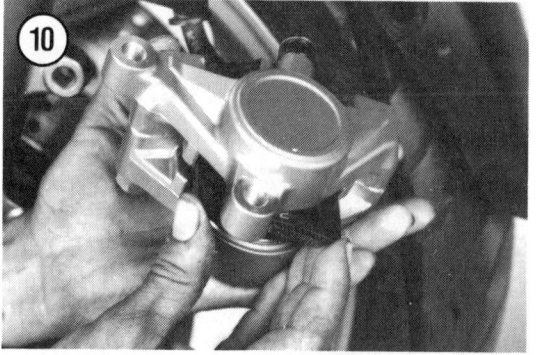

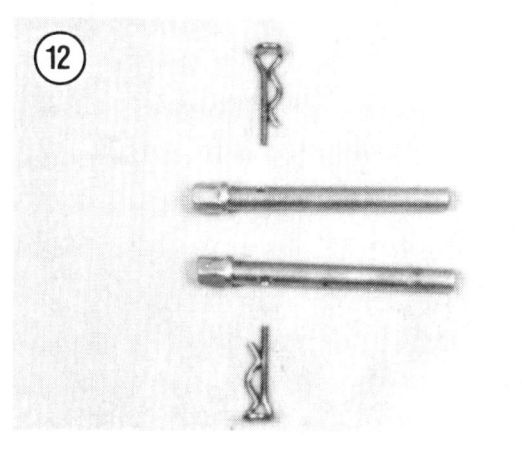

9. Check the pad spring (**Figure 13**) for fatigue or cracks.

10. Check the brake pad friction surface (**Figure 14**) for oil contamination or fraying. Check the pad plates for cracks or other damage. If the brake pads appear okay, measure the friction thickness with a vernier caliper (**Figure 15**). Replace the brake pads in a set if the friction thickness is too thin (**Table 1**).

WARNING
The brake pads must be replaced as set. When servicing front brakes, both the left- and right-hand calipers' brake pads must be replaced at the same time.

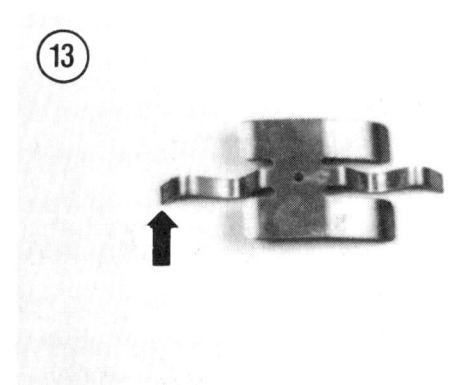

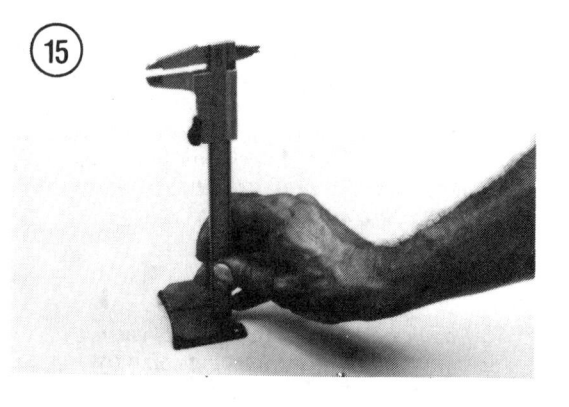

11. Remove the cap and diaphragm from the master cylinder. See **Figure 16** (front) or **Figure 17** (rear). Slowly push the pistons (**Figure 18**) into the caliper while checking the reservoir to make sure it doesn't overflow. The piston should move freely. You may need to use a C-clamp to push the piston back into the caliper. If the piston sticks, remove the caliper and rebuild it as described in this chapter.

12. *Rear brake caliper:* Install a shim onto each brake pad. Install the shim so that the arrow on the shim faces to the front of the bike.

13. Insert the pads through the bottom of the caliper housing. See **Figure 11** (inner) and **Figure 10** (outer).

NOTE
The friction material on both brake pads must face inward, toward the disc.

14. Install the pad spring (**Figure 19**) so that the end of the spring with the longer tang (**Figure 13**) faces to the front of the bike.

15. Install the front retaining pin (**Figure 8**) and rear retaining pin (**Figure 7**) so that the pins slide over the top of the pad spring tangs (**Figure 20**).

16. Install the retaining pin clips. See **Figure 5** and **Figure 6**.

17. Install the brake pad cover (**Figure 4**).

18. Carefully align the brake pads with the brake disc and install the caliper. Install the caliper bolts and tighten to the specifications in **Table 2**.

19. Support the motorcycle with either the front or rear wheel off the ground. Spin the wheel and pump the brake until the pads are seated against the disc.

20. Refill the master cylinder reservoir, if necessary, to maintain the correct fluid level. Install the diaphragm and top cap.

WARNING
Use brake fluid clearly marked DOT 3 from a sealed container. Other types may vaporize and cause brake failure. Always use the same brand name; do not intermix brake fluids, as many brands are not compatible.

WARNING
Do not ride the motorcycle until you are sure the brakes are working correctly.

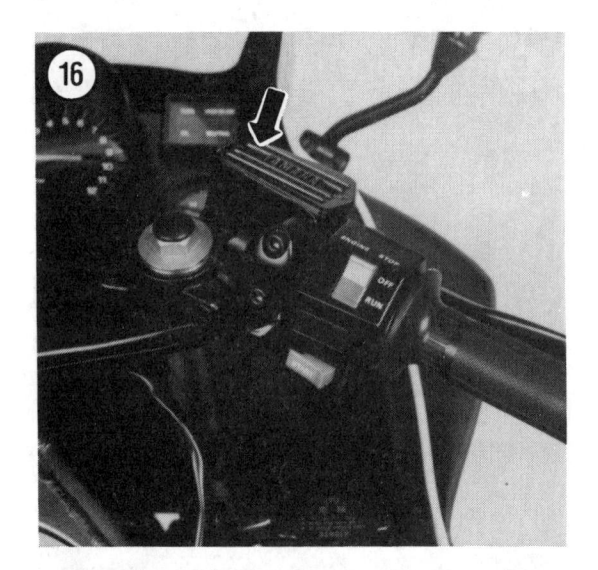

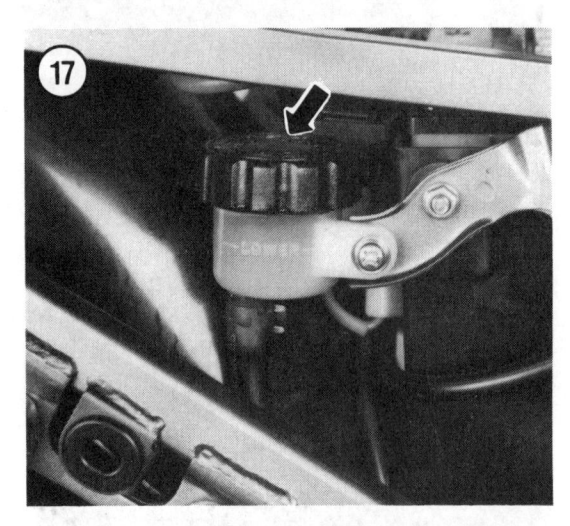

BRAKES

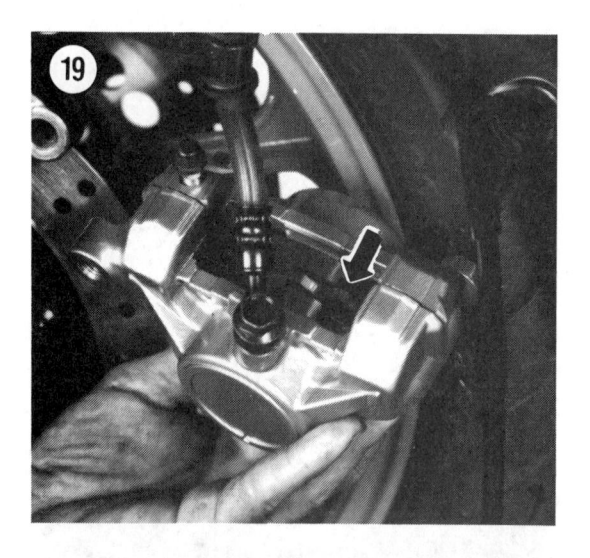

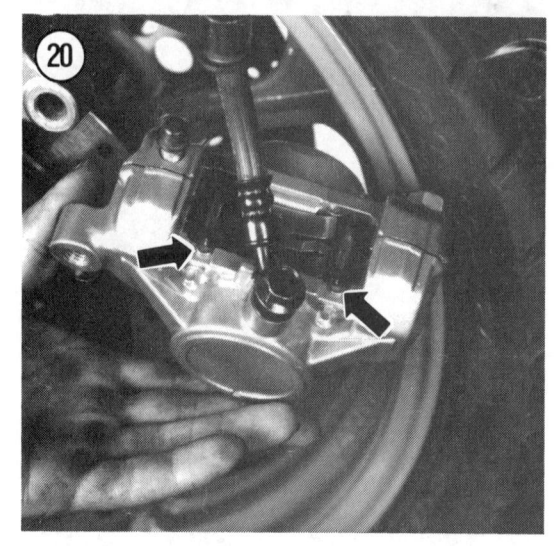

BRAKE CALIPERS

Front Caliper
Removal/Installation

Refer to **Figure 1**.

1. Drain the master cylinder as follows:
   a. Attach a hose to the brake caliper bleed screw (A, **Figure 21**).
   b. Place the end of the hose in a clean container (**Figure 22**).
   c. Open the bleed screw (A, **Figure 21**) and operate the brake lever to drain all brake fluid from the master cylinder reservoir.
   d. Close the bleed screw and disconnect the hose.
   e. Discard the brake fluid.
2. Remove the front brake pads as described in this chapter.
3. Remove the bolt and sealing washers attaching the brake hose to the caliper (B, **Figure 21**). To prevent the loss of brake fluid, cap the end of the brake hose and tie it up to the fender. Be sure to cap or tape the ends to prevent the entry of moisture and dirt.
4. Remove the bolts securing the brake caliper (C, **Figure 21**) to the front fork and remove the brake caliper.
5. Installation is the reverse of these steps. Note the following:
   a. Torque the caliper attaching bolts to specifications in **Table 2**.

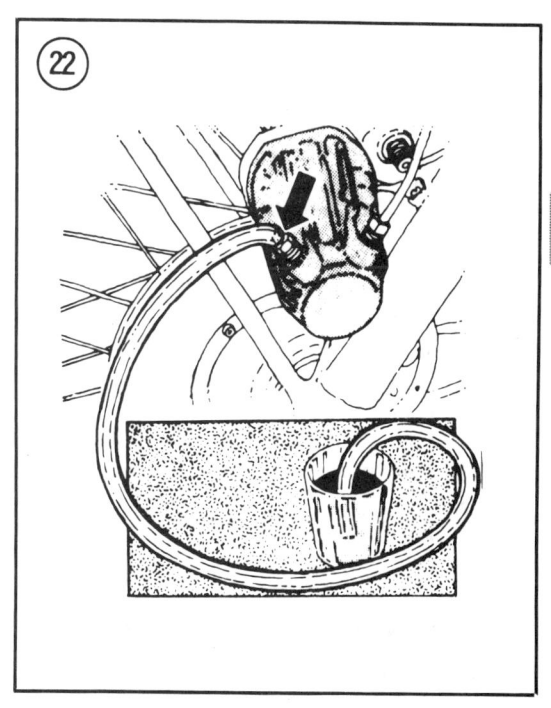

b. Install the brake hose using new washers (**Figure 23**).
   c. Tighten the brake hose banjo bolt to specifications in **Table 2**.
   d. Install the front brake pads as described in this chapter.
   e. Bleed the brakes as described under *Bleeding the System* in this chapter.

> **WARNING**
> *Do not ride the motorcycle until you are sure that the brakes are operating properly.*

Rear Caliper
Removal/Installation

Refer to **Figure 2**.
1. Drain the master cylinder as follows:
   a. Attach a hose to the brake caliper bleed screw (**Figure 24**).
   b. Place the end of the hose in a clean container (**Figure 24**).
   c. Open the bleed screw (**Figure 24**) and operate the brake pedal to drain all brake fluid from the master cylinder reservoir.
   d. Close the bleed screw and disconnect the hose.
   e. Discard the brake fluid.
2. Remove the rear brake pads as described in this chapter.
3. Remove the bolt and sealing washers attaching the brake hose to the caliper (A, **Figure 25**). To prevent the loss of brake fluid, cap the end of the brake hose and tie it up to the fender. Be sure to cap or tape the ends to prevent the entry of moisture and dirt.
4. Installation is the reverse of these steps. Note the following:
   a. Torque the caliper attaching bolts to specifications in **Table 2** (B, **Figure 25**).
   b. Install the rear brake pads as described in this chapter.
   c. Install the brake hose using new washers (**Figure 23**).
   d. Tighten the brake hose banjo bolt to specifications in **Table 2**.
   e. Bleed the brakes as described under *Bleeding the System* in this chapter.

> **WARNING**
> *Do not ride the motorcycle until you are sure that the brakes are operating properly.*

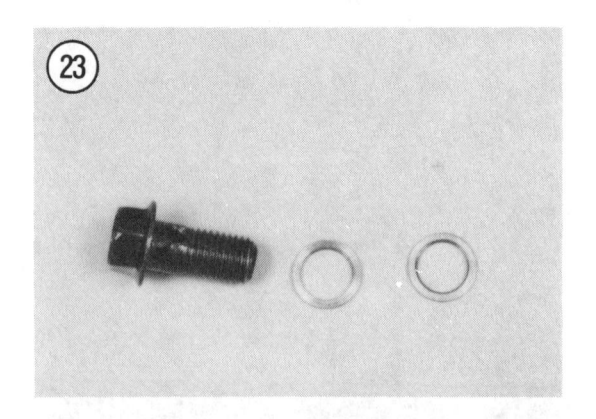

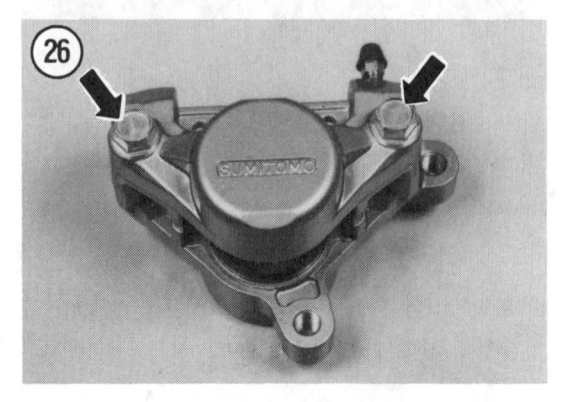

BRAKES

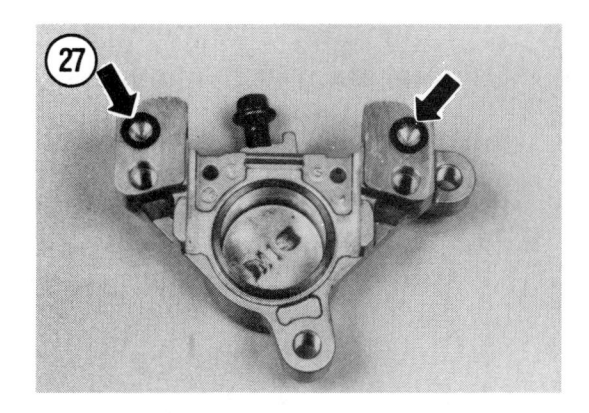

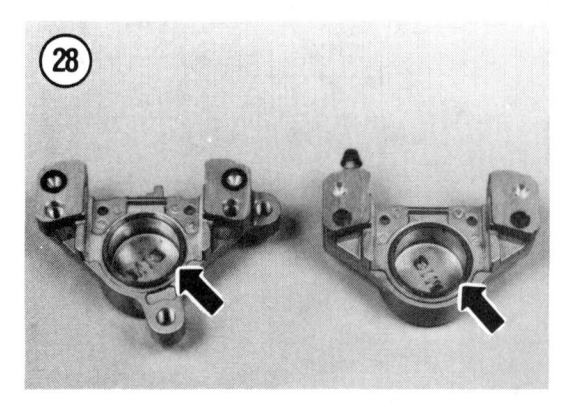

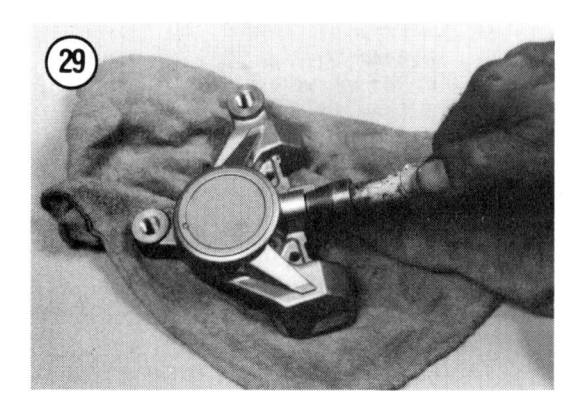

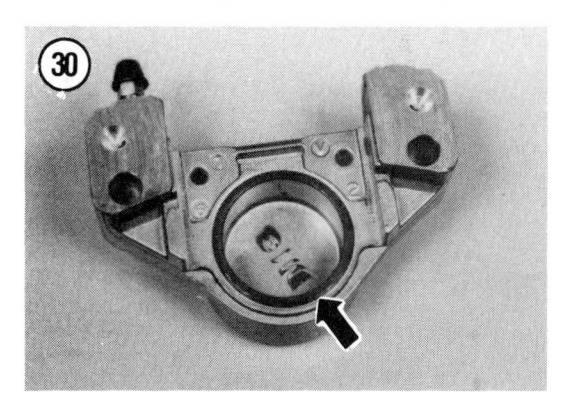

Caliper Rebuilding

Refer to **Figure 1** (front) or **Figure 2** (rear).
1. Remove the brake caliper as described in this chapter.
2. Remove the 2 caliper housing bolts (**Figure 26**) and separate the caliper housings.
3. Remove the 2 O-rings (**Figure 27**).

NOTE
*Compressed air will be required to remove the pistons (**Figure 28**).*

WARNING
Keep your fingers and hand out of the caliper bore area when removing the pistons in Step 4. The pistons will fly out of the bore with considerable force and could crush your fingers or hand.

4. Pad the piston with shop rags or wood blocks as shown in **Figure 29**. Block the exposed housing fluid port holes on the back of the caliper housing. Then apply compressed air through the caliper hose joint and force the piston out of the caliper (**Figure 30**).
5. Repeat for the opposite piston.
6. Remove the dust and piston seals from the caliper bore.
7. Clean all caliper parts (except brake pads) in new DOT 3 brake fluid. Place the cleaned parts on a lint-free cloth while performing the following inspection procedures.
8. Check the caliper bore for cracks, deep scoring or excessive wear. Measure the caliper inside diameter with a bore gauge. Replace the brake caliper if the inside diameter is too large (**Table 1**).
9. Check the caliper piston for deep scoring, excessive wear or rust.
10. Replace the caliper housing or piston if necessary.
11. The piston seal maintains correct brake pad to disc clearance. If the seal is worn or damaged, the brake pads will drag and cause excessive pad wear and brake fluid temperatures. Replace the piston and dust seals every time the caliper is disassembled.
12. Measure the brake pad friction thickness material with a vernier caliper (**Figure 15**). Replace both brake pads if any one pad is too thin (**Table 1**).

13. Assemble the caliper by reversing these steps. Note the following:
   a. Apply new DOT 3 brake fluid to the piston and seals before installation.
   b. Tighten the caliper housing bolts to the specifications in **Table 2**.

FRONT MASTER CYCLINDER

Removal/Installation

CAUTION
Cover the fuel tank, front fender and instrument cluster with a heavy cloth or plastic tarp to protect them from accidental spilling of brake fluid. Wash any spilled brake fluid off any painted or plated surfaces immediately, as it will destroy the finish. Use soapy water and rinse completely.

1. Drain the master cylinder as follows:
   a. Attach a hose to the brake caliper bleed screw (**Figure 22**).
   b. Place the end of the hose in a clean container (**Figure 22**).
   c. Open the bleed screw (**Figure 22**) and operate the brake lever to drain all brake fluid from the master cylinder reservoir.
   d. Close the bleed screw and disconnect the hose.
   e. Discard the brake fluid.
2. Disconnect the brake switch wires at the master cylinder.
3. Remove the bolt securing the brake hose to the master cylinder. Remove the brake hose and both sealing washers. Cover the end of the hose to prevent the entry of foreign matter and moisture. Tie the hose end up to the handlebar to prevent the loss of brake fluid.

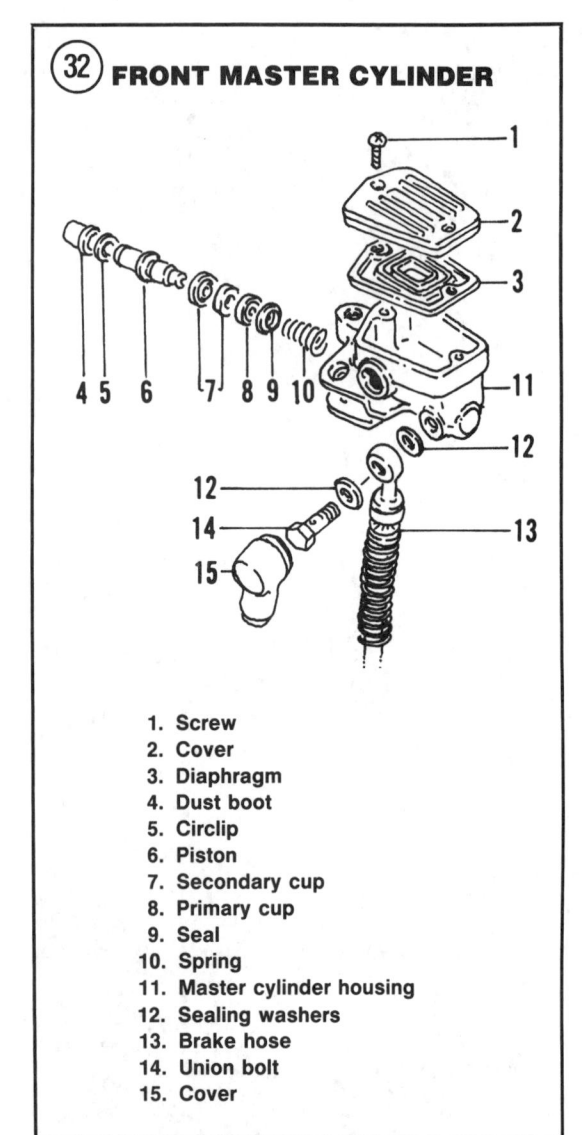

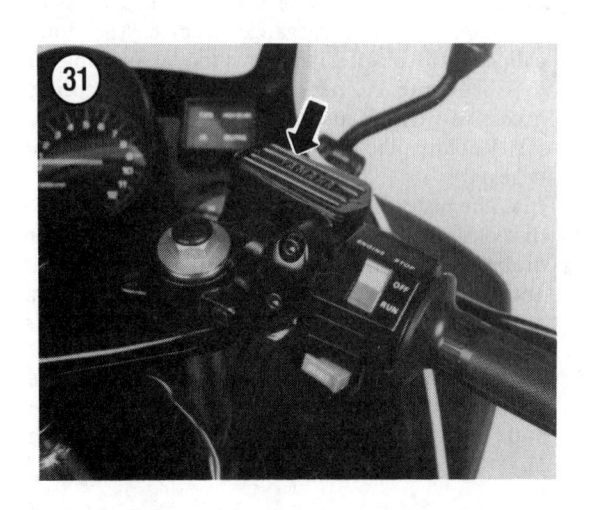

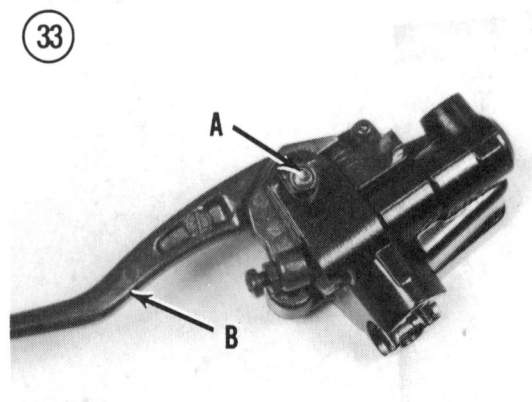

FRONT MASTER CYLINDER

1. Screw
2. Cover
3. Diaphragm
4. Dust boot
5. Circlip
6. Piston
7. Secondary cup
8. Primary cup
9. Seal
10. Spring
11. Master cylinder housing
12. Sealing washers
13. Brake hose
14. Union bolt
15. Cover

BRAKES

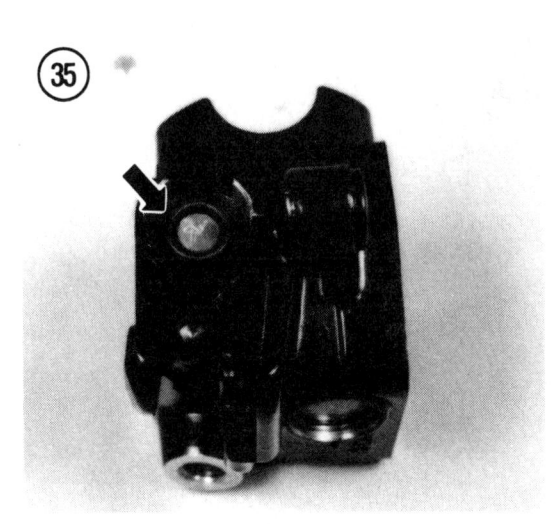

4. Remove the 2 clamping bolts and clamp securing the master cylinder to the handlebar and remove the master cylinder (**Figure 31**).
5. Install by reversing these removal steps. Note the following:
   a. Tighten the upper clamp bolt first, then the lower bolt to specifications in **Table 2**. There should be a gap at the lower part of the clamp after tightening.
   b. Install the brake hose onto the master cylinder. Be sure to place a sealing washer on each side of the hose fitting and install the banjo bolt (**Figure 23**). Tighten the banjo bolt to the specifications in **Table 2**.
   c. Bleed the brake system as described under *Bleeding the System* in this chapter.

WARNING
Do not ride the motorcycle until the front brake is operating correctly.

Disassembly

Refer to **Figure 32**.
1. Remove the master cylinder as described in this chapter.
2. Remove the screws securing the reservoir cap and diaphragm. Pour out the remaining brake fluid and discard it. *Never* reuse brake fluid.
3. Remove the nut and bolt (A, **Figure 33**) and remove the brake lever (B, **Figure 33**).
4. Remove the brake lever spring (**Figure 34**).
5. Pull the dust boot (**Figure 35**) out of the master cylinder housing.
6. Remove the circlip (A, **Figure 36**) with circlip pliers.
7. Remove the piston assembly (A, **Figure 37**) and spring (**Figure 38**).
8. Remove the seat (B, **Figure 37**) from the piston.

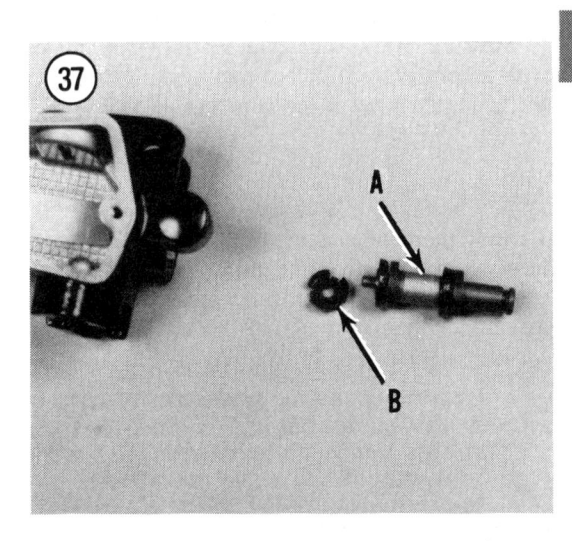

9. Remove the primary cup (A, **Figure 39**) from the piston.

CAUTION
*Do not remove the secondary cup (B, **Figure 39**) from the piston or damage to the secondary cup will occur.*

Inspection

1. Clean all parts (**Figure 40**) in fresh DOT 3 brake fluid. Place the master cylinder components on a clean lint-free cloth when performing the following inspection procedures.
2. Inspect the cylinder bore and piston contact surfaces for signs of wear or damage. If either part is less than perfect, replace it.
3. Check the end of the piston (C, **Figure 39**) for wear caused by the hand lever. Replace the entire piston assembly if any portion of it requires replacement. If the piston assembly is replaced, also replace the primary cup.
4. Check the secondary cup on the piston (B, **Figure 39**) for damage, softness or swelling. Replace the piston assembly if necessary.
5. Check the primary cup (A, **Figure 39**) for the same conditions as in Step 4. Replace the primary cup if necessary.
6. Inspect the pivot hole in the hand lever (**Figure 41**). If worn, it must be replaced.
7. Make sure the passages in the bottom of the brake fluid reservoir (**Figure 42**) are clear. Check the reservoir diaphragm (A, **Figure 43**) and cap (B, **Figure 43**) for damage and deterioration. Replace if necessary.
8. Inspect the condition of the threads in the master cylinderbody where the brake hose banjo bolt screws in. If the threads are damaged or partially stripped, replace the master cylinder.
9. Measure the master cylinder inside diameter with a bore gauge. Replace the master cylinder if the inside diameter is too large (**Table 1**).

Assembly

1. Soak the new caps in fresh brake fluid for at least 15 minutes to make them pliable. Coat the inside of the cylinder with fresh brake fluid prior to assembling the parts.

CAUTION
When installing the piston assembly, do not allow the cups to turn inside out as they will be damaged and allow brake fluid to leak within the cylinder bore.

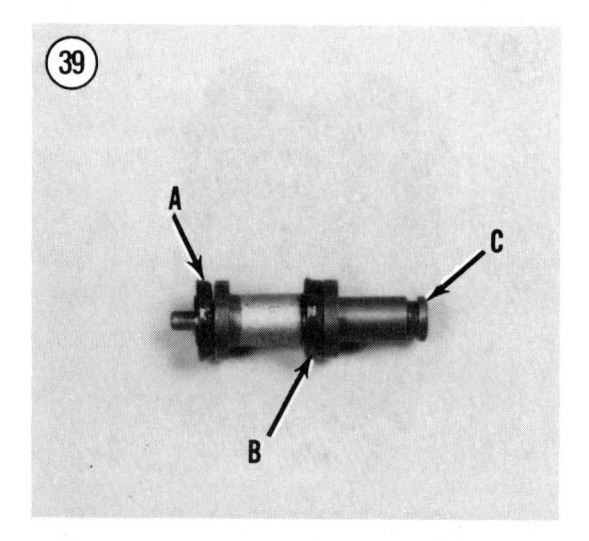

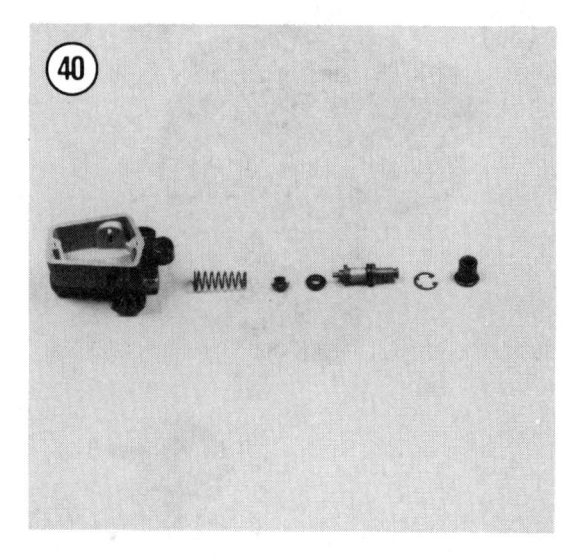

BRAKES

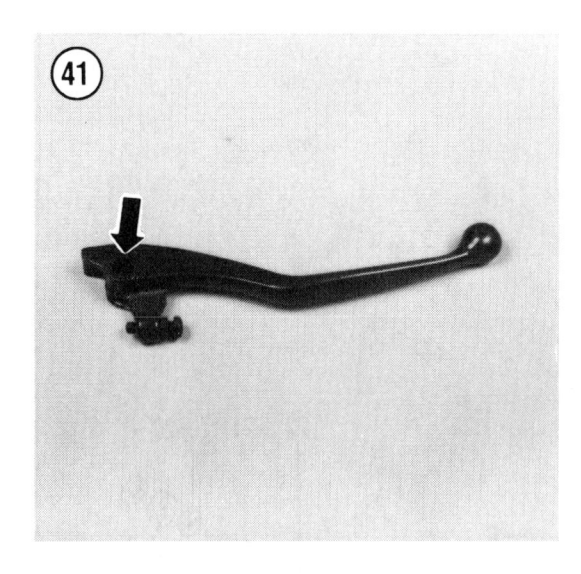

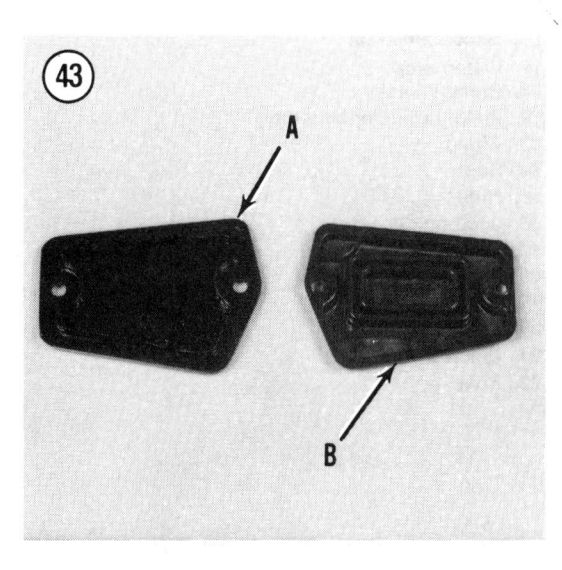

2. Slide the primary cup (A, **Figure 39**) onto the piston assembly. Install the primary cup so that the larger seal lip will face into the master cylinder first.
3. Install the piston seal.
4. Install the spring into the master cylinder housing (**Figure 38**) so that the small end of the spring faces the piston assembly.
5. Install the piston assembly into the master cylinder (**Figure 37**).
6. Compress the piston assembly and install the circlip (A, **Figure 36**) with circlip pliers.
7. Install the dust boot (B, **Figure 36**). Make sure the dust boot is firmly seated in the master cylinder.
8. Install the spring into the brake lever (**Figure 34**) and install the brake lever (B, **Figure 33**) onto the master cylinder. Install the pivot bolt and nut (A, **Figure 33**) and tighten the nut securely.
9. Install the diaphragm and cover onto the master cylinder until reinstallation.

REAR MASTER CYLINDER

Removal/Installation

Refer to **Figure 44** for this procedure.

CAUTION
Cover the swing arm with a heavy cloth or plastic tarp to protect it from accidental spilling of brake fluid. Wash any spilled brake fluid off any painted or plated surfaces immediately, as it will destroy the finish. Use soapy water and rinse completely.

1. Drain the master cylinder as follows:
   a. Attach a hose to the brake caliper bleed screw (**Figure 24**).
   b. Place the end of the hose in a clean container (**Figure 24**).
   c. Open the bleed screw (**Figure 24**) and operate the brake pedal to drain all brake fluid from the master cylinder reservoir.
   d. Close the bleed screw and disconnect the hose.
   e. Discard the brake fluid.
2. Remove the bolt securing the brake hose to the master cylinder (**Figure 44**). Remove the brake hose and both sealing washers. Cover the end of the hose to prevent the entry of foreign matter and moisture. Tie the hose end up to prevent the loss of brake fluid.

286

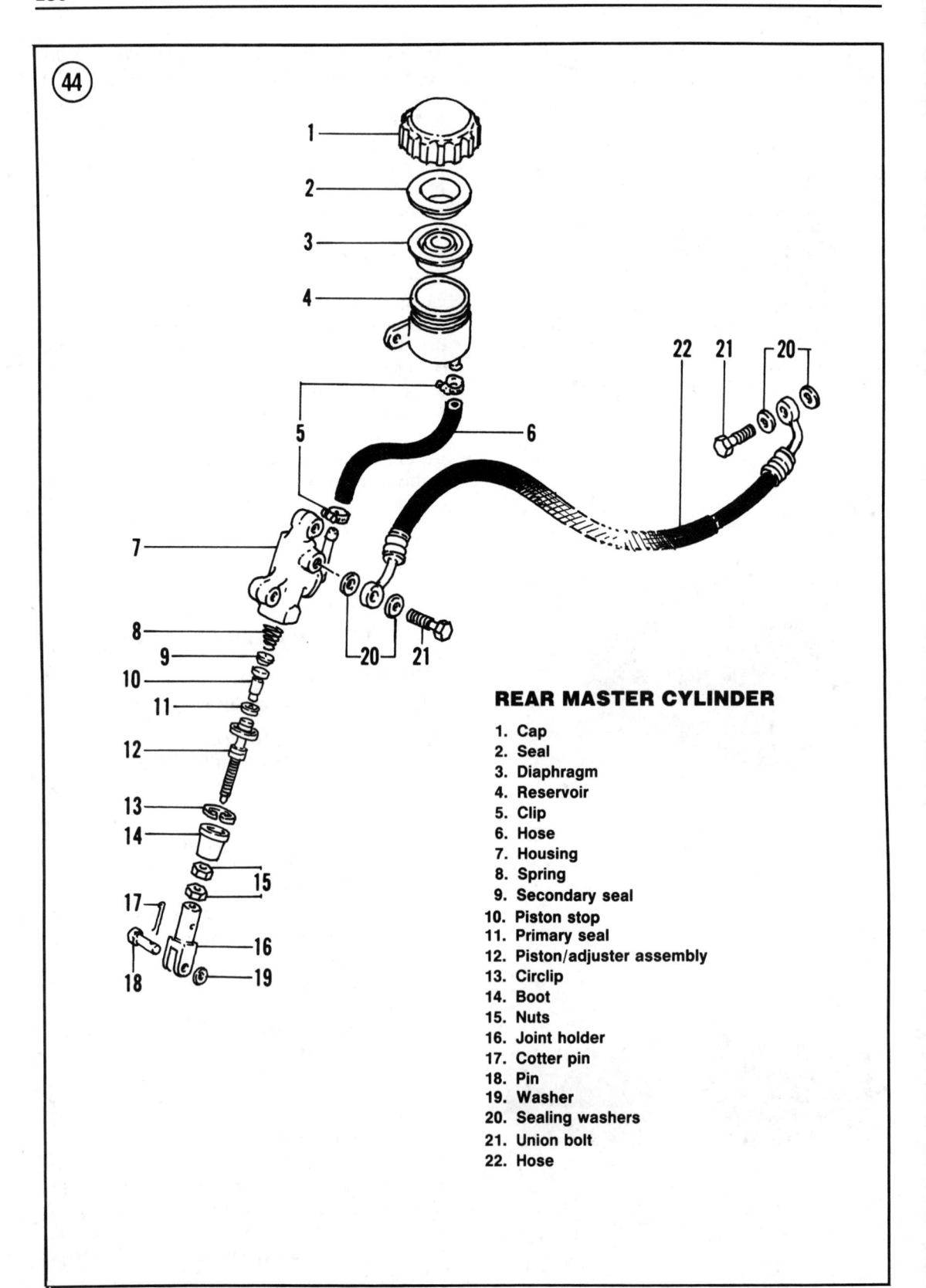

CHAPTER TWELVE

REAR MASTER CYLINDER

1. Cap
2. Seal
3. Diaphragm
4. Reservoir
5. Clip
6. Hose
7. Housing
8. Spring
9. Secondary seal
10. Piston stop
11. Primary seal
12. Piston/adjuster assembly
13. Circlip
14. Boot
15. Nuts
16. Joint holder
17. Cotter pin
18. Pin
19. Washer
20. Sealing washers
21. Union bolt
22. Hose

BRAKES

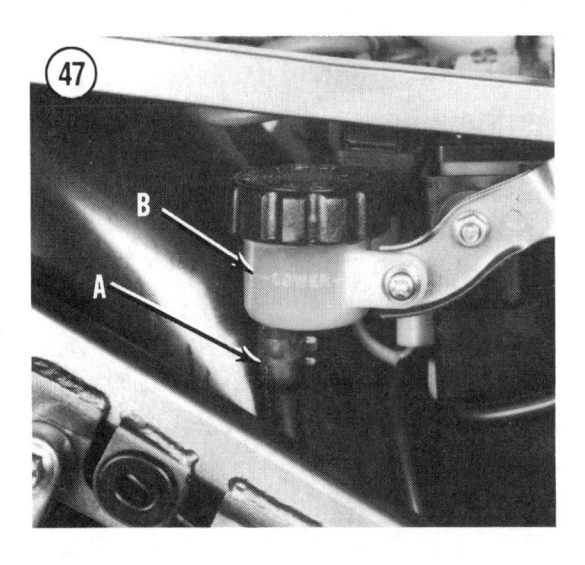

3. Disconnect cotter pin (**Figure 45**) and disconnect the brake pedal rod at the master cylinder push rod.

4. *FZ700 and FZ750:* Remove the footpeg bracket (**Figure 46**).

5. Disconnect the reservoir hose (**Figure 44**) at the master cylinder.

6. Remove the master cylinder bolts (**Figure 44**) and remove the master cylinder assembly.

7. Install by reversing these removal steps. Note the following:

   a. Install the brake hose into the U-shaped notch in the master cylinder. Be sure to place a sealing washer on each side of the hose fitting and install the banjo bolt. Tighten the banjo bolt to the specifications in **Table 2**.

   b. Insert the reservoir hose into the master cylinder and secure it.

   c. Tighten the master cylinder bolts to the specifications in **Table 2**.

   d. Bleed the brake system as described under *Bleeding the System* in this chapter.

   e. Adjust the rear brake pedal as described in Chapter Three; refer to *Rear Brake Pedal Height Adjustment* and *Rear Brake Light Switch Adjustment*.

WARNING
Do not ride the motorcycle until the rear brake is operating correctly.

Reservoir
Removal/Installation

The master cylinder reservoir can be removed by first draining the master cylinder as described under *Rear Master Cylinder Removal/Installation*. Disconnect the hose at the reservoir (A, **Figure 47**) and remove the reservoir (B, **Figure 47**). Reverse to install. Bleed the brake as described under *Bleeding the System* in this chapter.

Disassembly/Reassembly

Refer to **Figure 44**.

1. Remove the master cylinder as described in this chapter.
2. Remove the piston dust boot.
3. Remove the circlip with circlip pliers and remove the piston and spring.
4. Remove the primary and secondary cups from the piston assembly.
5. Inspect the master cylinder assembly as described in this chapter.
6. Assembly is the reverse of these steps. Note the following:

a. Soak the new caps in fresh brake fluid for at least 15 minutes to make them pliable. Coat the inside of the cylinder with fresh brake fluid prior to assembling the parts.

CAUTION
When installing the piston assembly, do not allow the cups to turn inside out as they will be damaged and allow brake fluid to leak within the cylinder bore.

b. Install the master cylinder piston assembly in the order shown in **Figure 44**.
c. Make sure the circlip seats in its groove completely.
d. Make sure the dust boot is firmly seated against the master cylinder.

Inspection

1. Clean all parts in fresh DOT 3 brake fluid. Place the master cylinder components on a clean lint-free cloth when performing the following inspection procedures.
2. Inspect the cylinder bore and piston contact surfaces for signs of wear or damage. If either part is less than perfect, replace it.
3. Check the end of the piston for wear caused by the piston stop. Replace the entire piston assembly if any portion of it requires replacement. If the piston assembly is replaced, also replace the primary cup.
4. Check the secondary cup for damage, softness or swelling. Replace the secondary cup if necessary.
5. Check the primary cup for the same conditions as Step 4. Replace the primary cup if necessary.
6. Inspect the piston stop and pushrod assembly for damage or bending. Replace if necessary.
7. Make sure the passages in the bottom of the brake fluid reservoir are clear. Check the reservoir cap and diaphragm for damage and deterioration. Replace if necessary.
8. Inspect the condition of the threads in the master cylinder body where the brake hose banjo bolt screws in. If the threads are damaged or partially stripped, replace the master cylinder body.
9. Measure the master cylinder inside diameter with a bore gauge; replace the master cylinder if the inside diameter is too large (**Table 1**).

BRAKE HOSE REPLACEMENT

A brake hose should replaced whenever it shows cracks, bulges or other damage. The deterioration of rubber by ozone and other atmospheric elements may require hose replacement every 4 years.

CAUTION
Cover components with a heavy cloth or plastic tarp to protect them from the accidental spilling of brake fluid. Wash any spilled brake fluid off of any painted or plated surface immediately, as it will destroy the finish. Use soapy water and rinse completely.

1. Before replacing a brake hose, inspect the routing of the old hose carefully, noting any guides and grommets the hose may go through.

BRAKES

2. Drain the master cylinder as described under *Front Master Cylinder Removal/Installation* or *Rear Master Cylinder Removal/Installation* in this chapter.

3. Disconnect the banjo bolts securing the hose at either end and remove the hose with its banjo bolts and 2 washers at both ends.

NOTE
On FZ700 and FZ750 models, it will be necessary to remove the fairing assembly to gain access to the front brake hose joint. See Chapter Thirteen.

4. To remove the front brake banjo joint (**Figure 48**), disconnect the hoses at the joint. Then remove the attaching bolts and remove the joint.

5. Install new brake hoses, sealing washers and bolts in the reverse order of removal. Be sure to install the new sealing washers in their correct positions. Tighten all banjo bolts to specifications in **Table 2**.

6. Refill the master cylinder(s) with fresh brake fluid clearly marked DOT 3. Bleed the brake as described under *Bleeding the System* in this chapter.

WARNING
Do not ride the motorcycle until you are sure that the brakes are operating properly.

BRAKE DISC

Inspection

It is not necessary to remove the disc from the wheel to inspect it. Small marks on the disc are not important, but deep radial scratches, deep enough to snag a fingernail, reduce braking effectiveness and increase brake pad wear. If these grooves are found, the disc should be resurfaced or replaced.

1. Measure the thickness around the disc at several locations with vernier calipers or micrometer (**Figure 49**). The disc must be replaced if the thickness at any point is less than the minimum specified in **Table 1**.

2. Make sure the disc bolts (**Figure 50**) are tight prior to performing this check. Check the disc runout with a dial indicator as shown in **Figure 51**. Slowly rotate the wheel and watch the dial indicator. If the runout is 0.15 mm (0.006 in.) or greater, the disc must be replaced.

3. Clean the disc of any rust or corrosion with spray brake cleaner. Never use an oil based solvent that may leave an oil residue on the disc.

Removal/Installation

1. Remove the front or rear wheel as described in Chapter Ten or Chapter Eleven.

NOTE
Place a piece of wood in the calipers in place of the disc. This way, if the brake lever is inadvertently squeezed, the piston will not be forced out of the cylinder. If this does happen, the caliper might have to be disassembled to reseat the piston and the system will have to be bled. By using the wood, bleeding the system is not necessary when installing the wheel.

2. Remove the bolts securing the disc to the wheel and remove the disc (**Figure 52**).

3. Install by reversing these removal steps. Note the following:
   a. Apply Loctite 242 (blue) to the bolts before installation.
   b. Tighten the disc bolts to the specifications in **Table 2**.

BLEEDING THE SYSTEM

This procedure is necessary only when the brakes feel spongy, there is a leak in the hydraulic system, a component has been replaced or the brake fluid has been replaced.

1. Flip off the dust cap from the brake bleeder valve.
2. Connect a length of clear tubing to the bleeder valve on the caliper. Place the other end of the tube into a clean container. Fill the container with enough fresh brake fluid to keep the end submerged. The tube should be long enough so that a loop can be made higher than the bleeder valve to prevent air from being drawn into the caliper during bleeding. See **Figure 53**.

CAUTION
Cover parts with a heavy cloth or plastic tarp to protect them from the accidental spilling of brake fluid. Wash any spilled brake fluid off of any painted or plated surface immediately, as it will destroy the finish. Use soapy water and rinse completely.

3. Clean the top of the master cylinder of all dirt and foreign matter. Remove the cap and diaphragm. Fill the reservoir to about 10 mm (3/8 in.) from the top. Install the diaphragm to prevent the entry of dirt and moisture.

WARNING
Use brake fluid clearly marked DOT 3 only. Others may vaporize and cause brake failure. Always use the same brand name; do not intermix the brake fluids, as many brands are not compatible.

4. Slowly apply the brake lever (front) or pedal (rear) several times. Hold the lever in the applied position and open the bleeder valve about 1/2 turn. Allow the lever to travel to its limit. When this limit is reached, tighten the bleeder screw. As the brake fluid enters the system, the level will drop in the master cylinder reservoir. Maintain the level at about 10 mm (3/8 in.) from the top of the reservoir to prevent air from being drawn into the system.

5. Continue to pump the lever or pedal and fill the reservoir until the fluid emerging from the hose is completely free of air bubbles.

NOTE
If bleeding is difficult, it may be necessary to allow the fluid to stabilize for a few hours. Repeat the bleeding procedure when the tiny bubbles in the system settle out.

6. Hold the lever or pedal in the applied position and tighten the bleeder valve. Remove the bleeder tube and install the bleeder valve dust cap.
7. If necessary, add fluid to correct the level in the master cylinder reservoir. It must be above the "LOWER" level line.
8. Install the cap. Tighten the screws on front master cylinders.

BRAKES

9. Test the feel of the brake lever or pedal. It should feel firm and should offer the same resistance each time it's operated. If it feels spongy, it is likely that air is still in the system and it must be bled again. When all air has been bled from the system, and the brake fluid level is correct in the reservoir, double-check for leaks and tighten all fittings and connections.

WARNING

Before riding the motorcycle, make certain that the brakes are operating correctly by operating the lever several times. Then make the test ride a slow one at first to make sure the brake is operating correctly.

Table 1 BRAKE SPECIFICATIONS

Brake fluid type	DOT 3
Front disc brake	
Disc diameter	
F2X700 & FZ700	267 mm (10.5 in.)
FZ750	235 mm (9.25 in.)
Disc thickness	
FTZ700 & FZ700	5.0 mm (0.197 in.)
FZ750	7.5 mm (0.3 in.)
Brake pad thickness	
New	5.5 mm (0.217 in.)
Wear limit	0.5 mm (0.0197 in.)
Master cylinder inside diameter	
FZX700 & FZ700	15.87 mm (0.63 in.)
FZ750	15.80 mm (0.62 in.)
Brake caliper inside diameter	45.4 mm (1.79 in.)
Rear disc brake	
Disc diameter	
F2X700 & FZ700	267 mm (10.5 in.)
FZ750	235 mm (9.25 in.)
Disc thickness	
F2X700 & FZ700	5.0 mm (0.197 in.)
FZ750	7.5 mm (0.3 in.)
Brake pad thickness	
New	5.5 mm (0.217 in.)
Wear limit	0.5 mm (0.0197 in.)
Master cylinder inside diameter	14.0 mm (0.55 in.)
Brake caliper inside diameter	42.8 mm (1.69 in.)

Table 2 BRAKE TIGHTENING TORQUES

Item	N-m	ft.-lb.
Caliper bolt (front and rear)	35	25
Brake hose banjo bolts	26	19
Front master cylinder clamp bolt	9	6.5
Brake disc bolts	20	14

CHAPTER THIRTEEN

FAIRING

This chapter contains removal and installation procedures for the fairing assembly on FZ700 and FZ750 models.

When removing a fairing component, it is best to reinstall all mounting hardware onto the removed part or store it in plastic bags taped to the inside of the fairing. After removal, fairing components should be placed away from the service area to prevent accidental damage.

LOWER FAIRING

Removal/Installation (FZ700)

1. Support the motorcycle on its side stand.
2. Remove the lower fairing mounting screws and remove the left- and right-hand lower fairing assemblies. See **Figure 1**.
3. Install by reversing these steps.

Removal/Installation (FZ750)

1. Park the motorcycle on its center stand.
2. Remove the lower fairing mounting screws and remove the left- and right-hand lower fairing assemblies. See **Figure 2**.
3. Install by reversing these steps.

UPPER FAIRING

Removal/Installation

1. Park the motorcycle on its center stand (FZ750) or sidestand (FZ700).
2. Remove the choke knob set screw and pull the knob (**Figure 3**) off of the choke shaft.
3. Remove the left-hand inner panel screws and remove the panel (**Figure 4**).

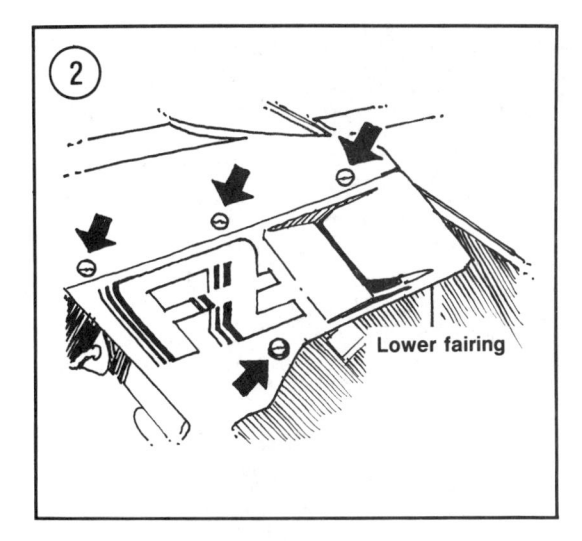

FAIRING

WARNING
Do not remove the radiator cap in Step 4 if the engine is hot. Scalding liquid may burn you.

4. Remove the radiator cap cover and remove the radiator cap.
5. Remove the right-hand inner panel screws and remove the panel (**Figure 5**).
6. Disconnect the speedometer cable (**Figure 6**).
7. Disconnect the electrical connectors that you can reach at this point.
8. Remove the mirror screws (**Figure 7**) and remove the mirrors.

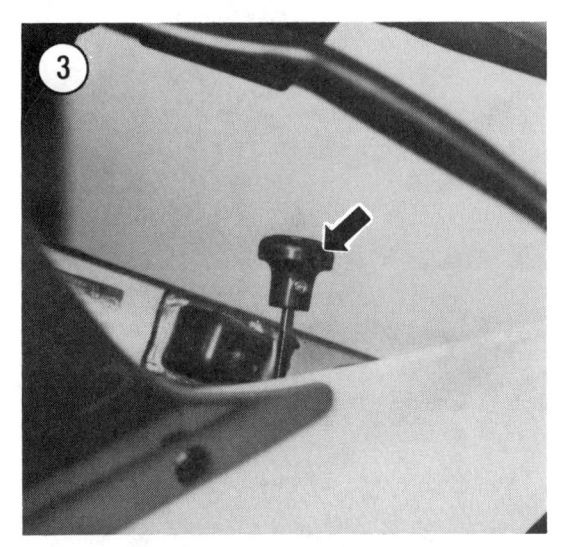

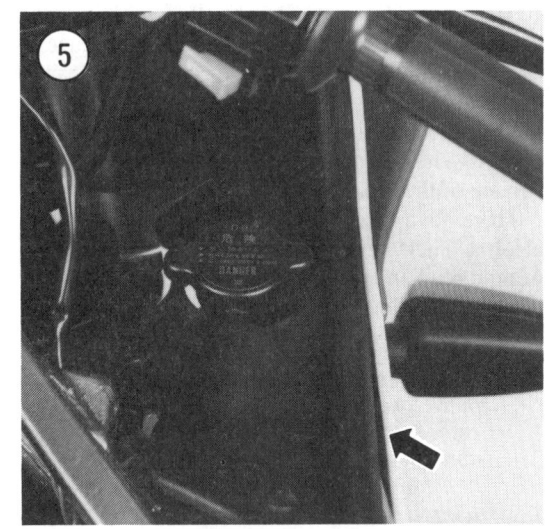

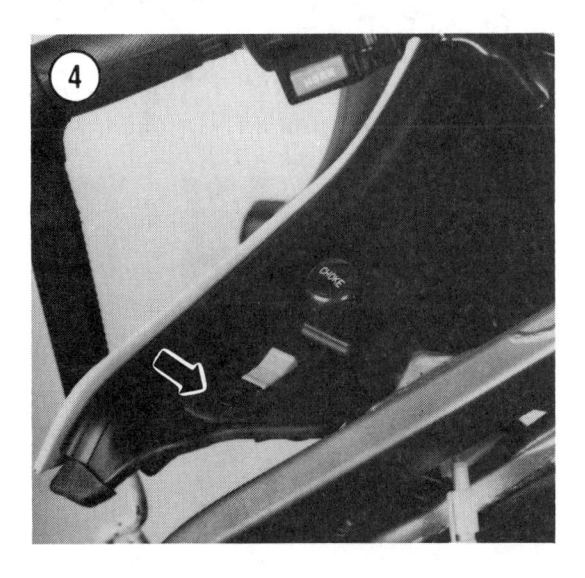

9. Remove the fairing mounting screws. On some screws, it will be necessary to use a long T-handle and socket (**Figure 8**) to reach them.

10. Pivot the upper fairing (**Figure 9**) forward. Check for any remaining attached electrical connectors or mounting screws and brackets (**Figure 10**). Remove the upper fairing assembly (**Figure 11**).

11. Install by reversing these steps. Check all controls to make sure the electrical connectors are properly attached and that the fairing does not alter throttle cable control.

WINDSHIELD

The windshield can be replaced by removing the mounting screws. Reverse to install.

Windshield Cleaning

Be very careful when cleaning the windshield as it can be scratched or damaged. Do not use a cleaner with an abrasive, a combination cleaner and wax or any solvent that contains ethyl or methyl alcohol. Never use gasoline or cleaning solvent. These products will scratch or destroy the surface of the windshield.

To remove oil, grease or road tar use isopropyl alcohol. Then wash the windshield with a solution of mild soap and water. Dry gently with a soft cloth or chamois—do not press hard.

NOTE
When removing road tar, make sure there are no small stones or sand embedded in it. Carefully remove any abrasive particles prior to rubbing with a cleaner. This will help minimize scratching.

Many commercial windshield cleaners are available. If using a cleaner, make sure it is safe for use on plastic and test it on a small area first.

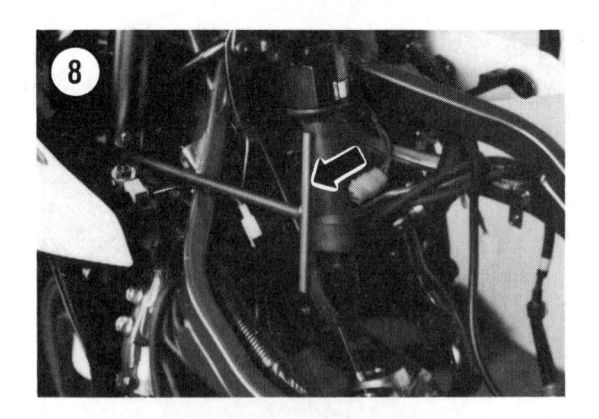

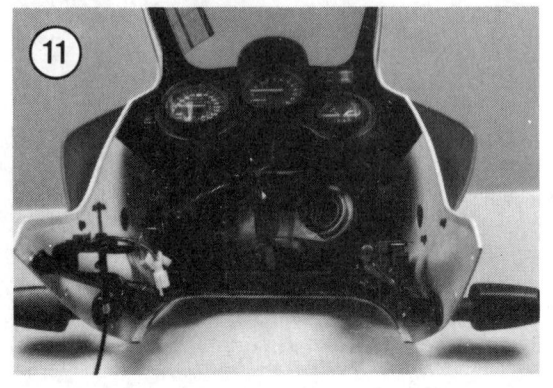

INDEX

A

Air cleaner 47-48
Air cleaner element 57

B

Battery 30-33
Brakes
  bleeding 290-291
  calipers 279-282
  disc 42, 274, 289-290
  fluid change 44
  fluid level 42-43
  hoses and seals 43
  hose replacement 288-289
  lever adjustment, front 44
  light switch adjustment,
    rear 45-46
  pad inspection 43-44
  pad replacement 275-278
  pedal height adjustment, rear 45
  problems 25

C

Cam case removal 93-94
Cam chain tensioner 91-92
Camshaft
  bearing clearance
    measurement 86-87
  case assembly 97-98
  case removal 95
  chain and sprockets
    inspection/replacement 87
  chain guides 87
  inspection 85-86
  installation 87-91, 98
  removal 83-85
Carburetor 66-67
Carburetor synchronization 67-68
Charging system 187-190
Choke cable adjustment 47

Clutch 23
  bleeding 151
  cover breather
    removal/installation 135-136
  cover removal/installation 135
  fluid level check 46
  hydraulic lines 46
  hydraulic system 146-147
  inspection 141-143
  installation 143-146
  removal 136-141
Compression test 62
Connecting rods 126-128
Coolant change 51-52
Coolant reservoir 216
Cooling inspection 215-216
Cooling system 50-51
Countershaft 159-160
Crankcase
  assembly 119-123
  ball bearings
    inspection/replacement 118-119
  disassembly 117-118
  inspection 118
Crankshaft
  inspection 123-124
  main bearing clearance
    measurement 124-126
  removal/installation 123
Cylinder block 103-106
Cylinder head inspection 96-97
Cylinder head cover 82-83

D

Drive chain 41-42, 256-257

E

Electrical components 208-212
Electrical problems 25
Electric starter 195-199
Emission control information 9

14

Emission control system 182-183
Engine
   break-in 130
   lubrication 23
   noises 23
   oil and filter change 34-37
   oil level check 33-34
   performance 21-23
   principles 72
   removal/installation
      (FZX700) 72-77
      (FZ700 and FZ750) 77-82
   servicing 72
   sprocket 154-155
Emission control system 182-183
Excessive vibration 25
Exhaust system 47, 184-185
External shift mechanism 155-157

F

Fairing 292-294
Fasteners 4-7, 53
Fork 240-247
Fork oil change 37-38
Fuel and vacuum line inspection 47
Fuel system
   carburetor 166-177
   filter 47, 181-182
   level 177-178
   level sender 181
   pump 182, 212-213
   tank 178-181
   valve 47, 181
Fuses 213

G

Gapping/installing
   spark plugs 63-64
Gears 157-159

H

Handlebars 234-236
Hoses 222-223
Hubs 229-230, 253-254

I

Ignition system 190-195
Ignition timing 66

L

Lighting system 199-203

Lubricants 7-8
Lubrication
   drive chain 40
   engine oil and
     filter change 34-37
   engine oil level check 33-34
   front fork oil change 37-38
   relay arm and connecting arm 39
   speedometer cable 39-40
   steering stem 40
   swing arm bearings 39
   throttle cable 39
   wheel bearings 40

M

Mainshaft 160-161
Maintenance 29
   air cleaner 47-48
   brake lever adjustment, front 44
   brake light switch
     adjustment, rear 45-46
   brake pedal height
     adustment,rear 45
   choke cable adjustment 47
   clutch fluid level check 46
   clutch hydraulic lines 46
   coolant change 51-52
   cooling system 50-51
   brake 42
   brake fluid change 44
   brake fluid level 42-43
   brake hoses and seals 43
   brake pad inspection 43-44
   drive chain 41-42
   exhaust system 47
   fuel and vacuum line
     inspection 47
   fuel valve/filter 47
   nuts, bolts and other
     fasteners 53
   steering play 48-50
   suspension, front 52
   suspension, rear 53
   throttle cable adjustment 46-47
Manual organization 1
Manufacturer's label 9
Master cylinder 147-148, 282-288
Mechanic's tips 14-16

N

Neutral switch 153-154
Noise emission control
   information 9

INDEX

O

Oil level switch	116
Oil pressure relief valve	115-116
Oil pump and strainer	110-115

P

Parts replacement	8-9
Pistons and piston rings	106-110

R

Radiator and fan	216-219

S

Safety	2
Service hints and notes	2-4, 159
Shift drum and forks	162-164
Shock absorber	257-262
Slave cylinder	148-151
Spark plug	
heat range	62-63
readings	64-66
Speedometer cable	39-40
Sprocket	
cover, front	153
coupling, rear	254-256
Starter clutch assembly	129-130
Steering	
head	237-240
play	48-50
stem	40
troubleshooting	25
Suspension, front	25, 52
Suspension, rear	53
Suspension adjustment	53-57
Swing arm	262-271
Swing arm bearings	40
Switches	203-208

T

Thermostat	219-220
Thermostat switch and water temperature sensor	223-224
Throttle cable	39, 46-47

Tires and Tools

Tires	29-30, 230-234
Tools	9-14, 57
Torque specifications	4
Transmission countershaft	
disassembly/assembly	159-160
gears	157-159
inspection	161-162, 164-165
mainshaft disassembly/assembly	160-161
service notes	159
shift drum and forks removal/installation	162-164
system	24
Troubleshooting	19-21
carburetor	25
instruments	19
Tune-up	
air cleaner element	57
carburetor	66-67
carburetor synchronization	67-68
compression test	62
gapping and installing the plugs	63-64
ignition timing	66
reading spark plugs	64-66
spark plug heat range	62-63
tools	57
valve clearance adjustment	59-61
valve clearance measurement	57-59

V

Valves and valve components	98-103
Valve clearance adjustment	59-61
Valve clearance measurement	57-59

W

Water pump	220-222
Wheels	225-228, 230, 249-253
Wheel bearings	40
Wiring connectors	208

1985 FZ750N AND 1986 FZ750S/FZ750SC

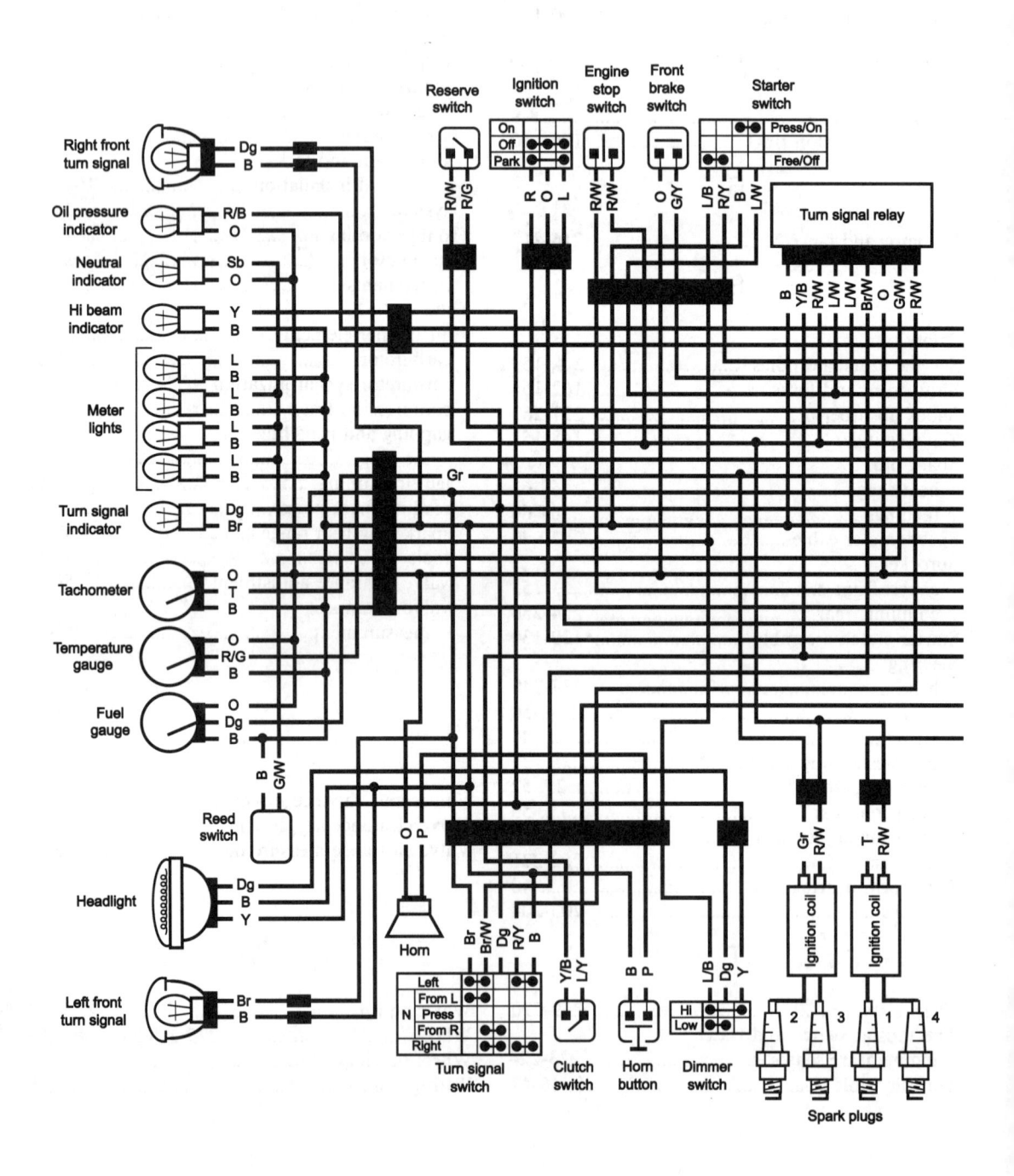

WIRING DIAGRAMS

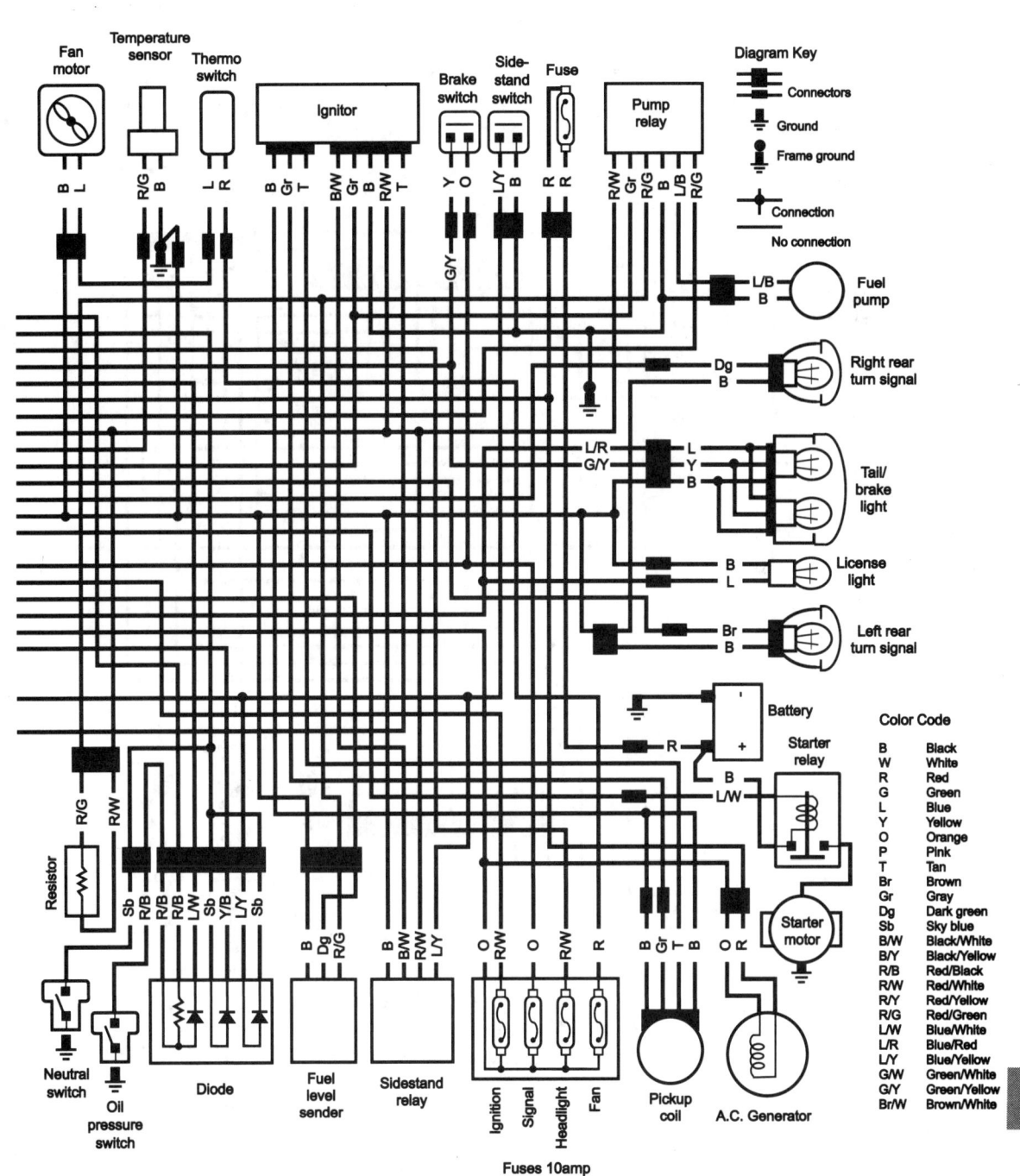

1986 FZX700S/FZX700SC AND 1987 FZX700T/FZX700TC

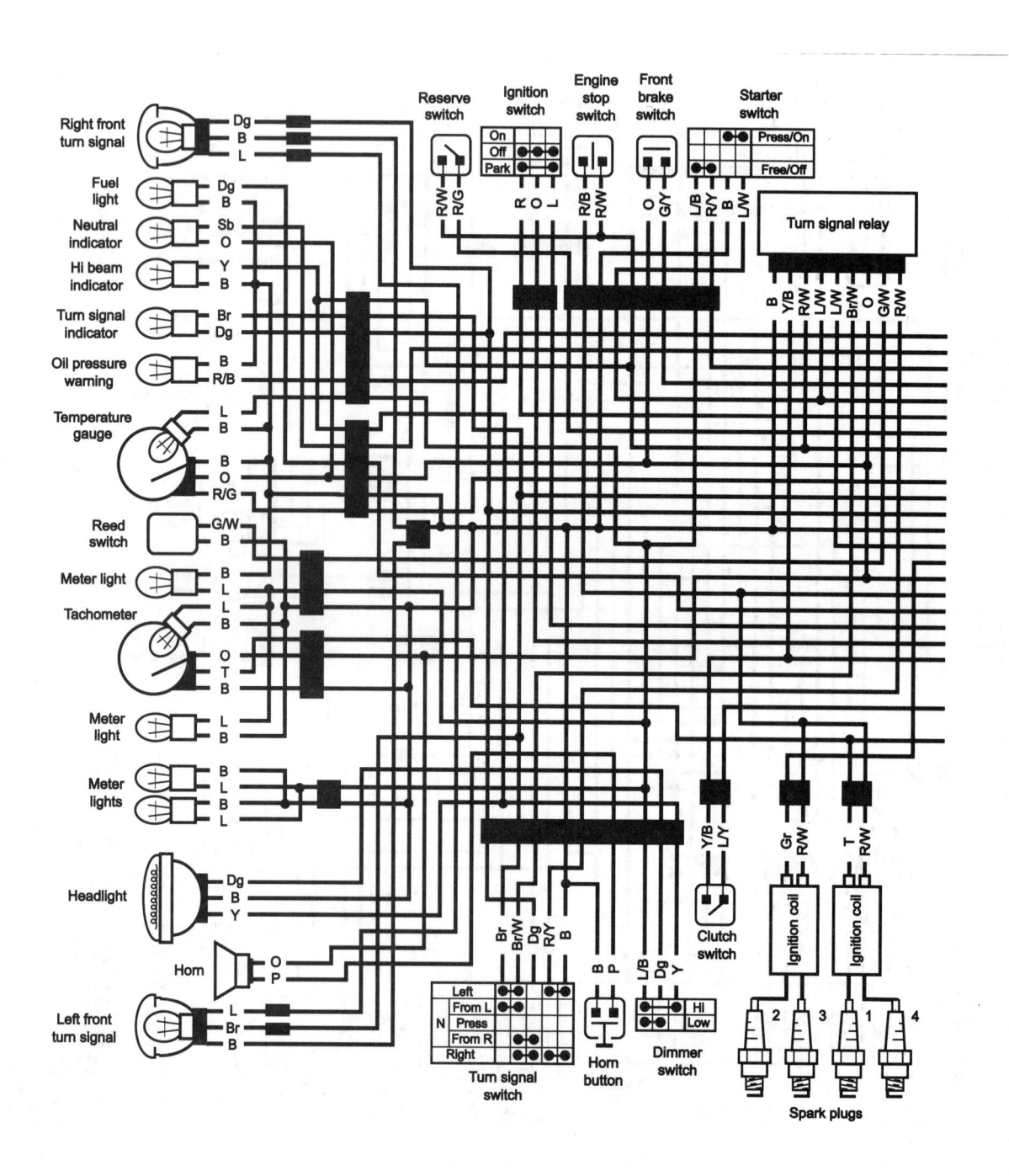

WIRING DIAGRAMS

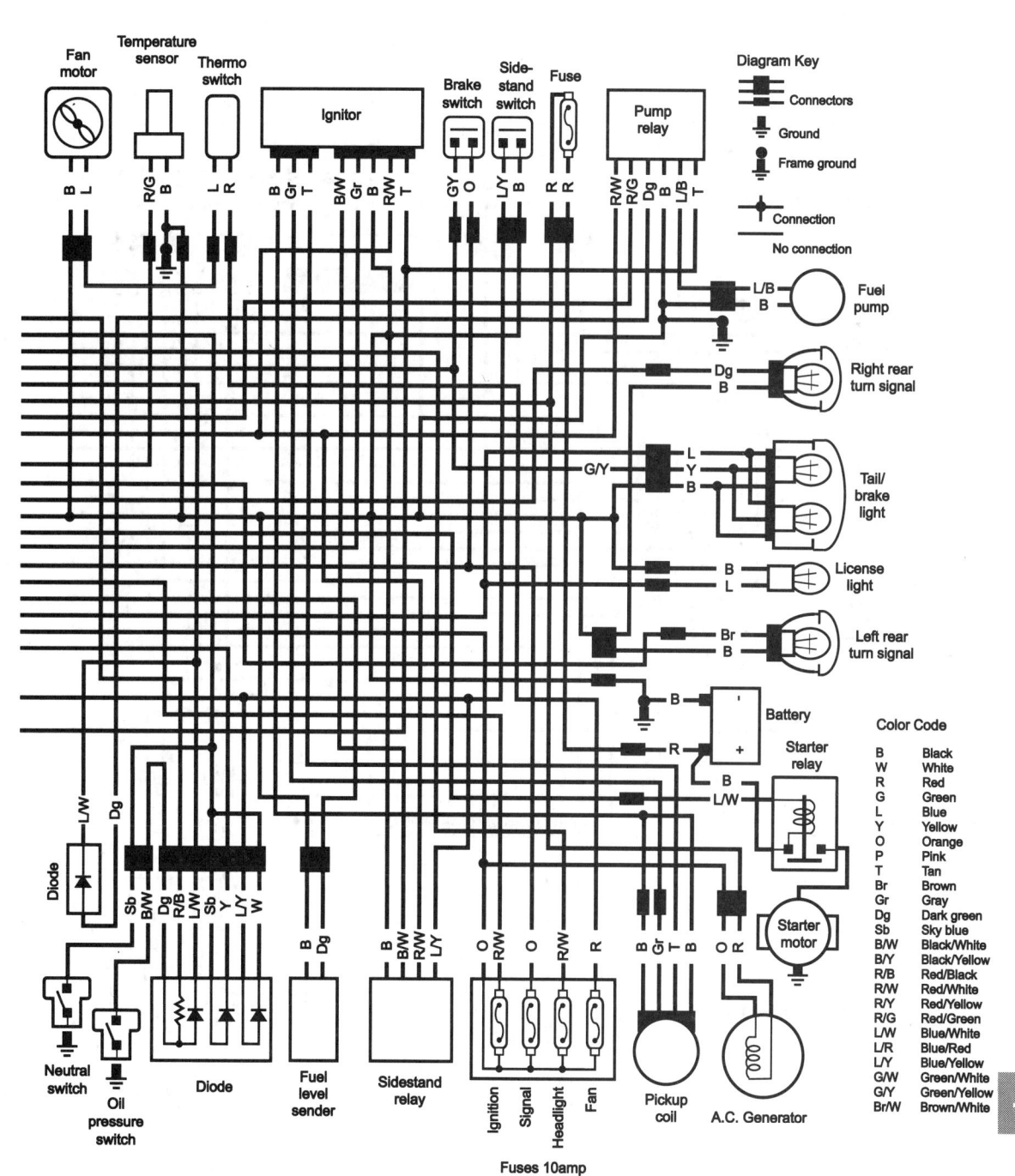

301

15

WIRING DIAGRAMS

1987 FZ700T/FZ700TC

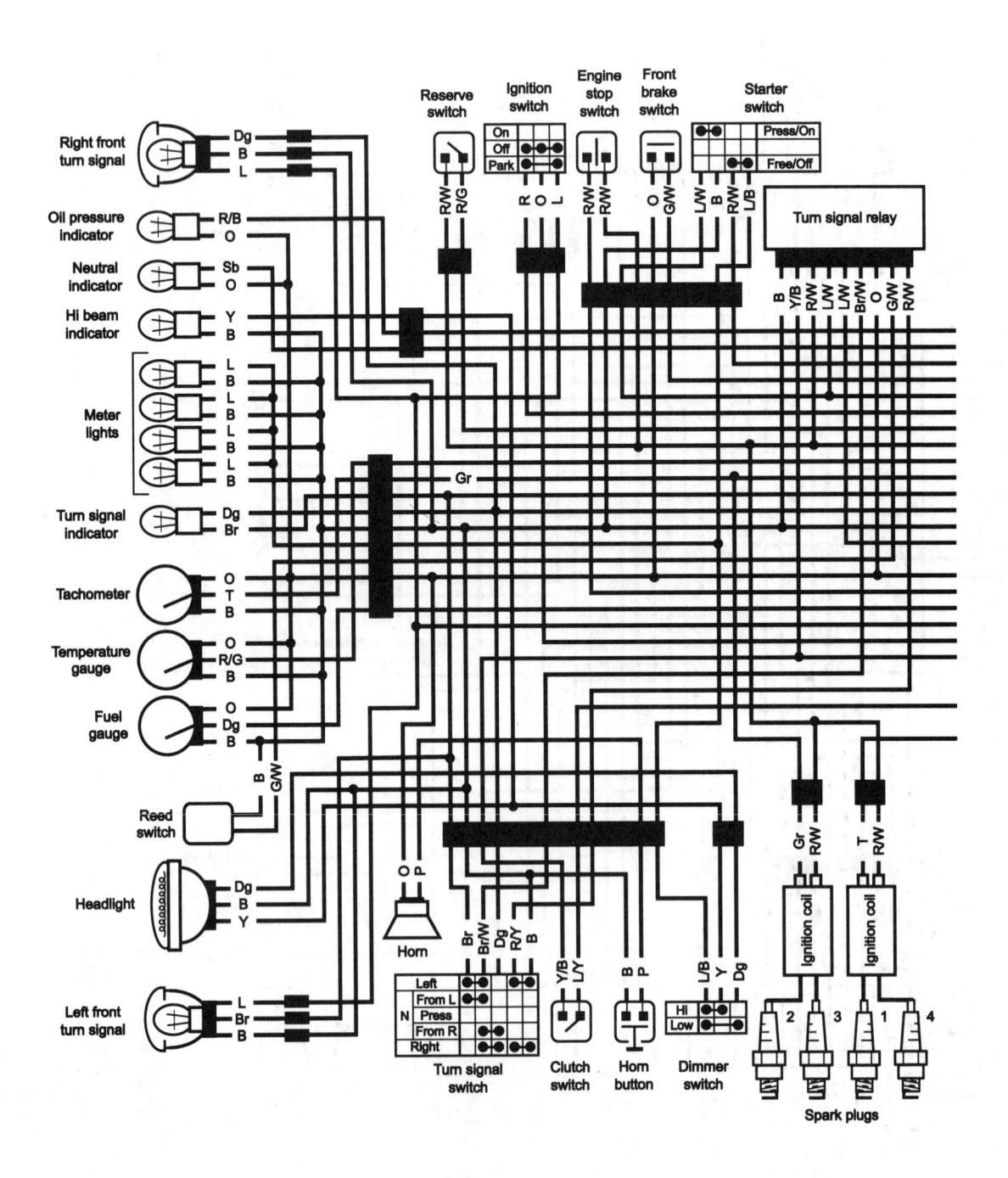

WIRING DIAGRAMS 303

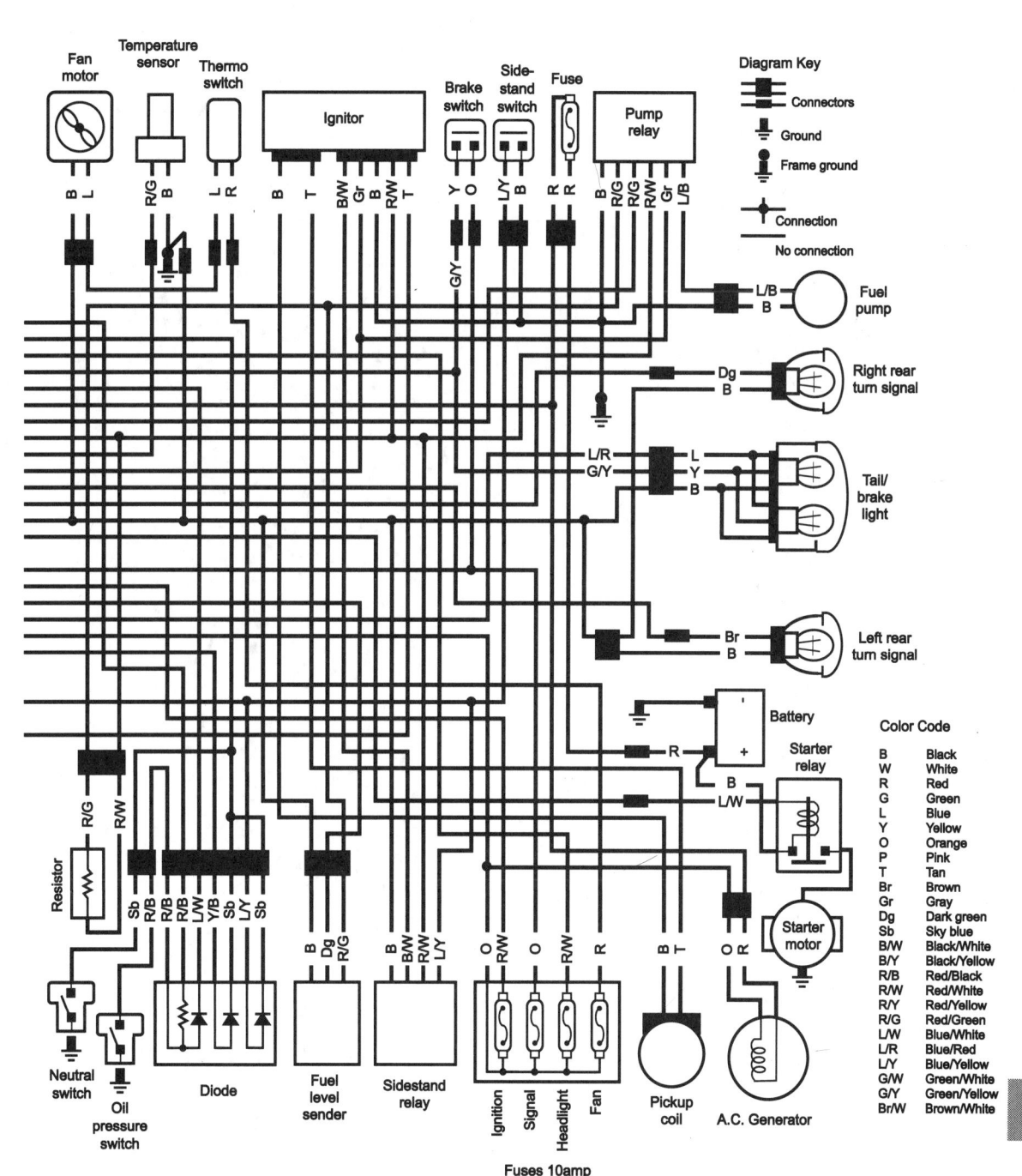

NOTES

NOTES

NOTES

MAINTENANCE LOG

Date	Miles	Type of Service

Check out *clymer.com* for our full line of powersport repair manuals.

BMW
- M308 500 & 600 CC twins, 55-69
- M502 BMW R-Series, 70-94
- M500 BMW K-Series, 85-95
- M503 R-850 & R-1100, 93-98

HARLEY-DAVIDSON
- M419 Sportsters, 59-85
- M428 Sportster Evolution, 86-90
- M429-3 Sportster Evolution, 91-02
- M418 Panheads, 48-65
- M420 Shovelheads, 66-84
- M421 FX/FL Softail Big-Twin Evolution, 84-94
- M422 FLT/FXR Big-Twin Evolution, 84-94
- M424 Dyna Glide, 91-95
- M425 Dyna Glide Twin Cam, 99-01

HONDA

ATVs
- M316 Odyssey FL250, 77-84
- M311 ATC, TRX & Fourtrax 70-125, 70-87
- M433 Fourtrax 90 ATV, 93-00
- M326 ATC185 & 200, 80-86
- M347 ATC200X & Fourtrax 200SX, 86-88
- M455 ATC250 & Fourtrax 200/250, 84-87
- M342 ATC250R, 81-84
- M348 TRX250R/Fourtrax 250R & ATC250R, 85-89
- M456 TRX250X 1987-1988, 91-92; TRX300EX 93-96
- M446 TRX250 Recon 1997-02
- M346-3 TRX300/Fourtrax 300 & TRX300FW/Fourtrax 4x4, 88-00
- M459 Fourtrax Foreman 95-98
- M454 TRX400EX 1999-02

Singles
- M310-13 50-110cc OHC Singles, 65-99
- M315 100-350cc OHC, 69-82
- M317 Elsinore, 125-250cc, 73-80
- M442 CR60-125R Pro-Link, 81-88
- M431-2 CR80R, 89-95, CR125R, 89-91
- M435 CR80, 96-02
- M457-2 CR125R & CR250R, 92-97
- M443 CR250R-500R Pro-Link, 81-87
- M432 CR250R & CR500R, 88-96
- M312-12 XL/XR75-100, 75-02
- M318 XL/XR/TLR 125-200, 79-87
- M328-2 XL/XR250, 78-00; XL/XR350R 83-85; XR200R, 84-85; XR250L, 91-96
- M320 XR400R, 96-00
- M339-6 XL/XR 500-650, 79-02

Twins
- M321 125-200cc, 64-77
- M322 250-350cc, 64-74
- M323 250-360cc Twins, 74-77
- M324-4 Rebel 250 & Twinstar, 78-87; Nighthawk 250, 91-97; Rebel 250, 96-97
- M334 400-450cc, 78-87
- M333 450 & 500cc, 65-76
- M335 CX & GL500/650 Twins, 78-83
- M344 VT500, 83-88
- M313 VT700 & 750, 83-87
- M460 VT1100C2 A.C.E. Shadow, 95-97
- M440 Shadow 1100cc V-Twin, 85-96

Fours
- M332 350-550cc 71-78
- M345 CB550 & 650, 83-85
- M336 CB650, 79-82
- M341 CB750 SOHC, 69-78
- M337 CB750 DOHC, 79-82
- M436 CB750 Nighthawk, 91-93 & 95-99
- M325 CB900, 1000 & 1100, 80-83
- M439 Hurricane 600, 87-90
- M441-2 CBR600, 91-98
- M434 CBR900RR Fireblade, 93-98
- M329 500cc V-Fours, 84-86
- M438 Honda VFR800, 98-00
- M349 700-1000 Interceptor, 83-85
- M458-2 VFR700F-750F, 86-97
- M327 700-1100cc V-Fours, 82-88
- M340 GL1000 & 1100, 75-83
- M504 GL1200, 84-87

Sixes
- M505 GL1500 Gold Wing, 88-92
- M506 GL1500 Gold Wing, 93-95
- M462 GL1500C Valkyrie, 97-00

KAWASAKI

ATVs
- M465 KLF220 Bayou, 88-95
- M466-2 KLF300 Bayou, 86-98
- M467 KLF400 Bayou, 93-99
- M470 KEF300 Lakota, 95-99
- M385 KSF250 Mojave, 87-00

Singles
- M350-9 Rotary Valve 80-350cc, 66-95
- M444 KX60-80, 83-90
- M351 KDX200, 83-88
- M447 KX125 & KX250, 82-91 KX500, 83-93
- M472 KX125, 92-98
- M473 KX250, 92-98

Twins
- M355 KZ400, KZ/Z440, EN450 & EN500, 74-95
- M360 EX500/GPZ500S, 87-93
- M356-2 700-750 Vulcan, 85-01
- M354 VN800 Vulcan 95-98
- M357 VN1500 Vulcan 87-98
- M471 VN1500 Vulcan Classic, 96-98

Fours
- M449 KZ500/550 & ZX550, 79-85
- M450 KZ, Z & ZX750, 80-85
- M358 KZ650, 77-83
- M359 900-1000cc Fours, 73-80
- M451 1000 &1100cc Fours, 81-85
- M452-3 ZX500 & 600 Ninja, 85-97
- M468 ZX6 Ninja, 90-97
- M469 ZX7 Ninja, 91-98
- M453 900-1100 Ninja, 84-93

POLARIS

ATVs
- M496 Polaris ATV, 85-95
- M362 Polaris Magnum ATV, 96-98
- M363 Scrambler 500, 4X4 97-00
- M365 Sportsman/Xplorer, 96-00

SUZUKI

ATVs
- M381 ALT/LT 125 & 185, 83-87
- M475 LT230 & LT250, 85-90
- M380 LT250R Quad Racer, 85-88
- M343 LTF500F Quadrunner, 98-00
- M483 Suzuki King Quad/ Quad Runner 250, 87-95

Singles
- M371 RM50-400 Twin Shock, 75-81
- M369 125-400cc 64-81
- M379 RM125-500 Single Shock, 81-88
- M476 DR250-350, 90-94
- M384 LS650 Savage Single, 86-88
- M386 RM80-250, 89-95

Twins
- M372 GS400-450 Twins, 77-87
- M481-3 VS700-800 Intruder, 85-01
- M482 VS1400 Intruder, 87-98
- M484-2 GS500E Twins, 89-00

Triple
- M368 380-750cc, 72-77

Fours
- M373 GS550, 77-86
- M364 GS650, 81-83
- M370 GS750 Fours, 77-82
- M376 GS850-1100 Shaft Drive, 79-84
- M378 GS1100 Chain Drive, 80-81
- M383-3 Katana 600, 88-96 GSX-R750-1100, 86-87
- M331 GSX-R600, 97-00
- M478-2 GSX-R750, 88-92 GSX750F Katana, 89-96
- M485 GSX-R750, 96-99
- M338 GSF600 Bandit, 95-00

YAMAHA

ATVs
- M394 YTM/YFM200 & 225, 83-86
- M487-2 YFM350 Warrior, 87-00
- M486-2 YFZ350 Banshee, 87-99
- M488-3 Blaster ATV, 88-01
- M489-2 Timberwolf ATV, 89-00
- M490-2 YFM350 Moto-4 & Big Bear, 87-99
- M493 YFM400FW Kodiak, 93-98

Singles
- M492 PW50 & PW80, BW80 Big Wheel 80, 81-98
- M410 80-175 Piston Port, 68-76
- M415 250-400cc Piston Port, 68-76
- M412 DT & MX 100-400, 77-83
- M414 IT125-490, 76-86
- M393 YZ50-80 Monoshock, 78-90
- M413 YZ100-490 Monoshock, 76-84
- M390 YZ125-250, 85-87 YZ490, 85-90
- M391 YZ125-250, 88-93 WR250Z, 91-93
- M497 YZ125, 94-99
- M498 YZ250, 94-98 and WR250Z, 94-97
- M491 YZ400F, YZ426F & WR400F, 98-00
- M417 XT125-250, 80-84
- M480-2 XT/TT 350, 85-96
- M405 XT500 & TT500, 76-81
- M416 XT/TT 600, 83-89

Twins
- M403 650cc, 70-82
- M395-9 XV535-1100 Virago, 81-99
- M495 XVS650 V-Star, 98-00

Triple
- M404 XS750 & 850, 77-81

Fours
- M387 XJ550, XJ600 & FJ600, 81-92
- M494 XJ600 Seca II, 92-98
- M388 YX600 Radian & FZ600, 86-90
- M396 FZR600, 89-93
- M392 FZ700-750 & Fazer, 85-87
- M411 XS1100 Fours, 78-81
- M397 FJ1100 & 1200, 84-93

VINTAGE MOTORCYCLES

Clymer® Collection Series
- M330 Vintage British Street Bikes, BSA, 500 & 650cc Unit Twins; Norton, 750 & 850cc Commandos; Triumph, 500-750cc Twins
- M300 Vintage Dirt Bikes, V. 1 Bultaco, 125-370cc Singles; Montesa, 123-360cc Singles; Ossa, 125-250cc Singles
- M301 Vintage Dirt Bikes, V. 2 CZ, 125-400cc Singles; Husqvarna, 125-450cc Singles; Maico, 250-501cc Singles; Hodaka, 90-125cc Singles
- M305 Vintage Japanese Street Bikes, Honda, 250 & 305cc Twins; Kawasaki, 250-750cc Triples; Kawasaki, 900 & 1000cc Fours